Highlights of this Study Guide

- Each Chapter of this **Study Guide** includes—
  - Chapter **Introduction**
  - Easy to Read & Understand, Comprehensive **Outline**
  - **True-False** Questions
  - **Fill-In** Questions
  - **Multiple-Choice** Questions
  - **Short Essay** Questions
  - **Issue Spotters**—hypothetical fact problems & black letter law questions on key issues
  - **Special Information for CPA Candidates**
- Most Chapters of this **Study Guide** include one or more questions based on past **CPA Exam Questions**
- Each Unit of this **Study Guide** ends with—
  - **Cumulative Hypothetical** & corresponding **Multiple-Choice** Questions
  - **Multiple-Choice** Questions covering *Focus on Legal Reasoning* & *Focus on Ethics* sections
- This **Study Guide** also contains an **Answer Appendix** with answers to all of the Questions & explanations of the Answers

Study Guide

to Accompany

West's Business Law: Alternate Edition

Text & Summarized Cases—Legal, Ethical, International, and E-Commerce Environment

Ninth Edition

GAYLORD A. JENTZ
Herbert D. Kelleher
Emeritus Professor in Business Law
University of Texas at Austin

ROGER LeROY MILLER
Institute for University Studies
Arlington, Texas

FRANK B. CROSS
Herbert D. Kelleher
Centennial Professor in Business Law
University of Texas at Austin

Prepared by

William Eric Hollowell
Member of
U.S. Supreme Court Bar
Minnesota State Bar
Florida State Bar

Roger LeRoy Miller
Institute for University Studies
Arlington, Texas

THOMSON
SOUTH-WESTERN
WEST

Australia · Canada · Mexico · Singapore · Spain · United Kingdom · United States

THOMSON
SOUTH-WESTERN
WEST

Study Guide to Accompany *West's Business Law: Alternate Edition*, Ninth Edition

By Gaylord A. Jentz, Roger LeRoy Miller, and Frank B. Cross

Editorial Director:
Jack Calhoun

Vice President/Editor-in-Chief:
George Werthman

Senior Acquisitions Editor:
Rob Dewey

Senior Developmental Editor:
Jan Lamar

Marketing Manager:
Steve Silverstein

Production Editors:
Bill Stryker and Anne Sheroff

Manufacturing Coordinator:
Rhonda Utley

Printer:
Victor Graphics

Printed in the United States of America
1 2 3 4 5 06 05 04

For more information
contact South-Western,
5191 Natorp Boulevard,
Mason, Ohio 45040.
Or you can visit our Internet site at:
http://www.westbuslaw.com

ISBN: 0-324-26998-6

Table of Contents

Preface

To the Student

This ***Study Guide*** is designed to help you read and understand ***West's Business Law: Alternate Edition,*** **Ninth Edition**.

How the *Study Guide* Can Help You

This *Study Guide* can help you maximize your learning, subject to the constraints and the amount of time you can allot to this course. There are at least six specific ways in which you can benefit from using this guide.

1. The *Study Guide* can help you decide which topics are the most important. Because there are so many topics analyzed in each chapter, many students become confused about what is essential and what is not. You cannot, of course, learn everything; this *Study Guide* can help you concentrate on the crucial topics in each chapter.

2. If you are forced to miss a class, you can use this *Study Guide* to help you learn the material discussed in your absence.

3. There is a possibility that the questions that you are required to answer in this *Study Guide* are representative of the types of questions that you will be asked during examinations.

4. You can use this *Study Guide* to help you review for examinations.

5. This *Study Guide* can help you decide whether you really understand the material. Don't wait until examination time to find out!

6. Finally, the questions in this *Study Guide* will help you develop critical thinking skills that you can use in other classes and throughout your career.

The Contents of the *Study Guide*

Business law sometimes is considered a difficult subject because it uses a specialized vocabulary and also takes most people much time and effort to learn. Those who work with and teach business law believe that the subject matter is exciting and definitely worthy of your efforts. Your text, ***West's Business Law: Alternate Edition,*** **Ninth Edition**, and this student learning guide have been written for the precise purpose of helping you learn the most important aspects of business law. We always try to keep you, the student, in mind.

Every chapter includes the following sections:

1. What This Chapter Is About: You are introduced to the main subject matter of each chapter in this section.

2. Chapter Outline: Using an outline format, the salient points in each chapter are presented.

3. True-False Questions: Ten true-false questions are included for each chapter. Generally, these questions test knowledge of terminology and principles. The answers are given at the back of the book. Whenever an answer is false, the reasons why it is false are presented at the back of the book also.

4. Fill-in Questions: Here you are asked to choose between two alternatives for each space that needs to be filled in. Answers are included at the back of the book.

5. Multiple-Choice Questions: Ten multiple-choice questions are given for each chapter. The answers, along with an explanation, are included at the back of this book.

6. Short Essay Questions: Two essay questions are presented for each chapter.

7. Issue Spotters: These questions alert you to certain principles within the chapter. Brief answers to these questions are included at the end of this text.

8. Special Information for CPA Candidates: This section alerts CPA candidates to principles within the chapter that are of special importance for the CPA exam and includes study tips of particular utility to these students.

How to Use this Study Guide

What follows is a recommended strategy for improving your grade in your business law class. It may seem like a lot of work, but the payoffs will be high. Try the entire program for the first three or four chapters. If you then feel you can skip some steps safely, try doing so and see what happens.

For each chapter we recommend you follow the sequence of steps below:

1. Read the What This Chapter Is About and Chapter Outline.

2. Read any of the Concept Summaries that may be included in the chapter you are studying in ***West's Business Law: Alternate Edition,*** **Ninth Edition**.

3. Read about half the textbook chapter (unless it is very long), being sure to underline only the most important topics (which you should be able to recognize after having read no more than two chapter outlines in this *Study Guide*). Put a check mark by the material that you do not understand.

4. If you find the textbook's chapter easy to understand, you might want to finish reading it. Otherwise, rest for a sufficient period before you read the second half of the chapter. Again, be sure to underline only the most important points and to put a check mark by the material you find difficult to understand.

5. After you have completed the entire textbook chapter, take a break. Then read only what you have underlined throughout the entire chapter.

6. Now concentrate on the difficult material, for which you have left check marks. Reread this material and *think about it*; you will find that it is very exciting to figure out difficult material on your own.

7. Now do the True-False Questions, Fill-In Questions, and Multiple-Choice Questions. Compare your answers with those at the back of this book. Make a note of the questions you have missed and find the pages in your textbook upon which these questions are based. If you still don't understand, ask your instructor.

8. If you still have time, do one or both of the essay questions.

9. Before your examination, study your class notes. Then review the chapter outline in the text. Reread the Chapter Outline in this *Study Guide*, then redo all of the questions within each chapter. Compare your answers with the answers at the back of this *Study Guide*. Identify your problem areas and reread the relevant pages in ***West's Business Law: Alternate Edition,* Ninth Edition**. Think through the answers on your own.

If you have followed the strategy outlined above, you should feel sufficiently confident and be relaxed enough to do well on your exam.

Study Skills for *West's Business Law: Alternate Edition,* Ninth Edition

Every student has a different way to study. We give several study hints below that we think will help any student to master the textbook ***West's Business Law: Alternate Edition,* Ninth Edition**. These skills involve outlining, marking, taking notes, and summarizing. You may not need to use all these skills. Nonetheless, if you do improve your ability to use them, you will be able to understand more easily the information in ***West's Business Law: Alternate Edition,* Ninth Edition**.

MAKING AN OUTLINE

An outline is simply a method for organizing information. The reason an outline can be helpful is that it shows how concepts relate to each other. Outlining can be done as part of your reading or at the end of your reading, or as a rereading of each section within a chapter before you go on to the next section. Even if you do not believe that you need to outline, our experience has been that the act of *physically* writing an outline for a chapter helps most students to improve greatly their ability to retain the material in ***West's Business Law: Alternate Edition,* Ninth Edition** and master it, thereby obtaining a higher grade in the class, with less effort.

To make an effective outline you have to be selective. Outlines that contain all the information in the text are not very useful. Your objective in outlining is to identify main concepts and to subordinate details to those main concepts. Therefore, your first goal is to *identify the main concepts in each section*. Often the large, first-level headings within your textbook are sufficient as identifiers of the major concepts within each section. You may decide, however, that you want to phrase an identifier in a way that is more meaningful to you. In any event, your outline should consist of several levels written in a standard outline format. The most important concepts are assigned a roman numeral; the second most important a capital letter; the third most important, numbers; and the fourth most important, lower-case letters. Even if you make an outline that is no more than the headings in the text, you will be studying more efficiently than you would be otherwise. As we stated above, the process of physically writing the words will help you master the material.

MARKING A TEXT

From kindergarten through high school you typically did not own your own textbooks. They were made available by the school system. You were told not to mark in them. Now that you own your own text for a course, your learning can be greatly improved by marking your text. There is a trade-off here. The more you mark up your textbook, the less you will receive from your bookstore when you sell it back at the end of the semester. The benefit is a better understanding of the subject matter, and the cost is the reduction in the price you receive for the resale of the text. Additionally, if you want a text that you can mark with your own notations, you necessarily have to buy a new one or a used one that has no markings. Both carry a higher price tag than a used textbook with markings. Again there is a trade-off.

Different Ways of Marking The most commonly used form of marking is to underline important points. The second most commonly used method is to use a felt-tipped highlighter, or marker, in yellow or some other transparent color. Marking also includes circling, numbering, using arrows, brief notes, or any other method that allows you to remember things when you go back to skim the pages in your textbook prior to an exam.

Why Marking Is Important Marking is important for the same reason that outlining is—it helps you to organize the information in the text. It allows you to become an *active* participant in the mastery of the material. Researchers have shown that the physical act of marking, just like the physical act of outlining, helps you better retain the material. The better the material is organized in your mind, the more you will remember. There are two types of readers—passive and active. The active reader outlines or marks. Active readers typically do better on exams. Perhaps one of the reasons that active readers retain more is because the physical act of outlining and/or marking requires greater concentration. It is through greater concentration that more is remembered.

Points to Remember When Marking

1. Read one section at a time before you do any extensive marking. You can't mark a section until you know what is important and you can't know what is important until you read the whole section.

2. Don't over mark. Just as an outline cannot contain everything that is in a text (or in a lecture), marking can't be of the whole book. Don't fool yourself into thinking you've done a good job just because each page is filled up with arrows, asterisks, circles, and underlines. When you go back to review the material you won't remember what was important. The key is *selective* activity. Mark each page in a way that allows you to see the most important points at a glance. You can follow up your marking by writing out more in your subject outline.

HOW TO STUDY AND TAKE EXAMS

There is basically one reason why you have purchased the *Study Guide*—to improve your exam grade. By using this *Study Guide* assiduously, you will have the confidence to take your mid-terms and final examinations and to do well. The *Study Guide*, however, should not just be used a day before each exam. Rather, the guide is most helpful if you use it at the time that you read the chapter. That is to say, after you read a chapter in ***West's Business Law: Alternate Edition,* Ninth Edition** you should directly go to the appropriate chapter in the *Study Guide*. This systematic review technique is the most effective study technique you can use.

Besides learning the concepts in each chapter as well as possible, there are additional strategies for taking exams. You need to know in advance what type of exam you are going to take—essay or objective or both. You need to know which reading materials and lectures will be covered. For both objective and essay exams (but more importantly for the former) you need to know if there is a penalty for guessing incorrectly. If there is, your strategy will be different: you will usually only mark what you are certain of. Finally, you need to know how much time will be allowed for the exam.

FOLLOWING DIRECTIONS

Students are often in a hurry to start an exam so they take little time to read the instructions. The instructions can be critical, however. In a multiple-choice exam, for example, if there is no indication that there is a penalty for guessing, then you should never leave a question unanswered. Even if there only remains a few minutes at the end of the exam, you should guess for those questions about which you are uncertain.

Additionally, you need to know the weight given to each section of an exam. In a typical multiple-choice exam, all questions have equal weight. In some exams, particularly those involving essay questions, different parts of the exam carry different weights. You should use these weights to apportion your time accordingly. If an essay part of an exam accounts for only 20 percent of the total points on the exam, you should not spend 60 percent of your time on the essay.

You need to make sure you are answering the question correctly. Some exams require a No. 2 lead pencil to fill in the dots on a machine-graded answer sheet. Other exams require underlining or circling. In short, you have to look at the instructions carefully.

Lastly, check to make sure that you have all the pages of the examination. If you are uncertain, ask the instructor or the exam proctor. It is hard to justify not having done your exam correctly because you failed to answer all the questions. Simply stating that you did not have them will pose a problem for both you and your instructor. Don't take a chance. Double check to make sure.

TAKING OBJECTIVE EXAMINATIONS

The most important point to discover initially with any objective test is if there is a penalty for guessing. If there is none, you have nothing to lose by guessing. In contrast, if a half-point is subtracted for each incorrect answer, then you probably should not answer any question for which you are purely guessing.

Students usually commit one of two errors when they read objective-exam questions: (1) they read things into the questions that don't exist, or (2) they skip over words or phrases.

Most test questions include key words such as:

- all
- always
- never
- only

If you miss these key words you will be missing the "trick" part of the question. Also, you must look for questions that are only *partly* correct, particularly if you are answering true/false questions.

Never answer a question without reading all of the alternatives. More than one of them may be correct. If more than one of them seems correct, make sure you select the answer that seems the most correct.

Whenever the answer to an objective question is not obvious, start with the process of elimination. Throw out the answers that are clearly incorrect. Even with objective exams in which there is a penalty for guessing, if you can throw out several obviously incorrect answers, then you may wish to guess among the remaining ones because your probability of choosing the correct answer is high.

Typically, the easiest way to eliminate incorrect answers is to look for those that are meaningless, illogical, or inconsistent. Often test authors put in choices that make perfect sense and are indeed true, but they are not the answer to the question under study.

Chapter 1
Introduction to Law and Legal Reasoning

WHAT THIS CHAPTER IS ABOUT

The first chapters in Unit 1 provide the background for the entire course. Chapter 1 sets the stage. From this chapter, you must understand that (1) the law is a set of general rules, (2) in applying these general rules, a judge cannot fit a case to suit a rule, but must fit (or find) a rule to suit the case, and (3) in fitting (or finding) a rule, a judge must also supply reasons for the decision.

CHAPTER OUTLINE

I. WHAT IS LAW?

Law consists of enforceable rules governing relationships among individuals and between individuals and their society.

II. SCHOOLS OF JURISPRUDENTIAL THOUGHT

Judges interpret and apply the law. When the law is expressed in general terms, there is some flexibility in interpreting it. This interpretation can be influenced by a judge's personal philosophy. Legal philosophies include the following.

A. THE NATURAL LAW SCHOOL

Natural law is a system of moral and ethical principles that are believed to be inherent in human nature and discoverable by humans through the use of their natural intelligence.

B. THE POSITIVIST SCHOOL

Legal positivists believe that there is no higher law than a nation's positive law (the law created by a particular society at a particular point in time). The law is the law and must be obeyed.

C. THE HISTORICAL SCHOOL

Followers of this school focus on legal principles that have been applied in past cases, emphasizing that those principles should be applied strictly in present cases.

D. LEGAL REALISM

Legal realists believe that in making decisions, judges are influenced by their own beliefs, the application of principles should be tempered by each case's circumstances, and extra-legal sources should be consulted.

III. BUSINESS ACTIVITIES AND THE LEGAL ENVIRONMENT

The law is split into different topics to make it easier to study, but more than one of those areas of the law can affect individual business decisions. Whether an activity is ethical is an important part of deciding whether to engage in it, but simply complying with the law may not meet all ethical obligations.

IV. SOURCES OF AMERICAN LAW

A. CONSTITUTIONAL LAW

The U.S. Constitution distributes power among the branches of government. It is the supreme law of the land. Any law that conflicts with it is invalid. The states also have constitutions, but the federal constitution prevails.

B. STATUTORY LAW

Statutes and ordinances are enacted by Congress and by state and local legislative bodies. Uniform laws (such as the Uniform Commercial Code) and model codes are created by panels of experts and scholars and adopted at the option of each state's legislature.

C. ADMINISTRATIVE LAW

Administrative law consists of the rules and regulations issued by administrative agencies, which derive their authority from the legislative and executive branches of government.

D. CASE LAW

Case law includes courts' interpretations of constitutional provisions, statutes, and administrative rules. Because statutes often codify common law rules, courts often rely on the common law as a guide to the intent and purpose of a statute. Case law governs all areas not covered by statutes.

V. THE COMMON LAW TRADITION

The American legal system, based on the decisions judges make in cases, is a common law system, which involves the application of principles applied in earlier cases with similar facts. This system comes from early English courts, which made a distinction between remedies at law and remedies in equity.

A. REMEDIES AT LAW AND REMEDIES IN EQUITY

As a rule, courts grant an equitable remedy only if the remedy at law is inadequate.

1. Remedies at Law

Remedies at law include awards of land, money, and items of value. A jury trial is available only in an action at law.

2. Remedies in Equity

Remedies in equity include decrees of specific performance, injunctions, and rescission. Decisions to award equitable remedies are guided by equitable maxims.

B. THE DOCTRINE OF *STARE DECISIS*

The use of precedent as binding authority in a common law system is the doctrine of *stare decisis*. *Stare decisis* makes the legal system more efficient, just, uniform, stable, and predictable.

1. When There Is No Precedent

When there is no precedent, a court may look at other legal principles and policies, social values, or scientific data.

2. When a Precedent Is Incorrect

A judge may decide that a precedent is incorrect if there have been changes in technology, business practices, or society's attitudes.

C. LEGAL REASONING

1. Issue-Rule-Application-Conclusion (IRAC)

Legal reasoning requires learning the facts of a case, identifying the issues and the relevant legal rules, applying the rules to the facts, and coming to a conclusion.

2. Forms of Legal Reasoning

In applying an old precedent or establishing a new one, judges use many forms of reasoning—deductive reasoning, linear reasoning, reasoning by analogy, and others—to harmonize theirs decisions with earlier cases.

VI. CLASSIFICATIONS OF LAW

A. SUBSTANTIVE AND PROCEDURAL LAW

Substantive law includes laws that define, describe, regulate, and create rights and duties. *Procedural law* includes rules for enforcing those rights.

B. CRIMINAL AND CIVIL LAW

Criminal law regulates relationships between individuals and society. *Civil law* regulates relationships between individuals.

C. PRIVATE AND PUBLIC LAW

Private law concerns relationships between private entities. *Public law* addresses the relationship between persons and their government.

D. CYBERLAW

Cyberlaw is the emerging body of law (court decisions, new and amended statutes, etc.) that governs cyberspace transactions.

VII. HOW TO FIND PRIMARY SOURCES OF THE LAW

A. FINDING STATUTORY LAW

1. Publication of Statutes

Federal statutes are arranged by date of enactment in *United States Statutes at Large*. State statutes are collected in similar state publications. Statutes are also published in codified form (the form in which they appear in the federal and state codes) in other publications.

2. Finding a Statute in a Publication

Statutes are usually referred to in their codified form. In the codes, laws are compiled by subject. For example, the *United States Code* (U.S.C.) arranges by subject most federal laws. Each subject is assigned a title number and each statute a section number within a title.

B. FINDING ADMINISTRATIVE LAW

1. Publication of Rules and Regulations

Rules and regulations adopted by federal administrative agencies are published initially in the *Federal Register*. They are also compiled by subject in the *Code of Federal Regulations* (C.F.R.).

2. Finding a Rule or Regulation in a Publication

In the C.F.R., rules and regulations are arranged by subject. Each subject is assigned a title number and each rule or regulation a section number within a title.

C. FINDING CASE LAW

1. Publication of Court Opinions

State appellate court opinions are often published by the state in consecutively numbered volumes. They may also be published in units of the *National Reporter System*, by West Publishing Company. Federal court opinions appear in other West publications.

2. Finding a Court Opinion in a Publication

After a decision is published, it is usually referred to by the name of the case and the volume, name, and page number of one or more reporters (which are often, but not always, West reporters). This information is called the citation.

VIII. HOW TO READ AND UNDERSTAND CASE LAW

A. THE PARTIES

1. Plaintiff v. Defendant

In the title of a case (*Alpha v. Beta*), the *v.* means versus (against). Alpha is the plaintiff (the party who filed the suit) and Beta the defendant. Some appellate courts place the name of the party appealing a decision first, so this case on appeal may be called *Beta v. Alpha*.

2. **Appellant v. Appellee**
The appellant is the party who appeals a case to another court or jurisdiction from the one in which the case was originally brought. An appellant may be referred to as a petitioner. The appellee is the party against whom an appeal is taken. An appellee may be referred to as a respondent.

B. THE COURT'S OPINION
The opinion contains the court's reasons for its decision, the rules of law that apply, and the judgment.

1. **Unanimous Opinion**
When more than one judge (or justice) decides a case, and they all agree, a unanimous opinion is written for the whole court.

2. **Majority Opinion**
If a decision is not unanimous, a majority opinion outlines the views of the majority.

3. **Concurring Opinion**
A concurring opinion is one in which a judge emphasizes a point that was not emphasized in the unanimous or majority opinion.

4. **Dissenting Opinion**
A dissenting opinion may be written by a judge who does not agree with the majority. A dissent may form the basis of arguments used years later in overruling the majority opinion.

TRUE-FALSE QUESTIONS

(Answers at the Back of the Book)

____ 1. Law is a body of enforceable rules governing relationships among individuals and between individuals and their society.

____ 2. Legal positivists believe that law should reflect universal moral and ethical principles that are part of human nature.

____ 3. The doctrine of *stare decisis* obligates judges to follow precedents established within their jurisdictions.

____ 4. Common law develops from rules of law announced in court decisions.

____ 5. Statutory law is legislation.

____ 6. The U.S. Constitution takes precedence over a conflicting provision in a state constitution.

____ 7. Congress enacted the Uniform Commercial Code for adoption by the states.

____ 8. Criminal law covers disputes between persons, and between persons and their governments.

____ 9. In most states, the same courts can grant legal or equitable remedies.

____ 10. A citation includes the name of the judge who decided the case.

FILL-IN QUESTIONS

(Answers at the Back of the Book)

The common law system, on which the American legal system is based, involves the application of principles applied in earlier cases ______________________________(with similar facts/whether or not the facts are similar). This use of previous case law, or ______________ (precedent/preeminent), is known as the doctrine of *stare decisis*, and ______________________________ (emphasizes a flexible/permits a predictable) resolution of cases.

MULTIPLE-CHOICE QUESTIONS

(Answers at the Back of the Book)

___ **1.** Adam is a legal positivist. Adam believes that

a. the law should be applied the same in all cases in all circumstances.
b. the law should reflect universal principles that are part of human nature.
c. the law should strictly follow decisions made in past cases.
d. the written law of a society at a particular time is most significant.

___ **2.** In a suit between Best Products, Inc., and Central Sales Corporation, the court applies the doctrine of *stare decisis.* This means that the court follows rules of law established by

a. all courts.
b. courts of higher rank only.
c. courts of lower rank only.
d. no courts.

___ **3.** In a suit between Delta Data Company and Eagle Information, Inc., the court applies the doctrine of *stare decisis.* This requires the court to find cases that, compared to the case before it, has

a. entirely different facts.
b. no facts, only conclusions of law.
c. precisely identical facts.
d. similar facts.

___ **4.** In a suit between Fine Manufacturing Company and Great Goods, Inc., the court orders a rescission. This is

a. an action to cancel a contract and return the parties to the positions they held before the contract's formation.
b. an award of damages.
c. an order to do or refrain from doing a particular act.
d. an order to perform what was promised.

___ **5.** In a given case, most courts may grant

a. equitable remedies only.
b. legal remedies only.
c. equitable or legal remedies, but not both.
d. equitable remedies, legal remedies, or both.

___ **6.** The U.S. Constitution takes precedence over

a. a provision in a state constitution or statute only.
b. a state supreme court decision only.
c. a state constitution, statute, and court decision.
d. none of the above.

___ **7.** Case law includes interpretations of federal and state

a. administrative rules and statutes only.
b. constitutions only.
c. administrative rules, statutes, and constitutions.
d. none of the above.

____ **8.** Civil law concerns

a. disputes between persons, and between persons and their governments.
b. only laws that define, describe, regulate, and create rights and duties.
c. only laws that establish methods for enforcing rights.
d. wrongs committed against society for which society demands redress.

____ **9.** Matt is a judge. To reason by analogy, Matt compares the facts in one case to

a. the facts in another case.
b. the defendant's arguments.
c. the plaintiff's hypothetical.
d. none of the above.

____ **10.** A concurring opinion, written by one of the judges who decides a case before a multi-judge panel, is

a. an opinion that is written for the entire court.
b. an opinion that outlines only the views of the majority.
c. a separate opinion that agrees with the court's ruling but for different reasons.
d. a separate opinion that does not agree with court's ruling.

SHORT ESSAY QUESTIONS

1. What is the primary function of law?

2. What is *stare decisis*? Why is it important?

ISSUE SPOTTERS

(Answers at the Back of the Book)

1. Under what circumstance might a judge rely on case law to determine the intent and purpose of a statute?

2. The First Amendment provides protection for the free exercise of religion. A state legislature enacts a law that outlaws all religions that do not derive from the Judeo-Christian tradition. Is this law valid within that state? Why or why not?

3. What is included in the citation of a case?

SPECIAL INFORMATION FOR CPA CANDIDATES

Those students planning to sit for the CPA examination will find it most helpful to learn, from the introductory material in this chapter, the terms that designate the different parties to a lawsuit. The general background provided in this chapter is, of course, helpful in understanding the specific concepts and principles set out in subsequent chapters. For that reason—and because much of that material includes information that a successful CPA candidate is expected to know—the background in this chapter is important.

Regarding general preparation for the examination—or for any exam, including ones in this course—CPA candidates and other students may find it helpful to review the significant material weekly. For concepts and principles that will be tested, some students find it helpful to make flashcards. Those cards can be reviewed weekly, together with whatever notes have been taken, and the relevant sections of this study guide.

Chapter 2
Courts and Alternative Dispute Resolution

WHAT THIS CHAPTER IS ABOUT

This chapter explains which courts have power to hear what disputes and when. The chapter also covers alternative dispute resolution, including online dispute resolution. Alternatives to litigation can be as binding to the parties as a court decree.

CHAPTER OUTLINE

I. THE JUDICIARY'S ROLE IN AMERICAN GOVERNMENT

Under the power of judicial review, the courts can decide whether the laws or actions of the executive branch and the legislative branch are constitutional.

II. BASIC JUDICIAL REQUIREMENTS

A. JURISDICTION

To hear a case, a court must have jurisdiction over (1) the defendant or the property involved and (2) the subject matter.

1. Jurisdiction over Persons or Property

A court has *in personam* (personal) jurisdiction over persons within the court's geographic area. Long arm statutes permit courts to exercise jurisdiction over persons outside that area who have *minimum contacts* within it (e.g., do business there). A court has *in rem* jurisdiction over property within its area.

2. Jurisdiction over Subject Matter

A court of general jurisdiction can decide virtually any type of case. A court's jurisdiction may be limited by the subject of a suit, the amount of money in controversy, or whether a proceeding is a trial or appeal.

3. Jurisdiction of the Federal Courts

a. Federal Questions

Any suit based on the Constitution, a treaty, or a federal law can originate in a federal court.

b. Diversity of Citizenship

Federal jurisdiction covers cases involving (1) citizens of different states, (2) a foreign government and citizens of a state or of different states, or (3) citizens of a state and citizens or subjects of a foreign government. The amount in controversy must be more than $75,000.

4. Exclusive v. Concurrent Jurisdiction

Exclusive: when cases can be tried only in federal courts or only in state courts. Concurrent: When both federal and state courts can hear a case.

B. JURISDICTION IN CYBERSPACE

Whether a court can compel the appearance of a party outside the geographic area of the court's jurisdiction depends on the amount of business the party transacts over the Internet with parties within the court's area ("sliding scale" test). Internationally, the minimum contacts test mentioned above generally applies.

C. VENUE

Venue is concerned with the most appropriate location for a trial.

D. STANDING TO SUE

Standing is the interest (injury or threat) that a plaintiff has in a case. A plaintiff must have standing to bring a suit, and the controversy must be justiciable (real, as opposed to hypothetical or purely academic).

III. THE STATE AND FEDERAL COURT SYSTEMS

A. STATE COURT SYSTEMS

1. Trial Courts

Trial courts are courts in which trials are held and testimony is taken.

2. Appellate Courts

Courts that hear appeals from trial courts look at *questions of law* (what law governs a dispute) but not *questions of fact* (what occurred in the dispute), unless a trial court's finding of fact is clearly contrary to the evidence. Decision of a state's highest court on state law is final.

B. THE FEDERAL COURT SYSTEM

1. U.S. District Courts

The federal equivalent of a state trial court of general jurisdiction. There is at least one federal district court in every state. Other federal trial courts include the U.S. Tax Court and the U.S. Bankruptcy Court.

2. U.S. Courts of Appeals

The U.S. (circuit) courts of appeals for twelve of the circuits hear appeals from the federal district courts located within their respective circuits. The court of appeals for the thirteenth circuit (the federal circuit) has national jurisdiction over certain cases.

3. United States Supreme Court

The highest level of the federal court system. The Supreme Court can review any case decided by any of the federal courts of appeals, and it has authority over some cases decided in state courts.

4. How Cases Reach the Supreme Court

To appeal a case to the Supreme Court, a party asks for a writ of *certiorari*. Whether the Court issues the writ is within its discretion.

IV. ALTERNATIVE DISPUTE RESOLUTION (ADR)

A. NEGOTIATION

Parties come together informally, with or without attorneys, to try to settle or resolve their differences without involving independent third parties. Forms of ADR associated with negotiation include—

1. Mini-trial

A private proceeding in which attorneys briefly argue each party's case. A third party indicates how a court would likely decide the issue.

2. Early Neutral Case Evaluation

Parties select a neutral third party (generally an expert) to evaluate their positions, with no hearing and no discovery. The evaluation is a basis for negotiating a settlement.

3. **Summary Jury Trial (SJT)**
Like a mini-trial, but a jury renders a nonbinding verdict. Negotiations follow. If no settlement is reached, either side can seek a full trial.

4. **Conciliation**
A conciliator assists disputing parties in negotiating, communicating offers, etc. Conciliators sometimes recommend solutions.

B. MEDIATION
Parties come together informally with a mediator, who is expected to propose solutions. A mediator is often an expert in a particular field.

C. ARBITRATION
An arbitrator—the third party hearing the dispute—decides the dispute. If the parties agree, the decision may be legally binding.

1. **Arbitration and the Courts**
Many courts require parties to try to settle their differences through arbitration before going to trial. The arbitrator's decision is not binding—if either party rejects the award, the case goes to trial.

2. **The Arbitration Process**
At an arbitration hearing, the parties make their arguments, present evidence, and call and examine witnesses, and the arbitrator makes a decision. The decision is called an **award,** even if no money is involved.

3. **Arbitration Clauses**
Disputes are often arbitrated because of an arbitration clause in a contract entered into before the dispute. Courts enforce such clauses.

4. **Arbitration Statutes**
Most states have statutes under which arbitration clauses are enforced. The Federal Arbitration Act (FAA) enforces arbitration clauses in contracts involving interstate commerce.

D. PROVIDERS OF ADR SERVICES
ADR services are provided by government agencies and private organizations, such as the American Arbitration Association and JAMS/Endispute.

V. ONLINE DISPUTE RESOLUTION
Many Web sites offer online dispute resolution (ODR) services to help resolve small- to medium-sized business liability claims.

A. WHAT LAW APPLIES IN AN ODR PROCEEDING?
Most ODR services do not apply the law of a specific jurisdiction. Results are based on general, common legal principles.

B. NEGOTIATION AND MEDIATION SERVICES

1. **Online Negotiation**
A settlement may be negotiated through blind bidding: one party submits an offer to be shown to the other party if it falls within a previously agreed range. There is a limited time to respond.

2. **Mediation Providers—SquareTrade**
SquareTrade resolves, as part of a free pilot program, disputes involving $100 or more between eBay customers. SquareTrade also resolves other disputes related to online transactions, using software to walk participants through a step-by-step resolution process.

C. ARBITRATION PROGRAMS

1. **Internet Corporation for Assigned Names and Numbers (ICANN)**
   The federal government set up ICANN as a nonprofit corporation to oversee the distribution of domain names. ICANN has issued rules and authorized organizations to resolve related disputes.

2. **Resolution Forum, Inc. (RFI)**
   RFI, a nonprofit entity associated with the Center for Legal Responsibility at South Texas College of Law, offers arbitration in an online conference room via a standard browser, using a password.

3. **Virtual Magistrate Project (VMAG)**
   VMAG resolves disputes involving users of online systems; victims of wrongful messages, postings and files; and system operators subject to complaints or similar demands. Online-related contract, intellectual property, property, and tort disputes. The goal is resolution within seventy-two hours. Appeal of a result may be made to a court.

VI. INTERNATIONAL DISPUTE RESOLUTION

To protect themselves, parties to international contracts may include special clauses, including a forum-selection clause (stating which jurisdiction will hear a dispute), a choice-of-law clause (stating which law applies), and an arbitration clause (stating that a dispute must go first to arbitration).

TRUE-FALSE QUESTIONS

(Answers at the Back of the Book)

____ 1. Under a long arm statute, a state court can compel someone outside the state to appear in the court.

____ 2. Doing substantial business in a jurisdiction over the Internet can be enough to support a court's jurisdiction over a nonresident defendant.

____ 3. The United States Supreme Court is the final authority for any case decided by a state court.

____ 4. Suits involving federal questions originate in federal district courts.

____ 5. Most lawsuits go to trial.

____ 6. In mediation, a mediator makes a decision on the matter in dispute.

____ 7. A party to an arbitration agreement may never be compelled to arbitrate a dispute.

____ 8. The jury verdict, in a summary jury trial, is binding.

____ 9. A major similarity between negotiation and mediation is that no third parties are involved.

____ 10. In binding arbitration, an arbitrator's decision is usually the final word.

FILL-IN QUESTIONS

(Answers at the Back of the Book)

Courts of original jurisdiction are ________________ (trial/reviewing) courts. Courts of appellate jurisdiction are ________________ (trial/reviewing) courts. Trial courts resolve disputes through determining ________________ (factual issues/the law) and applying ________________ (the facts to the law/ the law to the facts). Reviewing courts most commonly reverse cases on the basis of errors ________________ (of law but not of fact/of fact and of law) committed by lower courts within the same system.

MULTIPLE-CHOICE QUESTIONS

(Answers at the Back of the Book)

___ 1. Bob, who lives in Texas, advertises his business on the Web. Bob's page receives hundreds of "hits" by residents of Ohio. If a resident of Ohio files a suit against Bob in an Ohio state court, the court can compel Bob to appear, under the "sliding scale" test, if

a. Bob conducted substantial business with Ohio residents at his Web site.
b. there was any interactivity with any Ohio resident at Bob's Web site.
c. Bob's Web site was only a passive ad.
d. any of the above.

___ 2. General Business, Inc. (GBI), has its offices in Virginia, but owns property in Maryland, where Ann files a suit against GBI concerning that property. In this suit, Maryland has

a. diversity jurisdiction.
b. *in personam* jurisdiction.
c. *in rem* jurisdiction.
d. no jurisdiction.

___ 3. National Service Corporation was incorporated in Delaware, has its main office in California, and does business in New York. National is subject to the jurisdiction of

a. Delaware, California, or New York.
b. Delaware or California, but not New York.
c. Delaware or New York, but not California.
d. California or New York, but not Delaware.

___ 4. Ace Manufacturing, Inc., loses its suit against Best Products, Inc., and files an appeal. The appellate court is most likely to review the trial court's

a. application of the law.
b. consideration of the credibility of the evidence.
c. findings of fact.
d. interpretation of the conduct of the witnesses.

___ 5. The United States Supreme Court is required to hear John's suit against Kay if

a. it comes from a federal court.
b. it is an appeal.
c. John lost in a lower court.
d. none of the above.

___ 6. In Carol's suit against Don, before going to trial, the parties meet, with their attorneys, to try to resolve the dispute without a third party. This is

a. arbitration.
b. litigation.
c. mediation.
d. negotiation.

___ 7. Pat and Don submit their dispute to binding arbitration. A court can set aside the arbitrator's award if

a. Don is not satisfied with the award.
b. Pat is not satisfied with the award.
c. the award involves at least $75,000.
d. the award violates public policy.

____ 8. Small Business Company submits a claim against Medium Market Supplier, Inc., to an online dispute resolution forum. An appeal of this dispute may be made to a court by

a. Small only.
b. Medium only.
c. Small and Medium together only.
d. Small or Medium.

____ 9. Ann sues Carla in a state trial court. Ann loses the suit. If Ann wants to appeal, the most appropriate court in which to file the appeal is

a. the state appellate court.
b. the nearest federal district court.
c. the nearest federal court of appeals.
d. the United States Supreme Court.

____ 10. In Sara's suit against Tim, their attorneys present the case to a judge and jury. The jury renders an advisory verdict. The judge then meets with the parties to encourage a settlement. This is

a. a mini-trial.
b. a summary jury trial.
c. early neutral case evaluation.
d. mediation.

SHORT ESSAY QUESTIONS

1. What is jurisdiction? How does jurisdiction over a person or property differ from subject matter jurisdiction?

2. What permits a court to exercise jurisdiction based on contacts over the Internet?

ISSUE SPOTTERS

(Answers at the Back of the Book)

1. Ron wants to sue Art's Supply Company for Art's failure to deliver supplies that Ron needed to prepare his work for an appearance at a local Artists Fair. What must Ron establish before a court will hear the suit?

2. Carlos, a citizen of California, is injured in an automobile accident in Arizona. Alex, the driver of the other car, is a citizen of New Mexico. Carlos wants Alex to pay Carlos's $125,000 in medical expenses and car repairs. Can Carlos sue in federal court?

3. Jay is fired from his job and sues his employer. Jay loses the trial, and he appeals. The reviewing court affirms the decision of the trial court. Jay wants to appeal to the United States Supreme Court. Can the Supreme Court refuse to hear the case?

SPECIAL INFORMATION FOR CPA CANDIDATES

The procedural steps in a civil trial in an American court are not specifically tested on the CPA examination. A general understanding of the legal system will prove helpful, however, to comprehending other materials that are tested on the exam.

Chapter 3
Court Procedures

WHAT THIS CHAPTER IS ABOUT

After the decision to take a dispute to court, one of the most important parts of the judicial process is the application of procedural rules in the case. The goal of this chapter is to outline what happens before, during, and after a civil trial.

CHAPTER OUTLINE

I. PROCEDURAL RULES

The Federal Rules of Civil Procedure govern trials in federal district court. Each state has its own rules of procedure that apply in its courts, as well as to the federal courts within the state.

II. CONSULTING WITH AN ATTORNEY

The time and expense of litigation are important considerations when deciding what legal course to pursue. Attorney fees can be fixed, may accrue on an hourly or a contingency basis, or may be set by a judge.

III. PRETRIAL PROCEDURES

A. THE PLEADINGS

The pleadings inform each party of the claims of the other and specify the issues in the case. They include the complaint and answer (and counterclaim and reply).

1. The Plaintiff's Complaint

Filed by the plaintiff with the clerk of the trial court (with the proper venue). The complaint contains (1) a statement alleging the facts necessary for the court to take jurisdiction, (2) a short statement of the facts necessary to show that the plaintiff is entitled to a remedy, and (3) a statement of the remedy the plaintiff is seeking.

2. Service of Process

The complaint is delivered to the defendant, with a summons. The summons tells the defendant to answer the complaint and file a copy of the answer with the court and the plaintiff within a specified time (usually twenty to thirty days). Corporations receive service through their officers or registered agents.

3. The Defendant's Response to the Complaint

a. Answer

An answer admits the allegations in the complaint or denies them and sets out any defenses.

1) Affirmative Defense

Exists when the defendant admits the truth of the complaint but raises new facts to dismiss the action (for example, the time period for raising the claim has passed).

2) Counterclaim

The defendant's claim against the plaintiff, who will have to answer it with a reply, which has the same characteristics as an answer.

b. **Motion to Dismiss**
This motion alleges that even if the facts in the complaint are true, their legal consequences are such that there is no reason to go on with the suit and no need for the defendant to present an answer.

1) **Denial of the Motion**
If the court denies the motion, and the defendant does not file a further pleading, a judgment will be entered for the plaintiff.

2) **Grant of the Motion**
If the court grants the motion, the defendant is not required to answer the complaint. If the plaintiff does not file an amended complaint, a judgment will be entered for the defendant.

c. **No Response**
Results in a default judgment for the plaintiff (who is awarded the relief sought in the complaint).

B. DISMISSALS AND JUDGMENTS BEFORE TRIAL

1. **Motion to Dismiss**
(See above.) Either party may file a motion to dismiss if they have agreed to settle the case. A court may file such a motion on its own.

2. **Motion for Judgment on the Pleadings**
Any party can file this motion (after the complaint, answer, and any counterclaim and reply have been filed), when no facts are disputed and only questions of law are at issue. A court may consider only those facts stated in the pleadings.

3. **Motion for Summary Judgment**
Any party can file this motion, if there is no disagreement about the facts and the only question is which laws apply to those facts. A court can consider evidence outside the pleadings (for example, sworn statements by witnesses).

C. DISCOVERY

1. **What Discovery Is**
The process of obtaining information from the opposing party or from witnesses. Privileged material is safeguarded and only relevant matters are discoverable.

a. **Depositions**
Sworn testimony, recorded by a court official. Can be used as testimony, if a witness is unavailable, or to impeach (challenge the credibility of) a party or witness who testifies differently at trial.

b. **Interrogatories**
A series of written questions for which written answers are prepared and signed under oath. Interrogatories are directed to the plaintiff or the defendant.

c. **Request for Admissions**
A written request to a party for an admission of the truth of matters relating to the trial. Any matter admitted is considered to be true.

d. **Request for Documents, Objects, and Entry on Land**
A written request to examine documents and other items not in the party's possession.

e. **Request for Examinations**
Granted when a party's physical or mental condition is in question.

2. **What Discovery Does**
Allows both parties to learn as much as they can about what to expect at a trial and helps to narrow the issues so that trial time is spent on the main questions.

D. PRETRIAL CONFERENCE

After discovery, the attorneys may meet with the judge to discuss resolving the case or at least to clarify the issues and agree on such things as the number of expert witnesses or the admissibility of certain types of evidence.

E. JURIES

1. **The Right to a Jury Trial**
The Seventh Amendment to the U.S. Constitution guarantees the right to a jury trial for cases at law in federal courts when the amount in controversy exceeds $20. Most states have similar guarantees in their own constitutions (with a higher dollar-amount). The right to a trial by jury does not have to be exercised.

2. **Jury Selection**
Most civil matters can be heard by six-person juries. Some trials must be heard by twelve persons.

a. ***Voir Dire***
The process by which a jury is selected. The parties' attorneys ask prospective jurors questions to determine whether any are biased or have a connection with a party or a witness.

b. **Challenges**

1) **Peremptory Challenge**
Asking, without providing a reason, that an individual not be sworn in as a juror.

2) **Challenge for Cause**
Asking, for a specific reason, that an individual not be sworn in as a juror.

IV. THE TRIAL

A. OPENING STATEMENTS

Each side sets out briefly his or her version of the facts and outlines the evidence that will be presented. The plaintiff goes first.

B. PRESENTATION OF EVIDENCE

1. **Burden of Proof**
In a civil case, a plaintiff must prove his or her case by a **preponderance of the evidence** (the claim is more likely to be true than the defendant's). Some claims (such as fraud) must be proved by **clear and convincing evidence** (the truth of the claim is highly probable). Evidence includes the testimony of witnesses.

2. **Admissible Evidence**
Evidence that is relevant to the matter in question (tends to prove or disprove a fact in question or to establish that a fact or action is more probable or less probable than it would be without the evidence).

3. **Inadmissible Evidence**
Relevant evidence whose probative value is substantially outweighed by other considerations (the issue has been proved or disproved, or the evidence would mislead the jury, or cause the jury to decide the issue on an emotional basis). Hearsay is not admissible.

4. **Examination of Witnesses**

a. **Plaintiff's Side of the Case**
After the opening statements, the plaintiff calls and questions the first witness (direct examination); the defendant questions the witness (cross-examination); the plaintiff questions the witness again (redirect examination); the defendant follows (recross-examination). The plaintiff's other witnesses are then called.

b. **Defendant's Side of the Case**

1) **Motion for a Directed Verdict**
At the conclusion of the plaintiff's case, the defendant can ask the judge to direct a verdict for the defendant on the ground that the plaintiff presented no evidence that would justify granting the plaintiff relief. The judge grants the motion if there is insufficient evidence to raise an issue of fact.

2) **Defendant's Witnesses**
If the motion is denied, the defendant calls the witnesses for his or her side of the case (and there is direct, cross-, redirect, and recross-examination). At the end of the defendant's case, either side can move for a directed verdict.

c. **Rebuttal**
At the conclusion of the defendant's case, the plaintiff can present a rebuttal (additional evidence to refute the defendant's case).

d. **Rejoinder**
The defendant can refute the plaintiff's rebuttal in a rejoinder.

C. CLOSING ARGUMENTS
Each side summarizes briefly his or her version of the facts, outlines the evidence that supports his or her case, and reveals the shortcomings of the points made by the other party. The plaintiff goes first.

D. JURY TRIALS

1. **Jury Instructions**
In a jury trial, the judge instructs (charges) the jury in the law that applies to the case. The jurors may disregard the facts as stated in the charge, but they are not free to ignore the statements of law. (A reviewing court ordinarily remands a case for a new trial if a judge misstates the law in the jury instructions.)

2. **Jury Verdict**
In a jury trial, the jury specifies the factual findings and the amount of damages to be paid by the losing party. This is the verdict. After it is announced, the trial is ended, and the jurors are discharged.

V. POSTTRIAL MOTIONS

A. MOTION FOR A JUDGMENT IN ACCORDANCE WITH THE VERDICT
The prevailing party usually files this motion.

B. MOTION FOR A NEW TRIAL
This motion is granted if the judge believes that the jury erred but that it is not appropriate to grant a judgment for the other side (for example, the jury verdict resulted from a misapplication of the law or misunderstanding of the evidence, or there is newly discovered evidence, misconduct by the parties, or error by the judge).

C. MOTION FOR JUDGMENT *N.O.V.*
The defendant can file this motion, if he or she previously moved for a directed verdict (*n.o.v.* is from the Latin *non obstante veredicto,* "notwithstanding the verdict;" federal courts use "motion for

judgment as a matter of law"). The standards for granting this motion are the same as those for granting a motion to dismiss or a motion for a directed verdict.

VI. THE APPEAL

A. FILING THE APPEAL

The papers to be filed include—

1. **Notice of Appeal**
   The appellant (the losing party—or the winning party, if that party is dissatisfied with the relief obtained) must file a notice of appeal with the clerk of the trial court within a certain period of time.

2. **Record on Appeal**
   The appellant files in the reviewing court: (1) the pleadings, (2) a transcript of the trial and copies of the exhibits, (3) the judge's rulings on the parties' motions, (4) the arguments of counsel, (5) the jury instructions, (6) the verdict, (7) the posttrial motions, and (8) the judgment order from which the appeal is taken.

3. **Brief**
   The appellant files with the abstract a brief, which contains (1) a short statement of the facts; (2) a statement of the issues; (3) the rulings by the trial court that the appellant contends are erroneous and prejudicial; (4) the grounds for reversal of the judgment; (5) a statement of the applicable law; and (6) arguments on the appellant's behalf, citing applicable statutes and relevant cases.

4. **Reply**
   The appellee (respondent) may file an answering brief.

B. APPELLATE REVIEW

Appellate courts do not usually reverse findings of fact unless they are contradicted by evidence at the trial. An appellate court can **affirm, reverse,** or **modify** a trial court's decision, or **remand** the case to the trial court for further proceedings consistent with the appellate court's opinion.

C. FURTHER APPEALS

If the reviewing court is an intermediate appellate court, the case may be appealed to the state supreme court. The state supreme court can affirm, reverse, or remand. If a federal question is involved, the case may be appealed to the United States Supreme Court, which may agree to hear it. Otherwise, the case is ended.

VII. ENFORCING THE JUDGMENT

The court can order a sheriff to seize property owned by the defendant and hold it until the defendant pays the judgment owed to the plaintiff. If the defendant fails to pay, the property can be sold at an auction and the proceeds given to the plaintiff, or the property can be transferred to the plaintiff in lieu of payment.

TRUE-FALSE QUESTIONS

(Answers at the Back of the Book)

___ **1.** Pleadings consist of a complaint, an answer, and a motion to dismiss.

___ **2.** In ruling on a motion for summary judgment, a court cannot consider evidence outside the pleadings.

___ **3.** At a pretrial conference, the parties and the judge may set ground rules for the trial.

___ **4.** An answer may admit or deny the statements or allegations in a complaint.

___ 5. Before a trial, if there are no issues of fact, and only questions of law, a court may grant a summary judgment.

___ 6. Only a losing party may appeal to a higher court.

___ 7. To obtain documents in the hands of an opposing party in anticipation of a trial, a party uses the appeal process.

___ 8. In a jury trial, the parties have a right to conduct *voir dire*.

___ 9. In a civil case, a plaintiff must establish his or her case beyond a reasonable doubt.

___ 10. A motion for a new trial will be granted if a jury verdict is the obvious result of a misapplication of the law.

FILL-IN QUESTIONS

(Answers at the Back of the Book)

A motion ______________________ (to dismiss/for summary judgment) alleges that even if the facts in the complaint are true, their legal consequences are such that there is no reason to go on with the suit and no need for the defendant to present an answer. A motion ______________________ (to dismiss/for judgment on the pleadings) is properly filed after the complaint, answer, and any counterclaim and reply have been filed, when no facts are disputed and only questions of law are at issue. A motion for ______________________ (summary judgment/a new trial) is proper if there is no disagreement about the facts and the only question is which laws apply to those facts.

MULTIPLE-CHOICE QUESTIONS

(Answers at the Back of the Book)

___ 1. Consolidated Industries, Inc., is considering filing a suit against First City Bank. In deciding whether to sue, the considerations include

a. the cost of going to court.
b. the patience to follow a case through the judicial system.
c. alternatives to settling the dispute without going to court.
d. all of the above.

___ 2. Digital Computer Corporation initiates a lawsuit against Eagle Distribution Company. Digital's complaint should contain

a. a statement alleging jurisdictional facts.
b. a statement of facts entitling the complainant to relief.
c. a statement asking for a specific remedy.
d. all of the above.

___ 3. In Alpha Company's suit against Beta Corporation, before the trial Alpha can obtain from Beta access to

a. all related documents in Beta's files.
b. everything in Beta's files.
c. nothing in Beta's files.
d. only material in Beta's files that Beta is willing to make available.

____ **4.** In Doug's suit against Erin, Erin would like to file a motion to dismiss. This motion may be filed

a. only if the court lacks jurisdiction.
b. only if the complaint does not state a claim for which relief can be granted.
c. if the court lacks jurisdiction or if the complaint does not state a claim for which relief can be granted.
d. none of the above.

____ **5.** Grant serves a complaint on Lee. Lee files a motion to dismiss. Lee will also need to file an answer to the complaint if

a. the motion to dismiss is granted.
b. the motion to dismiss is denied.
c. Grant files a motion for judgment on the pleadings.
d. none of the above.

____ **6.** Jill and Ken are involved in an automobile accident. Lyle is a passenger in Ken's car. Jill wants to ask Lyle, as a witness, some questions concerning the accident. Lyle's answers to the questions are given in

a. a deposition.
b. a response to interrogatories.
c. a response to a judge's request at a pretrial conference.
d. none of the above.

____ **7.** Ace Manufacturing, Inc., loses its suit against Best Products, Inc., and files an appeal. The appellate court is most likely to review the trial court's

a. application of the law.
b. consideration of the credibility of the evidence.
c. findings of fact.
d. interpretation of the conduct of the witnesses.

____ **8.** Ron files a suit against Sue. At the trial, Ron calls and questions Tim. What happens next?

a. Ron calls his second witness.
b. Ron questions Tim again.
c. Sue calls her first witness.
d. Sue questions Tim.

____ **9.** The jury returns a verdict against Gamma Services Corporation, in its suit against Omega Equipment, Inc. Gamma can file a motion for

a. a directed verdict.
b. a judgment on the pleadings.
c. a new trial or for a judgment notwithstanding the verdict.
d. summary judgment.

____ **10.** ABC Sales Company wins its suit against Delta Products, Inc. After the entry of a judgment, who can appeal?

a. ABC only
b. Delta only
c. Either ABC or Delta
d. None of the above

SHORT ESSAY QUESTIONS

1. What is the primary consideration in deciding whether to settle a dispute or take the dispute to court?

2. What evidence is, and what evidence is not, admissible in a trial?

ISSUE SPOTTERS

(Answers at the Back of the Book)

Pat contracted with Dean to deliver a quantity of computers to Pat's Computer Store. They disagree over the amount, the delivery date, the price, and the quality.

1. At the trial, after Pat calls her witnesses, offers her evidence, and otherwise presents her side of the case, Dean has at least two choices between courses of actions. What might Dean do?

2. After the trial, the judge issues a judgment that includes a grant of relief for Pat, but the relief is not as much as Pat wanted. Neither Pat nor Dean are satisfied with this result. Can either party—or both—appeal to a higher court?

3. The appellate court upholds the lower court's judgment and rules against Dean, who decides not to appeal further. How can Pat enforce the judgment?

SPECIAL INFORMATION FOR CPA CANDIDATES

The procedural steps in a civil trial in a U.S. court are not specifically tested on the CPA examination, but it is assumed that some of these details are familiar. Also, as noted in the previous chapter, a general understanding of the legal system will prove helpful to comprehending other materials that are tested on the exam. In particular, understanding the procedural course of a trial will help in reading the case excerpts in this textbook and in understanding the course of trials and judgments in general.

Chapter 4
Constitutional Authority to Regulate Business

WHAT THIS CHAPTER IS ABOUT

This chapter emphasizes that the Constitution is the supreme law in this country and discusses some of the constitutional limits on the law. Neither Congress nor any state may pass a law that conflicts with the Constitution. To sustain a federal law or action, a specific federal power must be found in the Constitution. A state has inherent power to enact laws that have a reasonable relationship to the welfare of its citizens.

CHAPTER OUTLINE

I. THE CONSTITUTIONAL POWERS OF GOVERNMENT

A. FEDERAL FORM OF GOVERNMENT

In a federal form of government (the United States), the states form a union and sovereign power is divided between a central authority and the states.

1. Relation between State and Federal Powers

Neither the national government nor a state government is superior to the other except within areas of exclusive authority granted under the Constitution. The courts determine the nature and scope of state and federal powers.

2. Relations among the States

a. The Privileges and Immunities Clauses

The Constitution (Article IV, Section 2) requires each state to provide the citizens of other states the same privileges and immunities it provides its own citizens. A state cannot treat nonresidents engaged in basic, essential activities differently without substantial justification. The Fourteenth Amendment prohibits a state from infringing on the privileges or immunities (such as the right to travel) of U.S. citizens.

b. The Full Faith and Credit Clause

The Constitution (Article IV, Section 1) requires that property and contract rights established by the law in one state be honored by other states.

B. THE SEPARATION OF POWERS

Under the Constitution, the legislative branch makes the laws, the executive branch enforces the laws, and the judicial branch interprets the laws. Each branch has some power to limit the actions of the other two.

C. THE COMMERCE CLAUSE

The Constitution (Article I, Section 8) gives Congress the power to regulate commerce among the states.

1. The Commerce Power Today

The national government can regulate every commercial enterprise in the United States. The United States Supreme Court has held, however, that this does not justify regulation of areas that have "nothing to do with commerce."

2. **The Regulatory Powers of the States**
States possess police powers (the right to regulate private activities to protect or promote the public order, health, safety, morals, and general welfare). Statutes covering almost every aspect of life have been enacted under the police powers.

3. **The "Dormant" Commerce Clause**
When state laws impinge on interstate commerce, courts balance the state's interest in regulating a certain matter against the burden on interstate commerce. State laws that *substantially* interfere with interstate commerce violate the commerce clause.

D. THE SUPREMACY CLAUSE AND FEDERAL PREEMPTION
The Constitution (Article IV) provides that the Constitution, laws, and treaties of the United States are the supreme law of the land. When federal and state laws are in direct conflict, the state law is rendered invalid. If Congress chooses to act exclusively in an area in which states have concurrent power, the federal law takes precedence over a state law on the same subject. It can be difficult to predict how a court will interpret congressional intent, however.

E. THE TAXING AND SPENDING POWERS

1. **The Taxing Power**
The Constitution (Article I, Section 8) gives Congress the power to levy taxes, but Congress may not tax some states and exempt others. Any tax that is a valid revenue-raising measure will be upheld.

2. **The Spending Power**
The Constitution (Article I, Section 8) gives Congress the power to spend the money it raises with its taxing power. This involves policy choices, with which taxpayers may disagree. Congress can spend funds to promote any objective, so long as it does not violate the Bill of Rights.

II. BUSINESS AND THE BILL OF RIGHTS
The first ten amendments to the Constitution protect individuals and businesses against some interference by the federal government. Under the due process clause of the Fourteenth Amendment, many rights also apply to the states.

A. FREEDOM OF SPEECH
The First Amendment guaranty of freedom of speech applies to the federal and state governments.

1. **Protected Speech**
Includes symbolic speech—nonverbal expressions, such as gestures, articles of clothing, some acts and so on. Governments can regulate the time, place, and manner of speech.

2. **Speech with Limited Protection**

   a. **Commercial Speech**
   A state restriction on commercial speech, such as advertising, is valid as long as it (1) seeks to implement a substantial government interest, (2) directly advances that interest, and (3) goes no further than necessary to accomplish its objective.

   b. **Corporate Political Speech**
   States can prohibit corporations from using corporate funds for independent expressions of opinion about political candidates.

3. **Unprotected Speech**

   a. **Defamatory Speech**
   Speech that harms the good reputation of another. Such speech can take the form of libel (if it is in writing) or slander (if it is oral).

b. **Lewd and Obscene Speech**
States can ban child pornography. One court has banned lewd speech and pornographic pinups in the workplace.

c. **"Fighting Words"**
Words that are likely to incite others to violence.

d. **Online Obscenity**
Attempts to regulate obscene materials on the Internet have been challenged, and some have been struck, as unconstitutional.

B. FREEDOM OF RELIGION

Under the First Amendment, the government may not establish a religion (the establishment clause) nor prohibit the exercise of religion (the free exercise clause).

1. **The Establishment Clause**
The government cannot show a preference for one religion over another, but must accommodate all religions. Sunday "closing laws" (restrictions on commercial acts on Sunday) have been upheld on the ground it is a legitimate government function to provide a day of rest.

2. **The Free Exercise Clause**
A law that infringes on the free exercise of religion in public places must be justified by a compelling state interest. Employers must reasonably accommodate the religious practices of their employees.

C. SEARCHES AND SEIZURES

Under the Fourth Amendment, law enforcement and other government officers cannot conduct unreasonable searches or seizures.

1. **Search Warrant**
An officer must obtain a search warrant before searching or seizing private property. It must describe what is to be searched or seized.

a. **Probable Cause**
To obtain a warrant, the officer must convince a judge that there is **probable cause** (evidence that would convince a reasonable person a search or seizure is justified).

b. **General and Neutral Enforcement Plan**
To obtain a warrant to inspect business premises, government inspectors must have probable cause, but the standard is different: a general and neutral enforcement plan is enough.

2. **No Search Warrant**
No warrant is required for seizures of spoiled or contaminated food or searches of businesses in highly regulated industries. General manufacturing is not considered a highly regulated industry.

D. SELF-INCRIMINATION

Under the Fifth Amendment, no person can be compelled to give testimony that might subject him or her to a criminal prosecution.

1. **Sole Proprietors**
Individuals who own their own businesses and have not incorporated cannot be compelled to produce their business records.

2. **Partnerships and Corporations**
Partnerships and corporations *can* be compelled to produce their business records, even if the records incriminate the persons who constitute the business entity.

III. DUE PROCESS AND EQUAL PROTECTION

A. DUE PROCESS

Both the Fifth and the Fourteenth Amendments provide that no person shall be deprived "of life, liberty, or property, without due process of law."

1. Procedural Due Process

Any government decision to take away the life, liberty, or property of an individual must include procedural safeguards to ensure fairness.

2. Substantive Due Process

Substantive due process focuses on the content (substance) of legislation.

a. Compelling Interest Test

A statute can restrict an individual's fundamental right (such as all First Amendment rights) only if the statute promotes a compelling or overriding governmental interest.

b. Rational Basis Test

Restrictions on business activities must relate rationally to a legitimate government purpose. Most business regulations qualify.

B. EQUAL PROTECTION

The Fourteenth Amendment prohibits a state from denying any person "the equal protection of the laws." The due process clause of the Fifth Amendment applies the equal protection clause to the federal government.

1. What Equal Protection Means

Equal protection means that the government must treat similarly situated individuals in a similar manner. If a law distinguishes among individuals, the basis for the distinction (classification) is examined.

a. Strict Scrutiny

A law that inhibits some persons' exercise of a fundamental right or a classification based on a suspect trait must be necessary to promote a compelling state interest.

b. Intermediate Scrutiny

Laws using classifications based on gender or legitimacy must be substantially related to important government objectives.

c. The "Rational Basis" Test

In matters of economic or social welfare, the classification will be considered valid if there is any conceivable rational basis on which it might relate to any legitimate government interest.

2. The Difference between Substantive Due Process and Equal Protection

A law that limits the liberty of *all* persons to do something may violate substantive due process. A law that limits the liberty of only *some* persons may violate equal protection.

C. PRIVACY RIGHTS

There is no specific guarantee of this right, but it is derived from guarantees in the First, Third, Fourth, Fifth, and Ninth Amendments. There are a number of federal statutes that protect privacy in certain areas.

TRUE-FALSE QUESTIONS

(Answers at the Back of the Book)

___ 1. A federal form of government is one in which a central authority holds all power.

___ 2. The president can hold acts of Congress and of the courts unconstitutional.

___ 3. Congress can regulate any activity that substantially affects commerce.

___ 4. A state law that substantially impinges on interstate commerce is unconstitutional.

___ 5. When there is a direct conflict between a federal law and a state law, the federal law is invalid.

___ 6. If a tax is reasonable, it is within the federal taxing power.

___ 7. The Bill of Rights protects individuals against various types of interference by the federal government only.

___ 8. Any restriction on commercial speech is unconstitutional.

___ 9. Due process and equal protection are different terms for the same thing.

___ 10. A right to privacy is not specifically guaranteed in the U.S. Constitution.

FILL-IN QUESTIONS

(Answers at the Back of the Book)

Police power is possessed by the ______________________ (federal government/states). Police power refers to the right of the ______________________ (federal government/states) to regulate private activities to protect or promote the public order, health, safety, morals, and general welfare. Building codes, licensing requirements, and many other ______________________ (federal/state) statutes have been enacted under the police power.

MULTIPLE-CHOICE QUESTIONS

(Answers at the Back of the Book)

___ 1. Of the three branches of the federal government provided by the Constitution, the branch that makes the laws is

a. the administrative branch.
b. the executive branch.
c. the judicial branch.
d. the legislative branch.

___ 2. Under the commerce clause, Congress can regulate

a. any commercial activity in the United States.
b. any noncommercial activity in the United States.
c. both a and b.
d. none of the above.

___ 3. A business challenges a state law in court, claiming that it unlawfully interferes with interstate commerce. The court will consider

a. only the state's interest in regulating the matter.
b. only the burden that the law places on interstate commerce.
c. the state's interest in regulating the matter and the burden that the law places on interstate commerce.
d. none of the above.

___ **4.** A state statute that bans corporations from making political contributions individuals can make is likely unconstitutional under

a. the commerce clause.
b. the First Amendment.
c. the supremacy clause.
d. none of the above.

___ **5.** A state statute that bans certain advertising practices to prevent consumers from being misled is likely unconstitutional under

a. the commerce clause.
b. the First Amendment.
c. the supremacy clause.
d. none of the above.

___ **6.** Procedures that are used to decide whether to take life, liberty, or property are the focus of constitutional provisions covering

a. equal protection.
b. procedural due process.
c. substantive due process.
d. the right to privacy.

___ **7.** A law that limits the liberty of all persons to engage in a certain activity may violate constitutional provisions covering

a. equal protection.
b. procedural due process.
c. substantive due process.
d. the right to privacy.

___ **8.** A law that restricts most vendors from doing business in a heavily trafficked area might be upheld under constitutional provisions covering

a. equal protection.
b. procedural due process.
c. substantive due process.
d. the right to privacy.

___ **9.** Congress enacts a law covering airports. If a state enacts a law that directly conflicts with this federal law

a. both laws are valid.
b. neither law is valid.
c. the federal law takes precedence.
d. the state law takes precedence.

___ **10.** Under the First Amendment, protected speech includes

a. dissemination of obscene materials.
b. "fighting words."
c. speech that harms the good reputation of another.
d. none of the above.

SHORT ESSAY QUESTIONS

1. What is the effect of the supremacy clause?

2. What is the significance of the commerce clause?

ISSUE SPOTTERS

(Answers at the Back of the Book)

1. Can a state, in the interest of energy conservation, ban all advertising by power utilities if conservation could be accomplished by less restrictive means? Why or why not?

2. Would a state law imposing a fifteen-year term of imprisonment without allowing a trial on all businesspersons who appear in their own television commercials be a violation of substantive due process? Would it violate procedural due process?

3. Would it be a violation of equal protection for a state to impose a higher tax on out-of-state companies doing business in the state than it imposes on in-state companies if the only reason for the tax is to protect the local firms from out-of-state competition?

SPECIAL INFORMATION FOR CPA CANDIDATES

In the past, most of the information covered in this chapter has not been included in the CPA examination. Those who sit for the exam are expected to know, however, that states base their regulation of professional licensing on their police powers. Test-takers will also be expected to know that the Securities Exchange Commission bases its regulation of securities on the Constitution's commerce clause.

When confronted with a multiple-choice question on the exam that covers these areas of the law, it is important to attempt to answer the question, even if it is not clear what the answer is. This is because in grading the multiple-choice portion of the exam, there is no deduction for wrong answers. Scores are based only on the total number of correct answers.

CUMULATIVE HYPOTHETICAL PROBLEM FOR UNIT ONE—INCLUDING CHAPTERS 1–4

(Answers at the Back of the Book)

Computer Data, Inc. (CDI), incorporated and based in California, signs a contract with Eagle Manufacturing Corporation, incorporated and based in Arizona, to make and sell customized software to Eagle for resale to consumers. CDI ships defective software to Eagle, which causes losses estimated at $100,000.

____ 1. Eagle and CDI enter into mediation. In mediation, the parties

a. may come to an agreement by mutual consent.
b. must accept a winner-take-all result.
c. settle their dispute without the assistance of a third party.
d. submit their dispute to a mediator for a legally binding decision.

____ 2. Eagle could file a suit against CDI in

a. Arizona only.
b. California only.
c. a federal court only.
d. Arizona, California, or a federal court.

___ 3. Eagle files a suit against CDI, seeking the amount of its losses as damages. Damages is a remedy

a. at law.
b. in equity.
c. at law or in equity, depending on how the plaintiff phrases its complaint.
d. at law or in equity, depending on whether there was any actual "damage."

___ 4. Federal authorities file charges against CDI, alleging that the shipment of defective software violated a federal statute. CDI asks the court to exercise its power of judicial review. This means that the court can review

a. the actions of the federal authorities and declare them excessive.
b. the charges against CDI and declare them unfounded.
c. the statute and declare it unconstitutional.
d. the totality of the situation and declare it unethical.

___ 5. Arizona enacts a statute that restricts certain kinds of advertising by Eagle and other businesses to protect consumers from being misled. A court would most likely hold this statute to be

a. an unconstitutional restriction of speech.
b. constitutional under the First Amendment.
c. justified by the need to protect individual rights.
d. necessary to protect state interests.

QUESTIONS ON THE FOCUS ON LEGAL REASONING FOR UNIT ONE—*KASKY V. NIKE, INC.*

(Answers at the Back of the Book)

___ 1. In *Kasky v. Nike, Inc.*, in the majority's opinion, commercial speech is distinguished from other speech in part by

a. its capacity to inform the public.
b. its contribution to the marketplace of ideas.
c. its inherent worth.
d. the identity of the speaker.

___ 2. In the dissent's opinion, commercial speech should be distinguished from other speech by

a. its capacity to inform the public.
b. its content.
c. its inherent worth in the marketplace of ideas.
d. the identity of the speaker.

___ 3. According to the majority, its holding regarding the defendant would have a chilling effect on

a. commercial speech only.
b. public debate only.
c. commercial speech and public debate.
d. none of the above.

QUESTIONS ON THE FOCUS ON ETHICS FOR UNIT ONE—ETHICS AND THE LEGAL ENVIRONMENT OF BUSINESS

(Answers at the Back of the Book)

___ **1.** The managers of Standard Products Company (SPC) evaluate its sale of possibly defective goods in terms of its ethical obligations, if any. In other words, the managers are considering SPC's

a. legal liability.
b. maximum profitability.
c. optimum profitability.
d. right or wrong behavior.

___ **2.** Obstacles to ethical business behavior by SPC's managers include

a. co-workers' dissent to unethical decisions.
b. legislative determinations as to what is in society's best interest.
c. the accountability of SPC to society for the firm's actions.
d. the collectivity of corporate decision making.

___ **3.** If SPC conducts its operations ethically, there will be a likely increase in its

a. future profits, goodwill, and reputation.
b. future profits only.
c. good will only.
d. reputation only.

Chapter 5
Torts and Cyber Torts

WHAT THIS CHAPTER IS ABOUT

The law of **torts** is concerned with wrongful conduct by one person that causes injury to another. *Tort* is French for "wrong." For acts that cause physical injury or that interfere with physical security and freedom of movement, tort law provides remedies, typically damages (money).

This chapter outlines intentional torts, including torts that are more specifically related to business, and negligence. Strict liability, another part of tort law, is outlined in Chapter 6.

CHAPTER OUTLINE

I. THE BASIS OF TORT LAW
Tort law recognizes that some acts are wrong because they cause physical injuries to persons or property, interfere with others' security or freedom, or harm certain intangible interests, such as privacy or reputation.

II. INTENTIONAL TORTS AGAINST PERSONS AND BUSINESS RELATIONSHIPS
Intentional torts involve acts that were intended or could be expected to bring about consequences that are the basis of the tort. A tortfeasor (one committing a tort) must intend to commit an act, the consequences of which interfere with the personal or business interests of another in a way not permitted by law.

A. ASSAULT AND BATTERY

1. Assault
An intentional act that creates in another person a reasonable apprehension or fear of immediate harmful or offensive contact.

2. Battery
An intentional and harmful or offensive physical contact. Physical injury need not occur. Whether the contact is offensive is determined by the reasonable person standard.

3. Compensation
A plaintiff may be compensated for emotional harm or loss of reputation resulting from a battery, as well as for physical harm.

4. Defenses to Assault and Battery

a. Consent
When a person consents to an act that damages him or her, there is generally no liability for the damage.

b. Self-Defense
An individual who is defending his or her life or physical well-being can claim self-defense.

c. Defense of Others
An individual can act in a reasonable manner to protect others who are in real or apparent danger.

d. **Defense of Property**
Reasonable force may be used in attempting to remove intruders from one's home, although force that is likely to cause death or great bodily injury can never be used just to protect property.

B. FALSE IMPRISONMENT

1. What False Imprisonment Is
The intentional confinement or restraint of another person without justification. The confinement can be accomplished through the use of physical barriers, physical restraint, or threats of physical force.

2. The Defense of Probable Cause
In some states, a merchant is justified in delaying a suspected shoplifter if the merchant has probable cause. The detention must be conducted in a reasonable manner and for only a reasonable length of time.

C. INTENTIONAL INFLICTION OF EMOTIONAL DISTRESS
Infliction of emotional distress is an intentional act that amounts to extreme and outrageous conduct resulting in severe emotional distress to another (a few states require physical symptoms). Repeated annoyance, with threats (such as extreme methods of debt collection), is one way to commit this tort.

D. DEFAMATION
Defamation is wrongfully hurting another's good reputation through false statements. Doing it orally is slander; doing it in writing is libel.

1. The Publication Requirement
The statement must be published (communicated to a third party). Anyone who republishes or repeats a defamatory statement is liable.

2. Types of False Utterances that Are Torts *Per Se*
Proof of injury is not required when one falsely states that another has a loathsome communicable disease, has committed improprieties while engaging in a profession or trade, or has committed or been imprisoned for a serious crime, or that an unmarried woman is unchaste.

3. Defenses to Defamation

a. **Truth**
The statement is true. It must be true in whole, not in part.

b. **Privileged Speech**
The statement is privileged: absolute (made in a judicial or legislative proceeding) or qualified (for example, made by one corporate director to another and was about corporate business).

c. **Public Figures**
The statement is about a public figure, made in a public medium, and related to a matter of general public interest. To recover damages, a public figure must prove a statement was made with actual malice (knowledge of its falsity or reckless disregard for the truth).

E. INVASION OF PRIVACY
Four acts qualify as invasions of privacy:

1. The use of a person's name, picture, or other likeness for commercial purposes without permission. (This is appropriation—see below.)
2. Intrusion on an individual's affairs or seclusion.
3. Publication of information that places a person in a false light.

4. Public disclosure of private facts about an individual that an ordinary person would find objectionable.

F. APPROPRIATION

The use of one person's name or likeness by another, without permission and for the benefit of the user, is appropriation. An individual's right to privacy includes the right to the exclusive use of his or her identity.

G. FRAUDULENT MISREPRESENTATION

Fraud is the use of misrepresentation and deceit for personal gain. Puffery (seller's talk) is not fraud. The elements of fraudulent misrepresentation—

1. **Misrepresentation** of material facts or conditions with knowledge that they are false or with reckless disregard for the truth.
2. **Intent** to induce another to rely on the misrepresentation.
3. **Justifiable reliance** by the deceived party.
4. **Damages** suffered as a result of reliance.
5. **Causal connection** between the misrepresentation and the injury.

H. WRONGFUL INTERFERENCE

Torts involving wrongful interference with another's business rights generally fall into the two categories outlined here.

1. **Wrongful Interference with a Contractual Relationship**
   This occurs when one party induces another to break a contract. Simply reaping the benefits of a broken contract is not enough. Elements include:
   a. A **contract** between two parties.
   b. A third party's **knowledge** of the contract.
   c. The third party's intentionally causing either of the two parties to **break the contract**. The third party's bad faith or harmful intent is immaterial, but the purpose of the interference must be to advance the third party's economic interest.
2. **Wrongful Interference with a Business Relationship**
   If there are two shoe stores in a mall, placing an employee of Store A in front of Store B to divert customers to Store A is the tort of wrongful interference with a business relationship (an unfair trade practice).
3. **Defenses to Wrongful Interference**
   A person is not liable if the interference is justified or permissible (such as bona fide competitive behavior).

III. INTENTIONAL TORTS AGAINST PROPERTY

A. TRESPASS TO LAND

This occurs if a person, without permission, enters onto, above, or below the surface of land owned by another; causes anything to enter onto the land; or remains on the land or permits anything to remain on it.

1. **Trespass Criteria, Rights, and Duties**
   Posted signs *expressly* establish trespass. Entering onto property to commit an illegal act *impliedly* does so. Trespassers are liable for any property damage. Owners may have a duty to post notice of any danger.

2. **Defenses against Trespass to Land**
Defenses against trespass include that the trespass was warranted or that the purported owner had no right to possess the land in question.

B. **TRESPASS TO PERSONAL PROPERTY**
Occurs when an individual unlawfully harms the personal property of another or interferes with an owner's right to exclusive possession and enjoyment. Defenses include that the interference was warranted.

C. **CONVERSION**

1. **What Conversion Is**
An act depriving an owner of personal property without the owner's permission and without just cause. Conversion is the civil side of crimes related to theft. Buying stolen goods is conversion.

2. **Defenses**
Defenses to conversion include that the purported owner does not own the property or does not have a right to possess it that is superior to the right of the holder. Necessity is also a defense.

D. **DISPARAGEMENT OF PROPERTY**
Disparagement of property occurs when economically injurious falsehoods are made about another's product or ownership of property. It is a general term for torts that can be specifically referred to as slander of quality (product) or slander of title (ownership of property).

IV. NEGLIGENCE

A. **THE ELEMENTS OF NEGLIGENCE**

1. **What Negligence Is**
Someone's failure to live up to a required duty of care, causing another to suffer injury. The breach of the duty must create a risk of certain harmful consequences, whether or not that was the intent.

2. **The Elements of Negligence**
(1) A duty of care, (2) breach of the duty of care, (3) damage or injury as a result of the breach, and (4) the breach causes the damage or injury.

B. **THE DUTY OF CARE AND ITS BREACH**

1. **The Reasonable Person Standard**
The duty of care is measured by the reasonable person standard (how a reasonable person would have acted in the same circumstances).

2. **Duty of Landowners**
Owners are expected to use reasonable care (guard against some risks and warn of others) to protect persons coming onto their property.

3. **Duty of Professionals**
A professional's duty is consistent with his or her knowledge, skill, and intelligence, including what is reasonable for that professional.

4. **Factors for Determining a Breach of the Duty of Care**
The nature of the act (whether it is outrageous or commonplace), the manner in which the act is performed (cautiously versus heedlessly), and the nature of the injury (whether it is serious or slight). Note: Failing to rescue a stranger in peril is *not* a breach of a duty of care.

C. THE INJURY REQUIREMENT AND DAMAGES

To recover damages (receive compensation), the plaintiff must have suffered some loss, harm, wrong, or invasion of a protected interest. Punitive damages (to punish the wrongdoer and deter others) may also be awarded.

D. CAUSATION

1. Causation in Fact

The breach of the duty of care must cause the injury—that is, "but for" the wrongful act, the injury would not have occurred.

2. Proximate Cause

There must be a connection between the act and the injury strong enough to justify imposing liability. Generally, the harm or the victim of the harm must have been foreseeable in light of all of the circumstances.

E. DEFENSES TO NEGLIGENCE

1. Assumption of Risk

A plaintiff who voluntarily enters into a risky situation, knowing the risk, cannot recover. This does not include a risk different from or greater than the risk normally involved in the situation.

2. Superseding Cause

A superseding intervening force breaks the connection between the breach of the duty of care and the injury or damage. Taking a defensive action (such as swerving to avoid an oncoming car) does not break the connection. Nor does someone else's attempt to rescue the injured party.

3. Contributory Negligence

In some states, a plaintiff cannot recover for an injury if he or she was negligent. The last-clear-chance doctrine allows a negligent plaintiff to recover if the defendant had the last chance to avoid the damage.

4. Comparative Negligence

In most states, the plaintiff's and the defendant's negligence is compared and liability prorated. Some states allow a plaintiff to recover even if his or her fault is greater than the defendant's. In many states, the plaintiff gets nothing if he or she is more than 50 percent at fault.

F. SPECIAL NEGLIGENCE DOCTRINES AND STATUTES

1. *Res Ipsa Loquitur*

If negligence is very difficult to prove, a court may infer it, and the defendant must prove he or she was *not* negligent. This is only if the event causing the harm is one that normally does not occur in the absence of negligence and is caused by something within the defendant's control.

2. Negligence *Per Se*

A person who violates a statute providing for a criminal penalty is liable when the violation causes another to be injured, if (1) the statute sets out a standard of conduct, and when, where, and of whom it is expected; (2) the injured person is in the class protected by the statute; and (3) the statute was designed to prevent the type of injury suffered.

3. "Danger Invites Rescue" Doctrine

A person who endangers another is liable for injuries to third persons who attempt to rescue the endangered party.

4. Special Negligence Statutes

Good Samaritan statutes protect those who aid others from being sued for negligence. Dram shop acts impose liability on bar owners for injuries caused by intoxicated persons who are served by those owners. A statute may impose liability on social hosts for acts of their guests.

V. CYBER TORTS

A. DEFAMATION ONLINE

Under the Communications Decency Act of 1996, Internet service providers (ISPs) are not liable for the defamatory remarks of those who use their services.

B. SPAM

Spam is junk e-mail. Some states ban or regulate its use, which may constitute trespass to personal property. The First Amendment may also limit what the government can do to restrict it.

TRUE-FALSE QUESTIONS

(Answers at the Back of the Book)

____ 1. To commit an intentional tort, a person must intend the consequences of his or her act or know with substantial certainty that certain consequences will result.

____ 2. A reasonable apprehension or fear of harmful or offensive contact at some time in the future is an assault.

____ 3. A defamatory statement must be communicated to a third party to be actionable.

____ 4. Puffery is fraud.

____ 5. Depriving an owner of personal property without permission and without just cause, to place it in another's service, is conversion.

____ 6. To determine whether a duty of care has been breached, a judge asks how he or she would have acted in the same circumstances.

____ 7. Disparagement of property is another term for appropriation.

____ 8. Bona fide competitive behavior can constitute wrongful interference with a contractual relationship.

____ 9. Internet service providers are not normally liable for the defamatory remarks of those who use their services.

____ 10. The government cannot regulate spam.

FILL-IN QUESTIONS

(Answers at the Back of the Book)

1. Basic defenses to ______________________________ (negligence/intentional torts) include comparative negligence, contributory negligence, and assumption of risk.

2. One who voluntarily and knowingly enters into a risky situation normally cannot recover damages. This is the ____ (defense of contributory negligence/defense of assumption of risk).

3. When both parties' failure to use reasonable care combines to cause injury, in some states the injured party's recovery is precluded by his or her own negligence. This is the ______________________________ (comparative/contributory) negligence doctrine.

4. When both parties' failure to use reasonable care combines to cause injury, in most states damages are reduced by a percentage that represents the degree of the plaintiff's negligence. This is the ______________________________ (comparative/contributory) negligence doctrine.

MULTIPLE-CHOICE QUESTIONS

(Answers at the Back of the Book)

___ **1.** Driving his car negligently, Paul crashes into a telephone pole. The pole falls, smashing through the roof of a house onto Karl, who is sitting inside. Karl dies. But for Paul's negligence, Karl would not have died. Regarding Karl's death, Paul's crash is the

a. cause in fact.
b. intervening cause.
c. proximate cause.
d. superseding cause.

___ **2.** Joe shoves Kay, who falls and suffers a concussion. This is an intentional tort

a. if Joe had a bad motive for shoving Kay.
b. if Joe intended to shove Kay.
c. if Kay was afraid of Joe.
d. only if Joe intended that Kay suffer a concussion.

___ **3.** Alan, the owner of Beta Computer Store, detains Cathy, a customer, whom Alan suspects of shoplifting. This is false imprisonment if

a. Alan detains Cathy for an unreasonably long time.
b. Cathy did not shoplift.
c. Cathy has probable cause to suspect Alan of deceit.
d. Cathy protests her innocence.

___ **4.** Best Box Company advertises so effectively that National Products, Inc., stops doing business with Average Packages Corporation. Best is liable for

a. appropriation.
b. wrongful interference with a business relationship.
c. wrongful interference with a contractual relationship.
d. none of the above.

___ **5.** Gil sends a letter to Holly in which he falsely accuses her of embezzling from her employer. This is defamation only if the letter is read by

a. any third person.
b. Gil.
c. Holly.
d. Holly's employer.

___ **6.** Internet Services, Inc. (ISI), is an Internet service provider. ISI does not create, but disseminates, a defamatory statement by Jill, its customer, about Ron. Liability for the remark may be imposed on

a. ISI and Jill.
b. ISI or Jill, but not both.
c. ISI only.
d. Jill only.

___ **7.** Lee, a salesperson for Midsize Corporation, causes a car accident while on business. Lee and Midsize are liable to all persons

a. who are injured.
b. who do not have insurance to pay for their injuries.
c. whose injuries could have been reasonably foreseen.
d. with whom Lee was doing business.

___ **8.** Fred drives across Gail's land. This is a trespass to land only if

a. Fred damages the land.
b. Fred does not have Gail's permission to drive on her land.
c. Fred makes disparaging remarks about Gail's land.
d. Gail is aware of Fred's driving on her land.

___ **9.** To protect its customers and other business invitees, Grocers Market must warn them of

a. hidden dangers.
b. obvious dangers.
c. hidden and obvious dangers.
d. none of the above.

___ **10.** Online Services Company (OSC) is an Internet service provider. Ads Unlimited, Inc., sends spam to OSC's customers, some of whom then cancel OSC's services. Ads Unlimited is liable for

a. battery.
b. conversion.
c. infliction of emotional distress.
d. trespass to personal property.

SHORT ESSAY QUESTIONS

1. What is a *tort*?

2. Identify and describe the elements of a cause of action based on negligence.

ISSUE SPOTTERS

(Answers at the Back of the Book)

1. Adam kisses the sleeve of Eve's blouse, to which she did not consent and which she finds offensive. Is Adam guilty of a tort?

2. If a student takes another student's business law textbook as a practical joke and hides it for several days before the final examination, has a tort been committed?

3. After less than a year in business, Superior Club surpasses Ordinary Club in number of members. Superior's marketing strategies attract many Ordinary members, who then change clubs. Does Ordinary have any recourse against Superior?

SPECIAL INFORMATION FOR CPA CANDIDATES

Usually, the CPA examination tests your knowledge of torts in such situations as the following:

- Liability for damages and injuries caused by defective products (see Chapter 6).
- Employers' liability for the torts of their employees (see Chapter 32).
- Liability for the torts of corporate officers and directors committed in the course of their corporate duties (see Chapter 37).
- Liability of auditors, accountants, and other professionals (see Chapter 52).

Chapter 6
Strict Liability and Product Liability

WHAT THIS CHAPTER IS ABOUT

Strict liability is liability for injury imposed for reasons other than fault. Manufacturers, processors, and sellers may be liable to consumers, users, and bystanders for physical harm or property damage caused by defective goods. This is **product liability**.

CHAPTER OUTLINE

I. STRICT LIABILITY

A. ABNORMALLY DANGEROUS ACTIVITIES

The basis for imposing strict liability on an abnormally dangerous activity is that the activity creates an extreme risk. Balancing the risk against the potential for harm, it is fair to ask the person engaged in the activity to pay for injury caused by that activity.

B. OTHER APPLICATIONS OF STRICT LIABILITY

A person who keeps a dangerous animal is strictly liable for any harm inflicted by the animal. A significant application of strict liability is in the area of product liability (discussed below).

II. PRODUCT LIABILITY

Product liability may be based on negligence, misrepresentation, or strict liability. It may also be based on warranty law (see Chapter 23).

A. PRODUCT LIABILITY BASED ON NEGLIGENCE

If the failure to exercise reasonable care in the making or marketing of a product causes an injury, the basis of liability is negligence.

1. **Manufacturer's Duty of Care**
   Due care must be exercised in designing, assembling, and testing a product; selecting materials; inspecting and testing products bought for use in the final product; and placing warnings on the label to inform users of dangers of which an ordinary person might not be aware.

2. **Privity of Contract between Plaintiff and Defendant Is Not Required**

3. **Violation of Statutory Duty**
   Manufacturers have statutory duties, such as those relating to labeling. Violation of a statutory duty may be negligence *per se* (see Chapter 5).

B. PRODUCT LIABILITY BASED ON MISREPRESENTATION

If misrepresentation causes injury, there may liability if it (1) is of a material fact, (2) is intended to induce a buyer's reliance, and (3) the buyer relies on it.

1. **Proof of Defects Not Required**
   Plaintiff does not have to show product was defective or malfunctioned.

2. **Fraudulent Misrepresentation**
   Occurs when misrepresentation is done knowingly or with reckless disregard for the facts (such as intentionally concealing defects).

3. **Nonfraudulent Misrepresentation**
Occurs when a merchant innocently misrepresents the character or quality of goods (the misrepresentation need not be done knowingly).

III. STRICT PRODUCT LIABILITY

A defendant may be held liable for the result of his or her act regardless of intention or exercise of reasonable care (see Chapter 5).

A. PUBLIC POLICY

Public policy assumes that (1) consumers should be protected from unsafe products, (2) manufacturers and distributors should not escape liability solely for lack of privity, and (3) sellers and lessors are in a better position to bear the cost of injuries caused by their products.

B. THE REQUIREMENTS FOR STRICT PRODUCT LIABILITY

Under the *Restatement (Second) of Torts*, Section 402A—

1. **Product Is in a Defective Condition When the Defendant Sells It**

2. **Defendant Is Normally in the Business of Selling the Product**

3. **Defect Makes the Product Unreasonably Dangerous**
A product may be so defective if either—

   a. **Product Is Dangerous beyond the Ordinary Consumer's Expectation**
   There may have been a flaw in the manufacturing process that led to some defective products being marketed, or a perfectly made product may not have had adequate warning on the label.

   b. **There Is a Less Dangerous, Economically Feasible Alternative that the Manufacturer Failed to Use**
   A manufacturer may have failed to design a safe product.

4. **Plaintiff Incurs Harm to Self or Property by Use of the Product**

5. **Defect Is the Proximate Cause of the Harm**

6. **Product Was Not Substantially Changed After It Was Sold**
Between the time the product was sold and the time of the injury.

C. PRODUCT DEFECTS

The *Restatement (Third) of Torts: Products Liability* categorizes defects as—

1. **Manufacturing Defects**
A manufacturing defect occurs when a product departs from its intended design even though all possible care was taken (strict liability).

2. **Design Defects**
A design defect exists when a foreseeable risk of harm posed by a product could have been reduced by use of a reasonable alternative design and the omission makes the product unreasonably unsafe. A court would consider such factors as consumer expectations and warnings.

3. **Warning Defects**
A warning defect happens when a foreseeable risk of harm posed by a product could have been reduced by providing a reasonable warning and the omission makes the product unreasonably unsafe. Factors include the content and comprehensibility of a warning, and the expected users.

D. MARKET-SHARE LIABILITY

Some courts hold that all firms that manufactured and distributed DES (diethylstilbestrol) during a certain period are liable for injuries in proportion to the firms' respective shares of the market.

E. OTHER APPLICATIONS OF STRICT PRODUCT LIABILITY

1. Who May Be Liable
Sellers of goods, including manufacturers, processors, assemblers, packagers, bottlers, wholesalers, distributors, and retailers. Suppliers of component parts and lessors may be liable for injuries caused by defective products.

2. Strict Liability Extends to Bystanders
All courts extend strict liability to cover injured bystanders (limited in some cases to those whose injuries are reasonably foreseeable).

IV. DEFENSES TO PRODUCT LIABILITY

A. ASSUMPTION OF RISK
In some states, this is a defense if (1) plaintiff knew and appreciated the risk created by the defect and (2) plaintiff voluntarily engaged in the risk, event though it was unreasonable to do so.

B. PRODUCT MISUSE
The use must not be the one for which the product was designed, and the misuse must not be reasonably foreseeable.

C. COMPARATIVE NEGLIGENCE (FAULT)
Most states consider a plaintiff's actions in apportioning liability.

D. COMMONLY KNOWN DANGERS
Failing to warn against such a danger is not ground for liability.

E. STATUTES OF LIMITATIONS
A statute of limitations provides that an action must be brought within a specified period of time after the cause of action accrues (after some damage occurs or after a harmed party discovers the damage).

F. STATUTES OF REPOSE
A statute of repose limits the time in which a suit can be filed. It runs from an earlier date and for a longer time than a statute of limitations.

G. TYPE OF INJURY OR LOSS
Some courts limit recovery to personal injuries. Recovery for economic loss is rarely available.

H. TYPE OF GOODS OR LACK OF RECOGNITION
Some states limit the application of strict liability to new goods. Some states refuse to recognize the doctrine of strict liability.

TRUE-FALSE QUESTIONS

(Answers at the Back of the Book)

___ 1. Strict liability is imposed for reasons other than fault.

___ 2. Under the doctrine of strict liability, a defendant is liable for the results of his or her acts only if he or she intended those results.

___ 3. A product liability suit may be based on a warranty theory.

___ 4. Product liability is imposed only if a defect in the design or construction of a product causes an injury.

___ 5. Suppliers are generally required to design products that are safe when misused or that include some protective device.

___ 6. Privity of contract between the plaintiff and defendant is required to bring a product liability suit based on negligence.

____ 7. One of the requirements for a product liability suit based on strict liability is a failure to exercise due care.

____ 8. In many states, the plaintiff's negligence is a defense that may be raised in a product liability suit based on strict liability.

____ 9. A manufacturer has a duty to warn about risks that are obvious or commonly known.

____ 10. Assumption of risk can be raised as a defense in a product liability suit.

FILL-IN QUESTIONS

(Answers at the Back of the Book)

Statutes of limitations and statutes of repose restrict the time within which an action may be brought. A statute of ________________ (limitations/repose) typically provides a specified period after a cause of action accrues within which an action must be brought. Sometimes the running of this period ________________ (does not begin until/ends when) the injured party discovers, or should have discovered, the injury. A statute of ________________ (limitations/repose) provides a time limit on filing a claim, whether or not a cause of action has accrued, so that a defendant will not be vulnerable to a lawsuit indefinitely. Usually, a statute of ________________ (limitations/repose) begins to run at an earlier date and runs for a longer time than a statute of ________________ (limitations/repose).

MULTIPLE-CHOICE QUESTIONS

(Answers at the Back of the Book)

____ 1. A bridge's design is defective and soon after completion it begins to sway in the wind. Everyone stays off, except Carl, who wants to show off. Carl falls from the bridge and sues its manufacturer, who can raise the defense of

a. assumption of risk.
b. commonly known danger.
c. product misuse.
d. none of the above.

____ 2. Sport Supplies sells a treadmill to John without warning him of the fact, known to Sport, that the safety shut-off device does not work. In using the treadmill, John discovers the defect. Later, while running on the treadmill, John's shoelace is caught in the gears, which do not shut off, and his foot is injured. If John sues Sport on the ground of strict liability in a jurisdiction that recognizes comparative negligence, Sport may be

a. entirely liable, because Sport was comparatively negligent.
b. partially liable, because Sport was comparatively negligent.
c. entirely liable, because John was comparatively negligent.
d. not liable, because John was comparatively negligent.

____ 3. SmithCo supplies Jones, Inc., with components for its products. Jones assembles the components and sells the assembled products to consumers. Lee buys and uses one of the products and is injured due to a defective component. In a suit based on strict liability, Lee may recover damages from

a. SmithCo only.
b. Jones only.
c. either SmithCo or Jones.
d. none of the above.

___ **4.** Standard Manufacturing Corporation makes appliances. To satisfy its liability for injuries to consumers harmed by defective Standard appliances, Standard can pass the costs on to

a. consumers in the form of higher prices.
b. other makers of appliances in the form of market-share liability.
c. suppliers in the form of kickbacks.
d. the government in the form of direct payments.

___ **5.** Alpha Products, Inc., makes bicycles. Carla is injured while riding an Alpha bike and files a suit against the maker for product liability based on misrepresentation. To succeed, Carla must show that

a. Alpha did not use due care with respect to making the bike.
b. Alpha misrepresented a material fact regarding the bike, on which Carla relied.
c. Carla did not abuse or misuse the bike.
d. Carla was in privity of contract with Alpha.

___ **6.** Kitchen Products, Inc. (KPI), makes knives. Jay is injured while using a KPI knife, and sues the maker for product liability based on negligence. KPI could successfully defend against the suit by showing that

a. Jay's injury resulted from a commonly known danger.
b. Jay misused the knife in a foreseeable way.
c. KPI did not sell the knife to Jay.
d. the knife was not altered after KPI sold it.

___ **7.** Standard Tools, Inc., makes and sells tools. Tina is injured as a result of using a Standard tool. Tina sues Standard for product liability based on strict liability. To succeed, Tina must prove that Standard

a. was in privity of contract with Tina.
b. did not use care with respect to the tool.
c. misrepresented a material fact regarding the tool on which Tina relied.
d. none of the above.

___ **8.** Yard Work, Inc., makes and sells garden tools. Under the *Restatement (Second) of Torts*, a tool could be unreasonably dangerous

a. only if, in making the tool, Yard Work failed to use a less dangerous but economically feasible alternative.
b. only if the tool is dangerous beyond the ordinary consumer's expectation.
c. if, in making the tool, Yard Work failed to use a less dangerous but economically feasible alternative or if the tool is dangerous beyond the ordinary consumer's expectation.
d. none of the above.

___ **9.** Fran is in Green's Grocery store when a bottle of Hi Cola on a nearby shelf explodes, injuring her. She can recover from the manufacturer of Hi Cola only if she can show that

a. she did not assume the risk of the explosive bottle of Hi Cola.
b. she intended to buy the explosive bottle of Hi Cola.
c. she was injured due to a defect in the product.
d. the manufacturer failed to use due care in making the bottle of Hi Cola.

___ **10.** Omega Electronics, Inc., designs and makes CD players. In a product liability suit based on negligence, Omega could be liable for violating its duty of care with respect to a player's

a. design only.
b. manufacture only.
c. design or manufacture.
d. none of the above.

SHORT ESSAY QUESTIONS

1. What distinguishes strict liability as a theory for recovery in a product liability case from other bases for recovery?

2. How defective must a product be to support a cause of action in strict liability?

ISSUE SPOTTERS

(Answers at the Back of the Book)

1. Delta Corporation makes tire rims, which it sells to Eagle Vehicles, Inc., to put on its cars. One set of rims is defective, which an inspection would reveal. Eagle does not inspect the rims. The car is sold to Fast Auto Sales. Greg buys the car, which is soon in an accident caused by the defective rims and in which Greg is injured. Is Eagle liable?

2. Real Chocolate Company makes a box of candy, which it sells to Sweet Things, Inc., a distributor. Sweet sells the box to a Tasty Candy store, where Jill buys it. Jill gives it to Ken, who breaks a tooth on a stone the same size and color of a piece of the candy. If Real, Sweet, and Tasty were not negligent, can they be liable for the injury?

3. Good Lock Company makes automobile door locks. Premier Motors Corporation installs the locks on Premier cars. Doug buys a Premier car. While driving home, Doug does not wear a seat belt. In a one-car accident, he is thrown from the car when the door flies open and is killed. In a suit based on strict liability, could Good and Premier claim that Doug's failure to wear a seat belt contributed to his death?

SPECIAL INFORMATION FOR CPA CANDIDATES

The CPA examination has traditionally tested on three kinds of product liability actions: (1) UCC warranties (see Chapter 23), (2) negligence, and (3) strict liability. In particular, in a negligence or strict liability action, remember that no privity of contract is required. Keep in mind that the negligence may occur at any stage in a product's development, manufacture, and sale. Review the elements for an action in strict product liability. Also, don't forget relevant defenses, including assumption of risk and foreseeable misuse.

Chapter 7
Intellectual Property and Internet Law

WHAT THIS CHAPTER IS ABOUT

Intellectual property consists of the products of intellectual, creative processes. Many of these products (such as inventions, books, software, movies, and songs) are protected by the law of trademarks, patents, copyrights, and related concepts. The first parts of this chapter outlines the laws that protect these products. The last part of this chapter covers the protection of intellectual property in cyberspace.

CHAPTER OUTLINE

I. TRADEMARKS AND RELATED PROPERTY

A. TRADEMARKS

The Lanham Act protects trademarks at the federal level. Many states also have statutes that protect trademarks.

1. What a Trademark Is

A distinctive mark, motto, device, or emblem that a manufacturer stamps, prints, or otherwise affixes to the goods it produces to distinguish them from the goods of other manufacturers.

2. The Federal Trademark Dilution Act of 1995

Prohibits **dilution** (unauthorized use of marks on goods or services, even if they do not compete directly with products whose marks are copied).

3. Trademark Registration

A trademark may be registered with a state or the federal government. Trademarks do not need to be registered to be protected.

a. Requirements for Federal Registration

A trademark may be filed with the U.S. Patent and Trademark Office on the basis of (1) use or (2) the intent to use the mark within six months (which may be extended to thirty months).

b. Renewal of Federal Registration

Between the fifth and sixth years and then every ten years (twenty years for marks registered before 1990).

4. Requirements for Trademark Protection

The extent to which the law protects a trademark is normally determined by how **distinctive** the mark is.

a. Fanciful, Arbitrary, or Suggestive Trademarks

Generally considered the most distinctive trademarks.

b. Descriptive Terms, Geographic Terms, and Personal Names

Not inherently distinctive and not protected until they acquire a **secondary meaning** (which means that customers associate the mark with the source of a product)

c. Generic Terms

Terms such as *bicycle* or *computer* receive no protection, even if they acquire secondary meaning.

5. **Trademark Infringement**
When a trademark is copied to a substantial degree or used in its entirety by another, the trademark is infringed.

B. TRADE DRESS

Trade dress is the image and appearance of a product, and is subject to the same protection as trademarks.

C. SERVICE, CERTIFICATION, AND COLLECTIVE MARKS

The same policies and restrictions that apply to trademarks normally apply to service, certification, and collective marks.

1. **Service Marks**
Used to distinguish the services of one person or company from those of another. Registered in the same manner as trademarks.

2. **Certification Marks**
Used by one or more persons, other than the owner, to certify the region, materials, mode of manufacture, quality, or accuracy of the owner's goods or services.

3. **Collective Marks**
Certification marks used by members of a cooperative, association, or other organization.

D. TRADE NAMES

Used to indicate part or all of a business's name. Trade names cannot be registered with the federal government but may be protected under the common law if they are used as trademarks or service marks.

II. CYBER MARKS

A. ANTICYBERSQUATTING LEGISLATION

The Anticybersquatting Consumer Reform Act (ACRA) of 1999 amended the Lanham Act to make cybersquatting clearly illegal. Bad faith intent is an element (the ACRA lists "bad faith" factors). Damages may be awarded.

B. META TAGS

Words in a Web site's key-word field that determine the site's appearance in search engine results. Using others' marks as tags without permission constitutes trademark infringement.

C. DILUTION IN THE ONLINE WORLD

Using a mark, without permission, in a way that diminishes its distinctive quality. Tech-related cases have concerned the use of marks as domain names and spamming under another's logo.

III. PATENTS

A. WHAT A PATENT IS

A grant from the federal government that conveys and secures to an inventor the exclusive right to make, use, and sell an invention for a period of twenty years (fourteen years for a design).

B. REQUIREMENTS FOR A PATENT

An invention, discovery, or design must be genuine, novel, useful, and not obvious in light of the technology of the time. A patent is given to the first person to invent a product, not to the first person to file for a patent.

C. PATENT INFRINGEMENT

Making, using, or selling another's patented design, product, or process without the patent owner's permission. The owner may obtain an injunction, damages, destruction of all infringing copies, attorneys' fees, and court costs.

D. PATENTS FOR SOFTWARE

The basis for software is often a mathematical equation or formula, which is not patentable, but a patent can be obtained for a process that incorporates a computer program.

E. PATENTS FOR BUSINESS PROCESSES

Business processes are patentable (laws of nature, natural phenomena, and abstract ideas are not patentable).

IV. COPYRIGHTS

A. WHAT A COPYRIGHT IS

An intangible right granted by statute to the author or originator of certain literary or artistic productions. Protection is automatic; registration is not required.

B. COPYRIGHT PROTECTION

Automatic for the life of the author plus fifty years. Copyrights owned by publishing houses expire seventy-five years from the date of publication or a hundred years from the date of creation, whichever is first. For works by more than one author, copyright expires fifty years after the death of the last surviving author.

C. WHAT IS PROTECTED EXPRESSION?

To be protected, under Section 102 of the Copyright Act a work must meet these requirements—

1. Fit a Certain Category

It must be a (1) literary work; (2) musical work; (3) dramatic work; (4) pantomime or choreographic work; (5) pictorial, graphic, or sculptural work; (6) film or other audiovisual work; or (7) a sound recording. The Copyright Act also protects computer software and architectural plans.

2. Be Fixed in a Durable Medium

From which it can be perceived, reproduced, or communicated.

3. Be Original

A compilation of facts (formed by the collection and assembling of preexisting materials of data) is copyrightable if it is original.

D. WHAT IS NOT PROTECTED

Ideas, facts, and related concepts. If an idea and an expression cannot be separated, the expression cannot be copyrighted.

E. COPYRIGHT INFRINGEMENT

A copyright is infringed if a work is copied without the copyright holder's permission. A copy does not have to be exactly the same as the original—copying a substantial part of the original is enough.

1. Penalties

Actual damages (based on the harm to the copyright holder); damages under the Copyright Act, not to exceed $150,000; and criminal proceedings (which may result in fines or imprisonment).

2. Exception—Fair Use Doctrine

The Copyright Act permits the fair use of a work for purposes such as criticism, comment, news reporting, teaching (including multiple copies for classroom use), scholarship, or research.

F. COPYRIGHT PROTECTION FOR SOFTWARE

The Computer Software Copyright Act of 1980 provides protection.

1. What Is Protected

The binary object code (the part of a software program readable only by computer); the source code (the part of a program readable by people); and the program structure, sequence, and organization.

2. What May or May Not Be Protected
The "look and feel"—the general appearance, command structure, video images, menus, windows, and other displays—of a program.

V. COPYRIGHTS IN DIGITAL INFORMATION

Copyright law is important in cyberspace in part because the nature of the Internet means that data is "copied" before being transferred online.

A. THE COPYRIGHT ACT OF 1976

Copyright law requires the copyright holder's permission to sell a "copy" of a work. For these purposes, loading a file or program into a computer's random access memory (RAM) is the making of a "copy."

B. NO ELECTRONIC THEFT ACT OF 1997

Extends criminal liability to the exchange of pirated, copyrighted materials, even if no profit is realized from the exchange, and to the unauthorized copying of works for personal use.

C. DIGITAL MILLENNIUM COPYRIGHT ACT OF 1998

Imposes penalties on anyone who circumvents encryption software or other technological anti-piracy protection. Also prohibits the manufacture, import, sale, or distribution of devices or services for circumvention. ISP s are not liable for their customers' violations.

D. MP3 AND FILE-SHARING TECHNOLOGY

MP3 file compression and music file sharing occur over the Internet through peer-to-peer (P2P) networking. Doing this without the permission of the owner of the music's copyright is infringement.

VI. TRADE SECRETS

A. WHAT A TRADE SECRET IS

Customer lists, formulas, plans, research and development, pricing information, marketing techniques, production techniques, and generally anything that provides an opportunity to obtain an advantage over competitors who do not know or use it.

B. TRADE SECRET PROTECTION

Protection of trade secrets extends both to ideas and their expression. Liability extends to those who misappropriate trade secrets by any means. Trade secret theft is also a federal crime.

C. TRADE SECRETS IN CYBERSPACE

The nature of technology (especially e-mail) undercuts a firm's ability to protect its confidential information, including trade secrets.

VII. LICENSING

Permitting the use of a mark, copyright, patent, or trade secret for certain purposes. Use for other purposes is a breach of the license agreement. Licensing of computer information is discussed in Chapter 18.

VIII. INTERNATIONAL PROTECTION

A. THE BERNE CONVENTION

The Berne Convention is an international copyright treaty.

1. For Citizens of Countries That Have Signed the Berne Convention
If, for example, an American writes a book, the copyright in the book is recognized by every country that has signed the convention.

2. For Citizens of Other Countries
If a citizen of a country that has not signed the convention publishes a book first in a country that has signed, all other countries that have signed the convention recognize that author's copyright.

B. THE TRIPS AGREEMENT
Trade-Related Aspects of Intellectual Property Rights (TRIPS) Agreement is part of the agreement creating the World Trade Organization (WTO). Each member nation must not discriminate (in administration, regulation, or adjudication of intellectual property rights) against owners of such rights.

TRUE-FALSE QUESTIONS

(Answers at the Back of the Book)

___ **1.** To receive a patent, an applicant must show that an invention is genuine, novel, useful, and not obvious in light of current technology.

___ **2.** To obtain a copyright, an author must show that a work is genuine, novel, useful, and not a copy of a current copyrighted work.

___ **3.** In determining whether the use of a copyrighted work is infringement under the fair use doctrine, one factor is the effect of that use on the market for the copyrighted work.

___ **4.** A personal name is protected under trademark law if it acquires a secondary meaning.

___ **5.** A formula for a chemical compound is not a trade secret.

___ **6.** A trade name, like a trademark, can be registered with the federal government.

___ **7.** A copy must be exactly the same as an original work to infringe on its copyright.

___ **8.** Only the *intentional* use of another's trademark is trademark infringement.

___ **9.** Using another's trademark in a domain name without permission violates federal law.

___ **10.** Trademark dilution requires proof that consumers are likely to be confused by the unauthorized use of the mark.

FILL-IN QUESTIONS

(Answers at the Back of the Book)

Copyright protection is automatic for the life of the author of a work plus _______ (70/95/120) years. Copyrights owned by publishing houses expire _______ (70/95/120) years from the date of the publication of a work or _______ (70/95/120) years from the date of its creation, whichever is first. For works by more than one author, a copyright expires ______ (70/95/120) years after the death of the last surviving author.

MULTIPLE-CHOICE QUESTIONS

(Answers at the Back of the Book)

___ **1.** Alpha, Inc., makes computer chips identical to Beta Corporation's patented chip, except for slight differences in the "look," without Beta's permission. This is

a. copyright infringement.
b. patent infringement.
c. trademark infringement.
d. none of the above.

___ **2.** Omega, Inc., uses a trademark on its products that no one, including Omega, has registered with the government. Under federal trademark law, Omega

a. can register the mark for protection.
b. cannot register a mark that has been used in commerce.
c. is guilty of trademark infringement.
d. must postpone registration until the mark has been out of use for three years.

___ **3.** Ken invents a light bulb that lasts longer than ordinary bulbs and applies for a patent. If the patent is granted, the invention will be protected

a. for ten years.
b. for twenty years.
c. for Ken's life plus seventy years.
d. forever.

___ **4.** The graphics used in "Grave Raiders," a computer game, are protected by

a. copyright law.
b. patent law.
c. trademark law.
d. trade secrets law.

___ **5.** Production techniques used to make "Grave Raiders," a computer game, are protected by

a. copyright law.
b. patent law.
c. trademark law.
d. trade secrets law.

___ **6.** National Products Company uses USA Goods, Inc.'s trademark in National's advertising without USA's permission. This is

a. copyright infringement.
b. patent infringement.
c. trademark infringement.
d. none of the above.

___ **7.** Clothes made by workers who are members of the Clothes Makers Union are sold with tags that identify this fact. This is a

a. certification mark.
b. collective mark.
c. service mark.
d. trade name.

___ **8.** Tony owns Antonio's, a pub in a small town in Iowa. Universal Dining, Inc., opens a chain of pizza places in California called "Antonio's" and, without Tony's consent, uses "antoniosincalifornia" as part of the URL for the chain's Web site. This is

a. copyright infringement.
b. cybersquatting.
c. trademark dilution.
d. none of the above.

____ **9.** Data Corporation created and sells "Economix," financial computer software. Data's copyright in Economix is best protected under

a. the Berne Convention.
b. the Paris Convention.
c. the TRIPS Agreement.
d. none of the above.

____ **10.** International Media, Inc. (IMI), publishes *Opinion* magazine, which contains an article by Carl. Without Carl's permission, IMI puts the article into an online database. This is

a. copyright infringement.
b. patent infringement.
c. trademark infringement.
d. none of the above.

SHORT ESSAY QUESTIONS

1. What does a copyright protect?

2. What is a trade secret and how is it protected?

ISSUE SPOTTERS

(Answers at the Back of the Book)

1. Delta Company discovers that it can extract data from the computer of Gamma, Inc., its major competitor, by making a series of phone calls over a high-speed modem. When Delta uses its discovery to extract Gamma's customer list, without permission, what recourse does Gamma have?

2. Global Products develops, patents, and markets software. World Copies, Inc., sells Global's software without the maker's permission. Is this patent infringement? If so, how might Global save the cost of suing World for infringement and at the same time profit from World's sales?

3. Eagle Corporation began marketing software in 1990 under the mark "Eagle." In 2002, Eagle.com, Inc., a different company selling different products, begins to use "eagle" as part of its URL and registers it as a domain name. Can Eagle Corporation stop this use of "eagle"? If so, what must the company show?

SPECIAL INFORMATION FOR CPA CANDIDATES

The material in this chapter has not traditionally been part of the CPA examination.

When studying for the CPA exam, many students integrate their review of business law topics with their review of other topics that make up distinct subject matter on the exam. For example, when reviewing the law behind business organizations, it can be most helpful to review the accounting and reporting details behind businesses' financial statements. Which topics to integrate and how much time to spend on each depends in part on each student's knowledge and understanding of the individual topics, as well as the emphasis that should be placed on a topic because of its importance for the exam.

Chapter 8
Criminal Law and Cyber Crimes

WHAT THIS CHAPTER IS ABOUT

This chapter defines what makes an act a crime, describes crimes, lists defenses to crimes, and outlines criminal procedure. Sanctions for crimes are different from those for torts or breaches of contract. Another difference between civil and criminal law is that individuals can bring civil suits but only the government can prosecute criminals.

CHAPTER OUTLINE

I. CIVIL LAW AND CRIMINAL LAW

A. CIVIL LAW
Civil law consists of the duties that exist between persons or between citizens and their governments, excluding the duty not to commit crimes.

B. CRIMINAL LAW
A crime is a wrong against society proclaimed in a statute and, if committed, punishable by society through fines, imprisonment, or death. Crimes are offenses against society as a whole (some torts are also crimes) and are prosecuted by public officials, not victims. In a criminal trial, the state must prove its case beyond a reasonable doubt.

II. CLASSIFICATION OF CRIMES

Felonies are serious crimes punishable by death or by imprisonment in a federal or state penitentiary for more than a year. A crime that is not a felony is a misdemeanor—punishable by a fine or by confinement (in a local jail) for up to a year. Petty offenses are minor misdemeanors.

III. THE ESSENTIALS OF CRIMINAL LIABILITY

Two elements must exist for a person to be convicted of a crime:

A. THE CRIMINAL ACT (*ACTUS REUS*)
A criminal statute prohibits certain behavior—an act of commission (doing something) or an act of omission (not doing something that is a legal duty).

B. STATE OF MIND (INTENT TO COMMIT A CRIME, OR*MENS REA*)
The mental state required to establish criminal guilt depends on the crime.

IV. CORPORATE CRIMINAL LIABILITY

Corporations are liable for (1) crimes committed by their agents and employees within the course and scope of employment, (2) failing to perform a specific affirmative duty imposed by law, or (3) crimes authorized, commanded, committed, or recklessly tolerated by a firm's high managerial agents. Directors and officers are personally liable for crimes they commit and may be liable for the actions of employees under their supervision.

V. TYPES OF CRIMES

A. VIOLENT CRIME
These include murder, rape, assault and battery (see Chapter 5), and *robbery* (forcefully and unlawfully taking personal property from another). Classified by degree, depending on intent, weapon, and victim's suffering.

B. PROPERTY CRIME

Robbery could also be in this category.

1. Burglary

Unlawful entry into a building with the intent to commit a felony.

2. Larceny

Wrongfully taking and carrying away another's personal property with the intent of depriving the owner permanently of the property (without force or intimidation, which are elements of robbery).

a. Property

Property includes computer programs, computer time, trade secrets, cellular phone numbers, long-distance phone time, and natural gas.

b. Grand Larceny and Petit Larceny

In some states, grand larceny is a felony and petit larceny a misdemeanor. The difference depends on the value of the property taken.

3. Arson

The willful and malicious burning, by fire or explosion, of a building (and in some states, personal property) owned by another. Every state has a statute that covers burning a building to collect insurance.

4. Receiving Stolen Goods

The recipient need not know the identity of the true owner of the goods.

5. Forgery

Fraudulently making or altering any writing in a way that changes the legal rights and liabilities of another.

6. Obtaining Goods by False Pretenses

Obtaining goods through fraud or deceit.

C. PUBLIC ORDER CRIME

Examples: public drunkenness, prostitution, gambling, and illegal drug use.

D. WHITE-COLLAR CRIME

1. Embezzlement

Fraudulently appropriating another's property or money by one who has been entrusted with it (without force or intimidation).

2. Mail and Wire Fraud

a. The Crime

It is a federal crime to (1) mail or cause someone else to mail something written, printed, or photocopied for the purpose of executing (2) a scheme to defraud (even if no one is defrauded). Also a crime to use wire, radio, or television transmissions to defraud.

b. The Punishment

Fine of up to $1,000, imprisonment for up to five years, or both. If the violation affects a financial institution, the fine may be up to $1 million, the imprisonment up to thirty years, or both.

3. Bribery

a. Bribery of Public Officials

Attempting to influence a public official to act in a way that serves a private interest by offering the official a bribe. Committed when the bribe (anything the recipient considers valuable) is offered.

b. **Commercial Bribery**
Attempting, by a bribe, to obtain proprietary information, cover up an inferior product, or secure new business.

c. **Bribery of Foreign Officials**
Attempting, by bribing foreign officials, to obtain business contracts. Banned by the Foreign Corrupt Practices Act of 1977 (see Chapter 42).

4. **Bankruptcy Fraud**
Filing a false claim against a debtor; fraudulently transferring assets to favored parties; or fraudulently concealing property before or after a petition for bankruptcy is filed.

5. **Insider Trading**
Using inside information (information not available to the general public) about a publicly traded corporation to profit from the purchase or sale of the corporation's securities (see Chapter 40).

6. **Theft of Trade Secrets**
Under the Economic Espionage Act of 1996, it is a federal crime to steal trade secrets, or to knowingly buy or possess another's stolen secrets. Penalties include up to ten years' imprisonment, fines up to $500,000 (individual) or $5 million (corporation), and forfeiture of property.

E. ORGANIZED CRIME

1. **Money Laundering**
Transferring the proceeds of crime through legitimate businesses. Financial institutions must report transactions of more than $10,000.

2. **RICO**
Two offenses under the Racketeer Influenced and Corrupt Organizations Act (RICO) of 1970 constitutes "racketeering activity."

a. **Activities Prohibited by RICO**
(1) Use income from racketeering to buy an interest in an enterprise, (2) acquire or maintain such an interest through racketeering activity' (3) conduct or participate in an enterprise through racketeering activity, or 4) conspire to do any of the above.

b. **Civil Liability**
Civil penalties include divestiture of a defendant's interest in a business or dissolution of the business. Private individuals can recover treble damages, plus attorneys' fees, for business injuries.

c. **Criminal Liability**
RICO can be used to attack white-collar crime. Penalties include fines of up to $25,000 per violation, imprisonment for up to 20 years, or both.

VI. DEFENSES TO CRIMINAL LIABILITY

A. INFANCY
Cases involving persons who have not reached the age of majority are handled in juvenile courts. In some states, a child over a certain age (usually fourteen) and charged with a felony may be tried in an adult court.

B. INTOXICATION
Involuntary intoxication is a defense to a crime if it makes a person incapable of understanding that the act committed was wrong or incapable of obeying the law. *Voluntary* intoxication may be a defense if the person was so intoxicated as to lack the required state of mind.

C. INSANITY

1. **The *M'Naughten* Test**
   Some states use this test: a person is not responsible if at the time of the offense, he or she did not know the nature and quality of the act or did not know that the act was wrong.

2. **The Irresistible Impulse Test**
   Some states use this test: a person operating under an irresistible impulse may know an act is wrong but cannot refrain from doing it.

3. **The Model Penal Code Test**
   Most federal courts and some states use this test: a person is not responsible for criminal conduct if at the time, as a result of mental disease or defect, the person lacks substantial capacity either to appreciate the wrongfulness of the conduct or to conform his or her conduct to the law.

D. MISTAKE

1. **Mistake of Fact**
   Defense if it negates the mental state necessary to commit a crime.

2. **Mistake of Law**
   A person not knowing a law was broken may have a defense if (1) the law was not published or reasonably made known to the public or (2) the person relied on an official statement of the law that was wrong.

E. CONSENT

Defense if it cancels the harm that the law is designed to prevent, unless the law forbids an act without regard to the victim's consent. Normally applies only cases involving property crimes.

F. DURESS

1. **What Duress Is**
   When a person's threat induces another person to perform an act that he or she would not otherwise perform.

2. **When Duress Is a Defense**
   (1) The threat is one of serious bodily harm, (2) the threat is immediate and inescapable, (3) the threatened harm is greater than the harm caused by the crime, (4) the defendant is involved through no fault of his or her own, and (5) the crime is not murder.

G. JUSTIFIABLE USE OF FORCE

1. **Nondeadly Force**
   People can use as much nondeadly force as seems necessary to protect themselves, their dwellings, or other property or to prevent a crime.

2. **Deadly Force**
   Can be used in self-defense if there is a reasonable belief that imminent death or serious bodily harm will otherwise result, if the attacker is using unlawful force, and if the defender did not provoke the attack.

H. NECESSITY

A defendant may be relieved of liability if his or her criminal act was necessary to prevent an even greater harm.

I. ENTRAPMENT

When a law enforcement agent suggests that a crime be committed, pressures or induces an individual to commit it, and arrests the individual for it.

J. STATUTE OF LIMITATIONS

Provides that the state has only a certain amount of time to prosecute a crime. Most statutes of limitations do not apply to murder.

K. IMMUNITY

A state can grant immunity from prosecution or agree to prosecute for a less serious offense in exchange for information. This is often part of a plea bargain between the defendant and the prosecutor.

VII. CRIMINAL PROCEDURES

A. CONSTITUTIONAL SAFEGUARDS

Most of these safeguards apply not only in federal but also in state courts by virtue of the due process clause of the Fourteenth Amendment.

1. Fourth Amendment

Protection from unreasonable searches and seizures. No warrants for a search or an arrest can be issued without probable cause.

2. Fifth Amendment

No one can be deprived of "life, liberty, or property without due process of law." No one can be tried twice (double jeopardy) for the same offense. No one can be required to incriminate himself or herself.

3. Sixth Amendment

Guarantees a speedy trial, trial by jury, a public trial, the right to confront witnesses, and the right to a lawyer in some proceedings.

4. Eighth Amendment

Prohibits excessive bail and fines, and cruel and unusual punishment.

B. THE EXCLUSIONARY RULE

Evidence obtained in violation of the Fourth, Fifth, and Sixth Amendments, as well as all "fruit of the poisonous tree" (evidence derived from illegally obtained evidence), must be excluded.

C. THE *MIRANDA* RULE

1. Rights

A person in custody to be interrogated must be informed (1) he or she has the right to remain silent, (2) anything said can and will be used against him or her in court, (3) he or she has the right to consult with an attorney, and (4) if he or she is indigent, a lawyer will be appointed.

2. Exceptions

Rights can be waived. "Public safety" may warrant admissibility. If other evidence justifies a conviction, it will not be overturned if confession was coerced. A suspect must assertively state that he or she wants a lawyer, to exercise the right.

D. CRIMINAL PROCESS

1. Arrest

Requires a warrant based on probable cause (a substantial likelihood that the person has committed or is about to commit a crime). To make an arrest without a warrant, an officer must also have probable cause.

2. Indictment or Information

A formal charge is called an indictment if issued by a grand jury and an information if issued by a public prosecutor.

3. Trial

Criminal trial procedures are similar to those of a civil trial, but the standard of proof is higher: the prosecutor must establish guilt beyond a reasonable doubt.

4. **Federal Sentencing Guidelines**
Possible penalties for federal crimes. Sentence is based on a defendant's criminal record, seriousness of the offense, and other factors.

VIII. CYBER CRIME

A. CYBER THEFT
Computers make it possible for employees, and others, to commit crimes (such as fraud) involving serious financial losses. The Internet has made identity theft and crimes committed with stolen identities easier.

B. CYBER STALKING
Harassing a person in cyberspace (such as via e-mail). Prohibited by federal law and most states. Some states require a "credible threat" that puts the person in reasonable fear for his or her safety or the safety of the person's family.

C. HACKING
Using one computer to break into another. Often part of cyber theft.

D. CYBER TERRORISM
Exploiting computers for such serious impacts as the exploding of a "bomb" to shut down a central computer.

E. PROSECUTING CYBER CRIMES
Jurisdictional issues and the anonymous nature of technology can hinder the investigation and prosecution of crimes committed in cyberspace.

1. **The Computer Fraud and Abuse Act**
The Computer Access Device and Computer Fraud and Abuse Act of 1984 provides for criminal prosecution of a person who accesses a computer online, without authority, to obtain classified, restricted, or protected data (restricted government info, financial records, etc.), or attempts to do. Penalties include fines and up to five years' imprisonment.

2. **Other Federal Statutes**
Electronic Fund Transfer Act of 1978, Anticounterfeiting Consumer Protection Act of 1996, National Stolen Property Act of 1988, and more.

TRUE-FALSE QUESTIONS

(Answers at the Back of the Book)

____ 1. Only the government prosecutes criminal defendants.

____ 2. A crime punishable by imprisonment is a felony.

____ 3. Burglary involves taking another's personal property from his or her person or immediate presence.

____ 4. Embezzlement requires physically taking property for another's possession.

____ 5. Stealing a computer program is larceny.

____ 6. Offering a bribe is only one element of the crime of bribery.

____ 7. Receiving stolen goods is a crime only if the recipient knows the true owner.

____ 8. Generally, a person is not responsible for a criminal act if, as a result of a mental defect, he or she lacked substantial capacity to appreciate the wrongfulness of the act or to conform the conduct to the law.

___ 9. A person who accesses a computer online, without authorization, to obtain protected data commits a federal crime.

___ 10. RICO is often used to prosecute acts classified as white-collar crimes.

FILL-IN QUESTIONS

(Answers at the Back of the Book)

Specific constitutional safeguards for those accused of crimes apply in all federal courts, and most of them also apply in state courts under the due process clause of the Fourteenth Amendment. The safeguards include (1) the Fourth Amendment protection from ________________ (unexpected/unreasonable) searches and seizures, (2) the Fourth Amendment requirement that no warrants for a search or an arrest can be issued without ________________ (probable/possible) cause, (3) the Fifth Amendment requirement that no one can be deprived of "life, liberty, or property without ______________________________ (consent/due process of law)," (4) the Fifth Amendment prohibition against double ________________ (immunity/jeopardy), (5) the Sixth Amendment guaranties of a speedy ____________ (appeal/trial), ____________ ________________ (appeal to/trial by) a jury, a public trial, the right to confront ____________________ (counsel/witnesses), and the right to legal counsel, and (6) the Eighth Amendment prohibitions against excessive ______________________(bail/bail and fines) and cruel and unusual punishment.

MULTIPLE-CHOICE QUESTIONS

(Answers at the Back of the Book)

___ 1. Carl wrongfully takes a box from a Delta, Inc., shipping container, puts it in his truck, and drives away. This is

a. burglary.
b. embezzlement.
c. forgery.
d. larceny.

___ 2. Nora is charged with the commission of a crime. For a conviction, most crimes require

a. only a specified state of mind or intent on the part of the actor.
b. only the performance of a prohibited act.
c. a specified state of mind and performance of a prohibited act.
d. none of the above.

___ 3. Adam signs Beth's name, without her consent, to the back of a check payable to Beth. This is

a. burglary.
b. embezzlement.
c. forgery.
d. larceny.

___ 4. Owen, a bank teller, deposits into his account checks that bank customers give to him to deposit into their accounts. This is

a. burglary.
b. embezzlement.
c. forgery.
d. larceny.

____ **5.** Jay is charged with the commission of a crime. For a conviction, Jay must be found guilty beyond

a. a clear and convincing doubt.
b. all doubt.
c. a preponderance of doubt.
d. a reasonable doubt.

____ **6.** Nick is charged with the crime of mail fraud. For a conviction, Nick must be found to have

a. had a scheme to defraud.
b. used the mails.
c. had a scheme to defraud and used the mails.
d. none of the above.

____ **7.** Sue, a government agent, arrests Tim for the commission of a crime. Tim claims that Sue entrapped him. This is a valid defense if Sue

a. did not tell Tim that she was a government agent.
b. pressured Tim into committing the crime.
c. set a trap for Tim, who was looking to commit the crime.
d. was predisposed to commit the crime.

____ **8.** John is arrested on suspicion of the commission of a crime. Individuals who are arrested must be told of their right to

a. confront witnesses.
b. protection against unreasonable searches.
c. remain silent.
d. trial by jury.

____ **9.** While away from her business, Kate is arrested on suspicion of commission of a crime. At Kate's trial, under the exclusionary rule

a. biased individuals must be excluded from the jury.
b. business records must be excluded from admission as evidence.
c. illegally obtained evidence must be excluded from admission as evidence.
d. the arresting officer must be excluded from testifying.

____ **10.** Eve is arrested on suspicion of commission of a crime. A grand jury issues a formal charge against her. This is

a. an arraignment.
b. an indictment.
c. an information.
d. an inquisition.

SHORT ESSAY QUESTIONS

1. What are some of the significant differences between criminal law and civil law?

2. What constitutes criminal liability under the Racketeer Influenced and Corrupt Organizations Act (RICO) of 1968 and what are the penalties?

ISSUE SPOTTERS

(Answers at the Back of the Book)

1. Bob drives off in Fred's car mistakenly believing that it is his. Is this theft?

2. Ellen takes her roommate's credit card, intending to charge expenses that she incurs on a vacation. Her first stop is a gas station, where she uses the card to pay for gas. With respect to the gas station, has she committed a crime? If so, what is it?

3. Ben downloads consumer credit files from a computer of Consumer Credit Agency, without permission, over the Internet. Ben sells the data to Donna. Has Ben committed a crime? If so, what is it?

SPECIAL INFORMATION FOR CPA CANDIDATES

In the past, the CPA examination has not tested knowledge of specific crimes. Instead, the exam has asked for responses concerning liability in the context of corporate crime and in the area of accountants' liability. The first topic is covered in part in this chapter and in part in Chapter 40. Depending on the circumstances, corporate officers or directors may be liable for corporate crimes. An employer may also be liable for the crimes of his or her employees, although probably not in the absence of a specific statute setting out that liability. Accountants' criminal liability is covered in Chapter 52.

CUMULATIVE HYPOTHETICAL PROBLEM FOR UNIT TWO—INCLUDING CHAPTERS 5–8

(Answers at the Back of the Book)

Computer Data, Inc. (CDI), incorporated and based in California, signs a contract with Digital Products Corporation (DPC), incorporated and based in Arizona, to make and sell customized software for DPC to, in turn, sell to its clients.

___ **1.** To protect the rights that CDI has in the software it produces, CDI's best protection is offered by

a. criminal law.
b. intellectual property law.
c. tort law.
d. none of the above.

___ **2.** CDI ships defective software to DPC, which sells it to a customer, Eagle Distribution Corporation. The defective software causes losses that Eagle estimates at $100,000. With respect to Eagle, CDI has likely violated

a. criminal law.
b. intellectual property law.
c. tort law.
d. none of the above.

___ **3.** DPC's officers order some employees to access CDI's computers online to obtain its data without CDI's permission. This is

a. cyber fraud.
b. cyber theft.
c. cyber trespass.
d. none of the above.

____ **4.** During an investigation into DPC's activities, some of its officers are suspected of having committed crimes. As a corporation, DPC can

a. be fined or denied certain privileges if it is held criminally liable.
b. be imprisoned if it is held criminally liable.
c. be fined, denied privileges, or imprisoned if it is held criminally liable.
d. not be found to be criminally liable.

____ **5.** DPC's officers who are suspected of having committed crimes can

a. be fined or denied certain privileges if they are held criminally liable.
b. be imprisoned if they are held criminally liable.
c. be fined, denied privileges, or imprisoned if they are held criminally liable.
d. not be held criminally liable.

QUESTIONS ON THE FOCUS ON LEGAL REASONING FOR UNIT TWO—*PINSONNEAULT V. MERCHANTS & FARMERS BANK & TRUST CO.*

(Answers at the Back of the Book)

____ **1.** In *Pinsonneault v. Merchants & Farmers Bank & Trust Co.*, in the majority's opinion, a business must take security precautions if harm is foreseeable to

a. its employees.
b. its patrons.
c. members of the community.
d. passersby.

____ **2.** In the majority's opinion, under a negligence theory, the business in this case had

a. a duty and breached it.
b. a duty and satisfied it.
c. a duty but did not breach it or satisfy it.
d. no duty.

____ **3.** In the dissent's opinion, under a negligence theory, the business in this case had

a. a duty and breached it.
b. a duty and satisfied it.
c. a duty but did not breach it or satisfy it.
d. no duty.

QUESTIONS ON THE FOCUS ON ETHICS FOR UNIT TWO—ETHICS AND THE LEGAL ENVIRONMENT OF BUSINESS

(Answers at the Back of the Book)

____ **1.** Quality Info Company collects and sells personal data about individuals to businesses. This may violate

a. businesses' copyrights.
b. companies' freedom of speech.
c. individuals' privacy rights.
d. marketers' trademarks.

____ **2.** Macro Corporation makes and sells software. Nick operates a Web site under the domain name "macro-softwaresucks.com." In Macro's suit against Nick, his best defense is that this domain is protected by

a. copyright law.
b. Nick's freedom of speech.
c. Nick's privacy rights.
d. trademark law.

____ **3.** Don is the author of *E-Murder,* a cyberspace mystery. Fourteen years after Don dies, Fran prints copies of *E-Murder* and sells them for her own profit. This may violate Don's

a. copyright.
b. freedom of speech.
c. privacy rights.
d. trademark.

Chapter 9
Nature and Terminology

WHAT THIS CHAPTER IS ABOUT

Contract law concerns the formation and keeping of promises, the excuses our society accepts for breaking such promises, and what promises are considered contrary to public policy and therefore legally void. This chapter introduces the basic terms and concepts of contract law, including the rules for interpreting contract language.

CHAPTER OUTLINE

I. THE FUNCTION OF CONTRACT LAW

A. ENFORCE PROMISES

Contract law assures the parties to private agreements that the promises they make will be enforceable. Without the framework that the law provides, businesspersons could rely only on the good faith of others to keep their promises.

B. AVOID PROBLEMS

The rules of contract law are often followed in business agreements to avoid potential problems.

C. SUPPORT THE EXISTENCE OF A MARKET ECONOMY

Businesspersons can usually rely on the good faith of others to keep their promises, but when price changes or adverse economic factors make it costly to comply with a promise, good faith may not be enough.

II. DEFINITION OF A CONTRACT

A. WHAT A CONTRACT IS

A **contract** is a promise for the breach of which the law gives a remedy or the performance of which the law recognizes as a duty (that is, an agreement that can be enforced in court). A contract is formed by two or more parties who promise to perform or refrain from performing some act now or in the future.

B. THE OBJECTIVE THEORY OF CONTRACTS

Intention to enter into a contract is judged by objective (outward) facts as interpreted by a reasonable person, rather than by a party's subjective intention. Objective facts include (1) what the party said when entering into the contract, (2) how the party acted or appeared, and (3) the circumstances surrounding the transaction.

III. REQUIREMENTS OF A CONTRACT

A. THE ELEMENTS OF A CONTRACT

1. **Agreement**
   Includes an offer and an acceptance. One party must offer to enter into a legal agreement, and another party must accept the offer.

2. **Consideration**
   Promises must be supported by legally sufficient and bargained-for consideration.

3. **Contractual Capacity**
Characteristics that qualify the parties to a contract as competent.

4. **Legality**
A contract's purpose must be to accomplish a goal that is not against public policy.

B. DEFENSES TO THE ENFORCEABILITY OF A CONTRACT

1. **Genuineness of Assent**
The apparent consent of both parties must be genuine.

2. **Form**
A contract must be in whatever form the law requires (some contracts must be in writing).

IV. TYPES OF CONTRACTS

A. BILATERAL VERSUS UNILATERAL CONTRACTS

1. **Bilateral Contract**
A promise for a promise—to accept the offer, the offeree need only promise to perform.

2. **Unilateral Contract**
A promise for an act—the offeree can accept only by completing the contract performance. A problem arises when the promisor attempts to revoke the offer after the promisee has begun performance but before the act has been completed.

   a. **Revocation—Traditional View**
   The promisee can accept the offer only by performing fully. Offers are revocable until accepted.

   b. **Revocation—Modern View**
   The offer becomes irrevocable once performance begins. Thus, even though it has not yet been accepted, the offeror cannot revoke it.

B. EXPRESS VERSUS IMPLIED CONTRACTS

1. **Express Contract**
The terms of the agreement are fully and explicitly stated in words (oral or written).

2. **Implied-in-Fact Contract**
Implied from the conduct of the parties.

C. QUASI CONTRACTS—CONTRACTS IMPLIED IN LAW

In the absence of an actual contract, a quasi contract is imposed by a court to avoid the unjust enrichment of one party at the expense of another. Cannot be invoked if there is an actual contract that covers the area in controversy.

D. FORMAL VERSUS INFORMAL CONTRACTS

1. **Formal Contract**
Requires a special form or method of creation to be enforceable (such as a contract under seal, a formal writing with a special seal attached).

2. **Informal Contract**
All contracts that are not formal. Except for certain contracts that must be in writing, no special form is required.

E. EXECUTED VERSUS EXECUTORY CONTRACTS

1. **Executed Contract**
A contract that has been fully performed on both sides.

2. **Executory Contract**
A contract that has not been fully performed by one or more parties.

F. VALID, VOID, AND VOIDABLE CONTRACTS

1. **Valid Contract**
Has all the elements necessary for contract formation.

2. **Void Contract**
Has no legal force or binding effect (for example, a contract is void if its purpose was illegal).

3. **Voidable Contract**
Valid contract that can be avoided by one or more parties (for example, contracts by minors are voidable at the minor's option).

G. UNENFORCEABLE CONTRACTS
Contract that cannot be enforced because of certain legal defenses (for example, if a contract that must be in writing is not in writing).

V. INTERPRETATION OF CONTRACTS

Rules of contract interpretation provide guidelines for determining the meaning of contracts. The primary purpose of these rules is to determine the parties' intent from the language of their agreement and to give effect to that intent.

A. THE PLAIN MEANING RULE
When the writing is clear and unequivocal, it will be enforced according to its plain terms. The meaning of the terms is determined from the written document alone.

B. OTHER RULES OF INTERPRETATION
When the writing contains unclear terms, courts use the following rules—

1. A reasonable, lawful, and effective meaning is given to all terms.
2. A contract is interpreted as a whole; individual, specific clauses are considered subordinate to the contract's general intent. All writings that are part of the same transaction are interpreted together.
3. Terms that were negotiated separately are given greater consideration than standard terms and terms that were not negotiated separately.
4. A word is given its ordinary, common meaning, and a technical word its technical meaning, unless the parties clearly intended otherwise.
5. Specific, exact wording is given greater weight than general language.
6. Written or typewritten terms prevail over preprinted ones.
7. When the language has more than one meaning, it is interpreted against the party who drafted the contract.
8. Evidence of trade usage, prior dealing, and course of performance may be admitted to clarify meaning.

C. PLAIN-LANGUAGE LAWS
The federal government and most states require an agreement to be written clearly, coherently, and in words of common, everyday meaning.

TRUE-FALSE QUESTIONS

(Answers at the Back of the Book)

___ 1. All promises are legal contracts.

___ 2. An agreement includes an offer and an acceptance.

___ 3. A promisor is a person who makes a promise.

___ 4. A unilateral contract is accepted by a promise to perform.

___ 5. An oral contract is an implied contract.

___ 6. An unenforceable contract is a valid contract that can be avoided by at least one of the parties to it.

___ 7. Under the plain meaning rule, a court will enforce a contract in which the writing is clear and unequivocal.

___ 8. When the language in a contract has more than one meaning, it will be interpreted against the party who drafted the contract.

___ 9. An executory contract is one that has not been fully performed.

___ 10. A quasi contract arises from a mutual agreement between two parties.

FILL-IN QUESTIONS

(Answers at the Back of the Book)

Whether or not a party intended to enter into a contract is determined by the ____________ (objective/subjective) theory of contracts. The theory is that a party's intention to enter into a contract is judged by ____________ (objective/subjective) facts as they would be interpreted by a reasonable person. Relevant facts include: (1) what the party said; (2) what the party ____________ (did/secretly believed); and (3) the ____________ (circumstances surrounding/party's personal thoughts concerning) the transaction. Generally, courts examine facts in ____________ (a particular transaction/similar transactions) to determine whether the parties made a contract and, if so, what its terms are.

MULTIPLE-CHOICE QUESTIONS

(Answers at the Back of the Book)

___ 1. Bob files a suit against Carol, claiming that she freely entered into a contract with him. Freedom of contract is

a. a concept no longer followed by the courts.
b. a foundation for an ethical business practice.
c. a fundamental public policy in the United States.
d. a principle that describes contracting parties' intent.

___ 2. Dan, a doctor, renders aid to Eve, who is injured. Dan can recover the cost of from Eve

a. even if Eve was not aware of Dan's help.
b. only if Eve was aware of Dan's help.
c. only if Eve was not aware of Dan's help.
d. none of the above.

___ 3. National Supplies, Inc., agrees to deliver a truckload of paper to Office Products Company on Office's promise to pay for the paper. National delivers the paper. This contract is

a. executory on National's part.
b. executory on Office's part.
c. fully executed.
d. fully non-executed.

___ 4. Mary files a suit against Nick, alleging an implied-in-fact contract. The court will examine their conduct only to determine

a. the terms of the contract.
b. whether they intended to form a contract.
c. the terms of the contract and whether they intended to form a contract.
d. none of the above.

___ 5. Ann claims that she and Brian entered into a contract. The intent to enter into a contract is determined with reference to

a. the apparent theory of contracts.
b. the objective theory of contracts.
c. the personal theory of contracts.
d. the subjective theory of contracts.

___ 6. Rita calls Sam on the phone and agrees to buy his laptop computer for $500. This is

a. an express contract.
b. an implied-in-fact contract.
c. an implied-in-law contract.
d. a quasi contract.

___ 7. Owen files a suit against Pam, disputing the meaning of their contract. If the terms are unclear, under the common law rules of contract interpretation, the court will give effect to

a. the parties' intent as expressed in their contract.
b. what Owen claims was the parties' intent.
c. what Pam claims was the parties' intent.
d. what the parties commonly claim they intended.

___ 8. Lora files a suit against Mike, disputing the meaning of their contract. If the terms are unclear, the contract's express terms take priority over

a. course of performance only.
b. course of dealing only.
c. custom and usage of trade only.
d. course of performance, course of dealing, and custom and usage of trade.

___ 9. Adam's contract with Ben is voidable. This means that if the contract is avoided, with respect to the contract's obligations

a. both parties must perform.
b. neither party must perform.
c. only Adam must perform.
d. only Ben must perform.

___ **10.** Matt makes a promise to Nora. A promise is a declaration

a. only that one will do something in the future.
b. only that one will not do something in the future.
c. that one will or will not do something in the future.
d. none of the above.

SHORT ESSAY QUESTIONS

1. What are the basic elements of a contract?

2. What is the function of contract law?

ISSUE SPOTTERS

(Answers at the Back of the Book)

1. Jill signs and returns a letter from Kyle, referring to a book and its price. When Kyle delivers the book, Jill sends it back, claiming that they have no contract. Kyle claims they do. What standard determines whether these parties have a contract?

2. Ira receives from the local tax collector a notice of property taxes due. The notice is for tax on Jan's property, but Ira believes that the tax is his and pays it. Can Ira recover from Jan the amount paid?

3. Dora tells Ed that she will pay Ed $1,000 to set fire to Dora's store, so that she can collect money under a fire insurance policy. Ed sets fire to the store, but Dora refuses to pay. Can Ed recover?

SPECIAL INFORMATION FOR CPA CANDIDATES

Among the attributes for success on the CPA examination is a positive attitude. Preparation for the exam is a long process, and it can be difficult to keep one's mind focused on a successful conclusion. Because a positive attitude can make the difference between passing and failing, however, it is important that you stay refreshed, confident, and optimistic. To accomplish this, take time off from your studies once in a while. Spend an evening or an afternoon with friends; get some exercise; do some leisure reading; go to a movie—or do whatever else it takes, when your spirits sag, to regain a positive attitude.

Chapter 10
Agreement

WHAT THIS CHAPTER IS ABOUT

An agreement is the essence of every contract. The parties to a contract are the *offeror* (who makes an offer) and the *offeree* (to whom the offer is made). If, through the process of offer and acceptance, an agreement is reached, and the other elements are present (consideration, capacity, legality), a valid contract is formed.

A contract must contain reasonably definite terms. Generally, a contract must include, either expressed in the contract or capable of being reasonably inferred from it, the following terms: identification of the parties; identification of the contract's subject matter (also quantity); the consideration to be paid; and the time of performance.

CHAPTER OUTLINE

I. REQUIREMENTS OF THE OFFER

An offer is a promise or commitment to do or refrain from doing some specified thing in the future. An offer has three elements—

A. INTENTION

The offeror must intend to be bound by the offer.

1. How to Determine the Offeror's Intent

The offeror's intent is determined by what a reasonable person in the offeree's position would conclude the offeror's words and actions meant. Offers made in obvious anger, jest, or undue excitement do not qualify.

2. Nonoffers

What appears to be an offer may not be sufficient to form the basis of a contract. It is important to recognize what does not constitute an offer. Nonoffers include: (1) expressions of opinion, (2) statements of intention, (3) preliminary negotiations, and (4) advertisements, catalogues, price lists, and circulars. Auctions represent a special situation.

3. Agreements to Agree

Agreements to agree to a material term of a contract at some future date may be enforced if the parties clearly intended to be bound.

B. DEFINITENESS

1. Major Terms

All of the major terms must be stated with reasonable definiteness in the offer (or, if the offeror directs, in the offeree's acceptance).

2. Missing Terms

Courts are sometimes willing to supply a missing term when the parties have clearly manifested an intent to form a contract.

C. COMMUNICATION

The offer must be communicated to the offeree.

II. TERMINATION OF THE OFFER

A. TERMINATION BY ACTION OF THE PARTIES

1. Revocation of the Offer by the Offeror

The offeror usually can revoke the offer (even if he or she has promised to keep it open), by express repudiation or by performance of acts that are inconsistent with the offer and that are made known to the offeree.

a. Communicated to the Offeree

Revocation must be communicated to the offeree (or the offeree's agent) before the offeree accepts. A revocation becomes effective when the offeree or offeree's agent actually receives it.

b. Offers to the General Public

An offer made to the general public can be revoked in the same manner the offer was originally communicated.

2. Irrevocable Offers

a. Option Contract

1) What an Option Contract Is

A promise to hold an offer open for a specified period of time. A separate contract that takes away the offeror's power to revoke the offer for the period of time specified.

2) How Long an Offer Must Be Held Open

If no time is specified, a reasonable time is implied.

3) Death or Incompetence of a Party

Generally, the death or incompetence of a party does not terminate an option contract—unless the offeror's personal performance is essential to the fulfillment of the contract.

b. Detrimental Reliance

1) Promissory Estoppel

When the offeree justifiably relies on an offer to his or her detriment, this reliance may make the offer irrevocable.

2) Unilateral Contracts

Many courts will not allow the offeror to revoke the offer after the offeree has performed some substantial part of his or her duties under a unilateral contract. In effect, partial performance renders the offer irrevocable, giving the original offeree reasonable time to complete performance.

3. Rejection of the Offer by the Offeree

The offer may be rejected by the offeree by words or conduct evidencing an intent not to accept the offer.

a. Subsequent Attempt by the Offeree to Accept

Construed as a new offer.

b. Communicated to the Offeror

Rejection of an offer is effective only when it is actually received by the offeror or the offeror's agent.

c. Inquiring about an Offer

Asking about an offer is not rejecting it.

4. **Counteroffer by the Offeree**
The offeree's attempt to include different terms is a rejection of the original offer and a simultaneous making of a new offer. The mirror image rule requires the acceptance to match the offer exactly.

B. TERMINATION BY OPERATION OF LAW

1. **Lapse of Time**
An offer terminates automatically by law when the period of time specified in the offer has passed.

   a. **When the Time Begins to Run**
   When the offer is received by the offeree, not when it is sent. If the offer is delayed, the period begins to run from the date the offeree would have received the offer (if the offeree knows or should know that the offer is delayed).

   b. **If No Time Is Specified**
   If no time is specified, then a reasonable time is implied.

2. **Destruction of the Subject Matter**
An offer is automatically terminated.

3. **Death or Incompetence of the Offeror or Offeree**
An offeree's power of acceptance is terminated. Exceptions include irrevocable offers (see above).

4. **Supervening Illegality of the Proposed Contract**
When a statute or court decision makes an offer illegal, the offer is automatically terminated.

III. ACCEPTANCE

A. UNEQUIVOCAL ACCEPTANCE
The offeree must accept the offer unequivocally. This is the mirror image rule (see above).

B. SILENCE AS ACCEPTANCE
Ordinarily, silence cannot operate as an acceptance. Silence or inaction can constitute acceptance under the following circumstances—

1. **Receipt of Offered Services**
If an offeree receives the benefit of offered services even though he or she had an opportunity to reject them and knew that they were offered with the expectation of compensation.

2. **Prior Dealings**
The offeree had prior dealings with the offeror that lead the offeror to understand that silence will constitute acceptance.

C. COMMUNICATION OF ACCEPTANCE

1. **Bilateral Contract**
A contract is formed when acceptance is communicated. The offeree must use reasonable efforts to communicate the acceptance to the offeror.

2. **Unilateral Contract**
Communication is unnecessary (because acceptance is by performance), unless the offeror requests notice or has no adequate means of determining if the act has been performed, or the law requires notice.

D. MODE AND TIMELINESS OF ACCEPTANCE IN BILATERAL CONTRACTS

1. **Mode**

a. **Authorized Means of Acceptance**
If an offeree uses a mode of communication expressly or impliedly authorized by the offeror, acceptance is effective when sent. This is the *mailbox rule* (deposited acceptance rule).

1) **Express**
When an offeror specifies how acceptance should be made, a contract is not formed unless the offeree uses that mode of acceptance. If the offeree uses that mode, the acceptance is effective even if the offeror never receives it.

2) **Implied**
When an offeror does not specify how acceptance should be made or specifies that the acceptance will be effective only when received, the offeree may use any medium that is reasonable under the circumstances (which include the means used by the offeror to make the offer).

3) **Exception**
If the acceptance is not properly dispatched (for example, it is not correctly addressed), in most states it will not be effective until received by the offeror or the offeror's agent. (If timely sent and timely received, however, it is considered to have been effective on dispatch.)

b. **Unauthorized Means of Acceptance**

1) **Effective When Received**
If an offeree uses a mode of communication that was not authorized by the offeror, acceptance is effective when received.

2) **Effective When Sent**
If an acceptance is timely sent and timely received, however, despite the means by which it is sent, it is considered to have been effective when sent.

c. **Rejection and Acceptance**
Sometimes an offeree sends a rejection first, then later changes his or her mind and sends an acceptance. The first communication to be received by the offeror determines whether a contract is formed. If the rejection is received first, there is no contract.

2. **Timeliness**
Acceptance is timely if it is made before the offer is terminated.

E. TECHNOLOGY AND ACCEPTANCE RULES
Generally, on the Internet, the mailbox rule is not needed because online acceptances are instantaneous (see Chapter 18).

TRUE-FALSE QUESTIONS

(Answers at the Back of the Book)

____ **1.** An agreement is normally evidenced by an offer and an acceptance.

____ **2.** A contract does not need to contain reasonably definite terms to be enforced.

____ **3.** Rejection of an offer by the offeree will terminate it.

____ **4.** There are no irrevocable offers.

____ **5.** Under the mirror image rule, an offeree's acceptance does not need to adhere exactly to the terms of the offeror's offer to create a contract.

____ 6. It is not possible for an offeree to accept an offer in silence.

____ 7. An offer terminates when the time specified in the offer has passed and the offeror has given one last chance to the offeree to accept.

____ 8. Anyone who is aware of an offer can accept it and create a binding contract.

____ 9. Acceptance is timely if it is made before an offer terminates.

____ 10. Acceptance is effective when sent if the offeree uses a mode of communication authorized by the offeror.

FILL-IN QUESTIONS

(Answers at the Back of the Book)

The elements of an effective offer are (1) a ______________________________ (serious/subjective) intent by the ______________________________ (offeror/offeree) to be bound by the offer; (2) ______________________________ (detailed/reasonably definite) contractual terms; and (3) communication of the offer to the ______________________________ (offeror/offeree).

MULTIPLE-CHOICE QUESTIONS

(Answers at the Back of the Book)

____ 1. Owen mails Pete an offer to sell his computer, stating that Pete has ten days to accept by e-mail. The next day, Pete e-mails an acceptance. This acceptance is effective when

a. received.
b. sent.
c. received or sent, depending on what Owen decides later.
d. the tenth day ends.

____ 2. **Based on a Sample CPA Exam Question.** Before opening her new sports merchandise store, Kay places an ad in the newspaper showing cross-training shoes at certain prices. Within hours of opening for business, the store is sold out of some of the shoes. In this situation

a. Kay has made an offer to the people reading the ad.
b. Kay has made a contract with the people reading the ad.
c. Kay has made an invitation seeking offers.
d. Any customer who demands goods advertised and tenders the money is entitled to them.

____ 3. Alpha Properties, Inc., makes an offer in a letter to Bob to sell a certain lot for $5,000, with the offer to stay open for thirty days. Bob would prefer to pay $4,000, if Alpha would sell at that price. To leave room for negotiation without rejecting the offer, Bob should reply

a. "I will not pay $5,000."
b. "Will you take $4,000?"
c. "I will pay $4,000."
d. "I will pay $4,500."

____ 4. Beth offers to sell Chris a certain piece of land. Chris says, "Yes, but $3,000 more for the land and the quarter acre behind it." Chris has

a. accepted the offer.
b. rejected the offer only.
c. made a counteroffer only.
d. rejected the offer and made a counteroffer.

____ **5.** Bill makes an offer to Ann. If Bill dies before Ann can reply, the offer

a. remains open.
b. remains open until Ann learns of Bill's death.
c. remains open until An replies.
d. terminates immediately.

____ **6.** Lee offers to sell his car to Mike, stating that the offer will stay open for thirty days. Lee may revoke the offer

a. before Mike accepts the offer.
b. only after Mike accepts or rejects the offer.
c. only after thirty days.
d. within thirty days, whether or not Mike has accepted the offer.

____ **7.** Beta Computers advertises a sale of its inventory at public auction. At the auction, Beta's auctioneer holds up a router and asks, "What am I bid for this item?" Which of the following is TRUE?

a. Each bid is an acceptance subject to no higher bid being received.
b. Each bid is an offer that may be accepted or rejected.
c. Each bid is an offer that must be accepted if no higher bid is received.
d. The first bid is an acceptance subject to no other bid being received.

____ **8.** Ron sends to Sounds, Inc. (SI), a written order for a sound system to be specially manufactured, offering a certain amount of money. If SI does not respond, it can be considered to have accepted the offer

a. if Ron knows that SI accepts all offers unless it sends notice to the contrary.
b. only after a reasonable time has passed.
c. only when SI begins the work.
d. only when SI finishes the work.

____ **9.** Paul makes an offer to Lynn in a letter, saying nothing about how her acceptance should be sent. Lynn's acceptance is sent via the mail. This acceptance is effective when

a. Lynn decides to accept.
b. Lynn sends the letter.
c. Paul receives the letter.
d. the letter is midway between the parties.

____ **10.** Pat makes an offer to Neal in a fax. Neal indicates his acceptance in a return fax. Neal's acceptance is effective when

a. Neal decides to accept.
b. Neal sends the fax.
c. Pat receives the fax.
d. the fax is midway between the parties.

SHORT ESSAY QUESTIONS

1. What are the elements necessary for an effective offer?

2. What are the elements necessary for an effective acceptance?

ISSUE SPOTTERS

(Answers at the Back of the Book)

1. One morning, when Jane's new car—with an $18,000 market value—doesn't start, she yells in anger, "I'd sell this car to anyone for $500." If you drop $500 in her lap, is the car yours?

2. Joe advertises in the *New York Times* that he will pay $5,000 to anyone giving him information as to the whereabouts of Elaine. Max sees a copy of the ad in a Tokyo newspaper, in Japanese, and sends Joe the information. Does Max get the reward?

3. Alpha Corporation offers to hire Beth to replace Curt, who has given Alpha a month's notice. Alpha gives Beth a week to decide whether to accept. Two days later, Curt signs an employment contract with Alpha for another year. The next day, Curt tells Beth of the new contract. Beth immediately sends a letter of acceptance to Alpha. Do Alpha and Beth have a contract?

SPECIAL INFORMATION FOR CPA CANDIDATES

One of the points covered in this chapter and often tested on the CPA examination is the mailbox rule. Sometimes, the examination has included a problem in which the offeror specifies that an acceptance must be received before it is effective. In that circumstance, of course, the mailbox rule does not apply. It might be helpful to remember, too, that the mailbox rule is the only exception to the rule that a communication is effective only on receipt—offers, revocations, rejections, counteroffers, and acceptances not subject to the mailbox rule must be received to be effective.

Chapter 11
Consideration

WHAT THIS CHAPTER IS ABOUT

Good reasons for enforcing promises have been held to include something given as an agreed exchange, a benefit that the promisor received, and a detriment that the promisee incurred. These are referred to as "consideration." No contract is enforceable without it.

Consideration is the value given in return for a promise. For example, the value can consist of money given in return for a promise to deliver certain goods. Thus, when Roy pays for a computer to be delivered by Sam, there is consideration. This chapter outlines the concepts and principles of consideration.

CHAPTER OUTLINE

I. ELEMENTS OF CONSIDERATION

Consideration has two elements: (1) there must be a bargained-for exchange between the parties (if a party intends to make a gift, he or she is not bargaining) and (2) what is bargained for must have legal value.

II. LEGAL SUFFICIENCY OF CONSIDERATION

Something of legal value must be given in exchange for a promise. It may be a return promise. If it is performance, that performance may be (1) an act (other than a promise); or (2) a forbearance (refraining from an act).

III. ADEQUACY OF CONSIDERATION

Adequacy of consideration refers to the fairness of a bargain. Normally, a court will not question the adequacy of consideration unless it indicates fraud, duress, incapacity, undue influence, or a lack of bargained-for exchange.

IV. AGREEMENTS THAT LACK CONSIDERATION

Situations in which promises or acts do not qualify as consideration include—

A. PREEXISTING DUTY

A promise to do what one already has a legal duty to do is not constitute legally sufficient consideration.

1. Example

If a merchant contracts to sell a computer to a consumer, that duty cannot serve as consideration for a second contract with the consumer to raise the price.

2. Exceptions

a. Unforeseen Difficulties

When a party runs into extraordinary difficulties that were unforeseen at the time the contract was formed, some courts will enforce an agreement to pay more.

1) Ordinary Business Risks Not Included

2) **Typical Cases**
Cases involving unforeseen difficulties frequently arise under construction contracts and relate to soil conditions.

b. **Rescission and New Contract**
Two parties can agree to rescind their contract to the extent that it is executory.

1) **Preexisting Duties Discharged by Rescission**
There are three separate agreements—the initial agreement, the rescission agreement, and the later agreement. Preexisting duties are discharged by the rescission.

2) **When Rescission and New Contract Occur at the Same Time**
Some courts hold that the new agreement is unenforceable, on the ground of insufficient consideration, unless both contracting parties' duties are changed. Other courts hold that the consideration for the original agreement carries over into the new agreement.

B. PAST CONSIDERATION
Promises made with respect to events that have already taken place are unenforceable.

V. PROBLEM AREAS CONCERNING CONSIDERATION

A. UNCERTAIN PERFORMANCE
If the terms of a contract express such uncertainty of performance that the promisor has not definitely promised to do anything, the promise is illusory—without consideration and unenforceable.

1. **Example**
Tio's Restaurant promises to buy from Pizza King, Inc., "such pizza ingredients as we may wish to order from Pizza King." Tio's promise is illusory, because performance depends solely on the discretion of Tio's. There is no bargained-for consideration.

2. **Option-to-Cancel Clauses**
Reserving, in a contract, the right to cancel or withdraw at any time can be an illusory promise. If the right is at all restricted, however—such as by requiring thirty days' notice—there is consideration.

B. SETTLEMENT OF CLAIMS

1. **Accord and Satisfaction**
Accord and satisfaction deals with a debtor's offer of payment and a creditor's acceptance of a lesser amount than the creditor originally purported to be owed.

a. **Accord**
The agreement under which one of the parties undertakes to give or perform, and the other to accept, in satisfaction of a claim, something other than that which was originally agreed on.

b. **Satisfaction**
Satisfaction takes place when the accord is executed. There can be no satisfaction unless there is first an accord.

c. **Amount of the Debt Must Be Unliquidated (in Dispute)**

1) **Unliquidated Debt—Consideration**
When the amount of the debt is in dispute, acceptance of a lesser sum discharges the debt. Consideration is given by the parties' giving up a legal right to contest the amount of debt.

2) **Liquidated Debt—No Consideration**
Acceptance of less than the entire amount of a liquidated debt is not satisfaction, and the balance of the debt is still owed. No consideration is given by the debtor, because the debtor has a preexisting obligation to pay the entire debt.

2. **Release**
A release (a promise to refrain from suing on a valid claim) bars any further recovery beyond the terms stated in the release. Releases will generally be binding if they are (1) given in good faith, (2) stated in a signed writing, and (3) accompanied by consideration.

3. **Covenant Not to Sue**
The parties substitute a contractual obligation for some other type of legal action based on a valid claim (such as promising not to sue on a valid claim if the cost of all damage is paid). In this case, if all damage is not paid, an action can be brought for breach of contract.

C. PROMISES ENFORCEABLE WITHOUT CONSIDERATION

1. **Promises to Pay Debts Barred by a Statute of Limitations**
Creditors must sue within a certain period to recover debts. If a debtor promises to pay a debt barred by a statute of limitations (promise can be implied if debtor acknowledges debt by making part payment), a creditor can sue to recover the entire debt, or at least the amount promised.

2. **Detrimental Reliance and Promissory Estoppel**
In some states, the doctrine of promissory estoppel prevents a promisor from asserting a lack of consideration as a defense. This occurs when—

   a. **Justifiable Reliance**
   A promise given by one party induces another party to rely (justifiably) on that promise to his or her detriment.

   b. **Foreseeability**
   The promisor must have known or had reason to believe that the promisee would likely be induced to change position. The change usually must be of substantial nature.

   c. **Fairness**
   If injustice cannot be avoided, the promise will be enforced.

3. **Charitable Subscriptions**
Promises to make gifts to charitable institutions are unenforceable because they are not supported by legally sufficient consideration.

   a. **Specific Use**
   Consideration may be found if the promisor bargained for and received a promise that the gift would be used in a specific way.

   b. **Promissory Estoppel**
   Some courts enforce these promises under the doctrine of promissory estoppel if a charity changes its position in reliance on the promise.

TRUE-FALSE QUESTIONS

(Answers at the Back of the Book)

___ 1. Normally, courts evaluate the adequacy or fairness of consideration even if the consideration is legally sufficient.

___ 2. A promise to do what one already has a legal duty to do is not legally sufficient consideration under most circumstances.

___ 3. Past consideration is consideration.

___ 4. Rescission is the unmaking of a contract so as to return the parties to the positions they occupied before the contract was made.

___ 5. A promise has no legal value as consideration.

___ 6. A covenant not to sue is an agreement to substitute a contractual obligation for some other type of action.

___ 7. A covenant not to sue always bars further recovery.

___ 8. Only a liquidated debt can serve as consideration for an accord and satisfaction.

___ 9. Consideration is the value given in return for a promise.

___ 10. Promissory estoppel may prevent a party from asserting a lack of consideration as a defense.

FILL-IN QUESTIONS

(Answers at the Back of the Book)

The doctrine of promissory estoppel, or detrimental reliance, involves a ____________________ (promise/performance) given by one party that induces another party to rely on it to his or her ____________________ (benefit/detriment). When the ____________________ (promisor/promisee) can reasonably have expected the reliance, and injustice cannot otherwise be avoided, the ______________ (promise/benefit) will be ____________________ (enforced/awarded). In other words, the ____________________ (promisor/promisee) must have acted with justifiable reliance. Generally, the act must have been of a ____________________ (substantial/inconsequential) nature.

MULTIPLE-CHOICE QUESTIONS

(Answers at the Back of the Book)

___ 1. Eve questions whether there is consideration for her contract with Frank. Consideration has two elements—there must be a bargained-for exchange and the value of whatever is exchanged must be

a. legally sufficient.
b. economically sufficient.
c. both a and b.
d. none of the above.

___ 2. Dave offers to buy a book owned by Lee for $40. Lee accepts and hands the book to Dave. The transfer and delivery of the book constitute performance. Is this performance consideration for Dave's promise?

a. Yes, because performance always constitutes consideration.
b. Yes, because Dave sought it in exchange for his promise, and Lee gave it in exchange for that promise.
c. No, because performance never constitutes consideration.
d. No, because Lee already had a duty to hand the book to Dave.

___ 3. **Based on a Sample CPA Exam Question.** Jay is seeking to avoid performing a promise to pay Karen $150. Jay is claiming a lack of consideration on Karen's part. Jay will win if he can show that

a. before Jay's promise, Karen had already performed the requested act.
b. Karen's only claim of consideration was the relinquishment of a legal right.
c. Karen's asserted consideration is only worth $50.
d. the consideration to be performed by Karen will be performed by a third party.

____ **4.** Gail promises to pay Harry $400 to repair the roof on Gail's office building. Harry fixes the roof. The act of fixing the roof is

a. consideration that creates Gail's obligation to pay Harry.
b. not consideration because Gail had a legal duty to pay Harry.
c. not consideration because it is not goods or money.
d. not consideration unless Gail is entirely satisfied with the job.

____ **5.** Max agrees to supervise a construction project for Nora for a certain fee. In mid-project, Max asks for more money, claiming an increase in the ordinary business expenses to complete the project. Nora agrees. This agreement is

a. enforceable as an accord and satisfaction.
b. enforceable because of unforeseen difficulties.
c. unenforceable under the preexisting duty rule.
d. unenforceable as an illusory promise.

____ **6.** Sue contracts with Todd to build two warehouses on two lots. After constructing the first warehouse, they decide to build a store on the second lot. Sue and Todd

a. may rescind the original contract and make a new contract to build a store.
b. may rescind the original contract but cannot make a new one to build a store.
c. must perform the executory part of the original contract.
d. must perform the original contract completely.

____ **7.** Pat causes an accident in which Ruth is injured. Ruth accepts Pat's offer of $5,000 to release Pat from further liability. Later, Ruth learns that her injuries are more serious than she realized. Ruth's release of Pat will

a. not bar a suit against Pat to recover for the injuries.
b. not bar a suit against Pat to recover for the injuries if Pat is insured.
c. not bar a suit against Pat to recover for the injuries if Ruth is insured.
d. prevent Ruth from suing Pat.

____ **8.** Jim promises to pay Kay to work for Jim. Kay agrees and quits her job. Jim does not hire Kay. Jim is liable to Kay based on

a. the concept of accord and satisfaction.
b. the concepts of rescission and new contract.
c. the doctrine of promissory estoppel.
d. Jim's illusory promise.

____ **9.** Eve questions whether there is consideration for her contract with Frank. Consideration has two elements—there must be a bargained-for exchange and the value of whatever is exchanged must be

a. adequately sufficient.
b. economically sufficient.
c. legally sufficient.
d. reasonably sufficient.

____ **10.** Don has a cause to sue Edna in a tort action, but agrees not to sue her if she will pay for the damage. If she fails to pay, Ed can bring an action against her for breach of contract. This is

a. a covenant not to sue.
b. an accord and satisfaction.
c. a release.
d. an unenforceable contract.

SHORT ESSAY QUESTIONS

1. When is consideration legally sufficient?

2. What are the circumstances in which a court will question whether consideration is adequate?

ISSUE SPOTTERS

(Answers at the Back of the Book)

1. In September, Sharon agrees to work for Cole Productions, Inc., at $500 a week for a year beginning January 1. In October, Sharon is offered the same work at $600 a week by Quintero Shows, Ltd. When Sharon tells Cole about the other offer, they tear up their contract and agree that Sharon will be paid $575. Is the new contract binding?

2. Rick, the president of Standard Corporation, announces to Standard employees, "If you work hard, and profits remain high, you'll get a bonus, if management thinks it's warranted." Profits remain high, but no bonus is paid. If the employees sue, would a court enforce the promise?

3. Before Paula starts her first year of college, Ross promises to pay her $5,000 if she graduates. She goes to college, borrowing and spending more than $5,000. At the start of he last semester, she reminds Ross of the promise. Ross sends her a note that says, "I revoke the promise." Is Ross's promise binding?

SPECIAL INFORMATION FOR CPA CANDIDATES

On the CPA examination, questions concerning consideration have often concentrated on the modification of contracts. You might find it helpful to review those rules. In particular, remember that an agreement to pay less than the amount that is owed for an unliquidated debt is not binding without consideration. Under the UCC, however, consideration is not required to modify a contract (for a sale of goods). Other important points to keep in mind include that the consideration exchanged by the parties does not have to have equal value—it does not even have to be reasonable or fair.

Chapter 12
Capacity and Legality

WHAT THIS CHAPTER IS ABOUT

If a party to a contract lacks capacity, an essential element for a valid contract is missing, and the contract is void. Some persons have capacity to enter into a contract, but if they wish, they can avoid liability under the contract. Also, to be enforceable, a contract must not violate any statutes or public policy.

CHAPTER OUTLINE

I. CONTRACTUAL CAPACITY

A. MINORS

A minor can enter into any contract that an adult can enter into, as long as it is not prohibited by law (for example, the sale of alcoholic beverages).

1. Age of Majority, Marriage, and Emancipation

A person who reaches the age of majority (eighteen, in most states) is not a minor for contractual purposes. In some states, marriage terminates minority status. Minors, over whom parents have relinquished control, have full contractual capacity.

2. Right to Disaffirm

A minor can disaffirm a contract by manifesting an intent not to be bound. A contract can ordinarily be disaffirmed at any time during minority or for a reasonable time after a minor comes of age.

3. Obligation on Disaffirmance

A minor cannot disaffirm a fully executed contract without returning whatever goods have been received or paying their reasonable value.

a. What the Adult Recovers

1) In Most States

If the goods (or other consideration) are in the minor's control, the minor must return them (without added compensation).

2) In a Growing Number of States

If the goods have been used, damaged, or ruined, the adult must be restored to the position he or she held before the contract.

b. What the Minor Recovers

All property that a minor has transferred to an adult as consideration, even if it is in the hands of a third party. If the property cannot be returned, the adult must pay the minor its value.

4. Exceptions to the Right to Disaffirm

a. Misrepresentation of Age

1) In Most States

A minor who misrepresents his or her age can still disaffirm a contract. In some states, he or she is not liable for fraud, because indirectly that might force the minor to perform the contract.

2) **In Some States**
Some states prohibit disaffirmance; some courts refuse to allow minors to disaffirm executed contracts unless they can return the consideration; some courts allow a minor to disaffirm but hold the minor liable for damages for fraud.

b. **Contracts for Necessaries**
Necessaries are food, clothing, shelter, medicine, and hospital care—whatever a court believes is necessary to maintain a person's status. A minor may disaffirm a contract for necessaries but will be liable for the reasonable value.

c. **Insurance and Loans**
Some jurisdictions prohibit a minor's right to disaffirm insurance contracts. If a loan is for the express purpose of enabling the minor to buy necessaries and the lender makes sure the money is so spent, then the minor must repay.

5. **Ratification**
Ratification is the act of accepting and thereby giving legal force to an obligation that was previously unenforceable.

a. **Express Ratification**
When a person, after reaching the age of majority, states orally or in writing that he or she intends to be bound by a contract.

b. **Implied Ratification**
When a minor performs acts inconsistent with disaffirmance or fails to disaffirm an executed contract within a reasonable time after reaching the age of majority.

6. **Parents' Liability**
Generally, parents are not liable for contracts made by their minor children acting on their own.

B. INTOXICATION

1. **If a Person Is Sufficiently Intoxicated to Lack Mental Capacity**
Any contract he or she enters into is voidable at the option of the intoxicated person, even if the intoxication was voluntary.

2. **If a Person Understands the Legal Consequences of a Contract**
Despite intoxication, the contract is usually enforceable.

C. MENTAL INCOMPETENCE

1. **Persons Adjudged Mentally Incompetent by a Court**
If a person has been adjudged mentally incompetent by a court of law and a guardian has been appointed, a contract by the person is void.

2. **Incompetent Persons Not So Adjudged by a Court**

a. **Those Who Do Not Understand Their Contracts**
A contract is voidable (at the option of the person) if a person does not know he or she is entering into the contract or lacks the capacity to comprehend its nature, purpose, and consequences.

b. **Those Who Understand Their Contracts**
If a mentally incompetent person understands the nature and effect of entering into a certain contract, the contract will be valid.

II. LEGALITY

A. CONTRACTS CONTRARY TO STATUTE

1. **Usury**
Every state sets rates of interest charged for loans (exceptions are made for certain business deals). Charging a higher rate is usury—some states allow recovery of the principal plus interest; other states allow recovery of the principal but no interest; a few states permit no recovery.

2. **Gambling**
All states regulate gambling (any scheme that involves distribution of property by chance among persons who pay for the chance to receive the property). Some states do not enforce gambling debts.

3. **Sabbath (Sunday) Laws**

   a. **Prohibited Contracts**
   In some states, all contracts entered into on a Sunday are illegal. Other states prohibit only the sale of certain merchandise (such as alcoholic beverages) on a Sunday.

   b. **Exceptions**
   Contracts for necessities and works of charity; executed contracts.

4. **Licensing Statutes**

   a. **Professional Licenses**
   Members of certain professions (such as doctors) must be licensed.

   b. **Business Licenses**
   Business licenses provide a means of regulating and taxing certain businesses, and protecting the public. Lack of a business license can bar the enforcement of a work-related contract.

      1) **Illegal Contracts**
      If the statute's purpose is to protect the public, a contract with an unlicensed individual is illegal.

      2) **Enforceable Contracts**
      If the statute's purpose is to raise revenue, a contract with an unlicensed individual is enforceable.

5. **Contracts to Commit a Crime**
A contract to commit a crime is illegal. If the contract is rendered illegal by statute after it has been entered into, the contract is discharged.

B. CONTRACTS CONTRARY TO PUBLIC POLICY

1. **Contracts in Restraint of Trade**

   a. **Prohibited Contracts**
   Contracts that restrain trade, adversely affect the public, or violate an antitrust statute.

   b. **Covenant Not to Compete**
   Acceptable if reasonable, determined by the length of time and size of area in which the party agrees not to compete. (In the sale of a business, it must also be a separate agreement.)

2. **Unconscionable Contracts or Clauses**
A bargain that is unfairly one-sided is unconscionable.

   a. **Procedural Unconscionability**
   Relates to a party's lack of knowledge or understanding of contract terms because of small print, "legalese," etc. An adhesion contract (drafted by one party for his benefit) may be held unconscionable.

   b. **Substantive Unconscionability**
   Relates to the parts of a contract that are so unfairly one-sided they "shock the conscience" of the court.

3. **Exculpatory Clauses**

   a. **What an Exculpatory Clause Is**
   Contract that absolves a party of negligence or other wrong. Sometimes found in rental agreements and real property leases.

   b. **Legality**
   Often held to be unconscionable. In most real property leases, held to be contrary to public policy. Not enforced if the party seeking its enforcement is involved in a business important to the public as a matter of practical necessity (airlines, public utilities).

4. **Other Contracts Contrary to Public Policy**

   a. **Discriminatory Contracts**
   Contracts in which a party promises to discriminate in terms of color, race, religion, national origin, disability, or gender.

   b. **Contracts for the Commission of a Tort**

   c. **Contracts Injuring Public Service**
   Contracts that interfere with a public officer's duties or involve a conflict between duties and private interests.

   d. **Agreements Obstructing the Legal Process**

C. EFFECT OF ILLEGALITY

1. **The General Rule**
An illegal contract is void. No party can sue to enforce it and no party can recover for its breach.

2. **Exceptions**

   a. **Justifiable Ignorance of the Facts**
   A party who is innocent may recover benefits conferred in a partially executed contract or enforce a fully performed contract.

   b. **Members of Protected Classes**
   When a statute is designed to protect a certain class of people, a member of that class can enforce a contract in violation of the statute (the other party to the contract cannot enforce it).

   c. **Withdrawal from an Illegal Agreement**
   If the illegal part of an agreement has not been performed, the party rendering performance can withdraw and recover the performance or its value.

   d. **Fraud, Duress, or Undue Influence**
   A party induced to enter into an illegal bargain by fraud, duress, or undue influence can enforce the contract or recover for its value.

3. **Severable, or Divisible, Contracts**
A court may enforce the legal part of a contract, if the illegal part does not affect the essence of the bargain.

TRUE-FALSE QUESTIONS

(Answers at the Back of the Book)

___ 1. An adult may not generally disaffirm a contract entered into with a minor.

___ 2. In some states, a minor who disaffirms a contract must restore the adult party to the position he or she held before the contract was made.

____ **3.** An intoxicated person who enters into a contract can void it.

____ **4.** A minor can disaffirm his or her liability for tortious conduct.

____ **5.** A person who has been adjudged mentally incompetent by a court cannot enter into legally binding contracts on his or her own.

____ **6.** A contract clause that exculpates one party for negligence or other wrongdoing will usually be considered unconscionable.

____ **7.** An adhesion contract is a contract in which the dominant party dictates the terms.

____ **8.** If an illegal contract is executory, it may be enforced.

____ **9.** If the purpose of a licensing statute is to protect the public from unlicensed practitioners, a contract entered into with an unlicensed practitioner is enforceable.

____ **10.** Covenants not to compete are never enforceable because they are unreasonable restraints of trade.

FILL-IN QUESTIONS

(Answers at the Back of the Book)

The act of accepting and giving legal force to an obligation that previously was not enforceable is ____________________ (disaffirmance/ratification). In relation to contracts entered into by minors or persons who are intoxicated or mentally incompetent, this is an act or an expression in words by which the person, on or after reaching majority or regaining sobriety or mental competence, indicates intent to be bound by a contract.

Disaffirmance or ratification may be express or implied. For example, a person's continued use and payments on something bought when he or she was incompetent is inconsistent with a desire to ____________________ (disaffirm/ratify) and ____________________ (indicates/does not indicate) an intent to be bound by the contract. In general, any act or conduct showing an intent to affirm the contract will be deemed ____________________ (disaffirmance/ratification).

MULTIPLE-CHOICE QUESTIONS

(Answers at the Back of the Book)

____ **1.** **Based on a Sample CPA Exam Question.** Tom is minor who enters into a contract with Diane. All of the following are effective methods for Tom to ratify the contract EXCEPT

a. expressly ratifying the contract after Tom reaches the age of majority.
b. failing to disaffirm the contact within a reasonable time after Tom reaches the age of majority.
c. ratifying the contract before Tom reaches the age of majority.
d. impliedly ratifying the contract after Tom reaches the age of majority.

____ **2.** While intoxicated, Don agrees to sell his warehouse for half its assessed value. The contract is

a. enforceable even if Don did not understand its legal consequences.
b. enforceable only if Don understood its legal consequences.
c. unenforceable because it obviously favors the buyer.
d. unenforceable under any circumstances.

___ 3. Ed is adjudged mentally incompetent. Fran is appointed to act as Ed's guardian. Ed signs a contract to sell his house. The contract is enforceable

a. only if Ed knew he was entering into a contract.
b. only if Ed had the mental capacity to comprehend the consequences.
c. if Ed knew he was entering into a contract or had the mental capacity to comprehend the consequences.
d. none of the above.

___ 4. Eve, a sixteen-year-old minor, buys a car from Fine Autos and wrecks it. To disaffirm the contract and satisfy a duty of restitution, Eve must

a. only return the car.
b. only pay for the damage.
c. return the car and pay for the damage.
d. none of the above.

___ 5. Bob bets Carl on the outcome of the SuperBowl. Gambling on sports events is illegal in their state. Before the game is over, Bob's attempt to withdraw from the bet is

a. invalid if it comes in the second half.
b. invalid without Carl's consent.
c. invalid unless Bob's team was ahead at the time of the withdrawal.
d. valid.

___ 6. Jill sells her business to Kyle and, as part of the agreement, promises not to engage in a business of the same kind within thirty miles for one year. This promise is

a. an unreasonable restraint of trade.
b. unreasonable in terms of geographic area and time.
c. unreasonable in terms of Kyle's "goodwill" and "reputation."
d. valid and enforceable.

___ 7. Luke is an unlicensed contractor in a state that requires a license to protect the public from unauthorized contractors. Mary hires Luke to build an office building. This contract is

a. enforceable only after Mary learns of Luke's status.
b. enforceable only before Mary learns of Luke's status.
c. enforceable only if no problems arise.
d. unenforceable.

___ 8. Fred signs a covenant not to compete with his employer, General Sales Corporation. This covenant is enforceable if it

a. is not ancillary to the sale of a business.
b. is reasonable in terms of geographic area and time.
c. is supported by consideration.
d. requires both parties to obtain business licenses.

___ 9. Sam leases real property from Tina under an agreement that includes an exculpatory clause. This clause is likely unenforceable

a. as a matter of public policy.
b. if either party is in a business important to the public interest.
c. if the lease involves commercial property.
d. none of the above.

___ 10. Ann contracts with Bob, a financial planner who is required by the state to have a license. Bob does not have a license. Their contract is enforceable if

a. Ann does not know that Bob is required to have a license.
b. Bob does not know that he is required to have a license.
c. the purpose of the statute is to protect the public from unlicensed practitioners.
d. the purpose of the statute is to raise government revenue.

SHORT ESSAY QUESTIONS

1. Who has protection under the law relating to contractual capacity and what protection do they have?

2. What makes an agreement illegal? What is the effect of an illegal agreement?

ISSUE SPOTTERS

(Answers at the Back of the Book)

1. Tom, a minor, enters into a contract with Diane. How might Tom effectively ratify this contract?

2. Joan runs a business through which she sells stolen goods. Joan pays Kim, a police officer, not to shut down her operation. When the crimes are discovered, Joan and Kim are jailed. Joan sues Kim to recover her payments to him. How much can she recover?

3. International Airlines, Inc., prints on its tickets that it is not liable for any injury to a passenger caused by the airline's negligence. If the cause of an accident is found to be the airline's negligence, can it use the clause as a defense to liability?

SPECIAL INFORMATION FOR CPA CANDIDATES

The CPA examination has not generally tested heavily on capacity. Those points that it may be important to keep in mind include that a minor can disaffirm a contract for a reasonable time after reaching majority. The CPA exam recognizes the rule that for a minor to disaffirm, he or she must return whatever the minor received under the contract. Also, on the CPA exam, intoxication qualifies as a defense only if it was involuntary.

The CPA exam has often asked questions relating to covenants not to compete and to contracts that violate licensing statutes. A covenant not to compete is usually legal if it is part of the sale of a business. A covenant not to compete between an employer and an employee is legal if it is reasonable in length of time and geographic scope.

If a contracting party failed to comply with a licensing statute that has as its purpose the raising of revenue, the contract will likely still be enforceable. If the purpose of the statute is to regulate members of the profession of which the noncomplying party claims to be a part, however, the contract is not enforceable.

Chapter 13
Genuineness of Assent

WHAT THIS CHAPTER IS ABOUT

A contract may be unenforceable if the parties have not genuinely assented to its terms. Assent may be lacking because of mistakes, misrepresentation, undue influence, or duress. A party who has not truly assented can choose to avoid the transaction. Lack of assent is both a defense to the enforcement of a contract and a ground for rescission (cancellation) of a contract.

CHAPTER OUTLINE

I. MISTAKES

It is important to distinguish between mistakes made in judgment as to value or quality and mistakes made as to facts. Only the latter have legal significance.

A. MISTAKES OF FACT

1. Bilateral Mistake of Fact

If *both* parties are mistaken as to a *material fact*, the contract can be rescinded by either. This is also true if the parties attach different meanings to a term subject to more than one reasonable interpretation.

2. Unilateral Mistake

When *one* contracting party makes a mistake as to some material fact, he or she is *not* entitled to relief from the contract. Exceptions are—

a. Other Party's Knowledge

A contract may not be enforceable if the other party to the contract knows or should have known that a mistake was made.

b. Mathematical Mistakes

A contract may not be enforceable if a significant mistake in addition, subtraction, division, or multiplication was inadvertent and made without gross negligence.

B. MISTAKES IN VALUE

When *one or both* parties make a mistake as to the *market value* or quality of the object of a contract, the contract can be *enforced* by either party.

II. FRAUDULENT MISREPRESENTATION

When an innocent party is fraudulently induced to enter into a contract, the contract normally can be avoided because that party has not voluntarily consented to its terms.

A. THE ELEMENTS OF FRAUD

(1) Misrepresentation of a material fact, (2) an intent to deceive, and (3) an innocent party's justifiable reliance on the misrepresentation.

1. Misrepresentation Has Occurred

Misrepresentation can be in words or actions.

a. **Statements of Opinion**
Statements of opinion are generally not subject to claims of fraud. But when a naïve purchaser relies on an expert's opinion, the innocent party may be entitled to rescission or reformation.

b. **Misrepresentation by Conduct**
Misrepresentation can occur by, for example, concealment, which prevents the other party from learning of a material fact.

c. **Misrepresentation of Law**
Misrepresentation of law does not entitle a party to relief, unless the misrepresenting party is in a profession that is known to require greater knowledge of the law than the average person has.

d. **Misrepresentation by Silence**
Generally, no party to a contract has a duty to disclose facts. Exceptions include—

1) **Latent Defect**
If a serious defect is known to the seller but could not reasonably be suspected by the buyer, the seller may have a duty to speak.

2) **Fiduciary Relationship**
In a fiduciary relationship, if one party knows facts that materially affect the other's interests, they must be disclosed.

3) **Statutory Provisions**
Some statutes (for example, the Truth-in-Lending Act) provide exceptions to the rule of nondisclosure.

2. **Intent to Deceive (*Scienter*)**
A misrepresenting party must know that facts are falsely represented.

a. **When This Occurs**
If a party (1) knows a fact is not as stated; (2) makes a statement he or she believes not to be true or makes it recklessly, without regard to the truth; or (3) says or implies that a statement is made on a basis such as personal knowledge when it is not.

b. **When Proof of Fault Is Not Necessary**
In many cases (often involving sales of land or stock), a buyer need prove only a seller's representation was false, without regard to the seller's state of mind.

3. **Reliance on the Misrepresentation**
The misrepresentation must be an important factor in inducing the party to contract. Reliance is not justified if the party knows the true facts or relies on obviously extravagant statements, or the defect is obvious.

B. INJURY TO THE INNOCENT PARTY
To rescind a contract, most courts do not require proof of injury. To recover damages, proof of injury is required. In actions based on fraud, punitive damages are often granted, on the public-policy ground of punishing the defendant or setting an example to deter similar wrongdoing by others.

III. NONFRAUDULENT MISREPRESENTATION

A. INNOCENT MISREPRESENTATION
This occurs when a person misrepresents a material fact without the intent to defraud (he or she believes the statement to be true). A party who relies on the statement to his or her detriment can rescind the contract.

B. NEGLIGENT MISREPRESENTATION

This occurs when a person misrepresents a material fact by failing to exercise reasonable care in uncovering or disclosing the facts, or not using the skill and competence that his or her business or profession requires. In effect, this is treated as fraudulent misrepresentation.

IV. UNDUE INFLUENCE

Undue influence occurs when a contract enriches a party at the expense of another who is dominated by the enriched party. Such a contract is voidable.

A. LACK OF FREE WILL

The essential feature is that the party taken advantage of does not exercise free will.

B. CONFIDENTIAL OR FIDUCIARY RELATIONSHIPS

Undue influence often occurs in relationships in which one party can greatly influence another (attorney-client, parent-child). The dominant party is held to extreme or utmost good faith in dealing with the subservient party.

1. Presumption

When a contract between the parties favors the dominant party, a court will often presume that it was made under undue influence.

2. To Rebut the Presumption

The dominant party has to show that full disclosure was made, that consideration was adequate, and that the subservient party received independent and competent advice before completing the transaction.

V. DURESS

Duress involves conduct of a coercive nature.

A. WHAT DURESS IS

Forcing a party to enter into a contract by threatening the party with a wrongful or illegal act—threatening blackmail or extortion, for example.

B. WHAT DURESS IS NOT

Threatening to exercise a legal right; economic need (unless the party exacting the price also creates the need).

VI. ADHESION CONTRACTS AND UNCONSCIONABILITY

A. WHAT AN ADHESION CONTRACT IS

A contract written exclusively by one party (the dominant party, usually a seller or creditor) and presented to the other (buyer or borrower) on a take-it-or-leave-it basis. Typically, a standard form contract.

B. TO AVOID ENFORCEMENT OF THE CONTRACT

The adhering party must show that the parties had substantially unequal bargaining positions and that enforcement would be unfair or oppressive.

1. Unconscionability

Unconscionability under UCC 2–302 applies only to contracts for sales of goods. Many courts, however, apply the concept to other contracts.

2. Fraud, Undue Influence, and Duress

In states that have not adopted UCC 2–302, the courts rely on traditional notions of fraud, undue influence, and duress.

TRUE-FALSE QUESTIONS

(Answers at the Back of the Book)

___ 1. A unilateral mistake does not generally afford the mistaken party a right to relief from the contract.

___ 2. When parties to both sides of a contract are mistaken as to the same material fact, either party can rescind the contract.

___ 3. To commit fraud, one party must intend to mislead another.

___ 4. To rescind a contract for fraud, a plaintiff must prove that he or she suffered an injury.

___ 5. Threatening a civil suit does not normally constitute duress.

___ 6. A contract entered into under undue influence is voidable.

___ 7. Adhesion contracts are always enforced.

___ 8. If a person believes a statement to be true, he or she cannot be held liable for misrepresentation.

___ 9. A seller has no duty to disclose to a buyer a defect that is known to the seller but could not reasonably be suspected by a buyer.

___ 10. When both parties make a mistake as to the market value of the object of their contract, either party can rescind the contract.

FILL-IN QUESTIONS

(Answers at the Back of the Book)

Believing something is worth more than it is a mistake of ____________________(fact/value). When parties contract, their agreement establishes the worth of the object of their contract for the moment. The next moment, the worth may change. Either party may be mistaken as to what the change may be. This is a mistake of __________ (fact/value). Under such a mistake, a contract ______________________ (cannot/may) be avoided. Mistakes as to ______________________________ (value/fact) will almost never justify voiding a contract.

MULTIPLE-CHOICE QUESTIONS

(Answers at the Back of the Book)

___ 1. **Based on a Sample CPA Exam Question.** Metro Transport asks for bids on a construction project. Metro estimates that the cost will be $200,000. Most bids are about $200,000, but A&B Construction bids $150,000. In adding a column of figures, A&B mistakenly omitted a $50,000 item. Because Metro had reason to know of the mistake

a. A&B can avoid the contract because Metro knew of the errors.
b. A&B can avoid the contract because the errors were the result of negligence.
c. Metro can enforce the contract because the errors were unilateral.
d. Metro can enforce the contract because the errors were material.

___ 2. Adam persuades Beth to contract for his company's services by telling her that his employees are the "best and the brightest." Adam's statement is

a. duress.
b. fraud.
c. puffery.
d. undue influence.

___ 3. Carol sells to Dan ten shares of Eagle Corporation stock. Dan believes that it will increase in value, but it later drops in price. From Carol, Dan can most likely recover

a. the difference between the stock's purchase price and its later value.
b. the stock's later value only.
c. the stock's purchase price only.
d. none of the above.

___ 4. Fran is an eighty-year-old widow with no business experience. Fran's nephew Mark urges her to sell some of her stock at a price below market value to Tim, Mark's "business" partner. Fran, relying on Mark, agrees to sell the stock to Tim. She may avoid the contract on the ground of

a. duress.
b. fraud.
c. mistake.
d. undue influence.

___ 5. In offering to sell amplifiers to Eve for her theater, Fred intentionally misstates their capacity. In reliance, Eve buys the amplifiers. Frank's statement is

a. duress.
b. fraud.
c. puffery.
d. undue influence.

___ 6. Ken sells Larry a parcel of land, claiming that it is "perfect" for commercial development. Larry later learns that it is not zoned for commercial uses. Larry may rescind the contract only if

a. Ken knew about the zoning law.
b. Larry did not know about the zoning law.
c. the zoning law was not common knowledge.
d. none of the above.

___ 7. Energy Source, a chain of computer stores, presents its customer Joe with a form contract on a take-it-or-leave basis to finance his purchase. The contract is

a. not enforceable if enforcement would be unfair or oppressive.
b. not enforceable if the terms are fair but the customer does not want to pay.
c. not enforceable in states that have not adopted UCC 2–302.
d. enforceable under all circumstances.

___ 8. Ron contracts with Gail under what Ron later learns to have been misrepresented facts. Ron has not yet suffered an injury. He can

a. only obtain damages from Gail.
b. only rescind the contract.
c. either obtain damages or rescind the contract.
d. none of the above.

___ 9. To sell his house to Amy, Ray does not tell her that the foundation was built on unstable pilings. Amy may later avoid the contract on the ground of

a. duress.
b. fraud.
c. mistake.
d. undue influence.

___ 10. Lou and Paula enter into a contract. Lou later tells Paula that if she does not perform her part of the deal, he will sue her. Paula can avoid the contract on the basis of

a. duress.
b. fraudulent misrepresentation.
c. undue influence.
d. none of the above.

SHORT ESSAY QUESTIONS

1. Why are mistakes of value not accorded the same relief as mistakes of fact?

2. What are the elements of fraudulent misrepresentation?

ISSUE SPOTTERS

(Answers at the Back of the Book)

1. Mike, a famous and wealthy musician, dies. Mike's wife Jenny sells their farm to Carl, who asks what should be done with all the "junk" on the property. Jenny says that Carl can do whatever he wants with it. Unknown to Jenny or Carl, in a cabinet in the house are the master tapes for an unreleased album. Can Carl keep the tapes?

2. In selling a house, Matt tells Ann that the wiring, fixtures, and appliances are of a certain quality. Matt knows nothing about the quality, but it is not as specified. Ann buys the house. On learning the true quality, Ann confronts Matt, who says he wasn't trying to fool her, he was only trying to make a sale. Can she rescind the deal?

3. Julie, an accountant, certifies several audit reports to Olive Corporation, Julie's client, knowing that Olive intends to use the reports to obtain loans from Ace Credit Company. Julie believes that the reports are true and does not intend to deceive Ace, but does not check the reports before certifying them. Can Julie be held liable to Ace?

SPECIAL INFORMATION FOR CPA CANDIDATES

The CPA examination has traditionally covered at least four of the types of conduct mentioned in this chapter—fraudulent misrepresentation, nonfraudulent misrepresentation, undue influence, and duress. You may want to review the elements of those types of conduct, keeping in mind that each of these is interpreted according to the person defrauded, unduly influenced, or under duress (they are not interpreted according to what a reasonable person in the position of the innocent party would have believed). Remember, too, that the conduct must relate to a material fact, or otherwise be material, and it must truly result in the innocent party's assent.

Chapter 14
The Statute of Frauds

WHAT THIS CHAPTER IS ABOUT

Under the Statute of Frauds, certain types of contracts must be in writing to be enforceable. If there is no written evidence of a contract that falls under this statute, it is not void, but it may not be enforceable. This chapter covers contracts that fall under the Statute of Frauds and the parol evidence rule, which concerns the admissibility at trial of evidence that is external to written contracts.

CHAPTER OUTLINE

I. ORIGIN OF THE STATUTE OF FRAUDS

The English passed the Statute of Frauds in 1677. Today, every state has a statute that stipulates what types of contracts must be in writing (or evidenced by a writing) to be enforceable. If one of these contracts is not in writing, the contract is not void but the Statute of Frauds is a defense to its enforcement.

II. CONTRACTS FALLING WITHIN THE STATUTE OF FRAUDS

A. CONTRACTS INVOLVING INTERESTS IN LAND

Land includes all objects permanently attached, such as trees. Contracts to transfer interests in land (such as leases; see Chapter 48) must be in writing.

B. THE ONE-YEAR RULE

1. Performance Objectively Impossible Must Be in Writing

A contract must be in writing if performance is objectively impossible within a year of the date of the contract's formation.

2. Possibility of Performance Need Not Be in Writing

A contract need not be in writing if performance within one year is possible—even if it is improbable, unlikely, or takes longer.

C. COLLATERAL PROMISES

A promise ancillary to a principal transaction and made by a third party to assume the debts or obligations of the primary party (only if the primary party does not perform) must be in writing to be enforceable.

1. Exception—"Main Purpose" Rule

An oral promise to answer for the debt of another is enforceable if the guarantor's main purpose is to secure a personal benefit.

2. Estate Debts

Promises made by the administrator or executor of an estate to pay personally the estate debts must be in writing to be enforceable.

D. PROMISES MADE IN CONSIDERATION OF MARRIAGE

Prenuptial agreements must be in writing to be enforceable.

E. CONTRACTS FOR SALES OF GOODS

The Uniform Commercial Code (UCC) requires a writing for a sale of goods priced at $500 or more (see Chapter 19).

F. EXCEPTIONS TO THE STATUTE OF FRAUDS

1. Partial Performance

a. Contracts for the Transfer of Interests in Land

If a buyer pays part of the price, takes possession, and makes permanent improvements and the parties cannot be returned to their pre-contract status quo, a court may grant specific performance.

b. Contracts Covered by the UCC

Under the UCC, an oral contract is enforceable to the extent that a seller accepts payment or a buyer accepts delivery of the goods.

2. Admissions

In some states, if a party admits in pleadings, testimony, or in court that a contract was made, the contract will be enforceable.

3. Promissory Estoppel

An oral contract may be enforced if (1) a promisor makes a promise on which the promisee justifiably relies to his or her detriment, (2) the reliance was foreseeable to the promisor, and (3) injustice can be avoided only by enforcing the promise.

4. Special Exceptions under the UCC

Oral contracts that may be enforceable under the UCC include those for customized goods and those between merchants that have been confirmed in writing (see Chapter 19).

III. SUFFICIENCY OF THE WRITING

No formal writing is required, but there must be at least a memo that includes the following.

A. SIGNATURE OF THE PARTY TO BE CHARGED

The writing must be signed (initialed) by the party against whom enforcement is sought (the party who refuses to perform). The signature can be anywhere in the writing.

B. ESSENTIAL TERMS

1. Contracts Covered by the UCC

The writing must include a quantity term. Other terms need not be stated exactly, if they adequately reflect the parties' intentions.

2. Other Contracts

The writing must include the identity of the parties, subject matter, consideration, and essential terms (in a sale of land these would include the price and a description of the property).

IV. THE PAROL EVIDENCE RULE

A. THE RULE

If a written contract is the final expression of the parties' agreement, evidence of prior negotiations, prior agreements, or contemporaneous oral agreements that contradicts or varies the terms is not admissible at trial.

B. EXCEPTIONS

Parol evidence is admissible to show—

1. **Contract Subsequently Modified**
   Evidence of subsequent modification (oral or written) of a written contract is admissible (but oral modifications may not be enforceable if they bring the contract under the Statute of Frauds).

2. **A Contract Is Voidable or Void**

3. **Meaning of Ambiguous Terms**

4. **Essential Term Lacking in an Incomplete Contract**

5. **Prior Dealing, Course of Performance, or Usage of Trade**
   Under the UCC, evidence can be introduced to explain or supplement a contract by showing a prior dealing, course of performance, or usage of trade (see Chapter 19).

6. **Orally Agreed-on Condition**
   Proof of such a condition does not modify the written terms but involves the enforceability of the written contract.

7. **An Obvious or Gross Clerical Error**

TRUE-FALSE QUESTIONS

(Answers at the Back of the Book)

___ 1. A contract that cannot, by its own terms, possibly be performed within a year must be in writing to be enforceable.

___ 2. A promise to answer for the debt of another must always be in writing to be enforceable.

___ 3. A promise on which a promisee justifiably relies to his or her detriment will not be enforced unless it is in writing.

___ 4. In some states, if a party admits in pleadings that a contract was made, even if the contract was oral, it will be enforceable.

___ 5. Oral contracts that are *not* enforceable under the UCC include those for customized goods.

___ 6. A contract for a transfer of an interest in land need not be in writing to be enforceable under the Statute of Frauds.

___ 7. To be enforceable, a contract for a sale of goods priced at $300 or more must be in writing.

___ 8. An oral contract that should be in writing to be enforceable under the Statute of Frauds may be enforceable if it has been partially performed.

___ 9. The only writing sufficient to satisfy the Statute of Frauds is a printed form, with the heading "Contract," signed at the bottom by all parties.

___ 10. The parol evidence rule permits the introduction at trial of evidence of the parties' negotiations or agreements that contradicts or varies their contract.

FILL-IN QUESTIONS

(Answers at the Back of the Book)

A collateral promise is a promise that is ______________________ (superior/ancillary) to a ______________________ (primary/secondary) contractual relationship.

A promise by one person to pay the debts or discharge the duties of another person if the other fails to perform ____________________ (must/need not) be in writing to be enforceable under the Statute of Frauds. If the main purpose of a promise to pay another's debts or perform another's duties is to benefit the promisor, however, the agreement ____________________ (must/need not) be in writing to be enforceable.

MULTIPLE-CHOICE QUESTIONS

(Answers at the Back of the Book)

___ **1.** Jim orally promises to work for Pat, and Pat orally promises to employ Jim at a rate of $500 a week. This contract must be in writing to be enforceable if Jim promises to work for

a. his entire life.
b. at least five years.
c. five years but either party can terminate the contract on two weeks' notice.
d. both a and c.

___ **2.** Standard Business Company agrees to hire Tim as a sales representative for six months. Their contract is oral. This contract is enforceable by

a. Standard only.
b. Tim only.
c. Standard or Tim.
d. none of the above.

___ **3.** **Based on a Sample CPA Exam Question.** Under a written agreement, Adam sells a motel to Bill. When Adam removes the furniture, Bill sues. The court decides the written agreement includes everything the parties intended. Which of the following agreements about the furniture will be admissible?

a. A prior written agreement only
b. A subsequent oral agreement only
c. Either a prior written agreement or a subsequent oral agreement
d. None of the above

___ **4.** Alpha Properties and Beta Corporation enter into an oral contract for the sale of a warehouse. Before Beta takes possession, this contract is enforceable by

a. Alpha only.
b. Beta only.
c. Alpha or Beta.
d. none of the above.

___ **5.** ABC Distribution, Inc., orally contracts for a lease of its storage facilities to Delta Manufacturing Company. Delta pays part of the price, takes possession, and makes permanent improvements to the property. The contract is most likely enforceable against

a. ABC only.
b. Delta only.
c. ABC and Delta.
d. none of the above.

___ 6. Alpha Computers contracts with Engineers. Inc. (EI), to buy EI's circuit boards. The contract is most likely enforceable against EI if Alpha offers as proof of the agreement

a. a sales slip signed by EI.
b. a purchase order that sets out all the terms but is signed by neither party.
c. the sales slip signed by EI or the unsigned work order.
d. none of the above.

___ 7. Investors, Inc., contracts with J&J Properties to buy J&J's warehouse. The contract is most likely enforceable against J&J if Investors offers as proof of the agreement

a. a blank sheet of J&J's letterhead stationery only.
b. J&J's business card only.
c. a blank sheet of J&J's letterhead stationery or J&J's business card.
d. none of the above.

___ 8. Jay and Kim enter into a contract for Jay's sale to Kim of ten computers for $500 each. After Kim takes possession, but before she makes payment, this contract is enforceable

a. only if it is in writing.
b. only if it is oral.
c. whether it is oral or in writing.
d. none of the above.

___ 9. Ed borrows $1,000 from First State Bank. Fran orally promises the bank that she will repay the debt if Ed does not. This promise is enforceable by

a. Ed only.
b. First State Bank only.
c. Ed or First State Bank.
d. none of the above.

___ 10. Greg agrees to make bookshelves for Holly, who tells Ira that she will guarantee payment for whatever supplies Greg orders from Ira for the shelves. Holly's promise is enforceable

a. only if it is in writing.
b. only if it is oral.
c. whether it is oral or in writing.
d. none of the above.

SHORT ESSAY QUESTIONS

1. What is required to satisfy the writing requirement of the Statute of Frauds?

2. What is *not* admissible under the parol evidence rule?

ISSUE SPOTTERS

(Answers at the Back of the Book)

1. In selling an office building, Jill tells Kyle that the filing cabinets are included. The sales agreement, which says that it "supercedes all oral promises relating to the sale," says nothing about the filing cabinets. Are the cabinets a part of the deal?

2. Quality Goods, Inc. (QGI), and National Sales Corporation orally agree to a deal. QGI types up the essential terms on letterhead stationery and files it in QGI's office. If QGI later refuses to complete the transaction, is this memo a sufficient writing to enforce the contract against it?

3. GamesCo orders $800 worth of game pieces from Midstate Plastic, Inc. Midstate delivers, and GamesCo pays for, $450 worth. GamesCo then says it wants no more pieces from Midstate. GamesCo and Midstate have never dealt with each other before and have nothing in writing. Can Midstate enforce a deal for $350 more?

SPECIAL INFORMATION FOR CPA CANDIDATES

Among the details covered in this chapter, the CPA examination has asked questions about the types of contracts that fall within the Statute of Frauds, the enforceability of oral contracts that come under the Statute of Frauds, and the effect of an oral acceptance of a written offer. Sometimes, these details have been woven into questions are less direct. For example, a question might ask for a calculation of damages for the breach of an oral contract, which requires a consideration of the types of contracts subject to the Statute of Frauds.

Chapter 15
Third Party Rights

WHAT THIS CHAPTER IS ABOUT

A party to a contract can assign the rights arising from it to another or delegate the duties of the contract by having another perform them. A third party also acquires rights to enforce a contract when the contract parties intend the contract to benefit the third party (who is an intended beneficiary). When a contract only incidentally benefits a third party, he or she is an incidental beneficiary and cannot enforce it.

CHAPTER OUTLINE

I. ASSIGNMENTS AND DELEGATIONS

Assignment and delegation occur after the original contract is made, when one of the parties transfers to another party an interest or duty in the contract.

A. ASSIGNMENTS

1. What an Assignment Is

Parties to a contract have rights and duties. One party has a *right* to require the other to perform, and the other has a *duty* to perform. The transfer of the *right* to a third person is an assignment.

2. Effect of an Unconditional Assignment

(1) The rights of the assignor are extinguished; (2) the assignee has a right to demand performance from the obligor; and (3) the assignee's rights are subject to the defenses the obligor has against the assignor.

3. How Assignments Function

Assignments are involved in much business financing. The most common contractual right that is assigned is the right to the payment of money.

4. Form of an Assignment

An assignment can take any form, oral or written. Assignments covered by the Statute of Frauds must be in writing to be enforceable. Most states require contracts for the assignment of wages to be in writing.

5. Rights That Cannot Be Assigned

a. Statute Prohibits Assignment

(For example, statutes often prohibit assignment of future workers' compensation benefits.)

b. Contract Is Personal

The rights under the contract cannot be assigned unless all that remains is a money payment. (Personal services are unique to the person rendering them. Rights to receive personal services are likewise unique and cannot be assigned.)

c. Assignment Materially Increases or Alters Risk or Duties of Obligor

d. Contract Stipulates That It Cannot Be Assigned

Exceptions: a contract cannot prevent an assignment of—

1) A right to receive money.
2) Rights in real estate (restraint against alienation).
3) Rights in negotiable instruments (see Chapter 24).
4) A right to receive damages for breach of a sales contract or for payment of amount owed under it (even if contract prohibits it).

6. Notice of Assignment
An assignment is effective immediately, with or without notice.

a. Same Right Assigned to More Than One Party
If the assignor assigns the same right to different persons, in most states, the first assignment in time is the first in right. In some states, priority is given to the first assignee who gives notice.

b. Discharge before Notice
Until an obligor has notice, his or her obligation can be discharged by performance to the assignor. Once the obligor has notice, only performance to the assignee can act as a discharge.

B. DELEGATIONS
Duties are delegated. The party making the delegation is the delegator; the party to whom the duty is delegated is the delegatee.

1. Form of Delegation
No special form is required.

2. Duties That Cannot Be Delegated
Any duty can be delegated, unless (1) performance depends on the personal skill or talents of the obligor, or special trust has been placed in the obligor, (2) performance by a third party will vary materially from that expected by the obligee (the one to whom performance is owed) under the contract, or (3) the contract expressly prohibits it.

3. Effect of a Delegation
The obligee (the one to whom performance is owed) must accept performance from the delegatee, unless the duty is one that cannot be delegated. If the delegatee fails to perform, the delegator is still liable.

4. Liability of the Delegatee
If the delegatee makes a promise of performance that will directly benefit the obligee, there is an "assumption of duty." Breach of this duty makes the delegatee liable to the obligee, and the obligee can sue both the delegatee and the delegator.

C. ASSIGNMENT OF ALL RIGHTS
A contract that provides in general words for an assignment of all rights (for example, "I assign the contract" or "I assign all my rights under the contract") is both an assignment of rights and a delegation of duties.

II. THIRD PARTY BENEFICIARIES
Only intended beneficiaries acquire legal rights in a contract.

A. INTENDED BENEFICIARIES
An intended beneficiary is one for whose benefit a contract is made. If the contract is breached, he or she can sue the promisor.

1. Types of Intended Beneficiaries

a. Creditor Beneficiaries
A creditor beneficiary benefits from a contract in which a promisor promises to pay a debt that the promisee owes to him or her.

b. **Donee Beneficiaries**
A donee beneficiary benefits from a contract made for the express purpose of giving a gift to him or her. (The "modern view" is not to distinguish between types of intended beneficiaries.)

2. **Vesting of an Intended Beneficiary's Rights**
To enforce a contract against the original parties, the rights of the third party must first vest (take effect). The rights vest when (1) the third party manifests assent to the contract or (2) the third party materially alters his or her position in detrimental reliance

3. **Modification or Rescission of the Contract**
Until the third party's rights vest, the others can modify or rescind the contract without the third party's consent. If the contract reserves the power to rescind or modify, vesting does not terminate the power.

B. INCIDENTAL BENEFICIARIES
The benefit that an incidental beneficiary receives from a contract between other parties is unintentional. An incidental beneficiary cannot enforce a contract to which he or she is not a party.

C. INTENDED OR INCIDENTAL BENEFICIARY?

1. **Reasonable Person Test**
A beneficiary is intended if a reasonable person in his or her position would believe that the promisee intended to confer on the beneficiary the right to sue to enforce the contract.

2. **Other Factors Indicating an Intended Beneficiary**
(1) Performance is rendered directly to the third party, (2) the third party has the right to control the performance, or (3) the third party is expressly designated as beneficiary in the contract.

TRUE-FALSE QUESTIONS

(Answers at the Back of the Book)

___ 1. Third parties have no rights under contracts to which they are not parties.

___ 2. The party who makes an assignment is the assignee.

___ 3. Rights under a personal service contract normally can be assigned.

___ 4. All rights can be assigned.

___ 5. An assignee can compel an obligor with notice of the assignment to perform.

___ 6. A right to the payment of money may be assigned.

___ 7. An assignment is not effective without notice.

___ 8. No special form is required to create a valid delegation of duties.

___ 9. Only intended beneficiaries acquire legal rights in a contract.

___ 10. A delegation does not relieve the delegator of the obligation to perform if the delegatee fails to perform.

FILL-IN QUESTIONS

(Answers at the Back of the Book)

The transfer of rights to a third person is ______________________ (an assignment/a delegation) and the transfer of duties to a third person is ______________________ (an assignment/a delegation). Probably the most common contractual right that is ______________________ (assigned/delegated) is the right to the payment of money. For instance, Digital Computer Corporation sells its computers on credit. Digital has the right to installment payments from its customers. To obtain funds to buy more inventory, Digital can ______________ (assign/delegate) the right to the payments to a financing agency, which will pay Digital for the right.

MULTIPLE-CHOICE QUESTIONS

(Answers at the Back of the Book)

___ 1. Greg enters into a contract with Holly that indirectly benefits Ira, although neither Greg nor Holly intended that result. Ira is

a. a delegatee.
b. an assignee.
c. an incidental beneficiary.
d. an intended beneficiary.

___ 2. Dan and Eve sign a contract under which Dan agrees to repair Eve's computer for $150. Later, they agree that Eve will pay the $150 directly to Dan's creditor, First State Bank. The bank is

a. a delegatee.
b. an assignee.
c. an incidental beneficiary.
d. an intended beneficiary.

___ 3. Jim and Kay enter into a contract that intentionally benefits Lora. Lora's rights under this contract will vest

a. only if she manifests assent to it.
b. only if she materially alters her position in detrimental reliance on it.
c. if she manifests assent to it or if she materially alters her position in detrimental reliance on it.
d. none of the above.

___ 4. Jill insures her warehouse under a policy with Kappa Insurance Company. Jill assigns the policy to Lyle, who also owns a warehouse. Kappa's best argument against the assignment of the policy is that

a. it did not consent to the assignment.
b. it was not paid for the assignment.
c. the assignment will materially alter its risk.
d. this is a personal service contract.

___ 5. Nora signs a contract to provide lawn-mowing services to Owen. Nora delegates her duty under the contract to Pat. Owen can compel performance from

a. Nora only.
b. Pat only.
c. Pat or, if Pat does not perform, Nora.
d. none of the above.

____ **6.** Ron and Sue sign a contract. Tim, a third party, is an intended beneficiary to the contract if

a. performance is rendered directly to Tim.
b. there is an express designation in the contract.
c. Tim has the right to control the details of performance.
d. any of the above.

____ **7.** **Based on a Sample CPA Exam Question.** Dan assigns to Evan a contract to buy a used car from Fran. To be valid, the assignment must

a. be in writing and be signed by Dan.
b. be supported by adequate consideration from Evan.
c. not be revocable by Dan.
d. not materially increase Fran's risk or duty.

____ **8.** A contract for a sale of goods between John and Mary provides that the right to receive damages for its breach cannot be assigned. This clause

a. is effective only before the contract is executed.
b. is effective only after the contract is executed.
c. is effective under all circumstances.
d. is not effective.

____ **9.** Ellen unconditionally assigns to Fred her rights under a contract with Gil. Ellen's rights under the contract

a. are extinguished.
b. continue until the contract is fully executed.
c. continue until Gil performs his obligations under the contract.
d. continue until Fred receives Gil's performance.

____ **10.** Ann has a right to receive payment under a contract with Bill. Without notice, Ann assigns the right first to Carl and then to Diane. In most states, the party with priority to the right would be

a. Ann.
b. Bill.
c. Carl.
d. Diane.

SHORT ESSAY QUESTIONS

1. What is a third party beneficiary contract? What are the circumstances under which a third party can bring an action to enforce it?

2. Who are the parties in an assignment? What are their rights and duties?

ISSUE SPOTTERS

(Answers at the Back of the Book)

1. Brad owes Carol $100. Don tells Brad to give him the money and he will pay Carol. Brad gives the money to Don who does not pay Carol. Can Carol successfully sue Don for the money?

2. Alan owes Beth $100. Beth assigns her right to the money to Chuck. Can Chuck successfully sue Alan for the money?

3. Eagle Construction Company contracts to build a house for Frank. The contract states that "any assignment of this contract renders the contract void." After Eagle builds the house, but before Frank pays, Eagle assigns its right to payment to Good Credit Company. Can Good Credit enforce the contract against Frank?

SPECIAL INFORMATION FOR CPA CANDIDATES

It is important to remember for the CPA examination that only a creditor or donee beneficiary may recover from a promisor who fails to perform according to the contract—an incidental beneficiary has no enforceable rights under the contract. It is also important to remember that generally any contract can be assigned (unless the contract expressly prohibits it). There are more restrictions on delegations of duties. The point to remember in regard to delegation of duties is that when a duty is personal, it cannot be assigned.

Finally, it should be remembered that unless there is a release or a novation, the assignor remains liable on the contract despite its assignment. A party who, without notice of an assignment, pays an assignor will not later be liable to the assignee: the assignee should notify the obligor of the assignment.

Chapter 16
Performance and Discharge

WHAT THIS CHAPTER IS ABOUT

This chapter discusses performance and discharge of contracts. Performance of a contract (when the parties do what they agreed to do) discharges it. Discharging a contract terminates it. Discharge usually results from performance but can occur in other ways: (1) the occurrence or failure of a condition on which a contract is based, (2) breach of the contract, (3) agreement of the parties, and (4) operation of law.

CHAPTER OUTLINE

I. CONDITIONS

A **condition** is a possible future event, occurrence or nonoccurrence of which triggers performance of an obligation or terminates an obligation. If performance is contingent on a condition that is not satisfied, neither party has to perform.

A. CONDITION PRECEDENT

A condition that must be fulfilled before a party's performance can be required. Such conditions are common. For example, a real estate contract is usually conditioned on the buyer's ability to get financing.

B. CONDITION SUBSEQUENT

A condition that operates to terminate an obligation to perform. The condition follows a duty to perform. Such conditions are rare.

C. CONCURRENT CONDITION

When each party's duty to perform is conditioned on the other party's duty to perform. Occurs only when the parties are to perform their duties simultaneously (for example, paying for goods on delivery). No party can recover for breach unless he or she first tenders performance.

D. EXPRESS AND IMPLIED CONDITIONS

1. Express Condition

Provided for by the parties' agreement. Usually prefaced by the word "if," "provided," "after," or "when."

2. Implied-in-Fact Condition

Understood to be part of the agreement but not found in the express language of the agreement. The court infers them from the promises (notice is an implied condition to correct a defect under warranty).

II. DISCHARGE BY PERFORMANCE

Most contracts are discharged by the parties' doing what they promised to do.

A. TENDER OF PERFORMANCE

Discharge can be accomplished by **tender** (an unconditional offer to perform by one who is ready, willing, and able to do so). If performance has been tendered and the other party refuses to perform, the party making the tender can sue for breach.

B. TYPES OF PERFORMANCE

1. Complete Performance
Express conditions fully satisfied in all aspects.

2. Substantial Performance
Performance that does not vary greatly from the performance promised in the contract. If one party fulfills the terms of the contract with substantial performance, the other party is obligated to perform (but may obtain damages for the deviations).

3. Performance to the Satisfaction of One of the Parties
When the subject matter of the contract is personal, performance must actually satisfy the party (a condition precedent). Contracts involving mechanical fitness, utility, or marketability need only be performed to the satisfaction of a reasonable person.

4. Performance to the Satisfaction of a Third Party
When the satisfaction of a third party is required, most courts require the work to be satisfactory to a reasonable person.

C. MATERIAL BREACH OF CONTRACT
A breach of contract is the nonperformance of a contractual duty. It is material when performance is not at least substantial; the nonbreaching party is excused from performing. If a breach is minor (not material), the nonbreaching party's duty to perform may be suspended until the breach is remedied.

D. ANTICIPATORY REPUDIATION
Before either party has a duty to perform, one party refuses to perform.

1. Damages and a Similar Contract
This can discharge the nonbreaching party, who can sue to recover damages immediately and can also seek a similar contract elsewhere.

2. Retraction
Until the nonbreaching party treats repudiation as a breach, the repudiating party can retract his or her repudiation by proper notice.

E. TIME FOR PERFORMANCE
If a specific time is stated, the parties must usually perform by that time. If time is stated to be vital or construed to be "of the essence," it is a condition of the contract. If no time is stated, a reasonable time is implied, and a delay will not affect the performing party's right to payment.

III. DISCHARGE BY AGREEMENT

A. DISCHARGE BY RESCISSION
Rescission is the process by which a contract is canceled and the parties are returned to the positions they occupied prior to forming it.

1. Executory Contracts
Contracts that are executory on both sides can be rescinded.

a. Requirements
The parties must make another agreement, which must satisfy the legal requirements for a contract. Their promises not to perform are consideration for the second contract.

b. Form
A rescission agreement is enforceable if oral (even if the original agreement was in writing), except an agreement must be in writing if it is subject to the UCC and the contract requires written rescission.

2. **Executed Contracts**
Contracts that are executed on one side can be rescinded only if the party who has performed receives consideration to call off the deal.

B. **DISCHARGE BY NOVATION**
Occurs when the parties to a contract and a new party get together and agree to substitute the new party for one of the original parties. Requirements are (1) a previous valid obligation, (2) an agreement of all the parties to a new contract, (3) the extinguishment of the old obligation (discharge of the prior party), and (4) a new, valid contract.

C. **DISCHARGE BY SUBSTITUTED AGREEMENT**
Parties to a contract can execute a new agreement with different terms. The new agreement can either expressly or impliedly revoke and discharge the previous contract's obligations.

D. **DISCHARGE BY ACCORD AND SATISFACTION**
To discharge by accord and satisfaction, the parties must agree to accept performance that is different from the performance originally promised.

1. **Accord**
An accord is an executory contract to perform an act that will satisfy an existing duty. An accord suspends, but does not discharge, the duty.

2. **Satisfaction**
Satisfaction is the performance of the accord, which discharges the original contractual obligation.

3. **If the Obligor Refuses to Perform**
The obligee can sue on the original obligation or seek a decree for specific performance on the accord.

IV. DISCHARGE BY OPERATION OF LAW

A. **ALTERATION OF THE CONTRACT**
An innocent party can treat a contract as discharged if the other party materially alters a term (such as quantity or price) without consent.

B. **STATUTES OF LIMITATIONS**
Statutes of limitations limit the period during which a party can sue based on a breach of contract.

1. **UCC 2–725**
An action for the breach of a contract for a sale of goods must be commenced within four years after the breach occurs, whether the innocent party knows of the breach. The parties can shorten this period to one year but cannot extend it.

2. **New Promise to Perform Starts the Period Again**
If the party who owes the obligation makes a new promise to perform, the cause of action barred by the statute of limitations is revived.

C. **BANKRUPTCY**
A discharge in bankruptcy (see Chapter 30) will ordinarily bar enforcement of most of a debtor's contracts.

D. **IMPOSSIBILITY OR IMPRACTICABILITY OF PERFORMANCE**

1. **Objective Impossibility of Performance**
A contract may be discharged if, after it is made, performance becomes objectively impossible, as in the following: (1) death or incapacity of one of the parties, (2) specific subject matter of the contract is destroyed, or (3) change in the law that renders performance illegal.

2. **Commercial Impracticability**
   Performance may be excused if it becomes much more difficult or expensive than contemplated when the contract was formed.

3. **Frustration of Purpose**
   A contract will be discharged if supervening circumstances make it impossible to attain the purpose the parties had in mind.

4. **Temporary Impossibility**
   An event that makes it temporarily impossible to perform will suspend performance until the impossibility ceases.

TRUE-FALSE QUESTIONS

(Answers at the Back of the Book)

___ **1.** A promise to perform subject to obtaining financing is a condition precedent.

___ **2.** Complete performance occurs when a contract's conditions fully occur.

___ **3.** A material breach of contract does not excuse the nonbreaching party from further performance.

___ **4.** An executory contract cannot be rescinded.

___ **5.** Objective impossibility discharges a contract.

___ **6.** A condition can trigger the performance of a legal obligation.

___ **7.** If a contract does not require a certain time for performance, a reasonable time will be implied.

___ **8.** A party can treat a contract as discharged if the other party materially alters the quantity term without consent.

___ **9.** If, before either party to a contract has a duty to perform, one party refuses to do so, there is nothing the other party can do.

___ **10.** There is no limit to the time that a party can file a suit against another based on a breach of contract.

FILL-IN QUESTIONS

(Answers at the Back of the Book)

Most contracts are discharged by performance—by doing what was promised. Any contract can be discharged by agreement of the parties. ______________________ (Rescission/Novation) is the process by which a contract is canceled and the parties are returned to the positions they occupied before forming it. ______________________ (Rescission/Novation) substitutes a new party for an original party by agreement of all the parties. ______________________ (Substitution of a new contract/Accord and satisfaction) revokes and discharges a prior contract. ______________________ (A substitution/An accord) suspends a contractual duty that has not been discharged. Once the ______________________ (substitution/accord) is performed, the original contractual obligation is discharged.

MULTIPLE-CHOICE QUESTIONS

(Answers at the Back of the Book)

___ **1.** Don contracts to build a store for Pat for $500,000, with payments to be in installments of $50,000 as building progresses. Don finishes the store except for a cover over a compressor on the roof. A cover can be installed for $500. Pat refuses to pay the last installment. If Don's breach is not material

a. Don has a claim against Pat for $50,000.
b. Pat has a claim against Don for damages for Don's breach of his duty to put a cover over the compressor.
c. both a and b.
d. none of the above.

___ **2.** Ann enters a contract with Bill. Before either party performs, rescission of their contract requires

a. additional consideration.
b. a mutual agreement to rescind.
c. performance by both parties.
d. restitution.

___ **3.** Ron contracts to repair Joe's building for $30,000. Payment is to be made "on the satisfaction of Will, Joe's architect." To save money, Joe tells Will not to approve the repairs. If Ron sues Joe for $30,000, Ron will

a. win, because Will is Joe's architect.
b. win, because Joe is not acting reasonably.
c. lose, because Ron is not acting reasonably, honestly, and in good faith.
d. lose, because Will has not expressed satisfaction with the work.

___ **4.** Sam and Tony want to discharge their obligations under a prior contract by executing and performing a new agreement. They must execute and perform

a. an accord and satisfaction.
b. an assignment.
c. a novation.
d. a nullification.

___ **5.** On May 1, Val agrees to work for Babco, Inc., for four months beginning June 1. On May 15, Babco tells Val that it doesn't need her after all. Val's duty to work for Babco

a. was discharged on May 15.
b. was discharged on May 16.
c. will be discharged on June 1.
d. will be discharged on September 30.

___ **6.** Jim and Gail contract for the sale of 500 computers. The agreement states, "The obligations of the parties are conditional on Gail obtaining financing from First Bank by August 1." This clause is

a. a condition precedent.
b. a condition subsequent.
c. a concurrent condition.
d. none of the above.

___ 7. Lee and Mary want Nick to replace Lee as a party to their contract. They can best accomplish this by agreeing to

a. an accord and satisfaction.
b. an assignment.
c. a novation.
d. a nullification.

___ 8. Adam contracts with Beth to deliver Beth's goods to her customers. This contract will, like most contracts, be discharged by

a. accord and satisfaction.
b. agreement.
c. operation of law.
d. performance.

___ 9. **Based on a Sample CPA Exam Question.** Eve contracts with Frank to act as his personal financial planner. Eve's duties under this contract will be discharged if

a. Frank declares bankruptcy.
b. it becomes illegal for Eve to provide the service.
c. the cost of providing the service doubles.
d. none of the above.

___ 10. Tony and Carol contract for the sale of Tony's business. Carol gives Tony a down payment, and Tony gives Carol the keys to one of his stores. Before the contract is fully performed, however, they agree to return the down payment and keys, and cancel the sale. This is

a. an accord and satisfaction.
b. an alteration of contract.
c. a novation.
d. a rescission.

SHORT ESSAY QUESTIONS

1. How are most contracts discharged?

2. What effect does a material breach have on the nonbreaching party? What is the effect of a nonmaterial breach?

ISSUE SPOTTERS

(Answers at the Back of the Book)

1. Eagle Construction contracts with Fred to build a store. The work is to begin on May 1 and be done by November 1, so that Fred can open for the holiday buying season. Eagle does not finish until November 15. Fred opens but, due to the delay, loses some sales. Is Fred's duty to pay for the construction of the store discharged?

2. Red Tiger Foods contracts to buy from Bree Distributors 200 carloads of frozen pizzas. Before Red Tiger or Bree start performing, can they call off the deal? What if Bree has already shipped the pizzas?

3. Remington and Brandt agree to go into the house painting business together as Rem, Brandt & Company. They agree that the business will begin when they raise $10,000 in capital to buy supplies. What happens if they can't raise the money?

SPECIAL INFORMATION FOR CPA CANDIDATES

In the past, the CPA examination has tested heavily on discharge, agreements to discharge, and discharge by operation of law. For this reason, it would be good to review those topics. In particular, releases and novations are covered in connection with assignments (discussed in the previous chapter), and accord and satisfaction is tested. Discharge by operation of law should not be confused with termination of an offer by operation of law. For example, the death of an offeror will terminate an offer, but the death of a party to a contract will not necessarily discharge the contract. Other important points to remember, among those covered in this chapter, include what will discharge a party by frustration of purpose. Only something that was not expected will qualify (unusual weather, for example). A statute of limitations begins to run from the time of a breach, or when the breach should have been discovered.

Chapter 17
Breach of Contract and Remedies

WHAT THIS CHAPTER IS ABOUT

Breach of contract is the failure to perform what a party is under a duty to perform. When this happens, the nonbreaching party can choose one or more remedies. Unless damages would be inadequate, that is usually what a court will award.

CHAPTER OUTLINE

I. DAMAGES

Damages compensate a nonbreaching party for the loss of a bargain and, under special circumstances, for additional losses. Generally, the party is placed in the position he or she would have occupied if the contract been performed.

A. TYPES OF DAMAGES

1. Compensatory Damages

Damages compensating a party for the *loss* of a bargain—the difference between the promised performance and the actual performance.

a. Incidental Damages

Expenses that are caused directly by a breach of contract (such as those incurred to obtain performance from another source). Incidental damages are added to compensatory damages.

b. Measurement of Compensatory Damages

1) Contract for a Sale of Goods

The usual measure is the difference between the contract price and the market price. If the buyer breaches and the seller has not yet made the goods, the measure is lost profits on the sale.

2) Contract for a Sale of Land

a) Majority Rule

If specific performance (see below) is unavailable, or if the buyer breaches, the measure of damages is the difference between the land's contract price and its market price.

b) Minority Rule

If the seller breaches and the breach is not deliberate, the buyer recovers any down payment, plus expenses.

3) Construction Contracts

a) Owner's Breach Before, During, or After Construction

Contractor can recover (1) before construction: only profits (contract price, less cost of materials and labor); (2) during construction: profits, plus cost of partial construction; (3) after construction: the contract price, plus interest.

b) **Contractor's Breach**
Owner can recover for (1) failing to begin: cost, above contract price, to complete; (2) stopping mid-project: cost of completion; (3) late completion: costs related to loss of use; (4) substantial performance: cost of completion, if there would be no substantial economic waste (if cost to complete does not exceed value the extra work contributes.)

2. **Consequential Damages**
Damages giving an injured party the entire *benefit* of the bargain—foreseeable losses caused by special circumstances beyond the contract. The breaching party must know (or have reason to know) that special circumstances will cause the additional loss.

3. **Punitive Damages**
Damages punishing a guilty party and making an example to deter similar, future conduct. Awarded for a tort, but not for a contract breach.

4. **Nominal Damages**
Damages (such as $1) establishing, when no actual loss resulted, that a defendant acted wrongfully.

B. MITIGATION OF DAMAGES

An injured party has a duty to mitigate damages. For example, persons whose jobs have been wrongfully terminated have a duty to seek other jobs. The damages they receive are their salaries, less the income they received (or would have received) in similar jobs.

C. LIQUIDATED DAMAGES VERSUS PENALTIES

1. **Liquidated Damages Provision**
Specifies a certain amount to be paid in the event of a breach to the nonbreaching party for the loss. Such provisions are enforceable.

2. **Penalty Provision**
Specifies a certain amount to be paid in the event of a breach *to penalize the breaching party*. Such provisions are *not* enforceable.

3. **How to Determine If a Provision Will Be Enforced**
Ask: (1) when contract was made, was it clear damages would be difficult to estimate? (2) Was amount set as damages a reasonable estimate? If either answer is "no," provision will not be enforced.

II. RESCISSION AND RESTITUTION

A. RESCISSION

Rescission is an action to undo, or cancel, a contract—to return nonbreaching parties to the positions they occupied prior to the transaction. Rescission is available if fraud, mistake, duress, or failure of consideration is present. The rescinding party must give prompt notice to the breaching party.

B. RESTITUTION

To rescind a contract, the parties must make **restitution** by returning to each other goods, property, or money previously conveyed.

III. SPECIFIC PERFORMANCE

This remedy calls for the performance of the act promised in the contract.

A. WHEN SPECIFIC PERFORMANCE IS AVAILABLE

Damages must be an inadequate remedy. If goods are unique, a court will decree specific performance. Specific performance is granted to a buyer in a contract for the sale of land (every parcel of land is unique).

B. WHEN SPECIFIC PERFORMANCE IS NOT AVAILABLE

Contracts for sale of goods (other than unique goods) rarely qualify, because substantially identical goods can be bought or sold elsewhere. Courts normally refuse to grant specific performance of personal service contracts.

IV. REFORMATION

Used when the parties have imperfectly expressed their agreement in writing. Allows the contract to be rewritten to reflect the parties' true intentions.

A. WHEN REFORMATION IS AVAILABLE

(1) In cases of fraud or mutual mistake; (2) to prove the correct terms of an oral contract; (3) if a covenant not to compete is for a valid purpose (such as the sale of a business), but the area or time constraints are unreasonable, some courts will reform the restraints to make them reasonable.

B. WHEN REFORMATION IS NOT AVAILABLE

If the area or time constraints in a covenant not to compete are unreasonable, some courts will throw out the entire covenant.

V. RECOVERY BASED ON QUASI CONTRACT

When there is no enforceable contract, quasi contract prevents unjust enrichment. The law implies a promise to pay the reasonable value for benefits received.

A. WHEN QUASI-CONTRACTUAL RECOVERY IS USEFUL

A party has partially performed under a contract that is unenforceable. The party may recover the reasonable value (fair market value).

B. ELEMENTS TO RECOVER IN QUASI CONTRACT

The party seeking recovery must show (1) he or she conferred a benefit on the other party, (2) he or she had the reasonable expectation of being paid, (3) he or she did not act as a volunteer in conferring the benefit, and (4) the other party would be unjustly enriched by retaining it without paying.

VI. ELECTION OF REMEDIES

A nonbreaching party must choose which remedy to pursue. The purpose of the doctrine is to prevent double recovery. The doctrine has been eliminated in contracts for sales of goods—UCC remedies are cumulative [UCC 2–703, 2–711].

VII. WAIVER OF BREACH

Occurs when a nonbreaching party accepts defective performance.

A. EFFECT OF A WAIVER

A waiver keeps a contract going.

1. Past Breaches

A party waiving a breach cannot take later action based on the breach. In effect, the waiver erases the past breach.

2. Future Breaches

Normally, a waiver of one breach does not waive future breaches. It extends to future breaches, however, if a reasonable person would conclude that similar defective performance would be acceptable in the future.

B. LIABILITY FOR DAMAGES

A nonbreaching party can recover damages for defective performance.

VIII. CONTRACT PROVISIONS LIMITING REMEDIES

A. EXCULPATORY CLAUSES

A provision excluding liability for fraudulent or intentional injury or for illegal acts will not be enforced. An exculpatory clause for negligence contained in a contract made between parties who have roughly equal bargaining positions usually will be enforced.

B. LIMITATION-OF-LIABILITY CLAUSES

Provide that the only remedy for breach is replacement, repair, or refund of the purchase price (or some other limit). Such clauses may be enforced.

C. CONTRACTS FOR SALES OF GOODS

Remedies can be limited (see Chapter 22).

TRUE-FALSE QUESTIONS

(Answers at the Back of the Book)

____ 1. Damages are designed to compensate a nonbreaching party for the loss of a bargain.

____ 2. Punitive damages are usually not awarded in breach of contract actions.

____ 3. Nominal damages establish that a defendant acted wrongfully

____ 4. Liquidated damages are uncertain in amount.

____ 5. In rescinding a contract, the parties essentially return to the positions they were in before the contract was formed.

____ 6. Rescission is not available in a case involving fraud.

____ 7. On a breach of contract, the nonbreaching party has a duty to mitigate any damages that he or she suffers.

____ 8. Quasi-contractual recovery is possible only when there is an enforceable contract.

____ 9. Consequential damages are foreseeable damages that arise from a party's breach of a contract.

____ 10. Specific performance is the usual remedy when one party has breached a contract for a sale of goods.

FILL-IN QUESTIONS

(Answers at the Back of the Book)

The usual measure of compensatory damages under a contract for a sale of goods is the difference between ____________________ (the contract price and the market price/the market price and lost profits on the sale). The usual remedy for a seller's breach of a contract for a sale of real estate is ____________________ (specific performance/rescission and restitution). If this remedy is unavailable or if the buyer breaches, in most states the measure of damages is the difference between ____________________ (the contract price and the market price/the market price and lost profits on the sale).

MULTIPLE-CHOICE QUESTIONS

(Answers at the Back of the Book)

___ 1. Ann pays Bob $1,000 to design an intranet for her business office. The next day, Bob tells Ann that he has accepted a job with Computer Services, Inc., and cannot design her network, but he does not return her payment. Ann can recover

a. $1,000.
b. Bob's pay from Computer Services, Inc.
c. $1,000 plus Bob's pay from Computer Services, Inc.
d. nothing.

___ 2. Sue contracts to deliver Tom's products to his customers for $1,500, payable in advance. Tom pays the money, but Sue fails to perform. Tom can

a. rescind the contract.
b. obtain restitution of the $1,500 but not rescind the contract.
c. rescind the contract and obtain restitution of the $1,500.
d. none of the above.

___ 3. Eagle Corporation contracts to sell to Frosty Malts, Inc., six steel mixers for $5,000. When Eagle fails to deliver, Frosty buys mixers from Great Company, for $6,500. Frosty's measure of damages is

a. $6,500.
b. $5,000.
c. $1,500 plus incident al damages.
d. nothing.

___ 4. General Construction contracts to build a store for Home Stores for $1 million. In mid-project, Home repudiates the contract, and General stops working. General incurred costs of $600,000 and would have made a profit of $100,000. General's measure of damages is

a. $1 million.
b. $700,000.
c. $100,000.
d. nothing.

___ 5. Dave contracts with Paul to buy a computer for $1,000. Dave tells Paul that if it is not delivered on Monday, he will lose $2,000 in business. Paul ships the computer late. Dave can recover

a. $3,000.
b. $2,000.
c. $1,000.
d. nothing.

___ 6. Jay agrees to sell an acre of land to Kim for $5,000. Jay fails to go through with the deal, when the market price of the land is $7,000. If Kim cannot obtain the land through specific performance, Kim may recover

a. $7,000.
b. $5,000.
c. $2,000.
d. nothing.

___ **7.** Ken orally agrees to build three barns for Lora. He builds the first barn, but she fails to pay him. To redress the breach, Ken's best option is

a. damages.
b. quasi-contractual recovery.
c. rescission.
d. specific performance.

___ **8.** Sam agrees to deliver two tons of copper to United Conversion, Inc., under a contract that states delivery is to be within "15" days when the parties intend "50" days. If United will not amend the contract, Sam may obtain

a. reformation.
b. rescission.
c. specific performance.
d. nothing.

___ **9.** Brenda agrees to sell an office building to Carl. When Brenda refuses to complete the deal, Carl uses and recovers damages. Carl can also obtain

a. quasi-contractual recovery.
b. restitution.
c. specific performance.
d. none of the above.

___ **10.** **Based on a Sample CPA Exam Question.** Eagle Manufacturing, Inc., contracted with Digital Repair Services to maintain Eagle's computers. A "Liquidated Damages Clause" provides that Digital will pay Eagle $500 for each day that Digital is late in responding to a service request. If Digital is three days late in responding, and Eagle sues to enforce this clause, Eagle will

a. lose, because liquidated damages clauses violate public policy.
b. lose, unless the liquidated damages clause is determined to be a penalty.
c. win, because liquidated damages clauses are always enforceable.
d. win, unless the liquidated damages clause is determined to be a penalty.

SHORT ESSAY QUESTIONS

1. What are damages designed to do in a breach of contract situation?

2. What must parties do to rescind a contract?

ISSUE SPOTTERS

(Answers at the Back of the Book)

1. Greg contracts to build a storage shed for Holly, who pays Greg in advance, but Greg completes only half the work. Holly pays Ira $500 to finish the shed. If Holly sues Greg, what would be the measure of recovery?

2. Lyle contracts to sell his ranch to Mary, who is to take possession on June 1. Lyle delays the transfer until August 1. Mary incurs expenses in providing for livestock that she bought for the ranch. When they made the contract, Lyle had no reason to know of the livestock. Is Lyle liable for Mary's expenses in providing for the cattle?

3. Excel Engineering, Inc., signs a contract to design a jet for Flight, Inc. The contract excludes liability for errors in the design and construction of the jet. An error in design causes the jet to crash. Is the clause that excluded liability enforceable?

SPECIAL INFORMATION FOR CPA CANDIDATES

One of the points in this chapter covered in the past on the CPA examination has been that if damages are appropriate, specific performance will not be granted. Specific performance is granted most typically in cases involving unique goods. Also remember that liquidated damages must be reasonable in light of what could have been expected when the contract was made.

Chapter 18
E-Contracts

WHAT THIS CHAPTER IS ABOUT

E-contracts include any contract entered into in e-commerce, whether business to business (B2B) or business to consumer (B2C), and any contract involving the computer industry. This chapter reviews some of the problems of e-contracts.

CHAPTER OUTLINE

I. ONLINE CONTRACT FORMATION

Disputes arising from contracts entered into online concern the terms and the parties' assent to those terms.

A. ONLINE OFFERS

Terms should be conspicuous and clearly spelled out. On a Web site, this can be done with a link to a separate page that contains the details. Subjects include remedies, forum selection, statute of limitations, payment, taxes, refund and return policies, disclaimers, and privacy policies. A click-on acceptance box should also be included.

B. ONLINE ACCEPTANCES

A *shrink-wrap agreement* is an agreement whose terms are expressed inside a box in which a product is packaged. Usually, the agreement is not between a seller and a buyer, but a manufacturer and the product's user. Terms generally concern warranties, remedies, and other issues.

1. **Shrink-Wrap Agreements—Enforceable Contract Terms**
   Courts often enforce shrink-wrap agreements, reasoning that the seller proposed an offer that the buyer accepted after an opportunity to read the terms. Also, it is more practical to enclose the full terms of sale in a box.

2. **Shrink-Wrap Agreements—Proposals for Additional Terms**
   If a court finds that the buyer learned of the shrink-wrap terms *after* the parties entered into a contract, the court might conclude that those terms were proposals for additional terms, which were not part of the contract unless the buyer expressly agreed to them.

3. **Click-On Agreements**
   A *click-on agreement* is when a buyer, completing a transaction on a computer, indicates his or her assent to be bound by the terms of the offer by clicking on a button that says, for example, "I agree." The terms may appear on a Web site through which a buyer obtains goods or services, or on a computer screen when software is loaded.

4. **Browse-Wrap Terms**
   Browse-wrap terms do not require a user to assent to the terms before going ahead with an online transaction. Offerors of these terms generally assert that they are binding without the user's active consent. Critics argue that a user should at least be required to navigate past the terms before they should be considered binding.

II. E-SIGNATURES

How are e-signatures created and verified, and what is their legal effect?

A. E-SIGNATURE TECHNOLOGIES

Methods for creating and verifying e-signatures include—

1. **Digital Signatures**
Asymmetric (different) cryptographic keys provide private code for one party and public software for another party, who reads the code to verify the first party's identity. A cybernotary issues the keys.

2. **Signature Dynamics**
One party signs a digital pad with a stylus. A measurement of the signature, with time and date, is encrypted in a biometric token and attached to a document. Another party can use the token to verify the signature.

3. **Other Forms**
A smart card is a credit-card size device embedded with code that can be read by a computer to establish a person's identity or signature. Other possibilities include retina- and face-scanning.

B. STATE LAWS GOVERNING E-SIGNATURES
Most states have laws governing e-signatures, although the laws are not uniform. The Uniform Electronic Transactions Act (UETA), issued in 1999, was an attempt by the National Conference of Commissioners on Uniform State Laws and the American Law Institute to create more uniformity.

C. FEDERAL LAW ON E-SIGNATURES AND E-DOCUMENTS
In 2000, Congress enacted the Electronic Signatures in Global and National Commerce (E-SIGN) Act to provide that no contract, record, or signature may be denied legal effect solely because it is in an electronic form. Some documents are excluded (such as those governed by UCC Articles 3, 4, and 9.)

III. PARTNERING AGREEMENTS

Through a partnering agreement, a seller and a buyer agree in advance on the terms to apply in all transactions subsequently conducted electronically. These terms may include access and identification codes. A partnering agreement, like any contract, can prevent later disputes.

IV. THE UNIFORM ELECTRONIC TRANSACTIONS ACT

The UETA removes barriers to e-commerce by giving the same legal effect to e-records and e-signatures as to paper documents and signatures.

A. THE SCOPE AND APPLICABILITY OF THE UETA
The UETA applies only to e-records and e-signatures in a transaction (an interaction between two or more people relating to business, commercial, or government activities). The UETA does not apply to laws governing wills or testamentary trusts, the UCC (except Articles 2 and 2A), the UCITA, and other laws excluded by the states that adopt the UETA.

B. THE FEDERAL E-SIGN ACT AND THE UETA

1. **Does the E-SIGN Act Preempt the UETA?**
If a state enacts the UETA without modifying it, the E-SIGN Act does not preempt it. The E-SIGN Act preempts modified versions of the UETA to the extent that they are inconsistent with the E-SIGN Act.

2. **Can the States Enact Alternative Procedures or Requirements?**
Under the E-SIGN Act, states may enact alternative procedures or requirements for the use or acceptance of e-records or e-signatures if—

a. The procedures or requirements are consistent with the E-SIGN Act.
b. The procedures do not give greater legal effect to any specific type of technology.
c. The state law refers to the E-SIGN Act if the state adopts the alternative after the enactment of the E-SIGN Act.

C. HIGHLIGHTS OF THE UETA
Individual state versions of the UETA as enacted may vary.

1. **The Parties Must Agree to Conduct Their Transaction Electronically**
This agreement may be implied by the circumstances and the parties' conduct (for example, giving out a business card with an e-mail address on it). Consent may also be withdrawn.

2. **Parties Can "Opt Out"**
Parties can waive or vary any or all of the UETA, but the UETA applies in the absence of an agreement to the contrary.

3. **Attribution**
The effect of an e-record in a transaction is determined from its context and circumstances. Attribution refers to the identification of a party.

   a. **Names and "Signatures"**
   A person's name is not necessary to give effect to an e-record, but if, for example, a person types his or her name at the bottom of an e-mail purchase order, that typing qualifies as a "signature" and is attributed to the person.

   b. **Relevant Evidence**
   Any relevant evidence can prove that an e-record or e-signature is, or is not, attributable to a certain person.

   c. **Issues Arising outside the UETA**
   State laws other than the UETA apply to issues that relate to agency, authority, forgery, or contract formation.

4. **Notarization**
A document can be notarized by a notary's e-signature.

5. **The Effect of Errors**
If the parties agree to a security procedure and one party does not detect an error because it did not follow the procedure, the conforming party can avoid the effect of the error [UETA 10].

   a. **When Other State Laws Determine the Effect of an Error**
   Other state laws determine the effect if the parties do not agree on a security procedure.

   b. **To Avoid the Effect of an Error**
   A party must (1) promptly notify the other party of the error and of his or her intent not to be bound by it and (2) take reasonable steps to return any benefit or consideration received. If restitution cannot be made, the transaction may be unavoidable.

6. **Timing**

   a. **When Is an E-Record "Sent"?**
   When it is directed from the sender's place of business to the intended recipient in a form readable by the recipient's computer at the recipient's place of business with the closest relation to the deal (or either party's residence, if there is no place of business). Once an e-record leaves the sender's control or comes under the recipient's control, it is sent.

   b. **When Is an E-Record "Received"?**
   When it enters the recipient's processing system in a readable form—even if no person is aware of its receipt [UETA 15].

V. THE UNIFORM COMPUTER INFORMATION TRANSACTIONS ACT

UCC Article 2 could not be applied to most transactions involving software, so alternatives were proposed. The Uniform Computer Information Transactions Act (UCITA) was issued by the National Conference of Commissioners on Uniform State Laws and the American Law Institute.

A. THE SCOPE AND APPLICABILITY OF THE UCITA

The UCITA covers contracts to license or buy software, and contracts that give access to—or allow the distribution of—computer information ("information in electronic form obtained from or through use of a computer, or that is in digital or equivalent form capable of being processed by a computer" [UCITA 102(10)].

1. **The UCITA May Apply to Only Part of a Transaction**
If the primary subject matter of a deal is computer and information rights, the UCITA applies to the entire transaction. If this is not the primary subject matter, the UCITA applies only to the part involving computer information.

2. **Parties Can "Opt Out"**
The UCITA applies in the absence of an agreement to the contrary, but parties can waive or vary any or all of it. (Or parties can include contracts that would not otherwise be under the UCITA.)

B. **HIGHLIGHTS OF THE UCITA**
The UCITA includes general provisions like UCC Article 2 (for example, the UCITA has a statute of frauds, although it requires a writing when a contract is for $5,000 or more), as well as choice of law and choice of forum provisions, making it more comprehensive.

1. **Warranties**
These are the same as under UCC Article 2, but tailored for the UCITA's subject matter.

2. **Support and Service Contracts**
These are not required, but once made, the licensor must comply. When a contract is silent on an issue, the licensor must do whatever is reasonable in light of ordinary business standards.

3. **Authentication and Attribution**
The UCITA provides for the authentication of e-signatures. To authenticate means to sign a record, or with the intent to sign a record, to execute, or to adopt an electronic sound, symbol, or the like to link with the record. A record is retrievable information that is inscribed in a tangible medium or stored in an electronic or other medium. (The UCITA uses the word *record* instead of *writing*.)

4. **Mass-Market Licenses and Access Contracts**

a. **Mass-Market Licenses**
This is an electronic form contract usually presented with a purchased package of computer information (a shrink-wrap or click-on license (discussed above). A licensee has the right to return, and is entitled to reimbursement for the reasonable expense of returning, computer information, and these rights cannot be waived.

b. **Access Contracts**
This is "a contract to obtain by electronic means access to, or information from, an information processing system of another person, or the equivalent of such access" (for example, Internet access) [UCITA 102(a)(1)].

5. **Electronic Self-Help**
A licensor may cancel, repossess, prevent continued use, or take similar actions on a licensee's breach of a license. A licensor may enforce the licensor's rights through electronic means (for example, install a turn-off function in licensed software so it can be disabled if the license is violated). This is not allowed in mass-market licenses, or if the parties do not agree. The licensor must give fifteen days' notice and cannot use this means if the licensor knows it will harm third persons.

TRUE-FALSE QUESTIONS

(Answers at the Back of the Book)

___ 1. A shrink-wrap agreement is normally not enforced.

___ 2. A click-on agreement is normally enforced.

___ 3. State e-signature laws are not uniform.

___ 4. Under federal law, a signature may be denied legal effect simply because it is in electronic form.

___ 5. The Uniform Electronic Transactions Act (UETA) is a federal law.

___ 6. The UETA does not apply to a transaction unless the parties agree to apply it.

___ 7. Under the UETA, a person's name is not necessary to give effect to an electronic record.

___ **8.** Under the UETA, a contract is enforceable even if it is in electronic form.

___ **9.** The Uniform Computer Information Transactions Act (UCITA) covers contracts involving *computer information.*

___ **10.** The UCITA bans the use of "electronic self-help."

FILL-IN QUESTIONS

(Answers at the Back of the Book)

Parties do not need to participate in e-commerce to make binding contracts, according to the ________________ (UCITA only/UETA only/UCITA and the UETA). E-signatures are valid under the ______________ (UCITA only/UETA only/UCITA and the UETA). The ________________ (UCITA/UETA) supports all e-transactions, but does not create rules for them. The ______________ (UCITA/UETA) does not apply unless contracting parties agree to use e-commerce in their transactions.

MULTIPLE-CHOICE QUESTIONS

(Answers at the Back of the Book)

___ **1.** Alpha Corporation attempts to enter into shrink-wrap agreements with buyers of its products. A shrink-wrap agreement is an agreement whose terms are expressed

a. in code at the end of a computer program.
b. inside a box in which a product is packaged.
c. in small print at the end of a paper contract signed by both parties.
d. on a computer screen.

___ **2.** Beta, Inc., includes a shrink-wrap agreement with its products. A court would likely enforce this agreement if a buyer used the product

a. after having had an opportunity to read the agreement.
b. before having had an opportunity to read the agreement.
c. only after actually reading the agreement.
d. none of the above.

___ **3.** Gamma Company agrees to sell software to Holly from Gamma's Web site. To complete the deal, Holly clicks on a button that, with reference to certain terms, states, "I agree." The parties have

a. a binding contract that does not include the terms.
b. a binding contract that includes only the terms to which Holly later agrees.
c. a binding contract that includes the terms.
d. no contract.

___ **4.** Local Delivery Company and Regional Trucking, Inc., attempt to enter into a contract in electronic form. Under the Electronic Signatures in Global and National Commerce Act (E-SIGN Act), because this contract is in electronic form, it

a. may be denied legal effect.
b. may not be denied legal effect.
c. will be limited to certain terms.
d. will not be enforced.

___ **5.** International Investments, Inc., enters into contracts in e-commerce and in traditional commerce. The UETA applies, if at all, only to those transactions in which the parties agree to use

a. e-commerce.
b. traditional commerce.
c. e-commerce or traditional commerce.
d. none of the above.

___ **6.** American Sales Company and B2C Corporation enter into a contract over the Internet. The contract says nothing about the UETA. The UETA applies to

a. none of the contract.
b. only the part of the contract that does not involve computer information.
c. only the part of the contract that involves computer information.
d. the entire contract.

___ **7.** Digital Tech, Inc., e-mails an e-record, as part of a business deal, to E-Engineering Corporation. Under the UETA, an e-record is considered sent

a. only when it leaves the sender's control.
b. only when it comes under the recipient's control.
c. when it leaves the sender's control or comes under the recipient's control.
d. when it is midway between the sender and recipient.

___ **8.** New Software, Inc. (NSI), and Open Source Company (OSC) agree to follow a certain security procedure in transacting business. NSI fails to follow the procedure and, for this reason, does not detect an error in its deal with OSC. OSC can avoid the effect of the error

a. only if NSI's name is affixed to the e-record evidencing the error.
b. only if OSC takes reasonable steps to return any benefit or consideration received.
c. under any circumstances.
d. under no circumstances.

___ **9.** First Financial Corporation and Great Applications, Inc., enter into a contract involving software. The Uniform Computer Information Transactions Act (UCITA) covers contracts to

a. buy software only.
b. license software only.
c. buy or license software.
d. none of the above.

___ **10.** Delta Company and Epsilon, Inc., agree to a contract that expressly brings itself under the UCITA, which would not otherwise apply to this agreement. The UCITA covers

a. none of the contract.
b. only the part of the contract that does not involve computer information.
c. only the part of the contract that involves computer information.
d. the entire contract.

SHORT ESSAY QUESTIONS

1. Are shrink-wrap and click-on agreements enforceable?

2. What are some of the similarities between the UCITA and the UETA?

ISSUE SPOTTERS

(Answers at the Back of the Book)

1. Applied Products, Inc., does business with Best Suppliers, Inc., online. Under the UETA, what determines the effect of the electronic documents evidencing the parties' deal? Is a party's "signature" necessary?

2. Technical Support, Inc., and United Services Corporation enter into a contract that involves *computer information,* as that term is defined by the UCITA. For purposes of the UCITA, what is computer information?

3. Computer Applications Corporation and Digitized Data, Inc., agree to a contract in e-commerce. Assuming the deal falls under both the UETA and the UCITA, what are the differences between those uniform acts as they might apply in this situation?

SPECIAL INFORMATION FOR CPA CANDIDATES

The CPA examination covers some information technology (IT) topics, but not the law discussed in this chapter relating to e-contracts. The exam may require review of business information systems and the roles and responsibilities of personnel within an IT department. Those systems consist, of course, of hardware, software, and network components. Their use includes data structure, analysis, and manipulation, as well as transaction and application processing. It may also be useful to review IT control objectives, control activities and design, physical access controls and security, and disaster recovery and business continuity.

CUMULATIVE HYPOTHETICAL PROBLEM FOR UNIT THREE—INCLUDING CHAPTERS 9–18

(Answers at the Back of the Book)

Doe & Roe is a small accounting firm that provides bookkeeping, payroll, and tax services for small businesses. Java, Inc., is a small manufacturing firm, making and selling commercial espresso machines.

___ **1.** Java sends e-mail to Doe & Roe, offering to contract for Doe & Roe's services for a certain price. The offer is sent on June 1 and is seen by Doe on June 2. The offer states that it will be open until July 1. This offer

a. cannot be revoked because it is a firm offer.
b. cannot be revoked because it is an option contract.
c. could have been revoked only before Doe saw it.
d. may be revoked any time before it is accepted.

___ **2.** Java and Doe & Roe discuss terms for a contract, but nothing is put in writing. If a dispute develops later, and one party files a suit against the other, alleging breach of contract, the court will determine whether or not there is a contract between the parties by looking at

a. the fairness of the circumstances.
b. the offeree's subjective intent.
c. the parties' objective intent.
d. the parties' subjective intent.

___ **3.** Java and Doe & Roe sign a written contract for Doe & Roe's services. The contract includes a large arithmetical error. Java later files a breach of contract suit against Doe & Roe, which asserts the mistake as a defense. Doe & Roe will win

a. if Java wrote the contract.
b. if the mistake was unilateral and Java knew it.
c. only if the mistake was due to Java's negligence.
d. only if the mistake was mutual.

___ **4.** Java and Doe & Roe sign a written contract for Doe & Roe's services. Java later files a breach of contract suit against Doe & Roe. Doe & Roe could avoid liability on the contract if

a. the contract has been assigned.
b. there is an unexecuted accord between the parties.
c. Java has been discharged by a novation.
d. none of the above.

___ **5.** Java and Doe & Roe sign a written contract for Doe & Roe's services. Java later files a suit against Doe & Roe. Doe & Roe is held to be in breach of contract. The court is most likely to grant relief to Java in the form of

a. damages.
b. specific performance.
c. damages and specific performance.
d. none of the above.

QUESTIONS ON THE FOCUS ON LEGAL REASONING FOR UNIT THREE— *FORD V. TRENDWEST RESORTS, INC.*

(Answers at the Back of the Book)

___ **1.** Alpha Corporation enters into an agreement to hire Bob for employment at-will. If Alpha breaches the agreement, under the holding in *Ford v. Trendwest Resorts, Inc.*, Bob is most likely to be awarded

a. damages that represent future earnings.
b. damages that represent lost earnings.
c. nominal damages.
d. nothing.

___ **2.** Beta Company enters into an agreement to hire Carol for employment at-will. In the opinion of the majority in *Ford v. Trendwest Resorts, Inc.*, the agreement between Beta and Carol

a. does not change the at-will employment relation between the parties.
b. establishes a claim for lost wages if Beta breaches the agreement *after* Carol starts work.
c. establishes a claim for lost wages if Beta breaches the agreement *before* Carol starts work.
d. establishes a claim for lost wages if Beta breaches the agreement at any time.

___ **3.** Gamma, Inc., enters into an agreement to hire Dan for employment at-will. In the opinion of the dissent in *Ford v. Trendwest Resorts, Inc.*, the agreement between Gamma and Dan

a. does not change the at-will employment relation between the parties.
b. establishes a claim for lost wages if Gamma breaches the agreement *after* Dan starts work.
c. establishes a claim for lost wages if Gamma breaches the agreement *before* Dan starts work.
d. establishes a claim for lost wages if Gamma breaches the agreement at any time.

QUESTIONS ON THE FOCUS ON ETHICS FOR UNIT THREE— CONTRACT LAW AND THE APPLICATION OF ETHICS

(Answers at the Back of the Book)

___ **1.** Ann and Bill enter into a contract for Bill's services. Whether this contract is unconscionable is determined by

a. a court.
b. Ann only.
c. Bill only.
d. UCC 2–302.

___ **2.** Sam offers goods to Tina at less than half their market price, of which Sam is not aware. Tina knows the goods' value, but says nothing. Tina's silence could be justified by

a. a covenant not to compete.
b. the concept of unconscionability.
c. the doctrine of promissory estoppel.
d. the principle of freedom of contract.

___ **3.** To bid on a job, General Contractor, Inc. (GCI), relies on the promise of Standard Subcontracting Corporation (SSC) to perform certain work at a certain price. If SSC fails to perform, GCI may recover from SSC under

a. a covenant not to compete.
b. the concept of unconscionability.
c. the doctrine of promissory estoppel.
d. the principle of freedom of contract.

Chapter 19
The Formation of Sales and Lease Contracts

WHAT THIS CHAPTER IS ABOUT

This chapter introduces two parts of the Uniform Commercial Code: Article 2, which covers sales of goods, and Article 2A, which covers leases. The chapter also includes a section on contracts for international sales of goods.

CHAPTER OUTLINE

I. THE UNIFORM COMMERCIAL CODE

The UCC provides rules to deal with all phases of a commercial sale: Articles 2 and 2A cover contracts for sales or leases of goods; Articles 3, 4, and 4A cover payments by checks, notes, and other means; Article 7 covers warehouse documents; and Article 9 covers transactions that involve collateral.

II. THE SCOPE OF ARTICLE 2—SALES

Article 2 governs contracts for sales of goods.

A. WHAT IS A SALE?

A **sale** is "the passing of title from the seller to the buyer for a price" [UCC 2–106(1)]. The price may be payable in money, goods, services, or land.

B. WHAT ARE GOODS?

Goods are tangible and movable. Legal disputes concern the following—

1. Goods Associated with Real Estate

Goods include minerals or the like and structures, if severance from the land is by the seller (but not if the buyer is to do it); growing crops or timber to be cut; and other "things attached" to realty but capable of severance without material harm to the land [UCC 2–107].

2. Goods and Services Combined

a. General Rule

Services are not included in the UCC. If a transaction involves both goods and services, a court determines which aspect is dominant.

b. Special Cases

Serving food or drink is a sale of goods [UCC 2–314(1)]. Other goods include unborn animals and rare coins.

C. WHO IS A MERCHANT?

UCC 2–104: Special rules apply to those who (1) deal in goods of the kind involved; (2) by occupation, hold themselves out as having knowledge and skill peculiar to the practices or goods involved in the transaction; (3) employ a merchant as a broker, agent, or other intermediary.

III. THE SCOPE OF ARTICLE 2A—LEASES

Article 2A governs contracts for leases of goods.

A. DEFINITION OF A LEASE
A **lease agreement** is the bargain of the lessor and lessee, in their words and deeds, including course of dealing, usage of trade, and course of performance [UCC 2A–103(k)].

B. CONSUMER LEASES
Special provisions apply to leases involving (1) a lessor who regularly leases or sells, (2) a lessee who leases for a personal, family, or household purpose, and (3) total payments of less than $25,000 [UCC 2A–103(1)(e)].

C. FINANCE LEASES
A finance lease involves a lessor (financier) who buys or leases goods from a supplier and leases or subleases them to a lessee [UCC 2A–103(g)]. The lessee must perform, whatever the financier does [UCC 2A–407].

IV. THE FORMATION OF SALES AND LEASE CONTRACTS
The following summarizes how the UCC *changes* the common law of contracts.

A. OFFER
An agreement sufficient to constitute a contract can exist even if verbal exchanges, correspondence, and conduct do not reveal exactly when it became binding [UCC 2–204(2), 2A–204(2)].

1. Open Terms
A sales or lease contract will not fail for indefiniteness even if one or more terms are left open, as long as (1) the parties intended to make a contract and (2) there is a reasonably certain basis for the court to grant an appropriate remedy [UCC 2–204(3), 2A–204(3)].

a. Open Price Term

1) If the parties have not agreed on a price, a court will determine "a reasonable price at the time for delivery" [UCC 2–305(1)].

2) If either the buyer or the seller is to determine the price, the price is to be fixed in good faith [UCC 2–305(2)].

3) If a price is not fixed through the fault of one party, the other can cancel the contract or fix a reasonable price [UCC 2–305(3)].

b. Open Payment Term
When parties do not specify payment terms—

1) Payment is due at the time and place at which the buyer is to receive the goods [UCC 2–310(a)].

2) The buyer can tender payment in cash or a commercially acceptable substitute (a check or credit card) [UCC 2–511(2)].

c. Open Delivery Term
When no delivery terms are specified—

1) The buyer normally takes delivery at the seller's place of business [UCC 2–308(a)]. If the seller has no place of business, the seller's residence is used. When goods are located in some other place and both parties know it, delivery is made there.

2) If the time for shipment or delivery is not clearly specified, a court will infer a "reasonable" time [UCC 2–309(1)].

d. Duration of an Ongoing Contract
A party who wishes to terminate an indefinite but ongoing contract must give reasonable notice to the other party [UCC 2–309(2), (3)].

e. **Options and Cooperation Regarding Performance**

1) When no specific shipping arrangements have been made but the contract contemplates shipment of the goods, the seller has the right to make arrangements [UCC 2–311].

2) When terms relating to an assortment of goods are omitted, the buyer can specify the assortment [UCC 2–311].

f. **Open Quantity Term**
If parties do not specify a quantity, there is no basis for a remedy. Exceptions include [UCC 2–306]—

1) **Requirements Contract**
The buyer agrees to buy and the seller agrees to sell all or up to a stated amount of what the buyer needs or requires. There is consideration: the buyer gives up the right to buy from others.

2) **Output Contract**
The seller agrees to sell and the buyer agrees to buy all or up to a stated amount of what the seller produces. Because the seller forfeits the right to sell goods to others, there is consideration.

3) **The UCC Imposes a Good Faith Limitation**
The quantity under these contracts is the amount of requirements or output that occurs during a normal production year.

2. **Merchant's Firm Offer**
If a merchant gives assurances in a signed writing that an offer will remain open, the offer is irrevocable, without consideration, for the stated period, or if no definite period is specified, for a reasonable period (neither to exceed three months) [UCC 2–205, 2A–205].

a. The offer must be written and signed by the offeror. When a firm offer is contained in a form contract prepared by the offeree, a separate firm offer assurance must be signed as well.

b. The other party need not be a merchant.

B. ACCEPTANCE

1. **Methods of Acceptance**
When an offeror does not specify a means of acceptance, acceptance can be by any reasonable means [UCC 2–206(1), 2A–206(1)].

2. **Promise to Ship or Prompt Shipment**

a. **Promise or Shipment of Conforming Goods**
An offer to buy goods for current or prompt shipment can be accepted by a promise to ship or by a prompt shipment [UCC 2–206(1)(b)].

b. **Shipment of Nonconforming Goods**
Prompt shipment of nonconforming goods is both an acceptance and a breach, unless the seller (1) seasonably notifies the buyer that it is offered only as an accommodation and (2) indicates clearly that it is not an acceptance.

3. **Communication of Acceptance**
To accept a unilateral offer, the offeree must notify the offeror of performance if the offeror would not otherwise know [UCC 2–206(2)].

4. **Additional Terms**
If the offeree's response indicates a definite acceptance of the offer, a contract is formed, even if the acceptance includes terms in addition to, or different from, the original offer [UCC 2–207(1)].

a. **Subject to the Offeror's Assent**
If the offeree's additional terms are conditioned on the offeror's assent, the offeree's response is not an acceptance.

b. **Not Subject to the Offeror's Assent**
Does the contract include the additional terms?

1) **When One or Both Parties Are Nonmerchants**
Additional terms are considered proposals and not part of the contract. The contract is on the offeror's terms [UCC 2–207(2)].

2) **When Both Parties Are Merchants**
Additional terms are part of the contract unless (1) the offer expressly states no other terms; (2) they materially alter the original contract; or (3) the offeror objects to the modified terms in a timely fashion [UCC 2–207(2)].

3) **When the Parties Act As If They Have a Contract**
Regardless of what parties write down, they have a contract according to their conduct [UCC 2–207(3)]. If they do not act in accord with added terms, the terms are not part of a contract.

C. CONSIDERATION

An agreement modifying a sales or lease contract needs no consideration to be binding [UCC 2–209(1), 2A–208(1)].

1. **Modification Must Be Sought in Good Faith [UCC 1–203]**

2. **When Modification without Consideration Requires a Writing**

a. Contract prohibits changes except by a signed writing.

b. If a consumer (nonmerchant) is dealing with a merchant, and the merchant's form prohibits oral modification, the consumer must sign a separate acknowledgment [UCC 2–209(2), 2A–208(2)].

c. Any modification that brings a *sales* contract under the Statute of Frauds must be in writing to be enforceable [UCC 2–209(3)].

D. THE STATUTE OF FRAUDS

To be enforceable, a sales contract must be in writing if the goods are $500 or more and a lease if the payments are $1,000 or more [UCC 2–201, 2A–201].

1. **Sufficiency of the Writing**
A writing is sufficient if it indicates the parties intended to form a contract and is signed by the party against whom enforcement is sought. A sales contract is not enforceable beyond the quantity stated. A lease must identify and describe the goods and the lease term.

2. **Written Confirmation between Merchants**
The requirement of a writing is satisfied if one merchant sends a signed written confirmation to the other.

a. **Contents of the Confirmation**
The confirmation must indicate the terms of the agreement, and the merchant receiving it must have reason to know of its contents.

b. **Objection Within Ten Days**
Unless the merchant who receives the confirmation objects in writing within ten days, the confirmation is enforceable [UCC 2–201(2)].

3. **Exceptions**
An oral contract for a sale or lease that should otherwise be in writing will be enforceable in cases of [UCC 2–201(3), 2A–201(4)]—

a. **Specially Manufactured Goods**
The seller (or lessor) makes a substantial start on the manufacture of the goods, or makes commitments for it, and the goods are unsuitable for resale to others in the ordinary course of the business.

b. **Admissions**
The party against whom enforcement of a contract is sought admits in pleadings or court proceedings that a contract was made.

c. **Partial Performance**
Some payment has been made and accepted or some goods have been received and accepted (enforceable to that extent).

E. PAROL EVIDENCE

1. **The Rule**
If the parties to a contract set forth its terms in a writing intended as their final expression, the terms cannot be contradicted by evidence of any prior agreements or contemporaneous oral agreements.

2. **Exceptions [UCC 2–202, 2A–202]**
A court may accept evidence of the following—

a. **Consistent Additional Terms**
Such terms clarify or remove ambiguities in a writing.

b. **Course of Dealing and Usage of Trade**
The meaning of an agreement is interpreted in light of commercial practices and other surrounding circumstances [UCC 1–205].

c. **Course of Performance**
Conduct that occurs under the agreement indicates what the parties meant by the words in their contract [UCC 2–208(1), 2A–207(1)].

3. **Rules of Construction**
Express terms, course of performance, course of dealing, and usage of trade are to be construed together when they do not contradict one another. If that is unreasonable, the priority is: (1) express terms, (2) course of performance, (3) course of dealing, and (4) usage of trade [UCC 1–205(4), 2–208(2), 2A–207(2)].

F. UNCONSCIONABILITY
An unconscionable contract is so one-sided and unfair (when it is made) that enforcing it is unreasonable. A court can (1) refuse to enforce the contract, (2) enforce it without the unconscionable clause, or (3) limit the clause to avoid an unconscionable result [UCC 2–302, 2A–108].

V. CONTRACTS FOR THE INTERNATIONAL SALE OF GOODS
Contracts for the international sale of goods are governed by the 1980 United Nations Convention on Contracts for the International Sale of Goods (CISG).

A. APPLICABILITY OF THE CISG
The CISG is to international sales contracts what UCC Article 2 is to domestic sales contracts (except the CISG does not apply to consumer sales). The CISG applies when the parties to an international sales contract do not specify in writing the precise terms of their contract.

B. COMPARISON OF CISG AND UCC PROVISIONS

1. **Mirror Image Rule**
   The terms of the acceptance must mirror those of the offer [Art. 19].

2. **Irrevocable Offers**
   An offer is irrevocable if the offeror states that it is or if the offeree reasonably relies on it as being irrevocable. The offer is irrevocable even without a writing and consideration [Art. 16(2)].

3. **The Statute of Frauds**
   Article 11 does not include the requirements of the Statute of Frauds. (This accords with the law of most nations, in which contracts no longer need to meet formal requirements to be enforceable.)

4. **Price Term**
   Must be specified or be determinable from the contract.

5. **Time of Contract Formation**
   When an acceptance is sent, an offer becomes irrevocable, but the acceptance is not effective until it is received. Acceptance by performance does not require notice to the offeror.

C. SPECIAL PROVISIONS IN INTERNATIONAL CONTRACTS

1. **Choice of Language**
   Designates official language for interpreting contract in the event of disagreement. May indicate language for translations and arbitration.

2. **Choice of Forum**
   Designates forum, including specific court, for litigating a dispute. Clause is invalid if it denies one party an effective remedy, is the product of fraud or unconscionable conduct, causes substantial inconvenience to one party, or violates public policy.

3. **Choice of Law**
   Designates the applicable law. Under international law, there is no limit on parties' choice of law. If a choice is not specified, the governing law is that of the country of the seller's place of business.

4. ***Force Majeure* ("Impossible or Irresistible Force")**
   Stipulates that acts of God and other eventualities (government orders, regulations, embargoes, shortages of materials) may excuse a party from liability for nonperformance.

TRUE-FALSE QUESTIONS

(Answers at the Back of the Book)

___ 1. Article 2 of the UCC governs sales of goods.

___ 2. Under the UCC, a sale occurs when title passes from a seller to a buyer for a price.

___ 3. The UCC governs sales of services and real estate.

___ 4. Under the UCC, an agreement modifying a contract needs new consideration to be binding.

___ 5. If a contract for a sale of goods is missing a term, it will not be enforceable.

___ 6. An unconscionable contract is a contract so one-sided and unfair, at the time it is made, that enforcing it would be unreasonable.

___ 7. In effect, the CISG is to international sales contracts what Article 2 of the UCC is to domestic sales contracts.

___ 8. Under the UCC, an offer to buy goods can be accepted only by a prompt shipment of the goods.

___ 9. A lease agreement is the lessor and lessee's bargain.

___ 10. No oral contract is enforceable under the UCC.

FILL-IN QUESTIONS

(Answers at the Back of the Book)

______________________ (Course of dealing/Usage of trade) is a sequence of conduct between the parties that occurred before their agreement and establishes a common basis for their understanding. ______________ (Course of dealing/Usage of trade) is any practice or method of dealing having regularity of observance in a place, vocation, or ________ (deal/trade) so as to justify an expectation that it will be observed with respect to the transaction in question. The express terms of an agreement, the course of dealing, and the usage of trade will be construed to be __________(consistent/ inconsistent) with each other whenever reasonable. When that is not possible, the ______________________ (course of dealing/usage of trade/terms in the agreement) prevail.

MULTIPLE-CHOICE QUESTIONS

(Answers at the Back of the Book)

___ 1. Digital Computer Corporation and Electronic Data Systems, Inc., enter into a contract for a sale of goods. Under UCC Article 2, the price of a sale may be payable in

a. money only.
b. goods only.
c. money or goods only.
d. money, goods, services, or real estate.

___ 2. Alpha Electronics, Inc., sells computers, and some computer accessories, to persons who order them. Alpha is a merchant with respect to

a. computers only.
b. computer accessories only.
c. computers and computer accessories.
d. none of the above.

___ 3. A-One Products Corporation and Best Manufacturing, Inc., enter into a contract for a sale of goods that does not include a price term. In a suit between A-One and Best over this contract and the price, a court will

a. determine a reasonable price.
b. impose the lowest market price for the goods.
c. refuse to enforce the agreement.
d. return the parties to the positions they held before the contract.

___ 4. Apex Corporation sells two construction cranes to Baker Company, which leases one crane to Construction, Inc., and gives the other crane to Equipment, Inc. Article 2A of the UCC applies to

a. the gift only.
b. the lease only.
c. the sale only.
d. the gift, the lease, and the sale.

___ **5.** Mike and Rita orally agree to a sale of 100 pair of hiking boots at $50 each. Rita gives Mike a check for $500 as a down payment. Mike takes the check. At this point, the contract is enforceable

a. to the full extent because it is for specially made goods.
b. to the full extent because it is oral.
c. to the extent of $500.
d. none of the above.

___ **6.** Coastal Sales Corporation sends its purchase order form to Delta Products, Inc., for sixty display stands. Delta responds with its own form. Additional terms in Delta's form automatically become part of the contract unless

a. Coastal objects to the new terms within a reasonable period of time.
b. Coastal's form expressly required acceptance of its terms.
c. the additional terms materially alter the original contract.
d. any of the above.

___ **7.** Bob and Carol dispute the interpretation of an ambiguous clause in their contract. In a suit to determine the meaning of the clause, the court may accept evidence of

a. consistent additional terms only.
b. contradictory terms only.
c. consistent additional terms and contradictory terms.
d. none of the above.

___ **8.** **Based on a Sample CPA Exam Question.** Eagle Products, Inc., assures General Retail Corporation that its offer to sell its products at a certain price will remain open. This is a firm offer only if

a. General (the offeree) gives consideration for the offer.
b. General (the offeree) is a merchant.
c. the offer is made by Eagle (a merchant) in a signed writing.
d. the offer states the time period during which it will remain open.

___ **9.** Don enters a contract with Ed's Furniture Store. In a later suit, Don claims that a clause in the contract is unconscionable. If the court agrees, it may

a. enforce the contract without the clause.
b. limit the application of the clause to avoid an unconscionable result.
c. refuse to enforce the contract.
d. any of the above.

___ **10.** Digital Products, Inc., agrees to buy an unspecified quantity of microchips from Excel Corporation. Excel breaches the contract. Digital can probably

a. enforce the agreement to the amount of a reasonable quantity.
b. enforce the agreement to the amount of Digital's requirements.
c. enforce the agreement to the amount of Excel's output.
d. not enforce the agreement.

STARBUCKS COFFEE COMPANY INTERNATIONAL SALES CONTRACT APPLICATIONS

(Answers at the Back of the Book)

The following hypothetical situation and multiple-choice questions relate to your text's fold-out exhibit of the international sales contract used by Starbucks Coffee Company. In that contract, Starbucks orders five hundred tons of coffee at $10 per pound from XYZ Co.

___ **1.** Starbucks and XYZ would have an enforceable contract even if they did *not* state in writing

a. the amount of coffee ordered.
b. the price of the coffee.
c. both a and b.
d. none of the above.

___ **2.** If Starbucks and XYZ did not include a "DESCRIPTION" of the coffee as "High grown Mexican Altura," then the delivered coffee must meet

a. Starbuck's subjective expectations of their quality.
b. Starbuck's description of the goods in ads, on labels, and so on.
c. XYZ's description of the goods in ads, on labels, and so on.
d. XYZ's subjective belief in their quality.

___ **3.** Starbucks's incentive to pay on time, according to the terms of this contract, is the clause titled

a. CLAIMS.
b. GUARANTEE.
c. PAYMENT.
d. PRICE.

___ **4.** XYZ's incentive to deliver coffee that conforms to the contract is the clause titled

a. CLAIMS.
b. GUARANTEE.
c. PAYMENT.
d. PRICE.

___ **5.** Under this contract, until the coffee is delivered to its destination, the party who bears the risk of loss is

a. Bonded Public Warehouse.
b. Green Coffee Association
c. Starbucks.
d. XYZ.

SHORT ESSAY QUESTIONS

1. UCC Article 2 deals with sales of goods. What is a sale? What are goods?

2. In certain phases of sales transactions involving merchants, the UCC imposes special standards. For these purposes, who is a merchant?

ISSUE SPOTTERS

(Answers at the Back of the Book)

1. Ace Autos, a car dealer, writes to Beth, "I have a 1999 Honda Civic that I will sell to you for $4,000. This offer will be kept open for one week." Six days later, Carl tells Beth that Ace sold the car that morning for $5,000. Did Ace breach any contract?

2. E-Design, Inc., orders 150 computer desks. Fine Supplies, Inc., ships 150 printer stands. Is this an acceptance of the offer or a counteroffer? If it is an acceptance, is it a breach of the contract? What if Fine told E-Design it was sending printer stands as "an accommodation"?

3. Truck Parts, Inc. (TPI), often sells supplies to United Service Company (USC), which services trucks. Over the phone, they negotiate for the sale of eighty-four sets of tires. TPI sends a letter to USC detailing the terms and two weeks later ships the tires. Is there an enforceable contract between them?

SPECIAL INFORMATION FOR CPA CANDIDATES

Concepts introduced in this chapter that are important to keep in mind for the CPA examination include the differences between common law and the UCC. The UCC rules that apply in transactions between merchants have also been on the exam in the past (questions covering firm offers, for instance), as have questions about which contracts must be in writing and what satisfies the writing requirement. Remember, too, that although the UCC applies to any sale of goods, regardless of the amount, an agreement for a sale of goods priced under $500 need not be in writing to be enforceable.

Chapter 20
Title, Risk, and Insurable Interest

WHAT THIS CHAPTER IS ABOUT

The UCC has special rules involving title, which may determine the rights and remedies of the parties to a sales contract. In most situations, however, issues concerning the rights and remedies of parties to sales or lease contracts are controlled by three other concepts: (1) identification, (2) risk of loss, and (3) insurable interest.

CHAPTER OUTLINE

I. IDENTIFICATION

For an interest in goods to pass from seller to buyer or lessor to lessee, the goods must (1) exist and (2) be identified as the goods subject to the contract. **Identification** is designation of the goods as the subject matter of the contract.

A. SIGNIFICANCE OF IDENTIFICATION

Identification gives the buyer (1) the right to obtain insurance and (2) the right to obtain the goods from the seller.

B. WHEN IDENTIFICATION OCCURS

According to the parties' agreement [UCC 2–501, 2A–217]. If they do not specify a time and the goods are—

1. **Existing Goods**
   Identification occurs when the contract is made.

2. **Future Goods**
   If a sale involves unborn animals or crops to be harvested within twelve months of the contract (or, for crops, during the next harvest season, whichever is further in the future), identification occurs when the goods are conceived, planted, or begin to grow.

3. **Goods That Are Part of a Larger Mass**
   Identification occurs when—

   a. **Goods Are Marked, Shipped, or Otherwise Designated**

   b. **Exception—Fungible Goods**
   A buyer can acquire rights to goods that are alike by physical nature, agreement, or trade usage and that are held by owners in common by replacing the seller as owner [UCC 2–105(4)].

II. WHEN TITLE PASSES

Parties can agree on when and under what conditions title will pass. If they do not specify a time, title passes on delivery [UCC 2–401(2)]. Delivery terms determine when this occurs.

A. SHIPMENT CONTRACTS

If the seller is required or authorized to ship goods by carrier, title passes at time and place of shipment [UCC 2–401(2)(a)]. All contracts are shipment contracts unless they say otherwise.

B. DESTINATION CONTRACTS

If the seller is required to deliver goods to a certain destination, title passes when the goods are tendered there [UCC 2–401(2)(b)].

C. DELIVERY WITHOUT MOVEMENT OF THE GOODS

If a buyer is to pick up goods, passing title turns on whether a seller must give a document of title (bill of lading, warehouse receipt).

1. When a Document of Title Is Required

Title passes when and where the document is delivered. The goods do not need to move (for example, they can stay in a warehouse).

2. When No Document of Title Is Required

If the goods have been identified, title passes when and where the contract was made. If the goods have not been identified, title does not pass until identification [UCC 2–401(3)].

D. SALES OR LEASES BY NONOWNERS

Generally, a buyer acquires whatever title the seller has to the goods sold [UCC 2–402, 2–403]. A lessee acquires whatever title a lessor could transfer, subject to the lease [UCC 2A–303, 2A–304, 2A–305].

1. Void Title

If the seller or lessor stole the goods, the buyer or lessee acquires nothing; the real owner can reclaim the goods.

2. Voidable Title

Seller has voidable title if goods obtained by fraud, paid for with check that is later dishonored, bought on credit from insolvent seller, or bought from a minor. Real owner can reclaim, except goods in possession of good faith purchaser for value [UCC 2–403(3)].

3. Entrustment Rule

Entrustment includes both delivering goods to a merchant and leaving goods with a merchant for later delivery or pickup [UCC 2–403(3)].

a. Entrusting Goods to a Merchant Who Deals in Goods of the Kind

The merchant can transfer all rights to a buyer or sublessee in the ordinary course of business [UCC 2–403(2), 2A–305(2)].

b. What a Buyer or Sublessee in the Ordinary Course Gets

Only those rights held by the person who entrusted the goods.

III. RISK OF LOSS

The question of who suffers a financial loss if goods are damaged, destroyed, or lost (who bears the *risk of loss*) is determined by the parties' contract. If the contract does not state who bears the risk, the UCC has rules to determine it.

A. DELIVERY WITH MOVEMENT OF THE GOODS—CARRIER CASES

When goods are to be delivered by truck or other paid transport—

1. Contract Terms

a. **F.O.B.** (Free on board)—delivery is at seller's expense to a specific location. Risk passes at the location [UCC 2–319(1)].

b. **F.A.S.** (Free alongside)—seller delivers goods next to the ship that will carry them, and risk passes to buyer [UCC 2–319(2)].

c. **C.I.F. or C.&F.** (Cost, insurance, and freight)—seller puts goods in possession of a carrier before risk passes [UCC 2–320(2)].

d. **Delivery Ex-ship** (From the carrying vessel)—risk passes to buyer when goods leave the ship or are unloaded [UCC 2–322].

2. **Shipment Contracts**
Risk passes to the buyer or lessee when the goods are delivered to a carrier [UCC 2–509(1)(a), 2A–219(2)(a)].

3. **Destination Contracts**
Risk passes to the buyer or lessee when the goods are tendered to the buyer at the destination [UCC 2–509(1)(b), 2A–219(2)(b)].

B. DELIVERY WITHOUT MOVEMENT OF THE GOODS

When goods are to be picked up by the buyer or lessee—

1. **If the Seller or Lessor Is a Merchant**
Risk passes only on the buyer's or lessee's taking possession of the goods.

2. **If the Seller or Lessor Is Not a Merchant**
Risk passes on tender of delivery [UCC 2–509(3), 2A–219(c)].

3. **If a Bailee Holds the Goods**
Risk passes when (1) the buyer receives a negotiable document of title for the goods, (2) the bailee acknowledges the buyer's (or in the case of a lease, the lessee's) right to the goods, or (3) the buyer receives a nonnegotiable document of title, presents the document to the bailee, and demands the goods. If the bailee refuses to honor the document, the risk remains with the seller [UCC 2–503(4)(b), 2–509(2), 2A–219(2)(b)].

C. CONDITIONAL SALES

1. **Sale or Return (or Sale and Return)**
A seller delivers goods to a buyer who may retain any part and pay accordingly. The balance is returned or held by the buyer as a bailee.

a. **Title and Risk Pass to the Buyer with Possession**
Title and risk stay with the buyer until he or she returns the goods to the seller within the specified time. A sale is final if the buyer fails to return the goods in time. Goods in the buyer's possession are subject to the claims of the buyer's creditors.

b. **Consignment**
A consignment is a sale or return. Goods in the consignee's (buyer's) possession are subject to his or her creditors' claims [UCC 2–326(3)].

2. **Sale on Approval**
A seller offers to sell goods, and the buyer takes them on a trial basis. Title and risk remain with the seller until the buyer accepts the goods.

a. **What Constitutes Acceptance**
Any act inconsistent with the trial purpose or the seller's ownership; or by the buyer's choice not to return the goods on time.

b. **Return**
Return is at the seller's expense and risk [UCC 2–327(1)]. Goods are not subject to the claims of the buyer's creditors until acceptance.

D. RISK OF LOSS WHEN A SALES OR LEASE CONTRACT IS BREACHED

Generally, the party in breach bears the risk of loss.

1. **When the Seller or Lessor Breaches**
Risk passes to the buyer or lessee when the defects are cured or the buyer or lessee accepts the goods in spite of the defects. If, after acceptance, a buyer discovers a latent defect, acceptance can be revoked and the risk goes back to the seller [UCC 2–510(2), 2A–220(1)].

2. **When the Buyer or Lessee Breaches**
Risk shifts to the buyer or lessee (if the goods have been identified), where it stays for a commercially reasonable time after the seller or lessor learns of the breach. The buyer or lessee is liable to the extent of any deficiency in seller or lessor's insurance [UCC 2–510(3), 2A–220(2)].

IV. INSURABLE INTEREST

A party buying insurance must have a "sufficient interest" in the insured item. More than one party can have an interest at the same time.

A. INSURABLE INTEREST OF THE BUYER OR LESSEE

A buyer or lessee has an insurable interest in goods the moment they are identified, even before risk of loss passes [UCC 2–501(1), 2A–218(1)].

B. INSURABLE INTEREST OF THE SELLER OR LESSOR

A seller or lessor has an insurable interest in goods as long as he or she holds title or a security interest in the goods [UCC 2–501(2), 2A–218(3)].

V. BULK TRANSFERS

A *bulk transfer* is a transfer of more than half of a seller's inventory not made in the ordinary course of business [UCC 6–102(1)]. Subject to UCC Article 6, which, because of changes in the context in which bulk sales are made, has been repealed in most states.

TRUE-FALSE QUESTIONS

(Answers at the Back of the Book)

___ 1. Before an interest in specific goods can pass from a seller to a buyer, the goods must exist and be identified to the contract.

___ 2. Under all circumstances, title passes at the time and place that the buyer accepts the goods.

___ 3. Unless a contract provides otherwise, it is normally assumed to be a shipment contract.

___ 4. In a sale on approval, the buyer can set aside the deal by returning the goods.

___ 5. A buyer and a seller cannot both have an insurable interest in the same goods at the same time.

___ 6. A bulk transfer is a transfer of a major part of the inventory not made in the ordinary course of the transferor's business.

___ 7. In a sale on approval, the risk of loss passes to the buyer as soon as the buyer takes possession.

___ 8. An innocent buyer can acquire title to goods as a good faith purchaser from a thief.

___ 9. Under a destination contract, title passes at time and place of shipment.

___ 10. If a seller is a merchant, the risk of loss passes when a buyer takes possession of the goods.

FILL-IN QUESTIONS

(Answers at the Back of the Book)

_______________ (F.A.S./F.O.B.) means that delivery is at a seller's expense to a specific location—the place of shipment or a place of destination. When the term is _____________ (F.A.S./F.O.B.) place of *shipment*, risk passes when the seller puts the goods into a carrier's possession. When the term is _______________ (F.A.S./F.O.B.) place of *destination*, risk passes when the seller tenders delivery. _______________ (F.A.S./F.O.B.) requires a seller at his or her own expense and risk to deliver goods alongside the ship that will transport them at which point risk passes.

MULTIPLE-CHOICE QUESTIONS

(Answers at the Back of the Book)

___ **1.** Ron agrees to sell 1,000 pens to State University Book Store. Before an interest in the pens can pass from Ron to the book store, the pens must be

a. in existence only.
b. identified as the specific goods designated in the contract only.
c. in existence and identified as the goods in the contract.
d. none of the above.

___ **2.** **Based on a Sample CPA Exam Question.** Best Products Corporation agrees to ship one hundred calculators to International Engineering, Inc. (IEI). Before the calculators arrive at IEI's offices, they are lost. The most important factor in determining who bears the risk of loss is

a. how the calculators were lost.
b. the contract's shipping terms.
c. the method by which the calculators were shipped.
d. title to the calculators.

___ **3.** Stan buys a CD player from Tom, his neighbor, who agrees to keep the player until Stan picks it up. Before Stan can get it, the player is stolen. The loss is suffered by

a. Stan only.
b. Tom only.
c. Stan and Tom.
d. none of the above.

___ **4.** Retail Floor Stores buys tile from Superior Tile Corporation. Town Storage holds the tile in a warehouse. The tile is delivered to Retail by the transfer of a negotiable warehouse receipt. A fire later damages the tile. The loss is suffered by

a. Retail.
b. Superior.
c. Town.
d. none of the above.

___ **5.** Nora leaves her car with OK Auto Sales & Service for repairs. OK sells the car to Pete, who does not know that OK has no right to sell the car. Nora can recover from

a. OK only.
b. Pete only.
c. OK and Pete.
d. none of the above.

___ 6. Ed buys a sport utility vehicle (SUV) from Friendly Truck Sales, which agrees to keep the SUV until Ed picks it up. Before Ed can get it, it is stolen. The loss is suffered by

a. Ed only.
b. Friendly only.
c. Ed and Friendly.
d. none of the above.

___ 7. Omega Engineering, Inc., buys ten drafting tables from Quality Supply Corporation. They agree to ship the tables F.O.B. Omega via State Trucking Company. The tables are destroyed in transit. The loss is suffered by

a. Omega.
b. Quality.
c. State.
d. none of the above.

___ 8. New Products, Inc. (NPI), agrees to sell one hundred cell phones to Open Source Sales. NPI identifies the goods by marking the crate with red stripes. Before the crate is shipped, an insurable interest exists in

a. NPI only.
b. Open Source only.
c. NPI and Open Source.
d. none of the above.

___ 9. Standard Goods, Inc., ships fifty defective hard drives to Top Business Corporation. Top rejects the drives and ships them back to Standard, via United Transport, Inc. The drives are lost in transit. The loss is suffered by

a. Standard.
b. Top.
c. United.
d. none of the above.

___ 10. Red Apples Corporation agrees to sell forty cases of apples to Sweet Fruit, Inc., under a shipment contract. Red gives the apples to Refrigerated Trucking, Inc. (RTI), which delivers them to Sweet. Title passed when

a. Red agreed to sell the goods.
b. Red gave the goods to RTI.
c. RTI delivered the goods to Sweet.
d. none of the above.

SHORT ESSAY QUESTIONS

1. What is "risk of loss" under the UCC?

2. When does risk pass (a) under a shipment contract? (b) under a destination contract? (c) when the buyer is to pick up the goods and the seller is a merchant? (d) when the buyer is to pick up the goods and the seller is not a merchant? (e) when a bailee holds the goods?

ISSUE SPOTTERS

(Answers at the Back of the Book)

1. Under a contract between Great Products, Inc., in New York and National Sales Corporation in Dallas, if delivery is "F.O.B. New York," the risk passes when the Great Products puts the goods in a carrier's hands. If delivery is "F.O.B. Dallas," the risk passes when the goods reach Dallas. What if the contract says only that Great Products is "to ship goods at the seller's expense"?

2. Fine Farms in Washington sells Green Produce in Alaska a certain size of apples to be shipped "F.O.B. Seattle." The apples that Fine delivers to the shipping company for transport are too small. The apples are lost in transit. Who suffers the loss?

3. Chocolate, Inc., sells five hundred cases of cocoa mix to Dessert Company, which pays with a bad check. Chocolate does not discover that the check is bad until after Dessert sells the cocoa to Eden Food Stores, which suspects nothing. Can Chocolate recover the cocoa from Eden?

SPECIAL INFORMATION FOR CPA CANDIDATES

The most important concept in this chapter to master for the CPA examination is passage of the risk of loss. In most of the problems on the CPA examination, the party who bears the loss has traditionally been the party who breached the contract. You should bear in mind, however, that who ultimately bears the risk of loss is not necessarily the same party who has title or an insurable interest, nor does it depend on whether the buyer has paid for the goods or on whether some action by a party outside the contract contributed to the loss of the goods.

Other concepts discussed in this chapter may occur on the CPA exam. The concept of title is often tested in a context involving stolen goods, voidable title, or entrustment. The passage of title and risk may be at issue in questions on sales on approval and sales or return. Questions are also sometimes asked about bulk sales.

Chapter 21
Performance of Sales and Lease Contracts

WHAT THIS CHAPTER IS ABOUT

This chapter examines the basic obligations of a seller and a buyer under a sales contract. A seller has the obligation to deliver conforming goods, and the buyer has the obligation to accept and pay for those goods [UCC 2–301]. When a contract is unclear or its terms are indefinite and disputes arise, courts look to the UCC.

CHAPTER OUTLINE

I. THE GOOD FAITH REQUIREMENT

The obligations of good faith and commercial reasonableness underlie every contract within the UCC [UCC 1–203]. There is a higher standard for merchants: honesty in fact and the observance of reasonable commercial standards of fair dealing in the trade [UCC 2–103, 2A–516(1)].

II. OBLIGATIONS OF THE SELLER OR LESSOR

The seller or lessor must **tender** delivery (hold conforming goods at the disposal of the buyer or lessee and give whatever notice is reasonably necessary to enable the buyer or lessee to take delivery) [UCC 2–503(1), 2A–508(1)].

A. WHEN TENDER MUST OCCUR

At a reasonable hour, in a reasonable manner, and the goods must be kept available for a reasonable time [UCC 2–503(1)(a)]. Goods must be tendered in a single delivery unless parties agree otherwise [UCC 2–612, 2A–510] or, under the circumstances, a party can request delivery in lots [UCC 2–307].

B. PLACE OF DELIVERY

The parties may agree on a particular destination, or their contract or the circumstances may indicate a place.

1. Noncarrier Cases

a. Seller's Place of Business

If the contract does not designate a place of delivery, and the buyer is to pick up the goods, the place is the seller's place of business or if none, the seller's residence [UCC 2–308].

b. Identified Goods That Are Not at the Seller's Place of Business

Wherever they are is the place of delivery [UCC 2–308].

2. Carrier Cases

a. Shipment Contract

The seller must [UCC 2–504]—

1) Put the goods into the hands of a carrier.

2) Make a contract for the transport of the goods that is reasonable according to their nature and value.

3) Tender to the buyer any documents necessary to obtain possession of the goods from the carrier.

4) Promptly notify the buyer that shipment has been made.

5) If a seller fails to meet these requirements, and this causes a material loss or a delay, the buyer can reject the shipment.

b. **Destination Contract**
The seller must give the buyer appropriate notice and any necessary documents of title [UCC 2–503].

C. THE PERFECT TENDER RULE

A seller or lessor must deliver goods in conformity with every detail of the contract. If goods or tender fail in any respect, the buyer or lessee can accept the goods, reject them, or accept part and reject part [UCC 2–601, 2A–509].

D. EXCEPTIONS TO THE PERFECT TENDER RULE

1. **Agreement of the Parties**
Parties can agree in their contract that, for example, the seller can repair or replace any defective goods within a reasonable time.

2. **Cure**

a. **Within the Contract Time for Performance**
If nonconforming goods are rejected, the seller or lessor can notify the buyer or lessee of an intention to repair, adjust, or replace the goods and can then do so within the contract time for performance [UCC 2–508, 2A–513].

b. **After the Time for Performance Expires**
The seller or lessor can cure if there were reasonable grounds to believe the nonconformance would be acceptable.

c. **Substantially Restricts the Buyer's Right to Reject**
If the buyer or lessee refuses goods but does not disclose the nature of the defect, he or she cannot later assert the defect as a defense if it is one that could have been cured [UCC 2–605, 2A–514].

3. **Substitution of Carriers**
If, through no fault of either party an agreed manner of delivery is not available, a substitute is sufficient [UCC 2–614(1)].

4. **Installment Contracts**

a. **Substantial Nonconformity**
A buyer or lessee can reject an installment only if a nonconformity substantially impairs the value of the installment and cannot be cured [UCC 2–612(2), 2–307, 2A–510(1)].

b. **Breach of the Entire Contract**
A breach occurs if one or more nonconforming installments substantially impair the value of the whole contract. If the buyer or lessee accepts a nonconforming installment, the contract is reinstated [UCC 2–612(3), 2A–510(2)]

5. **Commercial Impracticability**
Delay or nondelivery is not a breach if performance is impracticable "by the occurrence of a contingency the nonoccurrence of which was a basic assumption on which the contract was made" [UCC 2–615(a)]. The seller must notify the buyer.

a. **Unforeseeability**
The unforeseen contingency (such as a sudden shortage of raw materials) must alter the essential nature of the performance.

b. **Partial Performance**
If a seller is able to fulfill a contract partially, the seller must allocate in a fair and reasonable manner deliveries among all contracted customers [UCC 2–615(b),(c)].

6. **Destruction of Identified Goods**
When goods are destroyed (through no fault of a party) before risk passes to the buyer, the parties are excused from performance [UCC 2–613(a)]. If goods are only partially destroyed, a buyer can treat a contract as void or accept damaged goods with a price allowance.

7. **Assurance and Cooperation**

a. **The Right of Assurance**
If a party has reasonable grounds to believe the other will not perform, he or she may "in writing demand adequate assurance."

1) **Suspension of Performance**
Until assurance is received, the party may "suspend" performance without liability.

2) **Between Merchants**
The grounds are determined by commercial standards [UCC 2–609, 2A–401]. If assurances are not provided within thirty days, this may be treated as a repudiation of the contract.

b. **The Duty of Cooperation**
When cooperation is not forthcoming, a party can suspend his or her performance and hold the uncooperative party in breach or perform in any reasonable manner [see UCC 2–311(3)(b)].

III. OBLIGATIONS OF THE BUYER OR LESSEE

The buyer or lessee must make payment at the time and place he or she receives the goods unless the parties have agreed otherwise [UCC 2–310(a), 2A–516(1)].

A. PAYMENT

Payment can be by any means agreed on between the parties [UCC 2–511].

B. RIGHT OF INSPECTION

The buyer or lessee can verify, before making payment, that the goods are what were contracted for. The buyer has no duty to pay if the goods are not what were ordered [UCC 2–513(1), 2A–515(1)].

1. **Time, Place, and Manner**
Inspection can be in any reasonable place, time and manner, determined by custom of the trade, practice of the parties, and so on [UCC 2–513(2)].

2. **C.O.D. Shipments**
If a buyer agrees to a C.O.D. shipment or to pay for goods on presentation of a bill of lading, no right of inspection exists [UCC 2–513(3)].

3. **Payment Due—Documents of Title (C.I.F. and C.&F. Contracts)**
Payment is required on receipt of documents of title, before inspection, and must be made unless the buyer knows the goods are nonconforming [UCC 2–310(b), 2–513(3)].

C. ACCEPTANCE

Acceptance is presumed if a buyer or lessee has a reasonable opportunity to inspect and fails to reject in a reasonable time [UCC 2–606, 2–602, 2A–515].

1. **How a Buyer or Lessee Can Accept**
A buyer or lessee can accept by words or conduct. Under a sales contract, a buyer can accept by any act (such as using or reselling the goods) inconsistent with the seller's ownership [UCC 2–606(1)(c)].

2. **A Buyer or Lessee Can Accept Only Some of the Goods**
But not less than a single commercial unit [UCC 2–601(c), 2A-509(1)].

IV. ANTICIPATORY REPUDIATION

The nonbreaching party can (1) treat the repudiation as a final breach by pursuing a remedy or (2) wait, hoping that the repudiating party will decide to honor the contract [UCC 2–610, 2A–402]. If the party decides to wait, the breaching party can retract the repudiation [UCC 2–611, 2A–403].

V. INTERNATIONAL CONTRACTS—LETTERS OF CREDIT

A. Principal Parties

The issuer (a bank) agrees to issue a letter of credit and to ascertain whether the beneficiary (seller) performs certain acts. The account party (buyer) promises to reimburse the issuer for amounts paid to the beneficiary.

B. Other Banks

There may be an advising bank that transmits information and a paying bank that expedites payment.

C. Issuer's Obligation

The issuer is bound to pay the beneficiary when the beneficiary complies with the terms of the letter (by presenting the required documents—typically a bill of lading).

TRUE-FALSE QUESTIONS

(Answers at the Back of the Book)

____ 1. The duties and obligations of the parties to a contract include those specified in their agreement.

____ 2. If a particular carrier is unavailable through no fault of either party, a commercially reasonable substitute may be used.

____ 3. Generally, under a sales or lease contract, all goods must be tendered in a single delivery.

____ 4. Unless the parties agree otherwise, a buyer or lessee must pay for goods in advance.

____ 5. A buyer or lessee can always reject delivered goods on discovery of a defect, regardless of previous opportunities to inspect.

____ 6. Merchants are held to the same standard of good faith as nonmerchants.

____ 7. A seller or lessor cannot consider a buyer or lessee in breach until the time for performance has past.

____ 8. If a buyer has a reasonable opportunity to inspect goods and fails to reject them within a reasonable time, acceptance is presumed.

____ 9. If a contract does not specify otherwise, the place for delivery of goods is the buyer's place of business.

____ 10. In an installment contract, a buyer can reject any installment for any reason.

FILL-IN QUESTIONS

(Answers at the Back of the Book)

A seller's obligations include holding ______________________ (conforming/nonconforming) goods at a buyer's disposal ______________ (and/or) giving notice reasonably necessary for the buyer to take delivery. The ______________ (seller/buyer) must make payment at the time and place of

____________ (delivery/receipt) of the goods ____________ (even if/unless) the parties have agreed otherwise.

MULTIPLE-CHOICE QUESTIONS

(Answers at the Back of the Book)

___ 1. Fine Poultry Corporation agrees to sell 600 frozen chickens to Fast Food, Inc., in three equal installments. In the first installment, 100 chickens are spoiled. Fast Food can

a. cancel the contract.
b. recover from Fine Poultry for breach of the entire contract.
c. reject the first installment only.
d. use the unspoiled chickens without payment.

___ 2. Smith Company in San Diego agrees to ship 500,000 plastic silver dollars to the Zenith Casino in Las Vegas. The goods are in a warehouse in Barstow. The agreement says that Zenith will pick up the goods, but says nothing about the place. The place of delivery is

a. Barstow.
b. San Diego.
c. Las Vegas.
d. none of the above.

___ 3. Pep Paints agrees to sell to Quality Painters Grade A-1 latex outdoor paint to be delivered May 8. On May 7, Pep tenders Grade B-2 paint. Quality rejects the Grade B-2 paint. If, two days later, Pep tenders Grade C-3 paint with an offer of a price allowance, Pep will have

a. additional, unlimited time to cure.
b. a reasonable time to cure.
c. one day to cure.
d. no time to cure.

___ 4. Family Game Town orders virtual reality helmets from Game Supplies, Inc. Game delivers, but Family rejects the shipment without providing a reason. If Game had known the reason, it could have corrected the problem within hours. If Family sues Game for damages, Family will

a. win, because Game's tender did not conform to the contract.
b. win, because Game made no attempt to cure.
c. lose, because Family's rejection was unjustified—Game could have cured.
d. lose, because a buyer cannot reject goods *and* sue for damages.

___ 5. Athletic Goods, Inc. (AGI), agrees to sell sports equipment to Bob's Sports Store. Before the time for performance, AGI tells Bob that it will not deliver. This is

a. anticipatory repudiation.
b. assurance and cooperation.
c. commercial impracticability.
d. perfect tender.

___ 6. Beth, a buyer in Canada, and Don, a seller in the United States, enter into a contract with a letter of credit. Don delivers the required documents to the issuing bank. The bank must

a. do nothing until Beth certifies the documents.
b. do nothing until Don delivers the goods to Beth.
c. pay Beth.
d. pay Don.

___ 7. **Based on a Sample CPA Exam Question.** Standard Office Products orders one hundred computers from National Suppliers. Unless the parties agree otherwise, National's obligation to Standard is to

a. deliver the computers to a common carrier.
b. deliver the computer's to Standard's place of business.
c. hold conforming goods and give notice for Standard to take delivery.
d. set aside conforming goods for Standard's inspection before delivery.

___ 8. Apple Farms contracts for a sale of fruit to Best Groceries, Inc. Apple can enforce its right to payment

a. only after Best has inspected the goods.
b. only after Best has had an opportunity to inspect the goods.
c. only before Best has inspected the goods.
d. whether or not Best has had the opportunity to inspect the goods.

___ 9. Computer Products ships ten monitors to Data Resources, Inc., per Data's request. Data can accept

a. only by telling the seller, "We accept."
b. only by unpacking the monitors and using them.
c. either by notifying the seller or by using the goods.
d. none of the above.

___ 10. Kay contracts to sell five laser printers to Lora under a shipment contract. Kay must

a. only make a reasonable contract for the transport of the goods.
b. only tender to Lora the documents needed to obtain possession of the goods.
c. make a reasonable contract for the transport of the goods and tender the documents needed to obtain the goods.
d. none of the above.

SHORT ESSAY QUESTIONS

1. What is a seller's right to cure? How does it affect a buyer's right to reject?

2. What is a buyer's right to inspect? How does it affect a seller's right to payment?

ISSUE SPOTTERS

(Answers at the Back of the Book)

1. Mike agrees to sell 1,000 espresso makers to Jenny to be delivered on May 1. Due to a strike in the last week of April, there is a temporary shortage of delivery vehicles. Mike can deliver the espresso makers 200 at a time over a period of ten days, with the first delivery on May 1. Does Mike have the right to deliver the goods in five lots?

2. Country Fruit Stand orders eighty cases of peaches from Citrus Farms. For no good reason, Citrus untimely delivers thirty cases instead of eighty. Does Country have the right to reject the shipment?

3. Great Images, Inc. (GI), agrees to sell Catalog Corporation (CC) 5,000 posters of celebrities, to be delivered on May 1. On April 1, GI repudiates the contract. CC informs GI that it expects delivery. Can CC sue GI without waiting until May 1?

SPECIAL INFORMATION FOR CPA CANDIDATES

A number of the concepts in this chapter often arise in the CPA examination, sometimes intertwined with the rules set out in other chapters covering Article 2 of the UCC. For example, a seller who does not tender delivery of conforming goods is in breach of the contract. Such a tender is also necessary for the risk of loss to pass.

It may be easiest to remember all of these rules by imagining a real sales contract situation and applying them to that situation. In particular, it can be helpful to sort out the rules in Article 2 that apply when one of the parties is a merchant and when both parties are merchants. The following topics (discussed in this chapter), as they relate to merchants, are often tested in the part of the CPA exam covering the UCC: risk of loss, the buyer's responsibility regarding rejected goods, the buyer's obligation to designate defects, sales on approval and sales or returns, and either party's right to assurance of performance.

Chapter 22
Remedies for Breach of Sales and Lease Contracts

WHAT THIS CHAPTER IS ABOUT

When a sales or lease contract is breached, the nonbreaching party has a number of remedies from which to choose. The general purpose is to put the party "in as good a position as if the other party had fully performed." This chapter sets out the remedies and the situations in which each is appropriate.

CHAPTER OUTLINE

I. REMEDIES OF THE SELLER OR LESSOR

A. WHEN THE GOODS ARE IN POSSESSION OF THE SELLER OR LESSOR

1. The Right to Cancel the Contract
A seller or lessor can cancel a contract (with notice to the buyer or lessee) if the other party breaches it [UCC 2–703(f), 2A–523(1)(a)].

2. The Right to Withhold Delivery
A seller or lessor can withhold delivery if a buyer or lessee wrongfully rejects or revokes acceptance, fails to pay, or repudiates [UCC 2–703(a), 2A–523(1)(c)]. If a buyer or lessee is insolvent, a seller or lessor can refuse to deliver unless a buyer pays cash [UCC 2–702(1), 2A–525(1)].

3. The Right to Resell or Dispose of the Goods

a. When a Seller or Lessor Can Resell or Lease to Another Party
A seller or lessor still has the goods and the buyer or lessee wrongfully rejects or revokes acceptance, fails to pay, or repudiates the contract [UCC 2–703(d), 2–706(1), 2A–523(1)(e), 2A–527(1)].

b. Unfinished Goods
A seller or lessor can (1) resell the goods as scrap or (2) finish and resell them (buyer or lessee is liable for any difference in price). The goal is to obtain maximum value [UCC 2–704(2), 2A–524(2)].

c. How to Conduct a Resale
In good faith and a commercially reasonable manner; give the original buyer notice, unless goods are perishable or will rapidly decline in value [UCC 2–706(2), (3)].

d. What the Seller or Lessor Can Recover
Any deficiency between the resale (or new lease) price and the contract price, plus incidental damages [UCC 2–706, 2–710, 2A–527].

4. The Right to Recover the Purchase Price or the Lease Payments Due
A seller or lessor can bring an action for the price if he or she is unable to resell [UCC 2–709(1), 2A–529(1)]. The buyer gets the goods, unless the seller or lessor disposes of them before collection of the judgment (with the proceeds credited to the buyer).

5. **The Right to Recover Damages**
If a buyer or lessee repudiates a contract or wrongfully refuses to accept, the seller or lessor can recover the difference between the contract price and the market price (at the time and place of tender), plus incidental damages. If the market price is less than the contract price, the seller or lessor gets lost profits [UCC 2–708, 2A–528].

B. WHEN THE GOODS ARE IN TRANSIT

A seller or lessor can stop delivery of goods if (1) buyer or lessee is insolvent or (2) buyer or lessee is solvent but in breach (if the quantity shipped is a carload, a truckload, or larger) [UCC 2–705, 2A–526]. This right is lost if—

1. Buyer or lessee has possession of the goods.
2. The carrier acknowledges rights of buyer or lessee.
3. A bailee other than a carrier acknowledges that he or she is holding the goods for buyer or lessee.
4. A document of title covering the goods is negotiated to the buyer.

C. WHEN THE GOODS ARE IN POSSESSION OF THE BUYER OR LESSEE

1. **The Right to Recover the Purchase Price or Lease Payments Due**
A seller or lessor can bring an action for the price if the buyer or lessee accepts the goods but refuses to pay [UCC 2–709(1), 2A–529(1)].

2. **The Right to Reclaim the Goods**

a. **Sales Contracts—Buyer's Insolvency**
If an insolvent buyer gets goods on credit, the seller can (within ten days) reclaim them. A seller can reclaim any time if a buyer misrepresents solvency in writing within three months before delivery [UCC 2–702(2)].

b. **Sales Contracts—A Buyer in the Ordinary Course of Business**
A seller cannot reclaim goods from such a buyer.

c. **Sales Contracts—Bars the Pursuit of Other Remedies**
A seller who reclaims gets preferential treatment over a buyer's other creditors (but cannot pursue other remedies) [UCC 2–702(3)].

d. **Lease Contracts**
A lessor can reclaim goods from a lessee in default [UCC 2A–525(2)].

II. REMEDIES OF THE BUYER OR LESSEE

A. WHEN THE SELLER OR LESSOR REFUSES TO DELIVER THE GOODS

When a seller or lessor fails to deliver or repudiates the contract, the buyer or lessee has the following rights.

1. **The Right to Cancel the Contract**
The buyer or lessee can rescind (cancel) the contract. On notice to the seller, the buyer or lessee is discharged [UCC 2–711(1), 2A–508(1)(a).

2. **The Right to Recover the Goods**
A buyer or lessee who paid for goods in the hands of the seller or lessor can recover them if the seller or lessor becomes insolvent within ten days of receiving payment and the goods are identified to the contract. Buyer or lessee must tender any unpaid balance [UCC 2–502, 2A–522].

3. **The Right to Obtain Specific Performance**
A buyer or lessee can obtain specific performance if goods are unique or damages would be inadequate [UCC 2–716(1), 2A–521(1)].

4. **The Right of Cover**
Buyer or lessee can obtain cover (substitute goods) and then sue for damages. The measure of damages is the difference between the cost of cover and the contract price, plus incidental and consequential damages, minus expenses saved by the breach [UCC 2–712, 2–715, 2A–518, 2A–520].

5. **The Right to Replevy the Goods**
Buyer or lessee can use, against the seller or lessor, replevin (an action to recover goods from a party wrongfully withholding them) if the buyer or lessee is unable to cover [UCC 2–716(3), 2A–521(3)].

6. **The Right to Recover Damages**
The measure of damages is the difference between the contract price and, when the buyer or lessee learned of the breach, the market price (at the place of delivery), plus incidental and consequential damages, minus expenses saved by the breach [UCC 2–713, 2A–519].

B. WHEN THE SELLER OR LESSOR DELIVERS NONCONFORMING GOODS

1. **The Right to Reject the Goods**
A buyer or lessee can reject the part of goods that fails to conform to the contract (and rescind the contract or obtain cover) [UCC 2–601, 2A–509].

   a. **Notice Required**
   Notice must be seasonable (timely), and a buyer or lessee must tell the seller or lessor what the defect is [UCC 2–602(1), 2–605, 2A–509(2), 2A–514].

   b. **Duties of a Merchant Buyer or Lessee**
   Follow the seller or lessor's instructions about the goods [UCC 2–603, 2A–511]. Without instructions, perishable goods can be resold; otherwise they must be stored or returned. A buyer or lessee is entitled to reimbursement for the cost.

   c. **The Right to Retain and Enforce a Security Interest**
   Buyers who rightfully reject or who justifiably revoke acceptance of goods in their possession have a security interest in the goods. A buyer can recover payments made for the goods and expenses to inspect, transport, and hold the goods, or can resell, withhold delivery, or stop delivery [UCC 2–711, 2–706].

2. **The Right to Revoke Acceptance**

   a. **Substantial Impairment**
   Any nonconformity must substantially impair the value of the goods *and* either not be seasonably cured or be difficult to discover [UCC 2–608, 2A–517].

   b. **Notice of a Breach Must Be within a Reasonable Time**
   Before the goods have undergone substantial change (not caused by their own defects, such as spoilage) [UCC 2–608(2), 2A–517(4)].

3. **The Right to Recover Damages for Accepted Goods**
Notice of a breach must be within a reasonable time [UCC 2–607, 2A–516]. The measure of damages is the difference between value of goods as accepted and value if they had been as promised [UCC 2–714(2), 2A–519(4)].

III. CONTRACTUAL PROVISIONS AFFECTING REMEDIES

Parties can provide for remedies in addition to or in lieu of those in the UCC, or they can change the measure of damages [UCC 2–719, 2A–503]. If a buyer or lessee is a consumer, limiting consequential damages for personal injuries on a breach of warranty is *prima facie* unconscionable.

IV. LEMON LAWS

If an automobile under warranty has a defect that significantly affects the vehicle's value or use, and the seller does not fix it within a specified number of opportunities, the buyer is entitled (after following certain procedures) to a new car, replacement of defective parts, or return of all consideration paid.

V. REMEDIES FOR INTERNATIONAL SALES CONTRACTS

The United Nations Convention on Contracts for the International Sale of Goods (CISG) provides remedies similar to those of the UCC, including, in the appropriate circumstances, damages (difference between contract and market prices), the right to avoid the contract, and the right to specific performance.

TRUE-FALSE QUESTIONS

(Answers at the Back of the Book)

___ 1. An award of damages is inappropriate if specific performance is possible.

___ 2. When a buyer accepts goods, if he or she fails to make proper and timely payment, the seller can sue to recover the price of the goods.

___ 3. When a seller discovers that a buyer has received goods on credit while insolvent, the seller can reclaim the goods.

___ 4. If a buyer or lessee wrongfully refuses to accept or pay for conforming goods, the seller or lessor can cancel the contract and recover damages.

___ 5. If a seller or lessor wrongfully refuses to deliver conforming goods, the buyer or lessee can cancel the contract and recover damages.

___ 6. A buyer cannot reject nonconforming goods once they have been delivered.

___ 7. When a seller is in breach, the buyer can cancel the contract, but he or she then loses all rights to any other remedy.

___ 8. A buyer or lessee who accepts a delivery of goods cannot withdraw the acceptance.

___ 9. If the seller has not yet delivered the goods, he or she can cancel the contract without liability.

___ 10. Remedies for the breach of international contracts are different from those available under the UCC.

FILL-IN QUESTIONS

(Answers at the Back of the Book)

Most states have lemon laws, which provide that if ______________________________________ (any automobile/an automobile under warranty) possesses a defect that significantly affects the vehicle's ______________________ (value/use/value or use), and the defect is not remedied by the seller ______________________________ (by a certain date/within a certain number of opportunities), the buyer is entitled to ____ (replacement of defective parts or return of all consideration paid/a new car, replacement of defective parts, or return of all consideration paid).

MULTIPLE-CHOICE QUESTIONS

(Answers at the Back of the Book)

___ 1. **Based on a Sample CPA Exam Question.** Digital Products Company agrees to sell to Eagle Manufacturing, Inc., a customized software system. If Eagle materially breaches the contract, the remedies available to Digital include the right

a. to cancel the contract only.
b. to recover damages only.
c. to cancel the contract and recover damages.
d. none of the above.

___ 2. Alpha Corporation agrees to buy one hundred hard drives from Beta, Inc. When Beta fails to deliver, Alpha is forced to cover. Alpha sues Beta. Alpha can recover from Beta

a. the cover price, minus the contract price, only.
b. incidental and consequential damages only.
c. the cover price, minus the contract price, plus incidental and consequential damages.
d. none of the above.

___ 3. Gamma Corporation agrees to sell the updated version of its word-processing software to Omega Company. Gamma delivers an outdated version of the program. Omega's remedies may include

a. recovering damages only.
b. rejecting part or all of the goods, or revoking acceptance only.
c. recovering damages, rejecting the goods, or revoking acceptance.
d. none of the above.

___ 4. Eagle Manufacturing, Inc., and Fine Furniture contract for the sale of thirty bookcases. They can agree

a. only to add to their UCC remedies.
b. only to substitute for their UCC remedies.
c. only to change the measure of damages under the UCC.
d. to add to or substitute for their UCC remedies, or to change the measure of damages under the UCC.

___ 5. Engineering, Inc. (EI), agrees to sell specially made parts to Precise Components Company. EI does not deliver. Due to a market shortage, Precise cannot obtain cover. The buyer's right to recover the parts from EI is

a. novation.
b. replevin.
c. rescission.
d. specific performance.

___ 6. ABC Market orders a truckload of apples from Hill Orchards. Hill can stop delivery of the apples in transit

a. only if ABC is insolvent.
b. only if ABC breaches the contract.
c. if ABC is insolvent or breaches the contract.
d. under no circumstances.

___ 7. Quantum Computers delivers sixty computers to Retail Sales, Inc., as per Retail's order. Retail does not reject or pay for the goods. Quantum can

a. only bring an action to recover the price.
b. only bring an action to reclaim the goods.
c. bring an action to recover the price or reclaim the goods.
d. none of the above.

___ 8. United Distribution Company contracts to buy goods from Variety Sales Corporation, which wrongfully fails to deliver. United can recover damages equal to the difference between the contract price and the market price

a. at the time the contract was made.
b. at the time and place of tender.
c. when United learned of the breach.
d. when United files a suit against Variety.

___ 9. Commercial Builders orders forty window frames from Delta Windows. Only half of the frames that Delta delivers conform to the contract. Commercial can reject the frames that do not conform and

a. cancel the contract, but not obtain cover.
b. obtain cover, but not cancel the contract.
c. cancel the contract or obtain cover.
d. none of the above.

___ 10. E-Equip, Inc., agrees to lease ten servers to Office Company. When E-Equip tries to deliver, Office refuses to accept. There is nothing wrong with the servers. E-Equip sues Office, seeking damages. E-Equip is entitled to the difference between

a. the contract price and the market price.
b. the market price and E-Equip's lost profits.
c. E-Equip's lost profits and the contract price.
d. none of the above.

SHORT ESSAY QUESTIONS

1. What can a seller do to protect itself on hearing that a buyer is in financial trouble?

2. What is the buyer's right of cover?

ISSUE SPOTTERS

(Answers at the Back of the Book)

1. Plain Clothes, Inc., contracts to sell to Fashion Outlets six hundred pairs of jeans, to be delivered and paid for in six monthly installments. Plain tenders the first installment. For no good reason, Fashion sends the shipment back to Plain without payment. Can Plain withhold delivery of the next installment?

2. Market Distributors, Inc., contracts to sell to National Motor Company (NMC) 10,000 cogwheels at $1 each to be delivered to NMC's factory in Detroit on May 1. Market knows that NMC will use the cogwheels to manufacture specialty motors and that NMC's operation will be at a standstill if it does not receive the goods. When Market fails to deliver, the price of cogwheels in Detroit is $1.20 each. NMC's operation shuts down. NMC sues Market. What is NMC entitled to?

3. Pizza King Corporation agrees to buy tomatoes from Quality Farms. When Quality tenders the goods, Pizza King wrongfully refuses to accept. Quality quickly sells the tomatoes to another buyer, for a lower price. Can Quality recover from Pizza King? If so, what's the measure of recovery?

SPECIAL INFORMATION FOR CPA CANDIDATES

The topics and details set out in this chapter have not been as heavily tested on the CPA examination as the concepts covered in other chapters in this unit. Knowing which remedies are available in which situations may prove useful, however.

Chapter 23
Sales and Lease Warranties

WHAT THIS CHAPTER IS ABOUT

Most goods are covered by some type of warranty designed to protect consumers. A warranty imposes a duty on the seller; a breach of warranty is a breach of the seller's promise. If the parties have not agreed to limit the remedies available to the buyer, the buyer can sue to recover damages or, sometimes, rescind the contract.

CHAPTER OUTLINE

I. WARRANTIES OF TITLE

A. GOOD TITLE
Sellers warrant that they have good and valid title and that the transfer of title is rightful [UCC 2–312(1)(a)].

B. NO LIENS
Sellers warrant that goods are free of a security interest of which the buyer has no knowledge [UCC 2–312(1)(b)]. Lessors warrant no third party will interfere with the lessee's use of the goods [UCC 2A–211(1)].

C. NO INFRINGEMENTS
Sellers warrant that the goods are free of any third person's patent, trademark, or copyright claims [UCC 2–312(3), 2A–211(2)].

1. **Sales Contract—If the Warranty Is Breached and the Buyer Is Sued**
The buyer must notify the seller. If the seller agrees in writing to defend and bear all costs, the buyer must let the seller do it (or lose all rights against the seller) [UCC 2–607(3)(b), (5)(b)].

2. **Lease—If the Warranty Is Breached and the Lessee Is Sued**
Same as above, except that a consumer who fails to notify the lessor within a reasonable time does not lose any rights against the lessor [UCC 2A–516(3)(b), (4)(b)].

D. DISCLAIMER OF TITLE WARRANTY
In a sales contract, a disclaimer can be made only by specific contractual language [UCC 2–312(2)]). In a lease, the disclaimer must be specific, in writing, and conspicuous [UCC 2A–214(4)].

II. EXPRESS WARRANTIES

A. WHEN EXPRESS WARRANTIES ARISE
A seller or lessor warrants that goods will conform to affirmations or promises of fact, descriptions, samples or models [UCC 2–313, 2A–210].

B. BASIS OF THE BARGAIN
An affirmation, promise, description, or sample must be part of the basis of the bargain: it must come at such a time that the buyer could have relied on it when agreeing to the contract [UCC 2–313, 2A–210].

C. STATEMENTS OF OPINION AND VALUE

1. **Opinions**
A statement relating to the value of goods or a statement of opinion or recommendation about goods is not an express warranty [UCC 2–313(2), 2A–210(2)], unless the seller or lessor who makes it is an expert and gives an opinion as an expert.

2. **Puffing**
Whether a statement is an express warranty or puffing is not easy to determine. Factors include the reasonableness of the buyer's reliance on the statement and the specificity of the statement.

III. IMPLIED WARRANTIES

An implied warranty is derived by implication or inference from the nature of a transaction or the relative situations or circumstances of the parties.

A. IMPLIED WARRANTY OF MERCHANTABILITY

A warranty automatically arises in every sale or lease of goods by a merchant who deals in such goods that the goods are merchantable [UCC 2–314, 2A–212].

1. **Merchantable Goods**

a. **Reasonably Fit for Ordinary Purposes**
Goods that are merchantable are "reasonably fit for the ordinary purposes for which such goods are used" [UCC 2–314(2)].

b. **Characteristics of Merchantable Goods**
Average, fair, or medium-grade quality; pass without objection in the market for goods of the same description; adequate package and label, as provided by the agreement; and conform to the promises or affirmations of fact made on the container or label.

c. **Merchant's Knowledge**
It makes no difference whether the merchant knew of or could have discovered a defect that makes a product unsafe.

2. **Merchantable Food**
Merchantable food is food that is fit to eat.

B. IMPLIED WARRANTY OF FITNESS FOR A PARTICULAR PURPOSE

Arises when seller or lessor (merchant or nonmerchant) knows or has reason to know the purpose for which buyer or lessee will use goods and knows he or she is relying on seller to select suitable goods [UCC 2–315, 2A–213]. Goods can be merchantable but unfit for a particular purpose.

C. IMPLIED WARRANTY—DEALING, PERFORMANCE, OR TRADE USAGE

When the parties know a well-recognized trade custom, it is inferred that they intended it to apply to their contract [UCC 2–314, 2A–212].

IV. OVERLAPPING WARRANTIES

A. WHEN WARRANTIES ARE CONSISTENT

They are cumulative [UCC 2–317, 2A–215].

B. WHEN WARRANTIES ARE INCONSISTENT

1. Express warranties displace inconsistent implied warranties (except fitness for a particular purpose).

2. Samples take precedence over inconsistent general descriptions.

3. Technical specs displace inconsistent samples or general descriptions.

V. WARRANTIES AND THIRD PARTIES

A. THE COMMON LAW REQUIRES PRIVITY

At common law, privity of contract must exist between a plaintiff and a defendant to bring any action based on a contract.

B. THE UCC ELIMINATES PRIVITY

The UCC includes three optional, alternative provisions eliminating privity with respect to certain types of injuries for certain beneficiaries. Each state may adopt one of the alternatives [UCC 2–318, 2A–216].

VI. WARRANTY DISCLAIMERS

A. EXPRESS WARRANTIES

A seller can avoid making express warranties by not promising or affirming anything, describing the goods, or using of a sample or model [UCC 2–313].

1. Oral Warranties

Oral warranties made during bargaining cannot be modified later.

2. Negating or Limiting Express Warranties

A written disclaimer—clear and conspicuous—can negate all warranties not in the written contract [UCC 2–316(1), 2A–214(1)].

B. IMPLIED WARRANTIES

1. General Language

Implied warranties can be disclaimed by the expression "as is" or a similar phrase [UCC 2–316(3)(a), 2A–214(3)(a)].

2. Specific Language

Fitness for a particular purpose—disclaimer must be in writing and conspicuous (word *fitness* is not required). Merchantability—disclaimer must mention *merchantability*; if in writing, must be conspicuous.

3. What Is Conspicuous

A term or clause that a reasonable person against whom it is to operate would notice (such as larger or contrasting type) [UCC 1–201(10)].

C. BUYER'S OR LESSEE'S EXAMINATION OF THE GOODS

If a buyer examines the goods before entering a contract, there is no implied warranty with respect to defects that a reasonable examination would reveal [UCC 2–316(3)(b), 2A–214(2)(b)]. The same is true if the buyer refuses to examine over the seller or lessor's demand.

D. UNCONSCIONABILITY

Courts view disclaimers with disfavor, especially when consumers are involved, and have sometimes held disclaimers unconscionable [UCC 2–302, 2A–108].

VII. STATUTE OF LIMITATIONS

An action for breach of contract under the UCC must be brought within four years after the cause of action accrues. In their contract, the parties can change the period to not less than one, and not more than four, years [UCC 2–725(1)].

A. WHEN A CAUSE OF ACTION FOR BREACH OF WARRANTY ACCRUES

When the seller tenders delivery, even if the nonbreaching party is unaware the cause has accrued [UCC 2–725(2)]. When a warranty extends to future performance, discovery of breach must await that time [UCC 2–725(2)], which is also when the statute of limitations begins to run.

B. WHEN THE LIMITATIONS PERIOD DOES NOT APPLY

When a buyer or seller brings suit on a legal theory unrelated to the UCC, the four-year period does not apply, even if the claim relates to the goods.

VIII. MAGNUSON–MOSS WARRANTY ACT

No seller is required to give a written warranty for consumer goods, but if a seller chooses to do so and the cost of the goods is more than—

A. $10

The warranty must be clearly labeled full or limited. A **full warranty** requires free repair or replacement of defective parts (there is no time limit). A **limited warranty** is any warranty that is not full.

B. $15

The seller must state (fully and conspicuously in a single document in "readily understood language") the seller's name and address, what is warranted, procedures for enforcing the warranty, any limitations on relief, and that the buyer has legal rights.

C. TIME LIMITS

Sellers can impose a time limit on the duration of an implied warranty, if it corresponds to the duration of the express warranty.

IX. WARRANTIES UNDER THE CISG

The United Nations Convention on Contracts for the International Sale of Goods (CISG) uses different language ("conformity of the goods" instead of "warranty"), but in effect provides for protection similar to the UCC's.

TRUE-FALSE QUESTIONS

(Answers at the Back of the Book)

____ 1. Promises of fact made during the bargaining process are express warranties.

____ 2. A contract cannot include both an implied warranty and an express warranty.

____ 3. A merchant cannot disclaim an implied warranty of merchantability.

____ 4. An express warranty can be limited.

____ 5. A clear, conspicuous, written statement brought to a buyer's attention when a contract is formed can disclaim all warranties.

____ 6. No seller is required to give a written warranty for consumer goods.

____ 7. A warranty of title can be disclaimed only by specific language in a contract.

____ 8. A seller's statement of opinion normally creates an express warranty.

____ 9. To disclaim the implied warranty of merchantability, a merchant must mention "merchantability."

____ 10. Whether or not a buyer examines goods before entering into a contract, there is an implied warranty with respect to defects an examination would reveal.

FILL-IN QUESTIONS

(Answers at the Back of the Book)

An express warranty ________________ (can/cannot) be disclaimed in writing if it is called to the buyer's attention. An implied warranty of fitness for a particular purpose ________________ (can/cannot) be disclaimed in writing. An implied warranty of merchantability ____________ (can/cannot) be disclaimed in writing. A disclaimer of the implied warranty of fitness for a particular purpose ______________ (must/need not) use the word "fitness." A disclaimer of the implied warranty of merchantability ______________ (must/need not) include the word merchantability.

MULTIPLE-CHOICE QUESTIONS

(Answers at the Back of the Book)

___ **1.** Eagle Skis, Inc., makes and sells skis. In deciding whether the skis are merchantable, a court would consider whether

a. Eagle violated any government regulations.
b. the skis are a quality product.
c. the skis are fit for the ordinary purpose for which such goods are used.
d. the skis are made in an efficient manner.

___ **2.** As a hobby, Tom converts old Volkswagens into off-road vehicles and sells them. During a sale, Wendy tells Dick that she knows nothing about off-road vehicles and wants Tom to pick a "good one" for her. On her first off-road drive, she is injured when the car's front axle snaps in two and the car rolls over. The axle would not have broken in ordinary driving. Tom is liable for breach of

a. an express warranty.
b. an implied warranty of merchantability.
c. an implied warranty of fitness for a particular purpose.
d. none of the above.

___ **3.** Great Furniture Company makes and sells furniture. To avoid liability for most implied warranties, their sales agreements should note that their goods are sold

a. "as is."
b. by a merchant.
c. for cash only.
d. in perfect condition.

___ **4.** Standard Manufacturing, Inc., sells a watch to Ted under a contract that includes an express warranty. Under the Magnuson-Moss Warranty Act, Standard can also disclaim

a. the implied warranty of merchantability only.
b. the implied warranty of fitness for a particular purpose only.
c. the implied warranties of merchantability and fitness for a particular purpose.
d. none of the above.

___ **5.** ABC Electronics sells electronic products. In sales to its customers, as a merchant ABC warrants that its title to the products is

a. bad.
b. fair.
c. good.
d. the best that money can buy at that price.

___ **6.** Quality Parts Company sells motor vehicle parts to dealers. In response to a dealer's order, Quality ships a crate with a label that reads, "Crate contains one 150-horsepower diesel engine." This is

a. an express warranty.
b. an implied warranty of merchantability.
c. an implied warranty of fitness for a particular purpose.
d. puffing.

___ 7. Alpha Offices, Inc., buys one hundred computer monitors from Beta Sales Corporation. There is no disclaimer of a title warranty. Regarding the transfer of title, Beta warrants that it is

a. rightful.
b. to the security interest of a third person.
c. the best that money can buy at that price.
d. wrongful.

___ 8. A-One Hardware sells tools. An A-One brochures states, "This drill bit will penetrate steel without dulling." This is

a. an express warranty.
b. an implied warranty of merchantability.
c. an implied warranty of fitness for a particular purpose.
d. puffing.

___ 9. Dealer Auto Sales sells cars, trucks, and other motor vehicles. A Dealer salesperson tells potential customers, "This is the finest car ever made." This is

a. an express warranty.
b. an implied warranty.
c. a warranty of title.
d. puffing.

___ 10. **Based on a Sample CPA Exam Question.** A sales representative for Fine Office Furniture shows swatches of upholstery fabric to a customer, who says he needs chairs for an office reception area. An example of an express warranty is a warranty of

a. conformity of goods to a sample.
b. fitness for a particular purpose.
c. merchantability.
d. usage of trade.

SHORT ESSAY QUESTIONS

1. What is the difference between the implied warranty of merchantability and the implied warranty of fitness for a particular purpose?

2. What is the general effect of a warranty disclaimer?

ISSUE SPOTTERS

(Answers at the Back of the Book)

1. Adam sells a car to Beth. Two months later, Consumer Credit, Inc., tells Beth that it has a security interest in the car, Adam missed three payments, and it is taking the car. Beth says, "I know nothing about any of this. You have to get your money from Adam. You can't take the car." Is Beth right?

2. Owen loves Phat Foods, which are cholesterol-rich. When Owen is diagnosed as suffering from heart disease, he sues Phat Foods Company, on the ground that its foods are not fit to eat in violation of the implied warranty of merchantability. Is it likely that the court will agree with Owen?

3. Ace Vehicles sells to Bob, a farmer, a used pick-up truck. The contract, in large type, states, "THE SALE OF THIS TRUCK IS 'AS IS.'" When the truck is delivered, it has no wheels. Can Ace use the statement in the contract to avoid liability for delivering a truck with no wheels?

SPECIAL INFORMATION FOR CPA CANDIDATES

The CPA examination does not cover the Magnuson-Moss Warranty Act (or similar state consumer protection legislation). The CPA exam does cover, however, the UCC's rules on warranty. These rules may be better applied if they are actually understood. That is, a rote memorization of the rules may not prove as useful as actual comprehension. To this end, it may be helpful to imagine their application in a real sales contract situation. In particular, remember that UCC warranty actions require privity of contract and that the warranty of merchantability applies only to merchants.

CUMULATIVE HYPOTHETICAL PROBLEM FOR UNIT FOUR—INCLUDING CHAPTERS 19–23

(Answers at the Back of the Book)

Alpha Engineering Corporation designs products for companies in the aerospace industry. Beta Computers, Inc. , makes and sells hard drives.

___ **1.** Alpha writes to Beta to order one hundred hard drives. Beta writes to accept but adds a clause providing for interest on any overdue invoices (a common practice in the industry). If there is no further communication between the parties

a. Beta has made a counteroffer.
b. there is a contract but without Beta's added term.
c. there is a contract that includes Beta's added term.
d. there is no contract because Alpha did not expressly accept the added term.

___ **2.** Beta tenders delivery of the hard drives to Alpha. Alpha says that it cannot take possession immediately but will do so later in the day. Before Alpha takes possession, the goods are destroyed in a fire. The risk of loss

a. passed to Alpha at the time the contract was formed.
b. passed to Alpha on Beta's tender of delivery.
c. remained with Beta, because Alpha had not yet taken possession.
d. remained with Beta, because title had not yet passed to Alpha.

___ **3.** Beta tenders delivery of the hard drives to Alpha. Alpha says that it had decided not to buy them. In Beta's suit against Alpha, Beta can recover the contract price if

a. Beta does not seek any damages in addition to the contract price.
b. Beta identified the goods to the contract and a reasonable effort to resell the goods would not succeed.
c. specific performance is not possible.
d. the goods have been destroyed and Beta's insurance is inadequate.

___ **4.** Alpha tries to put the hard drives into use, but they do not do what Beta promised. In the deal between Alpha and Beta, the most important factor in determining whether an express warranty was created is whether

a. Beta intended to create a warranty.
b. Beta made the promises in the ordinary course of business.
c. Beta's promises became part of the basis of the bargain.
d. Beta's statements were in writing.

___ **5.** Under the UCC, to be subject to an implied warranty of merchantability, Beta's hard drives do NOT need to be

a. adequately packaged and labeled.
b. fit for all of the purposes for which Alpha intends to use the goods.
c. in conformity with any affirmations of fact made on the package.
d. sold by a merchant.

QUESTIONS ON THE FOCUS ON LEGAL REASONING FOR UNIT FOUR—*PARKER TRACTOR & IMPLEMENT CO. V. JOHNSON*

(Answers at the Back of the Book)

___ **1.** Fast Pizza buys a delivery vehicle from Great Motors. The buyer later files a suit against the seller, on the basis of breach of warranty. Under the holding in *Parker Tractor & Implement Co. v. Johnson,* the buyer may be awarded damages even if there is uncertainty in

a. the amount.
b. the cause.
c. the purpose.
d. the reason.

___ **2.** Having no written records, Fast Pizza's proof in its suit against Great Motors consists almost entirely of the testimony of the owner and an expert. In the opinion of the majority in *Parker Tractor & Implement Co. v. Johnson,* Fast Pizza may obtain as damages

a. the loss shown by all of Fast Pizza's proof.
b. the loss shown by the owner's testimony only.
c. the loss shown by the expert's testimony only.
d. nothing.

___ **3.** According to the dissent in *Parker Tractor & Implement Co. v. Johnson,* Fast Pizza, in its suit against Great Motors, Fast Pizza may obtain as damages

a. the loss shown by all of Fast Pizza's proof.
b. the loss shown by the owner's testimony only.
c. the loss shown by the expert's testimony only.
d. nothing.

QUESTIONS ON THE FOCUS ON ETHICS FOR UNIT FOUR—DOMESTIC AND INTERNATIONAL SALES AND LEASE CONTRACTS

(Answers at the Back of the Book)

___ **1.** Eve and Fred enter into a contract for the sale of a computer. Even if not expressly stated, read into this contract is the concept of

a. advantage.
b. good faith.
c. impracticability.
d. unconscionability.

____ **2.** Gina and Harry enter into a contract for the sale of a DVD player. Either party's nonperformance may be excused, because of unforeseen circumstances, under the doctrine of commercial

a. advantage.
b. good faith.
c. impracticability.
d. unconscionability.

____ **3.** Ira and Jill enter into a contract for the sale of a personal data assistant. If the contract includes a clause that is perceived as grossly unfair to one party, its enforcement may be challenged under the doctrine of

a. advantage.
b. good faith.
c. impracticability.
d. unconscionability.

Chapter 24
The Function and Creation of Negotiable Instruments

WHAT THIS CHAPTER IS ABOUT

A **negotiable instrument** is a signed writing that contains an unconditional promise or order to pay an exact sum of money, when demanded or at an exact future time. This chapter outlines types of negotiable instruments and the requirements for negotiability.

CHAPTER OUTLINE

I. ARTICLES 3 AND 4 OF THE UCC

UCC Articles 3 and 4 apply to transactions involving negotiable instruments. Since 1990, most states have adopted revised versions of these articles. This outline refers to the revised articles. Both articles were also updated with proposed amendments in 2002 to comport with the Uniform Electronic Transactions Act and the needs of e-commerce.

II. THE FUNCTION OF INSTRUMENTS

A negotiable instrument can function as a substitute for money or as an extension of credit. To do so, it must be easily transferable without danger of being uncollectible.

III. TYPES OF INSTRUMENTS

A. DRAFTS AND CHECKS (ORDERS TO PAY)

The person who signs or makes an order to pay is the drawer. The person to whom the order is made is the drawee. The person to whom payment is ordered is the payee.

1. Draft

An unconditional written order by one person to another to pay money. The drawee must be obligated to the drawer either by an agreement or through a debtor-creditor relationship to honor the order.

a. Time Draft

Payable at a definite future time.

b. Sight Draft (Demand Draft)

Payable on sight (when presented for payment). A draft payable at a stated time after sight is both a time and a sight draft.

c. Trade Acceptance

A draft in which the seller is both the drawer and the payee. The draft orders the buyer to pay a specified sum of money to the seller, at a stated time in the future.

d. Banker's Acceptance

A draft drawn by a creditor against his or her debtor, who must pay it at maturity. Typically, the term is short.

2. **Check**
A draft drawn on a bank and payable on demand. A cashier's check is a draft in which the bank is both the drawer and drawee. A teller's check is a draft drawn by one bank on another bank [UCC 3–104(h)].

B. **PROMISSORY NOTES AND CDS (PROMISES TO PAY)**
A person who promises to pay is a maker. A person to whom the promise is made is a payee. A promissory note is a written promise by one party to pay money to another party. A certificate of deposit (CD) is a note made by a bank promising to repay a deposit of funds with interest on a certain date [UCC 3–104(j)].

IV. REQUIREMENTS FOR NEGOTIABILITY

To be negotiable, an instrument must meet all of the following requirements [UCC 3–104(a)]. The instrument must be—

A. **IN WRITING**
A writing can be on anything that (1) is permanent and (2) has portability [UCC 3–103(a)(6)].

B. **SIGNED BY THE MAKER OR DRAWER**
A signature can be any place on an instrument and in any form (a mark or rubber stamp) that purports to be a signature and authenticates the writing [UCC 1–201(39), 3–401(b)].

C. **AN UNCONDITIONAL PROMISE OR ORDER**

1. **Promise or Order**
A promise must be an affirmative written undertaking—more than a mere acknowledgment of a debt (an I.O.U. does not qualify; use of the words "I promise" or "Pay" qualifies) [UCC 3–103(a)(9)].

a. **Certificates of Deposit**
The bank's acknowledgment of a deposit and the other terms indicates a promise to repay a sum of money [UCC 3–104(j)].

b. **More Than One Payee**
An order may be addressed to more than one person, either jointly ("Pay Joe and Jan") or alternatively ("Pay Joe or Jan") [UCC 3–103(a)(6)].

2. **Unconditionality**
Payment cannot be conditional, and the promise or order cannot be subject to or governed by another writing, or be subject to rights or obligations stated in another writing [UCC 3–104(a), 3–106(a)]. Negotiability is not affected by—

a. **References to Other Writings [UCC 3–106(a)]**

b. **Payments Only out of a Particular Fund or Source [UCC 3–106(b)(ii)]**

c. **A Statement that an Instrument Is Secured by a Mortgage**
Destroys negotiability only if it stipulates that a promise to pay is subject to the terms of the mortgage [UCC 3–106(a)(ii)].

D. **AN ORDER OR PROMISE TO PAY A FIXED AMOUNT OF MONEY**
A negotiable instrument must state a fixed amount of money to be paid when the instrument is payable.

1. **Fixed Amount**

a. **References to Outside Sources**
Interest may be determined with reference to information not contained in the instrument but readily ascertainable by reference to a source described in the instrument [UCC 3–112(b)].

b. Variable Interest Rate Notes Can Be Negotiable
The fixed-amount requirement applies only to principal [UCC 3–104].

2. Payable in Money
Only instruments payable in money (not bonds, stock, gold, or goods) are negotiable [UCC 3–104(a)(3)]. *Money* is a medium of exchange recognized as the currency of a government [UCC 1–201(24)].

E. PAYABLE ON DEMAND OR AT A DEFINITE TIME

1. Payable on Demand
An instrument that is payable on sight or presentment or that does not state any time for payment [UCC 3–108(a)]. A check is payable on demand [UCC 3–104(f)]. Presentment occurs when a person presents an instrument to a person liable on it for payment or when a person presents a draft to a drawee for acceptance.

2. Payable at a Definite Time
Payable on or before a stated date or within a fixed period after sight, or on a date or time ascertainable at the time the instrument is issued [UCC 3–108(b)].

3. Acceleration Clause
Allows a holder to demand payment of entire amount due if a certain event occurs. Does not affect negotiability [UCC 3–108(b)(ii)]. A holder is "the person in possession if the instrument is payable to bearer, or in the case of an instrument payable to an identified person, if the identified person is in possession" [UCC 1–201(20)].

4. Extension Clause
The period of the extension must be specified if the right to extend is given to the maker. If the holder has the right, no period need be specified [UCC 3–108(b)(iii), (iv)].

F. PAYABLE TO ORDER OR TO BEARER
When it is issued or first comes into a holder's possession [UCC 3–104(a)(1)].

1. Order Instrument
May be payable "to the order of an identified person" or to "an identified person or order" (the person must be identified with certainty) [UCC 3–109(b)].

2. Bearer Instrument
Does not designate a specific payee (but an instrument payable to a nonexistent entity is not bearer paper) [UCC 3–109(a) and Comment 3]: "Payable to the order of bearer," "Pay to the order of cash," "Pay cash"

V. FACTORS NOT AFFECTING NEGOTIABILITY

A. NO DATE
Negotiability is affected only if a date is necessary to determine a definite time for payment [UCC 3–113(b)].

B. POSTDATING
Postdating an instrument does not affect negotiability [UCC 3–113(a)].

C. HANDWRITTEN WORDS
Handwritten words prevail typewritten words, which prevail over those that are printed (such as preprinted forms) [UCC 3–114].

D. DISCREPANCY BETWEEN WORDS AND NUMBERS
An amount stated in words outweighs a contradictory number [UCC 3–114].

E. UNSPECIFIED INTEREST RATE
If a rate is unspecified, interest will be at the *judgment rate* [UCC 3–112(b)].

F. NOTATION ON A CHECK THAT IT IS NONNEGOTIABLE
This has no effect on a check, but any other instrument is made nonnegotiable by the maker or drawer adding such a notation [UCC 3–104(d)].

TRUE-FALSE QUESTIONS

(Answers at the Back of the Book)

___ **1.** The person who signs or makes an order to pay is the drawer.

___ **2.** A negotiable instrument serves as a substitute for money.

___ **3.** A bearer instrument is payable to whoever possesses it.

___ **4.** To be negotiable, an instrument must be in writing.

___ **5.** An instrument can be negotiable even if it is not payable on demand or at a definite time.

___ **6.** An instrument including a clause that permits the date of maturity to be extended by the *maker* for "no more than a reasonable time" is negotiable.

___ **7.** An instrument payable to the order of a specific person is not negotiable.

___ **8.** To be negotiable, the terms of a promise or order must be included on the instrument.

___ **9.** To be negotiable, an instrument must include an unconditional promise to pay.

___ **10.** An instrument is not negotiable if reference must be made to foreign exchange rates when payment is due.

FILL-IN QUESTIONS

(Answers at the Back of the Book)

The person who signs or makes an order to pay is a ______________ (drawer/drawee). The person to whom an order to pay is made is a ______________ (drawee/payee). The person to whom payment is ordered is a ____________________ (payee/maker). A person who promises to pay a note is a ____________________ (payee/maker). A person to whom the promise to pay a note is made is a ____________________ (payee/drawee).

MULTIPLE-CHOICE QUESTIONS

(Answers at the Back of the Book)

___ **1.** **Based on a Sample CPA Exam Question.** Alex makes out an instrument that states Alex promises to pay $600 and gives it to Beth. To be negotiable, this instrument must

a. be payable to order or to bearer.
b. be signed by the payee.
c. contain references to all agreements between the parties.
d. contain necessary conditions of payment.

____ **2.** Bob makes out a check "Pay to the order of bearer." This is

a. a bearer instrument only.
b. an order instrument only.
c. a bearer and an order instrument.
d. none of the above.

____ **3.** Carl signs a promissory note payable to the order of Delta Loan Company. The note states simply that it is payable "with interest." This note is

a. negotiable.
b. nonnegotiable, because it does not specify a particular rate of interest.
c. nonnegotiable, because it is payable to Delta Loan Company.
d. nonnegotiable, because it states only that it is payable "with interest."

____ **4.** To pay for a new truck, Eagle Transport Company issues a draft in favor of Fine Motor Sales, Inc. A draft is

a. a promise to pay money.
b. a promise to deliver goods at a future date.
c. a conditional promise to pay money.
d. an unconditional written order to pay money.

____ **5.** Ira writes a check for $100 payable to Jan on Ira's account at First National Bank. Ira is

a. the drawee.
b. the drawer.
c. the holder.
d. the payee.

____ **6.** To pay for an office building, Kay executes a negotiable instrument in favor of Lee. They are the only two parties to the instrument. This is

a. a certificate of deposit.
b. a check.
c. a draft.
d. a promissory note.

____ **7.** Macro Industries, Inc., issues an instrument in favor of National Credit Corporation. To be negotiable, the instrument need *not*

a. be an unconditional promise or order to pay.
b. be payable on demand or at a specific time.
c. be signed by Macro Industries.
d. recite the consideration given in exchange for it.

____ **8.** Owen executes an instrument is favor of Paula. For the instrument to be negotiable, Owen's signature

a. may be anywhere on the instrument.
b. must be in the lower right hand corner.
c. must be on the back.
d. must not be on the instrument.

___ **9.** Quality Products, Inc., signs an instrument payable to Regional Distributors, Inc., that includes the notation "as per contract." This instrument is

a. negotiable.
b. nonnegotiable, because an obligation with respect to it is stated in another writing.
c. nonnegotiable, because it is governed by another writing.
d. nonnegotiable, because it states a condition to payment.

___ **10.** Sam signs a check payable to Tech Corporation. The check does not include a date. This check is

a. negotiable.
b. nonnegotiable, because it does not include a date.
c. nonnegotiable, because it is payable to Tech Corporation.
d. nonnegotiable, because it is signed by Sam.

SHORT ESSAY QUESTIONS

1. What are the primary functions of negotiable instruments?

2. What are the requirements for an instrument to be negotiable?

ISSUE SPOTTERS

(Answers at the Back of the Book)

1. After filling out her tax return, Pam wants to dramatize her feelings about the amount she has to pay. She writes on the back of her shirt, "Pay to the order of the IRS" and fills in the amount. For her signature, Pam uses a rubber stamp bearing her signature. Is the shirt negotiable?

2. Jill owes $600 to Ken, who asks Jill to sign an instrument for the debt. If included on that instrument, which of the following would prevent its negotiability—"I.O.U. $600," "I promise to pay $600," or an instruction to Jill's bank stating, "I wish you would pay $600 to Ken"?

3. Lisa writes out a check payable to the order of cash and gives it to Jeff. Is the check an order instrument or a bearer instrument?

SPECIAL INFORMATION FOR CPA CANDIDATES

For the CPA examination, the two most important concepts in the area of negotiable instruments are negotiability and holder in due course (HDC) (which is discussed in the next chapter). You should fully understand both concepts to be able to answer questions involving UCC Article 3. The significance of negotiability is that it facilitates the transfer and payment of money using a contractual obligation instead of cash. As you'll learn in the next chapter, if an instrument is negotiable, a holder can be an HDC. This is an important status because of the protection it provides.

Chapter 25
Transferability and Holder in Due Course

WHAT THIS CHAPTER IS ABOUT

A negotiable instrument is transferred more easily than a contract, and a person who acquires it is subject to less risk than the assignee of a contract. This chapter outlines the types and the effect of indorsements, defines *holder in due course* (HDC), and describes how a holder becomes an HDC.

CHAPTER OUTLINE

I. NEGOTIATION

On a transfer by negotiation, the transferee becomes a holder and receives the rights of the previous possessor (and possibly more) [UCC 3–201(a), 3–202(b), 3–203(b), 3–305, 3–306].

A. NEGOTIATING ORDER INSTRUMENTS
Order instruments are negotiated by delivery with indorsement [UCC 3–201(b)].

B. NEGOTIATING BEARER INSTRUMENTS
Bearer instruments are negotiated by delivery only [UCC 3–201(b)].

C. CONVERTING INSTRUMENTS
An instrument can be converted from a bearer to an order instrument, or vice versa, by indorsement. A check payable to "cash" subsequently indorsed "Pay to Bob" must be negotiated as an order instrument (by indorsement and delivery) [UCC 3–205(a)]. An instrument payable to a named payee ("Bob") and indorsed in blank is a bearer instrument [UCC 3–205(b)].

II. INDORSEMENTS

Indorsements are required to negotiate an order instrument. The person who indorses an instrument is an indorser; the person to whom the instrument is transferred is an indorsee.

A. WHAT AN INDORSEMENT IS
A signature with or without additional words or statements. Usually written on the back of an instrument but can be written on a separate piece of paper (an allonge) affixed (stapled) to it [UCC 3–204(a)].

B. BLANK INDORSEMENT
Specifies no particular indorsee and can consist of a mere signature [UCC 3–205(b)]. Converts an order instrument to a bearer instrument.

C. SPECIAL INDORSEMENT
Names the indorsee [UCC 3–205(a)]. No special words are needed. Converts a bearer instrument into an order instrument.

D. QUALIFIED INDORSEMENT
Disclaims or limits contract liability (see Chapter 19) (the notation "without recourse" is commonly used) [UCC 3–415(b)]. Often used by persons acting in a representative capacity.

1. No Payment Guarantee
Does not guarantee payment, but does transfer title. (Most blank and special indorsements are unqualified, guaranteeing payment and transferring title).

2. **Further Negotiation**
A *special* qualified indorsement makes an instrument order paper (and requires indorsement and delivery for negotiation). A *blank* qualified indorsement creates bearer paper (and requires only delivery).

E. RESTRICTIVE INDORSEMENTS

1. **Indorsement Prohibiting Further Indorsement**
Does not destroy negotiability [UCC 3–206(a)]. Has the same effect as a special indorsement.

2. **Conditional Indorsement**
Specifying an event on which payment depends does not affect negotiability. A person paying or taking the instrument for value can disregard the condition [UCC 3–206(b)]. (Conditional language on the face of an instrument, however, does destroy negotiability.)

3. **Indorsement for Deposit or Collection**
Making the indorsee (usually a bank) a collecting agent of the indorser (such as "For deposit only") locks the instrument into the bank collection process [UCC 3–206(c)].

4. **Trust Indorsement (Agency Indorsement)**
An indorsement by one who is to hold or use the funds for the benefit of the indorser or a third party [UCC 3–206(d), (e)]. To the extent the original indorsee pays or applies the proceeds consistently with the indorsement, he or she is a holder and can become a holder in due course (HDC). Any subsequent purchaser can qualify as an HDC (unless he or she knows the instrument was negotiated in breach of fiduciary duty).

III. MISCELLANEOUS INDORSEMENT PROBLEMS

A. FORGED OR UNAUTHORIZED SIGNATURES OR INDORSEMENTS
See Chapters 26 and 27.

B. MISSPELLED NAME
An indorsement should be the same as the name on the instrument. An indorsee whose name is misspelled can indorse with the misspelled name, the correct name, or both [UCC 3–204(d)].

C. MULTIPLE PAYEES
An instrument payable in the alternative ("Pay to the order of Bill or Joan") requires the indorsement of only one. An instrument payable jointly ("Pay to the order of Bill and Joan") requires the indorsements of both. If it is not clear how it is payable, it requires the indorsement of only one [UCC 3–110(d)].

D. AGENTS OR OFFICERS
An instrument payable to an entity ("Pay to the order of the YWCA") can be negotiated by the entity's representative. An instrument payable to a public officer ("Pay to the order of the County Tax Collector") can be negotiated by whoever holds the office [UCC 3–110(c)].

IV. HOLDER VERSUS HOLDER IN DUE COURSE (HDC)

A. HOLDER
A holder is "the person in possession if the instrument is payable to bearer, or in the case of an instrument payable to an identified person, if the identified person is in possession" [UCC 1–201(20)]. A holder is subject to the same defenses that could be asserted against the transferor (the party from whom the holder obtained the instrument).

B. HOLDER IN DUE COURSE
A holder who meets certain requirements becomes a holder in due course (HDC), and takes an instrument free of all claims to it and most defenses against payment that could be successfully asserted against the transferor.

V. REQUIREMENTS FOR HDC STATUS

To become an HDC, a person must be a holder and take an instrument (1) for value; (2) in good faith; and (3) without notice that it is overdue, that it has been dishonored, that any person has a defense against it or a claim to it, or that the instrument contains unauthorized signatures, alterations, or is so irregular or incomplete as to call into question its authenticity [UCC 3–302].

A. Taking for Value

A holder does not give value by receiving an instrument as a gift or inheriting it. A holder gives value by [UCC 3–303(a)]—

1. Performing a promise for which an instrument was issued or transferred.
2. Acquiring a security interest or other lien in the instrument (other than a lien obtained by a judicial proceeding).
3. Taking instrument in payment of, or as security for, an antecedent debt.
4. Giving a negotiable instrument as payment.
5. Giving an irrevocable commitment as payment.
6. **Special Situations**
   A holder can be limited to ordinary holder's rights by buying an instrument at a judicial sale or taking it under legal process; acquiring it when taking over an estate; or buying it as part of a bulk transfer [UCC 3–302(c)].

B. Taking in Good Faith

1. **What Good Faith Is**
   Good faith is "honesty in fact and the observance of reasonable commercial standards of fair dealing."
2. **How to Apply this Requirement**
   A purchaser must honestly believe that an instrument is not defective and observe reasonable commercial standards. This applies only to the holder—a person who in good faith takes an instrument from a thief may become an HDC.

C. Taking without Notice

A holder must acquire an instrument without knowing, or having reason to know, that it is defective.

1. **What Constitutes Notice?**
   Notice is (1) actual knowledge of a defect, (2) receipt of notice about a defect, or (3) reason to know that a defect exists [UCC 1–201(25)]. Knowledge of certain facts does not constitute notice [see UCC 3–302(b)].
2. **Overdue Instruments**
   a. **Demand Instruments—What Puts a Holder on Notice**
      If a holder takes an instrument knowing demand was made or takes it an unreasonable time after its issue (ninety days for a check; other instruments depend on the circumstances [UCC 3–304(a)]).
   b. **Time Instruments—What Puts a Holder on Notice**
      If a holder takes an instrument after its expressed due date. If, on an installment note or on a series of notes, the maker has defaulted on an installment or one of the notes [UCC 3–304(b)].
3. **Dishonored Instruments—What Puts a Holder on Notice**
   A holder has notice if he or she knows an instrument has been dishonored, or if he or she knows of facts that would lead him or her to suspect that an instrument has been dishonored [UCC 3–302(a)(2)].
4. **Notice of Claims or Defenses**
   A holder cannot be an HDC if he or she knows of a claim to the instrument or defense against it [UCC 3–302(a)]. Knowledge can be imputed if a claim or defense is apparent on the face of the instrument or if the purchaser otherwise had reason to know from facts surrounding the transaction.

a. **Incomplete Instruments—What Puts a Holder on Notice**
If an instrument is so incomplete that an element of negotiability is lacking (e.g., amount not filled in). Accepting an instrument without knowing it was incomplete when issued is not notice.

b. **Irregular Instruments—What Puts a Holder on Notice**
If an irregularity on the face of an instrument calls into question its validity or terms of ownership, or creates ambiguity as to who to pay.

c. **Voidable Obligations—What Puts a Holder on Notice**
Knowing a party to an instrument has a defense that entitles the party to avoid the obligation. Knowing of one defense bars HDC status to all defenses. Knowing that a fiduciary has wrongfully negotiated an instrument [UCC 3–307(b)].

VI. HOLDER THROUGH AN HDC

A. SHELTER PRINCIPLE
A person who does not qualify as an HDC but who acquires an instrument from an HDC or from someone with HDC rights receives the rights and privileges of an HDC [UCC 3–203(b)].

B. LIMITATIONS TO THE SHELTER PRINCIPLE
A holder who was a party to fraud or illegality affecting an instrument or who, as a prior holder, had notice of a claim or defense cannot improve his or her status by repurchasing it from a later HDC [UCC 3–203(b)].

VII. THE HDC CONCEPT IN THE INTERNATIONAL CONTEXT
The 1988 United Nations Convention on International Bills of Exchange and International Promissory Notes (CIBN) replaces the HDC doctrine with the concept of "protected holder."

A. DIFFERENT REQUIREMENTS
Good faith and value are not required for protected holder status. A party "without knowledge" of a defense against payment on an instrument qualifies. Every holder is presumed to be a protected holder.

B. SHELTER PRINCIPLE
The CIBN adopts the shelter principle, but the same limitations as under the UCC apply.

TRUE-FALSE QUESTIONS

(Answers at the Back of the Book)

___ **1.** A negotiable instrument can be transferred only by negotiation.

___ **2.** Indorsements are required to negotiate order instruments.

___ **3.** An instrument payable to a named payee and indorsed in blank is a bearer instrument.

___ **4.** Indorsements are required to negotiate bearer instruments.

___ **5.** Every person who possesses an instrument is a holder.

___ **6.** Anyone who takes an instrument for value, in good faith, and without notice is an HDC.

___ **7.** A holder has only those rights that his or her transferor had in the instrument.

___ **8.** All claims to an instrument can be successfully asserted against an HDC.

___ **9.** For HDC status, good faith means an honest belief that an instrument is not defective.

___ **10.** Knowing that an instrument has been dishonored prevents a holder from becoming an HDC.

FILL-IN QUESTIONS

(Answers at the Back of the Book)

A person who does not qualify as an HDC ______________ (can/cannot) acquire the rights of an HDC if a person who does not qualify as an HDC acquires an instrument from an HDC. A holder who was a party to fraud or illegality affecting an instrument ______________ (can/cannot) improve his or her status by repurchasing the instrument from a later HDC. A holder who, as a prior holder, had notice of a claim or defense against the instrument ______________ (can/cannot) improve his or her status by repurchasing it from a later HDC.

MULTIPLE-CHOICE QUESTIONS

(Answers at the Back of the Book)

___ **1.** Donna signs and delivers to Erin a $5,000 negotiable note payable to "Erin or bearer." Erin negotiates it to Frank, indorsing it on the back by signing "Erin." The note is

a. a bearer instrument, and Frank can convert it to order paper by writing "Pay to the order of Frank" above Erin's signature.
b. a bearer instrument, and it cannot be converted to an order instrument.
c. an order instrument, and it cannot be converted to a bearer instrument.
d. none of the above.

___ **2.** Alex makes out a check "Pay to the order of Beth." Beth indorses the check on the back. The check can now be negotiated by

a. delivery only.
b. indorsement only.
c. delivery and indorsement.
d. none of the above.

___ **3.** **Based on a Sample CPA Exam Question.** Lee accepts a promissory note from Mike. For Lee to be a holder in due course (HDC) of the note

a. all prior holders must have HDCs.
b. Lee must be the payee of the note.
c. the note must be negotiable.
d. the note must be "Payable to Bearer."

___ **4.** Jack writes out a check payable to the order of Kay. Kay receives the check but wants to negotiate it further to her friend Lee. Kay can negotiate the check further by

a. indorsing it only.
b. delivering it to the transferee only.
c. indorsing it and delivering it to the transferee.
d. none of the above.

___ **5.** Gail indorses a check, "Pay to Highway Equipment Corporation if they deliver the backhoe by June 1, 2003." This indorsement is

a. a blank indorsement.
b. a qualified indorsement.
c. a restrictive indorsement.
d. a special indorsement.

___ **6.** Sam issues a $5,000 note to Mark due six months from the date issued. One month later, Mark negotiates the note to Julie for $2,500 in cash and a negotiable check for $2,500. Julie is an HDC of the note to the extent of

a. $2,500.
b. $5,000.
c. $7,500.
d. none of the above.

___ **7.** Don signs a note that states, "Payable in thirty days." The note is dated March 2, which means it is due April 1. Joe buys the note on April 12. He is

a. an HDC to the extent that he paid for the note.
b. an HDC to the extent that the note is not yet paid.
c. not an HDC.
d. none of the above.

___ **8.** Steve opens an account at First National Bank with a $4,000 check drawn on another bank and payable to him. He indorses the check in blank. The bank credits his account and allows him to draw on the $4,000 immediately. The bank knows of no defense to the check. The bank is

a. an HDC to the extent that Steve draws against the $4,000 balance.
b. an HDC for the full amount of the check.
c. an HDC to the extent of any amount that is collected on the check.
d. not an HDC.

___ **9.** Pat writes out a check for $500, but does not specify a payee. Greg steals the check and makes it payable to himself. He negotiates the check to Nick, who takes it in good faith and without notice. Regarding payment, Pat is

a. not liable to Greg, because Greg is not a holder.
b. liable to Nick, because Nick is an HDC.
c. both a and b.
d. none of the above.

___ **10.** Ben contracts with Amy to fix her roof, and Amy writes Ben a check, but Ben never makes the repairs. Carl knows Ben breached the contract, but cashes the check anyway. Carl cannot attain HDC status as regards

a. any defense Amy might have against payment.
b. only any personal defense Amy might have against payment.
c. only Ben's breach, which is Amy's personal defense against payment.
d. none of the above.

SHORT ESSAY QUESTIONS

1. How are instruments negotiated?

2. How is a person who acquires a time instrument or a demand instrument put on notice that the instrument is overdue?

ISSUE SPOTTERS

(Answers at the Back of the Book)

1. Lynn writes a check for $100 payable to Mike. Negotiation occurs when Mike receives the check. How does Mike subsequently negotiate the check?

2. Tom gets a paycheck from his employer United Software Corporation, indorses the back ("Tom"), and goes to cash it at First State Bank. On the way, he loses the check. Victor finds it. Can Victor obtain payment on the check? How might Tom have avoided this loss?

3. Alan issues a $500 note to Bonnie due six months from the date issued. One month later, Bonnie negotiates the note to Carl for $250 in cash and a check for $250. To what extent is Carl an HDC of the note?

SPECIAL INFORMATION FOR CPA CANDIDATES

On the CPA exam, questions concerning negotiability and holders in due course are asked nearly every time. When testing on negotiability, the exam often includes instruments with a number of different indorsements. The CPA exam will not explain the indorsements for you. You will need to work through them and determine what they mean to respond to the question. (Remember that an indorsement in blank does not mean that there is no indorsement.) Negotiability is determined from the face of an instrument; whether an instrument is order paper or bearer paper can be affected by the front and the back of the instrument (and remember that this status can change). As regards holders in due course, memorize the requirements (holder, value, good faith, no notice). Review, too, the shelter rule, which is frequently covered on the exam and defenses, including breach of contract and fraud in the inducement, which are often on the exam.

Chapter 26
Liability, Defenses, and Discharge

WHAT THIS CHAPTER IS ABOUT

Two kinds of liability are associated with negotiable instruments: signature liability and warranty liability. This chapter outlines this liability, as well as the effects of certain defenses against holders and holders in due course (HDCs) and the ways in which parties can be discharged from liability on negotiable instruments.

CHAPTER OUTLINE

I. SIGNATURE LIABILITY

A person is liable for payment on an instrument if he or she, or his or her agent, signs it. A signature can consist of any name, including a trade or assumed name, or a word, mark, or symbol "executed or adopted by a person with the present intention to authenticate a writing" [UCC 1–209(39), 3–401(b)].

II. PRIMARY VERSUS SECONDARY LIABILITY

Every party (except a qualified indorser) who signs an instrument is either primarily or secondarily liable when it comes due [UCC 3–401(a)]. Each party is liable for the full amount to any later indorser or to any holder.

A. PRIMARY LIABILITY

A person who is primarily liable is absolutely required to pay, subject to certain defenses [UCC 3–305]. Primarily liable parties include—

1. Maker of a Note

If an instrument is incomplete when the maker signs it, the maker must pay it as completed if authorized or, if unauthorized, as completed to an HDC [UCC 3–407, 3–412, 3–413].

2. Acceptor of a Draft

When a drawee accepts a draft (by signing it), he or she becomes an acceptor and is primarily liable to all subsequent holders [UCC 3–409(a)]. (A drawee that refuses to accept a draft requiring the drawee's acceptance has dishonored the instrument.)

3. Issuer of a Draft Drawn on the Drawer

Such drafts include cashier's checks [UCC 3–412, 3–414].

B. SECONDARY LIABILITY

Drawers and unqualified indorsers are secondarily liable—they pay only if a party who is primarily liable does not pay. A drawer pays if a drawee does not; an indorser pays if a maker defaults. Secondary liability is triggered by proper presentment, dishonor, and notice of dishonor.

1. Proper Presentment

a. To the Proper Person

A note or CD is presented to the maker; a draft to the drawee for acceptance, payment, or both (whatever is required); a check to the drawee [UCC 3–501(a), 3–502(b)].

b. In the Proper Manner

Depending on the type of instrument [UCC 3–501(b)]: (1) any commercially reasonable means (oral, written, or electronic; but it is not effective until the demand is received); (2) a clearing-house procedure used by banks; or (3) at the place specified in the instrument.

c. **Timely**
Failure to present on time is the most common reason for improper presentment [UCC 3–414(f), 3–415(e), 3–501(b)(4)].

2. **Dishonor**
Occurs when payment or acceptance is refused or cannot be obtained within the prescribed time, or when required presentment is excused and the instrument is not accepted or paid [UCC 3–502(e), 3–504].

3. **Proper Notice**
On dishonor, to hold secondary parties liable, notice must be given within thirty days following the day on which a person receives notice of the dishonor (except a bank, which must give notice before midnight of the next banking day after receipt) [UCC 3–503].

C. ACCOMMODATION PARTIES

An accommodation party signs an instrument to lend his or her name as credit to another party on the instrument [UCC 3–419(a)].

1. **Primary or Secondary Liability?**
Primary liability: signing on behalf of a maker. Secondary liability: signing on behalf of a payee or other holder.

2. **Right of Recourse**
An accommodation party is never liable to the party accommodated.

D. AGENTS' SIGNATURES

Agents can sign negotiable instruments and thereby bind their principals [UCC 3–401(a)(ii), 3–402(a)].

1. **Authorized Agent—Liability of the Parties**

a. **When the Agent Clearly Names the Principal**
The principal is liable. The agent is not—if the signature shows that it is on behalf of the principal [UCC 3–402(b)(1)].

b. **Other Situations**
(1) If an agent signs his or her name only; (2) if an instrument is signed in both agent's and principal's names, but does not indicate agency relation; or (3) if an agent indicates agency status but fails to name the principal [UCC 3–402(b)(2)]—

1) **Agent's Liability**
Agent is personally liable to an HDC who has no notice that the agent was not intended to be liable. Agent is not liable to others if the original parties did not intend it.

2) **Principal's Liability**
Principal is liable if a party entitled to enforce the instrument can prove the agency.

2. **Unauthorized Agent—Liability of the Parties**
Agent's signature is ineffective except as the signature of the unauthorized signer [UCC 3–403(a)].

E. UNAUTHORIZED SIGNATURES

An unauthorized signature does not bind the person whose name is forged. (For liability of banks paying under forged signatures, see Chapter 27.)

1. **Two Exceptions**
(1) An unauthorized signature is binding if the person whose name is signed ratifies it [UCC 3–403(a)]; (2) a person can be barred, on the basis of negligence, from denying liability [UCC 3–115, 3–406, 4–401(d)(2)].

2. **Liability of the Signer**
An unauthorized signature operates as the signature of the *signer* in favor of an HDC [UCC 3–403(a)].

F. Special Rules for Unauthorized Indorsements

Generally, the loss falls on the first party to take the instrument. The loss falls on the maker or drawer in cases involving—

1. **Imposters**
An imposter is one who induces a maker or drawer to issue an instrument in the name of an impersonated payee.

2. **Effect of an Imposter's Indorsement**
Effective against the drawer, if the instrument is transferred to an innocent party [UCC 3–404(a)].

3. **Fictitious Payees**
A fictitious payee is one to whom an instrument is payable but who has no right to receive payment. (Often, dishonest employees issue such instruments or deceive employers into doing so.)

4. **Effect of a Fictitious Payee's Indorsement**
Not treated as a forgery; the employer can be held liable by an innocent holder [UCC 3–404(b)(2)]. The employer has recourse against the dishonest employee.

5. **Comparative Negligence Standard**
Comparative negligence applies in cases involving imposters and fictitious payees (thus, a bank may be partially liable) [UCC 3–404(d), 3–405(b)].

III. WARRANTY LIABILITY

A. Transfer Warranties

1. **The Warranties**
Any person who transfers an instrument for consideration warrants to the transferee and, if the transfer is by indorsement, to all later transferees and holders who take the instrument in good faith [UCC 3–416]—

   a. The transferor is entitled to enforce the instrument.

   b. All signatures are authentic and authorized.

   c. The instrument has not been altered.

   d. The instrument is not subject to a defense or claim that can be asserted against the transferor.

   e. The transferor has no knowledge of any insolvency proceedings against the maker, the acceptor, or the drawer of the instrument.

2. **To Whom the Warranties Extend**
With order instruments, the warranties run to any subsequent holder who takes the instrument in good faith. With bearer instruments, the warranties run only to the immediate transferee [UCC 3–416(a)].

3. **When to Sue for Breach of Warranty**
As soon as a transferee or holder who takes an instrument in good faith has reason to know of it [UCC 3–416(b), (c), (d)]. Notice of the claim must be given to the warrantor within thirty days.

4. **Disclaimer**
With respect to any instrument, except a check, include in the indorsement such words as "without warranties" [UCC 3–416(c)].

B. PRESENTMENT WARRANTIES

1. The Warranties
Any person who obtains payment or acceptance of an instrument warrants to any other person who in good faith pays or accepts the instrument [UCC 3–417(a), (d)]—

a. The person obtaining payment or acceptance is entitled or authorized to enforce the instrument (that is, there are no missing or unauthorized indorsements).

b. The instrument has not been altered.

c. The person obtaining payment or acceptance has no knowledge that the signature of the issuer of the instrument is unauthorized.

2. The Last Two Warranties Do Not Apply in Certain Cases
It is assumed, for example, that a drawer or a maker will recognize his or her own signature and that a maker or an acceptor will recognize whether an instrument has been materially altered.

3. When to Sue for Breach of Warranty
As soon as a transferee or holder who takes an instrument in good faith has reason to know of it [UCC 3–417(e)]. Notice of the claim must be given to the warrantor within thirty days.

4. Disclaimer
Valid with respect to any instrument except a check.

IV. DEFENSES

A. UNIVERSAL DEFENSES
Valid against all holders, including HDCs and holders who take by HDCs.

1. Forgery
Forgery of a maker's or drawer's signature cannot bind the person whose name is used (unless that person ratifies the signature or is precluded from denying it) [UCC 3–403(a)].

2. Fraud in the Execution
Defense is valid if a person is deceived into signing an instrument, believing that it is something else. Defense is not valid if a reasonable inquiry would have revealed the nature of the instrument.

3. Material Alteration
An alteration is material if it changes the contract terms between any two parties in any way (making any change in an unauthorized manner that relates to a party's obligation) [UCC 3–407(a)].

a. **Complete Defense against an Ordinary Holder**
A holder recovers nothing [UCC 3–407(a)]. (If an alteration is visible, a holder has notice and cannot be an HDC [UCC 3–302(a)(1)].)

b. **Partial Defense against an HDC**
If an instrument was originally incomplete and later completed in an unauthorized manner, an HDC can enforce it as completed [UCC 3–407(b)].

4. Discharge in Bankruptcy
Absolute defense [UCC 3–305(a)(1)].

5. Minority
A defense to the extent that state law recognizes it as a defense to a contract [UCC 3–305(a)(1)(i)] (see Chapter 12).

6. **Illegality**
   A defense if the law declares that an instrument executed in connection with illegal conduct is *void* [UCC 3–305(a)(1)(ii)].

7. **Mental Incapacity**
   An instrument issued by a person who has been adjudicated mentally incompetent by state proceedings is void [UCC 3–305(a)(1)(ii)].

8. **Extreme Duress**
   Extreme duress is an immediate threat of force or violence [UCC 3–305(a)(1)(ii)].

B. PERSONAL DEFENSES

Personal defenses avoid payment to an ordinary holder (but not an HDC).

1. **Breach of Contract or Breach of Warranty**
   If there is a breach of a contract for which an instrument was issued or a breach of warranty (see Chapter 23), the maker or drawer may not pay.

2. **Lack or Failure of Consideration [UCC 3–303(b), 3–305(a)(2)]**
   For example, when there is no consideration for the issuing of a note.

3. **Fraud in the Inducement (Ordinary Fraud)**
   If one issues an instrument based on false statements by the other party.

4. **Illegality**
   When a statute makes an illegal transaction *voidable*.

5. **Mental Incapacity**
   If a person drafts an instrument while mentally incompetent but before a court declares him or her so, the instrument is voidable.

6. **Others**
   Discharge by payment or cancellation; unauthorized completion of an incomplete instrument; nondelivery of an instrument; ordinary duress or undue influence.

C. FEDERAL LIMITATIONS ON HDC RIGHTS

A Federal Trade Commission rule (FTC Rule 433) effectively abolished HDC protection in consumer transactions.

1. **When the Rule Applies**
   As part of a consumer credit contract, a seller or lessor of consumer goods or services receives a promissory note from a consumer or arranges with a third party for a loan for a consumer to pay for the goods or services.

2. **What the Rule Requires**
   The seller or lessor must include in the contract a notice that all holders take subject to any defenses the debtor has against the seller or lessor.

3. **Effect of the Rule**
   There can be no HDC of an instrument that contains the notice (or a similar statement required by law) [UCC 3–106(d)]. A consumer can assert any defense he or she has against the seller of a product against a subsequent holder as well.

V. DISCHARGE

A. DISCHARGE BY PAYMENT OR TENDER OF PAYMENT

All parties are discharged if the party primarily liable pays to a holder the amount due in full [UCC 3–602, 3–603]. Payment by any other party discharges only that party and subsequent parties.

1. **Paying in Bad Faith**
A party is not discharged when paying in bad faith to a holder who got the instrument by theft or from someone who got it by theft (unless the holder has the rights of an HDC) [UCC 3–602(b)(2)].

2. **When Tender Is Refused**
Indorsers and accommodation parties with recourse against the party making tender are discharged to the extent of the tender [UCC 3–603(b)].

B. DISCHARGE BY CANCELLATION OR SURRENDER
A holder can discharge any party by intentionally destroying, mutilating, or canceling an instrument, canceling or striking out a party's signature, or adding words (such as "Paid") to the instrument indicating discharge [UCC 3–604]. A holder can also discharge by surrendering it to the person to be discharged.

C. DISCHARGE BY REACQUISITION
A person who reacquires an instrument that he or she held previously discharges all intervening indorsers against subsequent holders who do not qualify as HDCs [UCC 3–207].

D. DISCHARGE BY IMPAIRMENT OF RECOURSE OR OF COLLATERAL
If a holder adversely affects an indorser's right to recover payment from prior parties, the indorser is discharged [UCC 3–605].

TRUE-FALSE QUESTIONS

(Answers at the Back of the Book)

____ 1. Signature liability extends to any person who signs a negotiable instrument.

____ 2. Every party who signs an instrument is primarily liable for payment of it when it comes due.

____ 3. An authorized agent may be personally liable on an instrument on which the agent signs the agent's name but not the principal's name.

____ 4. Warranty liability does not bind parties who only present instruments for payment.

____ 5. An accommodation party who pays an instrument has a right of recourse against the accommodated party.

____ 6. Universal defenses can be raised to avoid payment to an HDC.

____ 7. A drawer can stop payment on a check in the possession of an innocent holder if the drawer was induced by an imposter to issue the check in the name of an impersonated payee.

____ 8. Personal defenses can be raised to avoid payment to an HDC.

____ 9. An unauthorized signature usually binds the person whose name is forged.

____ 10. A drawer is secondarily liable on an instrument.

FILL-IN QUESTIONS

(Answers at the Back of the Book)

There are three ______________ (presentment/transfer) warranties. Any person who seeks payment or acceptance of a negotiable instrument impliedly warrants to any other person who in good faith pays or accepts the instrument that: (1) the ______________ (presenter/transferor) has good title to the instrument or is authorized to obtain payment or acceptance on behalf of a one who has good title; (2) the ______________ (presenter/transferor) has no knowledge that the signature of

_______________ (any indorsee/the maker or the drawer) is unauthorized; and (3) the instrument has not been _______________ (materially altered/materially altered by the presenter/ materially altered by the transferor).

MULTIPLE-CHOICE QUESTIONS

(Answers at the Back of the Book)

___ 1. **Based on a Sample CPA Exam Question.** First National Bank is an HDC of a note for $1,000 on which there is the signature "Bob Adams." Bob has a defense against payment on the note to the bank if

a. Bob's signature was forged.
b. the note was issued based on the false statements of another party.
c. there was no consideration for issuing the note.
d. there was a breach of the contract for which the note was issued.

___ 2. Ron writes out a check for $50 to Sam. Sam alters the amount to $500. Although the alteration is clearly visible, Tina cashes the check for $500. Ron is liable to pay Tina for

a. $50.
b. $500.
c. $550.
d. none of the above.

___ 3. Gail writes a check on her account at First National Bank to Hal, a famous investor. The person purporting to be Hal is an imposter, however, named Ira. Ira negotiates the check to First National. Liability for the check is on

a. First National Bank.
b. Gail.
c. Hal.
d. Ira.

___ 4. Ann, who cannot read English, signs a note after Ben tells her that it is a credit application. If later sued by an HDC, Ann's best defense would be

a. duress.
b. mistake.
c. fraud in the inducement.
d. fraud in the execution.

___ 5. Beth gives a $500 note to Carl to deliver a load of apples to Beth's store. On delivery, the apples are spoiled. Beth may defend her decision not to pay the note based on

a. breach of warranty.
b. fraud in the inducement.
c. lack of consideration.
d. undue influence.

___ 6. Able Company writes a check to Baker Corporation that is drawn on Able's account at City Bank. Baker presents the check to the bank for payment. If the bank accepts the check, the bank is

a. not liable for payment.
b. primarily liable for payment.
c. secondarily liable for payment.
d. simultaneously liable for payment.

___ 7. Bill writes a check on his account at Community Bank to Donna to pay a preexisting debt. Donna negotiates the check to Ed by indorsement. Before Bill or Donna may be liable on the check, it must be

a. presented for payment only.
b. dishonored, for which notice must be given only.
c. presented for payment and dishonored, for which notice must be given.
d. none of the above.

___ 8. Delta Company writes a check to Eagle Credit, Inc., that is drawn on Delta's account at First Federal Bank. If the bank does not accept the check, liability for its amount is on

a. Delta.
b. Eagle.
c. First Federal.
d. no one.

___ 9. Frank signs a note payable to the order of Greg. Greg indorses the note and gives it to Holly as payment for a debt. Holly presents it to Frank, who pays it. Frank's payment discharges

a. all of the parties.
b. only Frank.
c. only Holly.
d. none of the above.

___ 10. United Business Corporation authorizes Vic to use company checks to buy office supplies. Vic writes a check to Wholesale Supplies, Inc., for $100 over the price of a purchase, for which the seller returns cash. When Wholesale presents the check for payment, it may recover

a. nothing.
b. the amount stated in the check.
c. the amount of the overpayment only.
d. the price of the supplies only.

SHORT ESSAY QUESTIONS

1. What are the similarities and differences between transfer and presentment warranties?

2. What are the two situations in which, when there is a forged or unauthorized indorsement, the burden of loss falls on the maker or drawer?

ISSUE SPOTTERS

(Answers at the Back of the Book)

1. Pat is an accountant with Quality Corporation, but has no authority to sign corporate checks. Pat orders office furniture from Retail Company and pays with a Quality check, signing "Quality Corp. by Pat, accountant." Retail does not know that Pat has no authority to sign the check. Can Quality refuse to pay it?

2. Dan issues a check for $100. Eve steals it and alters the amount to $1,000. She negotiates the check to Fred, who takes it in good faith, for value, and without notice of the alteration. Dan refuses to pay more than $100 on the check. Is Fred entitled to more from Dan?

3. Roy signs corporate checks for Standard Corporation. Roy makes a check payable to U-All Company, to whom Standard owes no money. Roy signs the check, forges U-All's indorsement, and cashes the check at First State Bank, the drawee. Does Standard have any recourse against the bank for the payment?

SPECIAL INFORMATION FOR CPA CANDIDATES

Questions can be constructed so that an apparently good faith party is liable on an instrument. This is particularly true in situations involving imposters, fictitious payees, and untrustworthy agents. You may find it helpful to review the rules concerning these culprits, and remember that a good faith party can be liable for a loss. There's one point that you may be able to forget, however: FTC Rule 433 has never been on the CPA exam.

Chapter 27
Checks, the Banking System, and E-Money

WHAT THIS CHAPTER IS ABOUT

This chapter outlines the duties and liabilities that arise when a check is issued and paid. UCC Articles 3 and 4 govern checks. If there is a conflict between the articles, Article 4 controls. This outline also covers electronic fund transfers, e-money, and online banking.

CHAPTER OUTLINE

I. CHECKS

A check is a draft drawn on a bank, ordering the bank to pay a fixed amount of money on demand [UCC 3–104(f)]. If a bank wrongfully dishonors any of the following special types of checks, the holder can recover expenses, interest, and consequential damages [UCC 3–411].

A. CASHIER'S CHECK

A check drawn by a bank on itself; negotiable on issue [UCC 3–104(g)].

B. TELLER'S CHECK

A draft drawn by a bank on another bank, or if drawn on a nonbank, payable at or through a bank [UCC 3–104(h)].

C. TRAVELER'S CHECK

A check on which a financial institution is both drawer and drawee. The buyer must sign it twice (buying it and using it) [UCC 3–104(i)].

D. CERTIFIED CHECK

A check accepted by the bank on which it is drawn [UCC 3–409(d)]. When a bank certifies a check, it immediately charges the drawer's account and transfers those funds to its own account. The effect of certification is to discharge the drawer and prior indorsers [UCC 3–414(c), 3–415(d)].

E. MISSING CASHIER'S, TELLER'S, AND CERTIFIED CHECKS

1. Who Can Claim a Refund?

The remitter or payee of a cashier's check or a teller's check, or the drawer of a certified check, can claim a refund if one of these types of checks is lost, destroyed, or stolen [UCC 3–312]. The claim becomes enforceable ninety days after the date of the check.

2. When Is the Bank Discharged?

If a person entitled to enforce the check presents it for payment, and the bank pays, the bank is discharged. If no one presents the check for payment, the bank's refund to the claimant discharges the bank.

II. THE BANK-CUSTOMER RELATIONSHIP

A. WHAT A BANK IS

A "person engaged in the business of banking, including a savings bank, savings and loan association, credit union or trust company" [UCC 4–105(1)]. Rights and duties of bank and customer are contractual.

B. WHAT A CUSTOMER IS

A customer is a creditor of the bank (and the bank, a debtor of the customer) when the customer deposits funds in his or her account. A bank acts as an agent for the customer when he or she writes a check drawn on the bank or deposits a check in his or her account for the bank to collect [UCC 4–201(a)].

III. HONORING CHECKS

If a bank dishonors a check for insufficient funds, it has no liability. The customer is liable to the payee or holder of the check in a civil suit. If intent to defraud is proved, the customer is also subject to criminal prosecution. If a bank wrongfully dishonors a check, however, it is liable to the customer [UCC 4–402].

A. OVERDRAFTS

1. Pay or Dishonor?

If there are insufficient funds in a customer's account, the bank can pay an item drawn on it or dishonor it. If the bank pays, it can charge the customer's account (if the customer has authorized payment) [UCC 4–401(a)]. If a check "bounces," a holder can resubmit it but must notify any indorsers of the first dishonor (or they are discharged).

2. Bank's Liability for Agreeing to Pay Overdrafts

Once a bank agrees to accept overdrafts, refusal to honor checks on an overdrawn account is wrongful dishonor [UCC 4–402(b)].

B. POSTDATED CHECKS

A bank can charge a postdated check against a customer's account if the customer does not give the bank enough notice. If the bank has notice but charges the check anyway, the bank is liable [UCC 4–401(c)].

C. STALE CHECKS

A bank is not obliged to pay an uncertified check presented for payment more than six months after its date [UCC 4–404]. If a bank pays in good faith, it can charge the customer's account for the amount.

D. DEATH OR INCOMPETENCE OF A CUSTOMER

Until a bank knows of the situation and has time to act, it is not liable for paying items [UCC 4–405]. If a bank knows of a death, for ten days after the date of death it can pay items drawn on or before the date of death (unless a person claiming an interest in the account orders a stop payment).

E. STOP-PAYMENT ORDERS

1. Who Can Order a Stop Payment and When Must It Be Received?

Only a customer or person authorized to draw on the account. Must be received in a reasonable time and manner [UCC 4–403(a), 4–405].

2. How Can a Stop Payment Be Given and How Long Is It Effective?

In most states, it can be given orally, but it is binding for only fourteen calendar days unless confirmed in writing. In writing, it is effective for six months, when it may be renewed [UCC 4–403(b)].

3. If the Bank Pays over an Order

It must recredit the customer's account for any loss, including damages for the dishonor of subsequent items [UCC 4–403(c)].

4. The Customer's Risks

Possible liability to payee for the amount of the item (and damages). Defense against payment to a payee may not prevent payment to a subsequent HDC [UCC 3–305, 3–306].

5. Cashier's Checks and Teller's Checks

Except in very limited circumstances, payment will not be stopped on a cashier's check or a teller's check. If the bank issuing such a check wrongfully refuses to pay it, the bank may be liable for expenses, loss of interest, and consequential damages [UCC 3–411(b)].

F. CHECKS BEARING FORGED SIGNATURES

1. The General Rule

A forged signature on a check has no legal effect as the signature of a drawer [UCC 3–403(a)]. If the bank pays, it must recredit the account.

2. Customer Negligence

If the customer's negligence substantially contributed to the forgery, the bank is not obligated to recredit the account [UCC 3–406(a)].

a. Reducing a Customer's Liability

A customer's liability may be reduced by a bank's negligence (if it substantially contributed to the loss) [UCC 3–406(b)].

b. Timely Examination of Bank Statements Required

The customer must examine the bank statement and canceled checks promptly and report any forged signatures [UCC 4–406(c)].

1) When There Is a Series of Forgeries by the Same Wrongdoer

To recover for all items, a customer must report the first forgery to the bank within *thirty* calendar days of receiving the statement and canceled checks [UCC 4–406(d)(2)].

2) When the Bank Is Also Negligent

If the bank fails to exercise ordinary care ("reasonable commercial standards"), it may have to recredit the customer's account for a portion of the loss (on the basis of comparative negligence) [UCC 4–406(e)].

c. Absolute Time Limit

Customer must report a forged signature within one year of the date the statement and canceled checks were available [UCC 4–406].

3. Other Parties from Whom the Bank May Recover

a. The Forger

A forged signature is effective as the signature of the unauthorized signer [UCC 3–403(a)].

b. The Customer or Collecting Bank Who Cashed the Check

The bank may recover from "the person to whom or for whose benefit payment was made" [UCC 4–207(a)(2), 3–418(a)(ii)]. The bank cannot recover from "a person who took the instrument in good faith and for value or who in good faith changed position in reliance on the payment or acceptance" [UCC 3–418(c)].

G. CHECKS BEARING FORGED INDORSEMENTS

1. The General Rule

If the bank pays a check with a forged indorsement, it must recredit the account (or be held liable for breach of contract) [UCC 4–401(a)].

2. Timely Examination of Bank Statements Required

The customer must examine the bank statement and canceled checks and report forged indorsements promptly. Failure to do so within three years relieves the bank of liability [UCC 4–111].

3. Parties from Whom the Bank May Recover

The bank can recover for breach of warranty from the bank that cashed the check [UCC 4–207(a)(2)]. Ultimately, the loss usually falls on the first party to take the instrument.

H. ALTERED CHECKS

If the bank fails to detect an alteration, it is liable to its customer for the loss [UCC 4–401(d)(1)].

1. **The Customer's Negligence**
If a bank traces its loss to the customer's negligence or, on successive altered checks, to the customer's failure to discover the first alteration, its liability is reduced (unless it was negligent) [UCC 4–401, 4–406].

2. **Parties from Whom the Bank May Recover**
The bank can recover from the transferor, for breach of warranty. Exceptions involve cashier's, teller's, and certified checks [UCC 3–417(a)(2), 4–208(a)(2), 4–207(a)(2)].

IV. ACCEPTING DEPOSITS

A. AVAILABILITY SCHEDULE FOR DEPOSITED CHECKS
Under the Expedited Funds Availability Act of 1987 and Regulation CC—

1. **Funds That Must Be Available the Next Business Day after Deposit**

a. **The First $100 of Any Deposit and the Next $400 of a Local Check**
The first $100 must be available for withdrawal on the opening of the next business day. The next $400 of a local check must be available by no later than 5:00 P.M. the next business day.

b. **Cash Deposits, Wire Transfers, and Certain Checks**
Funds must be available on the next business day for cash deposits, wire transfers, government checks, the first $100 of a day's check deposits, cashier's checks, certified checks, and checks for which the depositary and payor banks are the same institution.

2. **Funds That Must Be Available within Five Business Days**
All nonlocal checks and nonproprietary ATM deposits, including cash.

3. **Funds That Can Be Held for Eight Days or an Extra Four Days**
Eight days: funds in new accounts (open less than thirty days). Four days: deposits over $5,000 (except government and cashier's checks), accounts with many overdrafts, checks of questionable collectibility (the bank must tell the depositor it suspects fraud or insolvency).

B. INTEREST-BEARING ACCOUNTS
Under the Truth-in-Savings Act of 1991 and Regulation DD—

1. **When Must a Bank Pay Interest?**
On the full balance of a customer's account each day.

2. **What Must a Bank Tell New Customers?**
New customers must be told, in writing, the minimum to open an interest-bearing account, the interest in terms of the annual percentage yield, whether interest is calculated daily, and fees and other charges.

3. **What Must Be Included in a Monthly Statement?**
Interest earned, any fees that were charged, how the fees were calculated, and the number of days that the statement covers.

C. THE COLLECTION PROCESS

1. **Banks Involved in the Collection Process**
Depositary bank: first bank to receive a check for payment. *Payor bank*: bank on which a check is drawn. *Collecting bank*: bank (except payor bank) that handles a check for collection. *Intermediary bank*: any bank (except payor and depositary banks) involved in the collection process.

2. **Check Collection between Customers of the Same Bank**
An item payable by a depositary bank that is also the payor bank is an "on-us item." If the bank does not dishonor it by the second banking day, it is considered paid [UCC 4–215(e)(2)].

3. **Check Collection between Customers of Different Banks**
A depositary bank must arrange to present a check either directly or through intermediary banks to the appropriate payor bank.

a. **Midnight Deadline**
Each bank in the collection chain must pass a check on before midnight of the next banking day following receipt [UCC 4–202(b)].

b. **Deferred Posting and the Midnight Deadline**
Posting of checks received after a certain time can be deferred until the next day [UCC 4–108].

c. **Electronic Check Presentment**
Can be done the same day a check is deposited. The check may be kept at the place of deposit with only information about the check presented for payment under a Federal Reserve agreement, clearinghouse rule, or truncation agreement [UCC 4–110].

V. ELECTRONIC FUND TRANSFERS

A. TYPES OF ELECTRONIC FUND TRANSFER (EFT) SYSTEMS

1. **Automated Teller Machines (ATMs)**
Connected online to bank computers, ATMs accept deposits, dispense funds from accounts, make credit-card advances, and receive payments.

2. **Point-of-Sale Systems**
Connected online to bank computers, these systems allow consumers to transfer funds to merchants to pay for purchases. The merchant inserts the customer's card into a terminal to read the coded data on the card.

3. **Direct Deposits and Withdrawals**
Through an electronic terminal, a deposit may be made directly to a customer's account. An institution at which a customer's funds are on deposit can also make payments electronically to a third party.

4. **Pay-by-Telephone Systems**
These systems provide access to a financial institution's computer system by telephone to direct a transfer of funds.

B. CONSUMER FUND TRANSFERS

Under the Electronic Fund Transfer Act (EFTA) of 1978 and Regulation E (issued by the Federal Reserve Board of Governors)—

1. **Who Is Subject to the EFTA?**
Financial institutions that offer electronic fund transfers (EFTs) involving customer asset accounts established for personal, family, or household purposes. Telephone transfers are covered only if they are made pursuant to a prearranged plan involving periodic transfers.

2. **Disclosure Requirements**
The terms and conditions of EFTs involving a customer's account must be disclosed in readily understandable language at the time the customer contracts for services. Disclosures include—

a. **Customer Liability**
If a debit card is lost or stolen, and misused, a customer is liable for (1) \$50—if he or she notifies the bank within two business days of learning of the loss; (2) \$500—if he or she does not tell the bank until after the second day; or (3) unlimited amounts—if notice does not occur within sixty days after the transfer appears on the customer's statement.

b. **Errors on Monthly Statements**
Customer's and bank's responsibilities with respect to monthly statements: customer has sixty days to report an error, bank has ten days to respond or return any disputed amounts.

c. **Receipts**
Bank must furnish receipts for transactions made through electronic terminals,

d. **Periodic Statements**

1) **How Often They Must Be Provided**
Monthly statements are required for every month in which there is an electronic transfer of funds.

2) **What They Must Include**
The amounts and dates of transfers, the fees, identification of the terminals, names of third parties involved, and an address and phone number for inquiries and error notices.

e. **Stopping Preauthorized Transfers**
A customer may stop a transfer by notifying the institution orally or in writing up to three business days before the scheduled date of the transfer. The institution may require the customer to provide written confirmation with fourteen days of oral notification.

3. **Stopping Payment and Reversibility**
Except for preauthorized transfers, the EFTA does not provide for the reversal of an electronic transfer of funds, once it has occurred.

4. **Unauthorized Transfers**

a. **What an Unauthorized Transfer Is**
(1) A transfer is initiated by a person who has no actual authority to initiate the transfer; (2) the consumer receives no benefit from it; and (3) the consumer did not furnish the person "with the card, code, or other means of access" to his or her account.

b. **Criminal Sanctions**
Unauthorized use of an EFT system access device is a federal felony, subject to fines up to $10,000 and imprisonment up to ten years.

5. **Violations and Damages**
Banks are held to strict compliance. Penalties include—

a. **Civil**
A customer may recover actual damages, as well as punitive damages of not less than $100 and more than $1,000. In a class action suit, the punitive damages limit is the lesser of $500,000 or 1 percent of the institution's net worth.

b. **Criminal**
Sanctions included subjecting an institution or its officials to fines of up to $5,000 and imprisonment up to one year.

C. COMMERCIAL FUND TRANSFERS

In most states, UCC Article 4A clarifies the rights and liabilities of parties involved in fund transfers not subject to the EFTA or other federal or state statutes. In those states that have not adopted Article 4A, commercial fund transfers are governed by contract law and tort law.

VI. E-MONEY AND ONLINE BANKING

E-money has the potential to replace physical cash with virtual cash (e-money) in the form of electronic impulses, or digital cash.

A. STORED-VALUE CARDS

Plastic cards embossed with magnetic stripes containing encoded data. Can be used to buy specific goods and services offered by the issuer.

B. SMART CARDS

Contain microchips that hold more information than a magnetic stripe. Less prone to error, and carry and process security programming (such as a digital signature). Debits and credits are automatic and can be immediate.

1. Deposit Insurance for Smart-Card Balances

Most e-money is not covered by the Federal Deposit Insurance Corporation. If a bank becomes insolvent, an e-money holder is in the position of a general creditor.

2. Legal Protection for Smart Cards

Some statutes, such as the Federal Trade Commission Act (which prohibits unfair or deceptive practices), and common law principles (such as contract law) extend to e-money.

C. ONLINE BANKING SERVICES

These include bill consolidation and payment, transferring funds among accounts, and applying for loans. Depositing and withdrawing is not yet generally available over the Internet, but virtual banks do business through physical delivery systems.

D. REGULATORY COMPLIANCE

There are questions about the application of traditional banking regulations to online banks. For example, under the Community Reinvestment Act, a bank must define its market area. What is the market area of an Internet bank?

E. PRIVACY PROTECTION

1. Right to Financial Privacy Act of 1978

An issuer of e-money may be subject to this act if the issuer is deemed to be (1) a bank by virtue of its holding customer funds or (2) an entity that issues a physical card similar to a credit or debit card.

2. Financial Services Modernization Act (Gramm-Leach-Bliley Act) of 1999

This act proscribes the disclosure of financial institutions' customer data without notice and an opt-out opportunity.

VII. THE UNIFORM MONEY SERVICES ACT (UMSA)

The UMSA applies to traditional money services the same regulations that apply to other, traditional financial service businesses.

A. TRADITIONAL MONEY SERVICES

Money service businesses do not accept deposits, but issue money orders, traveler's checks, stored-value cards; exchange foreign currency; and cash checks.

B. INTERNET-BASED MONEY SERVICES

1. Systems Subject to the New Law

May include [UMSA 1–102(c)(21)]—

a. E-money and Internet payment mechanisms
b. Internet scrip
c. Stored-value products (smart, prepaid, and value-added cards)

2. What the UMSA Requires

Persons engaged in money transmission, check cashing, or currency exchange must obtain a license from a state, be examined by state officials, report on their activities to the state, and comply with certain record keeping requirements [UMSA 1–104].

3. **Rules That Govern Investments**
Money service businesses are covered by rules that govern investments, and must follow "safety and soundness rules," which concern the posting of bonds and annual auditing of their books [see UMSA 2–204].

TRUE-FALSE QUESTIONS

(Answers at the Back of the Book)

___ 1. A check is a draft drawn on a bank.

___ 2. If a bank fails to honor a customer's stop-payment order, it may be liable to the customer for more than the amount of the loss suffered by the drawer because of the wrongful payment.

___ 3. A bank's duty to honor its customer's checks is absolute.

___ 4. Generally, funds must be available on the next business day for cash deposits.

___ 5. A bank that fails to investigate an error and report its conclusion promptly to the customer is in violation of the Electronic Fund Transfer Act (EFTA).

___ 6. A customer must examine the statements provided by the institution handling his or her account and notify it of any errors within sixty days.

___ 7. The rights and duties of a bank and its customers are contractual.

___ 8. All funds deposited in all bank accounts must be available for withdrawal no later than the next business day.

___ 9. A bank that pays a customer's check bearing a forged indorsement must recredit the customer's account.

___ 10. A forged drawer's signature on a check is effective as the signature of the person whose name is signed.

FILL-IN QUESTIONS

(Answers at the Back of the Book)

A depositor is the ________________ (drawee/drawer) of a check. The depositor is the bank's ________________ (creditor/debtor) as to the amount on deposit in the depositor's account. The depositor is the bank's ________________ (agent/principal) in the deposit contract. The bank is the ________________ (drawee/drawer) of a check. The bank is the depositor's ________________ (creditor debtor) as to the amount on deposit in the depositor's account. The bank is the depositor's ________________ (agent/principal) in the handling of the account and in the collection process.

MULTIPLE-CHOICE QUESTIONS

(Answers at the Back of the Book)

___ 1. American Bank's cutoff hour is 2 P.M. The bank receives a check drawn on the account of Best Corporation, one of its customers, at 4 P.M. Monday, presented by Carol, not the bank's customer. The bank uses deferred posting. If it decides to dishonor the check, it must do so by midnight

a. Monday.
b. Tuesday.
c. Wednesday.
d. Thursday.

____ **2.** First National Bank pays a check on which has been forged the signature of the drawer, Gail, who is the bank's customer. The bank must recredit her account for the entire amount of the check if

a. Gail's negligence substantially contributed to the forgery.
b. the amount of the check was less than $50.
c. the amount of the check was more than $5,000.
d. the bank's negligence substantially contributed to the forgery.

____ **3.** Ann buys three television sets from Bob, paying with a check. When the sets prove defective, Ann orders City Bank, the drawee, to stop payment on the check. This order is valid for fourteen

a. years.
b. months.
c. weeks.
d. days.

____ **4.** First State Bank mistakenly pays one of Gary's checks with a forged indorsement. Gary can recover his loss from the bank if, after receipt of the bank statement, he notifies the bank within three

a. years.
b. months.
c. weeks.
d. days.

____ **5.** Eve writes a check for $600 drawn on her account at First Federal Bank and presents it to Greg. When Greg presents the check for payment, the bank dishonors it. Greg may sue

a. the bank for dishonoring the check.
b. Eve on the underlying obligation.
c. both the bank and Eve.
d. none of the above.

____ **6.** Delta Company issue a payroll check to Ed drawn on its account at First Community Bank. This check will be stale if Ed presents it for payment six

a. months after it is issued.
b. months after he indorses.
c. weeks after he receives it.
d. weeks after the pay period that it covers.

____ **7.** **Based on a Sample CPA Exam Question.** Jay is the holder and payee of check drawn by Karen on First National Bank. Jay takes the check to the bank to have it certified. After certification

a. Karen is discharged on the check.
b. Karen is primarily liable on the check.
c. the bank is discharged on the check.
d. the bank is secondarily liable on the check.

____ **8.** Dick loses his bank access card. He realizes his loss the next day but waits a week to call Eagle Bank, his bank. Meanwhile, Erin finds and uses Dick's card to withdraw $5,000 from his account. Dick is responsible for

a. $0.
b. $50.
c. $500.
d. $5,000.

___ 9. Adam pays for a purchase at Beta Computers with a check. Burt, the cashier, steals one of Adam's checks, forges his signature, and County Bank, Adam's bank, pays the check. Adam can recover from

a. no one.
b. Burt, but not County Bank.
c. County Bank, which can recover from Burt.
d. County Bank, which cannot recover from Burt.

___ 10. Web Funds, Inc., an e-money issuer, misrepresents the value of its products to the detriment of Jay and other consumers. Web Funds may be liable under

a. the Federal Trade Commission Act.
b. the Financial Services Modernization Act.
c. the Right to Financial Privacy Act.
d. the Uniform Money Services Act.

SHORT ESSAY QUESTIONS

1. Under what circumstances might a customer be unable recover from a bank that pays on a forged check drawn on the customer's account?

2. What are the principal features of the Electronic Fund Transfer Act (EFTA)?

ISSUE SPOTTERS

(Answers at the Back of the Book)

1. Lyn writes a check for $900 to Mac, who indorses the check in blank and transfers it to Nan. She presents the check to Omega Bank, the drawee bank, for payment. Omega does not honor the check. Is Lyn liable to Nan? Could Lyn be subject to criminal prosecution?

2. Hal steals a check from Irma, forges her signature, and transfers the check to Jay for value. Unaware that the signature is not Irma's, Jay presents the check to Local Bank, the drawee, which cashes the check. Irma discovers the forgery and insists that the bank recredit her account. Can the bank refuse to recredit the account? If not, can the bank recover the amount paid?

3. Ron writes a check for $700 to Sue. Sue indorses the check in blank and transfers it to Tim, who alters the check to read $7,000 and presents it to Union Bank, the drawee, for payment. The bank cashes it. Ron discovers the alteration and sues the bank. How much, if anything, can Ron recover? From whom can the bank recover this amount?

SPECIAL INFORMATION FOR CPA CANDIDATES

Typically, banking questions on the CPA exam concern the relationship between a bank and its customer. Remember in particular that there is no primarily liable party among the original three parties on a check; only the drawer can sue a drawee for wrongful dishonor (a payee cannot enforce a check against the drawee); and a drawee does not have to pay a stale check. Another specific matter tested on the exam has been the liability surrounding stop-payment orders. In that context, remember that a personal defense is no good against a holder in due course.

Electronic fund transfers are not tested on the CPA exam.

CUMULATIVE HYPOTHETICAL PROBLEM FOR UNIT FIVE—INCLUDING CHAPTERS 24–27

(Answers at the Back of the Book)

On May 15, 2002, Eve bought the following instrument from Beta Corporation for $1,700. Eve paid for the instrument with check. Eve knew that Alpha, Inc., disputed its liability on the instrument because of Beta's alleged breach of the computer purchase contract referred to on the face of the instrument. On May 20, First National Bank bought the instrument from Eve for $1,900. First National did not know that Alpha disputed its liability. On the back of the instrument is the indorsement "Pay to the order of First National Bank, without recourse [signed] *Eve*".

> May 1, 2001
>
> Alpha, Inc., promises to pay to Beta Corp. or bearer $2,000 on June 1, 2001, with interest at the rate of 8 % per year. Alpha may elect to extend the due date to July 1, 2001.
>
> Alpha, Inc.
>
> By *C.D. Jones*
>
> C.D. Jones, president
>
> Re: computer purchase order no. 123, dated May 1, 2001

___ **1.** This instrument is

a. a check.
b. a promissory note.
c. a sight draft.
d. a trade acceptance.

___ **2.** This instrument is

a. negotiable because it refers to the computer purchase agreement.
b. negotiable even though Alpha has the right to extend the due date.
c. nonnegotiable because Alpha has the right to extend the due date.
d. nonnegotiable because it refers to the computer purchase agreement.

___ **3.** First National Bank can negotiate the instrument

a. by delivery without indorsing it.
b. only by canceling Eve's indorsement.
c. only by indorsing it.
d. only by making it payable to the order of a specific individual.

___ **4.** First National demands payment on the instrument from Alpha. Alpha refuses, claiming that Beta breached the computer purchase agreement. First National

a. can collect from Alpha because First National is an HDC.
b. can collect from Eve, but not Alpha, because Eve knew of Alpha's claim.
c. cannot collect from Alpha because Eve was not an HDC.
d. cannot collect from Alpha because of Beta's breach.

___ **5.** Beta presents Eve's check for payment, but City Bank, the drawee, refuses to pay. The party with primary liability for payment of the check is

a. Beta.
b. City Bank.
c. Eve.
d. none of the above.

QUESTIONS ON THE FOCUS ON LEGAL REASONING FOR UNIT FIVE—*SCALISE V. AMERICAN EMPLOYERS INSURANCE CO.*

(Answers at the Back of the Book)

___ **1.** Dave delivers a check to Eagle Store, Inc., to pay for a DVD player. Eagle deposits the check in its account with First Federal Bank, which submits the check for collection to United Bank, the drawee bank, which clears the check. Under the holding in *Scalise v. American Employers Insurance Co.*, "payment" occurred when

a. Dave delivered the check.
b. Eagle deposited the check.
c. First Federal submitted the check for collection.
d. United cleared the check.

___ **2.** In the opinion of the majority in *Scalise v. American Employers Insurance Co.*, Dave's debt to Eagle for the DVD player was discharged when

a. Dave delivered the check.
b. Eagle deposited the check.
c. First Federal submitted the check for collection.
d. United cleared the check.

___ **3.** According to the reasoning of the dissent in *Scalise v. American Employers Insurance Co.*, it would be most fair to consider that "payment" occurred when

a. Dave delivered the check.
b. Eagle deposited the check.
c. First Federal submitted the check for collection.
d. United cleared the check.

QUESTIONS ON THE FOCUS ON ETHICS FOR UNIT FIVE—NEGOTIABLE INSTRUMENTS

(Answers at the Back of the Book)

___ **1.** Carol signs a promissory note in reliance on Don's assurance that it is not a note. Don negotiates the note to Friendly Collection Company, which takes it for value, in good faith, and without knowledge or notice of the circumstances by which it was executed. When Friendly tries to collect, Carol refuses to pay. Under the holder-in-due-course (HDC) doctrine, the loss falls on

a. Carol only.
b. Carol and Friendly equally.
c. Carol or Friendly, depending on who can most easily afford the loss.
d. Friendly only.

____ 2. First State Bank wrongfully dishonors a check issued by Greg, its customer, to Holly. On wrongful dishonor of a customer's check, a bank's liability may include

a. compensatory damages only.
b. consequential damages.
c. nominal damages only.
d. the amount of the check only.

____ 3. City Bank claims that Diane withdrew $5,000 from her account with the bank through its ATM. Diane denies making the withdrawal and offers proof that she was with Ed elsewhere at the time. In a suit to resolve the dispute, under the Electronic Fund Transfer Act (EFTA), the court may rule in favor of

a. City Bank only.
b. Diane only.
c. either City Bank or Diane.
d. none of the above.

Chapter 28
Secured Transactions

WHAT THIS CHAPTER IS ABOUT

This chapter covers transactions in which the payment of a debt is secured (guaranteed) by personal property owned by the debtor or in which the debtor has a legal interest. The importance of being a secured creditor cannot be overemphasized—secured transactions are as basic to modern business as credit.

CHAPTER OUTLINE

I. THE TERMINOLOGY OF SECURED TRANSACTIONS

UCC Article 9 applies to secured transactions.

A. SECURED TRANSACTION

Transaction in which payment of a debt is guaranteed by personal property owned by the debtor or in which the debtor has a legal interest.

B. SECURITY INTEREST, SECURED PARTY, COLLATERAL, AND DEBTOR

A *security interest* is the interest in the collateral that secures payment or performance of an obligation [UCC 1–201(37)]. A *secured party* is a creditor in whose favor there is a security interest in the debtor's collateral [UCC 9–102(a)(72)]. *Collateral* is the subject of a security interest [UCC 9–102(a)(12)]. *Debtor* is the party who owes payment [UCC 9–102(a)(28)].

II. CREATING A SECURITY INTEREST

A. TWO CONCERNS

A creditor's main concerns are, if a debtor fails to pay, (1) satisfaction of the debt through possession or sale of the collateral and (2) priority over other creditors to the collateral.

B. THREE REQUIREMENTS

A creditor's rights attach to collateral, creating an enforceable security interest against a debtor if the following requirements are met [UCC 9–203].

1. **Written Security Agreement**
   (1) It must be written or authenticated (which includes electronic media, or records), (2) describe the collateral, and (3) be signed or authenticated by the debtor [UCC 9–102, 9–108]. Or the secured party must possess the collateral.

2. **Secured Party Must Give Value**
   Value is any consideration that supports a contract [UCC 1–201(44)].

3. **Debtor Must Have Rights in the Collateral**
   The debtor must have an ownership interest or right (current or future legal interest) to obtain possession of the collateral.

III. PERFECTING A SECURITY INTEREST

Perfection is the process by which secured parties protect themselves against the claims of others who wish to satisfy their debts out of the same collateral.

A. PERFECTION BY FILING

Filing is the most common means of perfecting a security interest.

1. What a Financing Statement Must Contain

It must contain (1) the names of the debtor and the creditor (a trade name is not sufficient), and (3) a description of the collateral [UCC 9–502, 9–503, 9–506, 9–521].

2. Where to File a Financing Statement

Depending on how collateral is classified, filing is with a county (timber, fixtures, etc.) or a state (other collateral) [UCC 9–301(3), 9–502(b)]. The specific office depends on the debtor's location—

1) Individual debtors: the state of the debtor's residence.
2) Chartered entity (corporation): state of charter or filing.
3) Other: state in which business or chief executive office is.

B. PERFECTION WITHOUT FILING

1. Perfection by Possession

A creditor can possess collateral and return it when the debt is paid [UCC 9–310, 9–312(b), 9–313]. For some securities, instruments, and jewelry, this is the only way to perfect.

2. Automatic Perfection

a. Purchase-Money Security Interest (PMSI)

A PMSI is (1) retained in, or taken by a seller of, goods to secure part or all of the price, or (2) taken by a lender, such as a bank, as part of a loan to enable a debtor to buy the collateral [UCC 9–103(a)(2)].

b. Perfection of a PMSI

A PMSI in consumer goods is perfected automatically when it is created. The seller need do nothing more.

C. EFFECTIVE TIME DURATION OF PERFECTION

A financing statement is effective for five years [UCC 9–515]. A continuation statement filed within six months before the expiration date continues the effectiveness for five more years (and so on) [UCC 9–515(d), (e)].

IV. THE SCOPE OF A SECURITY INTEREST

A. PROCEEDS

Proceeds include whatever is received when collateral is sold or otherwise disposed of. A secured party has an interest in proceeds that perfects automatically on perfection of the security interest and remains perfected for twenty days after the debtor receives the proceeds. The interest remains perfected for more than twenty days if—

1. A filed financing statement covers the original collateral and the proceeds [UCC 9–315(c), (d)].
2. There is a filed statement that covers the original collateral and the proceeds are identifiable cash proceeds [UCC 9–315(d)(2)].

B. AFTER-ACQUIRED PROPERTY

A security agreement may provide for coverage of **after-acquired property** [UCC 9–204(a)]—collateral acquired by a debtor after execution of a security agreement.

C. FUTURE ADVANCES

A security agreement may provide that future advances against a line of credit are subject to a security interest in the collateral [UCC 9–204(c)].

D. THE FLOATING-LIEN CONCEPT

A *floating lien* is a security agreement that provides for the creation of a security interest in any (or all) of the above. The concept can apply to a shifting stock of goods—the lien can start with raw materials and follow them as they become finished goods and inventories and as they are sold, turning into accounts receivable, chattel paper, or cash.

V. PRIORITIES

When several creditors claim a security interest in the same collateral of a debtor, which interest has priority?

A. SECURED PARTIES V. UNSECURED PARTIES

Secured parties (perfected or not) prevail over unsecured creditors and creditors who have obtained judgments against the debtor but who have not begun the legal process to collect on those judgments [UCC 9–201(a)].

B. SECURED PARTIES V. BUYERS

1. The General Rule

A security interest in collateral continues even after the collateral has been sold unless the secured party authorized the sale.

2. Exception—Buyer in the Ordinary Course of Business

Takes goods free of any security interest (unless the buyer knows that the purchase violates a third party's rights) [UCC 9–320(a)].

3. Exception—Buyers of Consumer Goods Purchased outside the Ordinary Course of Business

The buyer must give value and not know of the security interest; the purchase must occur before the secured party perfects by filing [UCC 9–320(b)].

4. Exception—Buyers of Instruments, Documents, or Securities

A holder in due course, a holder to whom a negotiable instrument has been negotiated, and a bona fide purchaser of securities have priority over a previously perfected security interest [UCC 9–330(d), 9–331(a)].

5. Exception—Buyers of Farm Products

A buyer from a farmer has priority over a perfected security interest unless, in some states, the secured party has filed centrally an effective financing statement or the buyer has notice before the sale.

C. SECURED PARTIES V. OTHER SECURED PARTIES

1. The General Rule

The first interest to be filed or perfected has priority over other filed or perfected security interests. If none of the interests has been perfected, the first to attach has priority [UCC 9–322(a)(1), (3)].

2. Exception—Commingled or Processed Goods

When goods have lost their identity into a product or mass, security interests attach in a ratio of the cost of the goods to which each interest originally attached to the cost of the total product or mass [UCC 9–336].

3. Exception—Purchase-Money Security Interest (PMSI)

a. Inventory

A perfected PMSI prevails over a previously perfected security interest if the holder of the PMSI perfects and gives the holder of the other interest written notice of the PMSI before the debtor takes possession of the new inventory [UCC 9–324(b)].

b. **Software**
If software is used in goods subject to a PMSI, priority is according to the classification of the goods [UCC 9–103(c), 9–324(f)].

c. **Other Collateral**
A perfected PMSI prevails over a previously perfected security interest if the holder of the PMSI perfects before the debtor takes possession of the collateral or within twenty days [UCC 9–324(a)].

VI. RIGHTS AND DUTIES OF DEBTORS AND CREDITORS

A. INFORMATION REQUESTS
When filing, creditors and debtors can ask the filing officer to furnish a copy of the statement with the file number, the date, and the hour [UCC 9–523(a)]. Others (such as prospective creditors) can ask the filing officer to provide a certificate that gives information on possible perfected financing statements [UCC 9–523(c), 9–525(d)].

B. RELEASE, ASSIGNMENT, AND AMENDMENT
A secured party can release all or part of the collateral [UCC 9–512, 9–521(b)], or assign part or all of the security interest [UCC 9–514, 9–521(a)]. A filing can be amended, if both parties agree [UCC 9–512(a)].

C. CONFIRMATION OR ACCOUNTING REQUEST BY DEBTOR
When the debtor asks, the secured party must tell the debtor the amount of the unpaid debt (within two weeks of the debtor's request) [UCC 9–210].

D. TERMINATION STATEMENT
When a debt is paid, the secured party can send a termination statement to the debtor or file it with the original financing statement.

1. **If the Collateral Is Consumer Goods**
The statement must be filed within one month after the debt is paid, or—if the debtor requests the statement in writing—within twenty days of receipt of the request, whichever is earlier [UCC 9–513(b)].

2. **If the Collateral Is Other Goods**
The statement must be filed or furnished to the debtor within twenty days after a written request is made by the debtor [UCC 9–513(c)].

VII. DEFAULT
Default is whatever the parties stipulate in their agreement [UCC 9–601, 9–603]. Occurs most often when debtors fail to make payments or go bankrupt.

A. BASIC REMEDIES

1. **Take Possession of the Collateral**
A secured party can take possession of the collateral without a court order, if it can be done without a breach of the peace, [UCC 9–609(b)] and retain it for satisfaction of the debt [UCC 9–620] or resell it and apply the proceeds toward the debt [UCC 9–610] (see below).

2. **Execute and Levy**
A secured party can give up the security interest and proceed to judgment on the debt (this is done if the value of the collateral is less than the debt and the debtor has other assets) [UCC 9–601(a)].

3. **Proceed According to Local Real Estate Law**
If a security interest includes both real and personal property, a secured party can proceed against the personal property under UCC Article 9 or against all of the collateral under local real estate law [UCC 9–604(a)].

B. DISPOSITION OF COLLATERAL

1. Retention of Collateral by the Secured Party

a. Notice
A secured party must give written notice to the debtor. In all cases except consumer goods, notice must also be sent to any other secured party from whom the secured party has received notice of a claim.

b. If Debtor or Other Secured Party Objects within Twenty Days
The secured party must sell or otherwise dispose of the collateral [UCC 9–620(a), 9–621].

2. Consumer Goods
If the collateral is consumer goods with a PMSI and the debtor has paid 60 percent or more on the price or loan, the secured party must sell within ninety days [UCC 9–620(e), (f)].

3. Disposition Procedures
(1) Disposition must be in a commercially reasonable manner and (2) the debtor must be notified of the sale [UCC 9–610(b)].

a. Disposition
After default, a secured party may sell, lease, license, or otherwise dispose of any or all of the collateral. "Commercially reasonable" means the method, manner, time, place, and other terms.

b. The Secured Party Must Give Written Notice to the Debtor
In all cases except consumer goods, notice must also be sent to any other secured party from whom the secured party has received notice of a claim [UCC 9–611(b), (c)], unless the collateral is perishable or is customarily sold in a recognized market.

4. Proceeds from Disposition
Must be applied to (1) expenses stemming from retaking, storing, or reselling, (2) balance of the debt, (3) junior lienholders, and (4) surplus to the debtor [UCC 9–608(a); 9–615(a), (e)].

5. Deficiency Judgment
In most cases, if a sale of collateral does not repay the debt, the debtor is liable for any deficiency. A creditor can obtain a judgment to collect.

6. Redemption Rights
Before the secured party retains or disposes of the collateral, the debtor or any other secured party can take the collateral by tendering performance of all secured obligations and paying the secured party's expenses [UCC 9–623].

TRUE-FALSE QUESTIONS

(Answers at the Back of the Book)

____ 1. A financing statement is not effective if it is filed electronically.

____ 2. Attachment gives a creditor an enforceable security interest in collateral.

____ 3. A secured creditor's right to proceeds exists for twenty days after receipt only if the proceeds are forwarded to the secured party.

____ 4. To be valid, a financing statement does not need to contain a description of the collateral.

____ 5. When a secured debt is paid, the secured party does not need to file a termination statement in all cases.

___ 6. The security agreement determines most of the parties' rights and duties concerning the security interest.

___ 7. A secured party can release the collateral described in a financing statement even if the debtor has not paid the debt.

___ 8. Default occurs most commonly when a debtor fails to repay the loan for which his or her property served as collateral.

___ 9. After a default, and before a secured party disposes of the collateral, a debtor cannot exercise the right of redemption.

___ 10. When two secured parties have perfected security interests in the same collateral, generally the last to perfect has priority.

FILL-IN QUESTIONS

(Answers at the Back of the Book)

1. Generally, in a secured transaction, the ________________ (creditor/debtor) files a financing statement with the appropriate state office. When the debt is paid, the ________________ (creditor/debtor) may also send a termination statement to the officer with whom the financing statement was filed.

2. When two or more secured parties have perfected security interests in the same collateral, generally the ________ (first/last) to perfect has priority. When two conflicting security interests are unperfected, the ________ (first/last) to attach has priority.

MULTIPLE-CHOICE QUESTIONS

(Answers at the Back of the Book)

___ 1. Alpha Credit Corporation files a financing statement regarding a transaction with Beta Company. To be valid, the financing statement must contain all of the following *except*

a. a description of the collateral.
b. the debtor's name.
c. the reason for the transaction.
d. the secured party's name.

___ 2. Able Transport, Inc., buys a forklift, but does not make a payment on it for five months. The seller, Baker Equipment Company, repossesses it by towing it from a public street. Able sues Baker for breach of the peace. Able will likely

a. not prevail because Baker did not use judicial process.
b. not prevail because the repossession was not a breach of the peace.
c. prevail because Able did not default on the loan.
d. prevail because the repossession was a breach of the peace.

___ 3. Dan owns Eats Café, which he uses as collateral to borrow $10,000 from First State Bank. To be effective, the security agreement must include

a. a description that reasonably identifies the collateral only.
b. Dan's signature only.
c. a description that reasonably identifies the collateral and Dan's signature.
d. none of the above.

___ **4.** Great Trucks, Inc. (GTI), repossesses a truck (not a consumer good subject to a purchase-money security interest) from Highway Trucking Company, and decides to keep it instead of reselling it. GTI sends written notice of this intent to the debtor. GTI must also send notice to

a. only a junior lien claimant who has filed a statutory lien or security interest in the truck.
b. only a secured party from whom GTI has received notice of a claim in the truck.
c. any junior lien claimant who has filed a statutory lien or security interest and any secured party from whom GTI has received notice.
d. none of the above.

___ **5.** Irma, a debtor, wants to confirm the amount of his outstanding secured debt with Jiffy Loan Corporation. Irma can ask Jiffy to confirm her view of the debt, without charge, every

a. month.
b. six months.
c. twenty days.
d. year.

___ **6.** Kappa Credit, Inc., has a security interest in the proceeds from the sale of collateral owned by Local Stores Company. This interest may remain perfected for longer than twenty days after Local receives the proceeds

a. only if a filed financing statement covers the proceeds.
b. only if the proceeds are identifiable cash proceeds.
c. if a filed financing statement covers the proceeds or the proceeds are identifiable cash proceeds.
d. under any circumstances.

___ **7.** Nick borrows $5,000 from Modern Financial Corporation (MFC), which files a financing statement on May 1, but does not sign a security agreement until he receives the funds on May 5. He also borrows $5,000 from Omega Bank, which advances funds, files a financing statement, and signs a security agreement on May 2. He uses the same property as collateral for both loans. On his default, in a dispute over the collateral, MFC will

a. lose because Omega perfected first.
b. lose because Omega's interest attached first.
c. win because it filed first.
d. win because its interest attached first.

___ **8.** Peak Electronics Stores sell consumer products. To create a purchase-money security interest in a computer bought by Quinn, Peak must

a. assign to a collection agent a portion of Peak's accounts *payable*
b. assign to a collecting agent a portion of Peak's accounts *receivable*
c. extend credit for part or all of the purchase price of the computer.
d. refer Quinn to Rapid Cash Company, a third-party lender.

___ **9.** United Sales Company is incorporated in Virginia, with its chief executive office in Washington. Using its equipment as collateral, United borrows $5,000 from Zip Credit, Inc. To perfect its security interest, Zip should file its financing statement in

a. Virginia only.
b. Washington only.
c. Virginia and Washington.
d. the U.S. Federal Credit Agency office.

___ 10. Safe Loans, Inc., wants to perfect its security interest in collateral owned by Tech Corporation. Most likely, Safe should file a financing statement with

a. Tech's business agent's office.
b. the city manager.
c. the county clerk.
d. the secretary of state.

SHORT ESSAY QUESTIONS

1. What is the floating lien concept?

2. What are a secured party's rights on a debtor's default?

ISSUE SPOTTERS

(Answers at the Back of the Book)

1. Adam needs $500 to buy textbooks, and other supplies. Beth agrees to loan Adam $500, accepting as collateral Adam's computer. They put their agreement in writing. How can Beth let other creditors know of her interest in the computer?

2. Central Sales Company (CSC) borrows $1,000, using its inventory "present and after acquired" as collateral, from Delta Bank, which perfects its interest on May 1. On May 5, CSC buys from Excel Goods, Inc., new inventory in which CSC gives Excel a purchase-money security interest (PMSI). On the same day, Excel perfects its interest and notifies Delta. CSC takes possession of the new inventory on May 7. On June 1, CSC defaults on the loans. Whose security interest has priority?

3. First National Bank loans $5,000 to Gail to buy a car, which is used as collateral to secure the loan. Gail has paid less than 50 percent of the loan, when she defaults. First National could repossess and keep the car, but the bank does not want it. What are the alternatives?

SPECIAL INFORMATION FOR CPA CANDIDATES

The importance of the material in this chapter is evident in the number of questions that are devoted to it on the CPA examination. Traditionally, the UCC has made up about 25 percent of the exam, and of that 25 percent, about a third of the questions cover secured transactions. The concentration has been in four basic topics: attachment; perfection; priorities; and the rights of debtors, creditors, and others. Also frequently covered: purchase money security interests and the classification of goods as consumer goods, inventory, equipment, or farm products. All of these topics may be touched on in a single problem (or series of questions). To have a good grasp of how these topics interrelate, it may help to keep a diagram of the typical secured transaction in mind.

Chapter 29
Other Creditors' Remedies and Suretyship

WHAT THIS CHAPTER IS ABOUT

This chapter sets out the rights and remedies available to a creditor, when a debtor defaults, under laws other than UCC Article 9. Among those remedies are rights afforded by liens, and surety and guaranty agreements.

CHAPTER OUTLINE

I. LAWS ASSISTING CREDITORS

A. LIENS

A *lien* is a claim on a debtor's property that must be satisfied before the property is available to satisfy other creditor's claims. A lien has priority over an unperfected security interest. Mechanic's and artisan's liens have priority over perfected security interests.

1. Mechanic's Lien

Can be placed by a creditor on real property when a person contracts for labor, services, or materials to improve the property but does not pay.

a. When a Creditor Must File a Mechanic's Lien

Within a specific period, measured from the last date on which materials or labor were provided (usually within 60 to 120 days).

b. If the Owner Does Not Pay

The property can be sold to satisfy the debt. Notice of the foreclosure and sale must be given to the debtor in advance.

2. Artisan's Lien

A security device by which a creditor can recover from a debtor for labor and materials furnished in the repair of personal property.

a. The Creditor Must Possess the Property

Lien terminates if possession is voluntarily surrendered, unless the lienholder records notice of the lien in accord with state statutes.

b. If the Owner Does Not Pay

The property can be sold to satisfy the debt. Notice of the foreclosure and sale must be given to the debtor in advance.

3. Innkeeper's Lien

A security device placed on the baggage of guests for hotel charges that are not paid. The lien terminates when the charges are paid, or the baggage is returned or sold to satisfy the debt.

4. Judicial Liens

a. Attachment

Attachment is a court-ordered seizure and taking into custody of property before the entry of a final judgment for a past-due debt.

1) **After a Court Issues a Writ of Attachment**
A sheriff or other officer seizes nonexempt property. If the creditor prevails at trial, the property can be sold to satisfy the judgment.

2) **Limitations**
The due process clause of the Fourteenth Amendment limits a court's power to authorize seizure of a debtor's property without notice to the debtor or a hearing on the facts.

b. **Writ of Execution**
A *writ of execution* is an order, usually issued by a clerk of court, directing the sheriff to seize and sell any of the debtor's nonexempt property within the court's geographical jurisdiction.

1) **First, the Creditor Must Obtain a Judgment against the Debtor**
If the debtor does not pay, proceeds from the sale pay the judgment. The debtor can redeem the property any time before it is sold.

2) **Limitations**
Because of laws that exempt a debtor's homestead and designated items of personal property, many judgments are uncollectible.

B. GARNISHMENT
Garnishment is when a creditor collects a debt by seizing property of the debtor (such as wages or money in a bank account) that is being held by a third party (such as an employer or a bank), the garnishee.

1. **First, the Creditor Must Obtain a Judgment against the Debtor**
The garnishment judgment is then served on the garnishee so that, for example, part of the debtor's paycheck will be paid to the creditor.

2. **Limitations**
In some states, a creditor must go back to court for a separate order of garnishment for each pay period. Both federal and state laws limit the amount of money that can be garnished from a debtor's weekly take-home pay. State limits are often higher.

C. CREDITORS' COMPOSITION AGREEMENTS
A *creditors' composition agreement* is a contract between a debtor and his or her creditors for discharge of the debtor's liquidated debts on payment of a sum less than that owed.

D. MORTGAGE FORECLOSURE
A mortgagee can foreclose on the mortgaged property if the debtor defaults. The usual method is a judicial sale. The proceeds are applied to the debt.

1. **Equity of Redemption**
A mortgagor can redeem the property any time before the sale (and, in some states, within a certain period of time after the sale).

2. **Deficiency Judgment**
If the proceeds do not cover the foreclosure costs and the debt, the mortgagee can recover the difference from the mortgagor by obtaining a deficiency judgment (in a separate legal action after the foreclosure).

E. ASSIGNMENT FOR THE BENEFIT OF CREDITORS
A debtor may transfer title to his or her assets to a trustee or assignee, who sells them and pays each creditor in proportion to the debt. Each creditor may accept (and discharge the debt) or reject (and attempt to collect another way). Bankruptcy may supersede the assignment (see Chapter 30).

II. SURETYSHIP AND GUARANTY

A. SURETYSHIP

Suretyship is a promise by a third person to be responsible for a debtor's obligation. The promise does not have to be in writing. A surety is primarily liable—a creditor can demand payment from the surety the moment the debt is due.

B. GUARANTY

A *guaranty* is a promise to be secondarily liable for the debt or default of another. A guarantor pays only after the debtor defaults and the creditor has made an attempt to collect from the debtor. A guaranty must be in writing unless the main-purpose exception applies (see Chapter 14). A guaranty may be continuing (to cover a series of transactions), unlimited or limited in time and amount, and absolute (immediate liability on the debtor's default) or conditional (liability only a certain event).

C. DEFENSES OF THE SURETY AND THE GUARANTOR

To avoid payment, a surety (guarantor) may use the following defenses.

1. Material Change to the Contract between Debtor and Creditor

Without obtaining the consent of the surety (guarantor), a gratuitous surety is discharged completely and a compensated surety is discharged to the extent he or she suffers a loss.

2. The Principal Obligation Is Paid or Valid Tender Is Made

The surety (guarantor) is discharged from the obligation.

3. Most of the Defenses of the Principal Debtor

Defenses that cannot be used: the debtor's incapacity, bankruptcy, and the statute of limitations.

4. A Surety or Guarantor's Own Defenses

For example, fraud by the creditor to induce the surety (guarantor) to guarantee the debt (such as the creditor's failure to inform the surety of facts that would substantially increase the surety's risk).

5. A Creditor's Surrender or Impairment of the Collateral

Without the surety's (guarantor's) consent, releases the surety to the extent of any loss suffered from the creditor's actions.

D. RIGHTS OF THE SURETY AND THE GUARANTOR

If the surety (guarantor) pays the debt—

1. Right of Subrogation

The surety (guarantor) may pursue any remedies that were available to the creditor against the debtor.

2. Right of Reimbursement

The surety is entitled to receive from the debtor all outlays made on behalf of the suretyship arrangement.

3. Co-Sureties' Right of Contribution

A surety who pays more than his or her proportionate share on a debtor's default is entitled to recover from co-sureties.

III. PROTECTION FOR DEBTORS

A. EXEMPTIONS

1. Homestead

Each state allows a debtor to retain the family home (in some states only if debtor has a family) in its entirety or up to a specified amount.

2. **Personal Property**
Often exempt: household furniture up to a specified amount; clothing and other personal possessions; a vehicle (or vehicles) (up to a specified amount); certain animals, usually livestock but including pets; and equipment that the debtor uses in a business or trade.

B. **SPECIAL PROTECTION FOR CONSUMER DEBTORS**
A Federal Trade Commission rule limits the rights of a holder in due course (HDC) who holds a negotiable promissory note executed by a consumer as part of a consumer transaction (see Chapter 26). Other laws include the Truth-in-Lending Act, which protects consumers by requiring creditors to disclose certain information when making loans (see Chapter 44).

TRUE-FALSE QUESTIONS

(Answers at the Back of the Book)

___ 1. A mechanic's lien involves personal property.

___ 2. An employer can dismiss an employee due to garnishment for any one debt.

___ 3. A creditor's composition agreement discharges only the debtor's debts owed to those creditors who agree.

___ 4. An innkeeper's lien is placed on the baggage of guests for agreed-on hotel charges that remain unpaid.

___ 5. A writ of attachment is a court order to seize a debtor's property *before* the entry of a final judgment in a creditor's lawsuit against the debtor.

___ 6. A writ of execution is a court order to seize a debtor's property *after* the entry of a final judgment in a creditor's lawsuit against the debtor.

___ 7. Under an assignment for the benefit of creditors, the creditors must accept whatever payment is offered.

___ 8. A surety or guarantor is discharged from his or her obligation when the principal debtor pays the debt.

___ 9. To avoid liability on an obligation to a creditor, a surety cannot use any defenses available to the debtor.

___ 10. A surety cannot use the principal debtor's bankruptcy as a defense against the surety's payment of the debt.

FILL-IN QUESTIONS

(Answers at the Back of the Book)

A ______________ (contract of suretyship/guaranty contract) is a promise to a creditor made by a third person to be responsible for a debtor's obligation. A ______________ (guarantor/surety) is primarily liable: the creditor can hold the ______________ (guarantor/surety) responsible for payment of the debt when the debt is due, without first exhausting all remedies against the debtor. A ______________ (contract of suretyship/guaranty contract) also includes a promise to answer for a principal's obligation, but a ______________ (guarantor/surety) is secondarily liable—that is, the principal must first default, and ordinarily, a creditor must have attempted to collect from the principal, because ordinarily a debtor would not otherwise be declared in default.

MULTIPLE-CHOICE QUESTIONS

(Answers at the Back of the Book)

___ **1.** Fran leaves her necklace with Gold Jewelers to be repaired. When Fran returns for the necklace, she says, "I'll pay for the repair later." Gold can

a. keep the necklace for a reasonable time but must return it whether or not Fran pays.
b. keep the necklace until Fran pays.
c. keep the necklace whether or not Fran pays.
d. not keep the necklace.

___ **2.** Adam borrows money from Best Credit Company. If Adam defaults, to use attachment as a remedy Best must first

a. commence a suit against Adam.
b. succeed in a suit against Adam.
c. be unable to collect the amount of a judgment against Adam.
d. all of the above.

___ **3.** **Based on a Sample CPA Exam Question.** Ed's $2,500 debt to Owen is past due. To collect money from Ed's wages to pay the debt, Owen can use

a. an order of receivership.
b. a writ of attachment.
c. a writ of execution.
d. garnishment.

___ **4.** Eve owes Fred $200,000. A court awards Fred a judgment in the amount of the debt. To satisfy the judgment, Eve's home is sold at public auction for $150,000. The state homestead exemption is $50,000. Fred gets

a. $50,000.
b. $100,000.
c. $150,000.
d. nothing.

___ **5.** Great Company wants to borrow money from First State Bank. The bank insists that Hal, Great Company's president, agree to be personally liable for payment if Great defaults. If Hal agrees, he is

a. a guarantor only.
b. a surety only.
c. a guarantor and a surety.
d. none of the above.

___ **6.** Ira and Jill agree to act as guarantors on a loan made by Ken. Ken defaults on the payments and Jill refuses to pay. If Ira pays the debt, he can recover from

a. Ken and Jill under the right of reimbursement.
b. Ken and Jill under the right of proportionate liability.
c. Ken under the right of subrogation and Jill under the right of contribution.
d. none of the above.

___ 7. Aaron owes Barb $500 but refuses to pay. To collect, Barb files a suit against Aaron and wins. Aaron still refuses to pay. To collect the amount of the judgment, Barb can use

a. an assignment for the benefit of creditors.
b. a creditor's composition agreement.
c. a foreclosure.
d. a writ of execution.

___ 8. John owes First State Bank $40,000, secured by a mortgage on John's office building. John fails to make payments on the loan. To obtain the amount that is owed, the bank can use

a. an assignment for the benefit of creditors.
b. a creditor's composition agreement.
c. a foreclosure.
d. a writ of execution.

___ 9. Gail agrees to act, without compensation, as a surety for Mary's loan from Ace Credit. Later, without Gail's knowledge, Mary and Ace agree to extend the time for repayment and to increase the interest rate. Gail's obligation

a. remains the same.
b. changes to match Mary's obligation.
c. is discharged to the extent of any loss caused by the extension of time.
d. is discharged completely.

___ 10. Lee agrees to act, without compensation, as a guarantor for Paula's loan from Ron. Collateral for the loan is Paula's car, which Paula gives to Ron. Later, without Lee's knowledge, Paula and Ron agree to increase the interest rate and Ron returns the car to Paula. Lee's obligation

a. remains the same.
b. is discharged to the extent of the additional interest.
c. is discharged to the extent of any loss caused by surrender of the car.
d. is discharged completely.

SHORT ESSAY QUESTIONS

1. What is a lien? What are the four ways in which a lien can arise? What is a lienholder's priority compared to other creditors?

2. What are the differences between contracts of suretyship and guaranty contracts?

ISSUE SPOTTERS

(Answers at the Back of the Book)

1. Joe contracts with Larry of Midwest Roofing to fix Joe's roof. Joe pays half of the contract price in advance. Larry and Midwest complete the job, but Joe refuses to pay the rest of the price. What can Larry and Midwest do?

2. Pat wants to borrow $10,000 from Quality Loan Company to buy a new car, but Quality refuses to lend the money unless Ron cosigns the note. Ron cosigns and makes three of the payments when Pat fails to do so. Can Ron get this money from Pat?

3. Ann borrows $1,200 from Bill. Carol, Dian, and Ernie agree to act as co-sureties for the debt in equal proportions. Ann defaults and Bill collects all of the unpaid amount ($900) from Carol. Are Dian and Ernie discharged of any obligation? If not, how much do they owe and to whom do they owe it?

SPECIAL INFORMATION FOR CPA CANDIDATES

Suretyship is usually tested on the CPA examination in the section covering the relationship between debtors and creditors. Questions regarding suretyship have also been included in the contracts section as part of a Statute of Frauds question or a question concerning consideration. One common fact situation presented on the exam has involved a surety who is not paid for his or her suretyship. Consideration is usually present elsewhere in the question, however, and thus, its lack is not a defense for that surety. Another frequent scenario involves co-sureties—be certain that you grasp the rights of the parties in such circumstances.

Chapter 30
Bankruptcy Law

WHAT THIS CHAPTER IS ABOUT

This chapter covers bankruptcy law. Congressional authority to regulate bankruptcies comes from Article I, Section 8, of the U.S. Constitution. Bankruptcy law (1) protects a debtor by giving him or her a fresh start and (2) ensures equitable treatment to creditors competing for a debtor's assets.

CHAPTER OUTLINE

I. BANKRUPTCY PROCEEDINGS

Bankruptcy proceedings are held in federal bankruptcy courts. Current law is based on the Bankruptcy Reform Act of 1978 (the Bankruptcy Code, or the Code). Relief can be granted under the Code's Chapter 7, Chapter 11, Chapter 12, or Chapter 13.

II. LIQUIDATION PROCEEDINGS (CHAPTER 7)

This is the most familiar type of bankruptcy proceeding. A debtor declares his or her debts and gives all assets to a trustee, who sells the nonexempt assets and distributes the proceeds to creditors.

A. WHO CAN FILE FOR A LIQUIDATION

Any "person"—individuals, partnerships, and corporations (spouses can file jointly)—except railroads, insurance companies, banks, savings and loan associations, and credit unions.

B. FILING THE PETITION

1. Voluntary Bankruptcy

a. The Debtor Files a Petition with the Court

The petition includes schedules (lists) of (1) creditors and the debt to each, (2) the debtor's financial affairs, (3) the debtor's property, and (4) current income and expenses.

b. Filing of the Petition Constitutes an Order for Relief

The clerk of the court must give the trustee and creditors notice of the order within not more than twenty days.

c. Substantial Abuse

A court can dismiss a petition if granting it would constitute substantial abuse (if the debtor seeks only an advantage over creditors and his or her financial situation does not warrant a discharge of debts) [11 U.S.C. Section 707(b)].

2. Involuntary Bankruptcy

A debtor's creditors can force the debtor into bankruptcy proceedings.

a. Who Can Be Forced into Involuntary Proceedings

A debtor with twelve or more creditors, three or more of whom (with unsecured claims of at least \$11,625) file a petition. A debtor with fewer than twelve creditors, one or more of whom (with a claim of \$11,625) files. Not a farmer or a charitable institution.

b. When an Order for Relief Will Be Entered

If the debtor does not challenge the petition, the debtor is generally not paying debts as they come due, or a receiver, assignee, or custodian took possession of the debtor's property within 120 days before the petition was filed.

C. AUTOMATIC STAY

When a petition is filed, an automatic stay suspends all action by creditors against the debtor. The adequate protection doctrine protects secured creditors by requiring payments, or other collateral or relief, to the extent that the stay may cause the value of their collateral to decrease.

D. PROPERTY OF THE ESTATE

1. What Property Is Included in the Debtor's Estate

Interests in property presently held; community property; property transferred in a transaction voidable by the trustee; proceeds and profits; after-acquired property; interests in gifts, inheritances, property settlements, and life insurance death proceeds to which the debtor becomes entitled within 180 days after filing.

2. What Property Is Not Included

Property acquired after the filing of the petition except as noted above.

E. CREDITORS' MEETING AND CLAIMS

Within "not less than ten days or more than thirty days," the court calls a meeting of creditors, at which the debtor answers questions. Within ninety days of the meeting, a creditor must file a proof of claim. The proof lists the creditor's name and address, as well as the amount of the debt.

F. EXEMPTIONS

1. Federal Law

Exempts such property as interests in a residence to $17,425, a motor vehicle to $2,775, household goods to $9,300, and tools of a trade to $1,750, and the rights to receive Social Security and other benefits.

2. State Law

Most states preclude the use of federal exemptions; others allow a debtor to choose between state and federal. State exemptions may include different value limits and exempt different property.

G. THE TRUSTEE

After the order for relief, an interim trustee is appointed to preside over the debtor's property until the first meeting of creditors, when a permanent trustee is elected. A trustee's duty is to collect and reduce to money the property of the estate and distribute the proceeds.

1. Trustee's Powers

A trustee has the same rights as (1) a lien creditor with priority over an unperfected secured party and (2) a bona fide purchaser of real property from the debtor.

2. Voidable Rights

A trustee can use any reason (fraud, duress, etc.) that a debtor can use to obtain the return of property.

3. Preferences

A trustee can recover payments made or property transferred (or the value of the property if a preferred creditor has sold it to an innocent third party) by a debtor (1) within ninety days before the petition and (2) for a preexisting debt.

a. Insiders or Fraud

If a creditor is an insider (partner, corporate officer, relative) or a transfer is fraudulent, a trustee may recover transfers made within one year before filing.

b. **Transfers That Are Not Preferences**
Payment for services rendered within ten to fifteen days before the payment; payment received in the ordinary course of business (such as payment of a phone bill); transfer of property up to $600.

4. **Liens on Debtor's Property**
A trustee can avoid statutory liens that first became effective when the bankruptcy petition was filed or the debtor became insolvent, and any lien against a bona fide purchaser that was not enforceable on the date of the filing.

5. **Fraudulent Transfers**
A trustee can avoid fraudulent transfers made within one year of the filing of the petition or if they were made with the intent to delay, defraud, or hinder a creditor. Transfers for less than reasonably equivalent consideration may also be avoided if, by making them, the debtor became insolvent or was left in business with little capital.

H. DISTRIBUTION OF PROPERTY

Any amount remaining after the property is distributed to creditors is turned over to the debtor.

1. **Secured Creditors**
Within thirty days of the petition or before the first creditors' meeting (whichever is first), a debtor must state whether he or she will retain secured collateral (or claim it as exempt, etc.). The trustee must enforce the statement within forty-five days. If the collateral does not cover the debt, the secured creditor is an unsecured creditor for the difference.

2. **Unsecured Creditors**
Paid in the order of priority. Each class is paid before the next class is entitled to anything. The order of priority is—

a. Administrative expenses (court costs, trustee and attorney fees).
b. In an involuntary bankruptcy, expenses incurred by the debtor in the ordinary course of business from the filing of the petition to the appointment of the trustee or the issuance of an order for relief.
c. Unpaid wages, salaries, and commissions earned within ninety days of the petition, to $4,650 per claimant. A claim in excess is a claim of a general creditor (no. i below).
d. Unsecured claims for contributions to employee benefit plans, limited to services performed within 180 days before the petition and $4,650 per employee.
e. Claims by farmers and fishers, to $4,650, against storage or processing facilities.
f. Consumer deposits to $2,100 given to the debtor before the petition to buy, lease, or rent property or services that were not received.
g. Claims for paternity, alimony, maintenance, and support.
h. Taxes and penalties due to the government.
i. Claims of general creditors.

I. DISCHARGE

A discharge voids any judgment on a discharged debt and prohibits any action to collect a discharged debt. A co-debtor's liability is not affected.

1. **Exceptions—Debts That May Not Be Discharged**
Claims for back taxes, amounts borrowed to pay back taxes, goods obtained by fraud, debts that were not listed in the petition, alimony, child support, student loans, certain cash advances, and others.

2. **Objections—Debtors Who May Not Receive a Discharge**
Those who conceal property with the intent to hinder, delay, or defraud a creditor; who fail to explain a loss of assets; or who have been granted a discharge within six years of the filing of the petition.

3. Revocation of Discharge

A discharge may be revoked within one year if the debtor was fraudulent or dishonest during the bankruptcy proceedings.

J. REAFFIRMATION OF DEBT

A debtor's agreement to pay an otherwise dischargeable debt must be made before a discharge is granted and must usually be approved by the court. Can be rescinded within sixty days or before the discharge is granted, whichever is later.

III. REORGANIZATIONS (CHAPTER 11)

The creditors and debtor formulate a plan under which the debtor pays a portion of the debts, is discharged of the rest, and continues in business.

A. WHO IS ELIGIBLE FOR RELIEF UNDER CHAPTER 11

Any debtor (except a stockbroker or a commodities broker) who is eligible for Chapter 7 relief. Used most commonly by corporate debtors. The same principles apply that govern liquidation (automatic stay, etc.).

B. WHY A CASE MAY BE DISMISSED

Creditors may prefer a *workout* (a privately negotiated settlement) to bankruptcy proceedings, or there may be other reasons (inability to effect a plan, unreasonable delay by the debtor that is prejudicial to creditors, etc.).

C. DEBTOR IN POSSESSION

On entry of an order for relief, the debtor continues to operate his or her business as a debtor in possession (DIP).

1. If Gross Mismanagement Is Shown

The court may appoint a trustee (or receiver) to operate the business. This may also be done if it is in the best interests of the estate.

2. DIP's Role Is Similar to That of a Trustee in a Liquidation

The DIP can avoid pre-petition preferential payments and fraudulent transfers and decide whether to cancel pre-petition executory contracts.

3. Strong-Arm Clause

A DIP can avoid any obligation or transfer that could be avoided by (1) a creditor who extended credit at the time of bankruptcy and who consequently obtained (a) a lien or (b) a writ of execution that was returned unsatisfied; and (2) a bona fide purchaser of real property, if the transfer was perfected at the time of the bankruptcy.

D. COLLECTIVE BARGAINING AGREEMENTS

Can be rejected if the debtor first proposes modifications to the union and the union fails to adopt them without good cause. The debtor must (1) provide the union with information needed to evaluate the proposal and (2) confer in good faith to attempt a mutually satisfactory agreement.

E. CREDITORS' COMMITTEES

A committee of unsecured creditors is appointed to consult with the trustee or DIP. Other committees may represent special-interest creditors. Some small businesses can avoid creditors' committees.

F. THE REORGANIZATION PLAN

1. Who Can File a Plan

Only debtor within the first 120 days (100 days in some cases) after date of the order for relief. Any other party, if debtor does not meet the deadline or fails to obtain creditor consent within 180 days (or 160 days).

2. **What the Plan Must Do**
Conserve and administer the debtor's assets in the hope of a return to solvency; be fair and equitable ("in the best interests of the creditors"); designate classes of claims and interests; specify the treatment to be afforded the classes; and provide an adequate means for execution.

3. **The Plan Is Submitted to Creditors for Acceptance**
Each class adversely affected by a plan must accept it (two-thirds of the total claims must approve). If only one class accepts, the court may confirm it under the Code's cram-down provision if the plan does not discriminate unfairly against any creditors. The plan is binding on confirmation—the debtor is given a discharge from all claims not within the plan (except those that would be denied in a liquidation).

IV. INDIVIDUALS' REPAYMENT PLANS (CHAPTER 13)

A. WHO IS ELIGIBLE
Individuals (not partnerships or corporations) with regular income and unsecured debts of less than $290,525 or secured debts of less than $871,550.

B. VOLUNTARY FILING ONLY
A Chapter 13 case can be initiated by the filing of a voluntary petition only. A trustee is appointed.

C. AUTOMATIC STAY
On the filing of a petition, an automatic stay enjoins creditors from taking action against co-obligors of the debtor. If a creditor asks to vacate the stay against a co-debtor, unless written objection is filed, twenty days later the stay against the co-debtor is automatically terminated without a hearing.

D. THE REPAYMENT PLAN
The plan must provide for (1) turnover to the trustee of the debtor's future income, (2) full payment of all claims entitled to priority, and (3) the same treatment of each claim within a particular class.

1. **Filing and Confirming the Plan**
Only the debtor can file a plan, which the court will confirm if (1) the secured creditors accept it, (2) it provides that creditors retain their liens and the value of the property to be distributed to them is not less than the secured portion of their claims, or (3) the debtor surrenders the property securing the claim to the creditors.

2. **Payments under the Plan**
The time for payment must be less than three years (five years, with court approval). The payments must be timely, or the court can convert the case to a liquidation or dismiss the petition. Before completion of payments, the plan may be modified at the request of the debtor, the trustee, or an unsecured creditor.

3. **Objection to the Plan**
Over the objection of the trustee or an unsecured creditor, the court may approve a plan only if (1) the value of the property to be distributed is equal to the amount of the claims, or (2) all the debtor's disposable income during the plan will be used to make payments.

E. DISCHARGE
After completion of all payments, all debts provided for by the plan are discharged. A discharge obtained by fraud can be revoked within one year.

V. FAMILY-FARMER PLANS (CHAPTER 12)
Chapter 12 is nearly identical to Chapter 13. Eligible debtors include a family farmer whose gross income is at least 50 percent farm dependent and whose debts are at least 80 percent farm related (total debt must not exceed $1.5 million), and a partnership or closely held corporation (at least 50 percent owned by a farm family).

TRUE-FALSE QUESTIONS

(Answers at the Back of the Book)

___ 1. A debtor must be insolvent to file a voluntary petition under Chapter 7.

___ 2. The filing of a petition for bankruptcy will not stay most legal actions against the debtor.

___ 3. In a bankruptcy proceeding, any creditor's claim is allowed automatically unless contested by the trustee, the debtor, or another creditor.

___ 4. The same principles cover the filing of a liquidation petition and a reorganization proceeding.

___ 5. A bankruptcy may be commenced by involuntary petition under Chapter 13.

___ 6. Filing for bankruptcy under Chapter 13 is less expensive and less complicated than other bankruptcy proceedings.

___ 7. Under Chapter 13, a discharge obtained by fraud can be revoked within one year.

___ 8. When a business debtor files for Chapter 11 protection, the debtor is not allowed to continue in business.

___ 9. No small business can avoid creditors' committees under Chapter 11.

___ 10. Bankruptcy proceedings are held in federal bankruptcy courts.

FILL-IN QUESTIONS

(Answers at the Back of the Book)

Liquidation is the purpose of Chapter _______ (7/11/13). Reorganization is the purpose of Chapter _______ (7/11/13). Adjustment is the purpose of Chapter _______ (7/11/13). Under Chapter _______ (7/11/13), nonexempt property is sold, with proceeds distributed in a certain priority to classes of creditors, and dischargeable debts are terminated. Under Chapter _______ (7/11/13), a plan for reorganization is submitted, and if it is approved and followed, debts are discharged. Under Chapter _______ (7/11/13), a plan must be approved if the debtor turns over all disposable income for a three-year period, after which debts are discharged. The advantages of Chapter _______ (7/11/13) include the debtor's opportunity for a fresh start. The advantages of Chapter _______ (7/11/13) include the debtor's continuation in business under a plan that allows for reorganization of debts. The advantages of Chapter _____ (7/11/13) include the debtor's continuation in business and discharge of most debts.

MULTIPLE-CHOICE QUESTIONS

(Answers at the Back of the Book)

___ 1. Lora is the sole proprietor of Diners Cafe, which owes debts in an amount more than Lora believes she and the cafe can repay. The creditors agree that liquidating the business would not be in their best interests. To stay in business, Lora could file for bankruptcy under

a. Chapter 7 only.
b. Chapter 11 only.
c. Chapter 13 only.
d. Chapter 11 or Chapter 13.

___ 2. Mike's monthly income is $2,500, his monthly expenses are $2,100, and his debts are nearly $15,000. If he applied the difference between his income and expenses to pay off the debts, they could be eliminated within three years. The provision in the Bankruptcy Code that covers this plan is

a. Chapter 7.
b. Chapter 11.
c. Chapter 12.
d. Chapter 13.

___ 3. National Corporation has not paid any of its fifteen creditors, six of whom have unsecured claims of more than $8,000.The creditors can force National into bankruptcy under

a. Chapter 7 only.
b. Chapter 11 only.
c. Chapter 13 only.
d. Chapter 7 or Chapter 11.

___ 4. Owen files a bankruptcy petition under Chapter 7 to have his debts discharged. The debts most likely to be discharged include claims for

a. alimony and child support.
b. back taxes accruing within three years before the petition was filed.
c. certain fines and penalties payable to the government.
d. student loans, if the payment would impose undue hardship on Owen.

___ 5. Beth's monthly income is $2,000, her monthly expenses are $2,800, and her debts are nearly $40,000. A debtor in Beth's position who files for bankruptcy would most likely seek relief under

a. Chapter 7.
b. Chapter 11.
c. Chapter 12.
d. Chapter 13.

___ 6. **Based on a Sample CPA Exam Question.** Pat files a Chapter 7 petition for a discharge in bankruptcy. Pat may be denied a discharge if Pat

a. fails to explain a loss of assets.
b. fails to list a debt.
c. owes back taxes.
d. owes child support payments.

___ 7. Donna and Tom make down payments on goods to be received from Eagle Furniture Store. Before the goods are delivered, Eagle files for bankruptcy. Besides consumers like Donna and Tom, Eagle owes wages to its employees and taxes to the government. In what order will these debts be paid?

a. Unpaid wages, consumer deposits, taxes
b. Taxes, consumer deposits, unpaid wages
c. Consumer deposits, unpaid wages, taxes
d. Unpaid wages, taxes, consumer deposits

___ 8. Ann is appointed trustee of Bill's estate in bankruptcy. To collect the property of Bill's estate, Ann can set aside

a. a payment within the ordinary course of business only.
b. a transfer made within ninety days of the filing of the petition in preference to one creditor over others.
c. a payment with the course of business and a transfer within ninety days in preference to one creditor.
d. none of the above.

___ **9.** Regional Stores, Inc., files for bankruptcy. A corporation can file a petition for bankruptcy under

a. Chapter 7 only.
b. Chapter 11 only.
c. Chapter 13 only.
d. Chapter 7 or Chapter 11.

___ **10.** As a bankruptcy trustee, Dan has the power to avoid

a. fraudulent transfers only.
b. so-called preferential payments only.
c. transactions that the debtor could rightfully avoid, or cancel, only.
d. fraudulent transfers, preferences, and transactions that the debtor could rightfully avoid.

SHORT ESSAY QUESTIONS

1. Compare Chapters 7, 11, 12, and 13, discussing, for each chapter, the purpose or function, who is eligible for relief , whether proceedings can be initiated voluntarily or involuntarily, procedures leading to discharge, and the advantages.

2. How are secured creditors protected from losing the value of their security as a result of an automatic stay?

ISSUE SPOTTERS

(Answers at the Back of the Book)

1. Star Company's creditors include Town Bank with a perfected security interest in Star's building and equipment, United Construction with a mechanic's lien on the building that predates Town Bank's interest, and Variety Suppliers, Inc., with an unperfected security interest. Star files a petition for a Chapter 7 liquidation. In what order will the creditors be paid?

2. Adam is a vice president for Beta Company. On May 1, Adam loans Beta $10,000. On June 1, the company repays the loan. On July 1, Beta files for bankruptcy. Carl is appointed trustee. Can Carl recover the $10,000 paid to Adam on June 1?

3. After graduating from college, Tina works briefly as a salesperson before filing for bankruptcy. As part of her petition, Tina reveals her only debts as student loans, taxes accruing within the last year, and a claim against her based on misuse of customers' funds during her employment. Are these debts dischargeable in bankruptcy?

SPECIAL INFORMATION FOR CPA CANDIDATES

On the CPA examination, bankruptcy is tested as part of the section on creditors and debtors, which also tests on the material in the previous chapter. Topics that have been tested in the past include the requirements for filing for bankruptcy under Chapter 7, the basic steps of a bankruptcy, a general knowledge of Chapter 11 and Chapter 13, and specific coverage of preferential transfers, discharge, and debts that are not discharged in a bankruptcy proceeding. The priority of those with competing claims to the collateral is also usually included in questions on the exam.

CUMULATIVE HYPOTHETICAL PROBLEM FOR UNIT SIX—INCLUDING CHAPTERS 28–30

(Answers at the Back of the Book)

Omega Computers, Inc., sells computers to consumers.

___ **1.** Alan fixes the roof of Omega's office building, but Omega does not pay. Bob fixes one of Omega's trucks, but Omega does not pay. Bob does not return the truck to Omega. Alan and Bob place a mechanic's lien and an artisan's lien on Omega's property. Before foreclosure, notice must be given to Omega by

a. Alan only.
b. Bob only.
c. Alan and Bob.
d. none of the above.

___ **2.** In the course of business, Omega borrows money from First National Bank. Carol co-signs the loan as a surety. Omega defaults on the loan, and Carol pays the entire amount. To collect from Omega, Carol has the right of

a. contribution.
b. exemption.
c. exoneration.
d. subrogation.

___ **3.** Omega buys inventory from Beta Digital Products. Beta finances the purchase, accepts the inventory as security, and perfects its interest. Under UCC Article 9, perfection of a security interest will *not* affect the rights of

a. a buyer in the ordinary course of business.
b. a subsequent secured creditor.
c. the trustee in Omega's bankruptcy.
d. all of the above.

___ **4.** Omega files a voluntary petition in bankruptcy under Chapter 11. A reorganization plan is filed with the court. Normally, the court will confirm a Chapter 11 plan if it is accepted by

a. Omega.
b. Omega's secured creditors.
c. Omega's shareholders.
d. Omega's unsecured creditors.

___ **5.** Omega's Chapter 11 plan is confirmed, and a final decree is entered. Omega will

a. be discharged from all debts except as otherwise provided by the law.
b. be liquidated.
c. be operated in business by the bankruptcy trustee.
d. not be allowed to continue in the same business.

QUESTIONS ON THE FOCUS ON LEGAL REASONING FOR UNIT SIX—*IN RE STANTON*

(Answers at the Back of the Book)

___ **1.** Ann owns Beta Corporation. On Beta's behalf, Ann borrows money from Corporate Bank in exchange for a mortgage on Ann's house. Ann files for personal bankruptcy. Under the holding in *In re Stanton,* the bank's lien for the money could

a. be avoided by the bankruptcy trustee to the extent of the entire price of the house.
b. be avoided by the trustee to the extent of the full amount of the loan.
c. be avoided by the trustee to the extent of the unpaid amount of the loan.
d. not be avoided by the trustee.

___ **2.** In the previous question, suppose that the bank continually advanced money on the loan at its option, even after Ann files for bankruptcy. In the opinion of the majority in *In re Stanton,* the bank's post-petition advances would be

a. eliminated by the trustee.
b. equal to the trustee.
c. junior to the trustee.
d. senior to the trustee.

___ **3.** According to the reasoning of the dissent in *In re Stanton,* the bank's post-petition advances in the previous problem could

a. be avoided by the trustee to the extent of the entire price of the house.
b. be avoided by the trustee to the extent of full amount of the advances.
c. be avoided by the trustee to the extent of the unpaid amount of the entire loan.
d. not be avoided by the trustee.

QUESTIONS ON THE FOCUS ON ETHICS FOR UNIT SIX—CREDITORS' RIGHTS AND BANKRUPTCY

(Answers at the Back of the Book)

___ **1.** Ace Credit Collection, Inc., utilizes "self-help" repossession on its debtors' defaults. This remedy simplifies the process of repossession because

a. it can be done without judicial process.
b. it is less stressful for debtors.
c. it provides an incentive for confrontations with debtors.
d. the UCC clearly defines what constitutes "breach of the peace."

___ **2.** Best Credit Company lends money to Carl, a farmer. Carl secures the loan with his livestock's feed. If Best also obtains a security interest in the proceeds from the feed, and Carl defaults, Best can

a. not suffer any loss.
b. suffer a loss of no more than half of the value of the loan.
c. suffer a loss of no more than three-fourths of the value of the loan.
d. suffer a total loss.

____ 3. City Bank lends money to Don, taking a security interest in his assets. Later, Don files a bankruptcy petition. From the bank's point of view, once Don is in bankruptcy, his assets have

a. diminished value, or no value.
b. enhanced, or greater, value.
c. the same value as before the petition.
d. unique value.

Chapter 31
Agency Formation and Duties

WHAT THIS CHAPTER IS ABOUT

This chapter covers some of the aspects of agency relationships, including how they are formed and the duties involved. An agency relationship involves two parties: the principal and the agent. Agency relationships are essential to a corporation, which can function and enter into contracts only through its agents.

CHAPTER OUTLINE

I. AGENCY RELATIONSHIPS

In an agency relationship, the parties agree that the agent will act on behalf and instead of the principal in negotiating and transacting business with third persons.

A. EMPLOYER-EMPLOYEE RELATIONSHIPS

Normally, all employees who deal with third parties are deemed to be agents. Statutes covering workers' compensation and so on apply only to employer-employee relationships.

B. EMPLOYER–INDEPENDENT CONTRACTOR RELATIONSHIPS

Those who hire independent contractors have no control over the details of their physical performance. Independent contractors can be agents.

C. DETERMINING EMPLOYEE STATUS

The greater an employer's control over the work, the more likely it is that the worker is an employee. Another key factor is whether the employer withholds taxes from payments to the worker and pays unemployment and Social Security taxes covering the worker.

II. FORMATION OF THE AGENCY RELATIONSHIP

Consideration is not required. A principal must have capacity to contract, but anyone can be an agent. An agency can be created for any legal purpose.

A. AGENCY BY AGREEMENT

Normally, an agency must be based on an agreement that the agent will act for the principal. Such an agreement can be an express written contract or can be implied by conduct.

B. AGENCY BY RATIFICATION

A person who is not an agent (or who is an agent acting outside the scope of his or her authority) may make a contract on behalf of another (a principal). If the principal approves or affirms that contract by word or by action, an agency relationship is created by ratification (see Chapter 32).

C. AGENCY BY ESTOPPEL

1. The Principal's Actions

When a principal causes a third person to believe that another person is his or her agent, and the third person deals with the supposed agent, the principal is estopped to deny the agency relationship.

2. **The Third Party's Reasonable Belief**
The third person must prove that he or she reasonably believed that an agency relationship existed and that the agent had authority—that an ordinary, prudent person familiar with business practice and custom would have been justified in concluding that the agent had authority.

D. AGENCY BY OPERATION OF LAW
A court may find an agency relationship in the absence of a formal agreement. This may occur in family relationships or in an emergency, when the agent's failure to act outside the scope of his or her authority would cause the principal substantial loss.

III. DUTIES OF AGENTS AND PRINCIPALS
The principal-agent relationship is fiduciary.

A. AGENT'S DUTIES TO PRINCIPAL

1. **Performance**
An agent must use reasonable diligence and skill (the degree of skill of a reasonable person under similar circumstances), unless an agent claims special skills (such as those of an accountant), in which case the agent is expected to use those skills.

2. **Notification**
An agent must notify the principal of all matters concerning the agency. Notice to the agent is considered to be notice to the principal.

3. **Loyalty**
An agent must act solely for the benefit of the principal (not in the interest of the agent or a third party).

   a. **Confidentiality**
   Any information or knowledge acquired through the agency relationship is confidential. It cannot be disclosed during the agency or after its termination.

   b. **Agent's Loyalty Must Be Undivided**
   An agent employed by a principal to buy cannot buy from himself or herself, and an agent employed to sell cannot become the purchaser, without the principal's consent.

4. **Obedience**
When an agent acts on behalf of the principal, the agent must follow all lawful instructions of the principal. Exceptions include emergencies and instances in which instructions are not clearly stated.

5. **Accounting**
An agent must keep and make available to the principal an account of everything received and paid out on behalf of the principal. An agent must keep separate accounts for the principal's funds.

B. PRINCIPAL'S DUTIES TO AGENT

1. **Compensation**
A principal must pay an agent for services rendered (unless the agent does not act for money). Payment must be timely. If no amount has been agreed to, the principal owes the customary amount for such services.

2. **Reimbursement and Indemnification**
A principal must (1) reimburse the agent for money paid at the principal's request or for necessary expenses and (2) indemnify an agent for liability incurred because of authorized acts.

3. **Cooperation**
A principal must cooperate with and assist an agent in performing his or her duties. The principal must do nothing to prevent performance.

4. **Safe Working Conditions**
A principal must provide safe working conditions.

IV. RIGHTS AND REMEDIES OF AGENTS AND PRINCIPALS

If one party violates his or her duty to the other, remedies available to the party not in breach arise out of contract and tort law, and include damages, termination of the agency, injunction, and accounting.

A. AGENT'S RIGHTS AND REMEDIES AGAINST PRINCIPAL

For every duty of the principal, an agent has a corresponding right. Breach of a duty by the principal follows normal contract and tort remedies. If the relation is not contractual, an agent has no right to specific performance (but can recover for past services and future damages).

B. PRINCIPAL'S RIGHTS AND REMEDIES AGAINST AGENT

1. **Constructive Trust**
A court imposes a constructive trust if an agent retains benefits or profits that belong to the principal or takes advantage of the agency to obtain property the principal wants to buy. The court declares that the agent holds money or property on behalf of the principal.

2. **Avoidance**
If an agent breaches an agency agreement under a contract, the principal has a right to avoid any contract entered into with the agent.

3. **Indemnification**
A third party can sue a principal for an agent's negligence, and in certain situations the principal can sue the agent. The same is true if the agent violates the principal's instructions.

TRUE-FALSE QUESTIONS

(Answers at the Back of the Book)

___ 1. An agent can perform legal acts that bind his or her principal.

___ 2. Employees who deal with third parties are agents of their employers.

___ 3. An agent owes his or her principal a duty to act in good faith.

___ 4. An agent who fails to use reasonable diligence and skill in acting on behalf of his or her principal may be liable for breaching a duty of performance.

___ 5. In most states, a minor can be a principal but not an agent.

___ 6. Unless the parties agree otherwise, a principal must pay for an agent's services.

___ 7. A principal can never avoid a contract entered into with an agent.

___ 8. A third party cannot sue a principal for an agent's negligence.

___ 9. An agent must keep separate accounts for the principal's funds.

___ 10. Information obtained through an agency relationship is confidential.

FILL-IN QUESTIONS

(Answers at the Back of the Book)

An agent's use of reasonable diligence and skill is part of the agent's duty of ______________ (obedience/performance). Informing a principal of all material matters that come to the agent's attention concerning the subject matter of the agency is an aspect of the agent's duty of ______________ (accounting/notification). Acting solely for the benefit of the principal and not in the interest of the agent or a third party is part of the agent's duty of ________________ (loyalty/performance). Following all lawful and clearly stated instructions of the principal is an aspect of the agent's duty of ________________ (loyalty/obedience). If an agent is required to keep and make available to the principal a record of all property and money received and paid out on behalf of the principal, this is part of the agent's duty of ________________ (accounting/notification).

MULTIPLE-CHOICE QUESTIONS

(Answers at the Back of the Book)

___ 1. National Supplies Company hires Owen and Paula as employees to deal with third-party purchasers and suppliers. Owen and Paula are

a. agents only.
b. principals only.
c. agents and principals.
d. none of the above.

___ 2. Home Interiors, Inc. (HII), tells Jan, whose business is purchasing for others, to select and buy $200 worth of certain goods and ship them to HII's office. Jan buys the goods from Brand Name Products Store and ships them as directed, keeping an account for the expense in HII's name. HII and Jan

a. do not have an agency relationship, because Jan's business is buying for others.
b. do not have an agency relationship, because Jan did not indicate that she was acting for Baron.
c. do not have an agency relationship, because their agreement is not in writing.
d. have an agency relationship.

___ 3. **Based on a Sample CPA Question.** Doug agrees to act as an agent for Great Sales Corporation (GSC) on a commission basis. The agreement does not call for Doug to pay expenses out of his commission. GSC is required to

a. keep records, account to Doug, and pay Doug according to the agreement.
b. reimburse Doug for all authorized expenses.
c. both a and b.
d. none of the above.

___ 4. Greg, a salesperson at Home Electronics Company, tells Irma, a customer, "Buy your computer here, and I'll set it up for less than what Home would charge." Irma buys the computer, Greg sets it up, and Irma pays Greg, who keeps the money. Greg has breached the duty of

a. loyalty.
b. notification.
c. obedience.
d. performance.

___ 5. Carol is a salesperson who works for Delta Products, Inc. In determining whether Carol is Delta's employee or an independent contractor, the most important factor is

a. the degree of control that Delta exercises over Carol.
b. the distinction between Delta's business and Carol's occupation.
c. the length of the working relationship between Delta and Carol.
d. the method of payment.

___ 6. Standard Company and Tom wish to enter into an agency relationship for the purpose of buying computers for Standard's offices. This relationship requires

a. a written agreement only.
b. consideration only.
c. a written agreement and consideration.
d. none of the above.

___ 7. Ann gives Bill the impression that Carol is Ann's agent, when in fact she is not. Bill deals with Carol as Ann's agent. Regarding any agency relationship, Ann

a. can deny it.
b. can deny it to the extent of any injury suffered by Bill.
c. can deny it to the extent of any liability that might be imposed on Ann.
d. cannot deny it.

___ 8. Eagle Company hires Fran, who holds herself out as possessing special accounting skills, to act as its agent. As an agent, Fran must use the degree of skill or care expected of

a. an average, unskilled person.
b. a person having those special skills.
c. a reasonable person.
d. Eagle Company.

___ 9. Pat asks Quinn, a real estate broker, to sell her land. Quinn learns that Retail Mall Corporation (RMC) is willing to pay a high price for the land. Without telling Pat about RMC, Quinn says that he will buy the land himself. Instead, however, Pat sells the land to Sam. Quinn sues Pat. Quinn will

a. lose, because Pat was not Quinn's principal.
b. lose, because Quinn breached his duty to Pat.
c. win, because Pat breached her duty to Quinn.
d. win, because Quinn was never Pat's agent.

___ 10. Adam is an officer for Beta Corporation. When acting for Beta in ordinary business situations, Adam is

a. an agent.
b. a principal.
c. an agent and a principal.
d. none of the above.

SHORT ESSAY QUESTIONS

1. What are the chief differences among the relationships of principal and agent, employer and employee, and employer and independent contractor? What are the factors that indicate whether an individual is an employee or an independent contractor?

2. What are the ways in which a principal–agent relationship can be formed?

ISSUE SPOTTERS

(Answers at the Back of the Book)

1. Don contracts with Eve to buy a certain horse for Eve, who asks Don not to reveal her identity. Don makes a deal with Farm Stables, the owner of the horse, and makes a down payment. Eve fails to pay the rest of the price. Farm Stables sues Don for breach of contract. Can Don hold Eve liable for whatever damages he has to pay?

2. Alpha Corporation wants to build a new mall on a specific tract of land. Alpha enters into a contract with Beth to buy the land. When Beth learns the difference between the price that Alpha is willing to pay and the price at which the owner is willing to sell, she wants to buy the land and sell it to Alpha herself. Can she do this?

3. Carol is a booking agent, who agrees with performers to sign contracts with promoters and others on the performers' behalf. Dan is a truck driver for Entertainment Supplies Company (ESC). Dan does exactly what ESC tells him. Eve is a lighting technician who hires out on an *ad hoc* basis. Which of these is an employee? an independent contractor? an agent?

SPECIAL INFORMATION FOR CPA CANDIDATES

The material covered in this and the next chapter is always included in the CPA examination. Thus, while the concepts are basic and relatively simple, they are nevertheless essential. Agency concepts are applied in questions in the context of principal-agent relationships, partnership law, and corporation law.

Among the points to keep in mind are the rights and duties of the principal and agent, the fiduciary nature of the relationship, and how an agency relationship is formed. Its formation does not need to be contractual, but if it is, it must meet the requirements of a contract.

Chapter 32
Liability to Third Parties and Termination

WHAT THIS CHAPTER IS ABOUT

This chapter deals with the liability of principals and agents to third parties in contract and tort and principals' liability to third parties for agents' torts. The chapter concludes with a section on the termination of agency relationships.

CHAPTER OUTLINE

I. SCOPE OF AN AGENT'S AUTHORITY

A principal's liability in a contract with a third party arises from the authority given the agent to enter contracts on the principal's behalf.

A. EXPRESS AUTHORITY

1. Equal Dignity Rule

In most states, if the contract being executed is or must be in writing, the agent's authority must also be in writing.

a. Exception—Executive Officer Doing Ordinary Business

A corporate executive doing ordinary business does not need written authority from the corporation.

b. Exception—Agent Acting in the Presence of the Principal

In this case, the agent does not need written authority.

2. Power of Attorney

A power of attorney can be special or general. An ordinary power terminates on the incapacity or death of the person giving it. A durable power is not affected by the principal's incapacity.

B. IMPLIED AUTHORITY

Conferred by custom, can be inferred from the position an agent occupies, or is implied as reasonably necessary to carry out express authority.

C. APPARENT AUTHORITY AND ESTOPPEL

An agent has apparent authority when a principal, by word or action, causes a third party reasonably to believe that an agent has authority, though the agent has no authority. The principal may be estopped from denying it if the third party changes position in reliance.

D. EMERGENCY POWERS

If an emergency demands action by the agent, but the agent is unable to communicate with the principal, the agent has emergency power.

E. RATIFICATION

A principal can ratify an unauthorized contract or act, if he or she is aware of all material facts. Ratification can be done expressly or impliedly (by accepting the benefits of a transaction). An entire transaction must be ratified; a principal cannot affirm only part.

1. **Effect of Ratification Without Knowing All the Facts**
   If the third party acts in reliance to his or her detriment on the apparent ratification, the principal can repudiate but must reimburse the third party's costs.

2. **Effect of Ratification**
   Ratification binds the principal to the agent's act and treats it as if it had been authorized from the outset.

3. **Effect of No Ratification**
   There is no contract binding the principal; the third party's agreement with the agent is an unaccepted offer; the agent may be liable to the third party for misrepresenting his or her authority.

II. LIABILITY FOR CONTRACTS

Who is liable to third parties for contracts formed by an agent?

A. DEFINITIONS

1. **Disclosed Principal**
   A principal whose identity is known by the third party when the contract is made.

2. **Partially Disclosed Principal**
   A principal whose identity is not known by the third party, but the third party knows the agent is or may be acting for a principal when the contract is made.

3. **Undisclosed Principal**
   A principal whose identity is totally unknown by the third party, who also does not know that the agent is acting in an agency capacity at the time of the contract.

B. IF AN AGENT ACTS WITHIN THE SCOPE OF HIS OR HER AUTHORITY

1. **Disclosed Principal**
   If a principal's identity is known to a third party when an agent makes a contract, the principal is liable. The agent is not liable.

2. **Partially Disclosed Principal**
   The principal is liable. In most states, the agent is also liable (but is entitled to indemnification by the principal).

3. **Undisclosed Principal**
   The principal and the agent are liable. Exceptions—

   a. The principal was expressly excluded as a party in the contract.
   b. The contract is a negotiable instrument (check or note).
   c. The performance of the agent is personal to the contract.
   d. The third party would not have contracted with the principal had the third party known his or her identity, the agent or the principal knew this, and the third party rescinds the contract.

C. IF THE AGENT HAS NO AUTHORITY

The principal is not liable in contract to a third party. The agent is liable, for breach of the implied warranty of authority (not on breach of the contract), unless the third party knew the agent did not have authority.

D. ACTIONS BY E-AGENTS

E-agents include semi-autonomous computer programs capable of executing specific tasks. How much authority do e-agents have? Generally, any party who uses an e-agent is bound by the e-agent's operations whether or not the principal was aware of them.

III. LIABILITY FOR AGENT'S TORTS

An agent is liable to third parties for his or her torts. Is the principal also liable?

A. PRINCIPAL'S TORTIOUS CONDUCT

A principal may be liable for harm resulting from the principal's negligence or recklessness (giving improper instructions; authorizing the use of improper materials or tools; establishing improper rules; or failing to prevent others' tortious conduct while they are on the principal's property or using the principal's equipment, materials, or tools).

B. PRINCIPAL'S AUTHORIZATION OF AGENT'S TORTIOUS CONDUCT

A principal who authorizes an agent to commit a tortious act may be liable.

C. LIABILITY FOR AGENT'S MISREPRESENTATION

1. Fraudulent Misrepresentation

If a principal has given an agent authority to make statements and the agent makes false claims, the principal is liable. If an agent appears to be acting within the scope of authority in taking advantage of a third party, the principal who placed the agent in that position is liable.

2. Innocent Misrepresentation

When a principal knows that an agent does not have all the facts but does not correct the agent's or the third party's impressions, the principal is liable.

D. LIABILITY FOR AGENT'S NEGLIGENCE

Under the doctrine of *respondeat superior*, an employer is liable for harm caused (negligently or intentionally) to a third party by an employee acting within the scope of employment, without regard to the personal fault of the employer. This is known as *vicarious liability*.

1. Determining the Scope of Employment

a. Factors

In determining whether an act is within the scope of employment, a court considers—

1) the time, place, and purpose of the act.
2) whether the act was authorized by the employer.
3) whether the act is one commonly performed by employees on behalf of their employers.
4) whether the employer's interest was advanced by the act.
5) whether the private interests of the employee were involved.
6) whether the employer furnished the means by which an injury was inflicted.
7) whether the employer had reason to know that the employee would do the act in question.
8) whether the act involved the commission of a serious crime.

b. Travel and Commuting

The travel of those whose jobs require it is considered within the scope of employment for the duration of the trip, including the return. An employee going to and from work or meals is usually considered outside the scope of employment.

2. Employer's Liability for Agent's Torts outside the Scope of Employment

An employer who knows or should know that an employee has a propensity for committing tortious acts is liable for the acts even if they are outside the scope of employment. Also, an employer is liable for permitting an employee to engage in reckless acts that can injure others.

3. Agent's Liability for His or Her Own Torts

An employee is liable for his or her own torts. An employee who commits a tort at the employer's direction can be liable with the employer, even if he or she was unaware of the wrongfulness of the act.

IV. LIABILITY FOR INDEPENDENT CONTRACTOR'S TORTS

An employer is not liable for physical harm caused to a third person by the tortious act of an independent contractor (except in cases of hazardous activities such as blasting operations, the transportation of highly volatile chemicals, and the use of poisonous gases, in which strict liability is imposed).

V. LIABILITY FOR AGENT'S CRIMES

A principal is not liable for an agent's crime, unless the principal participated. In some jurisdictions, a principal may be liable for an agent's violating, in the course and scope of employment, such regulations as those governing sanitation, prices, weights, and the sale of liquor.

VI. LIABILITY FOR SUBAGENT'S ACTS

If an agent is authorized to hire subagents for the principal (to perform simple, definite duties; when it is the business custom; or for unforeseen emergencies), the principal is liable for the acts of the subagents.

VII. TERMINATION OF AN AGENCY

A. TERMINATION BY ACT OF THE PARTIES

1. Lapse of Time

An agency agreement may specify the time period during which the agency relationship will exist. If so, the agency ends when that time expires. If no definite time is stated, an agency continues for a reasonable time and can be terminated at will by either party.

2. Purpose Achieved

An agent can be employed to accomplish a particular objective. If so, the agency automatically ends when the objective is accomplished.

3. Occurrence of a Specific Event

An agency can be created to terminate on the occurrence of a certain event. If so, the agency automatically ends when the event occurs.

4. Mutual Agreement

Parties can cancel their agency by mutually agreeing to do so.

5. Termination by One Party

Both parties have the *power* to terminate an agency, but they may not have the *right* and may therefore be liable for breach of contract.

a. Agency at Will—Principal Must Give Reasonable Notice

To allow the agent to recoup expenses and, in some cases, to make a normal profit.

b. Agency Coupled with an Interest—Irrevocable

This agency is created for the benefit of the agent, who acquires a beneficial interest in the subject matter, and thus it is not equitable to permit a principal to terminate at will. Also, it is not terminated by the death of either the principal or the agent.

c. Not an Agency Coupled with an Interest—May Be Revocable

An agency coupled with an interest should not be confused with an agency in which the agent derives only proceeds or profits (such as a commission) from the sale of the subject matter. This is revocable by the principal, subject to any contract between the parties.

B. TERMINATION BY OPERATION OF LAW

1. Death or Insanity

Death or insanity of either party automatically and immediately ends an agency. Knowledge of the death is not required.

2. **Impossibility**
When the specific subject matter of an agency is destroyed or lost, the agency terminates. When it is impossible for the agent to perform the agency lawfully because of a change in the law, the agency terminates.

3. **Changed Circumstances**
When an event occurs that has such an unusual effect on the subject matter of the agency that the agent can reasonably infer that the principal will not want the agency to continue, the agency terminates.

4. **Bankruptcy**
Bankruptcy of the principal or the agent usually terminates an agency. In some circumstances, as when the agent's financial status is irrelevant to the purpose of the agency, the agency relationship may continue.

5. **War**
When the principal's country and the agent's country are at war with each other, the agency is terminated.

C. NOTICE REQUIRED FOR TERMINATION

1. **Notice Required**
If the parties themselves terminate the agency, the principal must inform any third parties who know of the agency that it has ended.

   a. **Agent's Authority Continues**
   An agent's actual authority continues until the agent receives notice of termination. An agent's apparent authority continues until the third person is notified (from any source).

   b. **What the Principal Must Do**
   The principal is expected to notify directly any third person the principal knows has dealt with the agent. For third persons aware of the agency but who have not dealt with the agent, constructive notice is sufficient.

   c. **Form of the Notice**
   No particular form of notice is required unless the agent's authority is written, in which case it must be revoked in writing, and the writing must be shown to all who saw the written authority.

2. **No Notice Required**
If an agency terminates by operation of law, there is no duty to notify third persons, unless the agent's authority is coupled with an interest.

TRUE-FALSE QUESTIONS

(Answers at the Back of the Book)

___ 1. If an agent acts within the scope of authority, a disclosed principal is liable to a third party for contracts made by the agent.

___ 2. A principal is not liable for an agent's torts committed within the scope of his or her employment.

___ 3. A principal is not bound to an unauthorized contract that he or she does not ratify.

___ 4. An undisclosed principal is liable to a third party for contracts made by an agent acting within the scope of his or her authority.

___ 5. In an ordinary agency relationship, the agency terminates automatically on the death of the principal.

___ **6.** An employer is liable for *any* harm caused to a third party by an employee acting within the scope of employment.

___ **7.** Both parties to an agency have the right to terminate the agency at any time.

___ **8.** When an agent enters into an authorized contract on behalf of a principal, the principal must ratify the contract to be bound.

___ **9.** When the specific subject matter of an agency is destroyed or lost, the agency terminates.

___ **10.** An e-agent is a person.

FILL-IN QUESTIONS

(Answers at the Back of the Book)

If an agent is authorized to hire subagents, the principal ____________ (is/is not) liable for the subagents' acts. An agent who hires for ____________________________ (a disclosed/an undisclosed) principal is responsible to the subagent in contract for such things as wages, but the __________________________ (disclosed/undisclosed) principal is generally liable for ____ (the subagent's crimes/tort injuries) under the doctrine of *respondeat superior.* An agent's unauthorized hiring of a subagent ____________________________________ (also results/generally does not result) in a legal relationship between principal and subagent.

MULTIPLE-CHOICE QUESTIONS

(Answers at the Back of the Book)

___ **1.** Java Company hires Ken to manage one of its stores. Although their employment agreement says nothing about Ken being able to hire employees to work in the store, Ken has this authority. This is

a. apparent authority.
b. express authority.
c. implied authority.
d. none of the above.

___ **2.** **Based on a Sample CPA Exam Question.** Kay acts within the scope of her authority to enter into a contract with First National Bank on behalf of Kay's undisclosed principal, Digital Engineering, Inc. Digital is

a. liable on the contract only if Digital ratifies the contract.
b. liable on the contract only if Digital's identity is later disclosed.
c. liable on the contract under the stated circumstances.
d. not liable on the contract.

___ **3.** Security Guns & Ammo, Inc., directs its salespersons never to load a gun during a sale. Bert, a salesperson, loads a gun during a sale. The gun fires, negligently injuring Kathy, who is in the store. Security is

a. not liable, because Bert was not acting within the scope of employment.
b. not liable, because employers are not responsible for their employees' torts.
c. liable under the doctrine of *respondeat superior.*
d. liable under the doctrine of *res ipsa loquitur.*

___ **4.** Ron orally engages Dian to act as his agent. During the agency, Ron knows that Dian deals with Mary. Ron also knows that Pete and Brad are aware of the agency but have not dealt with Dian. Ron decides to terminate the agency. Regarding notice of termination,

a. Dian need not be notified in writing.
b. Dian's actual authority terminates without notice to her of Ron's decision.
c. Dian's apparent authority terminates without notice to Mary.
d. Pete and Brad must be directly notified.

___ **5.** Smith Petroleum, Inc., contracts to sell oil to Jones Petrochemicals, telling Jones that it is acting on behalf of "a rich Saudi Arabian who doesn't want his identity known." Smith signs the contract, "Smith, as agent only." In fact, Smith is acting on its own. If the contract is breached, Smith may

a. not be liable, because Smith signed the contract as an agent.
b. not be liable, unless Jones knew Smith did not have authority to act.
c. be liable, unless Jones knew Smith did not have authority to act.
d. be liable, because Smith signed the contract as an agent.

___ **6.** Quality Products Company requires its customers to pay by check. Ray, a Quality agent, tells customers that they can pay him with cash. Quality learns of Ray's collections, but takes no action to stop them. Ray steals some of the cash. Quality may be liable for the loss under the doctrine of

a. apparent authority.
b. express authority.
c. implied authority.
d. none of the above.

___ **7.** Local Distribution Company employs Mary as an agent. To terminate Mary's authority, Local Distribution must notify

a. only Mary.
b. only third parties who know of the agency relationship.
c. Mary and third parties who know of the agency relationship.
d. none of the above.

___ **8.** National Manufacturing, Inc., employs Mark as an assembly worker. While attempting, without National's knowledge, to steal a forklift from National's property, Mark has an accident, negligently injuring Pam. Pam can recover from

a. National only.
b. Mark only.
c. National and Mark.
d. none of the above.

___ **9.** Standard Delivery Company employs Tina as a driver. While driving within the scope of employment, Tina causes an accident in which Vic is injured. Vic can recover from

a. Standard only.
b. Tina only.
c. Standard or Tina.
d. none of the above

____ **10.** American Grocers, Inc., employs Jill to buy and install a computer system for American's distribution network. When the system is set up and running, the agency

a. terminates automatically.
b. terminates after fourteen days.
c. continues for one year.
d. continues indefinitely.

SHORT ESSAY QUESTIONS

1. Identify and describe the categories of authority by which an agent can bind a principal and a third party in contract.

2. What are some of the situations in which a principal is liable for an agent's torts?

ISSUE SPOTTERS

(Answers at the Back of the Book)

1. Ann, owner of Best Goods Company, employs Cathy as an administrative assistant. In Ann's absence, and without authority, Cathy represents herself as Ann and signs a promissory note in Ann's name. In what circumstance is Ann liable on the note?

2. United Delivery Service employs Otis as a driver. One afternoon, United tells Otis to deliver a certain package within the hour. While making the delivery, to bypass a traffic jam, Otis recklessly drives onto the sidewalk, injuring Bea. Is United liable to Bea? Is Otis liable to Bea?

3. Great State Bank encourages its depositors to ask its advice concerning their investments. Holly, one of the bank's investment counselors, tells Ira to invest in Jiffy Corporation, although Holly knows its financial situation is precarious. If Ira loses money on the deal, can the bank be held liable?

SPECIAL INFORMATION FOR CPA CANDIDATES

The CPA examination covers agency principles in three contexts: agency law, partnership law, and corporation law. The scope of an agent's authority is virtually certain to be part of the exam. In particular, an agent's implied authority and an agent's apparent authority are among the most common topics on the test. It is thus important to be clear about the differences between these two concepts of authority. Implied authority is derived from express authority. Apparent authority arises from what a principal tells or shows a third party. Apparent authority can result from as little as the title or position that a principal gives an agent.

Another important point to keep in mind when applying these principles to questions on the exam is the size and type of the business at issue—the manager of a large store normally has more authority than the employee of a small store. Also, while a principal is ordinarily liable for the unintentional torts of his or her employees, the principal is not ordinarily liable for an employee's crimes.

On the termination of an agency relationship—as on the termination of a partnership—remember that actual notice must be given to creditors, but constructive notice is sufficient for others.

Chapter 33
Labor and Employment Law

WHAT THIS CHAPTER IS ABOUT

This chapter outlines the most significant laws regulating employment relationships. Other significant laws regulating the workplace—those prohibiting employment discrimination—are dealt with in Chapter 34.

CHAPTER OUTLINE

I. EMPLOYMENT AT WILL

Under the employment at-will doctrine, either the employer or the employee may terminate an employment relationship at any time and for any reason (unless a contract or the law provides to the contrary).

A. WRONGFUL DISCHARGE

An employer cannot fire an employee in violation of an employment contract or a federal or state statute. If so, the employee may bring an action for wrongful discharge.

B. EXCEPTIONS TO THE EMPLOYMENT-AT-WILL DOCTRINE

1. **Exceptions Based on Contract Theory**
   Some courts have held that an implied contract exists between an employer and an employee (if, for example, a personnel manual states that no employee will be fired without good cause). A few states have held all employment contracts contain an implied covenant of good faith.

2. **Exceptions Based on Tort Theory**
   Discharge may give rise to a tort action (based on fraud, for example) for wrongful discharge.

3. **Exceptions Based on Public Policy**
   An employer may not fire a worker for reasons that violate a public policy of the jurisdiction (for example, for refusing to violate the law). This policy must be expressed clearly in statutory law. Some state and federal statutes protect whistleblowers from retaliation. The False Claims Reform Act of 1986 gives a whistleblower 15 to 25 percent of proceeds recovered from fraud.

II. WAGE-HOUR LAWS

Davis-Bacon Act of 1931 requires "prevailing wages" for employees of some government contractors. Walsh-Healey Act of 1936 requires minimum wage and overtime for employees of some government contractors. Fair Labor Standards Act of 1938 (FLSA) covers all employees and regulates—

A. CHILD LABOR

Children under fourteen can deliver newspapers, work for their parents, and work in entertainment and agriculture. Children fourteen and older cannot work in hazardous occupations.

B. MAXIMUM HOURS

Employees who work more than forty hours per week must be paid no less than one and a half times their regular pay for all hours over forty. Executives, administrative employees, professional employees, and outside salespersons are exempt.

C. MINIMUM WAGE

A specified amount (periodically revised) must be paid to employees in covered industries. Wages include the reasonable cost to furnish employees with board, lodging, and other facilities.

III. LABOR UNIONS

A. FEDERAL LABOR LAWS

1. Norris-LaGuardia Act

Enacted in 1932. Restricts federal courts' power to issue injunctions against unions engaged in peaceful strikes, picketing, and boycotts.

2. National Labor Relations Act (NLRA) of 1935

Established rights to bargain collectively and to strike, and—

a. Unfair Employer Practices

Prohibits interfering with union activities, discriminating against union employees, refusing to bargain with union, other practices.

b. National Labor Relations Board (NLRB)

Created to oversee union elections, prevent employers from engaging in unfair practices, investigate employers in response to employee charges of unfair labor practices, issue cease-and-desist orders.

c. Workers Protected by the NLRA

Protected employees include job applicants, including those paid by a union to unionize the employer's work force.

3. Labor-Management Relations Act (LMRA) of 1947

Prohibits unions from refusing to bargain with employers, engaging in certain types of picketing, featherbedding, and other unfair practices. Preserves union shops, but allows states to pass right-to-work laws, which make it illegal to require union membership for employment.

4. Labor-Management Reporting and Disclosure Act (LMRDA) of 1959

a. Union Business

Requires elections of union officers under secret ballot; prohibits ex-convicts and Communists from holding union office; makes officials accountable for union property; allows members to participate in union meetings, nominate officers, vote in proceedings.

b. Hot-Cargo Agreements

Outlaws hot-cargo agreements (in which employers agree not to handle, use, or deal in non-union goods of other employers).

B. UNION ORGANIZATION

If a majority of workers sign authorization cards and the employer refuses to recognize the union, unionizers can petition the NLRB for an election.

1. Union Elections

For an election to be held, there must be support for the union by at least 30 percent of the workers. NLRB ensures secret voting.

2. Union Election Campaigns

Employers may limit campaign activities (fairly) and may campaign against union.

C. COLLECTIVE BARGAINING

The process by which labor and management negotiate terms and conditions of employment. Each side must bargain in good faith (be willing to meet and to consider the other's offers and proposals). Refusing to bargain in good faith without justification is an unfair labor practice.

D. STRIKES

A strike occurs when workers leave their jobs and refuse to work.

1. **Right to Strike**
Guaranteed by the NLRA, within limits. Strike activities, such as picketing, are protected by the First Amendment. Non-workers have a right to participate in picketing. Workers can also refuse to cross a picket line of fellow workers who are engaged in a lawful strike.

2. **Replacing or Rehiring Strikers**
An employer may hire substitute workers to replace strikers.

   a. **Economic Strikes over Working Conditions**
   Strikers have no right to return to their jobs, but must be given preference to any vacancies and also retain their seniority rights.

   b. **Employer Unfair Labor Practice Strikes**
   Strikers must be given their jobs back.

IV. WORKER HEALTH AND SAFETY

A. OCCUPATIONAL SAFETY AND HEALTH ACT OF 1970
Attempts to ensure safe and healthful work conditions for most employees.

1. **Enforcement Agencies**

   a. **Occupational Safety and Health Administration (OSHA)**
   Inspects workplaces and issues safety standards, including standards covering employee exposure to harmful substances.

   b. **National Institute for Occupational Safety and Health**
   Researches safety and health problems and recommends standards for OSHA to adopt.

   c. **Occupational Safety and Health Review Commission**
   Hears appeals from actions taken by OSHA administrators.

2. **Procedures and Violations**
Employees file complaints of OSHA violations (employers cannot retaliate); employers must keep injury and illness records; employers must file accident reports directly to OSHA. Penalties are limited.

B. STATE WORKERS' COMPENSATION LAWS
State laws establish procedure for compensating workers injured on the job.

1. **No State Covers All Employees**
Often excluded are domestic workers, agricultural workers, temporary employees, and employees of common carriers.

2. **Requirements for Recovery**
There must be an employment relationship, and the injury must be accidental and occur on the job or in the course of employment.

3. **Filing a Claim**
An employee must notify the employer of an injury (usually within thirty days), and file a claim with a state agency within a certain period (sixty days to two years) from the time the injury is first noticed.

4. **Acceptance of Workers' Compensation Benefits Bars Suits**
An employee's acceptance of benefits bars the employee from suing for injuries caused by the employer's negligence.

V. INCOME SECURITY

A. SOCIAL SECURITY

The Social Security Act of 1935 provides for payments to persons who are retired, widowed, disabled, etc. Employers and employees must contribute under the Federal Insurance Contributions Act (FICA).

B. MEDICARE

A health insurance program administered by the Social Security Administration for people sixty-five years of age and older and for some under sixty-five who are disabled.

C. PRIVATE PENSION PLANS

The Employee Retirement Income Security Act (ERISA) of 1974 empowers the Labor Management Services Administration of the U.S. Department of Labor to oversee operators of private pension funds.

1. Vesting

Generally, employee contributions to pension plans vest immediately; employee rights to employer contributions vest after five years.

2. Investing

Pension-fund managers must be cautious in investing and refrain from investing more than 10 percent of the fund in securities of the employer.

D. UNEMPLOYMENT COMPENSATION

The Federal Unemployment Tax Act of 1935 created a state system that provides unemployment compensation to eligible individuals.

VI. COBRA

The Consolidated Omnibus Budget Reconciliation Act (COBRA) of 1985 prohibits the elimination of a worker's medical, optical, or dental insurance on the termination of most workers' employment. Coverage must continue for up to 18 months (29 months in some cases). A worker pays the premium plus 2 percent.

VII. FAMILY AND MEDICAL LEAVE ACT (FMLA) OF 1993

Employers with fifty or more employees must provide them with up to twelve weeks of family or medical leave during any twelve-month period, continue health-care coverage during the leave, and guarantee employment in the same, or a comparable, position when the employee returns to work.

VIII. EMPLOYEE PRIVACY RIGHTS

A right to privacy has been inferred from constitutional guarantees provided by the First, Third, Fourth, Fifth, and Ninth Amendments to the Constitution. Tort law, state constitutions, and some federal and state statutes also provide some privacy rights.

A. ELECTRONIC MONITORING IN THE WORKPLACE

1. Laws Protecting Employee Privacy Rights

The Electronic Communications Privacy Act (ECPA) of 1986 bars the interception of any wire or electronic communication or the disclosure or use of information obtained by interception. Excepted is employers' monitoring of *business* telephone conversations.

2. Factors Considered by the Courts in Employee Privacy Cases

If an employee brings a tort action for invasion of privacy (see Chapter 5), a court may weigh the employee's reasonable expectation of privacy against the employer's need for surveillance. This may depend on whether the employee was aware of the monitoring.

3. Privacy Expectations and E-Mail Systems

In cases involving e-mail, it has not seemed to matter whether employees were aware of being monitored.

B. OTHER TYPES OF MONITORING

1. **Lie-Detector Tests**
Under the Employee Polygraph Protection Act of 1988, most employers cannot, among other things, require, request, or suggest that employees or applicants take lie-detector tests, except when investigating theft, including theft of trade secrets.

2. **Drug Testing**

    a. **Protection for the Privacy Rights of Private Employees**
    Some state constitutions may prohibit private employers from testing for drugs. State statutes may restrict drug testing by private employers. Other sources of protection include collective bargaining agreements and tort actions for invasion of privacy.

    b. **Protection for Government Employees**
    Constitutional limitations (the Fourth Amendment) apply. Drug tests have been upheld when there was a reasonable basis for suspecting employees of using drugs, or when drug use could threaten public safety.

3. **AIDS Testing**
Some state laws restrict AIDS testing. The federal Americans with Disabilities Act of 1990 and other statutes protect employees or applicants who have tested positive from discrimination.

4. **Genetic Testing**
This may violate the Americans with Disabilities Act of 1990 or other privacy provisions.

5. **Screening Procedures**
A key factor in determining whether preemployment screening tests violate privacy rights is whether there is a connection between the questions and the job for which an applicant is applying.

IX. EMPLOYMENT-RELATED IMMIGRATION LAWS

A. IMMIGRATION REFORM AND CONTROL ACT (IRCA)OF 1986
The IRCA prohibits employers from hiring illegal immigrants.

B. IMMIGRATION ACT OF 1990
Employers recruiting workers from other countries must complete a certification process, satisfy the U.S. Department of Labor that there is a shortage of qualified U.S. workers to perform the work, and show that bringing aliens into this country will not adversely affect the labor market.

TRUE-FALSE QUESTIONS

(Answers at the Back of the Book)

____ 1. Drug testing by private employers is permitted.

____ 2. There are no exceptions to the employment "at will" doctrine.

____ 3. Employers are required to establish retirement plans for their employees.

____ 4. Federal wage-hour laws cover all employers engaged in interstate commerce.

____ 5. Whistleblower statutes protect employers from workers' disclosure of the employer's wrongdoing.

____ 6. Under federal law, employers can monitor employees' personal communications.

____ 7. Employers can agree with unions not to handle, use, or deal in non-union-produced goods.

____ 8. Management serves as the representative of workers in bargaining with a union.

___ **9.** Federal labor law protects employees' rights to strike, to picket, and to boycott.

___ **10.** Employees have no right to engage in collective bargaining through elected representatives.

FILL-IN QUESTIONS

(Answers at the Back of the Book)

Under the employment-at-will doctrine, ____________ (either/neither) party may terminate an employment relationship at any time and for any reason ____________ (unless/even if) a contract provides to the contrary. An employee who is fired in violation of a federal or state statute ____________ (may/may not) bring an action for wrongful discharge. ____________ (Some/No) courts have held that an implied contract exists between an employer and an employee. ____________ (All/A few states) have held that all employment contracts contain an implied covenant of good faith. An employer ____________ (may/may not) fire a worker for reasons that violate a public policy of the jurisdiction.

MULTIPLE-CHOICE QUESTIONS

(Answers at the Back of the Book)

___ **1.** **Based on a Sample CPA Exam Question.** Fast Jack is a fast-food restaurant. To verify Fast Jack's compliance with statutes governing employees' wages and hours, personnel records should be checked against the provisions of

a. the Fair Labor Standards Act.
b. the Family and Medical Leave Act.
c. the National Labor Relations Act.
d. the Taft-Hartley Act.

___ **2.** Interstate Distributors, Inc., is investigating losses due to theft. Without violating employees' rights of privacy, Interstate may

a. monitor all employee phone conversations only.
b. require employees to take polygraph tests only.
c. monitor all employee phone conversations and require employees to take polygraph tests.
d. none of the above.

___ **3.** Ron, an employee of Standard Company, is injured. For Ron to receive *workers' compensation*, the injury must be

a. accidental and arise out of a preexisting disease or condition.
b. accidental and occur on the job or in the course of employment.
c. intentional and arise out of a preexisting disease or condition.
d. intentional and occur on the job or in the course of employment.

___ **4.** U.S. Goods, Inc. (USG), recruits workers from other countries to work in its U.S. plant. Under the Immigration Act of 1990, USG must show

a. only that bringing aliens into the country will not adversely affect the labor market in the area.
b. only that there is a shortage of qualified U.S. workers to perform the work.
c. that there is a shortage of qualified U.S. workers to perform the work and that bringing aliens into the country will not adversely affect the labor market in the area.
d. none of the above.

___ **5.** Mary is an employee of National Sales Company. Both Mary and National make contributions to the federal social security system under

a. the Employment Retirement Income Security Act.
b. the Federal Insurance Contributions Act.
c. the Federal Unemployment Tax Act.
d. none of the above.

___ **6.** Eagle, Inc., sets up a pension fund for its employees. Eagle's operation of the fund is regulated by

a. the Employment Retirement Income Security Act.
b. the Federal Insurance Contributions Act.
c. the Federal Unemployment Tax Act.
d. none of the above.

___ **7.** ABC Corporation provides health insurance for its 150 employees, including Dian. When Dian takes twelve weeks' leave to care for her child, she

a. can collect "leave pay" equal to twelve weeks' of health insurance coverage.
b. can continue her heath insurance at ABC's expense.
c. can continue her heath insurance at her expense.
d. loses her heath insurance immediately on taking leave.

___ **8.** Mega Corporation provides health insurance for its employees. When Mega closes one of its offices and terminates the employees, the employees

a. can collect "severance pay" equal to twelve weeks' of health insurance coverage.
b. can continue their heath insurance at Mega's expense.
c. can continue their heath insurance at their expense.
d. lose their heath insurance immediately on termination of employment.

___ **9.** Don works for Excel Tool Company. Don and other employees designate the Federated Machinists Union (FMU) as their bargaining representative. Without violating federal labor law, Excel can

a. only refuse to bargain with FMU.
b. only terminate Don for "choosing the wrong side."
c. refuse to bargain with FMU and terminate Don for "choosing the wrong side."
d. none of the above.

___ **10.** The Assembly Workers Union (AWU) represents the employees of Best Manufacturing, Inc. When AWU calls an economic strike, Best hires replacement workers. After the strike

a. the former strikers must be rehired without the termination of the replacement workers.
b. the replacement workers must be terminated whether or not the former strikers are rehired.
c. the former strikers must be rehired and the replacement workers must be terminated.
d. none of the above.

SHORT ESSAY QUESTIONS

1. What is the employment-at-will doctrine? What are its exceptions?

2. What are important federal laws concerning labor unions? What specifically does each law provide?

ISSUE SPOTTERS

(Answers at the Back of the Book)

1. Associated Services Company (ASC) issues an employee handbook that states employees will be discharged only for good cause. One day, Bob, an ASC supervisor, says to Carl, "I don't like your looks. You're fired." Is ASC liable for breach of contract?

2. Workers' compensation laws establish a procedure for compensating workers who are injured on the job. Instead of suing, an injured worker files a claim with the appropriate state agency. For the employee to obtain compensation, does the injury have to have been caused by the employer's negligence?

3. Ann applies for work with Beta Company, which tells her that it requires union membership as a condition of employment. Ann applies for work with Omega, Inc., which does not require union membership as a condition of employment but requires employees to join a union after six months on the job. Are these conditions legal?

SPECIAL INFORMATION FOR CPA CANDIDATES

The CPA examination has never covered the employment-at-will doctrine, the laws protecting whistle-blowers, the laws related to employee privacy rights, or labor law. FICA, FUTA, and the law governing workers' compensation have been often tested, however. FICA questions concern coverage and benefits; FUTA questions relate to the source of funds for unemployment compensation; workers' compensation questions often concern the basis for recovery under applicable laws. Some of the other material touched on in this chapter has been covered on recent CPA exams. This material includes FLSA, OSHA, and ERISA—their objectives, coverage, and application.

Chapter 34
Employment Discrimination

WHAT THIS CHAPTER IS ABOUT

The law restricts employers and unions from discriminating against workers on the basis of race, color, religion, national origin, gender, age, or handicap. A class of persons defined by one or more of these criteria is a *protected class*. This chapter outlines these laws.

CHAPTER OUTLINE

I. TITLE VII OF THE CIVIL RIGHTS ACT OF 1964

Prohibits employment discrimination against employees, applicants, and union members on the basis of race, color, national origin, religion, and gender.

A. WHO IS SUBJECT TO TITLE VII?

Employers with fifteen or more employees, labor unions with fifteen or more members, labor unions that operate hiring halls, employment agencies, and federal, state, and local agencies.

B. PROCEDURES UNDER TITLE VII

(1) A victim files a claim with the Equal Employment Opportunity Commission (EEOC); (2) the EEOC investigates and seeks a voluntary settlement; (3) if no settlement is reached, the EEOC may sue the employer; (4) if the EEOC chooses not to sue, the victim may file a lawsuit.

C. INTENTIONAL AND UNINTENTIONAL DISCRIMINATION

Title VII prohibits both intentional and unintentional discrimination.

1. Disparate-Treatment Discrimination

This is intentional discrimination by an employer against an employee.

a. *Prima Facie* Case—Plaintiff's Side of the Case

Plaintiff must show (1) he or she is a member of a protected class, (2) he or she applied and was qualified for the job, (3) he or she was rejected by the employer, (4) the employer continued to seek applicants or filled the job with a person not in a protected class.

b. Defense—Employer's Side of the Case

Employer must articulate a legal reason for not hiring the plaintiff. To prevail, the plaintiff must show that the employer's reason is a pretext and that discriminatory intent motivated the decision.

2. Disparate-Impact Discrimination

a. Types of Disparate-Impact Discrimination

Disparate-impact discrimination results if, because of a requirement or hiring practice—

1) an employer's work force does not reflect the percentage of members of protected classes that characterizes qualified individuals in the local labor market, or

2) members of protected class are excluded from employer's work force at substantially higher rate than nonmembers (under EEOC's "four-fifths rule," selection rate for protected class must be at least 80 percent of rate for group with the highest rate).

b. ***Prima Facie* Case—Plaintiff's Side of the Case**
Plaintiff must show a connection between a requirement or practice and a disparity; no evidence of discriminatory intent is needed.

D. DISCRIMINATION BASED ON RACE, COLOR, AND NATIONAL ORIGIN
Employers cannot effectively discriminate against employees on the basis of race, color, national origin, or religion (absent a substantial, demonstrable relationship between the trait and the job, etc.).

E. DISCRIMINATION BASED ON RELIGION
Title VII prohibits employers and unions from discriminating against persons because of their religions.

F. DISCRIMINATION BASED ON GENDER
Employers cannot discriminate against employees on the basis of gender (unless the gender of the applicant can be proved essential to the job, etc.). The Pregnancy Discrimination Act of 1978 amended Title VII: employees affected by pregnancy or related conditions must be treated the same as persons not so affected but similar in ability to work.

G. SEXUAL HARASSMENT

1. **Forms of Harassment**
(1) *Quid pro quo* harassment: when promotions, etc., are doled out on the basis of sexual favors; (2) hostile-environment harassment: when an employee is subjected to offensive sexual comments, etc.

2. **Harassment by Supervisors, Co-Workers, or Nonemployees**

a. **When an Employer May Be Liable**
If anyone (employee or nonemployee) harasses an employee, and the employer knew, or should have known, and failed to take immediate corrective action, the employer may be liable. To be liable for a supervisor's harassment, the supervisor must have taken a tangible employment action against the employee.

b. **Employer's Defense**
(1) Employer took "reasonable care to prevent and correct promptly any sexually harassing behavior," and (2) employee suing for harassment failed to follow employer's policies and procedures.

H. ONLINE HARASSMENT
Employers may avoid liability if they take prompt remedial action. Privacy rights must be considered if the action includes electronic monitoring of employees.

I. REMEDIES UNDER TITLE VII
Reinstatement, back pay, retroactive promotions, and damages.

1. **Damages**
Compensatory damages are available only in cases of intentional discrimination. Punitive damages are available only if an employer acted with malice or reckless indifference

2. **Limitations**
Total damages are limited to specific amounts against specific employers (from $50,000 against those with one hundred or fewer employees to $300,000 against those with more than five hundred employees).

II. EQUAL PAY ACT OF 1963
Prohibits gender-based discrimination in wages for equal work (work requiring equal skill, effort, and responsibility under similar conditions). Different wages are acceptable because of any factor but gender (seniority, merit, etc.).

III. DISCRIMINATION BASED ON AGE

A. AGE DISCRIMINATION IN EMPLOYMENT ACT (ADEA) OF 1967

Prohibits employment discrimination on the basis of age (including mandatory retirement), by employers with twenty or more employees, against individuals forty years of age or older. Administered by the EEOC, but private causes of action are also possible.

B. PRINCIPLES ARE SIMILAR TO TITLE VII

Requires the establishment of a *prima facie* case: plaintiff must show that he or she was (1) forty or older, (2) qualified for a position, and (3) rejected in circumstances that infer discrimination. The employer must articulate a legal reason; the plaintiff may show it is a pretext.

C. STATE EMPLOYEES

Under the Eleventh Amendment to the Constitution, a state is immune from suits brought by private individuals in federal court unless the state consents to the suit. A state agency sued by a state employee for age discrimination may have the suit dismissed on this ground.

IV. DISCRIMINATION BASED ON DISABILITY

Under the Americans with Disabilities Act (ADA) of 1990, an employer cannot refuse to hire a person who is qualified but disabled. Covered are all employers (except the states) with fifteen or more employees.

A. PROCEDURES AND REMEDIES UNDER THE ADA

1. Procedures

A plaintiff must show he or she (1) has a disability, (2) is otherwise qualified for a job and (3) was excluded solely because of the disability. A suit may be filed only after a claim is pursued through the EEOC (which may file a suit even if the employee agrees to arbitration).

2. Remedies

These include reinstatement, back pay, some compensatory and punitive damages (for intentional discrimination), and certain other relief. Repeat violators may be fined up to $100,000.

B. WHAT IS A DISABILITY?

"(1) [A] physical or mental impairment that substantially limits one or more of the major life activities . . . ; (2) a record of such impairment; or (3) being regarded as having such an impairment." Includes AIDS, morbid obesity, etc.; not homosexuality or kleptomania.

C. REASONABLE ACCOMMODATION

For a person with a disability, an employer may have to make a reasonable accommodation (more flexible working hours, new job assignment, different training materials or procedures)—but not an accommodation that will cause *undue hardship* ("significant difficulty or expense").

1. Job Applications

The application process must be accessible to those with disabilities.

2. Preemployment Physical Exams

Employers cannot require a disabled person to take a preemployment physical (unless all applicants do). Disqualification must be from problems that render a person unable to perform the job.

3. Dangerous Workers

An employer need not hire disabled workers who would pose a "direct threat to the health or safety" of co-workers or to themselves.

4. Substance Abusers

The ADA protects addicts who have completed or are in supervised rehabilitation, and alcoholics to the extent of equal treatment.

5. **Health-Insurance Plans**
   Workers with disabilities must be given equal access to insurance plans provided to other workers. If a plan includes a disability-based distinction, an employer must show (1) limiting coverage keeps the plan financially sound, (2) coverage would otherwise be too expensive for many workers, or (3) the distinction is justified by the risk and costs.

V. DEFENSES TO EMPLOYMENT DISCRIMINATION

The first defense is to assert that the plaintiff did not prove discrimination. If discrimination is proved, an employer may attempt to justify it as—

A. BUSINESS NECESSITY

An employer may show that there is a legitimate connection between a job requirement that discriminates and job performance.

B. BONA FIDE OCCUPATIONAL QUALIFICATION (BFOQ)

Another defense applies when discrimination against a protected class is essential to a job—that is, when a particular trait is a BFOQ. Generally restricted to cases in which gender is essential. Race can never be a BFOQ.

C. SENIORITY SYSTEMS

An employer with a history of discrimination may have no members of protected classes or disabled workers in upper-level positions. If no present intent to discriminate is shown, and promotions, etc., are distributed according to a fair seniority system, the employer has a good defense.

D. AFTER-ACQUIRED EVIDENCE

An employer who discovers, after discharging an employee, that the worker engaged in misconduct in applying for the job or while on the job may use that misconduct to limit the amount of damages to the plaintiff.

VI. AFFIRMATIVE ACTION

An affirmative action program attempts to make up for past discrimination by giving members of protected classes preferential treatment in hiring or promotion. Such an employment program cannot use quotas or preferences for unqualified persons, and once it has succeeded, it must be changed or dropped.

VII. STATE LAWS PROHIBITING DISCRIMINATION

Most states have statutes that prohibit the kinds of discrimination prohibited under federal law. Also, state laws often protect individuals, such as those under forty years of age or those who work at very small firms, who are not protected under federal law, and may provide for damages in addition to those allowed under federal law.

TRUE-FALSE QUESTIONS

(Answers at the Back of the Book)

____ 1. Once an affirmative action program has succeeded, it must be changed or dropped.

____ 2. In a sexual harassment case, an employer cannot be held liable for the actions of an employee.

____ 3. In a sexual harassment case, an employer cannot be held liable for the actions of a nonemployee.

____ 4. Women affected by pregnancy must be treated for all job-related purposes the same as persons not so affected but similar in ability to work.

____ 5. Employment discrimination against persons with a physical or mental impairment that substantially limits their everyday activities is prohibited.

___ 6. Discrimination complaints brought under federal law must be filed with the Equal Opportunity Employment Commission.

___ 7. If the Equal Employment Opportunity Commission decides not to investigate a claim, the victim has no other option.

___ 8. All employers are subject to Title VII of the Civil Rights Act of 1964.

___ 9. Disparate-treatment discrimination occurs when an employer intentionally discriminates against an employee.

___ 10. Title VII prohibits employers and unions from discriminating against persons because of their religions.

FILL-IN QUESTIONS

(Answers at the Back of the Book)

The Equal Employment Opportunity Commission (EEOC) monitors compliance with the federal antidiscrimination laws. The EEOC ______________________ (can/cannot) sue organizations that violate these laws. A victim files a claim with the EEOC, which investigates and ______________________ ______________________ (must sue/may sue if a settlement between the parties is not reached). If the EEOC does not sue, the victim may sue. On proof of discrimination, a victim may be awarded ______________________ ______________________ (reinstatement and back pay/reinstatement, back pay, and retroactive promotions).

MULTIPLE-CHOICE QUESTIONS

(Answers at the Back of the Book)

___ 1. Ann is an employee of Beta Communications Corporation. Ann attempts to resolve a gender-based discrimination claim with Beta, whose representative denies the claim. Ann's next best step is to

a. ask the Equal Opportunity Employment Commission whether a claim is justified.
b. file a lawsuit.
c. forget about the matter.
d. secretly sabotage company operations for revenge.

___ 2. Bob and Carol work for Delta Company. Bob is Carol's supervisor. During work, Bob touches Carol in ways that she perceives as sexually offensive. Carol resists the advances. Bob cuts her pay. Delta is

a. liable, because Bob's conduct constituted sexual harassment.
b. liable, because Carol resisted Bob's advances.
c. not liable, because Bob's conduct was not job-related.
d. not liable, because Carol resisted Bob's advances.

___ 3. **Based on a Sample CPA Exam Question.** Under the Age Discrimination in Employment Act of 1967, Alpha Corporation is prohibited from

a. committing unintentional age discrimination.
b. forcing an employee to retire.
c. terminating an employee between the ages of sixty-five and seventy for cause.
d. terminating an employee as part of a rational business decision.

____ **4.** Kay, who is hearing impaired, applies for a position with Local Company. Kay is qualified but is refused the job and sues Local. To succeed under the Americans with Disabilities Act, Kay must show that

a. Kay was willing to make a "reasonable accommodation" for Local.
b. Kay would not have to accept "significant additional costs" to work for Local.
c. Local refused to make a "reasonable accommodation" for Kay.
d. Local would not have to accept "significant additional costs" to hire Kay.

____ **5.** Omega Sales, Inc., promotes employees on the basis of color. Employees with darker skin color are passed over in favor of those with lighter skin color, regardless of their race. This is prohibited by

a. the Americans with Disabilities Act of 1990.
b. the Equal Pay Act of 1963.
c. Title VII of the Civil Rights Act of 1964.
d. none of the above.

____ **6.** Curt, personnel director for Digital Products, Inc., prefers to hire Asian Americans, because "they're smarter and work harder" than other minorities. This is prohibited by

a. the Age Discrimination in Employment Act of 1967.
b. the Americans with Disabilities Act of 1990.
c. Title VII of the Civil Rights Act of 1964 .
d. none of the above.

____ **7.** Greg and Holly work for Interstate Services, Inc. (ISI), as electrical engineers. Greg is paid more than Holly because, according to ISI, he is a man with a family to support. This is prohibited by

a. the Age Discrimination in Employment Act of 1967.
b. the Americans with Disabilities Act of 1990.
c. the Equal Pay Act of 1963.
d. none of the above.

____ **8.** Donna applies to Eagle Corporation for an administrative assistant's job, which requires certain typing skills. Donna cannot type but tells Eagle that she is willing to learn. Eagle does not hire Donna, who later sues. To successfully defend against the suit under Title VII, Eagle must show that

a. being a member of the majority is a BFOQ.
b. Donna was not willing to learn to type.
c. Eagle has a valid business necessity defense.
d. Eagle's work force reflects the same percentage of members of a protected class that characterizes qualified individuals in the local labor market.

____ **9.** Standard Corporation terminates Tom, who sues on the basis of age discrimination. To succeed under the Age Discrimination in Employment Act, Tom must show that at the time of the discharge, he was

a. forty or older.
b. forty or younger.
c. replaced with someone forty or older.
d. replaced with someone forty or younger.

____ **10.** National Company requires job applicants to pass certain physical tests. Only a few female applicants can pass the tests, but it they pass, they are hired. To successfully defend against a suit on this basis under Title VII, National must show that

a. any discrimination is not intentional.
b. being a male is a BFOQ.
c. passing the tests is a business necessity.
d. some men cannot pass the tests.

SHORT ESSAY QUESTIONS

1. Compare and contrast disparate-treatment discrimination and disparate-impact discrimination, and Title VII's response to each in the context of employment.

2. What does the Americans with Disabilities Act require employers to do?

ISSUE SPOTTERS

(Answers at the Back of the Book)

1. Phil applies for a job at Quality Corporation for which he is well qualified, but for which he is rejected. Quality continues to seek applicants and eventually fills the position with a person who is not a member of a minority. Could Phil succeed in a suit against Quality for discrimination?

2. Ruth is a supervisor for Subs & Suds, a restaurant. Tim is a Subs employee. The owner announces that some employees will be discharged. Ruth tells Tim that if he has sex with her, he can keep his job. Is this sexual harassment?

3. Paula, a disabled person, applies for a job at Quantity Corporation for which she is well qualified, but for which she is rejected. Quantity continues to seek applicants and eventually fills the position with a person who is not disabled. Could Paula succeed in a suit against Quantity for discrimination?

SPECIAL INFORMATION FOR CPA CANDIDATES

The CPA examination has included an occasional question on discrimination—what is prohibited and what individuals are protected. These questions have concerned the broad coverage of the law, rather than specific details.

CUMULATIVE HYPOTHETICAL PROBLEM FOR UNIT SEVEN—INCLUDING CHAPTERS 31–34

(Answers at the Back of the Book)

Donna, Earl, Frank, Gail, Hal, Ira, Jane, Karen, Larry, and Mike work for International Sales Corporation (ISC).

___ **1.** Donna, who works in ISC's warehouse, is injured on the job. Donna may NOT collect workers' compensation benefits if she

a. files a civil suit against a third party based on the injury.
b. intentionally caused her own injury.
c. was injured as a result of a co-worker's act.
d. worked for ISC for less than sixty days.

___ **2.** Earl retires from ISC at the age of sixty-five. Frank retires at sixty-seven. Because of a disability, Gail, after fifteen years, is unable to continue working for ISC. Hal is discharged from ISC as part of a reduction in force. All of the following benefits are part of Social Security EXCEPT

a. Earl's government retirement payments.
b. Frank's Medicare payments.
c. Gail's government disability payments.
d. Hal's unemployment benefits.

___ **3.** Ira works for ISC as a sales representative at a salary of $3,000 per month, plus a 10 percent commission. As ISC's agent, Ira

a. cannot be dismissed during the six-month period without cause.
b. cannot enforce the agency unless it is in writing and signed by Delta.
c. is an agent coupled with an interest.
d. must act solely in Delta's interest in matters concerning Delta's business.

___ **4.** Four employees file suits against ISC, alleging discrimination. Title VII of the Civil Rights Act of 1964 covers all of the following EXCEPT Jane's suit alleging discrimination on the basis of

a. age.
b. gender.
c. race.
d. religion.

___ **5.** Karen, an ISC manager, wants to institute a policy of mandatory retirement for all employees at age sixty-four. Larry, an ISC manager, wants to discharge Mike, who is age sixty-seven, for cause. Under federal anti-discrimination law

a. only Karen's wish can be granted.
b. only Larry's wish can be granted.
c. both Karen's and Larry's wishes can be granted.
d. none of the above.

QUESTIONS ON THE FOCUS ON LEGAL REASONING FOR UNIT SEVEN— *REDI-FLOORS, INC. V. SONENBERG CO.*

(Answers at the Back of the Book)

___ **1.** Nora contracts with Owen on behalf of Nora's principal Pat, without disclosing Pat's identity. Under the holding in *Redi-Floors, Inc. v. Sonenberg Co.*, Owen could pursue a breach of contract claim against

a. Nora only.
b. Pat only.
c. Nora and Pat jointly.
d. Nora or Pat, but not both.

___ **2.** In the previous question, suppose that Owen files claims jointly against Nora and Pat, and that this is unsuccessful. In the opinion of the majority in *Redi-Floors, Inc. v. Sonenberg Co.*, Owen might be able to maintain an action solely against Nora if the court

a. directed a verdict in Nora's favor.
b. directed a verdict in Pat's favor.
c. issued a written judgment order in Nora's favor.
d. issued a written judgment order in Pat's favor.

___ **3.** Under the facts in the previous questions, according to the reasoning of the dissent in *Redi-Floors, Inc. v. Sonenberg Co.*, Owen could not subsequently maintain an action solely against Nora because the court

a. directed a verdict in Nora's favor.
b. directed a verdict in Pat's favor.
c. issued a written judgment order in Nora's favor.
d. issued a written judgment order in Pat's favor.

QUESTIONS ON THE FOCUS ON ETHICS FOR UNIT SEVEN—AGENCY AND EMPLOYMENT

(Answers at the Back of the Book)

___ **1.** Eve is Fred's agent. Ethics would prevent Eve from

a. being loyal to Fred.
b. disclosing Eve's interest in property being bought by Fred.
c. profiting from the agency relation with Fred's consent
d. representing Gary in a transaction with Fred.

___ **2.** Harry is Irma's agent. Ethics might prescribe otherwise, but Harry's legal duties to Irma do not include

a. compensation.
b. cooperation.
c. loyalty.
d. reimbursement.

___ **3.** Jack offers Kay a job in a distant state. Kay accepts and moves her family. One month later, Kay is terminated without cause. Absent an employment contract or a personnel manual, Jack may be held to have violated

a. the employment-at-will doctrine.
b. the one-year exception to the employment-at-will doctrine.
c. the public-policy exception to the employment-at-will doctrine.
d. none of the above.

Chapter 35
Sole Proprietorships and Franchises

WHAT THIS CHAPTER IS ABOUT

This chapter briefly outlines the features of a sole proprietorship, the most common form of business, and discusses private franchises, which are widely used by entrepreneurs to seek profits.

CHAPTER OUTLINE

I. SOLE PROPRIETORSHIPS

The simplest form of business—the owner is the business.

A. ADVANTAGES

These include that the proprietor takes all the profits; this organization is easier to start than others (few legal forms involved); the form has more flexibility (the proprietor is free to make all decisions); and the owner pays only personal income tax on profits.

B. DISADVANTAGES

These include that the proprietor has all the risk (unlimited liability for all debts); there is limited opportunity to raise capital; and the business dissolves when the owner dies.

II. FRANCHISES

A franchise is any arrangement in which the owner of a trademark, a trade name, or a copyright has licensed others to use it in selling goods or services.

A. TYPES OF FRANCHISES

1. Distributorship

When a manufacturer licenses a dealer to sell its product (such as an automobile dealer). Often covers an exclusive territory.

2. Chain-Style Business Operation

When a franchise operates under a franchisor's trade name and is identified as a member of a group of dealers engaged in the franchisor's business (such as most fast-food chains). The franchisee must follow standardized or prescribed methods of operations, and may be obligated to obtain supplies exclusively from the franchisor.

3. Manufacturing or Processing-Plant Arrangement

When a franchisor transmits to the franchisee the essential ingredients or formula to make a product (such as Coca-Cola), which the franchisee makes and markets according to the franchisor's standards.

B. LAWS GOVERNING FRANCHISING

1. Federal Protection for Franchisees

a. **Automobile Dealers' Franchise Act of 1965**
Dealership franchisees are protected from manufacturers' bad faith termination of their franchises.

b. **Petroleum Marketing Practices Act (PMPA) of 1979**
Prescribes the grounds and conditions under which a gasoline station franchisor may terminate or decline to renew a franchise.

c. **Antitrust Laws**
May apply if there is an anticompetitive agreement (see Chapter 46).

d. **Federal Trade Commission (FTC) Franchise Rule**
Franchisors must disclose material facts necessary to a prospective franchisee's making an informed decision concerning a franchise. This must be in writing, and there must be a meeting between the parties at least ten business days before an agreement is signed or a payment made.

2. **State Protection for Franchisees**
Similar to federal law. State deceptive practices acts may apply, as may Article 2 of the Uniform Commercial Code.

C. **THE FRANCHISE CONTRACT**
A franchise relationship is created by a contract between the franchisor and the franchisee.

1. **Payment for the Franchise**
A franchisee pays (1) a fee for the franchise license, (2) fees for products bought from or through the franchisor, (3) a percentage of sales, and (4) a percentage of advertising and administrative costs.

2. **Business Premises**
The agreement may specify whether the premises for the business are leased or purchased and who is to supply equipment and furnishings.

3. **Location of the Franchise**
The franchisor determines the territory to be served and its exclusivity.

4. **Business Organization**
A franchisor may specify requirements for the form and capital structure of the franchisee's business.

5. **Quality Control**
A franchisor may specify standards of operation (such as quality standards) and personnel training methods. Too much control may result in a franchisor's liability for torts of a franchisee's employees.

6. **Pricing Arrangements**
A franchisor may require a franchisee to buy certain supplies from the franchisor at an established price. A franchisor may also suggest retail prices for the goods that the franchisee sells.

7. **Termination of the Franchise**
Determined by the parties. Usually, termination must be "for cause" (such as breach of the agreement, etc.) and notice must be given. A franchisee must be given reasonable time to wind up the business.

TRUE-FALSE QUESTIONS

(Answers at the Back of the Book)

____ 1. In a sole proprietorship, the owner and the business are entirely separate.

____ 2. In a sole proprietorship, the owner receives all of the profits.

____ 3. The income of a sole proprietorship is taxed to the owner as personal income.

____ 4. The death of the owner automatically dissolves a sole proprietorship.

____ 5. A court always determines the termination of a franchise.

____ 6. A franchise is an arrangement in which the owner of a trademark, a trade name, or a copyright has licensed others to use it in selling goods or services.

____ 7. A franchisee is not subject to the franchisor's control in the area of product quality.

____ 8. There is no state law covering franchises.

____ 9. There are no federal laws covering franchises.

____ 10. A franchisor may specify the form and capital structure of the franchisee's business.

FILL-IN QUESTIONS

(Answers at the Back of the Book)

An automobile dealership is an example of a ____________ (chain-style/distributorship/manufacturing) franchise. McDonald's is an example of a ____________ (chain-style/distributorship/manufacturing) franchise. Coca-Cola is an example of a ____________ (chain-style/distributorship/manufacturing) franchise.

MULTIPLE-CHOICE QUESTIONS

(Answers at the Back of the Book)

____ 1. Ann owns Beta Enterprises, a sole proprietorship. Ann's liability for the obligations of the business is

a. limited by state statute.
b. limited to the amount of his original investment.
c. limited to the total amount of capital Ann invests in the business.
d. unlimited.

____ 2. Adam invests in a franchise with Best Gas Stations, Inc. Best requires Adam to buy Best products for every phase of the operation. Adam's best argument to challenge this requirement is that it violates

a. an implied covenant of good faith and fair dealing.
b. antitrust laws.
c. the Federal Trade Commission's Franchise Rule.
d. the U.S. Franchise Agency's Purchase and Sale Regulations.

____ 3. Barb invests in a franchise with Copy Centers, Inc. The franchise agreement may require Barb to pay a percentage of Copy's

a. administrative expenses only.
b. advertising expenses only.
c. administrative and advertising expenses.
d. none of the above.

____ **4.** Dan wants the exclusive right to sell Excel Corporation software in a specific area. If Excel agrees, it may require Dan to pay

a. only a fee for a license to sell the software.
b. only a percentage of the receipts from sales of the software.
c. a fee for a license and a percentage of the receipts.
d. none of the above.

____ **5.** Fran buys a franchise from Global Services, Inc. In their agreement, Global may specify

a. requirements for the business form of the organization only.
b. standards of operation only.
c. requirements for the form of business and standards of operation.
d. none of the above.

____ **6.** Ron buys a franchise from Sports Club Corporation. If their agreement is like most franchise agreements, it will allow Sports Club to terminate the franchise

a. for any reason only with notice.
b. for any reason without notice.
c. for cause only.
d. under no circumstances.

____ **7.** Aaron invests in a franchise with Big Foods Corporation. With respect to the franchise, Aaron may have legal protection under

a. federal law only.
b. state law only.
c. federal and state law.
d. none of the above.

____ **8.** Donna, the owner of Eagle Sales, a sole proprietorship, wants to increase the business's capital without sacrificing control. This can be attained most successfully by

a. borrowing funds.
b. bringing in partners.
c. issuing stock.
d. selling the business.

____ **9.** Paul considers buying a franchise instead of developing and marketing his own products. A franchise could involve the licensing to Paul of

a. a copyright only.
b. a trademark or a trade name only.
c. a copyright, a trademark, or a trade name.
d. none of the above.

____ **10.** Alpha Communications Corporation grants a franchise to Ben. Ben is Alpha's

a. agent.
b. franchisee.
c. franchisor.
d. principal.

SHORT ESSAY QUESTIONS

1. What do franchise agreements generally provide with respect to a franchisee's location and form of doing business?

2. How do franchise agreements generally delegate price and quality controls over the franchisee's business?

ISSUE SPOTTERS

(Answers at the Back of the Book)

1. Frank plans to open a sporting goods store, and to hire Gail and Hal. Frank will invest only his own money. He does not expect to make a profit for at least eighteen months and to make little profit for the first three years. He hopes to expand eventually. Which form of business organization would be most appropriate?

2. American Bottling Company and U.S. Beverages, Inc., enter into a franchise agreement that provides it may be terminated at any time "for cause." American fails to meet the specified sales quota of U.S. Does this constitute "cause" for termination?

3. Merit Restaurants, Inc., sells franchises. Merit imposes on its franchisees standards of operation and personnel training methods. What is the potential pitfall to Merit if it exercises too much control over its franchisees?

SPECIAL INFORMATION FOR CPA CANDIDATES

For the CPA exam, it is most important to know the differences among the types of business organizations. Not traditionally tested on the exam are franchises. Of course, they may some day appear in a question on the test.

Chapter 36
Partnerships

WHAT THIS CHAPTER IS ABOUT

This chapter outlines the law of ordinary, or general, partnerships. Limited partnerships and limited liability partnerships are subject to different rules, which are set out in Chapter 41. Agency concepts (see Chapters 31 and 32) apply to all types of partnerships.

CHAPTER OUTLINE

I. THE LAW GOVERNING PARTNERSHIPS

A partnership arises from an agreement between two or more persons to carry on a business for profit. This agreement, the principles of agency law, and the Uniform Partnership Act (UPA) or the Revised Uniform Partnership Act (RUPA) govern partnerships.

II. DEFINITION OF PARTNERSHIP

A. ELEMENTS OF A PARTNERSHIP

"[A]n association of two or more persons to carry on as co-owners a business for profit" [UPA 6(1)]. There are three essential elements:

1. A sharing of profits or losses.
2. A joint ownership of the business.
3. An equal right in the management of the business.

B. SHARING PROFITS IS NOT ENOUGH

Sharing profits from a business does not imply a partnership, if the profits were received as payment of a debt by installments or interest on a loan, wages of an employee, rent to a landlord, an annuity to a widow or representative of a deceased partner, or a sale of goodwill of a business or property [UPA 7(4)]. Sharing profits from the joint ownership of property is not enough to create a partnership [UPA 7(2), (3)].

III. THE NATURE OF PARTNERSHIPS

A. PARTNERSHIP AS AN ENTITY

In many states, and under the UPA, the RUPA, and federal law, a partnership can be treated as an entity for certain purposes.

1. **Legal Capacity**
   Some states (and federal courts, when a federal question is at issue) permit a partnership to sue and be sued in the firm name; others allow a partnership to be sued as an entity but not to sue others in its firm name (it must use the names of the individual partners).

2. **Judgments**
   When a judgment is against a firm name, the liability is paid first out of partnership assets and then out of general partners' personal assets.

3. **Marshaling Assets**
Partnership creditors have first priority to the partnership's assets, and personal creditors of the individual partners have first priority to the individual assets of each partner.

4. **Bankruptcy**
In federal court, a bankruptcy in the firm name applies only to the partnership entity—it is not personal bankruptcy for the partners.

5. **Conveyance of Property**
A partnership can own property as an entity [UPA 8(3)] and can convey it without each individual partner's joining in the transaction.

B. AGGREGATE THEORY OF PARTNERSHIP
If a partnership is not regarded as a separate entity, it is treated as an aggregate of the individual partners.

IV. PARTNERSHIP FORMATION
A partnership agreement generally states the intention to create a partnership, contribute capital, share profits and losses, and participate in management.

A. FORMALITIES
A partnership agreement can be oral, written, or implied by conduct. Some must be in writing under the Statute of Frauds (see Chapter 14). Partners can agree to any terms that are not illegal or contrary to public policy.

B. DURATION

1. **Partnership for a Term**
The agreement can specify the duration of the partnership in terms of a date or the completion of a particular project. Dissolution without all partners' consent before expiration is a breach of the agreement.

2. **Partnership at Will**
No duration is set; any partner can dissolve a partnership at any time.

C. CAPACITY
Any person having capacity to enter a contract can become a partner. Minors and mentally incompetent persons can avoid their partnership contracts (see Chapter 12). If a partner is adjudicated mentally incompetent during the partnership, a court can decree dissolution.

D. A CORPORATION AS PARTNER
Many states (not the UPA) restrict the ability of corporations to become partners. In those states, courts sometimes validate such arrangements by characterizing them as joint ventures.

E. PARTNERSHIP BY ESTOPPEL
When parties who are not partners hold themselves out as partners and make representations that third persons rely on in dealing with them, liability is imposed on the alleged partner. A partner who consents to the misrepresentation is also liable to third persons extending credit in good faith reliance [UPA 16] (but the partnership is not).

V. PARTNERSHIP OPERATION

A. RIGHTS OF PARTNERS

1. **Management**

a. **Ordinarily, the Majority Rules**
"All partners have equal rights in the management and conduct of partnership business" [UPA 18(e)]. Each partner has one vote.

b. **When Unanimous Consent Is Required**
Unanimous consent is required to (1) alter the essential nature of the firm's business or capital structure; (2) admit new partners or enter a new business [UPA 18(g), (h)]; (3) assign property into a trust for the benefit of creditors; (4) dispose of the firm's goodwill; (5) confess judgment against the firm or submit firm claims to arbitration; (6) undertake any act that would make conduct of partnership business impossible [UPA 9(3)]; or (7) amend partnership articles.

2. **Interest in the Partnership**
Unless the partners agree otherwise, profits and losses are shared equally [UPA 18(a)].

3. **Compensation**
Doing partnership business is a partner's duty and not compensable. On the death of a partner, a surviving partner is entitled to compensation to wind up partnership affairs [UPA 18(f)].

4. **Inspection of Books**
A partner has a right to complete information concerning the conduct of partnership business [UPA 20]. Partnership books must be kept at the principal business office [UPA 19].

5. **Accounting**
A partner has a right to a formal accounting (1) on dissolution [UPA 22]; (2) when the partnership agreement provides for it; (3) when a partner is wrongfully excluded from the business, the books, or both; (4) when a partner withholds profits or benefits belonging to the partnership; or (5) when circumstances "render it just and reasonable."

6. **Property Rights**
A partner has an interest in the partnership, a right in partnership property, and a right to participate in management [UPA 24].

a. **Partner's Interest in the Firm**
A personal asset consisting of a proportionate share of the profits [UPA 26] and a return of capital. The interest can be assigned, and creditors can attach it by obtaining a charging order [UPA 28].

b. **Partnership Property**
A partner is co-owner with his or her partners of partnership property, holding it as a tenant in partnership [UPA 25(1)].

1) **If a Partner Dies**
Surviving partners, not the heirs of the deceased, have a right of survivorship to the property (they must account to the decedent's estate for the value [UPA 25(2)(d), (e)]).

2) **Each Partner Has Equal Rights**
Each partner can possess partnership property for business purposes or in satisfaction of firm debts, but cannot sell, assign, or deal with the property other than for partnership purposes [UPA 25(2)(a), (b)], without the consent of all of the partners.

B. DUTIES, POWERS, AND LIABILITIES OF PARTNERS

1. **Fiduciary Duties**
Partners (1) must act in good faith for the benefit of the partnership, (2) cannot engage in independent competitive activities without the other partners' consent, and (3) must account to the partnership for profits or benefits derived in a partnership transaction [UPA 21].

2. **General Agency Powers**
Each partner is an agent of every other partner and of the partnership in carrying out partnership business [UPA 9(1)].

   a. **Authority of Partners**
   Agency concepts apply to partners' authority (see Chapter 32).

   b. **Scope of Implied Powers**
   Implied authority is determined by the character and scope of the partnership business and the customary nature of the business. Normally, partners exercise all implied powers reasonably necessary to carry on the business [UPA 11].

3. **Joint Liability**
In most states, partners are jointly liable for partnership debts and contracts [UPA 15(b)] (each partner is liable for the entire debt; if one pays, the partnership or the other partners must reimburse that partner [UPA 18(b)]). To bring a successful claim against the partnership, a plaintiff must name all the partners as defendants.

4. **Joint and Several Liability**
In some states, partners are jointly and severally liable for partnership debts and contracts [see RUPA 306]. In all states, partners are jointly and severally liable for torts and breaches of trust [UPA 15(a)] (a partner who commits a tort must reimburse the partnership for any damages it pays). To bring a successful claim, a plaintiff need not name all the partners as defendants—a judgment against one partner does not extinguish the others' liability.

5. **Liability of Incoming Partner**
A newly admitted partner is liable for partnership debts incurred before his or her admission only to the extent of his or her interest in the partnership [UPA 17].

VI. PARTNERSHIP TERMINATION

Termination is caused by any change in the relations of the partners that demonstrates unwillingness or inability to carry on partnership business [UPA 29]. To continue the business, a partner can organize a new partnership.

A. DISSOLUTION

Occurs when a partner ceases to be associated with the carrying on of the business. Terminates the right of a partnership to exist as a going concern, but the partnership exists long enough to wind up its affairs.

1. **Dissolution by Acts of the Partners**

   a. **Dissolution by Agreement**
   The partnership agreement can stipulate events that will dissolve the firm. Partners can agree to dissolve the partnership early.

   b. **Partner's Power to Withdraw**
   No person can be compelled to be a partner. Under the UPA, a partner's withdrawal dissolves the partnership. Under the RUPA, dissolution results only if the partnership must be liquidated, not if a partner only quits the business [RUPA 601, 701, 801].

   c. **Admission of a New Partner**
   Admitting a new partner (without the consent of the others) causes dissolution. If the remaining or new partners continue the business, a new partnership arises (taking on the debts of the old [UPA 41]).

   d. **Transfer of a Partner's Interest**
   A transfer of a partner's interest or a sale of the interest for the benefit of creditors [UPA 28] leads to judicial dissolution (see below).

2. **Dissolution by Operation of Law**

   a. **Death**
   The death of a partner dissolves the firm, even if the partnership agreement provides for carrying on the business. (The surviving partners can form a new partnership.) Under the RUPA, death is not an automatic ground for dissolution [RUPA 601].

   b. **Bankruptcy**
   Bankruptcy of a partner (or the firm) will dissolve a partnership.

   c. **Illegality**
   Dissolution is caused by (1) an event that makes it unlawful for the partnership to continue, unless the partners decide to change the nature of the business and continue, or (2) an event that makes it illegal for any partner to carry on.

3. **Dissolution by Judicial Decree**
A court can dissolve a partnership for a partner's mental incompetency, incapacity, or improper conduct; impracticality of the firm's business (if it can be run only at a loss); or other circumstances [UPA 32].

4. **Notice of Dissolution**
The intent to dissolve (or to withdraw) must be communicated to each partner. Unless the other partners have notice, a withdrawing partner will continue to be bound as a partner to all contracts created for the firm. Notice must also be given to all affected third persons. A third person who has extended credit to the partnership must receive actual notice. For others, constructive notice is sufficient.

B. WINDING UP

Involves collecting and preserving partnership assets, paying debts, and accounting to each partner for the value of his or her interest.

1. **No New Obligations**
Once dissolution has occurred and partners have been notified, they cannot create new obligations on behalf of the partnership. Their only authority is to complete transactions begun but not finished at the time of dissolution and to wind up the business of the partnership.

2. **Interest of a Partner Who Violates the Partnership Agreement**
The other partners can buy out the interest and continue the business.

3. **If Dissolution Is Caused by the Death of a Partner**
All partnership assets vest in the surviving partners, who must settle partnership affairs and account to the estate of the deceased for the value of his or her interest. The surviving partners are entitled to payment for their services in winding up and for any costs [UPA 18(f)].

C. DISTRIBUTION OF ASSETS

1. **UPA Distribution**
Priority for the distribution of a partnership's assets is [UPA 40(b)]: (1) payment to third party creditors; (2) refund of loans made to or for the firm by a partner; (3) return of capital contribution to a partner; and (4) distribution of the balance, if any, to partners proportionate to their shares in the profits.

2. **RUPA Distribution**
Partner creditors are included among creditors who take first priority [RUPA 808]. Capital contributions and profits or losses are then calculated together to determine the amounts that the partners receive or the amounts that they must pay.

3. If the Partnership's Liabilities Are Greater Than Its Assets
Partners bear losses (in the absence of a contrary agreement) in the same proportion in which they shared profits. If the firm is insolvent, partners must still contribute their respective shares. If a partner does not contribute, the others must make the extra payments but have a right of contribution against whoever does not pay.

D. PARTNERSHIP BUY-SELL AGREEMENTS

1. UPA Buy-out
Partners may agree that one or more partners may buy out the others. The agreement may state who buys what, under what circumstances, and at what price, or that one or more partners will determine the value of the interest, and the others can decide whether to buy or sell.

2. RUPA Buy-out
If a partner's dissociation does not result in a dissolution of the partnership, a buy-out of the partner's interest is mandatory [RUPA 701] at basically the same price as he or she would get on dissolution.

VII. SPECIAL BUSINESS FORMS

A. JOINT VENTURE

A joint venture is an enterprise in which two or more persons combine their efforts or property for a single transaction or project, or a related series of transactions or projects. Unless otherwise agreed, joint venturers share profits and losses equally.

1. Characteristics
Same as a partnership except members have less implied and apparent authority than partners, and death of a member does not terminate a joint venture.

2. Duration
Depending on the circumstances: members specify the duration, the venture terminates when the project for which it is formed is completed, or any member can terminate the venture at will.

3. Duties, Rights, and Liabilities among Joint Venturers

a. Duties
Same as partners.

b. Conflicts When Members Are Competitors
(1) Each may face a choice between disclosing trade secrets to a competitor and breaching the duty to disclose, and (2) there is potential for violation of antitrust laws (see Chapter 46).

c. Rights
Each joint venturer has an equal right to manage the activities of the enterprise (though control may be given to one member).

d. Liability
Each joint venturer is liable to third parties for the actions of the other members in pursuit of the goal of the venture.

B. SYNDICATE

A group of individuals financing a project; may exist as a corporation, a partnership, or no legally recognized form.

C. JOINT STOCK COMPANY

Usually treated like a partnership (formed by agreement, members have personal liability, etc.), but members are not agents of one another, and has many characteristics of a corporation: (1) ownership by shares of stock, (2) managed by directors and officers, and (3) perpetual existence.

D. BUSINESS TRUST

Legal ownership and management of the property of the business is in one or more trustees; profits are distributed to beneficiaries, who are not personally responsible for the debts of the trust. Resembles a corporation.

E. COOPERATIVE

An association that is organized to provide an economic service to its members (or shareholders).

1. **Incorporated Cooperative**
   Subject to state laws governing nonprofit corporations. Distributes profits to owners on the basis of their transactions with the cooperative rather than on the basis of the amount of capital they contributed.

2. **Unincorporated Cooperatives**
   Often treated like partnerships. The members have joint liability for the cooperative's acts.

TRUE-FALSE QUESTIONS

(Answers at the Back of the Book)

___ 1. In most states, a partnership cannot exist unless a certificate of partnership is filed with a state.

___ 2. The liability of a partner for partnership debts is limited to the amount of capital he or she invests in the partnership.

___ 3. An assignment of a partner's interest causes the dissolution of the partnership.

___ 4. Unless a partnership agreement specifies otherwise, each partner has one vote in management matters.

___ 5. Creditors cannot use partnership property to satisfy the personal debts of a partner.

___ 6. Unless otherwise specified in the partnership agreement, profits in a partnership are shared in the same ratio as capital contributions.

___ 7. A syndicate may exist in the form of a corporation.

___ 8. A joint venture can be sued as an entity.

___ 9. A cooperative may take the form of a partnership or a corporation.

___ 10. The members of a joint venture have the same power as partners in a partnership to bind other members in the firm.

FILL-IN QUESTIONS

(Answers at the Back of the Book)

In most states, partners ________________ (are/are not) subject to joint liability on partnership debts, contracts, and torts. Joint liability means that if a third party sues a partner on a partnership ____________________________ (obligation/tort), the partner has the right to insist that the other partners be sued with him or her. If the third party does not sue all of the partners, those partners who are ________________ (not sued/sued) cannot be required to pay a judgment. In that circumstance, the assets of the partnership ________________________ (can/cannot) be used to satisfy the judgment. The third party's release of one partner ______________________________ (does not release/releases) the other partners. In most states, to bring a successful claim against a partnership on a debt or contract, a plaintiff ___________________ (may/must) name all the partners as defendants.

MULTIPLE-CHOICE QUESTIONS

(Answers at the Back of the Book)

___ **1.** Carl holds himself out as a partner of Delta Associates, a partnership, even though he has no connection to the firm. Carl obtains a personal loan based on this misrepresentation. Carl's default on the loan will result in liability on the part of

a. Carl only.
b. Delta only.
c. Carl and Delta jointly.
d. no one.

___ **2.** Ed and Fran are partners in Great Mines, which is in the process of dissolution. Ed wants to keep the firm's equipment. Ed

a. has no preference over Fran to the equipment.
b. is entitled to the equipment only if it was originally his idea to buy it.
c. is entitled to the equipment only if he asked for it before Fran.
d. is entitled to the equipment only if he bought it with partnership funds.

___ **3.** Holly owns International Imports. She hires Jay as a salesperson, agreeing to pay $10.00 per hour plus 10 percent of his sales. Holly and Jay are

a. partners for the duration of Jay's employment.
b. not partners, because Holly pays Jay an hourly wage.
c. not partners, because Jay does not have an ownership interest or management rights in the business.
d. not partners, because Jay receives a commission, not a share of the profits.

___ **4.** **Based a Sample CPA Exam Question.** Alan, Bill, and Carol are partners in ABC Accountants. Dissolution would be caused by

a. Alan joining another partnership.
b. Bill's interest in the partnership being attached by a court.
c. Carol being adjudicated bankrupt.
d. any partner being sued by the other partners for an accounting.

___ **5.** Owen and Pat are partners in Quality Investments, a partnership. Owen convinces Roy, a customer, to invest in a nonexistent gold mine. Owen absconds with Roy's money. If Roy sues Pat, Roy will

a. lose, because partners are not jointly and severally liable.
b. lose, because only partnership assets are available to pay the judgment.
c. win, because partners are jointly and severally liable.
d. win, because partnership assets are available to pay the judgment.

___ **6.** Vicky and Warren do business as a partnership under the name United Digital. United

a. is a tax-paying entity.
b. is required to file an information return but is not a tax-paying entity.
c. pays 1/2 of the taxes if there are only two partners.
d. pays 1/3 of the taxes if there are only two partners.

___ 7. Ann, Bert, and Carol are partners in an accounting firm. Ann tells Bert and Carol that effective immediately, she is quitting the firm. Later, Bert and Carol sign a contract with a supplier. The contract is binding on

a. Bert only.
b. Bert and Carol only.
c. Ann, Bert, and Carol.
d. none of the partners.

___ 8. **Based on a Sample CPA Exam Question.** Acme Corporation and U.S. Goods, Inc., form a joint venture to develop and market business software. A joint venture is

a. a corporate enterprise for a single undertaking of limited duration.
b. an association limited to no more than two persons in business for profit.
c. an association of persons engaged as co-owners in a single undertaking for profit.
d. an enterprise of numerous co-owners in a nonprofit undertaking.

___ 9. Evan and Frank form a syndicate to finance Great Offices, a real estate project. A syndicate

a. is similar to a corporation.
b. is similar to a partnership.
c. is a hybrid of a corporation and a partnership.
d. may exist as a partnership or a corporation.

___ 10. Gamma, Inc., and Omega Corporation pool their assets to form a business trust. A business trust is

a. similar to a corporation.
b. similar to a partnership.
c. a hybrid of a corporation and a partnership.
d. unlike a corporation or a partnership.

SHORT ESSAY QUESTIONS

1. What are the rights held by partners in terms of management, interest in the partnership, compensation, inspection of books, accounting, and property rights?

2. How do the concepts of joint liability, and joint and several liability, relate to partnerships?

ISSUE SPOTTERS

(Answers at the Back of the Book)

1. Dan and Eve are partners in a computer peripherals firm. When Dan dies, his widow claims that as Dan's heir, she is entitled to take his place as Eve's partner or she is entitled to a share of the firm's inventory. Is she right?

2. Fred and Gail are partners in a delivery business. When business is slow, without Gail's knowledge, Fred leases the delivery vehicles as moving vans. Because the vehicles would otherwise be sitting idle in a parking lot, can Fred keep the lease money?

3. Ace Construction and Bayside Developers form a joint venture. Central Processing and Delta Data form a joint stock company. Efficient Systems and Fast Products form an unincorporated cooperative. What do these forms of business organization have in common?

SPECIAL INFORMATION FOR CPA CANDIDATES

For the CPA exam, it is important to know the differences among the types of business organizations, including sole proprietorships and partnerships.

As of the time of this writing, the CPA examination tested candidates' knowledge of the UPA, not the RUPA. The UPA definition of *partnership* has frequently been on the exam. Remember that it represents an example of the aggregate theory (you may as well also review aspects of the entity theory). Keep in mind, too, that unless partners agree otherwise, they share profits, losses, and management rights equally, and that only surviving partners are entitled to a salary. Other important points include that partners are jointly and severally liable for torts committed by copartners carrying on the business but jointly liable for all partnership contracts.

For the CPA examination, an important point in the material in this chapter is the liability of partners to each other and to third parties—remember that every partner is an agent of the partnership and of the other partners. Review the liability of withdrawing partners and new partners.

Chapter 37
CORPORATIONS—
Formation and Financing

WHAT THIS CHAPTER IS ABOUT

This chapter covers corporate rights, powers, classifications, formation, and financing. Most corporations are formed under state law, and a majority of states follow some version of the Revised Model Business Corporation Act (RMBCA).

CHAPTER OUTLINE

I. THE NATURE OF THE CORPORATION

A. CORPORATE PERSONNEL
Shareholders elect a board of directors, which is responsible for overall management and hires corporate officers to run daily operations.

B. CORPORATE TAXATION
Corporate profits are taxed twice: as income to the corporation and, when distributed as dividends, as income to the shareholders.

C. CONSTITUTIONAL RIGHTS OF CORPORATIONS
A corporation is recognized as a "legal person" and, under the Bill of Rights, has the same rights as a natural person (see Chapter 4). A corporation is not a "natural citizen," however: only officers and employees have a right against self-incrimination, and the privileges and immunities clause does not protect corporations.

D. TORTS AND CRIMINAL ACTS
A corporation is liable for the torts committed by its agents within the course and scope of employment. A corporation may be held liable for the crimes of its employees and agents if the punishment for the crimes can be applied to a corporation.

E. CORPORATE SENTENCING GUIDELINES
The guidelines cover thirty-two levels of offenses. Punishment depends on the seriousness of a charge, the amount of money involved, and the extent to which corporate officers are involved. Sanctions are reduced when corporations cooperate to prevent, investigate, and punish wrongdoing.

II. CORPORATE POWERS

A. EXPRESS AND IMPLIED POWERS
Express powers are in (in order of priority) the U.S. Constitution, state constitution, state statutes, articles of incorporation, bylaws, and board resolutions. A corporation has the *implied* power to perform all acts reasonably appropriate and necessary to accomplish its purposes.

B. *ULTRA VIRES* DOCTRINE
Ultra vires acts are beyond the purposes stated in the articles. Most such acts have involved contracts (which generally are enforced [RMBCA 3.04]). Courts usually allow any legal action a firm takes to profit shareholders.

III. CLASSIFICATION OF CORPORATIONS

A. DOMESTIC, FOREIGN, AND ALIEN CORPORATIONS

A corporation is a domestic corporation in the state in which it incorporated, a foreign corporation in other states, and an alien corporation in other countries. A foreign corporation normally must obtain a certificate of authority to do business in any state except its home state.

B. PUBLIC AND PRIVATE CORPORATIONS

A public corporation is formed by the government to meet a political or governmental purpose (the U.S. Postal Service, AMTRAK). A private corporation is created for private benefit and is owned by private persons.

C. NONPROFIT CORPORATIONS

Corporations formed without a profit-making purpose (private hospitals, educational institutions, charities, and religious organizations).

D. CLOSE CORPORATIONS

To qualify as a close corporation, a firm must have a limited number of shareholders, and restrict its issue and transfer of stock.

1. Advantage

Exempt from most of the nonessential formalities of corporate operation (bylaws, annual meetings, etc. [RMBCA 7.32]).

2. Management

Resembles that of a sole proprietorship or a partnership—one or a few shareholders usually hold the positions of directors and officers.

3. Transfer of Shares

Often restricted by stipulating that shareholders offer their shares to the corporation or other shareholders before offering them to outsiders.

E. S CORPORATIONS

1. Requirements

Must be a domestic corporation; must not be a member of an affiliated group of corporations; shareholders must be individuals, estates, or certain trusts; must have thirty-five or fewer shareholders; can have only one class of stock; no shareholder can be a nonresident alien.

2. Advantages

Shareholders can use corporate losses to offset other income; only a single tax on corporate income is imposed at individual income tax rates at the shareholder level (whether or not it is distributed).

F. PROFESSIONAL CORPORATIONS

Generally subject to the law governing ordinary corporations.

1. Limited Liability

A shareholder in a professional corporation is protected from liability for torts (except malpractice) committed by other members.

2. Unlimited Liability

A court might regard a professional corporation as a partnership, in which each partner may be liable for the malpractice of the others.

IV. CORPORATE FORMATION

A. PROMOTIONAL ACTIVITIES

Promoters take the first steps in organizing a corporation: issue a prospectus (see Chapter 40) and secure the corporate charter (see below).

1. **Promoter's Liability**
Personally liable on preincorporation contracts, unless the contracting party agrees otherwise. This liability continues after incorporation unless the third party releases the promoter or the corporation assumes the contract by novation (see Chapter 16).

2. **Subscribers and Subscriptions**
Subscribers (who agree to buy stock in a future corporation) become shareholders as soon as the corporation is formed or as soon as it accepts their subscription agreement with the promoter.

   a. **Subscribers' Liability**
   A subscription is irrevocable for six months unless the parties agree otherwise [RMBCA 6.20]. In some states, a subscriber can revoke an offer to buy before the corporation accepts.

   b. **Corporation's Liability**
   Preincorporation subscriptions are continuing offers to buy stock. On or after its formation, a corporation can choose to accept the offer.

B. INCORPORATION PROCEDURES

1. **State Chartering**
Some states offer more advantageous tax or incorporation provisions.

2. **Articles of Incorporation**
The articles include basic information about the corporation and serve as a primary source of authority for its organization and functions.

   a. **Corporate Name**
   Cannot be the same as, or deceptively similar to, the name of a corporation doing business in the state.

   b. **Nature and Purpose**
   The intended business activities of the corporation must be specified. Stating a general corporate purpose is usually sufficient.

   c. **Duration**
   A corporation can have perpetual existence in most states.

   d. **Capital Structure**
   The amount of stock authorized for issuance; its valuation; and other information as to equity, capital, and credit must be outlined.

   e. **Internal Organization**
   Management structure can be described in bylaws later.

   f. **Registered Office and Agent**
   Usually, the registered office is the principal office of the corporation; the agent is a person designated to receive legal documents on behalf of the corporation.

   g. **Incorporators**
   Incorporators (some states require only one) must sign the articles when they are submitted to the state; often this is their only duty, and they need have no other interest in the corporation.

3. **Certificate of Incorporation (Corporate Charter)**
The articles of incorporation are sent to the appropriate state official (usually the secretary of state). Many states issue a certificate of incorporation authorizing the corporation to conduct business.

4. **First Organizational Meeting (After the Charter Is Granted)**

a. **Who Holds the Meeting**
The incorporators or the board; the business conducted depends on state law, the nature of the corporation's business, the provisions of the articles, and the wishes of the promoters.

b. **Adoption of the Bylaws**
This is the most important function of the first organizational meeting.

V. IMPROPER INCORPORATION

A. POSSIBLE RESULTS OF IMPROPER INCORPORATION
On the basis of improper incorporation—

1. **Shareholders May Be Personally Liable for Corporate Obligations**
A person attempting to enforce a contract or bring a tort suit against the corporation could seek to make the shareholders personally liable.

2. **Third Parties May Avoid Liability to the Corporation**
If a corporation seeks to enforce a contract, the defaulting party who learns of a defect in incorporation may be able to avoid liability.

B. *DE JURE* AND *DE FACTO* CORPORATIONS

1. ***De Jure* Existence**
Occurs if there is substantial compliance with all requirements for incorporation. In most states, the certificate of incorporation is evidence that all requirements have been met, and neither the state nor a third party can attack the corporation's existence.

2. ***De Facto* Existence**
The existence of a corporation cannot be challenged by third persons (except the state) if (1) there is a statute under which the firm can be incorporated, (2) the parties made a good faith attempt to comply with it, and (3) the firm has attempted to do business as a corporation.

C. CORPORATION BY ESTOPPEL
If an association that is neither an actual corporation nor a *de facto* or *de jure* corporation holds itself out as being a corporation, it will be estopped from denying corporate status in a suit by a third party.

VI. DISREGARDING THE CORPORATE ENTITY

A. PIERCING THE CORPORATE VEIL
A court may ignore the corporate structure (pierce the corporate veil) if—

1. A party is tricked or misled into dealing with the corporation rather than the individual.
2. The corporation is set up never to make a profit or always to be insolvent, or it is too thinly capitalized.
3. Statutory corporate formalities are not followed.
4. Personal and corporate interests are commingled to the extent that the corporation has no separate identity.

B. RESULT
Personal liability for corporate debts is imposed on shareholders.

VII. CORPORATE FINANCING

A. BONDS
Bonds are issued as evidence of funds that business firms borrow from investors. A lending agreement called a *bond indenture* specifies the terms (maturity date, interest). A trustee ensures that the terms are met.

B. STOCKS

The most important characteristics of stocks are: (1) investors need not be repaid, (2) stockholders receive dividends only when voted by the directors, (3) stockholders are the last investors to be paid on dissolution, and (4) stockholders vote for management and on major issues.

C. LOCATING POTENTIAL INVESTORS ONLINE

Services that match entrepreneurs with investors have expanded onto the Internet.

TRUE-FALSE QUESTIONS

(Answers at the Back of the Book)

___ 1. A shareholder can sue a corporation, and a corporation can sue a shareholder.

___ 2. A foreign corporation is a corporation formed in another country but doing business in the United States.

___ 3. Generally, a promoter is personally liable on a preincorporation contract.

___ 4. Any power set out in a corporation's charter or bylaws is *ultra vires.*

___ 5. To a corporation, stocks represent corporate ownership.

___ 6. To a corporation, bonds represent corporate debt.

___ 7. S corporations cannot avoid federal taxes at the corporate level.

___ 8. In some states, a close corporation can operate without formal shareholders' or directors' meetings.

___ 9. State corporation laws are completely uniform.

___ 10. A corporation is liable for the torts of its agents or officers committed within the course and scope of their employment.

FILL-IN QUESTIONS

(Answers at the Back of the Book)

Those who, for themselves or others, take the preliminary steps in organizing a corporation are ________________ (promoters/incorporators). These persons enter into contracts with professionals, whose services are needed in planning the corporation, and are personally liable on these contracts, ________________ (unless/even if) the third party issues a release or the corporation assumes the contract. A person who applies to the state on behalf of the corporation to obtain its certificate of incorporation is ________________ (a promoter/an incorporator). This person ________________ (must/need not) have any interest in the corporation.

MULTIPLE-CHOICE QUESTIONS

(Answers at the Back of the Book)

___ 1. Adam and Beth want to incorporate to sell computers. The first step in the incorporation procedure is to

a. file the articles of incorporation.
b. hold the first organizational meeting.
c. obtain a corporate charter.
d. select a state in which to incorporate.

___ 2. Alpha Company is a corporation. Alpha has the implied power to

a. amend the corporate charter.
b. declare dividends.
c. file a derivative suit.
d. perform all acts reasonably appropriate and necessary to accomplish its corporate purposes.

___ 3. Responsibility for the overall management of Beta, Inc., a corporation, is entrusted to

a. the board of directors.
b. the corporate officers and managers.
c. the owners of the corporation.
d. the promoters of the corporation.

___ 4. Delta Company is a private, for-profit corporation that (1) was formed for the purpose of marketing business office software, (2) is owned by ten shareholders, (3) is subject to double taxation, and (4) has made no public offering of its shares. Delta is

a. a close corporation.
b. a nonprofit corporation.
c. an S corporation.
d. a professional corporation.

___ 5. Eagle, Inc., issues bonds. Bonds

a. are issued by S corporations only.
b. are sometime referred to as "stock with preferences."
c. have fixed maturity dates.
d. require periodic interest payments from their owners.

___ 6. Like other corporations, Fine Services, Inc., issues securities most likely to

a. increase its market share.
b. increase its visibility.
c. obtain financing.
d. reduce its distribution costs.

___ 7. Great Goods, Inc., is a consumer products firm. As a source of authority for its organization and functions, its articles of incorporation are

a. a primary source.
b. a secondary source.
c. a source of final resort.
d. not a reliable source.

___ 8. Home Products Company issues common stock for sale to the public. If Ira buys ten shares of the stock, he has a proportionate interest with regard to

a. control only.
b. earnings and net assets only.
c. control, earnings, and net assets.
d. none of the above.

___ 9. Jiffy Corporation substantially complies with all conditions precedent to incorporation. Jiffy has

a. corporation by estoppel.
b. *de facto* existence.
c. *de jure* existence.
d. none of the above.

___ **10.** Kate is a shareholder of Local Delivery, Inc. A court might "pierce the corporate veil" and hold her personally liable for Local's debts if

a. Kate's personal interests are commingled with Local's interests to the extent that Local has no separate identity.
b. Local calls too many shareholders' meetings.
c. Local is overcapitalized.
d. none of the above.

SHORT ESSAY QUESTIONS

1. What is the significance of the following items as they relate to a company's articles of incorporation: (1) corporate name, (2) nature and purpose, (3) duration, (4) capital structure, (5) internal organization, (6) registered office and agent, and (7) incorporators?

2. Describe the features of nonprofit, close, S, and professional corporations.

ISSUE SPOTTERS

(Answers at the Back of the Book)

1. Macro Corporation is formed in one state, but does business through sales representatives in another state, in which it has no office or warehouse. Can the latter exercise jurisdiction over Macro?

2. Name Brand, Inc., is a small business. Twelve members of a single family own all of its stock. Ordinarily, corporate income is taxed at the corporate and shareholder levels. Is there a way for this firm to avoid this double income taxation?

3. The incorporators of Open Source, Inc., want their new firm to have the authority to transact virtually all types of business. Can they grant this authority to their firm?

SPECIAL INFORMATION FOR CPA CANDIDATES

Over time, the CPA examination has come to emphasize statutory principles (such as the MBCA and the RMBCA) and deemphasize common law principles (such as *de jure* and *de facto* corporations and the *ultra vires* doctrine—the most likely application of the latter is in a question that involves an executory contract).

Other important points to keep in mind include the liability of a promoter who organizes a new corporation (and how a promoter can avoid liability), the liability of the corporation in regard to preincorporation contracts, the relationship of the promoters to shareholders and the corporation, and the circumstances under which a shareholder may be liable for the debts of a corporation.

Chapter 38
CORPORATIONS—
Directors, Officers, and Shareholders

WHAT THIS CHAPTER IS ABOUT

This chapter outlines the rights and responsibilities of all participants—directors, officers, and shareholders—in a corporate enterprise. Also noted are the ways in which conflicts among these participants are resolved.

CHAPTER OUTLINE

I. ROLE OF DIRECTORS

The board of directors governs a corporation. Officers handle daily business.

A. ELECTION OF DIRECTORS

1. Number of Directors

Set in a corporation's articles or bylaws. Corporations with fewer than fifty shareholders can eliminate the board of directors [RMBCA 8.01].

2. How Directors Are Chosen

The first board (appointed by the incorporators or named in the articles) serves until the first shareholders' meeting. Shareholders by majority vote (see below) elect subsequent directors.

3. Removal of Directors

A director can be removed for cause by shareholder action (or the board may have the power). In most states, a director cannot be removed without cause unless shareholders have reserved the right.

B. BOARD OF DIRECTORS' MEETINGS

1. Formal Minutes and Notice

A board conducts business by holding formal meetings with recorded minutes. The dates for regular meetings are usually set in the articles and bylaws or by board resolution, and no other notice is required. Special meetings require notice to all directors. Telephone or e-conferencing is possible.

2. Quorum Requirements and Voting

Quorum requirements vary. If the firm specifies none, in most states a quorum is a majority of the number of directors authorized in the articles or bylaws. Voting is done in person, one vote per director.

C. RIGHTS OF DIRECTORS

1. Participation and Inspection

A director has a right to participate in corporate business. A director must have access to all corporate books and records to make decisions.

2. **Compensation and Indemnification**
Nominal sums may be paid to directors, and there is a trend to provide more. Most states permit a corporation to indemnify a director for costs and fees in defending against corporate-related lawsuits. Many firms buy insurance to cover indemnification.

D. MANAGEMENT RESPONSIBILITIES

1. **Areas of Responsibility**
Major policy and financial decisions; appointment, supervision, pay, and removal of officers and other managerial employees.

2. **Executive Committee**
Most states permit a board to elect an executive committee from among the directors to handle management between board meetings. The committee is limited to ordinary business matters.

II. ROLE OF CORPORATE OFFICERS AND EXECUTIVES

The board hires officers and other executive employees. Officers act as corporate agents (see Chapters 31 and 32).

A. QUALIFICATIONS

At the discretion of the firm; included in the articles or bylaws. A person can hold more than one office and also be a director.

B. RIGHTS AND DUTIES

The rights of corporate officers and other high-level managers are defined by employment contracts. Normally, the board can remove officers at any time (but the corporation could be liable for breach of contract). Officers' duties are the same as those of directors.

III. FIDUCIARY DUTIES OF DIRECTORS AND OFFICERS

Directors and officers are fiduciaries of the corporation.

A. DUTY OF CARE

Directors and officers must act in good faith, in what they consider to be the best interests of the corporation, and with the care that an ordinarily prudent person would exercise in similar circumstances.

1. **Duty to Make Informed and Reasonable Decisions**
Directors must be informed on corporate matters and act in accord with their knowledge and training. A director can rely on information furnished by competent officers, or others, without being accused of acting in bad faith or failing to exercise due care [RMBCA 8.30].

2. **Duty to Exercise Reasonable Supervision**
Directors must exercise reasonable supervision when work is delegated.

3. **Dissenting Directors**
Directors must attend board meetings; if not, he or she should register a dissent to actions taken (to avoid liability for mismanagement).

B. DUTY OF LOYALTY

Directors and officers cannot use corporate funds or confidential information for personal advantage. Specifically, they cannot—

1. Compete with the corporation.
2. Usurp a corporate opportunity.
3. Have an interest that conflicts with the interest of the corporation.
4. Engage in insider trading (see Chapter 40).

5. Authorize a corporate transaction that is detrimental to minority shareholders.

6. Sell control over the corporation.

C. CONFLICTS OF INTEREST

Directors and officers must disclose fully any conflict of interest that might occur in a deal involving the corporation. A contract may be upheld if it was fair and reasonable to the firm when it was made, there was full disclosure of the interest of the officers or directors involved, and it was approved by a majority of disinterested directors or shareholders.

IV. LIABILITY OF DIRECTORS AND OFFICERS

A. THE BUSINESS JUDGMENT RULE

Honest mistakes of judgment and poor business decisions do not make directors and officers liable to the firm for poor results, if the decision complies with management's fiduciary duties, has a reasonable basis, and is within managerial authority and the power of the corporation.

B. LIABILITY FOR TORTS AND CRIMES

Directors and officers are personally liable for their torts and crimes, and may be liable for those of subordinates (under the "responsible corporate officer" doctrine or the "pervasiveness of control" theory). The corporation is liable for such acts when committed within the scope of employment.

V. ROLE OF SHAREHOLDERS

A. SHAREHOLDERS' POWERS

Shareholders own the corporation, approve fundamental corporate changes, and elect and remove directors.

B. SHAREHOLDERS' MEETINGS

Regular meetings must occur annually; special meetings can be called to handle urgent matters.

1. Notice of Meeting Must be in Writing in Advance

Notice of a special meeting must state the purpose.

2. Proxies

Rather than attend a meeting, shareholders normally authorize third parties to vote their shares. A proxy may be revocable and may have a time limit. When a firm sends proxy materials to its shareholders, it must allow them to vote on pending policy proposals.

C. SHAREHOLDER VOTING

1. Quorum Requirements

At the meeting, a quorum must be present. A majority vote of the shares present is required to pass resolutions. Fundamental changes require a higher percentage.

2. Voting Techniques

Each common shareholder has one vote per share. The articles can exclude or limit voting rights.

a. Cumulative Voting

The number of members of the board to be elected multiplied by the total number of voting shares is the number of votes a shareholder has and can be cast for one or more nominees.

b. Shareholder Voting Agreements

A group of shareholders can agree to vote their shares together. A shareholder can vote by proxy. Any person can solicit proxies.

c. Voting Trust

Exists when legal title (recorded ownership on the corporate books) is transferred to a trustee who is responsible for voting the shares. The shareholder retains all other ownership rights.

VI. RIGHTS OF SHAREHOLDERS

A. STOCK CERTIFICATES

Notice of shareholder meetings, dividends, and corporate reports are distributed to owners listed in the corporate books, not on the basis of possession of stock certificates (which most states do not require).

B. PREEMPTIVE RIGHTS

Usually apply only to additional, newly issued stock sold for cash and must be exercised within a specified time (usually thirty days). When new shares are issued, each shareholder is given *stock warrants* (transferable options to acquire a certain number of shares at a stated price).

C. DIVIDENDS

Dividends can be paid in cash, property, or stock. Once declared, a cash dividend is a corporate debt. Dividends are payable only from (1) retained earnings, (2) current net profits, or (3) any surplus.

1. Illegal Dividends

A dividend paid when a corporation is insolvent is illegal and must be repaid. A dividend paid from an unauthorized account or causing a corporation to become insolvent may have to be repaid. In any case, the directors can be held personally liable.

2. If the Directors Fail to Declare a Dividend

Shareholders can ask a court to compel a declaration of a dividend, but to succeed, the directors' conduct must be an abuse of discretion.

D. INSPECTION RIGHTS

Shareholders (or their attorney, accountant, or agent) can inspect and copy corporate books and records for a proper purpose, if the request is made in advance [RMBCA 16.02]. This right can be denied to prevent harassment or to protect confidential corporate information.

E. TRANSFER OF SHARES

Any restrictions on transferability must be noted on the face of a stock certificate. Restrictions must be reasonable—for example, a right of first refusal remains with the corporation or the shareholders for only a specified time or a reasonable time.

F. RIGHTS ON DISSOLUTION

Shareholders can petition a court to dissolve a firm if [RMBCA 14.30]—

1. The directors are deadlocked, shareholders are unable to break the deadlock, and there is or could be irreparable injury to the firm.
2. The acts of the directors or those in control of the corporation are illegal, oppressive, or fraudulent.
3. Corporate assets are being misapplied or wasted.
4. The shareholders are deadlocked in voting power and have failed, for a specified period (usually two annual meetings), to elect successors to directors.

G. SHAREHOLDER'S DERIVATIVE SUIT

If directors fail to sue in the corporate name to redress a wrong suffered by the firm, shareholders can do so (after complaining to the board). Any recovery normally goes into the corporate treasury.

VII. LIABILITY OF SHAREHOLDERS

In most cases, if a corporation fails, shareholders lose only their investment. Exceptions include (see also Chapter 40)—

A. STOCK-SUBSCRIPTION AGREEMENTS

Once a subscription agreement is accepted, any refusal to pay is a breach, resulting in personal liability.

B. WATERED STOCK

In most cases, a shareholder who receives watered stock (stock sold by a corporation for less than par value) must pay the difference to the corporation. In some states, such shareholders may be liable to creditors of the corporation for unpaid corporate debts.

VIII. DUTIES OF MAJORITY SHAREHOLDERS

A single shareholder (or a few acting together) who owns enough shares to control the corporation owes a fiduciary duty to the minority shareholders and creditors when they sell their shares.

TRUE-FALSE QUESTIONS

(Answers at the Back of the Book)

___ **1.** The business judgment rule immunizes officers from liability for poor decisions that were made in good faith.

___ **2.** An officer is a fiduciary of a corporation.

___ **3.** Preemptive rights entitle shareholders to bring a derivative suit against the corporation.

___ **4.** Only certain funds are legally available for paying dividends.

___ **5.** Damages recovered in a shareholder's derivative suit are paid to the shareholder who brought the suit.

___ **6.** Generally, shareholders are not personally responsible for the debts of the corporation.

___ **7.** Directors, but not officers, owe a duty of loyalty to the corporation.

___ **8.** The business judgment rule makes a director liable for losses to the firm in most cases.

___ **9.** Shareholders may vote to remove members of the board of directors.

___ **10.** Par-value shares have a specific face value.

FILL-IN QUESTIONS

(Answers at the Back of the Book)

A stock certificate may be lost or destroyed, ______________________(and ownership is/but ownership is not) destroyed with it. A new certificate __________ (can/cannot) be issued to replace one that has been lost or destroyed. Notice of meetings, dividends, and operational and financial reports are all distributed according to the individual ______________________________________ (in possession of the certificate/recorded as the owner in the corporation's books).

MULTIPLE-CHOICE QUESTIONS

(Answers at the Back of the Book)

___ **1.** The board of directors of Consumer Goods Corporation announces a cash dividend. A cash dividend may *not* be paid from

a. accumulated surplus.
b. gross profits.
c. net profits.
d. retained earnings.

___ **2.** Jill is a shareholder of United Manufacturing Company. As a shareholder, Jill does *not* have a right to

a. compensation.
b. dividends.
c. inspect corporate books and records.
d. transfer shares.

___ **3.** Don and Eve are officers of Fine Products Corporation. As officers, their rights are set out in

a. Don and Eve's employment contracts.
b. international agreements.
c. state corporation statutes.
d. the firm's certificate of authority.

___ **4.** Fred is a director of Great Sales, Inc. As a director, Fred owes Great Sales a duty of

a. care only.
b. loyalty only.
c. care and loyalty.
d. none of the above.

___ **5.** **Based on a Sample CPA Exam Question.** The management of National Brands, Inc., is at odds with the shareholders over some recent decisions. The shareholders may file a shareholders' derivative suit to

a. compel dissolution of National.
b. compel payment of a properly declared dividend.
c. enforce a right to inspect corporate records.
d. recover damages from the management for an *ultra vires* act.

___ **6.** Jiffy Corporation uses cumulative voting in its elections of directors. Kay owns 3,000 Jiffy shares. At an annual meeting at which three directors are to be elected, Mary may cast for any one candidate

a. 1,000 votes.
b. 3,000 votes.
c. 9,000 votes.
d. 27,000 votes.

___ **7.** Local Business Corporation invests in intrastate businesses. In Local's state, as in most states, the minimum number of directors that must be present before its board can transact business is

a. all of the directors authorized in the articles.
b. a majority of the number authorized in the articles or bylaws.
c. any odd number.
d. none of the above.

___ **8.** Micro Manufacturing Company makes and sells computer chips. Like most corporations, Micro's officers are hired by the company's

a. directors.
b. incorporators.
c. officers.
d. shareholders.

___ **9.** Nora is a director of Open Source, Inc. Nora has a right to

a. compensation.
b. participation.
c. preemption.
d. none of the above.

___ **10.** Pat is a director of Quik Buy, Inc. Without informing Quik Buy, Pat goes into business with Fast Sales, Inc., to compete with Quik Buy. This violates

a. the business judgment rule.
b. the duty of care.
c. the duty of loyalty.
d. none of the above.

SHORT ESSAY QUESTIONS

1. How do the duty of care and the duty of loyalty govern the conduct of directors and officers in a corporation?

2. What are the rights of the shareholders of a corporation?

ISSUE SPOTTERS

(Answers at the Back of the Book)

1. Alpha Corporation's board of directors, who include Beth and Carl (officers of the firm), is deadlocked over whether to market a new product. Dan, a minority shareholder, suspects that Beth and Carl are taking advantage of the deadlock to use corporate assets (offices, equipment, supplies, staff time) to initiate a competing enterprise. Can Dan intervene?

2. Beta Corporation has an opportunity to buy stock in Gamma, Inc. The directors decide that, instead of Beta buying the stock, the directors will buy it. Frank, a Beta shareholder, learns of the purchase and wants to sue the directors on Beta's behalf. Can he do it?

3. Gail is Omega Corporation's majority shareholder. She owns enough stock in Omega that if she were to sell it, the sale would be a transfer of control of the firm. Does she owe a duty to Omega or the minority shareholders in selling her shares?

SPECIAL INFORMATION FOR CPA CANDIDATES

For the CPA examination, be sure that you understand the relationship of directors and officers to the corporation. These individuals have fiduciary duties and agency authority that shareholders do not have. Officers and directors must exercise reasonable care, subject to the business judgment rule (which absolves those who act in good faith).

Note that this is not the same as the due diligence standard of the Securities Exchange Commission (SEC) (see Chapter 40). For that reason, pay close attention to which standard a question involves. Regarding shareholders, you should know their rights, and in what circumstances a shareholder may be personally liable for the obligations of a corporation.

Chapter 39
CORPORATIONS—
Merger, Consolidation, and Termination

WHAT THIS CHAPTER IS ABOUT

This chapter covers corporate mergers, consolidations, purchase of another corporation's assets, and purchase of a controlling interest in another corporation. The chapter also touches on the reasons for, and methods used in, terminating a corporation.

CHAPTER OUTLINE

I. MERGER AND CONSOLIDATION

Whether a combination is a merger or a consolidation, the rights and liabilities of shareholders, the corporation, and its creditors are the same.

A. MERGER

1. What a Merger Is

A merger is the combination of two or more corporations, often by one absorbing the other. After a merger, only one of the corporations exists.

2. The Results of a Merger

The surviving corporation has all of the rights, assets, liabilities, and debts of itself and the other corporation. Its articles of incorporation are deemed amended to include changes stated in the articles of merger.

B. CONSOLIDATION

In a consolidation, two or more corporations combine so that each corporation ceases to exist and a new one emerges. The results of a consolidation are essentially the same as the results of a merger.

C. PROCEDURE FOR MERGER OR CONSOLIDATION

1. The Basic Steps

(1) Each board approves the merger or consolidation plan; (2) each firm's shareholders vote on the plan at a shareholders' meeting; (3) the plan is filed, usually with the secretary of state; and (4) the state issues a certificate of merger or consolidation.

2. Short-Form Mergers

A substantially owned subsidiary corporation can merge into its parent corporation without shareholder approval, if the parent owns at least 90 percent of the subsidiary's outstanding stock.

3. Appraisal Rights

If provided by statute, a shareholder can dissent from a merger, consolidation, sale of substantially all the corporate assets not in the ordinary course of business, and (in some states) amendments to articles.

a. Procedure

A shareholder must file written notice of dissent before the shareholders vote on the proposed transaction. If the transaction is approved, the shareholder must make a written demand for payment.

b. Fair Value
Fair value is the value on the day before the date the vote is taken [RMBCA 13.01]. The corporation must make a written offer to buy the shareholder's stock. If fair value cannot be agreed to, a court will set it.

II. PURCHASE OF ASSETS

A. IS SHAREHOLDER APPROVAL REQUIRED?
A corporation that buys all or substantially all of the assets of another corporation does not need shareholder approval. The corporation whose assets are acquired must obtain approval of its board and shareholders (and see the antitrust guidelines in Chapter 46).

B. ASSUMPTION OF LIABILITY
An acquiring corporation is not responsible for the seller's liabilities, unless there is (1) an implied or express assumption, (2) a sale amounting to a merger or consolidation, (3) a buyer retaining the seller's personnel and continuing the business, or (4) a sale executed in fraud to avoid liability.

III. PURCHASE OF STOCK
A purchase of a substantial number of the voting shares of a corporation's stock enables an acquiring corporation to control a target corporation. The acquiring corporation deals directly with shareholders to buy shares.

A. TENDER OFFERS
A tender offer is a public offer. The offer can turn on the receipt of a specified number of shares by a specified date.

1. The Price Offered for the Target's Stock
This price is generally higher than the stock's market price before the tender offer. It may involve an exchange of stock or cash for stock in the target.

2. Federal and State Laws
Federal securities laws control the terms, duration, and circumstances in which most tender offers are made. Most states also impose regulations.

B. TARGET RESPONSES

1. Good Faith Decision
The directors of the target firm must make a good faith decision as to whether the shareholders' acceptance or rejection of the offer would be most beneficial. The directors must fully disclose all material facts.

2. To Resist a Takeover
Among other tactics, a target may make a self-tender (offer to buy its own stock). A target may also sell its most desirable assets or take other defensive measures (such as a poison pill: give its shareholders the right to buy additional shares at low prices). A request for an injunction on the ground that a takeover will violate antitrust laws may also succeed.

IV. TERMINATION

A. DISSOLUTION

1. Voluntary Dissolution

a. To Initiate Dissolution
Shareholders can initiate dissolution by a unanimous vote. Directors may propose dissolution to the shareholders for a vote.

b. **To Dissolve**
The corporation files articles of dissolution with the secretary of state [RMBCA 14.03]. The effective date of dissolution will be the date of the articles. The corporation notifies its creditors and sets a date (at least 120 days following the date of dissolution) by which all claims against the corporation must be received [RMBCA 14.06].

2. **Involuntary Dissolution**

a. **By the State**
In an action brought by the secretary of state or the state attorney general, a corporation may be dissolved for [RMBCA 14.20]—

1) Failing to comply with corporate formalities or other statutory requirements.

2) Procuring a charter through fraud or misrepresentation.

3) Abusing corporate powers (*ultra vires* acts).

4) Violating the criminal code after a demand to discontinue the violation has been made by the secretary of state.

5) Failing to commence business operations.

6) Abandoning operations after starting up.

b. **By a Shareholder**
The articles of a close corporation may empower any shareholder to dissolve the corporation at will or on the occurrence of a certain event (such as the death of another shareholder).

c. **By a Court**
Courts can dissolve a corporation when a board is deadlocked or for mismanagement [RMBCA 14.30].

B. **LIQUIDATION**
Corporate assets are converted into cash and distributed among creditors and shareholders according to specific rules.

1. **Board Supervision**
If dissolution is by voluntary action, the members of the board act as trustees of the assets, and wind up the affairs of the corporation for the benefit of corporate creditors and shareholders.

2. **Court Supervision**
If dissolution is involuntary, the board does not wish to act as trustee, or shareholders or creditors can show why the board should not act as trustee, a court will appoint a receiver to wind up the corporate affairs.

TRUE-FALSE QUESTIONS

(Answers at the Back of the Book)

___ 1. In a short-form merger, the merging corporation's shareholders do not need to approve the merger.

___ 2. Appraisal rights are always available to shareholders.

___ 3. Shareholder approval is not required to amend articles of incorporation.

___ 4. Shareholder approval is not required when a corporation sells all of its assets to another company.

___ 5. A self-tender is a corporation's offer to buy stock from its own shareholders.

___ 6. Dissolution of a corporation cannot occur without the unanimous approval of its shareholders.

___ 7. In a consolidation, the new corporation inherits all of the rights of the consolidating corporations.

___ 8. A corporation that buys the assets of another corporation always assumes the debts of the selling corporation.

___ 9. In a merger, the surviving corporation inherits all of the disappearing corporation's preexisting rights.

___ 10. Appraisal rights are not normally available in sales of substantially all the corporate assets not in the ordinary course of business.

FILL-IN QUESTIONS

(Answers at the Back of the Book)

If provided by statute, a shareholder can dissent from any ______________(extraordinary/ordinary) fundamental changes in a corporation. To do so, the ______________ (corporation/shareholder) must file a written notice of dissent ______________ (after/before) the shareholders vote on the proposed change. If the change is approved, the shareholder must make a written demand for payment. The fair value of shares is usually their value on the day ______________ (after/before) the date on which ______________ (the change is made/the vote is taken).

MULTIPLE-CHOICE QUESTIONS

(Answers at the Back of the Book)

___ 1. National Sales, Inc., merges with Online Marketing Corporation. Only National remains. After the merger, National acquires Online's assets

a. automatically.
b. only after completing certain statutory procedures.
c. only if it was a specified result of the merger.
d. none of the above.

___ 2. Computer Company plans to consolidate with Software Corporation to form CS, Inc. This requires the approval of

a. their boards of directors only.
b. their shareholders only.
c. their boards and their shareholders.
d. none of the above.

___ 3. Alpha Corporation and Beta Company consolidate to form AB, Inc. AB assumes Alpha and Beta's

a. assets only.
b. liabilities only.
c. assets and liabilities.
d. none of the above.

___ 4. **Based on a Sample CPA Exam Question.** Digital Equipment, Inc., sells computer products. Which of the following may Digital's board of directors do without shareholder approval?

a. Amend the articles of incorporation
b. Buy substantially all of the assets of another corporation
c. Dissolve the corporation
d. Sell substantially all of the assets of Digital

___ 5. Gamma, Inc., is unprofitable. In a suit against Gamma, a court might order Gamma's dissolution if Gamma does not

a. declare a dividend.
b. make a profit this year.
c. pay its taxes.
d. any of the above.

___ 6. Spice Corporation and Sugar, Inc., combine so that only Spice remains, as the surviving corporation. This is

a. a consolidation.
b. a merger.
c. a purchase of assets.
d. a purchase of stock.

___ 7. Carl files a suit against Diners Company. While the suit is pending, Eats, Inc., merges with Diners. Eats absorbs Diners. After the merger, liability in the suit rests with

a. Carl.
b. Diners.
c. Eats.
d. none of the above.

___ 8. Macro Sales Corporation and Micro Products Company combine and a new organization, MM, Inc., takes their place. This is

a. a consolidation.
b. a merger.
c. a purchase of assets.
d. a purchase of stock.

___ 9. Tech Corporation and United Company plan to merge. Most likely, the articles of merger will be filed with

a. a county recording office.
b. the Securities and Exchange Commission.
c. the state secretary of state.
d. the U.S. Treasury Department.

___ 10. Vicky is a shareholder in Web Services, Inc. Vicky could typically exercise appraisal rights if Web was involved in

a. a consolidation only.
b. a merger only.
c. a consolidation or a merger.
d. none of the above.

SHORT ESSAY QUESTIONS

1. Discuss the following takeover defense terms: greenmail; Pac-man; poison pill; and white knight.
2. Describe the procedure for a merger or a consolidation.

ISSUE SPOTTERS

(Answers at the Back of the Book)

1. ABC Corporation combines with DEF, Inc. ABC ceases to exist. DEF is the surviving firm. Global Corporation and Local Company combine. Afterwards, Global and Local cease to exist. GL, Inc., a new firm, functions in their place. Which of these is a merger and which is a consolidation?

2. Interstate Corporation asks its shareholders to vote on a proposed merger with Regional, Inc. Jill, an Interstate shareholder, votes against it, but is outvoted by the other shareholders. Is there anything Jill can do to avoid being forced to go along with the transaction?

3. Mega Corporation makes a public offer to buy the stock of Mini, Inc. The price of the offer is higher than the market price of the stock, but Mini's board believes that it should be resisted. What can Mini do to retain control over itself?

SPECIAL INFORMATION FOR CPA CANDIDATES

One of the most important aspects of the material in this chapter, to remember for the CPA examination, is the role of shareholders. Note particularly the events that require shareholder approval (and those that don't). Also, review the section on appraisal rights: they are available *only* when specifically provided by statute.

Chapter 40
CORPORATIONS—Investor Protection and Online Securities Offerings

WHAT THIS CHAPTER IS ABOUT

The general purpose of securities laws is to provide sufficient, accurate information to investors to enable them to make informed buying and selling decisions about securities. This chapter provides an outline of federal securities laws.

CHAPTER OUTLINE

I. THE SECURITIES AND EXCHANGE COMMISSION (SEC)

The SEC administers the federal securities laws and regulates the sale and purchase of securities.

A. THE SEC'S BASIC FUNCTIONS

1. Require disclosure of facts concerning offerings of certain securities.
2. Regulate national securities trading.
3. Investigate securities fraud.
4. Regulate securities brokers, dealers, and investment advisers.
5. Supervise mutual funds.
6. Recommend sanctions in cases involving violations of securities laws. (The U.S. Department of Justice prosecutes violations.)

B. THE SEC'S EXPANDING REGULATORY POWERS

The SEC's powers include the power to seek sanctions against those who violate foreign securities laws; to suspend trading if prices rise and fall in short periods of time; to exempt persons, securities, and transactions from securities law requirements; and to require more corporate disclosure.

II. SARBANES-OXLEY ACT OF 2002

Imposes strict disclosure requirements and harsh penalties for violations of securities laws.

A. RESPONSIBLE PARTIES

Chief corporate executives (CEOs and CFOs) are responsible for the accuracy and completeness of financial statements and reports filed with the SEC [Sections 302 and 906]. Penalties for knowingly certifying a report or statement that does not meet statutory requirements include up to $1 million in fines and ten years imprisonment ($5 million and twenty years for "willful" certification). Altering or destroying documents is also subject to fines and imprisonment.

B. PUBLIC COMPANY ACCOUNTING OVERSIGHT BOARD

The SEC oversees this entity, which regulates and oversees public accounting firms (see Chapter 52).

C. LIMITATIONS ON PRIVATE ACTIONS

A private action for securities fraud must be brought within two years of the discovery of the violation or five years after the violation, whichever is earlier [Section 804].

III. SECURITIES ACT OF 1933

Requires that all essential information concerning the issuance (sales) of new securities be disclosed to investors.

A. WHAT IS A SECURITY?

1. Courts' Interpretation of the Securities Act

A security exists in any transaction in which a person (1) invests (2) in a common enterprise (3) reasonably expecting profits (4) derived *primarily* or *substantially* from others' managerial or entrepreneurial efforts.

2. A Security Is an Investment

Examples: stocks, bonds, investment contracts in condominiums, franchises, limited partnerships, and oil or gas or other mineral rights.

B. REGISTRATION STATEMENT

Before offering securities for sale, issuing corporations must (1) file a registration statement with the Securities and Exchange Commission (SEC) and (2) provide investors with a prospectus that describes the security being sold, the issuing corporation, and the investment or risk.

1. Contents of a Registration Statement

a. Description of the significant provisions of the security and how the registrant intends to use the proceeds of the sale.

b. Description of the registrant's properties and business.

c. Description of the management of the registrant; its security holdings; its remuneration and other benefits, including pensions and stock options; and any interests of directors or officers in any material transactions with the corporation.

d. Financial statement certified by an independent public accountant.

e. Description of pending lawsuits.

2. Twenty-Day Waiting Period after Registration

Securities cannot be sold for twenty days (oral offers can be made).

3. Advertising

During the waiting period, very limited written advertising is allowed. After the period, no written advertising unaccompanied by a prospectus is allowed, except a tombstone ad, which simply tells how to obtain a prospectus.

C. EXEMPT SECURITIES

Securities that can be sold (and resold) without being registered include—

1. Small Offerings under Regulation A

An issuer's offer of up to $5 million in securities in any twelve-month period (including up to $1.5 million in nonissuer resales) is exempt. The issuer must file with the SEC a notice of the issue and an offering circular (also provided to investors before the sale). A company can *test the waters* (determine potential interest) before preparing the circular.

2. Other Exempt Securities

a. All bank securities sold prior to July 27, 1933.

b. Commercial paper if maturity does not exceed nine months.

c. Securities of charitable organizations.

d. Securities resulting from a reorganization issued in exchange for the issuer's existing securities and certificates issued by trustees, receivers, or debtors in possession in bankruptcy (see Chapter 30).

e. Securities issued exclusively in exchange for the issuer's existing securities, provided no commission is paid (such as stock splits).

f. Securities issued to finance the acquisition of railroad equipment.

g. Any insurance, endowment, or annuity contract issued by a state-regulated insurance company.

h. Government-issued securities.

i. Securities issued by banks, savings and loan associations, farmers' cooperatives, and similar institutions.

D. EXEMPT TRANSACTIONS

Securities that can be sold without being registered include those sold in transactions that consist of—

1. Small Offerings under Regulation D

Offers that involve a small amount of money or are not made publicly.

a. Offerings Up to $1 Million
Noninvestment company offerings up to $1 million in a twelve-month period [Rule 504].

b. Blank-Check Company Offerings Up to $500,000
Offerings up to $500,000 in any one year by companies with no specific business plans are exempt if (1) no general solicitation or advertising is used, (2) the SEC is notified of the sales, and (3) precaution is taken against nonexempt, unregistered resales [Rule 504a].

c. Offerings Up to $5 Million
Private, noninvestment company offerings up to $5 million in a twelve-month period if (1) no general solicitation or advertising is used; (2) the SEC is notified of the sales; (3) precaution is taken against nonexempt, unregistered resales; and (4) there are no more than thirty-five unaccredited investors. If the sale involves any unaccredited investors, all investors must be given material information about the company, its business, the securities [Rule 505].

d. Private Offerings in Unlimited Amounts
Essentially the same requirements as Rule 505, except (1) there is no limit on the amount of the offering and (2) the issuer must believe that each unaccredited investor has sufficient knowledge or experience to evaluate the investment [Rule 506].

e. Offerings to Qualified Purchasers
Offerings up to $5 million per transaction to qualified purchasers (wealthy, sophisticated investors) only [Rule 1001].

2. Small Offerings to Accredited Investors Only

An offer up to $5 million is exempt if (1) no general solicitation or advertising is used; (2) the SEC is notified of the sales; (3) precaution is taken against nonexempt, unregistered resales; and (4) there are no unaccredited investors [Section 4(6)].

3. Intrastate Issues

Offerings in the state in which the issuer is organized and doing business are exempt [Rule 147] if, for nine months after the sale, no resale is made to a nonresident.

4. Resales ("Safe Harbors")

Most securities can be resold without registration. Resales of blank-check company offerings [Rule 504a], small offerings [Rule 505], private offerings [Rule 506], and offers to accredited investors only [Section 4(6)] are exempt from registration if—

a. The Securities Have Been Owned for Two Years or More

If seller is not an **affiliate** (in control with the issuer) [Rule 144].

b. The Securities Have Been Owned for at Least One Year

There must be adequate public information about the issuer, the securities must be sold in limited amounts in unsolicited brokers' transactions, and the SEC must be notified of the resale [Rule 144].

c. The Securities Are Sold Only to an Institutional Investor

The securities, on issue, must not have been of the same class as securities listed on a national securities exchange or a U.S. automated interdealer quotation system, and the seller on resale must take steps to tell the buyer they are exempt [Rule 144A].

E. VIOLATIONS OF THE 1933 ACT

If registration statement or prospectus contains material false statements or omissions, liable parties include anyone who signed the statement.

1. Defenses

Statement or omission was not material; plaintiff knew of misrepresentation and bought stock anyway; *due diligence* (Chapter 52).

2. Penalties

Fines up to $10,000; imprisonment up to five years; injunction against selling securities; order to refund profits; damages in civil suits.

IV. SECURITIES EXCHANGE ACT OF 1934

Regulates the markets in which securities are traded by requiring disclosure by Section 12 companies (corporations with securities on the exchanges and firms with assets in excess of $10 million and five hundred or more shareholders).

A. INSIDER TRADING—SECTION 10(b) AND SEC RULE 10b-5

Section 10(b) proscribes the use of "any manipulative or deceptive device or contrivance in contravention of such rules and regulations as the [SEC] may prescribe." Rule 10b-5 prohibits the commission of fraud in connection with the purchase or sale of any security (registered or unregistered).

1. What Triggers Liability

Any material omission or misrepresentation of material facts in connection with the purchase or sale of any security can trigger liability.

2. What Does Not Trigger Liability

Under the Private Securities Litigation Reform Act of 1995, financial forecasts and other forward-looking statements do not trigger liability if they include "meaningful cautionary statements identifying factors that could cause actual results to differ materially."

3. Who Can Be Liable

Those who take advantage of inside information when they know that it is unavailable to the person with whom they are dealing can be liable.

a. Insiders

These include officers, directors, majority shareholders, and persons having access to or receiving information of a nonpublic nature on which trading is based (accountants, attorneys).

b. **Outsiders**

1) **Tipper/Tippee Theory**
One who acquires inside information as a result of an insider's breach of fiduciary duty to the firm whose shares are traded can be liable, if he or she knows or should know of the breach.

2) **Misappropriation Theory**
One who wrongfully obtains inside information and trades on it to his or her gain can be liable, if a duty to the lawful possessor of information was violated and harm to another results.

B. **INSIDER REPORTING AND TRADING—SECTION 16(b)**
Officers, directors, and shareholders owning 10 percent of the securities registered under Section 12 are required to file reports with the SEC concerning their ownership and trading of the securities.

1. **Corporation Is Entitled to All Profits**
A firm can recapture *all* profits realized by an insider on *any* purchase and sale or sale and purchase of its stock in any six-month period.

2. **Applicability of Section 16(b)**
Section 16(b) applies to stock, warrants, options, and securities convertible into stock.

C. **PROXY STATEMENTS—SECTION 14(A)**
Section 14(a) regulates the solicitation of proxies from shareholders of Section 12 companies. Whoever solicits a proxy must disclose, in the proxy statement, all of the pertinent facts.

D. **VIOLATIONS OF THE 1934 ACT**

1. **Criminal Penalties**
Maximum jail term is twenty-five years; fines up to $5 million for individuals and $2.5 million for partnerships and corporations.

2. **Civil Sanctions**

a. **Insider Trading Sanctions Act of 1984**
SEC can bring suit in federal court against anyone violating or aiding in a violation of the 1934 act or SEC rules. Penalties include triple the profits gained or the loss avoided by the guilty party.

b. **Insider Trading and Securities Fraud Enforcement Act of 1988**
Enlarged the class of persons subject to civil liability for insider-trading violations, increased criminal penalties, and gave the SEC authority to (1) reward persons providing information and (2) make rules to prevent insider trading.

V. REGULATION OF INVESTMENT COMPANIES

The SEC regulates investment companies and mutual funds under the Investment Company Act of 1940, the Investment Company Act Amendments of 1970, the Securities Act Amendments of 1975, and later amendments.

A. **WHAT AN INVESTMENT COMPANY IS**
Any entity that (1) is engaged primarily "in the business of investing, reinvesting, or trading in securities" or (2) is engaged in such business and has more than 40 percent of the company's assets in investment securities. (Does not include banks, finance companies, and others).

B. **WHAT AN INVESTMENT COMPANY MUST DO**
Register with the SEC by filing a notification of registration and, each year, file reports with the SEC. All securities must be in the custody of a bank or stock exchange member.

C. WHAT AN INVESTMENT COMPANY CANNOT DO

No dividends may be paid from any source other than accumulated, undistributed net income. There are restrictions on investment activities.

VI. STATE SECURITIES LAWS

All states regulate the offer and sale of securities within individual state borders. Exemptions from federal law are not exemptions from state laws, which have their own exemptions. Under the National Market Securities Improvement Act of 1996, the SEC regulates most national securities activities.

VII. ONLINE SECURITIES OFFERINGS AND DISCLOSURES

Federal and state laws set out the requirements for online initial public offerings. Under SEC interpretations, there is no difference in the disclosure requirements, only in the medium of disclosure, for which there may be new avenues of liability. Also, an online prospectus may not qualify for a Regulation D exemption.

VIII. ONLINE SECURITIES FRAUD

Issues include the use of chat rooms to affect the price of securities, fictitious press releases, and illegal offerings. The First Amendment protects the use of chat rooms. Also, there is a distinction between statements of fact and opinion.

TRUE-FALSE QUESTIONS

(Answers at the Back of the Book)

____ 1. A security that does not qualify for an exemption must be registered before it is offered to the public.

____ 2. Before a security can be sold to the public, prospective investors must be provided with a prospectus.

____ 3. Stock splits are exempt from the registration requirements of the Securities Act of 1933, if no commission is paid.

____ 4. Sales of securities may not occur until twenty days after registration.

____ 5. Private offerings of securities in unlimited amounts that are not generally solicited or advertised must be registered before they can be sold.

____ 6. A proxy statement must fully and accurately disclose all of the facts that are pertinent to the matter on which shareholders are being asked to vote.

____ 7. All states have disclosure requirements and antifraud provisions that cover securities.

____ 8. *Scienter* is not a requirement for liability under Section 10(b) of the Securities Exchange Act of 1934.

____ 9. No one who receives inside information as a result of another's breach of his or her fiduciary duty can be liable under SEC Rule 10b-5.

____ 10. No security can be resold without registration.

FILL-IN QUESTIONS

(Answers at the Back of the Book)

The SEC can award "bounty" payments to persons providing information leading to the ________________________ (conviction/prosecution) of insider-trading violations. Civil penalties include ________________ (double/triple) the profits gained or the loss avoided. Criminal penalties include maximum jail terms of ______________ (ten/ twenty-five) years. Violators ____________ (may/may not) also be subject to multi-million-dollar fines.

MULTIPLE-CHOICE QUESTIONS

(Answers at the Back of the Book)

___ **1.** **Based a Sample CPA Question.** Under the Securities Exchange Act of 1934, the Securities and Exchange Commission is responsible for all of the following activities EXCEPT

a. investigating securities fraud.
b. prosecuting criminal violations of federal securities laws.
c. regulating the activities of securities brokers.
d. requiring disclosure of facts concerning offerings of securities listed on national securities exchanges.

___ **2.** Beth, a director of Alpha Company, learns that an Alpha engineer has developed a new, improved product. Over the next six months, Beth buys and sells Alpha stock for a profit. Of Beth's profit, Alpha may recapture

a. all of it.
b. half of it.
c. 10 percent of it.
d. none of it.

___ **3.** Central Brokerage Associates sells securities. The definition of a security does *not* include, as an element,

a. an investment.
b. a common enterprise.
c. a reasonable expectation of profits.
d. profits derived entirely from the efforts of the investor.

___ **4.** Superior, Inc., is a private, noninvestment company. In one year, Superior advertises a $300,000 offering. Concerning registration, this offering is

a. exempt because of the low amount of the issue.
b. exempt because it was advertised.
c. exempt because the issuer is a private company.
d. not exempt.

___ **5.** Huron, Inc., makes a $6 million private offering to twenty accredited investors and less than thirty unaccredited investors. Huron advertises the offering and believes that the unaccredited investors are sophisticated enough to evaluate the investment. Huron gives material information about itself, its business, and the securities to all investors. Concerning registration, this offering is

a. exempt because of the low amount of the issue.
b. exempt because it was advertised.
c. exempt because the issuer believed that the unaccredited investors were sophisticated enough to evaluate the investment.
d. not exempt.

___ **6.** Ontario, Inc., in one year, advertises two $2.25 million offerings. Buying the stock are twelve accredited investors. Concerning registration, this offering is

a. exempt because of the low amount of the issue.
b. exempt because it was advertised.
c. exempt because only accredited investors bought stock.
d. not exempt.

___ 7. Omega Corporation's registration statement must include

a. a description of the accounting firm that audits Omega.
b. a description of the security being offered for sale.
c. a financial forecast for Omega's next five years.
d. all of the above.

___ 8. Frank, an officer of Gamma, Inc., learns that Gamma has developed a new source of energy. Frank tells Gail, an outsider. They each buy Gamma stock. When the development is announced, the stock price increases, and they each immediately sell their stock. Subject to liability for insider trading is

a. Frank only.
b. Gail only
c. Frank and Gail.
d. none of the above.

___ 9. National Sales, Inc., wants to make an offering of securities to the public. The offer is not exempt from registration. Before National sells these securities, it must provide investors with

a. a prospectus.
b. a registration statement.
c. a tombstone ad.
d. none of the above.

___ 10. Great Lakes Company is a private, noninvestment company. Last year, as part of a $250,000 advertised offering, Great Lakes sold stock to John, a private investor. John would now like to sell the shares. Concerning registration, this resale is

a. exempt because of the low amount of the original issue.
b. exempt because the offering was advertised.
c. exempt because all resales are exempt.
d. not exempt.

SHORT ESSAY QUESTIONS

1. What is the process by which a company sells securities to the public?

2. How is insider trading regulated by Section 10(b), SEC Rule 10b-5, and Section 16(b)?

ISSUE SPOTTERS

(Answers at the Back of the Book)

1. When a corporation wishes to issue certain securities, it must provide sufficient information for an unsophisticated investor to evaluate the financial risk involved. Specifically, the law imposes liability for making a false statement or omission that is "material." What sort of information would an investor consider material?

2. Lee is an officer of Macro Oil, Inc. Lee knows that a Macro geologist has just discovered a new deposit of oil. Can Lee take advantage of this information to buy and sell Macro stock?

3. The Securities Act of 1933, the Securities Exchange Act of 1934, and other securities regulation is federal law. In-State Corporation incorporated in one state, does business exclusively in that state, and offers its securities for sale only in that state. Are there securities laws to regulate this offering?

SPECIAL INFORMATION FOR CPA CANDIDATES

Securities law is an important part of the CPA examination. Among the significant details you should pick up from your study of this chapter are the basic differences between the two federal securities acts, the definition of a security, and the requirements for selling securities that are not exempt—registration statement, prospectus, and the twenty-day waiting period. Among the regulations that exempt certain securities and transactions from the registration requirements, the most important for purposes of the CPA exam are Regulation A and Regulation D. These rules are consistently tested. In your study of the Securities Exchange Act of 1934, emphasize insider trading but be aware that other aspects of the act may be tested.

Chapter 41
Limited Liability Companies and Limited Partnerships

What This Chapter Is About

This chapter sets out the law relating to relatively new business organizations: limited liability companies (LLCs), limited liability partnerships (LLPs), limited partnerships, and limited liability limited partnerships (LLLPs). The chief features of these business forms are limited liability and tax advantages.

Chapter Outline

I. LIMITED LIABILITY COMPANIES

A limited liability company (LLC) is a hybrid form of business enterprise.

A. Governing Law

State statutes govern LLCs. Despite some similarities among these state laws, less than one-fourth of the states have adopted the Uniform Limited Liability Company Act (ULLCA).

B. Taxation of an LLC

An LLC is taxed as a partnership unless it chooses to be taxed as a corporation.

C. Foreign Investors

These may become LLC members.

D. The Nature of the LLC

An LLC offers the limited liability of a corporation [ULLCA 303]. Members can bring derivative actions on the LLC's behalf [ULLCA 101]. Courts may pierce the LLC veil.

E. LLC Formation

Articles of organization must be filed with the state. Certain information is required. Some states require that an LLC have at least two members.

F. Jurisdictional Requirements

An LLC is a citizen of every state of which its members are citizens.

G. Advantages of the LLC

Taxed as a partnership; liability of members is limited to the amount of their investment; members can participate in management; corporations, partnerships, and foreign investors can be members; no limit on the number of members (in many states, one is enough).

H. Disadvantages of the LLC

Statutory restrictions on the transfer of ownership; because the LLC is a new form, little case law exists; until uniform statutes are adopted by most states, an LLC with multistate operations may face difficulties.

I. The LLC Operating Agreement

Provisions relate to management, division of profits (equally if not specified otherwise), transfer of membership, what events trigger dissolution, and so on. The agreement does not have to be in writing. If there is no agreement, state statutes govern. If there is no statute, partnership law applies.

J. LLC MANAGEMENT

1. Member-Managed LLC
Unless members agree otherwise, all members participate in management and voting rights are usually proportional to capital contributions. An agreement may set governing procedures (in contrast to corporations, which are subject to specific state requirements).

2. Manager-Managed LLC
Members may designate a group to run the firm. If so, the members' interests in the firm may qualify as securities.

II. LIMITED LIABILITY PARTNERSHIPS

Professionals may organize as a limited liability partnership (LLP) to enjoy the tax advantages of a partnership, while avoiding personal liability for the wrongdoing of other partners.

A. LIABILITY IN AN LLP

In an LLP, professionals avoid personal liability for malpractice of other partners.

1. Liability outside the State of Formation
Most states apply the law of the state in which the LLP was formed.

2. Supervising Partner's Liability
A partner who commits a wrongful act is liable for the results. Also liable is the partner who supervises the party who commits the act. Some states provide that each partner is liable only up to the proportion of his or her responsibility for the result.

B. FAMILY LIMITED LIABILITY PARTNERSHIPS

This is a limited liability partnership (LLP) in which most of the partners are related. All partners must be natural persons or persons acting in a fiduciary capacity for natural persons. Family-owned farms may benefit from the use of the family limited liability partnership (FLLP) form.

III. LIMITED PARTNERSHIPS

Limited partnerships must include at least one general partner and one or more limited partners. General partners assume management responsibility and liability for all partnership debts.

A. FORMATION OF A LIMITED PARTNERSHIP

The partners sign a certificate of limited partnership, which requires information similar to that found in a corporate charter (see Chapter 36). The certificate is filed with the secretary of state [RULPA 101(7), 201].

B. RIGHTS AND LIABILITIES OF PARTNERS

1. Rights of Limited Partners
Essentially the same rights as general partners. Can generally assign their interests in the partnership [RULPA 702, 704]. Can also sue on behalf of the firm if general partners refuse [RULPA 1001].

2. Liabilities of Limited Partners

a. Limited Liability to Creditors of the Partnership
Liable to the extent of any contribution that is promised to the firm or any part of a contribution that was withdrawn [RULPA 502].

b. Personal Liability for Defects in Formation

1) If a Firm Is Organized in an Improper Manner
If the limited partner fails to withdraw on discovery of the defect, he or she can be personally liable to the firm's creditors.

2) If There Is a False Statement in the Partnership Certificate

If a limited partner knows of the statement, he or she may be liable to any person who relies on it [RULPA 207].

3) **How to Avoid Future Liability**
File an amendment or corrected certificate or renounce an interest in the profits of the partnership [RULPA 304].

3. **Limited Partners and Management**
Generally, participating in management results in personal liability for partnership debt, if creditors knew of participation [RULPA 303].

C. DISSOLUTION OF THE LIMITED PARTNERSHIP

1. **General Partners—Dissolution**
Retirement, death, or mental incompetence of a general partner dissolves the firm, unless continued by other general partners [RULPA 801]. Illegality, expulsion, or bankruptcy of general partner dissolves a firm.

2. **Limited Partners—No Dissolution**
Death or assignment of interest of a limited partner does not dissolve the firm [RULPA 702, 704, 705], nor does personal bankruptcy.

3. **Court Decree**
A limited partnership can be dissolved by court decree [RULPA 802].

4. **Priority to Assets on Dissolution**
(1) Creditors, including partners who are creditors; (2) partners and former partners receive unpaid distributions of partnership assets and, except as otherwise agreed, a return on their contributions and amounts proportionate to their share of distributions [RULPA 201(a)(10), 804].

IV. LIMITED LIABILITY LIMITED PARTNERSHIPS

This form is similar to a limited partnership, except that the liability of all partners in a limited liability limited partnership (LLLP) is limited to the amount of their investment in the firm.

V. MAJOR BUSINESS FORMS COMPARED

To decide which form of business organization is appropriate involves the consideration of such factors as the ease of creation, the liability of the owners, tax considerations, and the need for capital. Each form has advantages and disadvantages that indicate when it is most useful.

TRUE-FALSE QUESTIONS

(Answers at the Back of the Book)

___ 1. Most states require that a limited partnership file a certificate of limited partnership with the appropriate state office.

___ 2. The death of a limited partner will dissolve a limited partnership.

___ 3. A limited liability company must be formed and operated in compliance with federal law.

___ 4. A limited liability company is a citizen of every state of which its members are citizens.

___ 5. A limited liability company does not offer the limited liability of a corporation.

___ 6. A limited liability partnership does not limit in any way the liability of its partners.

___ 7. In a limited partnership, the liability of each partner is limited to the amount of capital he or she has invested in the partnership.

___ 8. In a limited liability limited partnership, the liability of each partner is limited to the amount of capital he or she has invested in the partnership.

___ 9. In a limited liability company, members do not have to participate in the management of the company.

___ 10. Most limited liability company (LLC) statutes provide that unless the members agree otherwise, all profits of the LLC will be divided equally.

FILL-IN QUESTIONS

(Answers at the Back of the Book)

Unless the participants agree otherwise, all of the ______________________ (members/limited partners) of a ______________________ (limited liability company/limited partnership) may participate in management without assuming liability for the obligations of the firm. In contrast, the ______________________ (members/limited partners) of a ______________________ (limited liability company/limited partnership) who participate in management may be personally liable for the debts of the firm.

MULTIPLE-CHOICE QUESTIONS

(Answers at the Back of the Book)

___ 1. **Based on a Sample CPA Question.** Ann is a limited partner in Beta Sales, a limited partnership. Credit Company, a Beta creditor, claims that Ann is subject to personal liability for Beta's debts because Ann has the right, as a limited partner to take control of the firm. Credit is correct about

a. Ann's liability only.
b. Ann's right to control the firm only.
c. Ann's liability and Ann's right to control the firm.
d. none of the above.

___ 2. Dave is a general partner in Eagle Investments, a limited partnership. Dave pays personal income taxes on

a. all of the firm's income.
b. his share of the firm's income.
c. only the amount of the firm's income that is actually paid to him.
d. none of the above.

___ 3. Adam and Beth form A&B, LLC, a limited liability company (LLC). One advantage of an LLC is that it may be taxed as

a. a corporation.
b. a partnership.
c. a sole proprietorship.
d. none of the above.

___ 4. Larry is a member of Macro Services, a limited liability company. Larry is liable for the firm's debts

a. in proportion to the total number of members in the firm.
b. to the extent of his capital contribution.
c. to the full extent of the debts.
d. none of the above.

___ 5. Carol and Don form E-Stuff as a limited liability company. They can participate in the firm's management

a. only to the extent that they assume personal liability for the firm's debts.
b. only to the extent of the amount of their investment in the firm.
c. to any extent.
d. to no extent.

___ 6. Jack and Jill form J&J, a limited partnership. Jack is a general partner. Jill is a limited partner. Dissolution of the firm would result from Jill's

a. assignment of her interest in the firm to a third party only.
b. bankruptcy or death only.
c. assignment of interest, bankruptcy, or death.
d. none of the above.

___ 7. Drs. Kay and Lyle are partners in a medical clinic, which is organized as a limited liability partnership. A court holds Lyle liable in a malpractice suit. Kay is liable

a. in proportion to the total number of partners in the firm.
b. to the extent of her capital contribution.
c. to the full extent of the liability.
d. none of the above.

___ 8. Mike, Nora, and Owen want to form a limited partnership. A limited partnership must have at least

a. one general partner and one limited partner.
b. one general partner and two limited partners.
c. two limited partners.
d. none of the above.

___ 9. Pete is a general partner, and Quinn is a limited partner in PQ Partners, a limited partnership. As regards PQ, Quinn has

a. fewer rights than Pete.
b. more rights than Pete.
c. the same rights as Pete.
d. none of the above.

___ 10. Ron and Sara form Top Goods, LLC, a limited liability company (LLC). A disadvantage of an LLC is that

a. its income is double taxed.
b. its members are subject to personal liability for the firm's debts.
c. state laws concerning limited liability companies are not yet uniform.
d. none of the above.

SHORT ESSAY QUESTIONS

1. What are the advantages of doing business as a limited liability company?

2. Describe the following characteristics of limited partnerships: creation, sharing of profits and loses, liability, capital contribution, management, duration, assignment, and priorities on liquidation.

ISSUE SPOTTERS

(Answers at the Back of the Book)

1. Carol, Donna, and Earl are partners in an accounting firm that is a limited liability partnership. Carol is Donna's supervising partner. Donna obtains $50,000 by committing fraud against Fred, one of the firm's clients. Who may be liable for the $50,000?

2. Olga is a limited partner, and Anton is a general partner of Platinum Fitness Club, a limited partnership. Anton manages the firm. Olga has some expertise in the area and believes that she could do a better job than Anton at managing, but she abstains from becoming actively involved. Why might she choose to keep away from management activities?

3. Greg, Harry, and Ida are members of Best Products, LLC (limited liability company). What are their options with respect to the management of Best Products?

SPECIAL INFORMATION FOR CPA CANDIDATES

For the CPA exam, it is most important to know the differences among the types of business organizations, including limited partnerships and limited liability companies.

Chapter 42
Ethics and Business Decision Making

WHAT THIS CHAPTER IS ABOUT

The concepts set out in this chapter include the nature of business ethics and the relationship between ethics and business. Ultimately, the goal of this chapter is to provide you with basic tools for analyzing ethical issues in a business context.

CHAPTER OUTLINE

I. BUSINESS ETHICS

Ethics is the study of what constitutes right and wrong behavior. Ethics focuses on morality and the application of moral principles in everyday life.

A. WHAT IS BUSINESS ETHICS?

Business ethics focuses on what constitutes ethical behavior in the world of business. Business ethics is *not* a separate kind of ethics.

B. WHY IS BUSINESS ETHICS IMPORTANT?

An understanding of business ethics is important to the long-run viability of a business, the well being of its officers and directors, and the welfare of its employees.

II. SETTING THE RIGHT ETHICAL TONE

Some unethical conduct is founded on the lack of sanctions.

A. THE IMPORTANCE OF ETHICAL LEADERSHIP

Management must set and apply ethical standards to which they are committed. Employees will likely follow their example. Ethical conduct can be furthered by not tolerating unethical behavior, setting realistic employee goals, and periodic employee review.

B. CREATING ETHICAL CODES OF CONDUCT

Most large corporations have codes of conduct that indicate the firm's commitment to legal compliance and to the welfare of those who are affected by corporate decisions and practices. Large firms may also emphasize ethics in other ways (for example, with training programs).

C. CORPORATE COMPLIANCE PROGRAMS

Components of a comprehensive corporate ethical-compliance program include an ethical code of conduct, an ethics committee, training programs, and internal audits to monitor compliance. These components should be integrated. The Sarbanes-Oxley Act of 2002 requires firms to set up confidential systems for employees to report suspected illegal or unethical financial practices.

D. CONFLICTS AND TRADE-OFFS

A firm's duty to its shareholders should be weighed against duties to others who may have a greater stake in a particular decision. For example, an employer should consider whether it has an ethical duty to loyal, long-term employees not to replace them with workers who will accept lower pay and whether this duty prevails over a duty to improve profitability by restructuring.

III. DEFYING THE RULES: THE ENRON CASE

Unethical conduct resulted in the single largest bankruptcy of a U.S. business firm.

A. THE UNETHICAL CONDUCT

Managers took advantage of accounting standards to overestimate future earnings, which resulted in inflated reports of current earnings. To maintain these exaggerations, the company created subsidiaries to which it could shift unreported losses and assets with inflated values. Many of these shifts occurred outside the U.S. to avoid federal income taxes. When questioned, management refused to investigate and reveal financial improprieties.

B. WHO WAS AFFECTED

This misconduct affected the firm's managers, employees, suppliers, and shareholders, and the community and society in general.

IV. BUSINESS ETHICS AND THE LAW

The minimal acceptable standard for ethical business behavior is compliance with the law. Ethical standards, such as those in a company's policies or codes of ethics, must also guide decisions.

A. LAWS REGULATING BUSINESS

Because there are many laws regulating business, it is possible to violate one without realizing it. Ignorance of the law is no excuse.

B. "GRAY AREAS"

There are many "gray areas" in which it is difficult to predict how a court will rule. For example, if a consumer's misuse of a product harms the consumer, should the manufacturer bear the responsibility? The best course is to act responsibly and in good faith.

C. TECHNOLOGICAL DEVELOPMENTS AND LEGAL UNCERTAINTIES

How laws apply in the context of cyberspace is not certain.

V. APPROACHES TO ETHICAL REASONING

Ethical reasoning is the process by which an individual examines a situation according to his or her moral convictions or ethical standards. Fundamental ethical reasoning approaches include the following.

A. DUTY-BASED ETHICS

1. Religious Ethical Standards

Religious standards provide that when an act is prohibited by religious teachings, it is unethical and should not be undertaken, regardless of the consequences. Religious standards also involve compassion.

2. Kantian Ethics

Immanual Kant believed that people should be respected because they are qualitatively different from other physical objects. Kant's *categorical imperative* is that individuals should evaluate their actions in light of what would happen if everyone acted the same way.

3. Principle of Rights

According to the principle that persons have rights (to life and liberty, for example), a key factor in determining whether a business decision is ethical is how that decision affects the rights of others, including employees, customers and society.

B. OUTCOME-BASED ETHICS

Utilitarianism is a belief that an action is ethical if it produces the greatest good for the greatest number. This approach is often criticized, because it tends to reduce the welfare of people to plus and minus signs on a cost-benefit worksheet.

VI. BUSINESS ETHICS ON A GLOBAL LEVEL

A. MONITORING THE EMPLOYMENT PRACTICES OF FOREIGN SUPPLIERS

Concerns include the treatment of foreign workers who make goods imported and sold in the United States by U.S. firms. Should a U.S firm refuse to deal with certain suppliers or monitor their workplaces to make sure that the workers are not being mistreated?

B. THE FOREIGN CORRUPT PRACTICES ACT

The Foreign Corrupt Practices Act (FCPA) of 1977 applies to—

1. U.S. Companies

Including their directors, officers, shareholders, employees, and agents.

a. What Is Prohibited

The FCPA prohibits the bribery of most foreign government officials to get an official to act in an official capacity to provide business opportunities.

b. What Is Permitted

The FCPA permits payments to (1) minor officials whose duties are ministerial, (2) foreign officials if the payments are lawful in the foreign country, or (3) private foreign companies or other third parties unless the U.S. firm knows payments will be made to a foreign government.

2. Accountants

a. What Is Required

All companies must (1) keep detailed records that "accurately and fairly" reflect the company's financial activities and (2) have an accounting system that provides "reasonable assurance" that all transactions are accounted for and legal.

b. What Is Prohibited

The FCPA prohibits false statements to accountants and false entries in accounts.

3. Penalties

Firms: fines up to $2 million. Officers or directors: fines up to $100,000 (cannot be paid by the company); imprisonment up to five years.

C. OTHER NATIONS

A treaty signed by members of the Organization for Economic Cooperation and Development makes the bribery of foreign officials a crime.

TRUE-FALSE QUESTIONS

(Answers at the Back of the Book)

____ 1. Ethics is the study of what constitutes right and wrong behavior.

____ 2. A background in business ethics is as important as knowledge of specific laws.

____ 3. The *minimal* acceptable standard for ethical behavior is compliance with the law.

____ 4. According to utilitarianism, it does not matter how many people benefit from an act.

____ 5. The best course towards accomplishing legal and ethical behavior is to act responsibly and in good faith.

____ 6. The ethics of a particular act is always clear.

___ 7. To foster ethical behavior among employees, managers should apply ethical standards to which they are committed.

___ 8. If an act is legal, it is ethical.

___ 9. The roles that women play in other countries can present ethical problems for U.S. firms doing business internationally.

___ 10. Bribery of public officials is only an ethical issue.

FILL-IN QUESTIONS

(Answers at the Back of the Book)

______________________________________ (Religious standards/ Kantian ethics/ The principle of rights) provide that when an act is prohibited by religious teachings, it is unethical and should not be undertaken, regardless of the consequences. According to ______________________________________ (religious standards/ Kantian ethics/ the principle of rights), individuals should evaluate their actions in light of what would happen if everyone acted the same way. According to ______________________________________ (religious standards/ Kantian ethics/ the principle of rights), a key factor in determining whether a business decision is ethical is how that decision affects the rights of others.

MULTIPLE-CHOICE QUESTIONS

(Answers at the Back of the Book)

___ 1. Beth is a marketing executive for Consumer Goods Company. Compared to Beth's personal actions, her business actions require the application of ethical standards that are

a. more complex.
b. simpler.
c. the same.
d. none of the above.

___ 2. Pat, an employee of Quality Products, Inc., takes a duty-based approach to ethics. Pat believes that regardless of the consequences, he must

a. avoid unethical behavior.
b. conform to society's standards.
c. place his employer's interest first.
d. produce the greatest good for the most people.

___ 3. Joy adopts religious ethical standards. These involve an element of

a. compassion.
b. cost-benefit analysis.
c. discretion.
d. utilitarianism.

___ 4. Eve, an employee of Fine Sales Company, takes an outcome-based approach to ethics. Eve believes that she must

a. avoid unethical behavior.
b. conform to society's standards.
c. place her employer's interest first.
d. produce the greatest good for the most people.

___ **5.** In a debate, Ed's best criticism of utilitarianism is that it

a. encourages unethical behavior.
b. fosters conformance with society's standards.
c. mandates acting in an employer's best interest.
d. results in human costs many persons find unacceptable.

___ **6.** In resolving an ethical problem, in most cases a decision by a business firm will have a negative effect on

a. one group as opposed to another.
b. the firm's competitors.
c. the government.
d. none of the above.

___ **7.** **Based on a Sample CPA Exam Question.** Ethical standards would most likely be considered to have been violated if Acme Services, Inc., represents to Best Production Company that certain services will be performed for a stated fee, but it is apparent at the time of the representation that

a. Acme cannot perform the services alone.
b. the actual charge will be substantially higher.
c. the actual charge will be substantially lower.
d. the fee is a competitive bid.

___ **8.** Tina, the president of United Sales, Inc., tries to ensure that United's actions are legal and ethical. To ensure this result, the best course of Tina and United is to act in

a. good faith.
b. ignorance of the law.
c. regard for the firm's shareholders only.
d. their own self interest.

___ **9.** Alan, an executive with Beta Corporation, follows the "principle of rights" theory, under which an action may be ethical depending on how it affects

a. the right determination under a cost-benefit analysis.
b. the right of Alan to maintain his dignity.
c. the right of Beta to make a profit.
d. the rights of others.

___ **10.** Gamma, Inc., a U.S. corporation, makes a side payment to the minister of commerce of another country for a favorable business contract. In the United States, this payment would be considered

a. illegal only.
b. unethical only.
c. illegal and unethical.
d. none of the above.

SHORT ESSAY QUESTIONS

What is the difference between legal and ethical standards? How are legal standards affected by ethical standards?

ISSUE SPOTTERS

(Answers at the Back of the Book)

1. If, like Robin Hood, a person robs the rich to pay the poor, does his or her benevolent intent make his or her actions ethical?

2. Delta Tools, Inc., markets a product that under some circumstances is capable of seriously injuring consumers. Does Delta owe an ethical duty to remove this product from the market, even if the injuries result only from misuse?

3. Acme Corporation decides to respond to what it sees as a moral obligation to correct for past discrimination by adjusting pay differences among its employees. Does this raise an ethical conflict between Acme's employees? Between Acme and its employees? Between Acme and its shareholders?

SPECIAL INFORMATION FOR CPA CANDIDATES

Ethics is tested in the business law and professional responsibilities portion of the CPA examination. The general outline provided in this chapter can serve as a jumping-off point for a more specific study of professional ethics. In the past, the CPA has covered the legal implications to CPAs, of certain business transactions, as well as the CPA's professional responsibility to clients and the accounting profession. The Foreign Corrupt Practices Act has been tested in the securities portion of the exam.

Specific topics in the area of professional responsibility can be divided into two categories: (1) the code of conduct and other professional responsibilities and (2) the law relating to CPA responsibilities. The first category can be further split into such topics as the code of professional conduct; proficiency and due care; consulting responsibilities; and tax practice responsibilities. The second category includes such topics as potential common law liability to clients and third parties, liability under federal statutes, and liability relating to working papers, privileged communications with clients, and confidentiality. These topics are covered in Chapter 52.

CUMULATIVE HYPOTHETICAL PROBLEM FOR UNIT EIGHT—INCLUDING CHAPTERS 35–42

(Answers at the Back of the Book)

Adam, Beth, and Carl are sole proprietors who decide to pool their resources to produce and maintain an Internet portal Web site, "i-World."

___ **1.** Adam, Beth, and Carl decide to form a partnership. They transfer their business assets and liabilities to the firm and start business on May 1, 2003. The parties execute a formal partnership agreement on July 1. The partnership began its existence

a. on May 1.
b. on July 1.
c. when each partner's individual creditors consented to the asset transfer.
d. when the parties initially decided to form a partnership.

___ **2.** After six months in operation, Adam, Beth, and Carl decide to change the form of their partnership to a limited partnership. To form a limited partnership, they must

a. accept limited liability for all of the partners.
b. create the firm according to specific statutory requirements.
c. designate one general partner to be a limited partner.
d. each make a capital contribution.

___ **3.** Adam, Beth, and Carl's i-World is very successful. In March 2004, they decide to incorporate. The articles of incorporation must include all of the following except

a. the name of a registered agent.
b. the name of the corporation.
c. the names of the incorporators.
d. the names of the initial officers.

___ **4.** In January 2005, Adam, Beth, and Carl decide to issue additional stock in i-World, Inc. The registration statement must include

a. a copy of the corporation's most recent proxy statement.
b. the names of prospective accredited investors.
c. the names of the current shareholders.
d. the principal purposes for which the proceeds from the offering will be used.

___ **5.** The issue of shares that i-World, Inc., plans to make qualifies under Rule 504 of Regulation D of the Securities Act of 1933. Under this rule, i-World

a. may not make the offering through general advertising.
b. may sell the shares to an unlimited number of investors.
c. must offer the shares for sale for more than twelve months.
d. must provide all prospective investors with a prospectus.

QUESTIONS ON THE FOCUS ON LEGAL REASONING FOR UNIT EIGHT— *IN RE MILLER*

(Answers at the Back of the Book)

___ **1.** Alan, a broker, commits securities fraud. According to the majority in *In re Miller*, to impute liability for the fraud under Section 20 of the Securities Exchange Act of 1934 on Alan's supervisor Ben and their employer Carol requires a finding of

a. agency.
b. bankruptcy.
c. partnership.
d. none of the above.

___ **2.** Under the facts in the previous question, according to the dissent in *In re Miller*, to impute liability for the fraud under Section 20 of the Securities Exchange Act of 1934 on Ben and Carol requires a finding of

a. agency.
b. bankruptcy.
c. partnership.
d. none of the above.

___ **3.** In the previous questions, suppose that liability for Alan's act is imputed under Section 20 on Ben and Carol, both of whom file for bankruptcy. In the opinion of the majority in *In re Miller*, a discharge of the debt represented by this liability could be obtained by

a. Ben only.
b. Carol only.
c. Ben and Carol.
d. neither Ben nor Carol.

QUESTIONS ON THE FOCUS ON ETHICS FOR UNIT EIGHT—BUSINESS ORGANIZATIONS

(Answers at the Back of the Book)

___ 1. Donna is an officer with Eagle, Inc. Donna finds herself in a position to acquire assets that would benefit Eagle if acquired in its name. If Donna usurps this opportunity, she may violate the duty of

a. acting in one's own interest.
b. agency.
c. care.
d. loyalty.

___ 2. Frank is a director of Great Sale Corporation. Ordinarily, Frank owes fiduciary duties only to

a. Great Sale's corporate personnel.
b. Great Sale's creditors.
c. Great Sale's shareholders.
d. himself.

___ 3. Burt is an employee of Cathy, a franchisee of Diners Restaurants, Inc. The franchisor may be liable for Burt's torts committed within the scope of his employment under the principles of

a. acting in one's own interest.
b. agency.
c. care.
d. loyalty.

Chapter 43
Administrative Law

WHAT THIS CHAPTER IS ABOUT

Federal, state, and local administrative agencies regulate virtually every aspect of a business's operation. Agencies' rules, orders, and decisions make up the body of administrative law. How agencies function is the subject of this chapter.

CHAPTER OUTLINE

I. AGENCY CREATION AND POWERS

Congress delegates some of its authority to make and implement laws, particularly in highly technical areas, to administrative agencies.

A. ENABLING LEGISLATION

To create an agency, Congress passes enabling legislation, which specifies the powers of the agency.

B. TYPES OF AGENCIES

1. Executive Agencies

Includes cabinet departments and their subagencies. Subject to the authority of the president, who can appoint and remove their officers.

2. Independent Regulatory Agencies

Includes agencies outside the major executive departments. Their officers serve for fixed terms and cannot be removed without just cause.

C. AGENCY POWERS AND THE CONSTITUTION

Agency powers include functions associated with the legislature (rulemaking), executive branch (enforcement), and courts (adjudication). Under Article I of the Constitution and the delegation doctrine, Congress has the power to establish agencies to create rules for implementing laws.

II. ADMINISTRATIVE PROCESS

Rulemaking, investigation, and adjudication make up the administrative process. The Administrative Procedure Act (APA) of 1946 imposes procedural requirements that agencies must follow.

A. RULEMAKING

Rulemaking is the formulation of new regulations. Legislative rules, or substantive rules, are as legally binding as the laws that Congress makes. Interpretive rules are not binding but indicate how an agency will apply a certain statute.

1. Notice of the Proposed Rulemaking

An agency begins by publishing, in the *Federal Register,* a notice that states where and when proceedings will be held, terms or subject matter of the proposed rule, and the agency's authority for making the rule.

2. Comment Period

Interested parties can express their views. An agency must respond to significant comments by modifying the final rule or explaining, in a statement accompanying the final rule, why it did not.

3. The Final Rule
The agency publishes the final rule in the *Federal Register*. The final rule has binding legal effect unless overturned by a court.

B. INVESTIGATION
Agencies must have knowledge of facts and circumstances pertinent to proposed rules. Agencies must also obtain information and investigate conduct to ascertain whether its rules are being violated.

1. Inspections and Tests
Through on-site inspections and testing, agencies gather information to prove a regulatory violation or to correct or prevent a bad condition.

2. Subpoenas
A subpoena *ad testificandum* is an order to a witness to appear at a hearing. A subpoena *duces tecum* is an order to a party to hand over records or other documents. Limits on agency demands for information through these subpoenas, and otherwise, include—

a. An investigation must have a legitimate purpose.

b. The information that is sought must be relevant.

c. Demands must be specific.

d. The party from whom the information is sought must not be unduly burdened by the request.

3. Search Warrants
A search warrant directs an officer to search a specific place for a specific item and present it to the agency.

a. Fourth Amendment
The Fourth Amendment protects against unreasonable searches and seizures by requiring that in most instances a physical search must be conducted under the authority of a search warrant.

b. Warrantless Searches
Warrants are not required to conduct searches in businesses in highly regulated industries, in certain hazardous operations, and in emergencies.

C. ADJUDICATION
Adjudication involves the resolution of disputes by an agency.

1. Negotiated Settlements
The purpose of negotiation is (1) for agencies: to eliminate the need for further proceedings and (2) for parties subject to regulation: to avoid publicity and the expense of litigation.

2. Formal Complaints
If there is no settlement, the agency may issue a formal complaint. The party charged in the complaint may respond with an answer. The case may go before an administrative law judge (ALJ).

3. The Role of an Administrative Law Judge (ALJ)
The ALJ presides over the hearing. The ALJ has the power to administer oaths, take testimony, rule on questions of evidence, and make determinations of fact. An ALJ works for the agency, but must be unbiased. Certain safeguards in the APA prevent bias and promote fairness.

4. Hearing Procedures
Procedures vary widely from agency to agency. Agencies exercise substantial discretion over the type of procedures used. A formal hearing resembles a trial, but more items and testimony are admissible in an administrative hearing.

5. **Agency Orders**
After a hearing, the ALJ issues an initial order. Either side may appeal to the commission that governs the agency and ultimately to a federal appeals court. If there is no appeal or review, the initial order becomes final.

III. LIMITATIONS ON AGENCY POWERS

Because of the concentration of so much authority in administrative agencies, the three branches of the government exercise control over agency powers.

A. JUDICIAL CONTROLS

The APA provides for judicial review of most agency decisions.

1. Requirements for Judicial Review

a. The action must be reviewable (under the APA, agency actions are presumed reviewable).

b. Under the ripeness doctrine, the case must be "ripe for review," which requires—

1) The party must have standing (a direct stake in the outcome).

2) The party must have exhausted all administrative remedies.

3) An actual controversy must be at issue.

2. Scope of Review

In most cases, a court defers to the facts as found in an agency proceeding. A court will review whether an agency has —

a. Exceeded its authority under its enabling legislation.

b. Improperly interpreted laws applicable to the action under review.

c. Violated any constitutional provisions.

d. Failed to act in accord with procedural requirements.

e. Taken actions that were arbitrary, capricious, or an abuse of discretion. (Actions taken willfully, unreasonably, and without considering the facts violate the "arbitrary and capricious" test.)

f. Reached conclusions not supported by substantial evidence.

B. EXECUTIVE CONTROLS

The president may veto enabling legislation or subsequent modifications to agency authority that Congress seeks to enact. The president appoints and removes many federal officers, including those in charge of agencies.

C. LEGISLATIVE CONTROLS

Congress can give power to an agency, take power away, reduce or increase agency finances, abolish an agency, investigate the implementation of the laws, investigate agencies, and affect policy through individual legislators' attempts to help their constituents deal with agencies.

IV. PUBLIC ACCOUNTABILITY

A. FREEDOM OF INFORMATION ACT (FOIA) OF 1966

The federal government must disclose certain records to any person on request. A failure to comply may be challenged in federal district court.

B. GOVERNMENT-IN-THE-SUNSHINE ACT OF 1976
Requires (1) that "every portion of every meeting of an agency" that is headed by a "collegial body" is open to "public observation" and (2) procedures to ensure that the public is provided with adequate advance notice of meetings and agendas (with exceptions).

C. REGULATORY FLEXIBILITY ACT OF 1980
Whenever a new regulation will have a "significant impact upon a substantial number of small entities," the agency must conduct a regulatory flexibility analysis. The analysis must measure the cost imposed by the rule on small businesses and must consider less burdensome alternatives.

D. SMALL BUSINESS REGULATORY ENFORCEMENT FAIRNESS ACT
Under this act, passed in 1996—

1. **Congress Reviews New Federal Regulations**
Congress reviews new regulations for at least sixty days before they take effect. Opponents have time to present arguments to Congress.

2. **Agencies Must Issue "Plain English" Guides**
Agencies must prepare guides that explain how small businesses can comply with their regulations.

3. **Regional Boards Rate Federal Agencies**
The National Enforcement Ombudsman receives comments from small businesses about agencies. Based on the comments, Regional Small Business Fairness Boards rate the agencies.

4. **Small Businesses May Recover Expenses and Fees**
Small businesses may recover expenses and legal fees from the government if an agency makes excessive demands for fines or penalties.

V. STATE ADMINISTRATIVE AGENCIES

A state agency often parallels a federal agency, providing similar services on a local basis. The supremacy clause requires that the federal agency's operation prevail over an inconsistent state agency's action. State court judicial review of state agency decisions parallels federal court review of federal agency decisions.

TRUE-FALSE QUESTIONS

(Answers at the Back of the Book)

___ 1. Enabling legislation specifies the powers of an agency.

___ 2. Most federal agencies are part of the executive branch of government.

___ 3. To create an agency, Congress enacts enabling legislation.

___ 4. Agency rules are not as legally binding as the laws that Congress enacts.

___ 5. After an agency adjudication, the administrative law judge's order must be appealed to become final.

___ 6. Congress has no power to influence agency policy.

___ 7. The Administrative Procedure Act provides for judicial review of most agency actions.

___ 8. When a new regulation will have a significant impact on a substantial number of small entities, an analysis must be conducted to measure the cost imposed on small businesses.

___ 9. State administrative agency operations prevail over federal agency actions.

___ 10. An agency cannot conduct a search without a warrant.

FILL-IN QUESTIONS

(Answers at the Back of the Book)

The rulemaking process begins with the publication in the ______________ (*Congressional Record/Federal Register*) of a notice of the proposed rulemaking. The agency may conduct a public hearing at which it presents evidence to justify the proposed rule, and ______________ (anyone/no one) may present opposing evidence. The agency ______________ (must/need not) respond to significant comments. After the hearing, the agency publishes the final draft of the rule in the ______________ (*Congressional Record/Federal Register*).

MULTIPLE-CHOICE QUESTIONS

(Answers at the Back of the Book)

___ 1. Ann, a congressperson, believes a new federal agency is needed to perform a certain function. Congress has the power to establish an agency to

a. adjudicate disputes arising from rules only.
b. make rules only.
c. adjudicate disputes arising from rules and make rules.
d. none of the above.

___ 2. Like other federal agencies, the Securities and Exchange Commission may obtain information concerning activities and organizations that it oversees by compelling disclosure through

a. a search only.
b. a subpoena only.
c. a search or a subpoena.
d. neither a search nor a subpoena.

___ 3. In making rules, the procedures of the Equal Employment Opportunity Commission and other federal agencies normally includes

a. notice and opportunity for comments by interested parties only.
b. publication of the final draft of the rule only.
c. notice and opportunity for comments by interested parties, and publication of the final draft of the rule.
d. none of the above.

___ 4. The Occupational Safety and Health Administration (OSHA) issues a subpoena for Alpha Corporation to hand over its files. Alpha's possible defenses against the subpoena include

a. OSHA cannot issue a subpoena.
b. OSHA is a federal agency, but Alpha only does business locally.
c. OSHA's request is not specific enough.
d. OSHA's request violates Alpha's right to privacy.

___ 5. The National Oceanic and Atmospheric Administration (NOAA) is a federal agency. To limit the authority of NOAA, the president can

a. abolish NOAA.
b. take away NOAA's power.
c. refuse to appropriate funds to NOAA.
d. veto legislative modifications to NOAA's authority.

___ **6.** The Federal Energy Regulatory Commission (FERC) wants to close a series of its meetings to the public. To open the meetings, a citizen could sue the FERC under

a. the Freedom of Information Act.
b. the Government-in-the-Sunshine Act.
c. the Regulatory Flexibility Act.
d. the Small Business Regulatory Enforcement Fairness Act.

___ **7.** The U.S. Fish and Wildlife Service orders Ed to stop using a certain type of fishing net from his boat. To appeal this order to a court, Ed must

a. appeal simultaneously to the agency and the court.
b. bypass all administrative remedies and appeal directly to the court.
c. exhaust all administrative remedies.
d. ignore the agency and continue using the net.

___ **8.** The Federal Trade Commission (FTC) issues an order relating to the advertising of Great Sales, Inc. Great Sales appeals the order to a court. The court may review whether the FTC's action is

a. arbitrary, capricious, or an abuse of discretion.
b. discourteous, disrespectful, or dissatisfying to one or more parties.
c. flippant, wanton, or in disregard of social norms.
d. impious, non-utilitarian, or in violation of ethical precepts.

___ **9.** The Environmental Protection Agency (EPA) publishes notice of a proposed rule. When comments are received about the rule, the EPA must respond to

a. all of the comments.
b. any significant comments that bear directly on the proposed rule.
c. only comments by businesses engaged in interstate commerce.
d. only comments by businesses that will be affected by the rule.

___ **10.** Mary is an administrative law judge (ALJ) for the National Labor Relations Board. In hearing a case, Mary has the authority to make

a. decisions binding on the federal courts.
b. determinations of fact.
c. new laws.
d. new rules.

SHORT ESSAY QUESTIONS

1. What are the conditions to judicial review of an agency enforcement action?

2. How does Congress hold agency authority in check?

ISSUE SPOTTERS

(Answers at the Back of the Book)

1. The Securities and Exchange Commission (SEC) makes rules regarding what disclosures must be made in a stock prospectus, prosecutes and adjudicates alleged violations, and prescribes punishment. This gives the SEC considerable power. What checks are there against this power?

2. The U.S. Department of Transportation (DOT) sometimes hears an appeal from a party whose contract with the DOT is canceled. An administrative law judge (ALJ), who works for the DOT, hears this appeal. What safeguards promote the ALJ's fairness?

3. The U.S. Department of Justice holds formal hearings concerning the deportation and exclusion of immigrants. How do such formal hearings resemble a trial? How are they different?

SPECIAL INFORMATION FOR CPA CANDIDATES

The material in this chapter has not been part of the CPA examination in the past. Regarding specific administrative agencies, however, you will be expected to know that the commerce clause supports the Securities Exchange Commission's regulation of interstate buying and selling of securities.

Although you should plan on taking the CPA examination as soon as possible after completing your undergraduate education (because the exam is an academic test, covering material that is part of the curriculum in the accounting programs in business schools), you should find some relief in the fact that the exam does not cover new law for at least one year after the law is enacted. If a question is posed on the test on a topic on which a new law has been enacted within the twelve months preceding the test, you will be given credit for answering the question in accord with the old law or the new law.

Chapter 44
Consumer Law

WHAT THIS CHAPTER IS ABOUT

Federal and state laws protect consumers from unfair trade practices, unsafe products, discriminatory or unreasonable credit requirements, and other problems related to consumer transactions. This chapter focuses on *federal* consumer law.

CHAPTER OUTLINE

I. DECEPTIVE ADVERTISING

The Federal Trade Commission Act of 1914 created the Federal Trade Commission (FTC) to prevent unfair and deceptive trade practices. *Deceptive advertising* is advertising that would mislead a consumer.

A. ADVERTISING THAT IS DECEPTIVE

Scientifically untrue claims; misleading half-truths; bait-and-switch ads (if a seller refuses to show an advertised item, fails to have adequate quantities on hand, fails to promise to deliver within a reasonable time, or discourages employees from selling the item.).

B. ADVERTISING THAT IS NOT DECEPTIVE

Puffing (vague generalities, obvious exaggeration).

C. ONLINE DECEPTIVE ADVERTISING

The same laws that apply to other forms of advertising apply to online ads, under FTC guidelines.

D. FTC ACTIONS AGAINST DECEPTIVE ADVERTISING

If the FTC believes that an ad is unfair or deceptive, it sends a complaint to the advertiser, who may settle. If not, the FTC can, after a hearing, issue a cease-and-desist order or require counteradvertising.

E. TELEMARKETING AND ELECTRONIC ADVERTISING

1. Telephone Consumer Protection Act (TCPA) of 1991

The TCPA prohibits (1) phone solicitation using an automatic dialing system or a prerecorded voice and (2) transmission of ads via fax without the recipient's permission. Consumers can recover actual losses or $500, whichever is greater, for each violation. If a defendant willfully or knowingly violated the act, a court can award treble damages.

2. Telemarketing and Consumer Fraud and Abuse Prevention Act of 1994

This act authorized the FTC to set rules for telemarketing and bring actions against fraudulent telemarketers. The FTC's Telemarketing Sales Rule of 1995 makes it illegal to misrepresent information and requires disclosure.

F. STATE LAWS

Most states also have laws regulating phone solicitation.

II. LABELING AND PACKAGING

A. FAIR PACKAGING AND LABELING ACT OF 1966

This act requires that product labels identify the product; net quantity of contents; quantity of servings, if the number of servings is stated; manufacturer; packager or distributor. The appropriate federal agency can require more (such as fat content).

B. OTHER FEDERAL LAWS

Other federal statutes included the Fur Products Labeling Act of 1951, the Wool Products Labeling Act of 1939, the Flammable Fabrics Act of 1953, and the Smokeless Tobacco Health Education Act of 1986.

III. SALES

Federal agencies that regulate sales include the FTC and the Federal Reserve Board of Governors (Regulation Z governs credit provisions in sales contracts). All states have some form of consumer protection laws.

A. DOOR-TO-DOOR SALES

States' "cooling-off" laws permit a buyer to rescind a door-to-door purchase within a certain time. The FTC has a three-day period. The FTC requires a seller to notify a buyer of the right to cancel (if the sale is in Spanish, notice must be in Spanish).

B. TELEPHONE AND MAIL-ORDER SALES

Consumers are partly protected by federal laws prohibiting mail fraud and by state law that parallels federal law.

1. FTC "Mail or Telephone Order Merchandise Rule" of 1993

For goods bought via phone lines or through the mail, merchants must ship orders within the time promised in their ads, notify consumers when orders cannot be shipped on time, and issue a refund within a specified time if a consumer cancels an order.

2. Postal Reorganization Act of 1970

Unsolicited merchandise sent by the mail may be retained, used, discarded, or disposed of, without obligation to the sender.

C. ONLINE SALES

The same federal and state laws that apply to other media generally protect consumers online.

IV. CREDIT PROTECTION

A. TRUTH-IN-LENDING ACT (TILA) OF 1968

The TILA, administered by the Federal Reserve Board, requires the disclosure of credit terms.

1. Who Is Subject to the TILA?

Creditors who, in the ordinary course of business, lend money or sell goods on credit to consumers, or arrange for credit for consumers, are subject to the TILA.

2. What Does the TILA Require?

Under Regulation Z, in any transaction involving a sales contract in which payment is to be made in more than four installments, a lender must disclose all the credit terms clearly and conspicuously.

3. Equal Credit Opportunity Act of 1974

This act prohibits (1) denial of credit on the basis of race, religion, national origin, color, sex, marital status, age and (2) credit discrimination based on whether an individual receives certain forms of income.

4. Credit-Card Rules

Liability of a cardholder is $50 per card for unauthorized charges made before the issuer is notified the card is lost. An issuer cannot bill for unauthorized charges if a card was improperly issued. To withhold payment for a faulty product, a cardholder must use specific procedures.

5. Consumer Leasing Act of 1988

Those who lease consumer goods in the ordinary course of their business, if the goods are priced at $25,000 or less and the lease term exceeds four months, must disclose all material terms in writing.

B. FAIR CREDIT REPORTING ACT (FCRA) OF 1970

1. **What the FCRA Provides**
   Consumer credit reporting agencies may issue credit reports only for certain purposes (extension of credit, etc.); a consumer who is denied credit, or is charged more than others would be, on the basis of a report must be notified of the fact and of the agency that issued the report.

2. **Consumers Can Have Inaccurate Information Deleted**
   If a consumer discovers that the report contains inaccurate information, the agency must delete it within a reasonable period of time.

C. FAIR DEBT COLLECTION PRACTICES ACT (FDCPA) OF 1977

Applies only to debt-collection agencies that, usually for a percentage of the amount owed, attempt to collect debts on behalf of someone else.

1. **What the FDCPA Prohibits**

   a. Contacting the debtor at the debtor's place of employment if the employer objects.

   b. Contacting the debtor during inconvenient times or at any time if an attorney represents the debtor.

   c. Contacting third parties other than the debtor's parents, spouse, or financial advisor about payment unless a court agrees.

   d. Using harassment, or false and misleading information.

   e. Contacting the debtor any time after the debtor refuses to pay the debt, except to advise the debtor of further action to be taken.

2. **What the FDCPA Requires**
   Collection agencies must give a debtor notice that he or she has thirty days to dispute the debt and request written verification of it.

3. **Remedies**
   A debt collector may be liable for actual damages, plus additional damages not to exceed $1,000 and attorneys' fees.

D. GARNISHMENT OF WAGES

To collect a debt, a creditor may use garnishment, which involves attaching a debtor's assets that are in the possession of a third party (employer, bank). The debtor must be notified and have an opportunity to respond. The amount that may be garnished is limited.

V. CONSUMER HEALTH AND SAFETY

A. FOOD AND DRUGS

The Federal Food, Drug, and Cosmetic Act (FFDCA) of 1938 sets food standards, levels of additives, classifications of food and food ads; regulates medical devices. Drugs must be shown to be effective and safe. Enforced by the Food and Drug Administration (FDA).

B. CONSUMER PRODUCT SAFETY

The Consumer Product Safety Act of 1972 includes a scheme for the regulation of consumer products and safety by the Consumer Product Safety Commission (CPSC). The CPSC—

1. Conducts research on product safety.

2. Sets standards for consumer products and bans the manufacture and sale of a product that is potentially hazardous to consumers.

3. Removes from the market any products imminently hazardous and requires manufacturers to report on any products already sold or intended for sale if the products have proved to be hazardous.

4. Administers other product safety legislation.

VI. STATE CONSUMER PROTECTION LAWS

State laws (typically directed at deceptive trade practices) may provide more protection for consumers than do federal laws. The Uniform Consumer Credit Code (UCCC) includes sections on truth in lending, fine-print clauses, and so on, but has been adopted in part in only a few states.

TRUE-FALSE QUESTIONS

(Answers at the Back of the Book)

___ 1. Advertising will be deemed deceptive if a consumer would be misled by the advertising claim.

___ 2. In general, labels must be accurate.

___ 3. A consumer cannot rescind a contract freely entered into.

___ 4. The TILA applies to creditors who, in the ordinary course of business, sell goods on credit to consumers.

___ 5. Misinformation in a consumer's credit file cannot be deleted.

___ 6. Consumers may have more protection under state laws than federal laws.

___ 7. The Fair Debt Collection Practices Act applies to anyone who attempts to collect a debt.

___ 8. There are no federal agencies that regulate sales.

___ 9. One who leases consumer goods in the ordinary course of business does not have to disclose any material terms in writing.

___ 10. An advertiser cannot fax ads to consumers without their permission.

FILL-IN QUESTIONS

(Answers at the Back of the Book)

The Truth-in-Lending Act contains provisions regarding credit cards. One provision limits the liability of the cardholder to __________ ($50/$500) per card for unauthorized charges made ________________ (after/before) the credit card issuer is notified that the card has been lost. Another provision ________________ (allows/prohibits) a credit card company ________________ (from billing/to bill) a consumer for any unauthorized charges ________________ (unless/if) the credit card was improperly issued by the company.

MULTIPLE-CHOICE QUESTIONS

(Answers at the Back of the Book)

___ 1. Rich Foods Company advertises that its cereal, "Fiber Rich," reduces cholesterol. After an investigation and a hearing, the FTC finds no evidence to support the claim. To correct the public's impression of Fiber Rich, the most appropriate action would be

a. a cease-and-desist order.
b. a civil fine.
c. a criminal fine.
d. counteradvertising.

___ **2.** ABC Corporation sells a variety of consumer products. Generally, the labels on its products must

a. only be accurate.
b. only use words as they are ordinarily understood by consumers.
c. be accurate and use words as they are ordinarily understood by consumers.
d. none of the above.

___ **3.** Maria speaks Spanish, but not English. Nick comes to her home and, after a presentation in Spanish, sells her a vacuum cleaner. He hands her a paper that contains only in English a notice of the right to cancel a sale within three days. This transaction is

a. proper, because the seller gave the buyer notice of her rights.
b. not proper, because the deal was in Spanish but the notice was in English.
c. proper, because ignorance of your rights is no defense.
d. not proper, because ignorance of your rights is a defense.

___ **4.** Ed takes out a student loan from First National Bank. After graduation, Ed goes to work, but he does not make payments on the loan. The bank agrees with Good Collection Agency (GCA) that if GCA collects the debt, it can keep a percentage of the amount. To collect the debt, GCA can contact

a. Ed at his place of employment, even if his employer objects.
b. Ed at unusual or inconvenient times or any time if he retains an attorney.
c. Ed only to advise him of further action that GCA will take.
d. third parties, including Ed's parents, unless ordered otherwise by a court.

___ **5.** The ordinary business of Ace Credit Company is to lend money to consumers. Ace must disclose all credit terms clearly and conspicuously in

a. all credit transactions.
b. any credit transaction in which payments are to be made in more than four installments.
c. any credit transaction in which payments are to be made in more than one installment.
d. no credit transaction.

___ **6.** Eve borrows money to buy a car and to pay for repairs to the roof of her house. She also buys furniture in a transaction financed by the seller whom she will repay in installments. If all of the parties are subject to the Truth-in-Lending Act, Regulation Z applies to

a. the car loan only.
b. the home improvement loan only.
c. the retail installment sale only.
d. the car loan, the home improvement loan, and the retail installment sale.

___ **7.** National Foods, Inc., sells breakfast cereals. National must include on the packages

a. the identity of the product only.
b. the net quantity of the contents and the number of servings only.
c. the identity of the product, the net quantity of the contents, and the number of servings.
d. none of the above.

___ **8.** General Tobacco Corporation (GTC) sells tobacco products. On the packages of its smokeless tobacco products, GTC must include warnings about health hazards associated with

a. cigarettes.
b. smokeless products.
c. tobacco products generally.
d. none of the above.

____ 9. Best Toy Company begins marketing a new toy that is highly flammable. The Consumer Product Safety Commission may

a. ban the toy's future manufacture and sale only.
b. order that the toy be removed from the market only.
c. ban the toy's future manufacture and sale, and order that the toy be removed from the market.
d. none of the above.

____ 10. Ann receives an unsolicited credit card in the mail and tosses it on her desk. Without Ann's permission, her roommate uses the card to buy new clothes for $1,000. Ann is liable for

a. $1,000.
b. $500.
c. $50.
d. none of the above.

SHORT ESSAY QUESTIONS

1. What are some of the more common deceptive advertising techniques and the ways in which the FTC may deal with such conduct?

2. What are the primary provisions of the Truth-In-Lending Act?

ISSUE SPOTTERS

(Answers at the Back of the Book)

1. Alpha Electronics, Inc., advertises Beta computers at a low price. Alpha keeps only a few in stock and tells its sales staff to switch consumers attracted by the price to more expensive brands. Alpha tells its staff that if all else fails, refuse to show the Betas, and if a consumer insists on buying one, do not promise delivery. Has Alpha violated a law?

2. Carol buys a notebook computer from Alpha Electronics. She pays for it with her credit card. When it proves defective, she asks Alpha to repair or replace it, but Alpha refuses. What can Carol do?

3. ABC Pharmaceuticals, Inc., believes it has developed a new drug that will be effective in the treatment of AIDS patients. The drug has had only limited testing, but ABC wants to make the drug widely available as soon as possible. To market the drug, what must ABC show the Food and Drug Administration?

SPECIAL INFORMATION FOR CPA CANDIDATES

The CPA examination generally does not test on the material covered in this chapter.

When studying for the CPA exam, many students integrate their review of business law topics with their review of other topics that make up distinct subject matter on the exam. For example, when reviewing the law behind business organizations, it can be most helpful to review the accounting and reporting details behind businesses' financial statements. Which topics to integrate and how much time to spend on each depends in part on each student's knowledge and understanding of the individual topics, as well as the emphasis that should be placed on a topic because of its importance for the exam.

Chapter 45
Environmental Law

WHAT THIS CHAPTER IS ABOUT

This chapter covers environmental law, which is the law that relates to environmental protection—common law actions and federal statutes and regulations.

CHAPTER OUTLINE

I. COMMON LAW ACTIONS

A. NUISANCE

Persons cannot use their property in a way that unreasonably interferes with others' rights to use or enjoy their own property. An injured party may be awarded damages or an injunction.

B. NEGLIGENCE AND STRICT LIABILITY

A business that fails to use reasonable care may be liable to a party whose injury was foreseeable. Businesses that engage in ultrahazardous activities are strictly liable for whatever injuries the activities cause.

II. STATE AND LOCAL REGULATION

States regulate the environment through zoning or more direct regulation. City, county, and other local governments control some aspects through zoning laws, waste removal and disposal regulations, aesthetic ordinances, and so on.

III. FEDERAL REGULATION

A. ENVIRONMENTAL REGULATORY AGENCIES

The Environmental Protection Agency (EPA) coordinates federal environmental responsibilities and administers most federal environmental policies and statutes. State and local agencies implement environmental statutes and regulations. Citizens can sue to enforce environmental regulations.

B. ENVIRONMENTAL IMPACT STATEMENTS

The National Environmental Policy Act (NEPA) of 1969 requires all federal agencies to consider environmental factors in making significant decisions.

1. **When an Environmental Impact Statement Must Be Prepared**
   Whenever a major federal action significantly affects the quality of the environment. An action qualifies as *major* if it involves a substantial commitment of resources (monetary or otherwise). An action is *federal* if a federal agency has the power to control it.

2. **What an EIS Must Analyze**
   (1) The impact on the environment that the action will have, (2) any adverse effects to the environment and alternative actions that might be taken, and (3) irreversible effects the action might generate.

3. **When an Agency Decides That an EIS Is Unnecessary**
   It must issue a statement supporting this conclusion.

C. OTHER FEDERAL LAWS

Other federal laws that require the consideration of environmental values in agency decision-making include the Fish and Wildlife Coordination Act of 1958 and the Endangered Species Act of 1973.

IV. AIR POLLUTION

The Clean Air Act of 1963 (and amendments) is the basis for regulation.

A. MOBILE SOURCES

Regulations governing air pollution from automobiles and other mobile sources specify standards and time schedules. For example, under the 1990 amendments to the Clean Air Act—

1. **New Automobiles' Exhaust**
   Manufacturers had to cut emission of nitrogen oxide by 60 percent and emission of other pollutants by 35 percent. Other sets of emission controls became or will become effective in 2004 and 2007.

2. **EPA Action**
   If a vehicle does not meet the standards, the EPA can order a recall and repair or replacement of pollution-control devices.

3. **Sport Utility Vehicles and Light Trucks**
   These vehicles are now subject to the same standards as cars.

4. **Gasoline**
   Service stations must sell gasoline with higher oxygen content.

5. **New Standards**
   The EPA attempts to update these and other standards when new scientific evidence is available.

B. STATIONARY SOURCES

The EPA sets air quality standards for stationary sources (such as industrial plants), and the states formulate plans to achieve them. For example, under the 1990 amendments to the Clean Air Act—

1. **Major New Sources**
   These must use the maximum achievable control technology (MACT) to reduce emissions from the combustion of fossil fuels (coal and oil).

2. **110 of the Oldest Coal-burning Power Plants in the United States**
   These were to cut emissions by 40 percent by the year 2001 to reduce acid rain.

3. **Utilities**
   Utilities were granted "credits" to emit certain amounts of sulfur dioxide, and those that emit less can sell their credits to other polluters.

4. **Other Factories and Businesses**
   These were to reduce emissions to cut ground-level ozone in 96 cities by 2005. Production of chlorofluorocarbons, carbon tetrachloride, and methyl chloroform (linked to depleting the ozone layer) must stop.

5. **Hazardous Air Pollutants**
   Industrial emissions of 189 specific hazardous air pollutants must be reduced through MACT. Certain landfills must install air-pollution collection and control systems.

C. PENALTIES

Civil penalties include assessments of up to $25,000 per day, or an amount equal to a violator's economic benefits from noncompliance, plus up to $5,000 per day for other violations. Criminal penalties include fines of up to $1 million and imprisonment of up to two years. Private citizens can sue.

V. WATER POLLUTION

A. NAVIGABLE WATERS

The Clean Water Act of 1972 amended the Federal Water Pollution Control Act (FWPCA) of 1948 to provide—

1. Goals

The goals of the statutes are to (1) make waters safe for swimming, (2) protect fish and wildlife, and (3) eliminate the discharge of pollutants into the water.

2. Limits on Discharges Based on Best Available Control Technology

Time schedules (extended by amendment in 1977 and by the Water Quality Act of 1987) limit discharges of pollutants.

3. Permits

Municipal and industrial polluters must obtain permits before discharging wastes into navigable waters, which include wetlands.

4. Penalties and Remedies

Civil penalties include assessments of from $10,000 per day (up to $25,000 per violation) to $25,000 per day. Criminal penalties include fines of $2,500 per day to $1 million total and one to fifteen years' imprisonment. Injunctions, damages, and clean-up costs can be imposed.

B. DRINKING WATER

The Safe Drinking Water Act of 1974 requires the EPA to set maximum levels for pollutants in public water systems. Operators must come as close as possible to the standards using the best available technology.

C. OCEAN DUMPING

The Marine Protection, Research, and Sanctuaries Act of 1972—

1. Radiological Waste and Other Materials

Dumping of radiological, chemical, and biological warfare agents, and high-level radioactive waste is prohibited. Transporting and dumping other materials (with exceptions) requires a permit.

2. Penalties

Civil penalties include assessments of not more than $50,000 or revocation or suspension of a permit. Criminal penalties include fines of up to $50,000, imprisonment for not more than a year, or both. Injunctions can be imposed.

D. OIL POLLUTION

The Oil Pollution Act of 1990 provides that any oil facility, oil shipper, vessel owner, or vessel operator that discharges oil may be liable for clean-up costs, damages, and fines of up to $25,000 per day.

VI. NOISE POLLUTION

Under Noise Control Act of 1972, the EPA sets maximum levels for noise. The act requires use of the best available technology. Injunctions may be imposed. Penalties include fines up to $50,000 per day and up to two years' imprisonment.

VII. TOXIC CHEMICALS

A. PESTICIDES AND HERBICIDES

1. Federal Insecticide, Fungicide, and Rodenticide Act (FIFRA) of 1947

a. Registration, Certification, and Use

Pesticides and herbicides must be (1) registered before they can be sold, (2) certified and used only for approved applications, and (3) used in limited quantities when applied to food crops.

b. Labels
Include directions for the use of a pesticide or herbicide, warnings to protect human health and the environment, a statement of treatment in the case of poisoning, and a list of the ingredients.

c. Penalties
For registrants and producers: suspension or cancellation of registration, up to a $50,000 fine, imprisonment up to one year. For commercial dealers: up to a $25,000 fine, imprisonment up to one year. For private users: a $1,000 fine, imprisonment up to thirty days.

2. "Reasonable Certainty of No Harm"
To remain on the market, a pesticide must have a "reasonable certainty of no harm" (one-in-a-million risk to people of cancer from exposure). Grocery stores must display brochures about pesticides in food.

B. TOXIC SUBSTANCES
Under the Toxic Substances Control Act of 1976, for substances that potentially pose an imminent hazard or an unreasonable risk of injury to health or the environment, the EPA may require special labeling, set production quotas, or limit or prohibit the use of a substance.

VIII. HAZARDOUS WASTES

A. RESOURCE CONSERVATION AND RECOVERY ACT (RCRA) OF 1976
The EPA determines which forms of solid waste are hazardous, and sets requirements for disposal, storage, and treatment. Penalties include up to $25,000 (civil) per violation, $50,000 (criminal) per day, imprisonment up to two years (may be doubled for repeaters), and up to $250,000 and fifteen years for knowingly violating the RCRA and endangering another's life.

B. SUPERFUND
The Comprehensive Environmental Response, Compensation, and Liability Act (CERCLA) of 1980 regulates the clean-up of leaking hazardous waste disposal sites. If a release or a threatened release occurs, the EPA can clean up a site and recover the cost from—

1. Potentially Responsible Parties
(1) The person who generated the wastes disposed of at the site, (2) the person who transported the wastes to the site, (3) the person who owned or operated the site at the time of the disposal, or (4) the current owner or operator.

2. Joint and Several Liability
One party can be charged with the entire cost (which that party may recover in a contribution action against others).

IX. GLOBAL ENVIRONMENTAL ISSUES

These include cross-border pollution and global warming. The Kyoto Protocol, which has been ratified by 160 nations (but not the United States), established reductions for different countries and regions in emissions of gases linked to global warming.

TRUE-FALSE QUESTIONS

(Answers at the Back of the Book)

___ **1.** No common law doctrines apply against polluters today.

___ **2.** Local governments can control some aspects of the environment through zoning laws.

___ **3.** Under federal environmental laws, there is a single standard for all polluters and all pollutants.

___ **4.** The Toxic Substances Control Act of 1976 regulates the clean up of leaking hazardous waste disposal sites.

___ **5.** The Environmental Protection Agency (EPA) can clean up a release of hazardous waste at a hazardous waste disposal site and recover the entire cost from the site's owner or operator.

___ **6.** States may restrict discharge of chemicals into the water or air.

___ **7.** A party who violates the Clean Air Act may realize economic benefits from the noncompliance.

___ **8.** The Environmental Protection Agency sets limits on discharges of pollutants into water.

___ **9.** A party who only transports hazardous waste to a hazardous waste disposal site cannot be held liable for any costs to clean up the site.

___ **10.** The Environmental Protection Agency sets maximum levels for noise.

FILL-IN QUESTIONS

(Answers at the Back of the Book)

The National Environmental Policy Act requires ______________ (federal/state and local) agencies to prepare environmental impact statements (EIS) when major ______________ (federal/state and local) actions significantly affect the quality of the environment. An EIS analyzes (1) the ______________ (environmental impact that an action will have/environment's impact on a project), (2) any adverse effects to the ______________ (environment/project) and alternative courses of action, and (3) irreversible effects that ______________ (an action might cause to the environment/the environment might cause to the project). If an agency decides that an EIS is unnecessary, it must issue a statement announcing that decision ______________ (and reasons/but it need not provide reasons) supporting the conclusion.

MULTIPLE-CHOICE QUESTIONS

(Answers at the Back of the Book)

___ **1.** The U.S. Department of the Interior's approval of coal mining operations in several eastern states requires an environmental impact statement

a. only because it affects the quality of the environment.
b. only because it is "major."
c. only because it is "federal."
d. because it affects the quality of the environment, is "major," and is "federal."

___ **2.** Standard Utility's new power plant burns fossil fuels. As a major new source of possible pollution, the plant must use

a. the all-pollution elimination control technology.
b. the best available control technology.
c. the maximum achievable control technology.
d. the most affordable control technology.

___ **3.** National Motors Corporation (NMC) makes sport utility vehicles (SUVs). Under the Clean Air Act, NMC is required to makes its SUVs comply with standards that, with respect to automobile exhaust emissions, are

a. different but neither more nor less strict.
b. less strict.
c. more strict.
d. the same.

___ **4.** Eagle Industries, Inc., fails to obtain a permit before discharging waste into navigable waters. Under the Clean Water Act, Eagle can be required

a. only to clean up the pollution.
b. only to pay for the cost of cleaning up the pollution.
c. to clean up the pollution or pay for the cost of doing so.
d. none of the above.

___ **5.** Petro, Inc., ships unlabeled containers of hazardous waste to off-site facilities for disposal. If the containers later leak, Petro could be found to have violated

a. the Comprehensive Environmental Response, Compensation, and Liability Act (CERCLA) only.
b. the Resource Conservation and Recovery Act (RCRA) only.
c. CERCLA and the RCRA.
d. none of the above.

___ **6.** Beta Company operates a hazardous waste storage facility. If Beta buries unlabeled containers without determining their contents and the containers leak, Beta could be found to have violated

a. the Comprehensive Environmental Response, Compensation, and Liability Act (CERCLA) only.
b. the Resource Conservation and Recovery Act (RCRA) only.
c. CERCLA and the RCRA.
d. none of the above.

___ **7.** The U.S. Department of the Interior approves minor landscaping around a federal courthouse in St. Louis. This does *not* require an environmental impact statement

a. only because it does not affect the quality of the environment.
b. only because it is not "major."
c. only because it is not "federal."
d. because it does not affect the quality of the environment, is not "major," and is not "federal."

___ **8.** **Based on a Sample CPA Exam Question.** Federated Industries' factories emit toxic air pollutants. Under the Clean Air Act and EPA regulations, Federated is required to

a. eliminate all air polluting emissions.
b. install emission control equipment on its products.
c. reduce emissions by installing the maximum achievable control technology.
d. remove all pollutants from its factories.

___ **9.** Alpha Development Company owns wetlands that it wants to fill in and develop as a site for homes. Under the Clean Water Act, before filling and dredging, Alpha must obtain a permit from

a. no one.
b. the Army Corps of Engineers.
c. the EPA.
d. the U.S. Department of the Navy.

___ **10.** Gamma Company owns a hazardous waste disposal site that it sells to Omega Properties, Inc. Later, the EPA discovers a leak at the site and cleans it up. The EPA can recover the cost from

a. Gamma only.
b. Omega only.
c. Gamma or Omega.
d. none of the above.

SHORT ESSAY QUESTIONS

1. What does the National Environmental Policy Act require?

2. What federal laws regulate toxic chemicals?

ISSUE SPOTTERS

(Answers at the Back of the Book)

1. ChemCorp generates hazardous wastes from its operations. Central Trucking Company transports those wastes to Intrastate Disposal, Inc., which owns a hazardous waste disposal site. Intrastate sells the property on which the disposal site is located to ABC Properties, Inc. If the EPA cleans up the site, from whom can it recover the cost?

2. ABC Company's plant emits smoke and fumes. ABC's operation includes a short railway system, and trucks enter and exit the grounds continuously. Constant vibrations from the trains and trucks rattle a nearby residential neighborhood. The residents sue ABC. Are there any reasons that the court might *refuse* to enjoin ABC's operation?

3. What federal agencies have authority to regulate environmental matters?

SPECIAL INFORMATION FOR CPA CANDIDATES

The CPA examination tests some concepts of environmental law. Environmental impact statements—their purpose and use—are one part of the material in this chapter that should be understood. You should have an awareness of the major environmental laws, too. Most important, however, is the Comprehensive Environmental Response, Compensation, and Liability Act (CERCLA) of 1980 (Superfund). Of specific significance is the use of the term "owner or operator" to subject many parties to liability for the clean-up costs of hazardous waste sites. In particular, you should remember the possibility that a lender may be held liable.

Chapter 46
Antitrust Law

WHAT THIS CHAPTER IS ABOUT

This chapter outlines aspects of the major antitrust statutes—the Sherman Act, the Clayton Act, and the Federal Trade Commission Act. The basis of the antitrust laws is a desire to foster competition (to result in lower prices and so on) by limiting restraints on trade (agreements between firms that have the effect of reducing competition in the marketplace).

CHAPTER OUTLINE

I. THE SHERMAN ANTITRUST ACT

The Sherman Antitrust Act of 1890 is one of the government's most powerful weapons to maintain a competitive economy.

A. MAJOR PROVISIONS OF THE SHERMAN ACT

Section 1 requires two or more persons; cases often concern agreements (written or oral) that have a wrongful purpose and lead to a restraint of trade. Section 2 cases deal with existing monopolies.

B. JURISDICTIONAL REQUIREMENTS

The Sherman Act applies to restraints that substantially affect interstate commerce. The act also covers activities by U.S. nationals abroad that have an effect on U.S. foreign commerce.

II. SECTION 1 OF THE SHERMAN ACT

Section 1 prohibits horizontal restraints and vertical restraints.

A. *PER SE* VIOLATIONS VERSUS THE RULE OF REASON

Some restraints are deemed *per se* violations. Others are subject to analysis under the rule of reason.

1. *Per Se* Violations

Agreements that are blatantly anticompetitive are illegal *per se.*

2. Rule of Reason

A court considers the purpose of an agreement, the power of the parties, the effect of the action on trade, and in some cases, whether there are less restrictive alternatives to achieve the same goals. If the competitive benefits outweigh the anticompetitive effects, the agreement is held lawful.

B. HORIZONTAL RESTRAINTS

Horizontal restraints are agreements that restrain competition between rivals in the same market.

1. Price Fixing

Any agreement among competitors to fix prices is a *per se* violation.

2. Group Boycotts

An agreement by two or more sellers to refuse to deal with a particular person or firm is a *per se* violation, if it is intended to eliminate competition or prevent entry into a given market.

3. Horizontal Market Division

An agreement between competitors to divide up territories or customers is a *per se* violation.

4. **Trade Associations**
Trade associations are businesses within the same industry or profession organized to pursue common interests. The rule of reason is applied.

5. **Joint Ventures**
A joint venture is an undertaking by two or more individuals or firms for a specific purpose. If price fixing or a market division is not involved, the agreement will be analyzed under the rule of reason.

C. VERTICAL RESTRAINTS
A restraint of trade that results from an agreement between firms at different levels in the manufacturing and distribution process.

1. **Territorial or Customer Restrictions**
This restriction consists of an agreement between a manufacturer and a distributor or retailer to restrict sales to certain areas or customers. It is judged under a rule of reason.

2. **Resale Price Maintenance Agreements**
In a resale price maintenance agreement between a manufacturer and a distributor or retailer, the manufacturer specifies the retail prices of its products. This is subject to the rule of reason.

3. **Refusals to Deal**
A firm is free to deal, or not, unilaterally, with whomever it wishes.

III. SECTION 2 OF THE SHERMAN ACT
Section 2 applies to individuals and to several people; cases concern the structure of a monopoly in the marketplace and the misuse of monopoly power. Section 2 covers two distinct types of behavior: monopolization and attempts to monopolize.

A. MONOPOLIZATION
This offense has two elements: (1) the possession of monopoly power in the relevant market and (2) the willful acquisition or maintenance of that power.

1. **Monopoly Power**
Monopoly power is sufficient power to control prices and exclude competition in an entire market.

   a. **Market-Share Test**
   A firm has monopoly power if its share of the relevant market is 70 percent or more.

   b. **The Relevant Market Has Two Elements—**

      1) **Relevant Product Market**
      This market includes all products with identical attributes and those that are sufficient substitutes for each other.

      2) **Relevant Geographical Market**
      If competitors sell in only a limited area, the geographical market is limited to that area.

2. **The Intent Requirement**
If a firm has market power as a result of a purposeful act to acquire or maintain that power through anticompetitive means, it is a violation of Section 2. Intent may be inferred from evidence that the firm had monopoly power and engaged in anticompetitive behavior.

B. ATTEMPTS TO MONOPOLIZE
Any action challenged as an attempt to monopolize (1) must be intended to exclude competitors and garner monopoly power and (2) must have a dangerous probability of success.

IV. THE CLAYTON ACT

Enacted in 1914, the Clayton Act is aimed at practices not covered by the Sherman Act. Conduct is illegal only if it substantially tends to lessen competition or create monopoly power.

A. SECTION 2—PRICE DISCRIMINATION

Price discrimination occurs when a seller charges different prices to competitive buyers for identical goods.

1. Elements

(1) The seller must be engaged in interstate commerce, (2) the effect of the price discrimination must be to substantially lessen competition or create a competitive injury, and (3) a seller's pricing policies must include a reasonable prospect of the seller's recouping its losses.

2. Exceptions

(1) When a lower price is charged temporarily and in good faith to meet another seller's equally low price to the buyer's competitor or (2) a buyer's purchases saved the seller costs in producing and selling goods.

B. SECTION 3—EXCLUSIONARY PRACTICES

1. Exclusive-Dealing Contracts

This is a contract under which a seller forbids a buyer to buy products from the seller's competitors. Prohibited if the effect is "to substantially lessen competition or tend to create a monopoly."

2. Tying Arrangements

This occurs when a seller conditions the sale of a product on the buyer's agreement to buy another product produced or distributed by the same seller. Legality depends on the agreement's purpose and its likely effect on competition in the relevant markets. Subject to the "soft" *per se* rule.

C. SECTION 7—MERGERS

A person or firm cannot hold stock or assets in another firm if the effect may be to substantially lessen competition. A crucial consideration in most cases is market concentration (percentage of market shares of firms in the relevant market).

1. Horizontal Mergers

These are mergers between firms competing with each other in the same market. If a merger creates an entity with a resulting significant market share, it may be presumed illegal. Factors include—

a. The degree of concentration in the relevant market.

b. The ease of entry into the relevant market.

c. Economic efficiency.

d. The financial condition of the merging firms.

e. The nature and prices of the products.

2. Vertical Mergers

This occurs when a company at one stage of production acquires a company at a higher or lower stage of production. Legality depends on market concentration, barriers to entry into that market, and the parties' intent.

3. Conglomerate Mergers

a. Market-Extension Merger

This occurs when a firm seeks to sell its product in a new market by merging with a firm already established in that market.

b. **Product-Extension Merger**
This is when a firm seeks to add a closely related product to its existing line by merging with a firm already producing that product.

c. **Diversification Merger**
This happens when a firm merges with another firm that offers a product or service wholly unrelated to the first firm's existing activities.

D. SECTION 8—INTERLOCKING DIRECTORATES
No person may be a director in two or more corporations at the same time if either firm has capital, surplus, or undivided profits of more than $18,193,000 or competitive sales of $1,819,300 or more (as of 2002).

V. ENFORCEMENT OF ANTITRUST LAWS

A. U.S. DEPARTMENT OF JUSTICE (DOJ)
The DOJ prosecutes violations of the Sherman Act as criminal or civil violations. Violations of the Clayton Act are not crimes; the DOJ can enforce it only through civil proceedings. Remedies include divestiture and dissolution.

B. FEDERAL TRADE COMMISSION (FTC)
The FTC enforces the Clayton Act; has the sole authority to enforce the Federal Trade Commission Act of 1914 (Section 5 condemns all forms of anticompetitive behavior that are not covered by other federal antitrust laws); issues administrative orders; can seek court sanctions.

C. PRIVATE PARTIES

1. **Treble Damages and Attorneys' Fees**
Private parties can sue for treble damages and attorneys' fees under the Clayton Act if they are injured by a violation of any federal antitrust law (except the FTC Act).

2. **Injunctions**
Private parties may seek an injunction to prevent an antitrust violation if it will injure business activities protected by the antitrust laws.

VI. EXEMPTIONS FROM ANTITRUST LAWS

A. LABOR ACTIVITIES
A labor union can lose its exemption if it combines with a nonlabor group.

B. AGRICULTURAL ASSOCIATIONS AND FISHERIES
Except exclusionary practices or restraints of trade against competitors.

C. INSURANCE COMPANIES
Exempt in most cases when state regulation exists.

D. FOREIGN TRADE
U.S. exporters may cooperate to compete with similar foreign associations (if it does not restrain trade in the U.S. or injure other U.S. exporters).

E. PROFESSIONAL BASEBALL
Other professional sports are not exempt.

F. OIL MARKETING
States set quotas on oil to be marketed in interstate commerce.

G. COOPERATIVE RESEARCH AND PRODUCTION
Cooperative research among small business firms is exempt.

H. JOINT EFFORTS TO OBTAIN LEGISLATIVE OR EXECUTIVE ACTION

Joint efforts by businesspersons to obtain executive or legislative action are exempt (*Noerr-Pennington* doctrine). Exception: an action is not protected if "no reasonable [person] could reasonably expect success on the merits" and it is an attempt to make anticompetitive use of government processes.

I. OTHER EXEMPTIONS

1. Activities approved by the president in furtherance of defense.
2. State actions, when the state policy is clearly articulated and the policy is actively supervised by the state.
3. Activities of regulated industries when federal commissions, boards, or agencies have primary regulatory authority.

VII. U.S. ANTITRUST LAWS IN THE GLOBAL CONTEXT

For U.S. courts to exercise jurisdiction over a foreign entity under U.S. antitrust laws, a violation must (1) have a substantial effect on U.S. commerce or (2) constitute a *per se* violation. Foreign governments and persons can also sue U.S. firms and persons for antitrust violations.

TRUE-FALSE QUESTIONS

(Answers at the Back of the Book)

___ 1. A horizontal restraint results from an agreement between firms at different levels in the manufacturing and distribution process.

___ 2. An agreement that restrains competition between rivals in the same market is a vertical restraint.

___ 3. Monopoly power is market power sufficient to control prices and exclude competition.

___ 4. An exclusive dealing contract is a contract under which competitors agree to divide up customers.

___ 5. Price discrimination occurs when a seller forbids a buyer to buy products from the seller's competitors.

___ 6. A horizontal merger results when a company at one stage of production acquires another company at a higher or lower stage in the chain of production and distribution.

___ 7. A merger between firms that compete with each other in the same market is a vertical merger.

___ 8. A relevant product market includes products that are sufficient substitutes for each other.

___ 9. An agreement that is inherently anticompetitive is illegal *per se*.

___ 10. An agreement between competitors to fix prices is a *per se* violation.

FILL-IN QUESTIONS

(Answers at the Back of the Book)

____________________ (Monopoly power/A restraint of trade) is any agreement that has the effect of reducing competition in the marketplace. ____________________ (Monopoly power/ Restraint of trade) is an extreme amount of market power. A firm that can raise its prices somewhat without too much concern for its competitors' response has some degree of market power. Determining whether such power is sufficient to call it ____________________ (monopoly power/ a restraint of trade) is one of the most difficult tasks in antitrust law.

MULTIPLE-CHOICE QUESTIONS

(Answers at the Back of the Book)

___ **1.** National Coal Association (NCA) is a group of independent coal mining companies. Demand for coal falls. The price drops. Coal Refiners Association, a group of coal refining companies, agrees to buy NCA's coal and sell it according to a schedule that will increase the price. This agreement is

a. a *per se* violation of the Sherman Act.
b. exempt from the antitrust laws.
c. subject to evaluation under the rule of reason.
d. none of the above.

___ **2.** International Sales, Inc. (ISI), is charged with a violation of antitrust law. ISI's conduct is a *per se* violation

a. if the anticompetitive harm outweighs the competitive benefits.
b. if the competitive benefits outweigh the anticompetitive harm.
c. if the conduct is blatantly anticompetitive.
d. only if it qualifies as an exemption.

___ **3.** Techno, Inc., sells its brand-name computer equipment directly to its franchised retailers. Depending on how existing franchisees do, Techno may limit the number of franchisees in a given area to reduce intrabrand competition. Techno's restrictions on the number of dealers is

a. a *per se* violation of the Sherman Act.
b. exempt from the antitrust laws.
c. subject to evaluation under the rule of reason.
d. none of the above.

___ **4.** Gamma Corporation is charged with a violation of antitrust law that requires evaluation under the rule of reason. The court will consider

a. only the effect of the conduct on trade.
b. only the power of the parties to accomplish what they intend.
c. only the purpose of the conduct.
d. the effect of the conduct, the power of the parties, and the purpose of the conduct.

___ **5.** Omega, Inc., controls 80 percent of the market for telecommunications equipment in the southeastern United States. To show that Omega is monopolizing that market in violation of the Sherman Act requires proof of

a. only the possession of monopoly power in the relevant market.
b. only the willful acquisition or maintenance of monopoly power.
c. the possession of monopoly power in the relevant market and the willful acquisition or maintenance of that power.
d. none of the above.

___ **6.** Handy Tools, Inc., charges Irma's Home Store five cents per item and Jack's Hardware ten cents per item for the same product. The two stores are competitors. If this substantially lessens competition, it constitutes

a. a market division.
b. an exclusionary practice.
c. price discrimination.
d. none of the above.

___ **7.** A group of foreign manufacturers organize to control the price for DVD players in the United States. Eagle Company, a U.S. firm, joins the group. If their actions have a substantial effect on U.S. commerce, a suit for violations of U.S. antitrust laws may be brought against

a. only Eagle.
b. only the foreign manufacturers.
c. Eagle and the foreign manufacturers.
d. none of the above.

___ **8.** Standard Company is charged with a violation of antitrust law subject to evaluation under the rule of reason. Standard's conduct is unlawful

a. if the anticompetitive harm outweighs the competitive benefits.
b. if the competitive benefits outweigh the anticompetitive harm.
c. if the conduct is blatantly anticompetitive.
d. only if it qualifies as an exemption.

___ **9.** Central Data Corporation and Digital, Inc., are competitors. They form a joint venture to research, develop, and produce new software for a particular line of computers. This joint venture is

a. a *per se* violation of the Sherman Act.
b. exempt from the antitrust laws.
c. subject to evaluation under the rule of reason.
d. none of the above.

___ **10.** Alpha, Inc., and Beta Corporation are competitors. They merge, and after the merger, Alpha is the surviving firm. To assess whether this is in violation of the Clayton Act requires a look at

a. market concentration.
b. market division.
c. market power.
d. none of the above.

SHORT ESSAY QUESTIONS

1. How does Section 1 of the Sherman Act deal with horizontal restraints?

2. How does the Clayton Act deal with exclusionary practices?

ISSUE SPOTTERS

(Answers at the Back of the Book)

1. Able Company, a bicycle manufacturer, refuses to deal with Baker Bikes, a retailer. In what circumstances might Able's refusal to deal with Baker violate antitrust law?

2. Under what circumstances would Pop's Market, a small store in a small, isolated town, be considered a monopolist? If Pop's is a monopolist, is it in violation of Section 2 of the Sherman Act?

3. Maple Corporation conditions the sale of its syrup on the buyer's agreement to buy Maple's pancake mix. What factors would a court consider to decide whether this arrangement violates the Clayton Act?

SPECIAL INFORMATION FOR CPA CANDIDATES

Most of the material in this chapter is not tested on the CPA examination. For the purposes of the exam, restraints of trade are acceptable in only two situations, both involving covenants not to compete (discussed in Chapter 13).

CUMULATIVE HYPOTHETICAL PROBLEM FOR UNIT NINE—INCLUDING CHAPTERS 43–46

(Answers at the Back of the Book)

Beta Chemical Corporation manufactures and sells chemical products to industrial customers and individual consumers.

___ **1.** Beta advertises its products as "the best in the market" and "everyone's top choice." Because of this advertising, the Federal Trade Commission may

a. issue a cease-and-desist order only.
b. require counteradvertising only.
c. issue a cease-and-desist order or require counteradvertising.
d. none of the above.

___ **2.** To determine whether Beta is violating regulations issued by the Environmental Protection Agency (EPA), the EPA may *not*

a. arbitrarily order Beta to shut its manufacturing site down.
b. conduct an on-site inspection of Beta's manufacturing site.
c. test Beta's products on its manufacturing site.
d. none of the above.

___ **3.** Beta's manufacturing process generates hazardous waste that is transported to Delta Company's disposal site by Kappa Trucking, Inc. If the EPA cleans up Delta's site, liability for the cost may be assessed against

a. Beta or Delta only.
b. Delta or Kappa only.
c. Beta or Kappa only.
d. Beta, Delta, or Kappa.

___ **4.** As a for-profit corporation that does business in interstate commerce, Beta may be subject to regulations issued by

a. federal administrative agencies only.
b. state administrative agencies in states in which Beta does business only.
c. federal agencies or state agencies in states in which Beta does business.
d. none of the above.

___ **5.** Beta charges National Refining, Inc., less per item than Beta charges International Export Corporation for the same product. The two buyers are competitors. This pricing difference violates antitrust law

a. if both buyers' customers pay the same price for the buyers' products.
b. if National and International know what each other pays.
c. if the pricing substantially lessens competition.
d. under no circumstances.

QUESTIONS ON THE FOCUS ON LEGAL REASONING FOR UNIT NINE— *PFENNIG V. HOUSEHOLD CREDIT SERVICES, INC.*

(Answers at the Back of the Book)

___ **1.** First Charge Company is a credit-card issuer. Greg is a First Charge cardholder. First Charge imposes a fee on Greg for granting his request to exceed the limit on his account. According to the majority in *Pfennig v. Household Credit Services, Inc.*, this fee is

a. a finance charge under Regulation Z.
b. a finance charge under the Truth-in-Lending Act (TILA).
c. not a finance charge under Regulation Z.
d. not a finance charge under the TILA.

___ **2.** Under the facts in the previous question, according to the dissent in *Pfennig v. Household Credit Services, Inc.*, the over-limit fee is

a. a finance charge under Regulation Z.
b. a finance charge under the Truth-in-Lending Act (TILA).
c. not a finance charge under Regulation Z.
d. not a finance charge under the TILA.

___ **3.** In the previous questions, suppose that the fee is a finance charge. According to the majority in *Pfennig v. Household Credit Services, Inc.*, this means that this fee, in relation to other terms in the parties' credit agreement, is subject to

a. equally conspicuous disclosure.
b. less conspicuous disclosure.
c. more conspicuous disclosure.
d. no disclosure.

QUESTIONS ON THE FOCUS ON ETHICS FOR UNIT NINE— GOVERNMENT REGULATION

(Answers at the Back of the Book)

___ **1.** The U.S. Fish and Wildlife Service (FWS) prohibits Victor from harvesting the timber on fifty acres of his land until it is clear that the timber is not a habitat for an endangered species. Victor files a suit against the FWS. The court is most likely to hold that this is

a. a compensatory "taking."
b. a "taking" but not compensatory.
c. compensatory but not a "taking."
d. not a compensatory "taking."

___ **2.** Ann owes a debt to Best Products, Inc. In an attempt to collect, Best contacts Ann's spouse Carl at his workplace. Under the Fair Debt Collection Practices Act, this contact is

a. permitted because Best is the creditor.
b. permitted because Carl is Ann's spouse.
c. prohibited because Best is the creditor.
d. prohibited because Carl is Ann's spouse.

___ **3.** Dave is a professional athlete. Not subject to the antitrust laws to the same extent as other professional sports is

a. baseball.
b. basketball.
c. football.
d. soccer.

Chapter 47
Personal Property and Bailments

WHAT THIS CHAPTER IS ABOUT

This chapter covers the nature of personal property, forms of property ownership, the acquisition of personal property, and bailments. Personal property can be tangible (such as a car) or intangible (such as securities or patents).

CHAPTER OUTLINE

I. PROPERTY CLASSIFICATION

Personal property can be tangible (a television set) or intangible (stocks, computer program). Real property consists of land and everything permanently attached to it.

II. FIXTURES

Personal property so closely associated with certain real property that it is viewed as part of it (such as plumbing in a building). Fixtures are included in a sale of land if the contract does not provide otherwise.

A. FACTORS IN DETERMINING THAT AN ITEM IS A FIXTURE

The intent of the parties, whether the item can be removed without damaging the real property, and whether the item is sufficiently adapted so as to have become a part of the real property.

B. TRADE FIXTURES

Installed for a commercial purpose by a tenant, whose property it remains, unless removal would irreparably damage the real property.

III. PROPERTY OWNERSHIP

Ownership can be viewed as the rights to possess property and to dispose of it.

A. FEE SIMPLE

A person who holds all of the rights is an owner in fee simple (see Chapter 48); on death, the owner's interest descends to his or her heirs.

B. CONCURRENT OWNERSHIP

1. Tenancy in Common

Each of two or more persons owns an *undivided* interest (each has rights in the whole—if each had rights in specific items, the interests would be *divided*). On death, a tenant's interest passes to his or her heirs. Most states presume that a co-tenancy is a tenancy in common unless there is a clear intention to establish a joint tenancy.

2. Joint Tenancy

Each of two or more persons owns an undivided interest in the property; a deceased joint tenant's interest passes to the surviving joint tenant or tenants. Can be terminated at any time before a joint tenant's death by gift, by sale, or by partition (divided into equal parts).

3. Tenancy by the Entirety

Created by a transfer of real property to a husband and wife; neither spouse can transfer separately his or her interest during his or her life. In some states, this tenancy has been effectively abolished. A divorce, either spouse's death, or mutual agreement will terminate this tenancy.

4. **Community Property**
Each spouse owns an undivided half interest in property acquired by either spouse during their marriage (except property acquired by gift or inheritance). Recognized in only some states, on divorce the property is divided equally in a few states and at a court's discretion in others.

IV. ACQUIRING OWNERSHIP OF PERSONAL PROPERTY

A. PURCHASE
Outlined in Chapters 19 through 23.

B. POSSESSION
An example of acquiring ownership by possession is the capture of wild animals. (Exceptions: (1) wild animals captured by a trespasser are the property of the landowner, and (2) wild animals captured or killed in violation of statutes are the property of the state.)

C. PRODUCTION
Those who produce personal property have title to it. (Exception: employees do not own what they produce for their employers.)

D. GIFT
A *gift* is a voluntary transfer of property ownership not supported by consideration.

1. The Three Requirements for an Effective Gift

a. Delivery

1) Constructive Delivery
If a physical object cannot be delivered, an act that the law holds to be equivalent to an act of real delivery is sufficient (a key to a safe-deposit box for the contents of the box, for example).

2) Delivery by a Third Person
If the person is the donor's agent, the gift is effective when the agent delivers the property to the donee. If the person is the donee's agent, the gift is effective when the donor delivers the property to the agent.

3) Giving Up Control
Effective delivery requires giving up control over the property.

b. Donative Intent
Determined from the language of the donor and the surrounding circumstances (relationship between the parties and the size of the gift in relation to the donor's other assets).

c. Acceptance
Courts assume a gift is accepted unless shown otherwise.

2. Gifts *Inter Vivos* and Gifts *Causa Mortis*
Gifts *inter vivos* are made during one's lifetime. Gifts *causa mortis* are made in contemplation of imminent death, do not become effective until the donor dies, and are automatically revoked if the donor does not die.

E. WILL OR INHERITANCE
Outlined in Chapter 51.

F. ACCESSION
Occurs when someone adds value to a piece of personal property by use of labor or materials. Ownership can be at issue in the following situations.

1. **When Accession Occurs without Permission of the Owner**
Courts tend to favor the owner over the one who improved the property (and deny the improver any compensation for the value added).

2. **When Accession Greatly Increases the Value or Changes the Identity**
The greater the increase, the more likely that ownership will pass to the improver who must compensate the original owner for the value of the property before the accession.

G. CONFUSION

Commingling goods so that one person's cannot be distinguished from another's. Frequently involves fungible goods. If goods are confused due to a wrongful act, the innocent party acquires all. If confusion is by agreement, mistake, or a third party's act, the owners share as tenants in common.

V. MISLAID, LOST, OR ABANDONED PROPERTY

A. MISLAID PROPERTY

Mislaid property is property that has been voluntarily placed somewhere by the owner and then inadvertently forgotten. When the property is found, the owner of the place where it was mislaid (not the finder) becomes the caretaker.

B. LOST PROPERTY

Lost property is property that is involuntarily left. A finder can claim title against the whole world, except the true owner. Many states require the finder to make a reasonably diligent search to locate the true owner. *Estray statutes* allow finders, after passage of a specified time, to acquire title to the property if it remains unclaimed.

C. ABANDONED PROPERTY

Abandoned property is property that has been discarded by the true owner, who has no intention of claiming title to it. A finder acquires title good against the whole world, including the original owner. A trespasser does not acquire title, however; the owner of the real property on which it was found does.

D. TREASURE TROVE

This is money, gold, silver, or bullion hidden in some private place, owner unknown. In the absence of a statute, a finder (who was not trespassing) has title to treasure trove against all but the true owner.

VI. BAILMENTS

The elements of a bailment are the following.

A. PERSONAL PROPERTY

Only personal property (tangible or intangible) is bailable.

B. DELIVERY OF POSSESSION (WITHOUT TITLE)

A bailee must (1) be given exclusive possession and control of the property and (2) knowingly accept it. Delivery may be actual or constructive.

C. AGREEMENT THAT THE PROPERTY BE RETURNED OR DISPOSED OF

The agreement must provide for the return of the property to the bailor or a third person, or for its disposal by the bailee.

VII. ORDINARY BAILMENTS

The three types of ordinary bailments are: (1) bailment for the sole benefit of the bailor, (2) bailment for the sole benefit of the bailee, and (3) bailment for their mutual benefit.

A. RIGHTS OF THE BAILEE

1. **Right of Possession**
This is temporary control and possession of property that ultimately is to be returned to the owner. During a bailment, a bailee can recover damages from any third persons for damage or loss to the property.

2. **Right to Use Bailed Property**
The extent to which bailees can use the property depends on the contract. If no provision is made, the extent depends on how necessary it is for the goods to be at the bailee's disposal.

3. **Right of Compensation**
A bailee has a right to be compensated as agreed and to be reimbursed for costs and services in the keeping of the property. To enforce this right, a bailee can place a lien on the property (see Chapter 29).

4. **Right to Limit Liability**
Bailees can limit their liability as long as—

   a. **Limitations Are Called to the Attention of the Bailor**
   Fine print on the back of a ticket stub is not sufficient.

   b. **Limitations Are Not Against Public Policy**
   Exculpatory clauses are carefully scrutinized by the courts and, in bailments, often held to be illegal. If a bailee attempts to exclude liability for his or her own negligence, the clause is unenforceable.

B. DUTIES OF THE BAILEE

1. **Duty of Care**
Bailees must exercise care over the property in their possession (or be liable in tort—see Chapter 5). The appropriate standard is—

   a. **Slight Care**
   In bailments for the sole benefit of the bailor, the bailee is liable only for gross negligence.

   b. **Great Care**
   In bailments for the sole benefit of the bailee, the bailee is liable for even slight negligence.

   c. **Ordinary Care**
   In bailments for the mutual benefit of both parties, the bailee is liable for a failure to use reasonable care.

2. **Duty to Return Bailed Property**
When a bailment ends, the bailee must relinquish the property. Failure to do so is a breach of contract and could constitute conversion.

   a. **Delivery of Goods to the Wrong Person**
   A bailee may be liable if the property is given to the wrong person.

   b. **Exceptions**
   The property is destroyed, lost, or stolen through no fault of the bailee, or given to a third party with a superior claim.

3. **Presumption of Negligence**
When the bailee has the property and damage occurs that normally results only from someone's negligence, the bailee's negligence is presumed. The bailee must prove that he or she was not at fault.

C. RIGHTS OF THE BAILOR

Complementary to the bailee's duties—

1. The property will be protected with reasonable care while in the bailee's possession.

2. The bailee will use the property as agreed (or not at all).

3. The property will be relinquished according to the bailor's directions.

4. The bailee will not alter the goods except as agreed.

5. The bailor will not be bound by any limitations on the bailee's liability unless these limitations are known and are enforceable by law.

6. Repairs or service will be done without defective workmanship.

D. DUTIES OF THE BAILOR

A bailor has a duty to provide the bailee with goods that are free from hidden defects that could injure the bailee.

1. Bailor's Duty Has Two Aspects

a. In a mutual-benefit bailment, bailor must notify bailee of all known defects and any hidden defects that the bailor knew of or could have discovered with reasonable diligence and proper inspection.

b. In a bailment for the sole benefit of the bailee, the bailor must notify the bailee of any known defects.

2. To Whom Does Liability Extend?

Liability extends to anyone who might be expected to come in contact with the goods. A bailor may also be liable under UCC Article 2A's implied warranties.

E. TERMINATION OF BAILMENTS

Bailments for a specific term end when the term ends. If no term is specified, a bailment can be terminated by mutual agreement of the parties, a demand by either party, completion of the bailment's purpose, an act by the bailee inconsistent with the terms of the bailment, or operation of law.

VIII. SPECIAL TYPES OF BAILMENTS

A. DOCUMENTS OF TITLE AND ARTICLE 7

Documents of title are subject to UCC Article 7 (unless federal law applies).

1. What a Document of Title Is

A document of title is a receipt for goods in the charge of a bailee-carrier or a bailee-warehouser and a contract for the shipment or storage of identified goods. These include bills of lading, warehouse receipts, and delivery orders.

2. Negotiability of a Document of Title

A document of title is negotiable if it specifies that goods be delivered to bearer or to the order of a named person. If so—

a. The possessor of the document is entitled to receive, hold, and dispose of the document and the goods it covers.

b. A good faith purchaser of the document may acquire greater rights to the document and the goods it covers than the transferor had or had the authority to convey (he or she may take free of the claims and defenses of prior parties).

3. **Due Negotiation**
Due negotiation means that the buyer of a document of title takes it (1) in good faith, for value, and without notice of a defense against or a claim to it, and (2) in the regular course of business or financing (not in settlement or payment of a money obligation).

4. **Goods Delivered According to a Thief's Instructions**
A bailee who receives goods from a thief and acts according to that individual's instructions is not liable to the goods' true owner (if he or she acted in good faith and observed reasonable commercial standards).

B. **COMMON CARRIERS**
Common carriers are publicly licensed to provide transportation services to the general public.

1. **Strict Liability**
Under UCC 7–309 and the common law, common carriers are strictly liable, regardless of negligence, for all loss or damage to goods in their possession, unless it is caused by an act of God, an act of a public enemy, an order of a public authority, an act of the shipper, or the nature of the goods.

2. **Limits to Liability**
Common carriers can limit their liability to an amount stated on the shipment contract. The shipper bears any loss occurring through its own fault or improper crating or packaging procedures.

3. **Connecting Carriers**
When connecting carriers are involved under a through bill of lading, the shipper can recover from the original carrier or any connecting carrier. Normally, the last carrier is presumed to have received the goods in good condition.

C. **WAREHOUSE COMPANIES**
Warehouse companies are liable for loss or damage to property resulting from negligence [UCC 7–204(1)]. A warehouse company can limit the dollar amount of liability, but the bailor must be given the option of paying an increased storage rate for an increase in the liability limit [UCC 7–204(2)].

D. **INNKEEPERS**
Those who provide lodging to the public for compensation as a regular business are strictly liable for injuries to guests (not permanent residents).

1. **Hotel Safes**
In many states, innkeepers can avoid strict liability for loss of guests' valuables by providing a safe. Statutes often limit the liability of innkeepers for articles that are not kept in the safe.

2. **Parking Facilities**
If an innkeeper provides parking facilities, and the guest's car is entrusted to the innkeeper, the innkeeper will be liable under the rules that pertain to parking lot bailees (ordinary bailments).

TRUE-FALSE QUESTIONS

(Answers at the Back of the Book)

____ 1. Generally, those who produce personal property have title to it.

____ 2. If goods are confused due to a wrongful act and the innocent party cannot prove what percentage is his or hers, the wrongdoer gets title to the whole.

____ 3. To constitute a gift, a voluntary transfer of property must be supported by consideration.

____ 4. If an accession is performed in good faith, the improver keeps the property as improved.

____ 5. One who finds abandoned property acquires title to it good against the true owner.

___ **6.** Any delivery of personal property from one person to another creates a bailment.

___ **7.** A bailee is not responsible for the loss of bailed property in his or her care.

___ **8.** A bailee's only duty is to surrender the property at the end of the bailment.

___ **9.** In some ordinary bailments, bailees can limit their liability.

___ **10.** Warehouse companies have the same duty of care as ordinary bailees.

FILL-IN QUESTIONS

(Answers at the Back of the Book)

A gift made during the donor's lifetime is a gift ______________ (*causa mortis/inter vivos*). A gift ______________ (*causa mortis/inter vivos*) is made in contemplation of imminent death. Gifts ______________ (*causa mortis/inter vivos*) do not become absolute until the donor dies from the contemplated illness or disease. A gift ______________ (*causa mortis/inter vivos*) is revocable at any time up to the death of the donor and is automatically revoked if the donor recovers. A gift ______________ (*causa mortis/inter vivos*) is revocable at any time before the donor's death.

MULTIPLE-CHOICE QUESTIONS

(Answers at the Back of the Book)

___ **1.** Eve designs an Internet home page to advertise her services as a designer of home pages. Tim hires her to design a homepage for his business. Eve has title to

a. her home page only.
b. Tim's home page only.
c. her homepage, Tim's home page, and any other home page she creates.
d. none of the above.

___ **2.** Nancy sells her boat to Chris and Nora. Chris and Nora are not married. The contract of sale says that the buyers each have a right of survivorship in the boat. Chris and Nora own the boat as

a. community property.
b. joint tenants.
c. tenants by the entirety.
d. tenants in common.

___ **3.** Meg wants to give Lori a pair of diamond earrings that Meg has in her safe-deposit box at First National Bank. Meg gives Lori the key to the box and tells her to go to the bank and take the earrings from the box. Lori does so. Two days later, Meg dies. The earrings belong to

a. Lori.
b. Meg's heirs.
c. First National Bank.
d. the state.

___ **4.** John is employed in remodeling homes bought and sold by Best Realty. In one of the homes, John finds an item of jewelry and takes it to Hall Gems, Inc., to be appraised. The appraiser removes some of the jewels. Best title to the jewels that were removed is with

a. John.
b. Hall Gems, Inc.
c. Best Realty.
d. John's employer.

___ 5. Jane, Mark, and Guy store their grain in three silos. Jane contributes half of the grain, Mark a third, and Guy a sixth. A tornado hits two of the silos and scatters the grain. If each can prove how much he or she deposited in the silos, how much of what is left belongs to each?

a. Jane owns half, Mark a third, and Guy a sixth
b. Because only a third is left, Mark owns it all
c. Because Jane and Mark lost the most, they split what is left equally
d. Jane, Mark, and Guy share what is left equally

___ 6. Doug wants to give Kim a notebook computer that is in a locker at the mall. Doug gives Kim the key to the locker and tells her to take the computer. Kim says that she doesn't want the computer and leaves the key on Doug's desk. The next day, Doug dies. The computer belongs to

a. Kim.
b. Doug's heirs.
c. the mall.
d. the state.

___ 7. Ann parks her car in an unattended lot behind Bob's store, which is closed. Ann locks the car and takes the keys. This is *not* a bailment because it does not involve

a. a transfer of possession.
b. a written contract.
c. money.
d. personal property.

___ 8. Marcy goes to Don's Salon for a haircut. Behind a plant on a table in the waiting area, Marcy finds a wallet containing $5,000. Possession of the wallet belongs to

a. Marcy because the money was lost.
b. Don because the money was mislaid.
c. the state under an estray statute.
d. the police under the local finders' law .

___ 9. Kay checks her coat at a restaurant. Hidden in the sleeve is her purse. By accepting the coat, the restaurant is a bailee of

a. the coat only.
b. the purse only.
c. both the coat and the purse.
d. none of the above.

___ 10. **Based on a Sample CPA Exam Question.** Adams Corporation ships goods via Baker Transport Company. Baker will *not* be liable for the loss of the goods if they are

a. crushed in a warehouse accident that is the fault of Baker's crane operator.
b. damaged because Adams failed to package the goods properly.
c. destroyed in a traffic accident that is the fault of Baker's truckdriver.
d. stolen by an unknown person.

SHORT ESSAY QUESTIONS

1. What are the principal features of the forms of concurrent property ownership: tenancies in common, joint tenancies, tenancies by the entirety, and community property?

2. What are the three elements involved in creating a valid gift?

ISSUE SPOTTERS

(Answers at the Back of the Book)

1. Alpha Corporation sends important documents to Beta, Inc., via Speedy Messenger Service. While the documents are in Speedy's care, a third party causes an accident to Speedy's delivery vehicle that results in the loss of the documents. Does Speedy have a right to recover from the third party for the loss of the documents?

2. Bob leaves his clothes with Corner Dry Cleaners to be cleaned. When the clothes are returned, some are missing and others are greasy and smell bad. Is Corner liable?

3. Omega Corporation ships a load of goods via Peak Transport Company. The load is lost in a hurricane in Florida. Who suffers the loss?

SPECIAL INFORMATION FOR CPA CANDIDATES

The CPA examination has questions that involve personal property ownership, including such aspects as the acquisition of ownership (especially gifts) and the types of ownership. Fixtures are covered (remember that the more difficult it is to remove an item, the more likely it will be regarded as a fixture). Trade fixtures are judged differently—be sure that you understand the difference.

Personal property, its ownership, and its transfer may also be at issue on such parts of the exam as those that test on sales of goods under the Uniform Commercial Code, sales involving the common law of contracts, commercial paper (negotiable instruments), securities law, secured transactions, and bailments (the subject of the next chapter). You may find it helpful to briefly review those topics from the frame of reference of the principles in this chapter.

Bailments are also tested on the CPA examination. You should be thoroughly familiar with what degree of care (slight, great, or reasonable) is required in which type of bailment (gratuitous for the bailor, gratuitous for the bailee, or mutual). The concepts related to documents of title may also be included in the questions on this part of the CPA exam.

Chapter 48
Real Property

WHAT THIS CHAPTER IS ABOUT

This chapter covers ownership rights in real property, including the nature of those rights and their transfer. The chapter also outlines the right of the government to take private land for public use, zoning laws, and other restrictions on ownership.

CHAPTER OUTLINE

I. THE NATURE OF REAL PROPERTY

Real property consists of land and the buildings, plants, and trees on it.

A. LAND

Includes the soil on the surface of the earth, natural products or artificial structures attached to it, the water on or under it, and the air space above.

B. AIR AND SUBSURFACE RIGHTS

Limitations on air rights or subsurface rights normally have to be indicated on the deed transferring title at the time of purchase.

1. Air Rights

Flights over private land do not normally violate the owners' rights.

2. Subsurface Rights

Ownership of the surface can be separated from ownership of the subsurface. In excavating, if a subsurface owner causes the land to subside, he or she may be liable to the owner of the surface.

C. PLANT LIFE AND VEGETATION

A sale of land with growing crops on it includes the crops, unless otherwise agreed. When crops are sold without a sale of the land, they are personal property.

II. OWNERSHIP INTERESTS IN REAL PROPERTY

A. FEE SIMPLE

A *fee simple absolute* owner has the most rights possible—to give the property away, sell it, transfer it by will, use it for virtually any purpose, and possess it to the exclusion of all the world—potentially forever.

B. LIFE ESTATES

Lasts for the life of a specified individual ("to A for his life"). A life tenant can use the land (but cannot commit waste), mortgage the life estate, and create liens, easements, and leases (but not longer than the life defining the estate).

C. LEASEHOLD ESTATES

Created when an owner or landlord conveys the right to possess and use property to a tenant for a certain period of time. The rights and duties of landlord and tenant are outlined in Chapter 49.

1. **Tenancy for Years**
Created by contract (which can sometimes be oral) by which property is leased for a specific period (a month, a year, a period of years). At the end of the period, the lease ends (without notice). If the tenant dies during the lease, the lease interest passes to the tenant's heirs.

2. **Periodic Tenancy**
Created by a lease that specifies only that rent is to be paid at certain intervals. Automatically renews unless terminated. Can arise if a landlord allows a tenant for years to hold over. Terminates, at common law, on one period's notice.

3. **Tenancy at Will**
A tenancy for as long as the landlord and tenant agree. Exists when a tenant for years retains possession after termination with the landlord's consent before payment of the next rent (when it becomes a periodic tenancy). Terminates on the death of either party.

4. **Tenancy at Sufferance**
Possession of land without right (without the owner's permission).

D. NONPOSSESSORY INTERESTS

1. **Easements and Profits**
Easement: the right of a person to make limited use of another person's land without taking anything from the property. *Profit*: the right to go onto another's land and take away a part or product of the land.

   a. **Creation of an Easement or Profit**
   By deed, will, contract, implication, necessity, or prescription.

   b. **Effect of a Sale of Property**
   The benefit of an easement or profit goes with the land. The burden goes with the land only if the new owner recognizes it, or knew or should have known of it.

   c. **Termination of an Easement or Profit**
   Terminates when deeded back to the owner of the land that is burdened; its owner becomes the owner of the property burdened; or it is abandoned with the intent to relinquish the right to it.

2. **Licenses**
A license is the revocable right of a person to come onto another person's land.

III. TRANSFER OF OWNERSHIP

A. DEEDS

Possession and title to land can be passed by deed without consideration.

1. **Requirements**
(1) Names of the grantor and grantee, (2) words evidencing an intent to convey, (3) legally sufficient description of the land, (4) grantor's (and usually the spouse's) signature, and (5) delivery of the deed.

2. **Warranty Deed**
Provides the most protection against defects of title—covenants that the grantor has title to, and the power to convey, the property; that the buyer will not be disturbed in his or her possession of the land; and that transfer is made without unknown adverse claims of third parties.

3. **Special Warranty Deed**
Warrants only that the grantor held good title during his or her ownership of the property, not that there were no title defects when others owned it. If all liens and encumbrances are disclosed, the seller is not liable if a third person interferes with the buyer's ownership.

4. **Quitclaim Deed**
Warrants less than any other deed. Conveys to the grantee only whatever interest the grantor had.

5. **Grant Deed**
By statute, may impliedly warrant that the grantor owns the property and has not encumbered it or conveyed it to another.

6. **Sheriff's Deed**
Gives ownership rights to a buyer at a sheriff's sale.

7. **Recording Statutes**
Require transfers to be recorded in public records (generally in the county in which the property is located) to prevent fraud. Many states require the grantor's signature and two witnesses' signatures.

   a. **Race Statute**
   The first person to record a deed has superior rights to the property, whether he or she knew of another previous, unrecorded transfer.

   b. **Pure Notice Statute**
   A person who does not know of a previous, unrecorded transfer can claim priority, whether or not he or she records first.

   c. **Notice-Race Statute**
   A person who does not know of a previous, unrecorded transfer and who files first can claim priority.

B. CONTRACTS FOR THE SALE OF REAL ESTATE

The steps in a sale of real estate include the formation of the contract, a title search, financing negotiations, a property inspection, and the closing.

1. **Formation of the Contract**
An offer to buy includes a deposit of earnest money (forfeited if the offer is withdrawn). Normally, the contract must be in writing to be enforceable; the writing should identify the parties, describe the property, and state the price.

   a. **Marketable Title**
   A contract for a sale of land includes an implied warranty that the seller will deliver marketable title. Defects that render title unmarketable include breaks in the chain of title and liens. Buyers buy title insurance against the risk of undiscovered defects.

   b. **Risk of Loss**
   Unless the parties agree otherwise, in most states the risk is on the buyer until title passes. The buyer must pay the contract price even if the property is destroyed (unless the destruction is due to the seller's negligence).

2. **Escrow**
The seller may give the deed to an escrow agent to deliver to the buyer when the conditions of sale are met, and the closing occurs. Once those conditions are met, passage of title relates back to the time of delivery of the deed to escrow (thus, if the grantor dies, title still passes).

3. **Financing**
A *mortgage* is a loan for which real property is given as security. If payments are not made, the mortgagee loses the right to title.

4. **Fitness of the Property**

   a. ***Caveat Emptor***
   In a few states, the seller makes no warranties with respect to fitness (unless the deed or contract specifies otherwise). The buyer takes the property "as is."

b. **Implied Warranty of Habitability**
In most states, the seller of a new house impliedly warrants that it will be fit for human habitation (in reasonable working order and of reasonably sound construction). In a few states, a later buyer can recover from the original builder under this warranty.

c. **Duty to Disclose**
In most states, sellers must disclose any known defect that materially affects the value of the property and that the buyer could not reasonably discover.

C. TRANSFER BY INHERITANCE
Outlined in Chapter 51.

D. ADVERSE POSSESSION
A person who possesses another's property acquires title good against the original owner if the possession is (1) actual and exclusive; (2) open, visible, and notorious; (3) continuous and peaceable for a statutorily required period of time; and (4) hostile, as against the whole world.

IV. LIMITATIONS ON THE RIGHTS OF PROPERTY OWNERS

A. EMINENT DOMAIN
The government can take private property for public use. To obtain title, a condemnation proceeding is brought. The Fifth Amendment requires that just compensation be paid for a taking; thus, in a separate proceeding a court determines the land's fair value (usually market value) to pay the owner.

B. ZONING
Under its police power, a state can pass zoning laws to regulate uses of land without having to compensate the landowner.

1. **Limits on the State Land-Use Regulation**
Regulation cannot be (1) confiscatory (or the owner must be paid just compensation); (2) arbitrary or unreasonable (taking without due process under the Fourteenth Amendment); or (3) discriminatory, under the Fourteenth Amendment.

2. **Variances**
An owner can obtain a variance if (1) it is impossible to realize a reasonable return on the land as zoned, (2) the ordinance adversely affects only the owner (and not all owners), and (3) granting a variance will not substantially alter the essential character of the zoned area.

C. RESTRICTIVE COVENANTS

1. **Covenants Running with the Land**
A covenant runs with the land (the original parties and their successors are entitled to its benefit or burdened with its obligation) if—

   a. It is created in a written agreement (usually the document that conveys the land).

   b. Parties intend that it run with the land (agreement states that all promisor's "successors, heirs, or assigns" will be bound).

   c. Covenant touches and concerns the land (limits on burdened land must have some connection to the land).

   d. Original parties are in privity of estate when covenant is created.

2. **Illegal Restrictive Covenants**
A covenant cannot be discriminatory.

TRUE-FALSE QUESTIONS

(Answers at the Back of the Book)

___ 1. A fee simple absolute is potentially infinite in duration and can be disposed of by deed or by will.

___ 2. The owner of a life estate has the same rights as a fee simple owner.

___ 3. An easement allows a person to use land and take something from it, but a profit allows a person only to use land.

___ 4. Deeds offer different degrees of protection against defects of title.

___ 5. The government can take private property for *public* use without just compensation.

___ 6. The government can take private property for *private* uses only.

___ 7. A periodic tenancy is a tenancy for a specified period of time, such as a month, a year, or a period of years.

___ 8. To obtain a variance, a landowner must show that his or her alternative use of the land would substantially alter its essential character.

___ 9. In most states, the seller of a new house impliedly warrants that it will be fit for human habitation.

___ 10. A license is a revocable right of a person to come onto another person's land.

FILL-IN QUESTIONS

(Answers at the Back of the Book)

The deed that provides the most protection against defects of title is the ____________________ (warranty/special warranty/quitclaim) deed. Among other things, it covenants that the transfer is made without any unknown adverse claims of third parties. The deed that warrants only that the grantor has done nothing to lessen the value of the property is the ______________________________ (warranty/special warranty/quitclaim) deed. Under this deed, the seller may not be liable if a third person interferes with the buyer's ownership. The deed that warrants less than any other deed is the _____________________ (warranty/special warranty/quitclaim) deed. This deed conveys to the grantee only whatever interest the grantor had.

MULTIPLE-CHOICE QUESTIONS

(Answers at the Back of the Book)

___ 1. Lou owns two hundred acres next to Brook's lumber mill. Lou sells to Brook the privilege of removing timber from his land to refine into lumber. The privilege of removing the timber is

a. a license.
b. an easement.
c. a profit.
d. none of the above.

___ 2. Evan owns an apartment building in fee simple. This means that Evan can

a. give the building away, but not sell it or transfer it by will.
b. sell the building or transfer it by a will, but cannot give it away.
c. give the building away, sell it, or transfer it by will.
d. none of the above.

____ **3.** Gina conveys her warehouse to Sam under a warranty deed. Later, Rosa appears, holding a better title to the warehouse than Sam. Rosa proceeds to evict Sam. Sam can recover from Gina

a. the purchase price of the property only.
b. damages from being evicted only.
c. the purchase price of the property and damages from being evicted.
d. none of the above.

____ **4.** Jan sells the eastern half of her land to Ken. According to the deed, Ken agrees to maintain a fence along the common boundary. Later, Jan sells the rest of her land to Ed, and Ken sells his land to Tina. Under the deed, Tina agrees to maintain the fence. If Ed sues Tina to repair the fence, Ed will

a. win, because the covenant runs with the land to Ed and Tina through Jan and Ken.
b. win, because Ed bought his half of Jan's land before Tina bought her half.
c. lose, because the original covenant was in the deed given by Jan to Ken.
d. lose, because there is no privity between Ed and Tina.

____ **5.** Dan owns a half-acre of land fronting on Blue Lake. Rod owns the property behind Dan's land No road runs to Dan's land, but Rod's driveway runs between a road and Dan's property, so Dan uses Rod's driveway. The right-of-way that Dan has across Rod's property is

a. a license.
b. an easement.
c. a profit.
d. none of the above.

____ **6.** **Based on a Sample CPA Exam Question.** Dave owns an office building. Dave sells the building to P&I Corporation. To be valid, the deed that conveys the property from Dave to P&I must include

a. only a description of the property.
b. only the purchase price.
c. a description of the property and the purchase price.
d. none of the above.

____ **7.** Susan signs a lease for an apartment, agreeing to make rental payments before the fifth of each month. The lease does not specify a termination date. This tenancy is

a. a periodic tenancy.
b. a tenancy at sufferance.
c. a tenancy at will.
d. a tenancy for years.

____ **8.** Rick sells his property to Ben, a good faith purchaser, on Monday. Rick sells the same property to Jill, also a good faith purchaser, on Tuesday. Ben records his interest on Wednesday. Jill records her interest on Thursday. The property is in a state with a notice-race statute. The property is owned by

a. Ben.
b. Jill.
c. Rick.
d. the state.

____ **9.** Home Corporation builds a new house, constructing the roof improperly. Before buying the house, Lee asks Pat (Home's sales agent) about the roof. Pat says that it was carefully constructed. Lee buys the house. The roof blows off in the first storm. Lee may successfully sue Home for

a. breach of an implied warranty of habitability only.
b. misrepresentation or fraud only.
c. breach of an implied warranty of habitability, misrepresentation, or fraud.
d. none of the above.

___ 10. Ann owns a cabin on Long Lake. Bob takes possession of the cabin without Ann's permission and puts up a sign that reads "No Trespassing by Order of Bob, the Owner." The statutory period for adverse possession is ten years. Bob is in the cabin for eleven years. Ann sues to remove Bob. She will

a. win, because Ann sued Bob after the statutory period for adverse possession.
b. win, because Bob did not have permission to take possession of the cabin.
c. lose, because Bob acquired the cabin by adverse possession.
d. lose, because the no-trespassing sign misrepresented ownership of the cabin.

SHORT ESSAY QUESTIONS

1. Describe the power of eminent domain and the process by which private property is condemned for a public purpose.

2. What does the implied warranty of habitability require, and when does it apply?

ISSUE SPOTTERS

(Answers at the Back of the Book)

1. Gary owns a commercial building in fee simple. Gary transfers temporary possession of the building to Holding Corporation (HC). Can HC transfer possession for even less time to Investment Company?

2. Charles sells his house to Diane under a warranty deed. Later, Carol appears, holding a better title to the house than Diane. Carol wants Diane off the property. What can Diane do?

3. Metro City designates certain areas within its limits for industrial, commercial, residential, and mixed uses. Nick owns a small plot of land in a mixed-use area. Can Metro limit only Nick's land to residential use?

SPECIAL INFORMATION FOR CPA CANDIDATES

Real property and property interests are covered on the CPA examination.

Of the material in this chapter, you should know the basic rights and interests of real property ownership, including the different types of tenancies. Regarding deeds, you should know the priorities of competing claims under the recording statutes and the differences among a warranty deed, a special warranty deed, and a quitclaim deed. You should also know the elements of adverse possession.

Life estates are included in questions about trusts (see Chapter 51). Other material to review in relation with this chapter for the real property questions on the exam include the types of property ownership, especially joint tenancy with the right of survivorship (Chapter 47); the law of landlord and tenant (Chapter 49); mortgage law (see Chapter 29); and insurance (Chapter 50).

Chapter 49
Landlord-Tenant Relationships

WHAT THIS CHAPTER IS ABOUT

This chapter outlines laws behind the landlord-tenant relationship, including contract doctrines, and state and local statutes and ordinances. More than one-fourth of the states have adopted the Uniform Residential Landlord and Tenant Act (URLTA).

CHAPTER OUTLINE

I. CREATING THE LANDLORD-TENANT RELATIONSHIP

A. FORM OF THE LEASE

To ensure the validity of a lease, it should be in writing and—

1. Express an intent to establish the relationship.
2. Provide for transfer of the property's possession to the tenant at the beginning of the term.
3. Provide for the landlord to retake possession at the end of the term.
4. Describe the property.
5. Indicate the length of the term and the amount and due dates of rent.

B. ILLEGALITY

A landlord cannot discriminate against tenants on the basis of race, color, religion, national origin, or gender. A tenant cannot promise to do something counter to these laws. There may be other state or local restrictions.

C. UNCONSCIONABILITY

Some jurisdictions (and URLTA 1.303) apply UCC 2–302, under which a court may declare an entire contract or any of its clauses unconscionable and thus illegal (see Chapters 12 and 13).

II. PARTIES' RIGHTS AND DUTIES

A. POSSESSION

1. **Landlord's Duty to Deliver Possession**
   A landlord must give a tenant possession of the property that the tenant has agreed to lease. Many states require a landlord to provide physical possession. Some require only the legal right to possession.

2. **Tenant's Right to Retain Possession**
   The tenant retains possession exclusively until the lease expires, unless the lease provides otherwise or the tenant defaults. A landlord can come onto the property for some purposes—for example, repairs.

3. **Covenant of Quiet Enjoyment**
   The landlord promises that during the lease term no one having superior title to the property will disturb the tenant's use and enjoyment of it. If so, the tenant can sue for damages for breach.

4. **Eviction**
If the landlord deprives the tenant of possession of the property or interferes with his or her use or enjoyment of it, the tenant can (1) sue for damages or possession or (2) stop paying rent or terminate the lease.

5. **Constructive Eviction**
This can result from a landlord's failure to perform adequately his or her duties under the lease.

6. **Retaliatory Eviction**
This occurs when a landlord evicts a tenant for complaining to a government agency about the premises' condition.

B. USE OF THE PREMISES

Unless the parties agree otherwise, a tenant may make any use of the property (but no waste), so long as it is legal, relates to the purpose for which the property is adapted or ordinarily used, does not injure the landlord's interest (no alterations without consent), and does not create a nuisance.

C. MAINTAINING THE PREMISES

1. **Statutory Requirements**
A landlord must comply with safety and health standards. In most states, a landlord must repair damage not caused by the tenant. A landlord is responsible for maintaining common areas, including defects the landlord knows of and those the landlord should know of.

2. **Implied Warranty of Habitability**
In most states, a landlord must furnish residential premises that are habitable. This applies to substantial defects that the landlord knows or should know about and has had a reasonable time to repair. In deciding whether a defect is sufficiently substantial, courts ask—

   a. Whether the tenant caused the defect.

   b. How long the defect has existed.

   c. The age of the building.

   d. The defect's impact on the tenant's health and safety.

   e. Whether a defect violates housing, building, or sanitation statutes.

3. **Remedies for Landlord's Failure to Maintain Leased Property**
In some circumstances, a tenant may withhold rent, pay for a repair and deduct the amount from the rent, cancel the lease, or sue for damages.

D. RENT

A tenant must pay rent even if he or she refuses to occupy the property or moves out (if the refusal or move is unjustified).

1. **Security Deposits and Late Charges**
These are legal. A landlord may withhold an amount from the deposit to cover damages.

2. **Rent Escalation and Property Taxes**
Unless the lease states otherwise, a landlord cannot raise rent during the term or charge the tenant for property taxes.

3. **Landlord's Remedies for Tenant's Failure to Pay Rent**
If a tenant fails to pay rent or refuses to give up wrongful possession of leased property, the landlord can resort to—

a. **Landlord's Lien**
In some states, a landlord can exercise a lien on the tenant's personal property (and sell it to recoup unpaid rent).

b. **Lawsuit**
In some states, a landlord must wait for up to ten days after the rent is due (and give notice) before suing for damages or termination.

c. **Recovery of Possession**
A landlord may bring an action in ejectment or, in most states, an unlawful detainer action (shorter and faster than ejectment).

4. **Landlord's Duty to Mitigate Damages**
In many states, even if a tenant vacates leased property unjustifiably, the landlord must make a reasonable attempt to lease the property to another party.

III. LIABILITY FOR INJURIES ON THE PREMISES

Liability usually depends on who controls the area where the injury occurred; the standard is reasonable care under all circumstances (see Chapter 5).

A. LANDLORD'S LIABILITY

1. **Injuries Caused by Defects on the Premises**
A landlord is liable for injuries resulting from a dangerous condition that the landlord knew about or should have known about, when the landlord fails to tell the tenant about it or actually conceals it. (Exception: obvious conditions or conditions the tenant knows about.)

2. **Common Areas**
A landlord is liable for injuries occurring on property within the landlord's control (common areas, such as hallways and elevators). This includes a duty to inspect and repair. (Exception: areas where people could not be reasonably expected to go.)

3. **Injuries Caused by Crimes of Third Persons**
If crimes are reasonably foreseeable and the landlord takes no steps to prevent them, he or she may be liable for negligence if an injury results. Foreseeability may depend on recent, prior, similar, criminal activity.

B. TENANT'S LIABILITY

A tenant must maintain in a reasonably safe condition those areas under his or her control. Under a commercial lease, the tenant's duty may coincide with the landlord's (and both may be liable).

IV. TRANSFERRING RIGHTS TO LEASED PROPERTY

A. TRANSFERRING THE LANDLORD'S INTEREST

A landlord can sell, give away, or otherwise transfer his or her real property (see Chapter 47), or transfer only the lease, only the reversionary interest, only the rent, or any of these rights in combination. If complete title is transferred, the tenant becomes the tenant of the new owner.

B. TRANSFERRING THE TENANT'S INTEREST

Before a tenant can assign or sublet his or her interest, the lease may require the landlord's consent (it cannot be unreasonably withheld). If the assignee or sublessee later defaults, the tenant must pay the rent.

V. TERMINATION OR RENEWAL OF THE LEASE

A. TERMINATION

On termination, a tenant is no longer liable for rent and is no longer entitled to possession of the property. A lease terminates when its term ends or by—

1. **Notice**
A periodic tenancy (see Chapter 47) will renew automatically unless one of the parties gives timely notice of termination.

2. **Release and Merger**
If a landlord conveys his or her interest in the property to the tenant, the transfer is a release, and the tenant's interest in the property merges into the title to the property (which he or she holds).

3. **Surrender by Agreement**
The parties may agree to end a tenancy before it would otherwise terminate.

4. **Abandonment**
A landlord may treat a tenant's moving out with no intent of returning before the end of the term as an offer of surrender. The landlord's retaking of possession relieves the tenant of the duty to pay rent.

5. **Forfeiture**
If a tenant fails to fulfill a condition under the lease, the tenant may forfeit his or her interest in it. Generally, if neither the lease nor a statute provides for forfeiture, a landlord may claim only damages.

6. **Destruction of the Property by a Cause beyond the Landlord's Control**
Usually, a landlord is not obligated to restore the premises. Depending on the terms of a lease, a commercial tenant may be responsible for restoring the premises, however.

B. **RENEWAL**
If a lease does not contain an option for renewal and the parties have not agreed that the tenant may stay on, the tenant has no right to remain.

TRUE-FALSE QUESTIONS

(Answers at the Back of the Book)

____ 1. Under the covenant of quiet enjoyment, a tenant will not be disturbed in the possession of the premises.

____ 2. If the covenant of quiet enjoyment is breached, the tenant can sue the landlord for damages.

____ 3. Generally, a tenant must pay rent when he or she moves out, if the move is unjustifiable.

____ 4. On termination, a tenant is entitled to possession of the property until a new tenant arrives.

____ 5. A tenant can withhold the rent if there is anything wrong with leased property.

____ 6. In most states, a tenant can alter leased premises without the landlord's consent.

____ 7. A landlord is liable for injuries occurring on property within the landlord's control.

____ 8. A tenant is liable for injuries occurring on property within the tenant's control.

____ 9. When a landlord sells leased premises to a third party, any existing leases terminate automatically.

____ 10. When a tenant assigns a lease to a third party, the tenant's lease obligations terminate automatically.

FILL-IN QUESTIONS

(Answers at the Back of the Book)

In many states, judicial decisions or statutes impose a duty on a landlord who leases ____________________ (commercial/residential) property to furnish premises that are habitable and to make repairs not caused by the ____________________ (landlord's/tenant's) actions. Under most circumstances, a ____________________ (commercial/residential) tenant is not required to make such major repairs as replacing a roof or a foundation. Thus, without a lease clause under which the ____________________ (commercial/residential) tenant assumes a duty to maintain the leased property, the tenant is under no obligation to do so. Normally, the tenant is liable for repairs required only as a result of the ____________________ (landlord's/tenant's) intentional or negligent actions.

MULTIPLE-CHOICE QUESTIONS

(Answers at the Back of the Book)

___ **1.** **Based on a Sample CPA Exam Question.** Paul leases a house from Quinn for a two-year term. To be enforceable, their lease must include

a. a description of the premises.
b. a due date for the payment of the property taxes.
c. a requirement that John will perform any structural repairs to the property.
d. a requirement that Paul carry liability insurance.

___ **2.** Lyle leases an apartment from Maria. With Maria's consent, Lyle assigns the lease to Nora for the last two months of the term, after which Nora exercises an option under the original lease to renew for three months. One month later, Nora moves out. Regarding the rent for the rest of the term

a. Lyle can be held liable.
b. Maria is liable.
c. no one is liable.
d. only Nora is liable.

___ **3.** Sue leases an apartment from Tom. The lease provides that Tom is not liable for any injury if the heating system fails to function. In January, the system breaks down. Sue becomes seriously ill. If Sue sues Tom, she will

a. win, because Sue is the tenant.
b. win, because the clause absolving Tom of liability is unconscionable.
c. lose, because the lease absolves Tom of responsibility.
d. lose, because Tom is the landlord.

___ **4.** Jill reports housing code violations in her apartment to local authorities. In retaliation, her landlord Ken changes the lock on her door, refuses to give her a new key, and starts eviction proceedings. If Jill sues Ken, she will

a. win, because Jill is the tenant.
b. win, because Ken is attempting a retaliatory eviction.
c. lose, because Ken is attempting a retaliatory eviction.
d. lose, because Tom is the landlord.

___ 5. National Corporation leases an office from Office Properties, Inc. (OP). Before the end of the lease term, National does not pay the rent for three months and then, without justification, vacates the office. OP can

a. do nothing until the lease term expires.
b. retake possession of the office only.
c. sue the tenant for the unpaid rent only.
d. retake possession of the office and sue the tenant for unpaid rent.

___ 6. Ace Sales leases a store from Best Mall, Inc. While installing trade fixtures, Ace's workers damage some floor tiles and fail to fix them. Later, Carl, a customer, trips on a tile and injures himself. If Carl sues Ace, he will

a. lose, because Best Mall is liable, not Ace.
b. lose, because Carl failed to exercise reasonable care.
c. win, because Ace failed maintain an area under its control.
d. win, because Carl was injured.

___ 7. Ruth signs a one-year lease for an apartment. Sam is the landlord. Six months later, Ruth moves out of the apartment with no intent of returning. Ruth has no more obligation to pay rent if Sam

a. does not ask for the rent.
b. does nothing.
c. enters the apartment to make a repair.
d. moves into the apartment.

___ 8. Ben leases an apartment from Carol. The lease states that Ben assumes liability for any injury to him while is in the apartment. Carol does not maintain the heating pipes. One cold night, they burst, discharging water into Ben's apartment. Ben slips in the water and breaks his leg. Carol is

a. liable for Ben's injury because of her negligence.
b. not liable because Ben assumed liability for his injury in the lease.
c. not liable because Ben's living room is not a common area.
d. only liable if prior tenants were injured in similar circumstances.

___ 9. Donna leases an apartment from Earl. Two months later, Donna moves out, and arranges with Fred to move in and pay the rent to Earl for the rest of the term. This is

a. an assignment.
b. an eviction.
c. a release and merger.
d. a sublease.

___ 10. Curt operates Diners Cafe in space that he leases in Eagle Mall, which is owned by Fine Property Company. Fine sells the mall to Great Investments, Inc. For the rest of the lease term, Curt owes rent to

a. Diners Cafe.
b. Fine Property.
c. Great Investments.
d. no one.

SHORT ESSAY QUESTIONS

1. In what circumstances is the landlord liable for injuries on the leased premises?

2. What are the ways in which a lease may be terminated?

ISSUE SPOTTERS

(Answers at the Back of the Book)

1. Ann leases an apartment from Bob. When Ann arrives to take possession, Cathy, the previous tenant, is still on the premises. Ann asks Bob to get rid of Cathy. Bob says that Cathy is Ann's problem. Is Bob right?

2. Lou owns a building in an area in which there have been auto thefts. A break-in occurs in Lou's building. He installs an alarm and hires a security guard. If more crimes occur in the building and an injury results, is Lou liable?

3. Quik Stop leases space in Ridge Mall, which is owned by Suburban Holdings, Inc. Suburban sells the mall to Town Properties, Inc. Is Quik Stop now Town's tenant? If so, is Town bound by the terms of the original lease?

SPECIAL INFORMATION FOR CPA CANDIDATES

The section of the CPA examination on property law includes questions on landlord-tenant law. Of the material covered in this chapter, it is important for you to know that a tenant is entitled to exclusive possession of the premises for the term of the lease. Eviction may result for using the property for illegal or prohibited purposes or for failing to pay the rent. You should the difference between an assignment and a sublease (the former involves the tenant's entire interest under the lease; the later involves all or part of the premises for a shorter term). Unless the lease prohibits it, a tenant can assign or sublet without the landlord's consent.

Material in other chapters that you may wish to review for the exam includes the types of tenancies covered in Chapter 47.

On the contracts section of the exam, there may be a question about a lease that cannot be completed within a year. Of course, any such lease must be in writing to be enforceable under the Statute of Frauds.

CUMULATIVE HYPOTHETICAL PROBLEM FOR UNIT TEN—INCLUDING CHAPTERS 47–49

(Answers at the Back of the Book)

As joint tenants, Eve and Frank own twenty acres of land, on which there is a warehouse surrounded by a fence.

____ 1. In determining whether the fence is a fixture, the most important factor is

a. the adaptability of the fence to the land.
b. the intent of Eve and Frank.
c. the manner in which the fence is attached to the land.
d. the value of the fence.

____ 2. Frank wants to sell the land and the warehouse. He executes and delivers a deed to Greg. Eve will

a. own all of the land and the warehouse because she did not sign the deed.
b. own exactly twenty acres and half a warehouse.
c. retain a 1/2 undivided interest in the property.
d. share ownership of the property with Greg as a joint tenant.

____ 3. For the deed between Frank and Greg to be effective, one of the conditions is that the deed must

a. be delivered by Frank with the intent to transfer title.
b. be recorded within certain statutory time limits.
c. include the sale price.
d. include the signatures of both Frank and Greg.

___ **4.** Before Greg records the deed, Frank deeds the same interest in the property to Helen. Helen is aware of the prior transfer to Greg and records her deed first. Under a race-notice recording statute, the prevailing party is

a. Eve.
b. Frank.
c. Greg.
d. Helen.

___ **5.** International Sales, Inc. (ISI), rents the warehouse from the owners, under a two-year lease that requires ISI to pay the property taxes. At the start of the second year, ISI agrees with J&J Transport to allow it to occupy the warehouse and pay rent to ISI. No one pays the property taxes for the second year. In a suit to collect, the owners would most likely

a. lose and have to pay the taxes themselves.
b. prevail against ISI because the agreement with J&J was a sublease.
c. prevail against ISI and J&J because they are jointly and severally liable.
d. prevail against J&J because the lease was assigned to J&J.

QUESTIONS ON THE FOCUS ON LEGAL REASONING FOR UNIT TEN—*TAHOE-SIERRA PRESERVATION COUNCIL, INC. V. TAHOE REGIONAL PLANNING AGENCY*

(Answers at the Back of the Book)

___ **1.** Washington County imposes a moratorium on building until the completion of the county's land-use plan. According to the majority in *Tahoe-Sierra Preservation Council, Inc. v. Tahoe Regional Planning Agency*, this moratorium is most likely

a. a taking and must be compensated.
b. a taking but does not require compensation.
c. not a taking and does not require compensation.
d. not a taking but must be compensated.

___ **2.** Under the facts in the previous question, according to the dissent in *Tahoe-Sierra Preservation Council, Inc. v. Tahoe Regional Planning Agency*, the moratorium is

a. a taking and must be compensated.
b. a taking but does not require compensation.
c. not a taking and does not require compensation.
d. not a taking but must be compensated.

___ **3.** Suppose that the moratorium in the previous questions is not a taking. According to the majority in *Tahoe-Sierra Preservation Council, Inc. v. Tahoe Regional Planning Agency*, this means that any costs associated with undeveloped land must be borne by

a. the county government.
b. the courts.
c. the federal government.
d. the landowner.

QUESTIONS ON THE FOCUS ON ETHICS FOR UNIT TEN—PROPERTY

(Answers at the Back of the Book)

___ **1.** Alpha Credit Company institutes a garnishment proceeding against Beta Services, Inc., a domain name registrar, to force a sale of Consumer Corporation's domain name. The court is most likely to rule that garnishment in this context is not possible because

a. domain names are not commonly sold in the market.
b. domain names do not have value.
c. the right to use a domain name is bound to the registrar's service.
d. the right to use a domain name is unique to the party whose actual name resembles the domain.

___ **2.** Dale finds a laptop computer. The laptop's true owner is Flo. As a finder, Dale can acquire good title to the laptop against

a. everyone except Flo.
b. everyone including Flo.
c. Flo but no one else.
d. no one.

___ **3.** Ross gives his silver trophies to United Awards, Inc., to hold temporarily. While in United's possession, the trophies are destroyed. United may be liable for the loss if this was a bailment for

a. no one's benefit.
b. Ross's sole benefit.
c. United's sole benefit.
d. the mutual benefit of both parties.

Chapter 50
Insurance

WHAT THIS CHAPTER IS ABOUT

Insurance is a contract in which one party agrees to compensate the other for any future loss on a specified subject by a specified peril. Essentially, insurance is an arrangement for managing—transferring and allocating—risk. This chapter covers the law relating to insurance.

CHAPTER OUTLINE

I. TERMINOLOGY AND CONCEPTS

A. RISK MANAGEMENT
Risk management consists of plans to protect personal and financial interests should an event undermine their security. The most common method is to transfer risk from a business or individual to an insurance company.

B. INSURANCE TERMINOLOGY
An insurance company is an *underwriter* or an *insurer;* the party covered by insurance is the *insured;* an insurance contract is a *policy;* consideration paid to an insurer is a *premium;* policies are obtained through an *agent* or *broker*.

C. RISK POOLING
Insurance companies spread the risk among a large number of people—the pool—to make the premiums small compared with the coverage offered.

D. CLASSIFICATIONS OF INSURANCE
Insurance is classified according to the nature of the risk involved.

E. INSURABLE INTEREST
To obtain insurance, one must have a sufficient interest in what is insured.

1. Life Insurance
One must have a reasonable expectation of benefit from the continued life of another. The benefit may be related to money or may be founded on a relationship (by blood or affinity).

a. Key-Person Insurance
An organization (partnership, corporation) can insure the life of a person who is important to that organization (partner, officer).

b. When the Insurable Interest Must Exist
An interest in someone's life must exist *when the policy is obtained.*

2. Property Insurance
One has an insurable interest in property when one would sustain a pecuniary loss from its destruction. An insurable interest in property must exist *when the loss occurs.*

II. THE INSURANCE CONTRACT
Policies generally are standard; in some states, this is required.

A. APPLICATION FOR INSURANCE

The application is part of the contract. Misstatements can void a policy, especially if the insurer shows that it would not have issued the policy if it had known the facts.

B. EFFECTIVE DATE OF COVERAGE

A policy is effective when (1) a binder is written, (2) the policy is issued, (3) a certain time elapses, or (4) a specified condition is met.

1. When a Policy Is Obtained from a Broker

A broker is the agent of the applicant. Until the broker obtains a policy, the applicant is normally not insured.

2. When a Policy Is Obtained from an Agent

An agent is the agent of the insurer. One who obtains a policy from an agent can be protected from the moment the application is made (under a binder), or the parties may agree to delay coverage until a policy is issued or some condition is met (such as a physical exam).

C. PROVISIONS AND CLAUSES

Some important clauses include—

1. Provisions Mandated by Statute

A court will deem that a policy contains such a clause even if it is not actually included in the language of the contract.

2. Incontestability Clause

After a life or health policy has been in force for a certain time (two or three years), the insurer cannot cancel the policy or avoid a claim on the basis of statements made in the application.

3. Coinsurance Clause

A standard provision in fire insurance policies; applies only in cases of *partial* loss. If an owner insures property up to a specified percentage (usually 80 percent) of its value, he or she will recover any loss up to the face amount of the policy. If the insurance is for less than this percentage, the owner is responsible for a proportionate share.

4. Appraisal and Arbitration Clauses

If insurer and insured disagree about the value of a loss, they can demand separate appraisals, to be resolved by a third party (*umpire*).

5. Multiple Insurance Coverage

If policies with several companies cover the same risk and the amount of coverage exceeds the loss, the insured collects from each insurer its proportionate share of the liability to the total amount of insurance.

6. Antilapse Clause

Provides grace period for insured to pay an overdue premium.

D. INTERPRETING PROVISIONS

Words in an insurance contract have their ordinary meanings. If there is an ambiguity or uncertainty, it is interpreted against the insurer.

E. CANCELLATION

A policy may be canceled for nonpayment of premiums, fraud or misrepresentation, conviction for a crime that increases the hazard insured against, or gross negligence that increases the hazard insured against. An insurer may be required to give advance written notice.

F. BASIC DUTIES AND RIGHTS

Parties must act in good faith and disclose all material facts. If there is a claim, the insurer must investigate. Insurer and insured must fulfill the terms of the policy.

G. DEFENSES AGAINST PAYMENT
Fraud, misrepresentation, violation of warranties, and actions that are against public policy or that are otherwise illegal.

III. TYPES OF INSURANCE

A. LIFE INSURANCE
A fixed amount is paid to a beneficiary on an insured's death.

1. Types of Life Insurance
Basic types: *whole life* has cash surrender value that grows at a predetermined rate and can be used as collateral for a loan; *term* provides protection for a specified period; has no cash surrender value.

2. Liability
Unless excluded, any cause of death is the insurer's risk. Typical exclusions: death by suicide, when the insured is a passenger in a commercial vehicle, in military action in war, or execution by the government.

3. Misstatement of Age
This does not void a policy, but premiums or benefits are adjusted.

4. Assignment
An insured can change beneficiaries, with notice to the insurer.

5. Creditors' Rights
Generally, a judgment creditor can reach an insured's interest in life insurance. The creditor cannot compel the insured to obtain cash surrender value or change the beneficiary to the creditor.

6. Termination
Usually occurs only on default in premium payments (policy lapses), payment of benefits, expiration of term, or cancellation by insured.

B. FIRE INSURANCE
Protects the homeowner against fire, lightning, and damage from smoke and water caused by the fire or the fire department.

1. Liability
Usually, recovery is limited to losses resulting from hostile fires. In some cases, the insured must file proof of a loss as a condition for recovery. In most cases, premises must be occupied at the time of loss, unless the parties agree otherwise.

2. Assignment
Not assignable without the insurer's consent (it would materially change the insurer's risk).

C. HOMEOWNERS' INSURANCE

1. Property Coverage
Included are the garage; house; other private buildings; personal possessions at home, in travel, or at work; and expenses for living away from home because of a fire or some other covered peril.

2. Liability Coverage
Covered are injuries occurring on the insured's property; damage or injury by the insured to others or their property, except for professional malpractice.

D. AUTOMOBILE INSURANCE

1. Liability Insurance
Covers bodily injury and property damage.

2. **Collision Insurance**
   Covers damage to the insured's car in any type of collision. Most people agree to pay a deductible before the insurer becomes liable.

3. **Comprehensive Insurance**
   Covers loss, damage, and destruction by fire, hurricane, hail, vandalism, and theft.

4. **Uninsured Motorist Insurance**
   Covers the driver and passengers against injury caused by any driver without insurance or by a hit-and-run driver. Some states require it all automobile policies sold to drivers.

5. **Other-Driver Coverage**
   Protects vehicle owner and anyone who drives the vehicle with owner's permission.

6. **No-fault Insurance**
   Provides that claims arising from an accident are made against the claimant's own insurer, regardless of whose fault the accident was.

E. BUSINESS LIABILITY INSURANCE

1. **Key-person Insurance**
   See above (I, E, 1, a).

2. **General Liability Insurance**
   Covers as many risks as the insurer agrees to cover. Policies can be drafted to meet special needs, such as specific risks of product liability (see Chapter 6).

3. **Professional Malpractice Insurance**
   Protects professionals against malpractice claims.

4. **Workers' Compensation Insurance**
   Covers payments to employees who are injured in accidents occurring on the job or in the course of employment (see Chapter 33).

TRUE-FALSE QUESTIONS

(Answers at the Back of the Book)

____ 1. Risk management involves the transfer of risk from an individual or a business to an insurance company.

____ 2. Insurance is classified by the nature of the person or interest protected.

____ 3. An insurance broker is always an agent of an insurance company.

____ 4. An insurance applicant is usually protected from the time an application is made, if a premium is paid.

____ 5. A person can insure anything in which he or she has an insurable interest.

____ 6. An application for insurance is not part of the insurance contract.

____ 7. An insured can change beneficiaries under a life insurance policy without the insurer's consent.

____ 8. A coinsurance clause in a fire insurance policy always reduces the amount of the insured's recovery.

____ 9. More than one party can have an insurable interest in, for example, the same property.

____ 10. Under an antilapse clause, an insurance policy lapses unless the insured pays a premium on time.

FILL-IN QUESTIONS

(Answers at the Back of the Book)

The words used in an insurance contract have their ______________ (ordinary/special) meaning and are interpreted by the courts in light of the ______________ (insured's conduct/nature of the coverage) involved. When there is an ambiguity in a policy, a provision is interpreted against the ______________ (insurance company/insured). When it is unclear whether an insurance contract actually exists because the written policy has not been delivered, the uncertainty will be determined against the ______________(insurance company/insured). A court presumes the policy _______ (is/is not) in effect unless the ______________ (insurance company/insured) can show otherwise.

MULTIPLE-CHOICE QUESTIONS

(Answers at the Back of the Book)

___ 1. Pam states, on her application to Quality Insurance, Inc., for a life insurance policy, that she has not been hospitalized within the last five years, forgetting that two years earlier she was hospitalized briefly. One year later, Pam dies for a cause unrelated to the earlier hospitalization. Quality denies payment. If Pam's beneficiary sues Quality, the beneficiary will

a. lose, because Pam's misstatement concerned a material fact.
b. lose, because an insurer can use any misstatement on an application to avoid payment.
c. win, because an insurer cannot use a misstatement on an application to avoid payment.
d. win, because Pam's misstatement did not concern a material fact.

___ 2. Ruth applies to Standard Insurance Company for a fire insurance policy for her warehouse. To obtain a lower premium, she misrepresents the age of the property. The policy is granted. After the warehouse is destroyed by fire, Standard learns the true facts. Standard can

a. not refuse to pay, because an application is not part of an insurance contract.
b. not refuse to pay, because fire destroyed the warehouse.
c. refuse to pay on the ground of fraud in the application.
d. refuse to pay on the ground that fire destroyed the warehouse.

___ 3. Carl is an executive with DigiCom, Inc. Because his death would cause a financial loss to the firm, it insures his life. Later, he resigns to work for a competitor, E-Tech Corporation. Six months later, Carl dies. Regarding payment for the loss, DigiCom can

a. collect, because the firm's insurable interest existed when the policy was obtained.
b. collect if the firm suffered a financial loss when Carl resigned.
c. not collect, because the firm's insurable interest did not exist when a loss occurred.
d. not collect, because the firm suffered no financial loss from Carl's death.

___ 4. **Based on a Sample CPA Exam Question.** Tom buys a house and obtains from Union Insurance Company a fire insurance policy on the property. If fire destroys the house, to collect payment under the policy, Tom's insurable interest

a. exists only if the property is owned by Tom or a related individual.
b. exists only if the property is owned in fee simple.
c. must exist when the loss occurs.
d. must exist when Union issues the policy and when the loss occurs.

___ 5. Satellite Communications, Inc., takes out an insurance policy on its plant with United Insurance, Inc. United could cancel the policy

a. for any reason.
b. if any of Satellite's drivers have their driver's licenses suspended.
c. if Satellite begins using grossly careless manufacturing practices.
d. if Satellite's president appears as a witness in a case against United.

___ 6. Deb takes out a fire insurance policy with Eagle Insurance Company on her $200,000 warehouse. The policy contains a coinsurance clause with a specified percentage of 80 percent. Deb insures the property for $160,000. In a fire, she suffers a $100,000 loss. She can recover

a. $200,000.
b. $160,000.
c. $100,000.
d. $80,000.

___ 7. Tech Corporation makes computers. To insure its products to cover injuries to consumers if the products prove defective, Tech should buy

a. group insurance.
b. liability insurance.
c. major medical insurance.
d. term life insurance.

___ 8. Fine Company has insurance policies with General Insurance, Inc., and InsurCorp covering the risk of loss of Fine's building in a fire. Each policy has a multiple insurance clause. If the building is partially destroyed in a fire, Fine can collect from each insurer

a. each insurer's proportionate share of the loss to the total amount of insurance.
b. half of the amount of the loss.
c. the full amount of the loss.
d. nothing.

___ 9. Ace Manufacturing, Inc., has property insurance with Best Insurer, Inc. Ace suffers a loss in a burglary, but Ace and Best cannot agree on the amount of recovery. Under an appraisal and arbitration clause

a. Ace can demand an appraisal that Best must pay.
b. Best can demand an appraisal that Ace must accept.
c. each party can demand separate appraisals to be resolved by a third party.
d. the government sets the value of the loss which both parties must accept.

___ 10. Alan buys BizNet, a company that provides Internet access, and takes out property insurance with InsCo to cover a loss of the equipment. Two years later, Alan sells BizNet. Six months after the sale, BizNet's equipment is stolen. Under InsCo's policy, Alan can recover

a. InsCo's proportionate share of the loss to the total amount of insurance.
b. the total amount of the insurance.
c. the total amount of the loss.
d. nothing.

SHORT ESSAY QUESTIONS

1. What is the concept of insurable interest, and what is its effect on insurance payments?

2. What are some of the types of insurance policies that businesses carry to protect themselves from risk?

ISSUE SPOTTERS

(Answers at the Back of the Book)

1. Why is an insurance premium small relative to the amount of coverage that an insurance company offers?

2. Adam is divorced and owns a house. He has no reasonable expectation of benefit from the life of Beth, his ex-spouse, but applies for insurance on her life anyway. He obtains a fire insurance policy on the house and then sells the house. Ten years later, Beth dies and fire destroys the house. Can Adam obtain payment for these events?

3. Umbrella insurance policies are bought separately from regular insurance coverage and can provide coverage for as much as $5 million. Under what circumstances might an individual want to buy umbrella insurance coverage?

SPECIAL INFORMATION FOR CPA CANDIDATES

Insurance is part of the property section of the CPA examination. The most important points for your review are the warranties that an insured makes when applying for a policy, the workings of coinsurance clauses, and the concept of insurable interest. When must a party have an insurable interest to obtain insurance? Can more than one party have an insurable interest in, for example, the same property? (Yes.) Does a coinsurance clause apply in a case of total loss? Except for questions concerning insurable interest, the CPA exam does not cover automobile or life insurance.

Chapter 51
Wills, Trusts, and Elder Law

WHAT THIS CHAPTER IS ABOUT

This chapter covers some of the laws governing the succession of property. (See also Chapter 47 on joint tenancy and Chapter 50 on insurance.) A person can direct the passage of property after death by will. If no valid will has been executed, state intestacy laws apply. A person can also transfer property with a trust. Elder law, which relates to the needs of older persons, is also covered in this chapter.

CHAPTER OUTLINE

I. WILLS

A *will* is a declaration of how a person wants property disposed of after death; a formal instrument that must follow the statutory requirements to be effective.

A. TERMINOLOGY OF WILLS

A *testator* is a person who makes a will; a *probate court* oversees the administration of a will by an *executor* (appointed by the testator in the will) or by an *administrator* (appointed by the court).

B. LAWS GOVERNING WILLS

Vary from state to state. Some of the law includes—

1. Uniform Probate Code (UPC)

The UPC codifies principles and procedures for the resolution of conflicts in settling estates and relaxes some of the requirements for a will.

2. Revised UPC

In 1990, the UPC was revised to further relax formal will requirements and to provide for the interpretation of will substitutes and other *inter vivos* transfers (see below).

C. TYPES OF GIFTS

A gift of real estate by will is a *devise*; the recipient is a *devisee*. A gift of personal property is a *bequest* or *legacy*; a recipient is a *legatee*. Gifts can be specific, general, or residuary. If there are not enough assets to pay all general bequests, an *abatement* reduces the gifts.

D. REQUIREMENTS FOR A VALID WILL

1. A Testator Must Have Capacity

When a will is made, the testator must be of legal age (in most states, at least eighteen years old) and sound mind (a person can be adjudged mentally incompetent or have delusions about certain subjects and, during lucid moments, still be of sound mind).

2. A Testator Must Have Intent

A testator must (1) intend a document to be his or her will, (2) understand the property being distributed, and (3) remember the "natural objects of his or her bounty" (family members and others for whom the testator has affection).

3. A Will Must Be in Writing

An outside document can be incorporated by reference if it exists when the will is executed and is identified in the will. In a few states, an oral (nuncupative) will is valid to pass personal property below a certain value if made in the expectation of imminent death.

4. **A Will Must Be Signed by the Testator**
The testator must sign with the intent to validate the will; the signature need not be at the end.

5. **A Will Must Be Witnessed**
The number of witnesses, their qualifications, and the manner in which it must be done vary from state to state.

6. **In a Few States, a Will Must Be "Published"**
Publication is an oral declaration by the maker to the witnesses that the document they are about to sign is his or her will.

E. REVOCATION OF WILLS
A will is revocable, in whole or in part, by its maker any time during the maker's lifetime by physical act (intentionally obliterating or destroying a will, or directing someone else to do so); by a document (a codicil, a new will); or by operation of law (marriage, divorce, annulment, birth of child).

F. RIGHTS UNDER A WILL
A surviving spouse can renounce the amount given by will and elect a forced share, if the share is larger than the gift. In most states, a forced share is one-third of an estate or an amount equal to a spouse's share under intestacy laws (see below). A beneficiary can renounce his or her share.

G. PROBATE PROCEDURES
Probate: establish the validity of a will and administer the estate. The UPC includes rules and procedures for resolving conflicts in settling estates and relaxes some of the will requirements.

1. **Informal Probate**
In some states, cars, bank accounts, etc., can pass by filling out forms, or property can be transferred by affidavit. Most states allow heirs to distribute assets themselves after a will is admitted to probate.

2. **Formal Probate**
For large estates, a probate court supervises distribution.

3. **Property Transfers outside the Probate Process**
Will substitutes include living trusts (see below), life insurance, and joint tenancies.

II. INTESTACY LAWS
Statutes of descent and distribution regulate how property is distributed when a person dies without a valid will. The rules vary widely from state to state, but typically, the debts of the decedent are satisfied out of his or her estate, and the remaining assets pass to the surviving spouse and children.

A. SURVIVING SPOUSE AND CHILDREN

1. **Legitimate Heirs**
The spouse usually receives a share of the estate (such as one-half if there is a surviving child); the children receive the rest. If no children or grandchildren survive, the spouse succeeds to the entire estate.

2. **Illegitimate Children**
In some states, intestate succession between a parent and an illegitimate child can occur only if the child is legitimized by ceremony or was acknowledged by the parent.

B. ORDER OF DISTRIBUTION

1. **Lineal Descendants**
If there is no surviving spouse or child, grandchildren are next in line, then parents. Generally, title descends (to children, etc.) before it ascends (to parents, etc.).

2. **Collateral Heirs**
If there are no lineal descendants, brothers, sisters, nieces, nephews, aunts, and uncles inherit. If none survive, property goes to collateral heirs' next of kin (relatives by marriage are not considered kin).

3. **Methods of Distribution**
Per stirpes: a class or group of distributees take the share that their deceased parent would have been entitled to had that parent lived. *Per capita*: each person takes an equal share of the estate.

III. TRUSTS

Trusts are arrangements by which a grantor (settlor) transfers legal title to the trust property to a trustee, who administers the property as directed by the grantor for the benefit of the beneficiaries.

A. ESSENTIAL ELEMENTS

1. A designated beneficiary.
2. A designated trustee.
3. A fund sufficiently identified to enable title to pass to the trustee.
4. Actual delivery to the trustee with the intention of passing title.

B. EXPRESS TRUSTS

1. **Living Trust (or *Inter Vivos* Trust)**
Created by trust deed to exist during the settlor's lifetime.

2. **Testamentary Trust**
Created by will to come into existence on the settlor's death (if the will is invalid, the trust is invalid). If not named in the will, a trustee is appointed by a court. Trustee's actions are subject to judicial approval.

3. **Charitable Trust**
Designed to benefit a segment of the public or the public in general, usually for charitable, educational, religious, or scientific purposes. Identities of the beneficiaries are uncertain.

4. **Spendthrift Trust**
Prevents a beneficiary's transfer of his or her right to future payments of income or capital by expressly placing restraints on the alienation of trust funds.

5. **Totten Trust**
Created when one person deposits money in his or her own name as trustee. Revocable at will until the depositor dies or completes the gift (for example, by delivery of the funds to the beneficiary).

C. IMPLIED TRUSTS

1. **Constructive Trust**
A constructive trust is an equitable remedy that enables plaintiffs to recover property (and sometimes damages) from defendants who would otherwise be unjustly enriched. A court declares the legal owner of the property to be a trustee for parties entitled to the benefit of the property.

2. **Resulting Trust**
A resulting trust arises when the conduct of the parties raise an inference that the party holding legal title to the property does so for the benefit of another.

D. THE TRUSTEE

Anyone capable of holding title to, and dealing in, property can be a trustee.

1. **Trustee's Duties**
Preserve the trust property; make the trust property productive; and if required by the terms of the trust agreement, pay income to the beneficiaries.

a. **General Duties**
Honesty, good faith, and prudence in administering the trust for the exclusive interest of the beneficiary; invest and manage trust assets as a prudent investor would manage his or her assets.

b. **Specific Duties**

1) **Keep Accurate Accounts of the Trust's Administration**
Furnish complete information to the beneficiary. Keep trust assets separate from his or her assets. Pay to an income beneficiary the net income of the trust at reasonable intervals.

2) **Invest the Trust Property**
Distribute the risk of loss from investments by diversification and dispose of assets that do not represent prudent investments.

2. **Trustee's Powers**
Whatever the settlor prescribes. State law applies only to the extent that it does not conflict with the terms of the trust.

a. **If State Law Applies**
May restrict the investment of trust funds, confining trustees to investments in conservative debt securities.

b. **Discretion to Distribute the Principal or Invest the Income**
Subject to trust purposes, a trustee may make adjustments in annual distributions to provide the beneficiary with predictable income.

3. **Allocations between Principal and Income**
Ordinary receipts and expenses (rent, royalties) are chargeable to income; extraordinary receipts and expenses (proceeds from the sale of property, stock dividends) are allocated to principal.

E. TRUST TERMINATION

Typically, a trust instrument specifies a termination date. If the trust's purpose is fulfilled before that date, a court may order the trust's termination. If no date is specified, a trust terminates when its purpose is fulfilled (or becomes impossible or illegal).

IV. ESTATE ADMINISTRATION

The procedure used to collect and distribute assets when a person dies, subject to the oversight of a probate court. Rules vary from state to state.

A. BASIC STEPS

(1) Did the decedent leave a will? (2) Does it name a executor? If so, the court must approve; if not, the court appoints an administrator.

B. DUTIES OF A PERSONAL REPRESENTATIVE

1. **What to Do with the Decedent's Assets**
Inventory and collect them; if necessary, have them appraised; manage them during administration to avoid waste or depletion.

2. **What to Do with Claims**
Pay federal and state income taxes, estate or inheritance taxes, and the valid claims of creditors.

a. **Federal Estate Tax**
Tax on the total value of the estate (not the beneficiaries) after debts, expenses, and exemptions (including gifts to charity). The lowest tax rates are applied to a surviving spouse and the children of the decedent.

b. **State Inheritance Tax**
Generally, imposed on the recipient of a bequest (not the estate). Tax rates are graduated according to the relationship between the beneficiary and decedent (lowest rates and largest exemptions are applied to a surviving spouse and children).

3. **Other Duties**
Post a bond, if required (the will can waive it). Distribute the estate pursuant to court order. Render an accounting to the court.

V. ELDER LAW

A. PLANNING FOR DISABILITY

In anticipation of becoming incapacitated, persons sometimes plan for others to manage their affairs.

1. **Durable Power of Attorney**
Authorizes a person to act on behalf of an incompetent person when he or she becomes incapacitated.

2. **Health-Care Power of Attorney**
Designates a person to choose medical treatment for a person who is unable to make such a choice.

3. **Living Will**
Designates whether or not a person wants certain life-saving procedures to be taken if they will not result in a reasonable quality of life.

B. MEDICAID

In anticipation of the cost of long-term care, persons sometimes plan to meet the requirements of Medicaid so their assets can go to others.

1. **What Medicaid Is**
Health-care services for the poor of all ages. Administered by state agencies; regulations vary from state to state. At the federal level, administered by the Health Care Financing Administration.

2. **Planning for Medicaid**
A person who accepts Medicaid pays his or her income to the state. Exceptions include a home, a car, and assets up to $75,000. Assets may also be transferred to others, but not within a certain period. A penalty "waiting period" may apply.

3. **Advising Others to Plan for Medicaid**
It is a crime for an attorney to advise elderly clients to give away assets to get Medicaid coverage of nursing-home costs, but at least one court has ruled that the law is unconstitutional.

TRUE-FALSE QUESTIONS

(Answers at the Back of the Book)

___ 1. A will is revocable only after the testator's death.

___ 2. The testator generally must sign a will.

___ 3. If a person dies without a will, all of his or her property automatically passes to the state.

___ 4. An *inter vivos* trust is a trust created by a grantor during his or her lifetime.

___ **5.** A testamentary trust is created by will to begin on the settlor's death.

___ **6.** A will can only distribute property.

___ **7.** If a person marries *after* executing a will, the spouse gets nothing on the person's death.

___ **8.** A beneficiary can renounce his or her share of property under a will.

___ **9.** A trustee has a duty to dispose of trust assets that do not represent prudent investments.

___ **10.** A trust terminates on the trustee's death.

FILL-IN QUESTIONS

(Answers at the Back of the Book)

When a person dies, a personal representative settles the decedent's affairs. A personal representative named in a will is an ________________ (administrator/executor). A personal representative appointed by a court for a decedent who dies without a will, who fails to name a personal representative in a will, who names a personal representative lacking the capacity to serve, or who writes a will that the court refuses to admit to probate is an ________________(administrator/executor).

MULTIPLE-CHOICE QUESTIONS

(Answers at the Back of the Book)

___ **1.** Adam's will provides for specific items of property to be given to certain individuals, including employees of his business. The will also provides for certain sums of money to be given to his daughters, Carol and Dian. Because Adam's assets are insufficient to pay in full all of the bequests

a. all of the property must be sold and the proceeds distributed to the heirs.
b. Carol and Dian get nothing.
c. the employees, who are not in a blood relationship with Adam, get nothing.
d. the gifts to Carol and Dian will be reduced proportionately.

___ **2.** **Based on a Sample CPA Exam Question.** Eve dies without a will, but is survived by her brother Frank, her child Gail, and her parents. The party with the first priority to receive Eve's estate is

a. her brother Frank.
b. her child Gail.
c. her parents.
d. the state.

___ **3.** Holly executes a will that leaves all of her property to Ira. Two years later, Holly executes a will that leaves all of her property to Jill. The second will does not expressly revoke the first will. Holly dies. The property passes to

a. Ira, because he was given the property in the first will.
b. Ira, because the second will did not expressly revoke the first will.
c. Jill, because the first will was revoked by the second will.
d. Jill, because two years separated the execution of the wills.

____ **4.** Kelly dies intestate, survived by Lisa, her mother; Mike, her spouse; Nick and Owen, their sons; and Pam, the daughter of Ruth, their daughter, who predeceased her mother. Under intestacy laws

a. Lisa and Mike receive equal portions of Kelly's estate.
b. Mike receives all of Kelly's estate.
c. Mike receives one-third of Kelly's estate, and Nick, Owen, and Pam receive equal portions of the rest.
d. Nick and Owen receive half of Kelly's estate, and Mike receives the rest.

____ **5.** Sam wants Tony and Vic, his sons, to get the benefit of Sam's farm when he dies. Sam can provide for them to get the farm's income, under another party's management, by setting up

a. a constructive trust.
b. an interstate trust.
c. a resulting trust.
d. a testamentary trust.

____ **6.** Alan's will provides, "I leave all my computer equipment to my good friend, Bob." When Alan dies, the personal representative gives Bob the computer equipment. Bob is

a. a devisee.
b. a legatee.
c. a residuary.
d. none of the above.

____ **7.** Ellen believes that probate is too time-consuming and costly, and wishes that her assets pass to her heirs as quickly and inexpensively as possible. To avoid probate most successfully, Ellen can

a. create a testamentary trust.
b. draft a will and not sign it.
c. have her heirs decide among themselves who will get what on her death.
d. hold the assets in joint tenancy.

____ **8.** Don is the trustee of a testamentary trust. The trust grants Don discretion to invest the assets. In most states, this means that Don

a. is entitled to invest the assets as he sees fit.
b. must confine trust investments to conservative securities.
c. must invest according to the prudent person rule.
d. must invest as aggressively as possible.

____ **9.** Kim is the trustee of a testamentary trust. Ordinary trust expenses, such as the rent for Kim's office, are chargeable to

a. Kim.
b. the court that oversees Kim's administration.
c. trust income.
d. trust principal.

____ **10.** Ann is Bill's adult daughter. Bill decides that he wants Ann to act on his behalf if he becomes incapacitated by old age. Bill should arrange for Ann to have

a. a living trust.
b. a durable power of attorney.
c. a power of trustee.
d. his Medicare benefits.

SHORT ESSAY QUESTIONS

1. What requirements must be satisfied to create a valid will?

2. In what ways may a will be revoked?

ISSUE SPOTTERS

(Answers at the Back of the Book)

1. Sheila makes out a will, leaving her property in equal thirds to Mark and Paula, her children, and Carol, her niece. Two years later, Sheila is adjudged mentally incompetent, and that same year, she dies. Can Mark and Paula have Sheila's will revoked, on grounds that she did not have the capacity to make a will?

2. Dick dies. Dick's will provides for specific property to be given to certain individuals, including Dick's family and employees. The will also provides for certain amounts of money to be given to Emily, Fred, and Greg. The estate's assets are not quite enough to pay Emily, Fred, and Greg in full. Who gets what?

3. When Bob dies, it is discovered that he has no will. He does have, however, many relatives—a spouse, children, adopted children, sisters, brothers, uncles, aunts, cousins, nephews, and nieces. What determines who gets what?

SPECIAL INFORMATION FOR CPA CANDIDATES

The CPA examination has not traditionally asked questions about the requirements or validity of a will. The exam has covered, however, estate and trust administration. You should know what makes up an estate (property that is part of the estate for tax purposes may not be part of the estate under the will—for example, property held in joint tenancy is subject to estate taxes but is not subject to a will).

In the property section of the exam, trusts have been much emphasized. You should know the essential elements of a trust, and the difference between *inter vivos* and testamentary trusts. You should be familiar with the definition of a spendthrift trust. Also important are the fiduciary duties of the trustee, who must, among other responsibilities, make allocations between principal and income. Finally, you should know what terminates a trust.

Chapter 52
Liability of Accountants and Other Professionals

WHAT THIS CHAPTER IS ABOUT

This chapter outlines the potential common law liability of professionals, the potential liability of accountants under securities laws and the Internal Revenue Code, and the duty of professionals to keep their clients' communications confidential.

CHAPTER OUTLINE

I. COMMON LAW LIABILITY TO CLIENTS

A. LIABILITY FOR BREACH OF CONTRACT
For a professional's breach of contract, a client can recover damages, including expenses incurred to secure another professional to provide the services and other reasonable and foreseeable losses.

B. LIABILITY FOR NEGLIGENCE
Professionals must exercise the standard of care, knowledge, and judgment generally accepted by members of their professional group.

1. Accountant's Duty of Care

a. Comply with Accounting Principles and Standards
Accountants must comply with generally accepted accounting principles (GAAP) and generally accepted auditing standards (GAAS) (though compliance does not guarantee relief from liability). Violation of either is *prima facie* evidence of negligence. Note: there may be a higher state law standard.

b. Act in Good Faith
If an accountant conforms to GAAP and acts in good faith, he or she will not be liable to a client for incorrect judgment.

c. Investigate Suspicious Financial Transactions
An accountant who uncovers suspicious financial transactions and fails to investigate the matter fully or to inform his or her client of the discovery can be held liable to the client for the resulting loss.

d. Designate Financial Statements as Unaudited
An accountant may be liable for failing to designate a balance sheet as "unaudited." An accountant may also be liable for failing to disclose to a client facts that give reason to believe misstatements have been made or fraud has been committed.

e. Defenses to Negligence

1) The accountant was not negligent.

2) If the accountant was negligent, the negligence was not the proximate cause of the client's loss.

3) The client was also negligent.

f. **Qualified Opinions and Disclaimers**
An accountant is not liable for damages resulting from whatever is qualified or disclaimed.

2. **Attorney's Duty of Care**

a. **General Duty**
All attorneys owe a duty to provide competent and diligent representation. The standard is that of a reasonably competent general practitioner of ordinary skill, experience, and capacity.

b. **Specific Responsibilities**
Attorneys must be familiar with well-settled principles of law applicable to a case, discover law that can be found through a reasonable amount of research, and investigate and discover facts that could materially affect the client's legal rights.

C. LIABILITY FOR FRAUD

1. **Actual Fraud**
A professional may be liable if he or she intentionally misstates a material fact to mislead his or her client and the client justifiably relies on the misstated fact to his or her injury.

2. **Constructive Fraud**
A professional may be liable for constructive fraud whether or not he or she acted with fraudulent intent (for example, an accountant who is grossly negligent; gross negligence includes the intentional failure to perform a duty in reckless disregard of the consequences).

II. LIABILITY TO THIRD PARTIES

Most courts hold that auditors can be held liable to third parties for negligence.

A. THE *ULTRAMARES* RULE

1. **The Privity Requirement**
An accountant owes a duty only to a third person with whom he or she has a direct contractual relationship (privity) or a relationship "so close as to approach that of privity."

2. **The "Near Privity" Rule**
In a few states, if a third party has a sufficiently close relationship or nexus with an accountant, the *Ultramares* privity requirement may be satisfied without establishing an accountant-client relationship.

B. THE *RESTATEMENT* RULE

Most courts hold accountants liable for negligence to persons whom the accountant "intends to supply the information or knows that the recipient intends to supply it" and persons whom the accountant "intends the information to influence or knows that the recipient so intends" [*Restatement (Second) of Torts*, Section 552].

C. LIABILITY TO REASONABLY FORESEEABLE USERS

A few courts hold accountants liable to any users whose reliance on an accountant's statements or reports was reasonably foreseeable.

III. THE SARBANES-OXLEY ACT OF 2002

This act imposes requirements on a public accounting firm that provides auditing services to an *issuer* (a company that has securities registered under Section 12 of the Securities Exchange Act of 1934; that is required to file reports under Section 15(d) of the 1934 act; or that files—or has filed—a registration statement not yet effective under the Securities Act of 1933).

A. THE PUBLIC COMPANY ACCOUNTING OVERSIGHT BOARD

This board, which reports to the Securities and Exchange Commission, oversees the audit of public companies subject to securities laws to protect public investors and ensure that public accounting firms comply with the provisions of the Sarbanes-Oxley Act.

B. APPLICABILITY TO PUBLIC ACCOUNTING FIRMS

Public accounting firms are firms and associated persons that are "engaged in the practice of public accounting or preparing or issuing audit reports."

1. Nonaudit Services

It is unlawful to perform for an issuer both audit and nonaudit services, which include bookkeeping for an audit client, financial systems design and implementation, appraisal services, fairness opinions, management functions, and investment services.

2. Audit Services

A public accounting firm cannot provide audit services to an issuer if the lead audit partner or the reviewing partner provided those services to the issuer in each of the prior five years, or if the issuer's chief executive officer, chief financial officer, chief accounting officer, or controller worked for the auditor and participated in an audit of the issuer within the preceding year.

3. Reports to an Issuer's Audit Committee

These reports must be timely and indicate critical accounting policies and practices, as well as alternatives discussed, and other communications, with the issuer's management.

C. DOCUMENT DESTRUCTION

The act prohibits destroying or falsifying records to obstruct or influence a federal investigation or in relation to a bankruptcy. Penalties include fines and imprisonment up to twenty years.

IV. LIABILITY OF ACCOUNTANTS UNDER SECURITIES LAWS

A. LIABILITY UNDER THE SECURITIES ACT OF 1933

1. Section 11—Misstatements or Omissions in Registration Statements

An accountant may be liable for misstatements and omissions of material facts in registration statements (which they often prepare for filing with the Securities and Exchange Commission (SEC) before an offering of securities—see Chapter 40).

a. To Whom an Accountant May Be Liable

An accountant may be liable to anyone who acquires a security covered by the statement. A plaintiff must show that he or she suffered a loss on the security. There is no requirement of privity or proof of reliance.

b. Due Diligence Defense

An accountant may avoid liability by showing that, in preparing the financial statements, he or she had—

1) Reasonable Grounds to Believe that the Statements Were True

After a reasonable investigation, the accountant believed that the statements were true and omitted no material facts.

2) Followed GAAP and GAAS

Failure to follow GAAP and GAAS is proof of a lack of due diligence.

3) Verified Information Furnished by Officers and Directors

This defense requires that accountants verify information furnished by the offering firm's officers and directors.

c. Other Defenses to Liability

1) There were no misstatements or omissions.

2) The misstatements or omissions were not of material facts.

3) The misstatements or omissions had no causal connection to the purchaser's loss.

4) The purchaser invested in the securities knowing of the misstatements or omissions.

2. **Section 12(2)—Misstatements or Omissions in Other Communications in an Offer**
Anyone offering or selling a security may be liable for fraud for communicating to an investor a misstatement or omission [Section 12(2)].

3. **Penalties and Sanctions for Violations**
The U.S. Department of Justice brings criminal actions against willful violators. Penalties: fines up to $10,000; imprisonment up to five years. The SEC can seek an injunction and other relief (such as an order to refund profits).

B. LIABILITY UNDER THE SECURITIES EXCHANGE ACT OF 1934

1. **Section 18—False or Misleading Statements in Certain SEC Documents**
An accountant may be liable for making or causing to be made in an application, report, document, or registration statement filed with the SEC a statement that at the time and in light of the circumstances was false or misleading with respect to any material fact.

a. **To Whom an Accountant May Be Liable**
Only sellers and purchasers who can prove (1) the statement affected the price of the security and (2) they relied on the statement and were unaware of its inaccuracy.

b. **Defenses**

1) **Proof of Good Faith**
Proof that the accountant did not know the statement was false or misleading. This can be refuted by showing the accountant's (1) intent to deceive or (2) reckless conduct and gross negligence.

2) **Buyer or Seller Knew the Statement Was False or Misleading**

3) **Statute of Limitations Tolled**
An action must be brought within one year after the discovery of facts constituting the cause and within three years after the cause accrues.

2. **Section 10(b) and Rule 10b-5—Misstatements or Omissions**
These laws cover written and oral statements.

a. **Section 10(b)**
Makes it unlawful for any person to use, in connection with the purchase or sale of any security, any manipulative or deceptive device or contrivance in contravention of SEC rules and regulations.

b. **Rule 10b-5**
Makes it unlawful for any person, by use of any means or instrumentality of interstate commerce, to—

1) Employ any device, scheme, or artifice to defraud.

2) Make any untrue statement of a material fact or to omit to state a material fact necessary to make the statements made, in light of the circumstances, not misleading.

3) Engage in any act, practice, or course of business that operates or would operate as a fraud or deceit on any person, in connection with the purchase or sale of any security.

c. **To Whom An Accountant May Be Liable**
Only to sellers or purchasers. Privity is not required. To recover, a plaintiff must prove (1) *scienter*, (2) a fraudulent action or deception, (3) reliance, (4) materiality, and (5) causation.

C. THE PRIVATE SECURITIES LITIGATION REFORM ACT OF 1995

1. **Adequate Procedures and Disclosure**
An auditor must use adequate procedures in an audit to detect any illegal acts. If something is detected, the auditor must disclose it to the board, audit committee, or SEC, depending on the circumstances.

2. **Proportionate Liability**
A party is liable only for the proportion of damages for which he or she is responsible.

3. **Aiding and Abetting**
An accountant who knows that he or she is participating in an improper activity and knowingly aids the activity (even by silence) is guilty of aiding and abetting. The SEC may obtain an injunction or damages.

V. POTENTIAL CRIMINAL LIABILITY OF ACCOUNTANTS

A. THE SECURITIES ACTS
An accountant may be subject to imprisonment of up to five years and a fine of up to $10,000 under the 1933 act and up to $100,000 under the 1934 act. Under the Sarbanes-Oxley Act, for a securities filing accompanied by an accountant's false or misleading certified audit statement, the accountant may be fined up to $5 million and imprisoned up to twenty years.

B. THE INTERNAL REVENUE CODE

1. **Aiding or Assisting in the Preparation of a False Tax Return**
A felony punishable by a fine of $100,000 ($500,000 in the case of a corporation) and imprisonment for up to three years [Section 7206(2)].

2. **Understatement of a Client's Tax Liability**
Liability is limited to one penalty per taxpayer per tax year.

a. **Negligent or Willful Understatement**
A tax preparer is subject to a penalty of $250 per return for negligent understatement and $1,000 for willful understatement or reckless or intentional disregard of rules or regulations [Section 6694].

b. **Aiding and Abetting an Individual's Understatement**
$1,000 per document ($10,000 in corporate cases) [Section 6701].

3. **Other Liability Related to Tax Returns**
A tax preparer may be subject to penalties for failing to furnish the taxpayer with a copy of the return, failing to sign the return, or failing to furnish the appropriate tax identification numbers [Section 6695].

C. STATE LAW
Most states impose criminal penalties for knowingly certifying false or fraudulent reports; falsifying, altering, or destroying books of account; and obtaining property or credit through the use of false financial statements.

VI. WORKING PAPERS

In some states, working papers are the accountant's property. The client has a right of access to them, and they cannot be transferred to another accountant or otherwise disclosed without the client's permission (or a court order). Unauthorized disclosure is a ground for a malpractice suit. Under the Sarbanes-Oxley Act, accountants are required, in some circumstances, to maintain working papers relating to an audit or review for five years. A knowing violation may result in a fine and imprisonment for up to ten years.

VII. CONFIDENTIALITY AND PRIVILEGE

A. ATTORNEY-CLIENT

The law protects the confidentiality of attorney-client communications. The client holds the privilege, and only the client may waive it.

B. ACCOUNTANT-CLIENT

In response to a federal court order, an accountant must provide the information sought; there is no privilege. In most states, on a court order, an accountant must disclose information about his or her client. In a few states, no disclosure is allowed (even in a court) without the client's permission.

VIII. LIMITING PROFESSIONALS' LIABILITY

Professionals may limit their liability for misconduct of other professionals with whom they work by organizing as a professional corporation (see Chapter 37) or a limited liability partnership (see Chapter 41).

TRUE-FALSE QUESTIONS

(Answers at the Back of the Book)

____ 1. Professionals must exercise the standard of care, knowledge, and judgment observed by their peers.

____ 2. A violation of GAAP and GAAS is *prima facie* evidence of negligence.

____ 3. Compliance with GAAP and GAAS will relieve an accountant of liability.

____ 4. In all states, an accountant is liable to anyone who relies on the accountant's negligently prepared reports.

____ 5. Accountants are not subject to criminal penalties under federal securities laws.

____ 6. A tax preparer may be subject to penalties under the Internal Revenue Code for assisting in filing a false tax return.

____ 7. There is no penalty under the Internal Revenue Code for failing to give the taxpayer a copy of the return.

____ 8. State-provided rights to confidentiality of accountant-client communications are not recognized in federal cases.

____ 9. Under the Private Securities Litigation Reform Act of 1995, a party is liable only for the proportion of damages for which he or she is responsible.

____ 10. For an accountant to be liable to a seller or purchaser for misstatements or omissions under SEC Rule 10b-5, there must be privity.

FILL-IN QUESTIONS

(Answers at the Back of the Book)

Accountants must comply with generally accepted accounting principles (GAAP) and generally accepted auditing standards (GAAS). An accountant who conforms to GAAP and acts in good faith ____________ (may/will not) be liable to a client for incorrect judgment. An accountant who uncovers suspicious financial transactions but fails to investigate fully or to inform the client ____________ (may/will not) be liable. If a client suffers a loss due to fraud that an accountant negligently fails to discover, the accountant ____________ (may/will not) be liable.

MULTIPLE-CHOICE QUESTIONS

(Answers at the Back of the Book)

___ **1.** Ann, an accountant, accumulates working papers in performing an audit for her client, Beta Corporation. Ann can release those papers

a. only on the request of another accountant.
b. only with Beta's permission.
c. under any circumstances.
d. under no circumstances.

___ **2.** **Based on a Sample CPA Exam Question.** Digital, Inc., asks Ed, an accountant, to prepare its financial statements. Ed conducts the audit negligently. The firm uses the statements to obtain a loan from First National Bank. The loan is not repaid. In most states, Ed is

a. liable only to Digital for the negligent audit.
b. liable to any possible foreseeable user of the statements.
c. liable to the bank if Ed knew the bank would rely on the statements.
d. liable to the bank only if it was in privity of contract with Ed.

___ **3.** Fine Distribution, Inc., includes financial statements prepared by Greg, an accountant, in a registration statement filed with the SEC as part of a public stock offer. Holly buys 100 shares and later suffers losses due to misstatements of fact in the statements. Holly sues Greg under the Securities Act of 1933. Holly will

a. lose, because Holly relied on the statements.
b. lose, if Greg and Holly were not in privity.
c. win, if Greg prepared the statements with knowledge of the misstatements.
d. win, if the misstatements were material.

___ **4.** Dick, an accountant, audits financial statements for Eagle Corporation and issues an unqualified opinion on them. Fran buys 100 shares of Eagle stock and later suffers losses due to misrepresentations in the statements. Fran sues Dick under the Securities Exchange Act of 1934. Fran will

a. lose, because Fran relied on the statements.
b. lose, if Dick and Fran were not in privity.
c. win, if Dick prepared the statements with knowledge of the misstatements.
d. win, if the misstatements were material.

___ **5.** Jack is an accountant. In most states, Jack can be compelled to disclose a client's communication

a. only on a court order.
b. only with the client's permission.
c. under any circumstances.
d. under no circumstances.

___ 6. In auditing Great Sales Corporation's books, Hal is assisted by Ira, a Great Sales employee. Hal does not discover Ira's theft of Great Sales money because Ira hides records that would reveal it. When Ira absconds with the money, Great Sales sues Hall. Great Sales will

a. lose, because Hal could not reasonably have been expected to discover the theft.
b. lose, because Hal is not liable for the results once she has performed.
c. win, because Hal did not discover the theft.
d. win, because Hal did not inform Great Sales of the theft.

___ 7. Carol, an accountant, breaches her contract with Diners Cafe, a local restaurant. Damages that Diners may recover include

a. only penalties imposed for failing to meet deadlines.
b. only the cost to secure the contracted-for services elsewhere.
c. penalties for missing deadlines and the cost to secure services elsewhere.
d. none of the above.

___ 8. Lily is injured in an auto accident, but Mega Insurance, Inc., refuses to pay her claim. She hires Nick, an attorney, who fails to file a suit against Mega before the time for filing runs out. Lily sues Nick. She will

a. lose, because clients are ultimately responsible for such deadlines.
b. lose, because Nick could not reasonably have been expected to file on time.
c. win, because Nick committed malpractice.
d. win, because the insurance company refused to pay her claim.

___ 9. Ace Auto Repairs hires Ben, an accountant, to perform an audit, in the course of which Ben accumulates several hundred pages of notes, computations, and other memoranda. After the audit

a. Ace has the right to retain all working papers.
b. Ben has the right to retain all working papers.
c. the working papers are filed with the SEC.
d. the working papers must be destroyed.

___ 10. Jane is an accountant whom Kay, a former client, charges with negligence. Jane's defenses include

a. only that she was not negligent.
b. only that if she was negligent, it was not the proximate cause of Kay's loss.
c. that she was not negligent, and if she was negligent, it was not the proximate cause of Kay's loss.
d. none of the above.

SHORT ESSAY QUESTIONS

1. Contrast an accountant's past and present potential common law liability to third persons.

2. What is the difference between the attorney-client privilege and the accountant-client privilege?

ISSUE SPOTTERS

(Answers at the Back of the Book)

1. What is a professional liable for, at common law, if he or she *un*intentionally misstates a material fact that misleads a client?

2. Dave, an accountant, prepares a financial statement for Excel Company, a client, knowing that Excel will use the statement to obtain a loan from the First National Bank. Dave makes negligent omissions in the statement that result in a loss to the bank. Can the bank successfully sue Dave?

3. Nora, an accountant, prepares a financial statement as part of a registration statement that Omega, Inc., files with the Securities and Exchange Commission before making a public offering of securities. In the statement is a misstatement of material fact not attributable to Nora's fraud or negligence. Pat relies on the misstatement, buys some of the securities, and suffers a loss. Can Nora be held liable to Pat?

SPECIAL INFORMATION FOR CPA CANDIDATES

Of course, the material in this chapter is part of the CPA examination. Among the most important points for you to know for the test are the accountant's potential tort liability to third parties—of the three basic approaches to liability, the CPA exam has in the past followed the *Ultramares* rule. With respect to liability under the Securities Acts, "mere" negligence is a defense under the 1934 act (which, as you may recall, requires "gross" negligence for liability). With respect to the possible criminal penalties, the CPA exam expects you to know them. Also keep in mind that unless a state provides for an accountant-client privilege, there is none. Related material on professional responsibility tested in the business law portion of the exam is covered in your auditing course.

Chapter 53
International and Comparative Law

WHAT THIS CHAPTER IS ABOUT

This chapter notes sources of international law, some of the ways in which U.S. businesspersons do business in foreign countries, and how that business is regulated. This chapter also compares the legal systems of various nations and specific legal concepts and principles related to contracts, torts, and employment relationships.

CHAPTER OUTLINE

I. INTERNATIONAL LAW

To facilitate commerce, sovereign nations agree to be governed in certain respects by international law.

A. SOURCES OF INTERNATIONAL LAW

1. **International Customs**
These are customs that evolved among nations in their relations with each other. "[E]vidence of a general practice accepted as law" [Article 38(1) of the Statute of the International Court of Justice].

2. **Treaties and International Agreements**
A treaty is an agreement or contract between two or more nations that must be authorized and ratified by the supreme power of each nation. A bilateral agreement occurs when only two nations form an agreement; multilateral agreements are those formed by several nations.

3. **International Organizations and Conferences**
Composed mainly of nations (such as the United Nations); usually established by treaty; such entities adopt resolutions that require particular behavior of nations (such as the 1980 United Nations Convention on Contracts for the International Sale of Goods).

B. LEGAL PRINCIPLES AND DOCTRINES

The following are based on courtesy and respect and are applied in the interest of maintaining harmony among nations.

1. **The Principle of Comity**
One nation defers and gives effect to the laws and judicial decrees of another country, so long as those laws and judicial decrees are consistent with the law and public policy of the accommodating nation.

2. **The Act of State Doctrine**
A doctrine under which the judicial branch of one country will not examine the validity of public acts committed by a recognized foreign government within its own territory. Often used in cases involving—

   a. **Expropriation**
   This occurs when a government seizes a privately owned business or goods for a proper public purpose and pays just compensation.

   b. **Confiscation**
   This occurs when a government seizes private property for an illegal purpose or without just compensation.

3. **The Doctrine of Sovereign Immunity**
Exempts foreign nations from the jurisdiction of domestic courts. In the United States, the Foreign Sovereign Immunities Act (FSIA) of 1976 exclusively governs the circumstances in which an action may be brought against a foreign nation.

a. **When Is a Foreign State Subject to U.S. Jurisdiction?**
When it has waived its immunity, or when the action is based on commercial activity in the U.S. by the foreign state [Section 1605].

b. **What Entities Fall within the Category of Foreign State?**
A political subdivision and an instrumentality (an agency or entity acting for the state) [Section 1603].

c. **What Is a Commercial Activity?**
Courts decide whether an activity is governmental or commercial.

II. DOING BUSINESS INTERNATIONALLY

A. INTERNATIONAL BUSINESS OPERATIONS

1. **Exporting**
The simplest way to do business internationally is to export to foreign markets. *Direct exporting*: signing a sales contract with a foreign buyer. *Indirect exporting*: selling directly to consumers through a foreign agent or foreign distributor.

2. **Manufacturing Abroad**
A domestic firm can establish a manufacturing plant abroad by—

a. **Licensing**
A firm may license its technology to a foreign manufacturer to avoid the process, product, or formula being pirated. The foreign firm agrees to keep the technology secret and to pay royalties for its use.

b. **Franchising**
Franchising (see Chapter 35) is a form of licensing in which the owner of a trademark, trade name, or copyright conditions its use in the selling of goods or services.

c. **Investing in a Wholly Owned Subsidiary or a Joint Venture**
When a wholly owned subsidiary is established, the domestic firm retains ownership of the foreign facilities and control over the entire operation. In a joint venture, a domestic firm and one or more foreign firms share responsibilities, profits, and liabilities.

B. REGULATION OF INTERNATIONAL BUSINESS ACTIVITIES

1. **Investing**
For property confiscated by a government without just compensation, few remedies are available. Many countries guarantee compensation to foreign investors in their constitutions, statutes, or treaties. Some countries provide insurance for their citizens' investments abroad.

2. **Export Control**

a. **Restricting Exports**
Under the Constitution, Congress cannot tax exports, but may set quotas. Under the Export Administration Act of 1979, restrictions can be imposed on the flow of technologically advanced products and technical data.

b. **Stimulating Exports**
Devices to stimulate exports include incentives and subsidies.

3. **Import Control**
Laws prohibit, for example, importing illegal drugs and agricultural products that pose dangers to domestic crops or animals.

a. **Quotas and Tariffs**
Quotas limit how much can be imported. Tariffs are taxes on imports (a percentage of the value or a flat rate per unit).

b. **Antidumping Duties**
A tariff (duty) may be assessed on imports to prevent dumping (sales of imported goods at "less than fair value," usually determined by prices in the exporting country).

4. **International Organizations and Agreements**

a. **World Trade Organization (WTO)**
This the principal instrument for regulating international trade. Each member country agrees to grant *most-favored-nation status* to other members (the most favorable treatment with regard to trade).

b. **European Union (EU)**
The EU is a regional trade association that minimizes trade barriers among its European member nations.

c. **North American Free Trade Agreement (NAFTA)**
NAFTA created a regional trading unit consisting of Mexico, the United States, and Canada. The goal is to eliminate tariffs in the region on substantially all goods over a period of fifteen to twenty years, while retaining tariffs on goods imported from other countries.

III. COMPARATIVE LAW
Comparative law is the study of legal systems and laws across nations.

A. COMPARATIVE LEGAL SYSTEMS

1. **Common Law and Civil Law Systems**
Legal systems are generally divided into common law and civil law systems.

a. **Common Law Systems**
Common law systems are based on case law. These systems exist in countries that were once a part of the British Empire (such as Australia, India, and the United States). The judges of different common law nations have produced differing common law principles.

b. **Civil Law Systems**
Civil law systems are based on codified law (statutes). Courts interpret the code and apply the rules without developing their own laws. Civil law systems exist in most European nations, in Latin American, African, and Asian countries that were colonies of those nations; Japan; South Africa; Muslim countries; and Louisiana.

c. **Similarities between Common and Civil Law Systems**
Much of the law in a common law system is statutory. In a civil law system, judges must develop some law because codes cannot address every issue.

d. **Differences among Common Law Systems**
The judges of different common law nations have produced differing common law principles. For example, the principles governing contracts differ in the United States and India.

e. **Differences among Civil Law Systems**
The French code sets out general principles of law; the German code is more specific. In some Middle Eastern countries, the code is grounded in religious, Islamic directives, known as *shari'a*. This makes it difficult to change.

B. JUDGES AND PROCEDURES
In all countries, the primary function of judges is the resolution of litigation.

1. **Differences among Judges**
In the United States, a judge normally does not actively participate in a trial, but in many countries, judges are involved, such as by questioning witnesses. In the United States, a federal judge is less likely to be influenced by politics (he or she serves for life and cannot be removed by impeachment except in extreme cases). In India, judges ruling contrary to the prime minister have been transferred or demoted.

2. **Differences among Procedures**
The procedures employed to resolve cases varies from country to country. For example, in Saudi Arabia, a defendant can "demand the oath"—swear before God that he did not do what he is charged with doing—and be released.

C. NATIONAL LAWS COMPARED
Even when statutory language is similar, application of the law varies among nations.

1. **Tort Law**
Tort law allows persons to recover damages for harms or injuries caused by the wrongful actions of others (see Chapters 5 and 6).

a. **Failure to Act**
In Germany, one is normally not liable for failing to rescue someone in distress. Some nations provide liability for negligent omissions.

b. **Damages**
Swiss and Turkish courts reduce damages if an award of full damages would cause undue hardship to a party who was found negligent. In some nations of northern Africa, different amounts of damages are awarded depending on the type of tort.

c. **Statutes of Limitations**
Generally, the period is longer than in the United States.

d. **Burden of Proof**
In the United States, the burden of proof is on the plaintiff. In Russia, the defendant must prove that he or she was not at fault.

2. **Contract Law**
For requirements of contracts in the United States, see Chapters 10–14.

a. **United Nations Convention for the International Sale of Goods**
Some contract law has been internationalized through the CISG (see Chapter 19), but parties can agree to apply other law.

b. **Agreement (Offer and Acceptance)**
In Germany, a written offer must be held open for a reasonable time, unless the offer states otherwise. Oral offers must be accepted immediately or they expire. In Mexico, if a time for acceptance is not stated in an offer, the offer is deemed held open for three days (plus whatever time is necessary for the mails).

c. **Consideration**
In Germany, consideration is not required for a contract to be binding—agreements to make gifts may thus be enforceable by the recipient. In India, some contracts are lawful in the absence of consideration, such as promises in exchange for a past act.

d. **Remedies**
Germany's typical remedy for breach of contract is specific performance (breaching party does what was promised). In the United States, this is granted only if the remedy of damages (money) is inadequate.

e. **Defenses**
Defenses include lack of a writing (United States, Saudi Arabia) or witnesses (Saudi Arabia), and lack of consideration (India).

3. **Employment Law**
Under the employment-at-will doctrine (see Chapter 33), employers can hire and fire employees "at will" (for any reason or no reason).

a. **Reasons for Discharging Employees**
Employers may fire employees without notice only for causes such as violence, imprisonment, excessive absenteeism, or lying on a job application (Taiwan), or if the worker commits a criminal offense, loses a license or other employment qualification, or seriously breaches his or her duties (Poland).

b. **Discharge Procedures**
In some countries, to discharge an employee for cause, an employer must first submit the proposed discharge to mediators (France) or a committee (Egypt).

c. **Wages and Benefits**
Wages are typically lower in other countries, but workers are often entitled to more paid time off.

d. **Equal Employment Opportunity**
In Indonesia, Japan, and Mexico, employers cannot discriminate against employees or job applicants on some bases. Discrimination is not prohibited in Argentina, Brazil, Egypt, or Turkey.

D. CULTURAL AND BUSINESS TRADITIONS

1. **Communication**
Language differences and different understandings of body movements, gestures, facial expressions, colors, and numbers can confound efforts to do business abroad. For example, advertising slogans translated word-for-word may be nonsense in other languages.

2. **Ethics**

a. **Gift Giving and Bribery**
In many countries, gift giving is common among companies or between companies and government. U.S. firms are prohibited from offering payments to foreign officials to secure favorable contracts (see Chapter 42). Payments to minor officials to, for example, facilitate paperwork are not prohibited.

b. **Women in Business**
Some countries reject any role for women professionals. Others impose cultural restrictions. For this reason, a U.S. company may be reluctant to assign women to work overseas. Equal employment opportunity is a basic policy in the United States, however (see Chapter 34).

TRUE-FALSE QUESTIONS

(Answers at the Back of the Book)

___ 1. All nations must give effect to the laws of all other nations.

___ 2. Under the act of state doctrine, foreign nations are subject to the jurisdiction of U.S. courts.

___ 3. Under the doctrine of sovereign immunity, foreign nations are subject to the jurisdiction of U.S. courts.

___ 4. The Foreign Sovereign Immunities Act states the circumstances in which the United States can be sued in foreign courts.

___ 5. A member of the World Trade Organization must usually grant other members most-favored nation status, with regard to trade.

___ 6. U.S. firms are prohibited from offering payments to foreign officials to secure favorable contracts.

___ 7. Legal systems are generally divided into criminal law and civil law systems.

___ 8. In all countries, the primary function of judges is the resolution of litigation.

___ 9. All international contracts are subject exclusively to the CISG.

___ 10. Congress cannot tax exports.

FILL-IN QUESTIONS

(Answers at the Back of the Book)

________________ (A confiscation/An expropriation) occurs when a national government seizes a privately owned business or privately owned goods for a proper public purpose. ________________ (A confiscation/An expropriation) occurs when the taking is made for an illegal purpose. When ________________ (a confiscation/an expropriation) occurs, the government pays just compensation. When ________________ (a confiscation/an expropriation) occurs, the government does not pay just compensation.

MULTIPLE-CHOICE QUESTIONS

(Answers at the Back of the Book)

___ 1. Kenya issues bonds to finance the construction of an international airport. Kenya sells some of the bonds in the United States to Larry. A terrorist group destroys the airport, and Kenya refuses to pay interest or principal on the bonds. Larry files suit in a U.S court. The court will hear the suit if Kenya

a. in effect confiscated Larry's funds when it refused to pay on the bonds.
b. in effect expropriated Larry's funds when it refused to pay on the bonds.
c. is a "foreign state" and selling bonds is a "commercial activity."
d. none of the above.

___ 2. To install new computers in government offices, Mexico accepts bids from U.S. firms, including Alpha, Inc., and Beta Corporation. Alpha wins the contract. Beta sues Alpha in a U.S. court, on the ground that its sole shareholder is the brother of the wife of Mexico's minister of commerce. The U.S. court

a. cannot rule on the legality of the contract under the act of state doctrine.
b. cannot rule on the legality of the contract under the principle of commercial relations.
c. must hold the contract illegal under the act of state doctrine.
d. must hold the contract illegal under the principle of commercial relations.

___ **3.** A U.S. buyer breaches a contract with a Polish seller. The seller sues in a Polish court and wins damages, but the buyer's assets are in the United States. A U.S. court may enforce the judgment under

a. the act of state doctrine.
b. the doctrine of sovereign immunity.
c. the principle of comity.
d. the principle of commercial relations.

___ **4.** Digital, Inc., makes supercomputers that feature advanced technology. To inhibit Digital's export of its products to other countries, Congress can

a. confiscate all profits on exported supercomputers.
b. expropriate all profits on exported supercomputers.
c. set quotas on exported supercomputers.
d. tax exported supercomputers.

___ **5.** MotorCorp manufactures cars in the United States. To boost the sales of MotorCorp and other domestic car manufacturers, Congress can

a. only set quotas on imported vehicles.
b. only tax imported vehicles.
c. set quotas and tax imports.
d. none of the above.

___ **6.** The United States has a common law legal system. Common law systems are based on

a. administrative rules and regulations.
b. case law.
c. codified law.
d. executive pronouncements.

___ **7.** France has a civil law legal system. Civil law systems are based on

a. administrative rules and regulations.
b. case law.
c. codified law.
d. executive pronouncements.

___ **8.** Nora is a judge in the United States. As a U.S. judge, Nora normally

a. actively participates in a trial.
b. does not actively participate in a trial.
c. is expected to question witnesses in a trial.
d. is influenced by politics.

___ **9.** Adam and Beth are citizens of different countries. A dispute arises between the two parties concerning their contract. In the area of contract law

a. some of the basic principles are similar among nations, but some are very different.
b. there are so few differences among nations that the law is, for all practical purposes, uniform.
c. there are no basic principles that any two nations share.
d. there is a law enforced by the United Nations that applies to all international contracts.

____ **10.** Maria believes that she is a victim of employment discrimination. Discrimination in employment is

a. not prohibited in any country.
b. prohibited in all countries.
c. prohibited in some countries.
d. required in all countries.

SHORT ESSAY QUESTIONS

1. In what ways may a company conduct international business?

2. How does the Foreign Sovereign Immunities Act affect commercial activities by foreign governments?

ISSUE SPOTTERS

(Answers at the Back of the Book)

1. Cafe Rojo, Ltd., a Colombian firm, agrees to sell coffee beans to Java Corporation, a U.S. company. Java accepts the beans, but refuses to pay. Cafe Rojo sues Java in a Colombian court and is awarded damages, but Java's assets are in the United States. Under what circumstances would a U.S. court enforce the Colombian court's judgment?

2. Hi-Cola Corporation, a U.S. company, markets a popular soft drink. The formula is secret, but with careful chemical analysis, its ingredients could be discovered. What can Hi-Cola do to prevent its product from being pirated abroad?

3. Gems International, Ltd., is a foreign firm that has a 12-percent share of the U.S. market for diamonds. To capture a larger share, Gems offers its products at a below-cost discount to U.S. buyers (and inflates the prices in its own country to make up the difference). How can this attempt to undersell U.S. businesses be defeated?

SPECIAL INFORMATION FOR CPA CANDIDATES

Most of the material in this chapter is not covered in the CPA examination (although in the business world, an accountant will likely encounter many aspects of international business and law). The Foreign Corrupt Practices Act has been tested in the securities portion of the exam.

The CPA examination is designed to test technical competence in at least three areas: (1) technical knowledge and the application of this knowledge, (2) an understanding of professional responsibilities, and (3) the exercise of good judgment. The material in this chapter can contribute to an understanding of the law as it applies in all three of these areas. This chapter provides background to a study of business law by underscoring the point that the law is not static. This material illustrates that the law changes—from time to time and from place to place within a given time. Basic principles may change only slowly and over relatively long periods of time, but there is otherwise the same fluidity in the law as there is in any other field of knowledge.

Overall, in the past, the CPA exam has tested heavily in the following areas of business law: contracts, sales, commercial paper, bankruptcy, agency, partnerships, corporations, securities, accountant's professional liability, and real and personal property. The CPA exam has tested less heavily in these areas: documents of title, secured transactions, suretyship, employment laws, insurance, and estates and trusts.

Chapter 54
Law for Small Business

WHAT THIS CHAPTER IS ABOUT

For entrepreneurs, business law takes on special significance, in part because of the small size of most entrepreneurial businesses. This chapter covers some aspects of the law as it applies in that context.

CHAPTER OUTLINE

I. THE IMPORTANCE OF LEGAL COUNSEL

A. FINDING AN ATTORNEY
Sources include friends, business associates, other entrepreneurs, business networks (chambers of commerce or bar organizations), Yellow Pages, *Martindale-Hubbell Law Directory* (available in libraries or at http://www.martindale.com).

B. INTERVIEWING AND EVALUATING ATTORNEYS
Ask: did the attorney seem knowledgeable about what you need? Did he or she seem willing to investigate the relevant law? Did you communicate well with each other? Did the attorney perceive what issues were of foremost concern and address those issues?

C. RETAINING AN ATTORNEY
Benefits of retaining an attorney include the lawyer's contacts (such as potential investors), business expertise, confidentiality of attorney-client communications, and flexibility of payment plans (for example, regular monthly billing, as opposed to one-time lump sum).

D. RETAINING AN ACCOUNTANT
A professional accountant is more expensive than bookkeeping software, but may be more accurate and adds to credibility with investors.

II. SELECTING AN APPROPRIATE BUSINESS FORM

Factors to consider when choosing a business form (see Chapters 35–41) include:

A. LIMITATIONS ON LIABILITY
Some business forms limit liability if, for example, a court awards damages to a customer injured on the premises (the owner is not personally liable). Corporations, limited partnerships, limited liability corporations (LLCs), and limited liability partnerships (LLPs) limit personal liability.

B. TAX CONSIDERATIONS

1. Sole Proprietorships
A sole proprietor pays taxes on business income as an individual.

2. Partnerships
Partnerships do not pay tax, but the partners pay income tax on the firm's profits.

3. Corporations
Most corporations pay double taxes (the corporation pays tax on profits, and the shareholders pay tax on distributions). S corporations and LLCs are taxed like partnerships.

C. Continuity of Life

In most cases, corporations survive their owners. In a partnership, the death or withdrawal of a partner may terminate the partnership unless the partners have expressly provided otherwise. A sole proprietorship ends with the death of the sole proprietor.

D. Legal Formality and Expense

1. Benefits of Formal Business Arrangements

These include an agreement setting out ownership rights if a dispute arises, and the advantages (or disadvantages) provided by existing statutes and case law relating to particular business forms.

2. Forms That Avoid Formality and Expense

Sole proprietorships and general partnerships avoid formalities and expense of incorporating or creating a limited partnership.

3. All Businesses

Any business must meet such legal requirements as business name registration, occupational licensing, state tax registration, health and environmental permits, zoning and building codes, import/export regulations, and laws governing the workplace.

III. CREATING THE BUSINESS ENTITY

There are no special requirements for creating a sole proprietorship. A general partnership requires only an agreement between the partners. Forming a limited partnership or corporation (see Chapter 34) is more complicated.

A. Choosing a Corporate Name

The name must be different from those of existing businesses (even unincorporated businesses) and should include the word *corporation, company,* or *incorporated*. It should be filed with the appropriate state office (usually secretary of state) to protect it as a trade name in the state.

B. Articles of Incorporation, Bylaws, and Initial Meetings

1. Articles of Incorporation

States vary with respect to what provisions must be included in the articles. S corporations must file additional forms with the IRS and (in most states) with the appropriate state agency.

2. Bylaws

Include provisions for the dates on which annual meetings will be held, terms for voting quorums, and other rules.

3. Initial Meeting

Directors adopt bylaws, appoint corporate officers and define their authority, issue stock, open bank accounts, take other necessary steps.

C. Creating a Corporate Records Book

Organizes important documents, such as articles of incorporation and minutes of director and shareholder meetings. Stock certificates may need to be created and a corporate seal may need to be obtained.

IV. INTELLECTUAL PROPERTY

Protecting rights in intellectual property (see Chapter 7) is a central concern to some new businesses, such as software companies.

A. Choosing and Protecting a Trademark

A trademark cannot be too similar to another mark or mislead customers to think that someone else made a product. Generally, the first to use a trademark owns it.

1. **Choosing a Trademark**
   A mark should be distinctive (for example, a made-up word such as Exxon or Kodak). Name-consulting companies help in selecting marks, but may be too expensive for small business entrepreneurs.

2. **Undertaking a Trademark Search**
   To ensure that a mark is not too similar to existing marks, check the Yellow Pages in the relevant area, consult *Gale's List of Tradenames*, look at the federal and state trademark registers, etc.

3. **Registering a Trademark**
   A trademark can be registered with the U.S. Patent and Trademark Office (PTO). This provides nationwide protection for a mark that is in use or will be within six months. If a logo consists of a distinctive name as well as a graphic, each can be registered independently.

4. **Protecting a Trademark**

   a. **Symbols to Put Others on Notice**
      If a mark is federally registered, the symbol ® may be used. If a mark is not registered, the symbol ™ can be used.

   b. **Renewal of Registration**
      Five years after the initial registration, registration may be renewed, and every ten years thereafter.

   c. **Abandonment**
      Allowing others to use a mark without restrictions or without protest can constitute abandonment. Abandonment is presumed if a mark registered with the PTO is not used for two years.

B. PROTECTING TRADE SECRETS

1. **What a Trade Secret Is**
   Trade secrets (see Chapter 7) are anything that makes an individual company unique and that would have value to a competitor.

2. **What a Firm Can Do to Protect Its Trade Secrets**
   Require employees to agree not to (1) divulge trade secrets, and (2) work for a competitor, or set up a competing business, in which the company's trade secrets will likely be disclosed.

V. RAISING FINANCIAL CAPITAL

A. LOANS

Capital can be raised through a bank loan, but this may not be possible for many entrepreneurs. Loans may be available from the Small Business Administration (SBA).

B. VENTURE CAPITAL

Most new businesses raise capital by exchanging ownership rights (equity) in the firm for capital (the investor may be called a venture capitalist).

1. **Procedure**
   Plan describing company, products, and anticipated performance is presented; investor examines the firm's books and assets (the investor should sign a confidentiality agreement not to disclose trade secrets).

2. **Points for Negotiation**
   These include the terms of financing, how much ownership and control the venture capitalist will receive, type and quantity of stock, and related issues.

C. SECURITIES REGULATION

When an investor exchanges capital for an interest in an enterprise and the interest consists of shares of stock (or otherwise qualifies as a security—see Chapter 40), it is subject to securities laws.

1. Private Offering

A limited amount of money can be raised from a limited number of investors without registering shares as securities with the Securities and Exchange Commission.

2. Public Offering

Making shares available for purchase by members of the public is highly regulated (but may raise a lot of capital). The securities must be registered. A simplified registration form for small businesses is the Small Corporate Offering Registration (SCOR).

VI. BUY-SELL AGREEMENTS AND KEY-PERSON INSURANCE

For any enterprise, a written agreement establishes what happens if partners or shareholders die, go bankrupt, get divorced, have their ownership interest attached, become disabled, or are so at odds that they cannot work together.

A. BUY-SELL AGREEMENT (KEY TERM OF SHAREHOLDER AGREEMENT)

Enables buy-out of a shareholder and provides for the price to be paid. Might include (1) a right of first refusal (prevents sale to a third party without first giving the other owners a right to buy), or (2) a "take-along" right (allows an investor to participate in sale of shares to a third party).

B. KEY-PERSON INSURANCE

This protects against the risk that a key person (manager, for example) may become disabled or die and (see Chapter 50) helps to cover losses caused by the death or disability.

VII. CONTRACT LAW AND THE ENTREPRENEUR

A. BASIC CONTRACT PRINCIPLES APPLY

Basic contract law (see Chapters 9 through 18) applies to leases and sales of real property and equipment. A contract should be in writing in case of a dispute, or in some cases (see Chapter 14) so it can be enforced.

B. AGENCY PRINCIPLES APPLY

If a firm is organized in a form other than a sole proprietorship, persons who sign contracts or negotiable instruments (Chapter 26) on its behalf will want to do so as agents to avoid personal liability.

VIII. CREDIT AND PAYMENT

A. FREE SHIPPING AND PRICE DISCOUNTS

To encourage prompt payment or payment in advance, a firm may offer free shipping or price discounts.

B. LATE CHARGES AND INTEREST

To get customers to pay on time, a firm may assess late charges. If a firm charges interest on overdue balances, the Truth-in-Lending Act may require certain disclosures (see Chapter 44).

C. COLLECTION OF OVERDUE DEBTS

A contract may provide that a buyer is responsible for all costs to collect overdue payments. State debt-collection laws typically prevent the use of abusive efforts, such as threatening individuals.

IX. EMPLOYMENT ISSUES

A. HIRING EMPLOYEES

Some important considerations are:

1. **Disclosure of Trade Secrets**
Employees should not disclose trade secrets of former (or current) employers.

2. **Promises of Job Security**
Employees should not unintentionally be promised job security. (Such promises can be implied from statements in employment manuals.) All terms could be put in writing (for example, that employment is at-will—see Chapter 33), including grounds for termination.

3. **Screening Applicants**
If appropriate, an applicant may be required to take a drug test. Credentials and job experience should be verified (to avoid a negligent-hiring lawsuit—for example, hiring someone as a driver who has no driver's license).

4. **Compliance with INS Requirements**
The Immigration and Naturalization Service (INS) has certain requirements with respect to employing noncitizens.

B. EMPLOYEE COMPENSATION

1. **Fair Labor Standards Act (FLSA)**
The FLSA applies to businesses with $500,000 or more in sales or engaged in interstate commerce and requires minimum wage, plus time-and-a-half for overtime (with exceptions), and wage and hour records.

2. **State Law**
May require a meal break or rest breaks.

C. WORKERS' COMPENSATION INSURANCE

In most states, an employee injured in the course of employment receives workers' compensation (and cannot sue the employer for more). Employers pay premiums for this insurance based in part on their safety records.

D. UNEMPLOYMENT COMPENSATION

Unemployment compensation (see Chapter 33) tax rates are based in part on the size of a payroll and the number of claimants. Compensation is not payable if an employee quits a job or is fired for misconduct.

E. FIRING EMPLOYEES

1. **Wrongful Termination**

a. **Employment Contracts**
Unless otherwise specified, an employee can be fired for any reason. If termination is in bad faith, an employee may bring an action for wrongful discharge. Defense: having good cause for termination.

b. **Antidiscrimination Laws**
Employers with fewer than fifteen employees are not covered by federal antidiscrimination laws, but may be covered by state laws.

2. **Severance Pay**
Severance pay is not required, but most states specify when an employee must be given his or her final paycheck.

3. **Employer's False Statements to Others**
An employer may be liable for (1) defamation if a negative false statement is made to others (such as other employers) about the reason for an employee's termination, or (2) misrepresentation if a positive false statement is made about the employee.

F. COVENANTS NOT TO COMPETE
Covenants not to compete (see Chapter 12) are generally enforceable so long as they are not unreasonably restrictive in terms of time or geographic area.

G. USING INDEPENDENT CONTRACTORS
Independent contractors are not employees (see Chapter 31) and an employer cannot control how they do their work.

1. **Taxes**
Income taxes and Social Security/Medicare taxes do not have to be withheld or paid. Employers need not pay premiums for workers' compensation insurance or unemployment insurance.

2. **Antidiscrimination Laws**
An independent contractor cannot sue an employer for discrimination.

3. **Misclassification of Employees as Independent Contractors**
If a government agency determines that workers are employees, not independent contractors, there may be tax liability and penalties.

TRUE-FALSE QUESTIONS

(Answers at the Back of the Book)

____ 1. The most important factor is choosing an attorney is the price.

____ 2. In most cases, corporations survive their owners.

____ 3. A corporation's name can be the same as that of another existing business.

____ 4. Allowing others to use a trademark without protesting that use can constitute abandonment of the mark.

____ 5. No money can be raised through an offering of stock without registering the shares as securities with the Securities and Exchange Commission.

____ 6. Key-person insurance helps to cover business losses caused by the death or disability of an essential employee.

____ 7. No contract needs to be in writing to be enforceable.

____ 8. To charge interest on an overdue account, a business must make certain disclosures relating to those charges before entering into the contract.

____ 9. An employer's promises of job security are never binding.

____ 10. If appropriate, a job applicant can be required to take a drug test.

FILL-IN QUESTIONS

(Answers at the Back of the Book)

An employer must withhold and pay federal and state income taxes and Social Security/Medicare taxes for ____________________ (employees/independent contractors/employees and independent contractors). An employer must pay premiums for workers' compensation insurance and unemployment insurance to cover ____________________ (employees/independent contractors/employees and independent contractors). An employer can be sued for discrimination by ____________________ (employees/independent contractors/employees and independent contractors).

MULTIPLE-CHOICE QUESTIONS

(Answers at the Back of the Book)

___ 1. Ann is starting a financial planning business. She hires Bob, an attorney, to handle the initial paperwork. The advantages of retaining an attorney at this point in a business include the lawyer's

a. business contacts only.
b. confidentiality only.
c. legal and business expertise only.
d. business contacts, confidentiality, and legal and business expertise.

___ 2. Carol is starting a business to design and maintain Web sites on the Internet. Carol can avoid all business-related legal requirements if she organizes the business as

a. a partnership only.
b. a sole proprietorship only.
c. a partnership or a sole proprietorship.
d. none of the above.

___ 3. Dave and Earl decide to open a restaurant and operate the business as a corporation. At the directors' initial meeting, the directors may

a. adopt articles of incorporation only.
b. adopt bylaws only.
c. choose a corporate name only.
d. adopt articles of incorporation and bylaws and choose a corporate name.

___ 4. Fran starts a business to market nationally an exercise package called Fran's Fitness. Registering her trademark with the U.S. Patent and Trademark Office provides nationwide protection for the mark

a. only if the mark is currently in use.
b. only if the mark is not yet in use but will be within six months.
c. if the mark is currently in use or will be in use within six months.
d. under any circumstances.

___ 5. Gary designs a new baseball bat and incorporates Big G Bats, Inc., to make and market it. To sell a limited number of shares of stock in Big G Bats to the public, Gary must register the shares with

a. an attorney with securities law expertise.
b. a venture capitalist.
c. the Securities and Exchange Commission.
d. no one.

___ 6. **Based on a Sample CPA Exam Question.** Adam goes into business as Best Goods, Inc., to sell goods throughout the United States. The Fair Labor Standards Act regulates

a. only Best's employees' minimum wages and overtime pay.
b. only the records of the hours in Best's employees' workweek.
c. Best's employees' minimum wages, overtime pay, and recorded hours.
d. none of the above.

___ **7.** Holly's job is to buy supplies for Interstate Corporation. To avoid personal liability for contracts signed on Interstate's behalf, Holly must sign

a. as an agent only.
b. as a party to the contract only.
c. as an agent and a party to the contract.
d. none of the above.

___ **8.** To encourage its customers to pay on time, Alpha Company may provide in its contracts that

a. Alpha may resort to abusive efforts to collect overdue accounts.
b. the customer is responsible for all collection costs on overdue accounts.
c. both a and b.
d. none of the above.

___ **9.** Beta, Inc., fires Carl, who applies to Gamma Company for a job. Gamma asks Beta to make a statement about the reason for Carl's termination. Beta might be held liable for making

a. a negative statement only.
b. a positive statement only.
c. a negative statement or a positive statement.
d. none of the above.

___ **10.** The four shareholders of Delta, Inc., want to prevent each other from selling the shares to third parties without first being given the opportunity to buy them. The shareholders can provide for this in

a. a buy-sell agreement that includes a "take-along" clause.
b. a buy-sell agreement that includes a right of first refusal.
c. a key-person clause that specifies who can sell what to whom.
d. none of the above.

SHORT ESSAY QUESTIONS

1. What are the primary factors to consider when choosing a business form?

2. What are some of the important considerations in discharging an employee?

ISSUE SPOTTERS

(Answers at the Back of the Book)

1. Dian has been running Eagle Services as a sole proprietorship, but would now like to limit her liability for the firm's obligations. What organizational form might Dian want to adopt for Eagle?

2. Omega, Inc., sells parts and service to local Internet access providers. How can Omega prevent its employees from revealing its customer lists and pricing policies if the employees go to work for a competitor or go into the same business for themselves?

3. Adam opened his first Bagels & Coffee shop four years ago. To open shops in more locations, Adam needs capital and wants to attract investors. How can he do this?

SPECIAL INFORMATION FOR CPA CANDIDATES

The CPA requires knowledge of some of the concepts discussed in this chapter. Many of these topics are discussed in more detail in other chapters. For example, for the exam, it is important to understand the differences among the basic forms of business organizations. These forms and their differences are discussed in more detail in Chapters 35 through 41. Securities law is an important part of the exam and is covered in detail in Chapter 40. Employment topics that may be part of the exam include unemployment compensation, workers' compensation, and the Fair Labor Standards Act (see Chapter 33). For specific information about the relevance, as regards the CPA exam, of other topics discussed in other chapters, see those chapters.

CUMULATIVE HYPOTHETICAL PROBLEM FOR UNIT ELEVEN—INCLUDING CHAPTERS 50–54

(Answers at the Back of the Book)

Earl, in his will, establishes a trust and designates First National Bank to be the trustee. The property of the trust includes warehouses and other commercial property.

___ **1.** On a warehouse, the trustee obtains a $300,000 fire insurance policy from American Insurance Company that includes an 80 percent coinsurance clause. At the time, the warehouse is valued at $400,000. When the warehouse is valued at $500,000, it sustains fire damage of $60,000. Recovery under the policy is

a. $45,000.
b. $60,000.
c. $75,000.
d. $300,000.

___ **2.** While operating as the trustee, the bank incurs charges that include ordinary expenses and extraordinary expenses. These are allocated

a. entirely to income.
b. entirely to principal.
c. extraordinary expenses to income and ordinary expenses to principal.
d. ordinary expenses to income and extraordinary expenses to principal.

___ **3.** On behalf of the trust, the trustee loans money to General Sales, Inc. (GSI). Hugh, an accountant, audited GSI's financial statements. The bank files a suit against Hugh based on fraud. Hugh's best defense is

a. a disclaimer included with the financial statements.
b. contributory negligence on the part of GSI.
c. lack of privity between Hugh and the trust.
d. lack of reliance on the statements on the part of the bank.

___ **4.** The bank retains Irma, an outside accountant, to prepare the trust's federal tax forms. The bank asks Irma to help it evade some of the taxes by providing false information. If Irma helps the bank, she may be subject to

a. federal criminal prosecution only.
b. an injunction prohibiting her from acting as a tax preparer only.
c. federal criminal prosecution and an injunction.
d. none of the above.

___ **5.** Jill, an accountant, prepares financial statements for a registration statement for Mega Industries, Inc. To be successful against Jill in a civil action under the Securities Act of 1933 for misleading statements in the registration statement, the trustee must prove

a. Jill's intent to deceive only.
b. the bank's reliance on the registration statement only.
c. Jill's intent to deceive and the bank's reliance on the registration statement.
d. none of the above.

QUESTIONS ON THE FOCUS ON LEGAL REASONING FOR UNIT ELEVEN— *OVERTON V. CONSOLIDATED INSURANCE CO.*

(Answers at the Back of the Book)

___ **1.** Dan believes that his property may be polluted and buys a property insurance policy from Eagle Insurance Company. Later, he learns that the property is polluted and must be cleaned up. He files a claim under the policy. According to the majority in *Overton v. Consolidated Insurance Co.*, Eagle

a. must pay the entire claim.
b. must pay the part of the claim that represents Dan's part of the pollution.
c. must pay the part of the claim that previous owners' insurers do not pay.
d. need not pay any part of the claim.

___ **2.** Under the facts in the previous question, according to the dissent in *Overton v. Consolidated Insurance Co.*, Eagle

a. must pay the entire claim.
b. must pay the part of the claim that represents Dan's part of the pollution.
c. must pay the part of the claim that previous owners' insurers do not pay.
d. need not pay any part of the claim.

___ **3.** Suppose that in the previous questions, Eagle is not charged with paying Dan's claim. This means that the clean-up costs must be borne by

a. Dan only.
b. the federal or state government only.
c. the property's prior owners only.
d. the responsible parties, which may include Dan and the prior owners.

QUESTIONS ON THE FOCUS ON ETHICS FOR UNIT ELEVEN— SPECIAL TOPICS

(Answers at the Back of the Book)

___ **1.** Standard Insurance Company includes in its policies a clause that states the insurer cannot contest statements made in the application after the policy has been in force for two years. This is

a. a limitations clause.
b. a misrepresentation clause.
c. an incontestability clause.
d. a non-repudiation clause.

____ **2.** Paul is an insurance agent. As an agent, Paul is liable for failing to advise a client of

a. every possible insurance option.
b. every reasonable insurance option.
c. every significant insurance option.
d. none of the above.

____ **3.** Eve is an accountant. As an accountant, Eve may be liable for violations of

a. consumer protection statutes only.
b. securities laws only.
c. tax laws only.
d. consumer protection statutes, securities laws, and tax laws.

Business Law for the Uniform CPA Examination

THE UNIFORM CPA EXAMINATION

To obtain a Certified Public Accountant (CPA) certificate or license, accountants must meet certain requirements. State boards of accountancy set these requirements. In every state, one of the requirements is passing the Uniform CPA Examination. The Board of Examiners of the American Institute of Certified Public Accountants (AICPA) is responsible for the preparation and advisory grading of the Uniform CPA Examination. The examination, which is given over a two-day period twice a year (in May and November), contains four sections: business law and professional responsibilities, auditing, accounting and reporting (taxation, managerial, and governmental not-for-profit organizations), and financial accounting and reporting.

The business law and professional responsibilities portion of the examination is given on the first day of the examination—Wednesday—from 9 A.M. until noon. The format consists of questions in a multiple-choice or other objective format and essay or problem-type questions. The multiple-choice questions are similar to some of the multiple-choice questions in this *Study Guide*. Normally, essay questions have two or more parts that test candidates' knowledge of different business law topics. Generally, an essay question consists of a fact situation involving a number of legal issues. Candidates are expected to discuss these issues and should provide reasons for their conclusions.

Distinctions about subject matter are not always clear-cut. That is, there may be some overlap of subjects within the four sections of the examination and within the seven areas of the business law section of the examination. For instance, the factual situation in a business law question may require knowledge of accounting or auditing, and the answers may involve a response based in part on this knowledge.

THE SUBJECT MATTER OF THE UNIFORM CPA EXAMINATION

Knowledge of business law is necessary to pass the test. Detailed information about the subject matter of the examination and the approximate percentage of the examination devoted to each of seven broad topics is provided in specifications adopted by the Board of Examiners of the AICPA. The business law and professional responsibilities section tests the candidates' knowledge of the legal implications of business transactions, particularly as they relate to accounting and auditing, and candidates' knowledge of the CPA's professional responsibilities to the public and the profession.

As outlined by the Board of Examiners of the AICPA, the section includes a CPA's professional responsibilities, business organizations, contracts, debtor-creditor relationships, government regulation of business, the Uniform Commercial Code, and property. The subjects on the examination normally are covered in standard textbooks on business law, auditing, taxation, and accounting. Candidates are expected to recognize the existence of legal implications and the applicable basic legal principles, and they are usually asked to indicate the probable result of the application of such basic principles.

The business law and professional responsibilities section is chiefly conceptual in nature and is broad in scope, as determined by the Board of Examiners of the AICPA. The examination is not intended to test competence to practice law or expertise in legal matters, but is intended to determine that the candidates' knowledge is sufficient (1) to recognize relevant legal issues, (2) to recognize the legal implications of business situations, (3) to apply the underlying principles of law to accounting and auditing situations, and (4) to seek legal counsel or recommend that it be sought.

The section deals with federal and widely adopted uniform laws. If there is no federal or applicable uniform law on a subject, the questions ask for knowledge of the majority rules. Federal tax elements may be covered in the overall context of a question.

Writing skills are assessed on selected essay responses. Five percent of the total points for the business law and professional responsibilities portion will be allocated to writing skills. Writing skills include such characteristics as the ability to organize a response coherently, brevity, clarity, use of standard English, responsiveness to the requirements of the question, and appropriateness for the reader. Standard English is the language of business and the professions.

STUDY TIP ☞ Effective Writing Skills

In answering essay questions on the Uniform CPA Examination, responses should be organized in short paragraphs, each limited to the explanation of a single main point, with short sentences. Short sentences and simple wording also demonstrate the ability to write concisely—that is, the ability to express an important point in as few words as possible. Clarity involves using words of precise meaning in well-constructed sentences. These words include terms that are appropriate for the subject being tested. Correct grammar—including punctuation, capitalization, spelling, and word usage—enhance clarity. In responding to a question, do not broadly discuss general subject matter. Address a question directly.

THE BUSINESS LAW CONTENT OF THE EXAMINATION

The specific content of the Business Law and Professional Responsibilities portion of the Uniform CPA Examination is as follows:[1]

I. Professional and Legal Responsibilities (15 percent)

- A. Code of Professional Conduct
- B. Proficiency, Independence, and Due Care
- C. Responsibilities in Other Professional Services
- D. Disciplinary Systems within the Profession
- E. Common Law Liability to Clients and Third Parties
- F. Federal Statutory Liability
- G. Privileged Communications and Confidentiality
- H. Responsibilities of CPAs in Business and Industry, and in the Public Sector

II. Business Organizations (20 percent)

- A. Agency
  1. Formation and Termination
  2. Duties of Agents and Principals
  3. Liabilities and Authority of Agents and Principals
- B. Partnerships, Joint Ventures, and Other Unincorporated Associations
  1. Formation, Operation, and Termination
  2. Liabilities and Authority of Partners and Joint Owners
- C. Corporations
  1. Formation and Operation
  2. Stockholders, Directors, and Officers
  3. Financial Structure, Capital, and Distributions
  4. Reorganization and Dissolution
- D. Estates and Trusts
  1. Formation, Operation, and Termination
  2. Allocation between Principal and Income
  3. Fiduciary Responsibilities
  4. Distributions

III. Contracts (10 percent)

- A. Formation
- B. Performance
- C. Third Party Assignments
- D. Discharge, Breach, and Remedies

---

[1] This and other information pertaining to the CPA examination is available at the Web site of the American Institute of Certified Public Accountants (AICPA) at **http://www.aicpa.org**.

IV. Debtor-Creditor Relationships (10 percent)

A. Rights, Duties, and Liabilities of Debtors and Creditors

1. Liabilities and Defenses
2. Release of Parties
3. Remedies of Parties

B. Rights, Duties, and Liabilities of Guarantors

1. Liabilities and Defenses
2. Release of Parties
3. Remedies of Parties

C. Bankruptcy

1. Voluntary and Involuntary Bankruptcy
2. Effects of Bankruptcy on Debtor and Creditors
3. Reorganizations

V. Government Regulation of Business (15 percent)

A. Federal Securities Acts

1. Securities Registration
2. Reporting Requirements
3. Exempt Securities and Transactions

B. Employment Regulation

1. Payroll Taxes
2. Employee Safety
3. Employment Discrimination
4. Wage and Hour
5. Pension and Other Fringe Benefits

C. Environmental Regulation

VI. Uniform Commercial Code (20 percent)

A. Negotiable Instruments

1. Types of Negotiable Instruments
2. Requisites of Negotiability
3. Transfer and Negotiation
4. Holders and Holders in Due Course
5. Liabilities, Defenses, and Rights
6. Discharge

B. Sales

1. Contracts Covering Goods
2. Warranties
3. Product Liability
4. Risk of Loss
5. Performance and Obligations
6. Remedies and Defenses

C. Secured Transactions

1. Attachment of Security Interests
2. Perfection of Security Interests
3. Priorities
4. Rights of Debtors, Creditors, and Third Parties

D. Documents of Title

VII. Property (10 percent)

A. Real Property

1. Types of Ownership
2. Lessor-Lessee
3. Deeds, Recording, Title Defects, and Title Insurance
4. Mortgages and Other Liens
5. Fixtures
6. Environmental Liability

B. Personal Property, Bailments, and Computer Technology Rights

1. Types of Ownership
2. Bailments
3. Computer Technology Rights

Cross References: Business Law Subjects in the Uniform CPA Examination— Chapters in *Business Law Today, Comprehensive Edition, Sixth Edition*

SUBJECTS	CHAPTERS
PROFESSIONAL AND LEGAL RESPONSIBILITIES	
A. Code of Professional Conduct	42, 52
B. Proficiency, Independence, and Due Care	42, 52
C. Responsibilities in Other Professional Services	42, 52
D. Disciplinary Systems Imposed by the Profession and State Regulatory Bodies	42, 52
E. Common Law Liability to Clients and Third Parties	42, 52
F. Federal Statutory Liability	42, 52
G. Privileged Communications and Confidentiality	42, 52
H. Responsibilities of CPAs in Business and Industry, and in the Public Sector	42, 52
BUSINESS ORGANIZATIONS	
A. Agency	31, 32
B. Partnerships, Joint Ventures, and Other Unincorporated Associations	35, 36, 41
C. Corporations	37, 38, 39 40
D. Estates and Trusts	51
CONTRACTS	
A. Formation	9, 10, 11, 12, 13, 14
B. Performance	16
C. Third-Party Assignments	15
D. Discharge, Breach, and Remedies	16, 17
DEBTOR-CREDITOR RELATIONSHIPS	
A. Rights, Duties, and Liabilities of Debtors and Creditors	29
B. Rights, Duties, and Liabilities of Guarantors	29
C. Bankruptcy	30
GOVERNMENT REGULATION OF BUSINESS	
A. Federal Securities Acts	40
B. Employment Regulation	33, 34
C. Environmental Regulation	45
UNIFORM COMMERCIAL CODE	
A. Negotiable Instruments	24, 25, 26, 27
B. Sales	19, 20, 21, 22, 23
C. Secured Transactions	28
D. Documents of Title	47
PROPERTY	
A. Real Property, including Insurance	48, 50
B. Personal Property, including Bailments and Computer Technology Rights	7, 47

PROPOSED CONTENT FOR THE BUSINESS LAW PORTION OF THE EXAMINATION

The AICPA Board of Examiners has proposed changes to the content of the Business Law portion of the Uniform CPA Examination to be implemented by November 2003. This new content is as follows

I. ETHICS AND PROFESSIONAL AND LEGAL RESPONSIBILITIES

   A. Code of Professional Conduct
   B. Proficiency, Independence, and Due Care
   C. Ethics and Responsibilities in Tax Practice
   D. Licensing and Disciplinary Systems Imposed by the Profession and State Regulatory Bodies
   E. Legal Responsibilities and Liabilities

      1. Common Law Liability to Clients and Third Parties
      2. Federal Statutory Liability

   F. Privileged Communications and Confidentiality

II. BUSINESS LAW

   A. Agency

      1. Formation and Termination
      2. Duties and Authority of Agents and Principals
      3. Liabilities and Authority of Agents and Principals

   B. Contracts

      1. Formation
      2. Performance
      3. Third Party Assignments
      4. Discharge, Breach, and Remedies

   C. Debtor-Creditor Relationships

      1. Rights, Duties, and Liabilities of Debtors, Creditors, and Guarantors
      2. Bankruptcy

   D. Government Regulation of Business

      1. Federal Securities Acts
      2. Other Government Regulation (Antitrust, Pension and Retirement Plans, Union and Employee Relations, and Legal Liability for Payroll and Social Security Taxes)

   E. Uniform Commercial Code

      1. Negotiable Instruments and Letters of Credit
      2. Sales
      3. Secured Transactions
      4. Documents of Title and Title Transfer

   F. Real Property, including Insurance

UNIFORM CPA EXAMINATION DATES

Uniform CPA Examinations are scheduled for the following dates:

2002—	May 8, 9 November 6, 7	2004—	May 5, 6 November 3, 4
2003—	May 7, 8 November 5, 6	2005—	May 4, 5 November 2, 3

Students who plan to sit for any of the Uniform CPA Examinations should obtain copies of *Information for Uniform CPA Examination Candidates* issued by the AICPA.[2]

---

[2] Copies may be obtained by writing to:

American Institute of Certified Public Accountants, Inc.
1211 Avenue of the Americas
New York, New York 10036-8775

Answers

Chapter 1

True-False Questions

1. T
2. F. Legal positivists believe that there can be no higher law that a nation's positive law (the law created by a particular society at a particular point in time). The belief that law should reflect universal moral and ethical principles that are part of human nature is part of the natural law tradition.
3. T
4. T
5. T
6. F. Each state's constitution is supreme within each state's borders, so long as it does not conflict with the U.S. Constitution.
7. F. The National Conference of Commissioners on Uniform State Laws drafted the Uniform Commercial Code (and other uniform laws and model codes) and proposed it for adoption by the states.
8. F. This is the definition of civil law. Criminal law relates to wrongs against society as a whole and for which society has established sanctions.
9. T
10. F. A citation may contain the names of the parties, the year in which the case was decided, and the volume and page numbers of a reporter in which the opinion may be found, but it does not include the name of the judge who decided the case.

Fill-in Questions

with similar facts; precedent; permits a predictable

Multiple-Choice Questions

1. D. Legal positivists believe that there can be no higher law than the written law of a given society at a particular time. They do not believe in "natural rights."
2. B. The use of precedent—the doctrine of *stare decisis*—permits a predictable, relatively quick, and fair resolution of cases. Under this doctrine, a court must adhere to principles of law established by higher courts.
3. D. The doctrine of *stare decisis* attempts to harmonize the results in cases with similar facts. When the facts are sufficiently similar, the same rule is applied. Cases with identical facts could serve as binding authority, but it is more practical to expect to find cases with facts that are not identical but similar—as similar as possible.
4. A. An order to do or refrain from a certain act is an injunction. An order to perform as promised is a decree for specific performance. These remedies, as well as rescission, are equitable remedies. An award of damages is a remedy at law.

5. D. Equity and law provide different remedies, and at one time, most courts could grant only one type. Today, most states do not maintain separate courts of law and equity, and a judge may grant either or both forms of relief. Equitable relief is generally granted, however, only if damages (the legal remedy) is inadequate.
6. C. The U.S. Constitution is the supreme law of the land. Any state or federal law or court decision in conflict with the Constitution is unenforceable and will be struck. Similarly, provisions in a state constitution take precedence over the state's statutes, rules, and court decisions.
7. C. In establishing case law, or common law, the courts interpret and apply state and federal constitutions, rules, and statutes. Case law applies in areas that statutes or rules do not cover. Federal law applies to all states, and preempts state law in many areas.
8. A. This is a definition of civil law. As for the other answer choices, law that defines, describes, regulates, or creates rights or duties is substantive la w. Law that establishes methods for enforcing rights established by substantive law is procedural law. Criminal law governs wrongs committed against society for which society demands redress.
9. A. In reasoning by analogy, a judge compares the facts in one case to the facts in another case and to the extent that the facts are similar, applies the same legal principle. If the facts can be distinguished, different legal rules may apply. In either case, a judge will ordinarily state his or her reasons for applying a certain principle and arriving at a certain conclusion.
10. C. A concurring opinion makes or emphasizes a point different from those made or emphasized in the majority's opinion. An opinion written for the entire court is a unanimous opinion. An opinion that outlines only the majority's views is a majority opinion. A separate opinion that does not agree with the majority's decision is a dissenting opinion.

Issue Spotters

1. Case law includes courts' interpretations of statutes, as well as constitutional provisions and administrative rules. Statutes often codify common law rules. For these reasons, a judge might rely on the common law as a guide to the intent and purpose of a statute.
2. No. The U.S. Constitution is the supreme law of the land, and applies to all jurisdictions. A law in violation of the Constitution (in this question, the First Amendment to the Constitution) will be declared unconstitutional.
3. A case citation includes the names of the parties, the year in which the case was decided, and the volume and page number of at least one reporter in which the opinion may be found. A citation always indicates the court in which the case was decided, but does not include the name of the judge or judges who decided it.

Chapter 2

True-False Questions

1. T
2. T
3. F. The decisions of a state's highest court on all questions of state law are final. The United States Supreme Court can overrule only those state court decisions that involve questions of federal law.
4. T
5. F. Most lawsuits—as many as 95 percent—are dismissed or settled before they go to trial. Courts encourage alternative dispute resolution (ADR) and sometimes order parties to submit to ADR, particularly mediation, before allowing their suits to come to trial.
6. F. In mediation, a mediator assists the parties in reaching an agreement, but not by deciding the dispute. The mediator emphasizes points of agreement, helps the parties evaluate their positions, and proposes solutions.
7. F. If an arbitration agreement covers the subject matter of a dispute, a party to the agreement can be compelled to arbitrate the dispute. A court would order the arbitration without ruling on the basic controversy.
8. F. The jury verdict after a summary jury trial (SJT) is not binding. SJT is a form of alternative dispute resolution in which the parties' attorneys present their cases to a jury, but no witnesses are called, and the verdict is advisory only.
9. F. Negotiation typically does not involve a third party. The major difference between negotiation and mediation is that mediation does involve the presence of a third party—a mediator—who assists the parties in reaching an agreement and who often suggests solutions towards that end.
10. T

Fill-in Questions

trial; reviewing; factual issues; the law to the facts; of law but not of fact

Multiple-Choice Questions

1. A. On a "sliding scale" test, a court's exercise of personal jurisdiction depends on the amount of business that an individual or firm transacts over the Internet. Jurisdiction is most likely proper when there is substantial business, most likely improper when a Web site is no more than an ad, and may or may not be appropriate when there is some interactivity.

"Any" interactivity with "any resident" of a state would likely not be enough, however.

2. C. A corporation is subject to the jurisdiction of the courts in any state in which it is incorporated, in which it has its main office, or in which it does business. In the suit in this question, the court may exercise *in rem* jurisdiction.

3. A. As noted above, a corporation is subject to the jurisdiction of the courts in any state in which it is incorporated, in which it has its main office, or in which it does business. The court may be able to exercise personal jurisdiction or *in rem* jurisdiction, or the court may reach a defendant corporation with a long arm statute. In the right circumstances, this firm might also be involved in a suit in a federal court, if the requirements for federal jurisdiction are met.

4. A. An appellate court examines the record of a case, looking mostly at questions of law for errors by the court below. If it determines that a retrial is necessary, the case is sent back to the lower court. For this reason, an appellant's best ground for an appeal focuses on the law that applied to the issues in the case, not questions concerning the credibility of the evidence.

5. D. The United States Supreme Court is not required to hear any case. The Court has jurisdiction over any case decided by any of the federal courts of appeals and appellate authority over cases decided by the states' highest courts if the latter involve questions of federal law. But the Court's exercise of its jurisdiction is discretionary, not mandatory.

6. D. Negotiation is an informal means of dispute resolution. Generally, unlike mediation and arbitration, no third party is involved in resolving the dispute. In those two forms, a third party may render a binding or nonbinding decision. Arbitration is a more formal process than mediation or negotiation. Litigation involves a third party—a judge—who renders a legally binding decision.

7. D. Neither the amount involved nor the parties' satisfaction is relevant. An arbitrator's award will be set aside if it violates pubic policy. Other grounds on which an award may be set aside arise from the arbitrator's conduct—for example, if his or her bad faith substantially prejudices the rights of one of the parties, or if he or she decides issues that the parties did not agree to submit to arbitration.

8. D. Online dispute resolution (ODR) is a new type of alternative dispute resolution. Most ODR forums resolve disputers informally and come to nonbonding resolutions. Any party to a dispute being considered in ODR may discontinue the process and appeal to a court at any time.

9. A. Every state has at least one court of appeals, which may be an intermediate appellate court or the state's highest court. If a federal or constitutional issue is involved, the case may ultimately be appealed to the United States Supreme Court.

10. B. In a summary jury trial, the jury's verdict is not binding, as it would otherwise be in a court trial. In a mini-trial, the attorneys argue a case and a third party renders an opinion, but the opinion discusses how a court would decide the dispute. Early neutral case negotiation is what its name suggests, involving a third party who evaluates the disputing parties' positions.

Issue Spotters

1. Before a court will hear a case, it must be established that the court has subject matter and personal jurisdiction and that the matter at issue is justiciable. The party bringing the suit must also have standing to sue.

2. Yes. Whenever a suit involves citizens of different states, diversity of citizenship exists, and the suit can be brought in a federal court. In diversity of citizenship suits, Congress has set an additional requirement—the amount in controversy must be more than $75,000.

3. Yes. There is no absolute right of appeal to the United States Supreme Court. A party may ask the Supreme Court to issue a writ of *certiorari* (an order to a lower court to send the Court the record of the case for review), but the Court may deny the request.

Chapter 3

True-False Questions

1. F. Pleadings inform each party of the other's claims and specify the issues. Pleadings consist of a complaint and an answer, not a motion to dismiss.

2. F. In ruling on a motion for summary judgment, a court can consider evidence outside the pleadings, such as answers to interrogatories.

3. T

4. T

5. T

6. F. A losing party may appeal an adverse judgment to a higher court, but the party in whose favor the judgment was issued may also appeal if, for example, he or she is awarded less than sought in the suit.

7. F. The process that involves obtaining access to documents and other materials in the hands of an opposing party prior to trial is the *discovery* process.

8. T

9. F. The plaintiff in a civil case must prove a case by a preponderance of the evidence (the claim is more likely to be true than the defendant's). Some claims (such as fraud) must be proved by clear and convincing evidence (the truth of the claim is highly probable). The standard in a criminal trial is *beyond a reasonable doubt*.

10. T

Fill-in Questions

to dismiss; for judgment on the pleadings; summary judgment

Multiple-Choice Questions

1. D. The considerations for whether to take a case to court involve primarily time and money. Even settling out of court for less than you are owed may be wise in terms of future expenses, time waiting, time lost, and frustration.
2. D. A complaint contains a statement alleging jurisdictional facts, a statement of facts entitling the complainant to relief, and a statement asking for a specific remedy. It is filed with the court that has proper jurisdiction and venue. A copy of the complaint is served, with a summons, on the defendant named in the complaint.
3. A. This is part of discovery. Discovery saves time, and the trend is toward more, not less, discovery. Discovery is limited, however, to relevant materials. A party cannot obtain access to such data as another's trade secrets or, in testimony, an admission concerning unrelated matters.
4. C. A defendant may file a motion to dismiss if he or she is not properly served with the complaint, if the court lacks personal or subject matter jurisdiction, if the venue is improper, if the complaint does not state a claim for which relief can be granted, or other specific reasons.
5. B. If a motion to dismiss is filed before a defendant answers a complaint and the motion is granted, the case is at an end. If the motion is denied, the defendant must file an answer, or a default judgment will be entered against him or her.
6. A. An important part of the discovery process is a deposition, which is sworn testimony. Interrogatories are a series of written questions for which written answers are prepared and signed under oath by the plaintiff or defendant. A pretrial conference involves the plaintiff, the defendant, their attorneys, and judge.
7. A. An appeals court examines the record of a case, looking mostly at questions of law for errors by the court below. If it determines that a retrial is necessary, the case is sent back to the lower court. For this reason, an appellant's best ground for an appeal focuses on the law that applied to the issues in the case, not questions concerning the credibility of the evidence.
8. D. After a plaintiff calls and questions the first witness on direct examination, the defendant questions the witness on cross-examination. The plaintiff may then question the witness again (redirect examination), and the defendant may follow (recross-examination). Then the plaintiff's other witnesses are called, and the defendant presents his or her case.
9. C. After a verdict, the losing party can move for a new trial or for a judgment notwithstanding the verdict. If these motions are denied, he or she can appeal.
10. C. For obvious reasons, a losing party may wish to appeal a judgment. A winning party has the same right to appeal if he or she is dissatisfied with the relief granted.

Issue Spotters

1. Dean can call his first witness. Or Dean could file a motion for a directed verdict. This motion asks the judge to direct a verdict for Dean on the ground that Pat presented no evidence that would justify granting Pat relief. The judge grants the motion if there is insufficient evidence to raise an issue of fact.
2. This is not necessarily the end of their case. Either a plaintiff or a defendant, or both, can appeal a judgment to a higher court. An appellate court can affirm, reverse, or remand a case, or take any of these actions in combination. To appeal successfully, it is best to appeal on the basis of an error of law, because appellate courts do not usually reverse on findings of fact.
3. Pat can ask the court to order a sheriff to seize property owned by Dean and hold it until Dean pays the judgment. If Dean fails to pay, the property can be sold at a public auction and the proceeds given to Pat, or the property can be transferred to Pat in lieu of payment.

Chapter 4

True-False Questions

1. F. A federal form of government is one in which separate states form a union and divide sovereign power between themselves and a central authority. The United States has a federal form of government.
2. F. The president does not have this power. Under the doctrine of judicial review, however, the courts can hold acts of Congress and of the executive branch unconstitutional.
3. T
4. T
5. F. Under the supremacy clause, when there is a direct conflict between a federal law and a state law, the federal law takes precedence over the state law, and the state law is rendered invalid.
6. T
7. F. The protections in the Bill of Rights limit the power of the federal government. Most of these protections also apply to the states through the due process clause of the Fourteenth Amendment.
8. F. Commercial speech (advertising) can be restricted as long as the restriction (1) seeks to implement a substantial government interest, (2) directly advances that interest, and (3) goes no further than necessary to accomplish its objective.

9. F. Due process relates to the limits that the law places on the liberty of *everyone*. Equal protection relates to the limits that the law places on only *some people*.
10. T

Fill-in Questions

states; states; state

Multiple-Choice Questions

1. D. Under Articles I, II, and III of the Constitution, the legislative branch makes the law, the judicial branch interprets the law, and the executive branch enforces the law.
2. A. Under the commerce clause, Congress has the power to regulate every commercial enterprise in the United States. Recently, the United States Supreme Court has struck down federal laws, to limit this power somewhat, in areas that have "nothing to do with commerce," including noneconomic, criminal conduct.
3. C. State laws that impinge on interstate commerce are not always struck down, nor are they always upheld. A court will balance the state's interest in regulating a certain matter against the burden that the law places on interstate commerce. If the law does not substantially interfere, it will not be held to violate the commerce clause.
4. B. The First Amendment provides corporations with significant protection of corporate political speech. As another example, a law that forbids a corporation from using inserts in its bills to its customers to express its views on controversial issues would also violate the First Amendment.
5. D. Commercial speech does not have as much protection under the First Amendment as noncommercial speech. Commercial speech that is misleading may be restricted if the restriction (1) seeks to advance a substantial government interest, (2) directly advances that interest, and (3) goes no further than necessary.
6. B. Aspects of the Fifth and Fourteenth Amendments that cover procedural due process concern the procedures used to make any government decision to take life, liberty, or property. These procedures must be fair, which generally mean that they give an opportunity to object.
7. C. Substantive due process focuses on the content (substance) of a law under the Fifth and Fourteenth Amendments. Depending on which rights a law regulates, it must either promote a compelling or overriding government interest or be rationally related to a legitimate governmental end.
8. A. Equal protection means that the government must treat similarly situated individuals in a similar manner. The equal protection clause of the Fourteenth Amendment applies to state and local governments, and the due process clause of the Fifth Amendment guarantees equal protection by the federal government. Generally, a law regulating an economic matter is considered valid if there is a "rational basis" on which the law relates to a legitimate government interest.
9. C. Under the supremacy clause, if Congress chooses to act exclusively in an area in which states have concurrent power, Congress is said to preempt the area. The federal law takes precedence over a state law on the same subject.
10. D. Dissemination of obscene materials is a crime. Speech that harms the good reputation of another, or defamatory speech, is not protected under the First Amendment. "Fighting words," which are words that are likely to incite others to respond with violence, are not constitutionally protected. Other unprotected speech includes other speech that violates criminal laws, such as threats.

Issue Spotters

1. No. Even if commercial speech is not related to illegal activities nor misleading, it may be restricted if a state has a substantial interest that cannot be achieved by less restrictive means. In this case, the interest in energy conservation is substantial, but it could be achieved by less restrictive means. That would be the utilities' defense against the enforcement of this state law.
2. Yes, the law would violate both types of due process. The law would be unconstitutional on substantive due process grounds, because it abridges freedom of speech. The law would be unconstitutional on procedural due process grounds, because it imposes a penalty without giving an accused a chance to defend his or her actions.
3. Yes. The tax would limit the liberty of some persons (out of state businesses), so it is subject to a review under the equal protection clause. Protecting local businesses from out-of-state competition is not a legitimate government objective. Thus, such a tax would violate the equal protection clause.

Cumulative Hypothetical Problem for Unit One—Including Chapters 1–4

1. A. Mediation involves the a third party, a mediator. The mediator does not decide the dispute but only assists the parties to resolve it themselves. Although the mediator does not render a legally binding decision, any agreement the parties reach may be legally binding.
2. D. These state and federal courts would all have jurisdiction over the defendant. The customer's state could exercise jurisdiction over the firm through its long arm statute. The firm's state would have juris-

diction over it as a resident. A federal court could hear the case under its diversity jurisdiction: the parties are residents of different states and the amount in controversy is at least $75,000.

3. A. Damages, or money damages, is a remedy at law. Remedies in equity include injunctions, specific performance, and rescission. The distinction arose because the law courts in England could not always grant suitable remedies, and so equity courts were created to grant other types of relief. The U.S. legal system derives from the English system.

4. C. The power of judicial review is the power of any state or federal court to review a statute and declare it unconstitutional. Courts can also review the actions of the executive branch, which includes administrative agencies, to determine their constitutionality. A statute or rule that is declared unconstitutional is void. The power of judicial review is not expressly stated in the Constitution but is implied.

5. B. A state may restrict commercial speech if the state has a substantial interest that cannot be achieved by less restrictive means. Protecting the interests of consumers is a substantial state interest. Preventing consumers from being misled by certain kinds of advertising is an interest that may arguably not be achievable by any less restrictive means than an outright ban.

Questions on the Focus on Legal Reasoning for Unit One—*Kasky v. Nike, Inc.*

1. D. The majority set out a three-part test for determining whether speech is commercial. The three elements included the speaker, the intended audience, and the content of the message. The court seemed to emphasized the source of the speech as the dominant element. None of the other answer choices were mentioned.

2. B. The dissent argued that commercial speech should be distinguished by its content only, not by its content, the identity of the speaker, and the intended audience, as the majority held. The dissent asserted in part that "the inherent worth of the speech in terms of its capacity for informing the public does not depend upon the identity of its source" and that corporate and other business speakers contribute to the types of ideas that the First Amendment "seeks to foster."

3. D. The majority felt that its holding would have no chilling effect on commercial speech or public debate. Because commercial speech is based on a profit motive, it is "more hardy than noncommercial speech" and not likely to be much inhibited by this case. The dissent disagreed, arguing that this case "would have an undoubted chilling effect on speech," inhibiting businesses' ability to participate in debates over matters of public concern.

Questions on the Focus on Ethics for Unit One—Ethics and the Legal Environment of Business

1. D. Ethics is the study of what constitutes right or wrong behavior. It focuses on the application of moral principles to conduct. In a business context, ethics involves the application of moral principles to business conduct. Legal liability is a separate question and may, or may not, indicate unethical behavior. Profitability is also a separate issue. *Optimum* profitability is the *maximum* profitability that a business may attain within the limits of the law *and* ethics.

2. D. The *lack* of meaningful dissent to unethical decisions, or enthusiasm for them, could be an obstacle to more ethical choices, but the existence of dissent to unethical selections is not likely to encourage more of the same. Statutes that declare a priority for society's interests are also unlikely to foster unethical business behavior, as is holding a business firm accountable for its unethical actions. The corporate setting, however, in which dissent to unethical behavior may be stifled and in which a decision maker may be removed from the effects of his or her decisions, can be an obstacle to ethical decisions.

3. A. If a business firm does not conduct its operations ethically, its goodwill, reputation, and future profits likely suffer. A firm that shows a commitment to ethical behavior often receives benefits greater than any advantages it may have sacrificed to do "what's right." A firm that is perceived as ethical may also attract investors.

Chapter 5

True-False Questions

1. T

2. F. A reasonable apprehension or fear of *immediate* harmful or offensive contact is an assault.

3. T

4. F. Puffery is seller's talk—the seller's *opinion* that his or her goods are, for example, the "best." For fraud to occur, there must be a misrepresentation of a *fact*.

5. T

6. F. To establish negligence, the courts apply a reasonable person standard to determine whether certain conduct resulted in a breach of a duty of care.

7. F. Disparagement of property is a general term for torts that can be more specifically referred to as slander of quality or slander of title.

8. F. This is not misconduct, in terms of a wrongful interference tort. Bona fide competitive behavior is permissible, whether or not it results in the breaking of a contract or other business relation.

9. T

10. F. Some states have statutes prohibiting or regulating the use of spam. Also, the sending of spam may constitute trespass to personal property, and could be curtailed by private lawsuits. What the government can do to restrict spam may be limited by the First Amendment's protection for freedom of speech, however.

Fill-in Questions

1. negligence;
2. defense of assumption of risk
3. contributory;
4. comparative

Multiple-Choice Questions

1. A. To satisfy the elements of a negligence cause of action, a breach of a duty of care must cause the harm. If an injury would not have occurred without the breach, there is causation in fact. Causation in fact can usually be determined by the but-for test: but for the wrongful act, the injury would not have occurred.
2. B. Joe committed a battery and may have committed an assault. For an intentional tort, what matters is the actor's intent regarding the consequences of an act or his or her knowledge with substantial certainty that certain consequences will result. Motive is irrelevant, and the other person's fear is not a factor in terms of the actor's intent.
3. A. To delay a customer suspected of shoplifting, a merchant must have probable cause (which requires more than a mere suspicion). A customer's concealing merchandise in his or her bag and leaving the store without paying for it would constitute probable cause. Even with probable cause, a merchant may delay a suspected shoplifter only for a reasonable time, however.
4. D. Advertising is bona fide competitive behavior, which is not a tort even if it results in the breaking of a contract. Obtaining more customers is one of the goals of effective advertising. Taking unethical steps to interfere with others' contracts or business relations could constitute a tort, however.
5. A. The basis of the tort of defamation is publication of a statement that holds an individual up to contempt, ridicule, or hatred. Publication means that statements are made to or within the hearing of persons other than the defamed party, or that a third party reads the statements. A secretary reading a letter, for example, meets this requirement. But the statements do not have to be read or heard by a specific third party. (Whether someone is a public figure is important only because a public figure cannot recover damages for defamation without proof of actual malice.)
6. D. Under the Communications Decency Act, an Internet service provider (ISP) may not be held liable for defamatory statements made by its customers online. Congress provided this immunity as an incentive to ISPs to "self-police" the Internet for offensive material.
7. C. To commit negligence, a breach of a duty of care must cause harm. If an injury was foreseeable, there is causation in fact. This can usually be determined by the but-for test: but for the wrongful act, the injury would not have occurred. Thus, an actor is not necessarily liable to all who are injured. Insurance coverage and business dealings are not factors.
8. B. Trespass to land occurs when a person, without permission, enters onto another's land, or remains on the land. An owner does not need to be aware of an act before it can constitute trespass, and harm to the land is not required. A trespasser may have a complete defense, however, if he or she enters onto the land to help someone in danger.
9. A. The standard of a business that invites persons onto its premises is a duty to exercise reasonable care. Whether conduct is unreasonable depends on a number of factors, including how easily the injury could have been guarded against. A landowner has a duty to discover and remove hidden dangers, but obvious dangers do not need warnings.
10. D. Trespass to personal property is intentional physical contact with another's personal property that causes damage. Sending spam through an Internet service provider (ISP) is intentional contact with the ISP's computer systems. A negative impact on the value of the ISP's equipment, by using its processing power to transmit e-mail, constitutes damage (the resources are not available for the ISP's customers). Also, service cancellations harm an ISP's business reputation and goodwill.

Issue Spotters

1. Yes. Adam is guilty of battery—an unexcused, harmful, or offensive physical contact intentionally performed. A battery may involve contact with any part of the body and anything (a blouse, in this problem) attached to it.
2. Yes. Trespass to personal property occurs when an individual unlawfully harms another's personal property or otherwise interferes with the owner's right to exclusive possession and enjoyment.
3. No. As long as competitive behavior is bona fide, it is not tortious even if it results in the breaking of a contract. The public policy that favors free competition in advertising outweighs any instability that bona fide competitive activity causes in contractual or business relations. To constitute wrongful interference with a contractual relationship, there must be (1) a valid, enforceable contract between two parties; (2) the knowledge of a third party that this contract exists; and (3) the third party's intentionally causing the breach of the contract (and damages) to advance the third party's interest.

Chapter 6

True-False Questions

1. T
2. F. A defendant may be liable for the result of his or her act regardless of intent—that is part of the basis of the doctrine of strict liability. Similarly, it usually does not matter whether the defendant exercised reasonable care. Strict liability is liability without regard to fault or intent.
3. T
4. F. Product liability may be imposed for defects in the design or construction of products that cause injuries, but it may also be imposed for a failure to include a reasonable warning.
5. T
6. F. An action based on negligence does not require privity of contract. At one time, there was a requirement of privity in product liability actions based on negligence, but this requirement began to be eliminated decades ago. Privity of contract is also not a requirement to bring a suit based on strict product liability.
7. F. In an action based on strict liability, a plaintiff does not have to prove that there was a failure to exercise due care. That distinguishes an action based on strict liability from an action based on negligence, which requires proof of a lack of due care. A plaintiff must show, however, that (1) a product was defective, (2) the defendant was in the business of distributing the product, (3) the product was unreasonably dangerous due to the defect, (4) the plaintiff suffered harm, (5) the defect was the proximate cause of the harm, and (6) the goods were not substantially changed from the time they were sold.
8. T
9. F. There is no duty to warn about such risks. Warnings about such risks do not add to the safety of products and could make other warnings seem less significant. In fact, a plaintiff's action in the face of such a risk can be raised as a defense in a product liability suit.
10. T

Fill-in Questions

limitations; does not begin until; repose; repose; limitations

Multiple-Choice Questions

1. A. Assumption of risk is a defense in an action based on product liability if the plaintiff knew and appreciated the risk created by the defect and voluntarily undertook the risk, even though it was unreasonable to do so.
2. B. The manufacturer was clearly negligent to sell a product with a defective safety switch. As a defendant in a product liability suit on the ground of negligence, the manufacturer would be liable. The plaintiff knew about the defect, however, and used the treadmill anyway. Under the defense of comparative negligence, the amount of the defendant's liability may be reduced in proportion to the amount by which the plaintiff's injury was the result of the plaintiff's own negligence.
3. C. The doctrine of strict liability extends to suppliers of component parts as well as the manufacturers, sellers, and distributors of the products made with those components.
4. A. In terms of spreading the costs, manufacturers and others who might be liable typically have insurance to cover any losses. To pay for the insurance, the insured may simply raise its prices to its customers. Partly for this reason, manufacturers and sellers of products are in a better position to bear the costs associated with injuries caused by their products, which is one of the public policy reasons for imposing strict liability generally. Other reasons include that consumers should be protected against unsafe products, and that manufacturers and distributors should not escape liability for faulty products simply because they are not in privity of contract with the ultimate users of those products.
5. B. If the plaintiff can prove these elements (material fact, misrepresentation, reliance, and injury), liability could be based on the circumstance that the manufacturer, when it sold its product, misrepresented the character of the product.
6. A. A manufacturer may be held liable if its product is unsafe as a result of negligence in the manufacture or if the design makes it unreasonably dangerous for the use for which it is made. A manufacturer also has a duty to warn and to anticipate reasonably foreseeable misuses. An injury must not have been due to a change in the product after it was sold, but there is no requirement of privity. There is no liability, however, with respect to injuries caused by commonly known dangers, even if the manufacturer does not warn against them.
7. D. In a product liability action based on strict liability, the plaintiff does not need to prove that anyone was at fault. Privity of contract is also not an element of an action in strict liability. A plaintiff does have to show, however, in a suit against a seller, that the seller was a merchant engaged in the business of selling the product on which the suit is based. Note that recovery is possible against sellers who are processors, assemblers, packagers, bottlers, wholesalers, distributors, retailers, or lessors, as well as against manufacturers.
8. C. These choices concern the defective condition of a product that causes harm to a plaintiff. A product may be unreasonably dangerous due to a flaw in the

manufacturing process, a design defect, or an inadequate warning.
9. C. All courts extend the doctrine of strict liability to injured bystanders. A defendant does not have to prove that the manufacturer or seller failed to use due care, nor is there a requirement of privity (or "intent" with regard to entering into privity). The defense of assumption of risk does not apply, because one cannot assume a risk that one does not know about.
10. C. If a manufacturer fails to use due care to make a product safe, the manufacturer may be liable for product liability based on negligence. This care must be used in designing the product, selecting the materials, producing the product, inspecting and testing any components, assembling the product, and placing warnings on the product.

Issue Spotters

1 Yes. The manufacturer is liable for the injuries to the user of the product. A manufacturer is liable for its failure to exercise due care to any person who sustains an injury proximately caused by a negligently made (defective) product. In this problem, the failure to inspect is a failure to use due care. Of course, the maker of the component part may also be liable.
2. Yes. Under the doctrine of strict liability, persons may be liable for the results of their acts regardless of their intentions or their exercise of reasonable care (that is, regardless of fault). There is no requirement of privity.
3. Yes. Most courts will consider a plaintiff's negligence in apportioning liability, resulting in an application of the doctrine of comparative negligence in strict liability cases.

Chapter 7

True-False Questions

1. T
2. F. A copyright is granted automatically when a qualifying work is created, although a work can be registered with the U.S. Copyright Office.
3. T
4. T
5. F. Anything that makes an individual company unique and would have value to a competitor is a trade secret. This includes a list of customers, a formula for a chemical compound, and other confidential data.
6. F. Trade names cannot be registered with the federal government. They are protected, however, under the common law (when used as trademarks or service marks) by the same principles that protect trademarks.
7. F. A copy does not have to be the same as an original to constitute copyright infringement. A copyright is infringed if a substantial part of a work is copied without the copyright holder's permission.
8. F. A trademark may be infringed by an intentional or unintentional use of a mark in its entirety, or a copy of the mark to a substantial degree. In other words, a mark can be infringed if its use is intended or not, and whether the copy is identical or similar. Also, the owner of the mark and its unauthorized user need not be in direct competition.
9. T
10. F. Proof of a likelihood of confusion is not required in a trademark dilution action. The products involved do not even have to be similar. Proof of likely confusion is required in a suit for trademark infringement, however.

Fill-in Questions

70; 95; 120; 70

Multiple-Choice Questions

1. B. A firm that makes, uses, or sells another's patented design, product, or process without the owner's permission commits patent infringement. It is not required that an invention be copied in its entirety. Also, the object that is copied does not need to be trademarked or copyrighted, in addition to being patented.
2. A. The user of a trademark can register it with the U.S. Patent and Trademark Office, but registration is not necessary to obtain protection from trademark infringement. A trademark receives protection to the degree that it is distinctive. A fanciful symbol is the most distinctive mark.
3. B. Ten years is the period for later renewals of a trademark's registration. The life of a creator plus seventy years is a period for copyright protection. No intellectual work is protected forever, at least not without renewal. To obtain a patent, an applicant must satisfy the U.S. Patent and Trademark Office that the invention or design is genuine, novel, useful, and not obvious in light of contemporary technology. A patent is granted to the first person to create whatever is to be patented, rather than the first person to file for a patent.
4. A. Copyright protects a specific list of creative works, including literary works, musical works, sound recordings, and pictorial, graphic, and sculptural works. Although there are exceptions for "fair use," a work need not be copied in its entirety to be infringed. Also, to make a case for infringement, proof of consumers' confusion is not required, and the owner and unauthorized user need not be direct competitors.
5. D. Business processes and information that cannot be patented, copyrighted, or trademarked are protected against appropriation as trade secrets. These processes and information include production techniques, as well as a product's idea and its expression.

6. C. Trademark law protects a distinctive symbol that its owner stamps, prints, or otherwise affixes to goods to distinguish them from the goods of others.
7. B. A collective mark is a certification mark used by members of a cooperative, association, or other organization (a union, in this problem). A certification mark certifies the region, materials, method of manufacture, quality, or accuracy of goods or services. A service mark distinguishes the services of one person or company from those of another. A trade name indicates part or all of a business's name.
8. D. This is not copyright infringement because no copyright is involved. This is not cybersquatting because no one is offering to sell a domain name to a trademark owner. (It is also unlikely that this violates the Anticybersquatting Consumer Protection Act because there is no indication of "bad faith intent.") Trademark dilution occurs when a trademark is used, without the owner's without permission, in a way that diminishes the distinctive quality of the mark. That has not happened here.
9. C. The Berne Convention provides some copyright protection, but its coverage and enforcement was not as complete or as universal as that of the TRIPS (Trade-Related Aspects of Intellectual Property Rights) Agreement. The Paris Convention allows parties in one signatory country to file for patent and trademark protection in other signatory countries.
10. A. Publishers cannot put the contents of their periodicals into online databases and other electronic resources, including CD-ROMs, without securing the permission of the writers whose contributions are included.

Issue Spotters

1. The owner of the customer list can sue its competitor for the theft of trade secrets. Trade secrets include customer lists. Liability extends to those who misappropriate trade secrets by any means, including modems.
2. This is patent infringement. A software maker in this situation might best protect its product, save litigation costs, and profit from its patent by the use of a license. In the context of this problem, a license would grant permission to sell a patented item. (A license can be limited to certain purposes and to the licensee only.)
3. Yes. This may be an instance of trademark dilution. Dilution occurs when a trademark is used, without permission, in a way that diminishes the distinctive quality of the mark. Dilution does not require proof that consumers are likely to be confused by a connection between the unauthorized use and the mark. The products involved do not have to be similar. Dilution does require, however, that a mark be famous when the dilution occurs.

Chapter 8

True-False Questions

1. T
2. F. Felonies are crimes punishable by imprisonment of a year or more (in a state or federal prison). Crimes punishable by imprisonment for lesser periods (in a local facility) are classified as misdemeanors.
3. F. These are elements of the crime of robbery. (Robbery also involves the use of force or fear.) Burglary requires breaking and entering a building with the intent to commit a crime. (At one time, burglary was defined to cover only breaking and entering the dwelling of another at night to commit a crime.)
4. F. This is an element of larceny. The crime of embezzlement occurs when a person entrusted with another's property fraudulently appropriates it. Also, unlike robbery, embezzlement does not require the use of force or fear.
5. T.
6. F. The crime of bribery occurs when a bribe is offered. Accepting a bribe is a separate crime. In either case, the recipient does not need to perform the act for which the bribe is offered for the crime to exist. Note, too, that a bribe can consist of something other then money.
7. F. The recipient of the goods only needs to know that the goods are stolen. The recipient does not need to know the identity of the thief or of the true owner to commit this crime. Thus, not knowing these individuals' identities is not a defense.
8. T
9. T
10. T

Fill-in Questions

unreasonable; probable; due process of law; jeopardy; trial; trial by; witnesses; bail and fines

Multiple-Choice Questions

1. D. A person who wrongfully or fraudulently takes and carries away another's personal property commits larceny. Unlike burglary, larceny does not involve breaking and entering. Unlike embezzlement, larceny requires that property be taken and carried away from the owner's possession. Unlike forgery, larceny does not require the making or altering of a writing. Unlike robbery, larceny does not involve force or fear.
2. C. The elements of most crimes include the performance of a prohibited act and a specified state of mind or intent on the part of the actor.
3. C. Fraudulently making or altering a writing in a way that changes another's legal rights is forgery. Forgery also includes changing trademarks, counter-

feiting, falsifying public documents, and altering other legal documents.

4. B. Embezzlement involves the fraudulent appropriation of another's property, including money, by a person entrusted with it. Unlike larceny, embezzlement does not require that property be taken from its owner.

5. D. The standard to find a criminal defendant guilty is beyond a reasonable doubt. This means that each juror must be convinced, beyond a reasonable doubt, of the defendant's guilt. The standard in most civil cases is a preponderance of the evidence.

6. C. The federal crime of mail fraud has two elements: a scheme to defraud by false pretenses, and mailing, or causing someone else to mail, a writing for the purpose of executing the scheme. It would also be a crime to execute the scheme by wire, radio, or television transmissions.

7. B. In considering the defense of entrapment, the important question is whether a person who committed a crime was pressured by the police to do so. Entrapment occurs when a government agent suggests that a crime be committed and pressure an individual, who is not predisposed to its commitment, to do it.

8. C. A person in police custody who is to be interrogated must be informed that he or she has the right to remain silent; anything said can and will be used against him or her in court; and he or she has the right to consult with an attorney. The person also must be told that if he or she is indigent, a lawyer will be appointed. These rights may be waived if the waiver is knowing and voluntary.

9. C. If, for example, a confession is obtained after an illegal arrest, the confession is normally excluded. Under the exclusionary rule, all evidence obtained in violation of the constitutional rights spelled out in the Fourth, Fifth, and Sixth Amendments normally is excluded, as well as all evidence derived from the illegally obtained evidence. The purpose of the rule is to deter police misconduct.

10. B. A formal charge issued by a grand jury is an indictment. A charge issued by a magistrate is called an information. In either case, there must be sufficient evidence to justify bringing a suspect to trial. The arraignment occurs when the suspect is brought before the trial court, informed of the charges, and asked to enter a plea.

Issue Spotters

1. No. A mistake of fact, as opposed to a mistake of law, will constitute a defense if it negates the mental state required for the crime. The mental state required for theft involves the knowledge that the property is another's and the intent to deprive the owner of it.

2. Yes. With respect to the gas station, she has obtained goods by false pretenses. She might also be charged with forgery, and most states have special statutes covering illegal use of credit cards.

3. Yes. The National Information Infrastructure Protection Act of 1996 amended the Counterfeit Access Device and Computer Fraud and Abuse Act of 1984. The statute provides that a person who accesses a computer online, without permission, to obtain classified data (such as consumer credit files in a credit agency's database) is subject to criminal prosecution. The crime has two elements: accessing the computer without permission and taking data. It is a felony if done for private financial gain. Penalties include fines and imprisonment for up to twenty years. The victim of the theft can also bring a civil suit against the criminal to obtain damages and other relief.

Cumulative Hypothetical Problem for Unit Two—Including Chapter s 5–8

1. B. Intellectual property law protects such intangible rights as copyrights, trademarks, and patents, which include the rights that an individual or business firm has in the products it produces. Protection for software comes from patent law and from copyright law. Protection for the distinguishing trademarks on the software come from, of course, trademark law.

2. C. Of these choices, the firm most likely violated tort law, which includes negligence and strict liability, both as distinct torts and as a part of product liability. Negligence requires proof of intent. Strict liability does not. These firms may also have breached their contracts and their warranties, topics which are discussed in the next Unit.

3. B. This is cyber theft. Accessing a computer online, without authority, to obtain classified, restricted, or protected data, or attempting to do so is prohibited by the National Information Infrastructure Protection Act of 1996. Penalties include fines and imprisonment for up to twenty years.

4. A. A corporation can be held liable for the crimes of its employees, officers, or directors. Imprisonment is not possible, in a practical sense, as a punishment for a corporation. A business firm can be fined or denied certain privileges, however.

5. C. Corporate officers can be held personally liable for the crimes they commit, whether or not the crimes were committed for their personal benefit or on their firm's behalf. Also, corporate officers can be held liable for the actions of employees under their supervision. Furthermore, a court can impose criminal liability on a corporate officer in those circumstances regardless of whether he or she participated in, directed, or even knew about a given crime.

Questions on the Focus on Legal Reasoning for Unit Two—*Pinsonneault v. Merchants & Farmers Bank & Trust Co.*

1. C. The majority stated that "business owners are in the best position to appreciate the crime risks that are posed on their premises." They have no general duty to protect all others from the criminal acts of third persons, but "they do have a duty to implement reasonable measures to protect their patrons from criminal acts when those acts are foreseeable."

2. B. The majority and the dissent agreed that in this case, the bank owed a duty to its patrons to take security steps against the reasonably foreseeable criminal acts of third parties. The majority concluded, after a review of the lower court's record, that the bank had met its duty.

3. A. As noted in the previous answer, the dissent agreed with majority that the bank owed a duty to its patrons to protect them from the reasonably foreseeable criminal acts of third parties. The dissent concluded, however, after a review of the trial court record, that the bank had not met this duty. The basis for the disagreement was the dissent's different interpretation of the facts.

Questions on the Focus on Ethics for Unit Two—Ethics and the Legal Environment of Business

1. C. The collection, buying, and selling of consumers' personal information may violate the individuals' privacy rights. A business should formulate a privacy policy and inform those whose data the firm collects. Copyrights and trademarks are not infringed in this problem. A business is not protected by the freedom of speech in the buying and selling of personal information.

2. B. This problem presents a cybergriper. A cybergriper uses another's trademark to protest, or otherwise complain about, in good faith and usually without profit, the owner's product or policy. Courts have held that this use of a mark is protected by the freedom of speech. The business's mark is not infringed because the public is not likely to be confused by the cybergriper's use.

3. A. Protection under copyright law for creative products, including books, extend for at least the life of the author plus seventy years. Exploiting a protected work before that protection expires would be a violation of copyright. Privacy rights, trademarks, and the freedom of speech can be violated in other contexts.

Chapter 9

True-False Questions

1. F. All contracts involve promises, but all promises do not establish contracts. (A contract is an agreement that can be enforced in court.) Contract law reflects which promises society believes should be legally enforced, and assures parties to private contracts that the agreements they make will be enforceable.
2. T
3. T
4. F. A bilateral contract is accepted by a promise to perform. A unilateral contract is formed when the offeree (the party who receives the offer) completes the requested act or other performance.
5. F. An oral contract is an express contract, which may be written or oral. In an express contract, the terms are fully stated in words. In an implied contract, it is the conduct of the parties that creates and defines the terms.
6. F. An unenforceable contract is a valid contract that cannot be enforced due to certain defenses. A voidable contract is a valid contract in which one or both of the parties has the option of avoiding his or her legal obligations.
7. T
8. T
9. T
10. F. A quasi contract is imposed by a court to avoid the unjust enrichment of one party at the expense of another. Quasi contracts are not true contracts.

Fill-in Questions

objective; objective; did; circumstances surrounding; a particular transaction

Multiple-Choice Questions

1. C. Freedom of contract refers to the law's recognition that most every individual may enter freely into contractual arrangements. This freedom is expressed in Article I, Section 10 of the U.S. Constitution.

2. A. An obligation to pay will be imposed by law to prevent one party from being unjustly enriched at another's expense. This is the doctrine of quasi contract. The doctrine will not be applied, however, if there is a contract covering the matter in dispute. Also, there are some circumstances in which parties will not be forced to pay for benefits "thrust" on them, particularly if this is done over their protest.

3. B. One party has performed; the other has not. The contract is executed on the one side and executory on the other, and classified as executory. Once the delivered goods are paid for, the contract will be fully executed.

4. C. In considering an implied-in-fact contract, a court looks at actions leading up to what happened. If, for example, the plaintiff furnished services, expecting to be paid, which the defendant should have known, and the defendant had a chance to reject the services and did not, the court would hold that the parties had an enforceable implied-in-fact contract.

5. B. According to the objective theory of contracts, a party's intent to enter into a contract is judged by outward, objective facts as they would be interpreted by a reasonable person, rather than by the party's own subjective intentions. A reasonable person in the position of a party receiving an offer can know what is in

the offer only from what is offered. A court might consider the circumstances surrounding a transaction, and the statements of the parties and the way they acted when they made their contract.

6. A. An express contract is a contract in which the terms are fully expressed in words, but those words do not necessarily have to be in writing. A contract that is implied from conduct is an implied-in-fact contract. Implied-in-law, or quasi, contracts are not actual contracts but are imposed on parties by courts.

7. A. The primary purpose of the rules for the interpretation of contracts is to determine the parties' intent from the language used in their agreement and to give effect to that intent. A court will not ordinarily interpret a contract according to what the parties later claim was their intent when they contracted.

8. D. One of the rules for the interpretation of contracts is that evidence of course of performance, course of dealing, and custom and usage of trade may be admitted to clarify the meaning of ambiguous terms. This evidence is given weight (or priority) in that order.

9. B. A voidable contract is a valid contract that can be avoided at the option of one or both of the parties. If a party with the option chooses to avoid the contract, both parties are released from their obligations under it. If a party with the option elects to ratify the contract, both parties must perform.

10. C. Like the definition of a promise, a contract can be defined as an agreement to do or refrain from doing some legal act now or in the future. Mutual promises can make up an agreement, and an agreement that can be enforced in a court is a contract.

Issue Spotters

1. Under the objective theory of contracts, if a reasonable person would have thought that the offeree accepted the offeror's offer when the offeree signed and returned the letter, a contract was made, and the offeree is bound. This depends in part on what was said in the letter (was it a valid offer?) and what was said in response (was it a valid acceptance?). Under any circumstances, the issue is not whether either party subjectively believed that they did, or did not, have a contract.

2. Yes. A person who is unjustly enriched at the expense of another can be required to account for the benefit under the theory of quasi contract. The parties here did not have a contract, but the law will impose one to avoid the unjust enrichment.

3. No. This "contract," although not fully executed, is for an illegal purpose and therefore void. A void contract gives rise to no legal obligation on the part of any party. A contract that is void is no contract. There is nothing to enforce.

Chapter 10

True-False Questions

1. T

2. F. One of the elements for a valid offer is that the terms be definite enough to be enforced by a court. This is so a court can determine if a breach had occurred and, if so, what the appropriate remedy would be. An offer might invite a specifically worded acceptance.

3. T

4. F. Irrevocable offers (offers that must be kept open for a period of time) include option contracts. Other irrevocable offers include a merchant's firm offer and, under the doctrine of promissory estoppel, an offer on which an offeree has changed position in reliance.

5. F. The mirror image rule requires that the terms of an offeree's acceptance must exactly match the terms of the offeror's offer to form a valid contract. Any other response effectively rejects the offer, terminating it. An offeree may, of course, include a counteroffer with his or her rejection.

6. F. Normally, silence does not operate as an acceptance, but it can be an acceptance when: an offeree takes the benefit of offered goods or services (even though he or she had an opportunity to reject and knew that they were offered with the expectation of compensation); the parties have had prior dealings in which the offeree has led the offeror reasonably to understand that the offeree will accept all offers unless he or she sends notice to the contrary; or if one has agreed that his or her failure to respond will constitute acceptance.

7. F. An offer terminates automatically when the time specified in the offer has passed. The offeree does not need to be given "one last chance" to accept for the offer to lapse.

8. F. Except in certain special circumstances, only the person to whom an offer is made can accept it.

9. T

10. T

Fill-in Questions

serious; offeror; reasonably definite; offeree

Multiple-Choice Questions

1. B. In these circumstances, the rule of acceptance on dispatch (the mailbox rule) dictates that the acceptance is effective when sent. When an offeree uses a method of communication expressly authorized by an offeror, acceptance is effective on dispatch.

2. C. In general, ads are treated as invitations to negotiate, not offers. This question and answer are based on a question that appeared in the CPA exam in May 1981.

3. B. This statement makes a second offer without rejecting the first offer. An offeree may make an offer without rejecting the original offer, in which case two offers exist, each capable of acceptance.

4. D. When an acceptance is made conditional, it constitutes a rejection, but the conditions state a counteroffer. A counteroffer is both a rejection of an original offer and a simultaneous making of a new offer.

5. D. An offer terminates on the offeror's death.

6. A. Generally, an offer may be revoked any time before acceptance. Most offers are revocable, even if they say that they are not, as long as the revocation is communicated to the offeree before acceptance. This may be done by express repudiation or by acts that are inconsistent with the offer and that are made known to the offeree (such as a sale to someone else about which the offeree learns).

7. B. In an auction with reserve, the bidder is the offeror. The auctioneer may reject a bid before the auctioneer strikes the hammer, which constitutes acceptance of the bid.

8. A. Silence can constitute acceptance in only a few circumstances, as is the case when the parties expect it—if, for example, a prior course of dealing indicates that notice is not required.

9. B. Under the mailbox rule, if an offeree uses a mode of communication expressly or impliedly authorized by the offeror, acceptance is effective when sent. Here, the mode was impliedly authorized because the offeror did not specify a particular mode. In such circumstances, whatever mode the offeror used to make the offer is reasonable to use to accept.

10. B. Traditional rules of contract apply to new forms of communication. Under the mailbox rule, using a mode of communication impliedly authorized by the offeror makes an acceptance effective when sent. Here, the offeror did not specify a certain mode, so the mode the offeror used to make the offer was a reasonable means of acceptance.

Issue Spotters

1. No. Taking into account Jane's frustration and the obvious difference between the value of her car and the purchase price, a reasonable person would declare that her offer was not made with serious intent and that you did not have an agreement.

2. Yes. An offer must be communicated to the offeree, so that the offeree knows it. For example, a reward must be communicated so that the offeree knows of it. If so, the offeree can claim the reward for doing whatever the reward was offered for doing.

3. No. The offer was revoked before it was accepted. Revocation of an offer may be implied by conduct inconsistent with the offer. When the corporation hired someone else, and the offeree learned of the hiring, the offer was revoked. The acceptance was too late.

Chapter 11

True-False Questions

1. F. Ordinarily, courts will not evaluate the adequacy of consideration, unless it is grossly inadequate or so unfair as to indicate the existences of fraud, duress, incapacity, undue influence, or a lack of bargained-for exchange.

2. T

3. F. Promises based on past consideration—that is, promises made with respect to events that have already happened—are unenforceable. They lack the element of bargained-for consideration.

4. T

5. F. A promise does have value as consideration. Consideration may consist of goods, money, performance, or a promise.

6. T

7. F. Unlike a release, a covenant not to sue does not always bar further recovery. If one party does not do what he or she promised, the other party can file a suit for breach of contract.

8. F. When a debt is liquidated, it is not in dispute—it is a preexisting obligation. A preexisting obligation cannot be consideration. For an accord and satisfaction, a debt must be disputed. The consideration is the parties' giving up their legal right to contest the amount of debt.

9. T

10. T

Fill-in Questions

promise; detriment; promisor; promise; enforced; promisee; substantial

Multiple-Choice Questions

1. A. To constitute consideration, the value of whatever is exchanged for the promise must be legally sufficient. Its economic value (its "adequacy") is rarely the basis for a court's refusal to enforce a contract.

2. B. Consideration must be bargained for. Performance or a promise is bargained for if, as in this problem, the promisor seeks it in exchange for his or her promise and the promisee gives it in exchange for that promise.

3. A. Past consideration is no consideration. Promises made with respect to past consideration are not enforceable. This question and answer are based on a question that appeared in the May 1995 CPA exam.

4. A. The promisee was not legally obligated to undertake the act, and the promisor was not legally obligated to pay the promisee until the performance was completed. The act undertaken was both detrimental to the promisee and beneficial to the promisor. Also, consideration must be bargained for. Performance or a promise is bargained for if, as in this problem, the promisor seeks it in exchange for his or her promise and the promisee gives it in exchange for that promise.
5. C. Generally, a promise to do what one already has a legal duty to do is not legally sufficient consideration, because no legal detriment or benefit has been incurred or received. This is the preexisting duty rule. Unforeseen difficulties may qualify as an exception to this rule, but an increase in ordinary business expenses, which is a type of risk usually assumed in doing business, does not qualify as an unforeseen difficulty.
6. A. Two parties can mutually agree to rescind their contract, at least to the extent that it is executory, and agree to a new contact. If the rescission and the making of the new contract are simultaneous, and a dispute later arises, the court may have to decide whether to apply the preexisting duty rule, but that seems unlikely in the circumstances described in this problem.
7. D. The injured party signed a valid, enforceable release. No fraud was involved. Consideration was given in the form of the uninjured party's promise to pay in return for the injured party's promise not to sue for a larger amount.
8. C. A person who reasonably relies on the promise of another to that person's detriment can recover under the doctrine of promissory estoppel (also called detrimental reliance). There must be (1) a promise, (2) reliance on the promise, (3) reliance of a substantial, definite nature, and (4) justice in the enforcement of the promise.
9. A. To constitute consideration, the value of whatever is exchanged for the promise must be legally sufficient. Its economic value (its "adequacy") is rarely the basis for a court's refusal to enforce a contract.
10. A. In a covenant not to sue, the parties substitute a contractual obligation for some other type of legal action, such as a tort. A covenant not to sue does not always bar further recovery, unlike a release.

Issue Spotters

1. Yes. The original contract was executory. The parties rescinded it and agreed to a new contract. If the employee had broken the contract to accept a contract with another employer, she might have been held liable for damages for the breach.
2. No. The promise is illusory, because performance is uncertain—it depends solely on the discretion of management. There is no bargained-for consideration, and thus, there is no enforceable promise.
3. Yes. Under the doctrine of detrimental reliance, or promissory estoppel, the promisee is entitled to payment of $5,000 from the promisor on graduation. There was a promise, on which the promisee relied, the reliance was substantial and definite (the promisee went to college for the full term, incurring considerable expenses, and will likely graduate), and it would only be fair to enforce the promise.

Chapter 12

True-False Questions

1. T
2. T
3. F. A person who enters into a contract when he or she is intoxicated can avoid the contract only if he or she was so intoxicated as to fail to comprehend the legal consequences of entering into the deal. Note, though, that the intoxication need not have been involuntary.
4. F. A minor is personally liable for his or her torts. In some circumstances, the minor's parents may also be held liable, if, for example, the tort was malicious or committed at the direction of the parent.
5. T
6. T
7. T
8. F. An illegal contract is void. A court will not enforce it on behalf of any party to it.
9. F. A contract with an unlicensed practitioner may be enforceable if the purpose of the statute is to raise government revenues, but not if the statute's purpose is to protect the public from unlicensed practitioners.
10. F. A covenant not to compete may be upheld if the length of time and the size of the geographic area in which the party agrees not to compete are reasonable. A court may in fact reform these terms to make them reasonable and then enforce them as reformed.

Fill-in Questions

ratification; disaffirm; indicates; ratification

Multiple-Choice Questions

1. C. Ratification is accepting and thus giving legal force to an obligation that was previously unenforceable. Most contracts with minors are not fully enforceable until the minor reaches the age of majority. Similarly, a minor cannot effectively ratify a contract until he or she attains majority. This question and answer are based on a question that appeared in the May 1993 CPA exam.
2. B. If a person was intoxicated enough to lack mental capacity, the contract is voidable at his or her option. Being intoxicated enough to lack mental capacity means being so impaired as not to comprehend

the consequences of entering into a contract. Otherwise, the contract is enforceable. Under no circumstances would the contract be void.

3. D. Only a guardian can enter into legally binding contracts on a person's behalf if the person has been adjudged mentally incompetent by a court. Any contract entered by the incompetent person is void. If the person has not been so adjudged, however, a contract may be enforceable if the person either knew it was a contract or understood its legal consequences.

4. C. To disaffirm a contract, a minor must return whatever he or she received under it. In a state in which there is also an obligation to return the other party to the position he or she was in before the contract, the minor must also pay for any damage to the goods.

5. D. The general rule is that an illegal contract is unenforceable. Thus, if an illegal agreement is executory, with the illegal part not yet performed, the party whose performance has not been rendered can withdraw. The person cannot be held in breach, and the contract cannot be enforced.

6. D. This promise (a covenant not to compete) is enforceable, because it is no broader than necessary for the other party's protection. Such promises may be considered contracts in restraint of trade, illegal on grounds of public policy, when they are broader than necessary (particularly in terms of geographic area and time), or are not accompanied by a sale of a business.

7. D. A contract with an unlicensed party is illegal and not enforceable by either party to it if the purpose of the licensing statute is to protect the public from unauthorized practitioners. If the purpose of the statute is to raise government revenues, however, the contract is enforceable.

8. B. The reasonableness of a covenant not to compete, accompanied by the sale of a business or included in an employment contract, is determined by the length of time and the size of the area in which the party agrees not to compete. In some cases, a court might even reform overly restrictive terms to prevent any undue burdens or hardships.

9. A. An exculpatory clause (a contract clause attempting to absolve a party of negligence or other wrongs) is often held unconscionable, especially in a case involving a lease of real property, or in which an employer is attempting to avoid liability for injury to an employee, or in which a business important to the public interest is seeking its enforcement.

10. D. A contract with an unlicensed individual may be enforceable depending on the nature of the applicable licensing statute. If the statute bars the enforcement of such contracts, of course they are not enforceable. They are also not enforceable if the statute's purpose is to protect the public from unlicensed practitioners. Otherwise, if the statute is intended only to raise revenue, such contracts may be enforceable.

Issue Spotters

1. A minor may effectively ratify a contract after he or she reaches the age of majority either expressly or impliedly. Failing to disaffirm an otherwise enforceable contract within a reasonable time after reaching the age of majority would also effectively ratify it. Nothing a minor does before attaining majority, however, will ratify a contract.

2. The criminal in this problem can recover none of the payments to the law enforcement official. Their contract was an illegal contract and, as such, unenforceable by either party to it and neither party can recover damages or the relief if the contract has been executed.

3. No. Generally, An exculpatory clause (a clause attempting to absolve parties of negligence or other wrongs) is not enforced if the party seeking its enforcement is involved in a business that is important to the public as a matter of practical necessity, such as an airline. Because of the essential nature of these services, they have an advantage in bargaining strength and could insist that anyone contracting for their services agree not to hold them liable.

Chapter 13

True-False Questions

1. T
2. T
3. T
4. F. Proof of an injury is not needed to rescind a contract for fraud. Proof of an injury is required, however, to recover damages on the basis of fraud.
5. T
6. T
7. F. If the parties to the contract had substantially unequal bargaining positions and enforcement would be unfair or oppressive, the contract will not be enforced. A court may base its decision on the doctrine of unconscionability, or on traditional concepts of fraud, undue influence, or duress.
8. F. A person can misrepresent a material fact without intending to defraud. This is known as innocent misrepresentation. A party who contracts with the person in reliance on the statement may be able to rescind the contract.
9. F. If a defect is serious (such as the risks of a medical procedure), it must be disclosed. The general rule is, however, that neither party to a contract has a duty to speak. Also, if a defect is obvious, a buyer cannot justifiably rely on a seller's representations.
10. F. When both parties to a contract make a mistake as to the market value or quality of the object of their deal, the contract can be *enforced* by either party. Mutual mistakes of *material fact* permit rescission by either party.

Fill-in Questions

value; value; cannot; value

Multiple-Choice Questions

1. A. Generally, a unilateral mistake—a mistake on the part of only one of the parties—does not give the mistaken party any right to relief. There are two exceptions. One of the exceptions is that the rule does not apply if the other party knew or should have known that a mistake was made. This question and answer are based a question that appeared in the CPA exam in May 1995.
2. C. This statement is none of the other choices because it is a statement of opinion, and thus is not generally subject to a claim of fraud or any of the other causes of action listed here. A fact is objective and verifiable. Puffery often involves vague assertions of quality. Affirmatively concealing a material fact, failing to respond when asked, and in some cases failing to volunteer pertinent facts may constitute fraud, however. Taking advantage of a party with whom one is in a confidential relationship to influence their entering into a "good deal" might constitute undue influence. Threats of physical harm may amount to duress.
3. D. When parties contract, their agreement establishes the value of the object of their transaction for the moment. Each party is considered to assume the risk that the value will change or prove to be different from what he or she thought. In this case, the buyer assumed the risk of a drop in the price. If instead the mistake had involved a material fact and had been mutual, the buyer may have been able to avoid the contract (or enforce it).
4. D. The contract may be avoided on the ground of undue influence. The inexperienced seller is justified, in these circumstances, in assuming that her nephew will not act in a manner inconsistent with her best interests.
5. B. The problem states the elements of fraudulent misrepresentation: misrepresentation of a material fact, intent to deceive, and the innocent party's justifiable reliance on the misrepresentation. The misrepresentation must be an important factor in inducing the party to contract—reliance is not justified if the party knows or should know the truth. The defrauded may elect to rescind or enforce the contract. Damages are recoverable on proof of injury.
6. D. Fraud involves misrepresentation that is intended to mislead another. The perpetrator must know or believe that the assertion is not true. Representations of future facts, statements of opinion, and most laypersons' statements about the law are generally not subject to claims of fraud. People are assumed to know the law. An exception occurs when the misrepresenting party is in a profession known to require a greater knowledge of the law than the average person possesses.
7. A. An adhesion contract (which is what a standard form contract often is) may not be enforced if the adhering party (the buyer, in this problem) shows that the parties had substantially unequal bargaining positions and enforcement would be unfair or oppressive. Such a contract may be avoided on grounds of unconscionability (the most likely possibility here), fraud, undue influence, or duress.
8. B. Proof of an injury is required to recover damages on the ground of misrepresentation. Proof of an injury is not generally required to rescind a contract on that basis.
9. B. Normally, a party to a contract does not have a duty to disclose defects. If a serious defect is known to the seller that is not known or could not be reasonably suspected by the buyer, however, the contract may be avoided by the buyer on the basis of misrepresentation.
10. D. Threatening to exercise a legal right, such as the right to sue to enforce a contract, is not duress. It is also not misrepresentation or undue influence.

Issue Spotters

1. No. When parties base their contract on a common assumption about a material fact that proves false, the transaction may be avoided if because of the mistake a different exchange of values occurs from the exchange of values that the parties contemplated. In other words, what the buyer actually found on the property was not part of the bargain between the buyer and the seller.
2. Yes. Rescission may be granted on the basis of fraudulent misrepresentation. The elements of fraudulent misrepresentation include intent to deceive, or *scienter*. *Scienter* exists if a party makes a statement recklessly, without regard to whether it is true or false, or if a party says or implies that a statement is made on some basis such as personal knowledge or personal investigation when it is not.
3. Yes. The accountant may be liable on the ground of negligent misrepresentation. A misrepresentation is negligent if a person fails to exercise reasonable care in disclosing material facts or does not use the skill and competence required by his or her business or profession.

Chapter 14

True-False Questions

1. T
2. F. A promise ancillary to a principal transaction and made by a third party to assume the debts or obligations of the primary party must generally be in writing to be enforceable. But there is an exception: an

oral promise to answer for the debt of another is enforceable if the guarantor's main purpose is to secure a personal benefit.

3. F. Under the doctrine of promissory estoppel, an oral contract may be enforced if a promisor makes a promise on which the promisee justifiably relies to his or her detriment, the reliance was foreseeable to the promisor, and injustice can be avoided only by enforcing the promise..

4. T

5. F. A contract for customized goods may be enforceable under the UCC even if it is only oral. Also, oral agreements between merchants that have been confirmed in writing may be enforceable.

6. F. The Statute of Frauds requires that contracts for all transfers of interests in land be in writing to be enforceable. Included are sales, mortgages, leases, and other transfers.

7. F. The UCC's Statute of Frauds requires that contracts for sales of goods priced at $500 or more must be in writing to be enforceable. Of course, there are exceptions. Oral contracts for customized goods, for example, may be enforced in some circumstances, as may oral contracts between merchants that have been confirmed in writing.

8. T

9. F. A writing sufficient to satisfy the Statute of Frauds may be an invoice, a confirmation memo, a letter, or a combination of documents, typewritten, imprinted, or handwritten. Generally, such a writing must state the essential terms and be signed by the party against whom the contract is being enforced (although the requirements vary with the type of contract).

10. F. Under the parol evidence rule, if the parties' contract is completely integrated into a writing (which they intend to be the embodiment of their agreement), evidence of their prior negotiations, prior agreements, or contemporaneous oral agreements that contradicts or varies the terms of their contract is not admissible at trial.

Fill-in Questions

ancillary; primary; must; need not

Multiple-Choice Questions

1. B. A contract that cannot be performed within one year must be in writing to be enforceable. This contract could not be performed within one year so it must be in writing, or evidenced by a writing. (The contracts in answer choices *a* and *c* are of uncertain duration and thus could terminate within a year.)

2. C. Either party can enforce this oral contract. A contract that cannot be performed within one year must be in writing to be enforceable. Because the employee was hired to work for six months, the contract can be performed within a year and does not need to be in writing to be enforced.

3. B. Under the parol evidence rule, if a writing that is determined to constitute a contract includes everything that the parties intended, no evidence of prior negotiations, prior agreements, or contemporaneous oral negotiations may be used to change the terms. A later oral agreement is admissible, however. This question and answer are based on a question that appeared as part of the CPA exam in May 1995.

4. D. Under the Statute of Frauds, a contract for the sale of an interest in land must be in writing to be enforceable. A party to an oral contract involving an interest in land cannot force the other party to buy or sell the property.

5. C. This is an exception to the rule that a contract for a transfer of an interest in land is not enforceable unless it is in writing. If a buyer pays part of the price, takes possession, and makes permanent improvements and the parties cannot be returned to their precontract status quo, a court may grant specific performance of an oral contract for the transfer of an interest in land.

6. A. The Statute of Frauds requires only a writing signed by the party against whom enforcement is sought. Thus, a signed sales receipt may be enough. A purchase order that is not signed by either party would not qualify, regardless of the details that are included on the form.

7. D. Letterhead stationery, and even a business card, might qualify as a signed writing. But neither would be sufficient proof on which to enforce a contract without proof of the necessary terms—parties, subject matter, price, and consideration. In the case of a sale of property, in some states those terms include price and a description of the property.

8. C. Under the UCC, an oral contract for goods priced at $500 or more is enforceable to the extent that the buyer accepts delivery of the goods (or the seller accepts payment). Note that there must be delivery or payment for this exception to the Statute of Frauds to apply.

9. D. A collateral promise must be in writing to be enforceable unless the main purpose of the party making the promise is to secure a benefit for himself or herself. Here, the problem does not include such a purpose. (A collateral promise is a secondary, or ancillary, promise to a primary, or principal, contractual relationship—a third party's promise to assume the debt of a primary party to a contract, for example.)

10. C. If the main purpose of a guarantor in accepting secondary liability is to serve a benefit for himself or herself, the contract need not be in writing to be enforceable. Here, the guaranty is to serve the guarantor's purpose, so it does not need to be in writing to be enforced.

Issue Spotters

1. No. Under the parol evidence rule, if a writing that is determined to constitute a contract includes a clause that no oral statements are incorporated, then no evidence of prior negotiations, prior agreements, or contemporaneous oral statements may be used to change the terms.
2. Yes. Letterhead stationery can constitute a signature. If the memo names the parties, the subject matter, the consideration, and the quantity involved in the transaction, it may be sufficient to be enforced against the party whose letterhead appears on it.
3. No. Under the UCC, a contract for a sale of goods priced at $500 or more must be in writing to be enforceable. In this case, the contract is not enforceable beyond the quantity already delivered and paid for.

Chapter 15

True-False Questions

1. F. Intended beneficiaries have legal rights in contracts under which they benefit. An intended beneficiary is a party whom the contracting parties intended to benefit. Third parties who benefit from a contract only incidentally (incidental beneficiaries) normally do not have rights under the contract.
2. F. In an assignment, the party assigning the rights is the *assignor*. The *obligor* is the party who was originally obligated to perform for the assignor. The party who receives the rights on an assignment is the *assignee* (who may also be the *obligee*). In a delegation, the party delegating the duties is the *delegator* (also the *obligator*) and the party assuming the duties is the *delegatee*.
3. F. A right under a personal service contract cannot normally be assigned. Also, a right cannot ordinarily be assigned if a statute expressly prohibits its assignment, a contract stipulates that it cannot be assigned, or assignment would materially increase or alter the risk of the obligor.
4. F. Rights that cannot be assigned are listed in the answer to the previous question. A right cannot be assigned if (1) a statute expressly prohibits its assignment; (2) a contract stipulates that it cannot be assigned; (3) it is under a contract that is uniquely personal; or (4) assignment would materially increase or alter the risk of the obligor.
5. T
6. T
7. F. An assignment is effective with or without notice. Until the obligor has notice of the assignment, however, the obligor can discharge his or her obligation by performance to the assignor. Also, if the same right is assigned without notice to more than one party, there may be a question as to who has priority.
8. T
9. T
10. T

Fill-in Questions

an assignment; a delegation; assigned; assign

Multiple-Choice Questions

1. C. An incidental beneficiary cannot enforce a contract between two other parties. An example of such a contract would be a consumer's agreement to buy a new car from an auto dealer. The car's manufacturer would indirectly benefit under this contract, but could not enforce it if, for example, the consumer refused to pay the dealer.
2. B. The party originally entitled to the payment of the money is the assignor, the party who agreed to pay is the obligor, and the party who receives the right to the payment is the assignee. An assignee has a right to demand performance from an obligor, but the assignee takes only those rights that the assignor originally had, and these rights are subject to defenses that the obligor has against the assignor. The obligor's consent is not necessary for an effective assignment.
3. C. The rights of an intended third party beneficiary to a contract vest when the original parties cannot rescind or change the contract without the third party's consent. This occurs when the beneficiary learns of the contract and manifests assent to it. This also occurs when the beneficiary changes position in reliance on the contract.
4. C. A right cannot normally be assigned if the assignment would materially increase or alter the risk of the obligor (the different circumstances represented by different persons with different property alter the risk in this problem). A right under a personal service contract cannot normally be assigned, but this is not a personal service contract, which requires a service unique to the person rendering it (an insurance policy is unlikely to qualify).
5. C. Delegating a duty does not normally free the delegator of the obligation to perform if the delegatee does not do so. Ordinarily, if a delegatee fails to perform, the delegator remains liable to the obligee. Of course, the obligee must accept performance from the delegatee if it is forthcoming. Note that here, this is not a personal service contract, which would prohibit its delegation, nor is its delegation prohibited by any other circumstance.
6. D. The presence of one or more of any of these factors strongly indicates that a third party is an intended, rather than an incidental, beneficiary.
7. D. An assignment is not valid if it materially increases or alters the risk or duties of the obligor. An assignment is also invalid if a statute prohibits it, if it involves a contract for personal services, or if, with some exceptions, the contract stipulates that it cannot

be assigned. This question and answer are based on a question that appeared in the CPA exam in May 1995.

8. D. An anti-assignment contract clause is generally effective, but there are exceptions. One of those exceptions concerns the right to receive damages for the breach of a sales contract. The assignment of such a right is valid, even if the contract prohibits it.

9. A. The effect of an unconditional assignment is to extinguish the rights of the assignor. Such an assignment also gives the assignee a right to demand performance from the obligor. Of course, the assignee's rights are subject to the defenses the obligor has against the assignor.

10. C. An assignment does not require notice. When an assignor assigns the same right to different persons, in most states the first to receive the assignment is the first in right.

Issue Spotters

1. Yes. When one person makes a promise with the intention of benefiting a third person, the third person can sue to enforce it. This is a third party beneficiary contract. The third party (the one to whom, in this problem, the money is owed) is the intended beneficiary.

2. Yes. When an assignor successfully assigns a right to receive payment, the assignor's right to the payment is extinguished, and the assignee acquires the right to enforce payment from the obligor.

3. Yes. Generally, if a contract makes it clear that a right is not assignable, no assignment will be effective, but there are exceptions, and assignment of the right to receive money cannot be prohibited.

Chapter 16

True-False Questions

1. T
2. T
3. F. A material breach of contract (which occurs when performance is not at least substantial) excuses the nonbreaching party from performance of his or her contractual duties and gives the party a cause of action to sue for damages caused by the breach. A *minor* breach of contract does not excuse the nonbreaching party's duty to perform, however, although it may affect the extent of his or her performance and, like any contract breach, allows the nonbreaching party to sue for damages.

4. F. An executory contract can be rescinded. If it is executory on both sides, it can be rescinded solely by agreement. In any case, the parties must make a new agreement, and this agreement must qualify as a contract. (The parties' promises not to perform are consideration for the new contract.)

5. T
6. T
7. T
8. T
9. F. A contracting party's refusal to perform, before either party is required to do so, constitutes anticipatory repudiation and can discharge the nonbreaching party, who can sue to recover damages immediately. The nonbreaching party can also seek a similar contract elsewhere.

10. F. Statutes of limitations limit the period during which a party can sue based on a breach of contract. UCC 2–725, for example, limits this time to four years.

Fill-in Questions

Rescission; Novation; Substitution of a new contract; An accord; accord

Multiple-Choice Questions

1. C. A breach of contract entitles the nonbreaching party to damages, but only a material breach discharges the nonbreaching party from his or her duty to perform under the contract. In this problem, the builder has a claim for the amount due on the contract, but the buyer is entitled to have set off the difference in the value of the building as constructed (that is, to subtract the expense to finish the construction).

2. B. For mutual rescission, the parties must make a contract that satisfies the legal requirements, which include consideration. Promises not to perform as originally agreed can constitute consideration when a contract is executory. If it is executed on one side, however, additional consideration or restitution is necessary.

3. B. Contracts that involve construction need only be performed to the satisfaction of a reasonable person. When a contract requires performance to the satisfaction of a third party, a minority of courts require the personal satisfaction of the third party (who must act honestly and in good faith). A majority of courts require the work to be satisfactory to a reasonable person. In this problem, if the work would satisfy a reasonable person, it must be paid for, regardless of the subjective motivation of the party to whom performance was rendered.

4. A. An accord is an executory contract to perform an act to satisfy a contractual duty that has not been discharged (that is, to provide and accept performance different from what was originally promised). An accord suspends the original obligation. A satisfaction is the performance of the accord. If a party does not perform under an accord, the nonbreaching party can bring an action based on either the accord or the original contract.

5. A. Reneging on an employment contract before the employment starts is anticipatory repudiation of the contract and discharges the nonbreaching party from performance. The nonbreaching party can treat the anticipatory breach as a material breach and sue for damages immediately.

6. A. A condition that must be fulfilled before a party is required to perform is a condition precedent. In other words, the condition precedes the absolute duty to perform.

7. C. A novation substitutes a new party for an original party, by agreement of all the parties. The requirements are a previous valid obligation, an agreement of all the parties to a new contract, extinguishment of the old obligation, and a new contract (which must meet the requirements for a valid contract, including consideration).

8. D. Accord and satisfaction, agreement, and operation of law are valid bases on which contracts are discharged, but most contracts are discharged by the parties' doing what they promised to do. A contract is fully discharged by performance when the contracting parties have fully performed what they agreed to do (exchange services for payment, for example).

9. B. This contract would thus be discharged by objective impossibility of performance. On this basis, a contract may be discharged if, for example, after it is made, performance becomes objectively impossible because of a change in the law that renders that performance illegal. This is also the result if one of the parties dies or becomes incapacitated, or the subject matter of the contract is destroyed. This question and answer is based on a question in the May 1995 CPA exam.

10. D. Contracts that have not been fully performed on either side can be rescinded. The parties must make another agreement (which must satisfy the legal requirements for a contract). The parties' promises not to perform are consideration for the new agreement. A contract that has been fully performed on one side can be rescinded only if the party who has performed receives additional consideration to call off the deal.

Issue Spotters

1. No. The builder has substantially performed its duties under the contract. Assuming this performance was in good faith, the builder could thus successfully sue for the value of the work performed. For the sake of justice and fairness, the buyer will be held to the duty to pay, less damages for the deviation from the contract deadline.

2. Contracts that are executory on both sides—contracts on which neither party has performed—can be rescinded solely by agreement. Contracts that are executed on one side—contracts on which one party has performed—can be rescinded only if the party who has performed receives consideration for the promise to call off the deal.

3. The raising of capital is a condition precedent to performance of the contract. If it is not satisfied, the obligations of the parties are discharged. In other words, under this contract, if the money is not raised, neither party needs to do anything.

Chapter 17

True-False Questions

1. T
2. T
3. F. An award of nominal damages, though usually small inn amount, establishes that a breaching party acted wrongfully. Also, nominal damages may be awarded when no actual loss results from a breach of contract (but the breach must still be proved).

4. F. Liquidated damages are certain amounts of money estimated in advance of, and payable on, a breach of contract. *Liquidated* means determined, settled, or fixed.

5. T

6. F. Rescission is available in cases involving fraud, mistake, duress, or failure of consideration. Both parties must make restitution to each other by returning whatever benefit was conveyed in execution of their contract. If the actual item cannot be returned, an equivalent amount in money must be paid.

7. T

8. F. There can be no enforceable contract if the doctrine of quasi contract is to be applied. Under this doctrine, to prevent unjust enrichment, the law implies a promise to pay the reasonable value for benefits received in the absence of an enforceable contract. This recovery is useful when one party has partially performed under a contract that is unenforceable.

9. T

10. F. Damages is the usual on breach of contracts for sales of goods. To obtain specific performance, damages must *not* be an adequate remedy. If goods are unique, or a contract involves a sale of land, damages would not adequately compensate an innocent party for a breach of contract, so specific performance is available.

Fill-in Questions

the contract price and the market price; specific performance; the contract price and the market price

Multiple-Choice Questions

1. A. The failure of one party to perform under a contract entitles the other party to rescind the contract. Both parties, however, must make restitution (return goods, property, or money previously conveyed). Here, on breaching the contract, which entitled the employer to rescind the deal, the contractor did not return the amount of the employer's payment.

2. C. A breach of contract by failing to perform entitles the nonbreaching party to rescind the contract, and the parties must make restitution by returning whatever benefit they conferred on each other, particularly when the breaching party would otherwise be unjustly enriched.
3. C. Under a contract for a sale of goods, the usual measure of compensatory damages is the difference between the contract price and the market price, plus incidental damages. On a seller's breach, the measure includes the difference between what the seller would have been owed if he or she had performed and what the buyer paid elsewhere for the goods.
4. B. The measure of damages on breach of a construction contract depends on which party breaches and when the breach occurs. If, as in this problem, the owner (buyer) breaches during construction, normally the contractor (seller) may recover its profit plus the costs incurred up to the time of the breach.
5. B. On the seller's breach of a contract, the buyer is entitled to be compensated for the loss of the bargain. Here, the buyer will receive what was contracted for, but it will be late. When, as in this problem, a seller knew that the buyer would lose business if the goods were not delivered on time, the loss of the bargain is the consequential damages (the amount lost as a foreseeable consequence of the breach).
6. C. Specific performance is an award of the act promised in a contract. This remedy is granted when the legal remedy (damages) is inadequate. Damages are generally inadequate for a buyer on the breach of a contract for a sale of land, because every piece of land is considered unique. If specific performance is not available, however, as when the land cannot be sold by the contracting seller, damages are possible, and their measure is the benefit of the buyer's bargain (the difference between the contract price and the market price of the land at the time of the breach).
7. B. A quasi contract may be imposed when a party has partially performed under a contract that is unenforceable. (An oral contract, the terms of which cannot be performed within one year, is unenforceable under the one-year rule of the Statute of Frauds.) To obtain quasi-contractual relief, a party must show that (1) he or she conferred a benefit on another, (2) he or she conferred the benefit with the reasonable expectation of being paid, (3) he or she did not act as a volunteer in conferring the benefit, and (4) the party receiving the benefit would be unjustly enriched by retaining the benefit without paying for it.
8. A. Reformation permits a contract to be rewritten to reflect the parties' actual intentions when they have imperfectly expressed their agreement in writing. This often applies in a case of fraud or mutual mistake (in a land sale contract, for example, when the property's legal description is erroneous). To prevent hardship, a court may also reform a covenant not to compete to convert its unreasonable terms into reasonable ones.
9. D. Under the election of remedies doctrine, a nonbreaching party must choose which remedy to pursue. Here, the innocent party chose damages. The purpose of the doctrine is to prevent double recovery: a party may not recover twice for the same harm. This doctrine has been eliminated in contracts for sales of goods, however. In other words, under the UCC, double recovery is not possible, but remedies are cumulative (choosing to pursue one remedy does not foreclose the pursuit of others).
10. D. If the clause is determined to be a penalty clause, it will be unenforceable. To determine whether a clause is a liquidated damages clause or a penalty clause, consider first whether, when the contract was made, damages would clearly be difficult to estimate in the event of a breach. Second, consider whether the amount set as damages is a reasonable estimate. Two "yeses" mean the clause is enforceable. One "no" means the provision is an unenforceable penalty. This question and answer are based on a question that was in the May 1993 CPA exam.

Issue Spotters

1. A nonbreaching party is entitled to his or her benefit of the bargain under the contract. Here, the innocent party is entitled to be put in the position she would have been in if the contract had been fully performed. The measure of the benefit is the cost to complete the work ($500). These are compensatory damages.
2. No. To recover damages that flow from the consequences of a breach but that are caused by circumstances beyond the contract (consequential damages), the breaching party must know, or have reason to know, that special circumstances will cause the nonbreaching party to suffer the additional loss. That was not the circumstance in this problem.
3. This clause is known as an exculpatory clause. In many cases, such clauses are not enforced, but to be effective in any case, all contracting parties must have consented to it. A clause excluding liability for negligence may be enforced if the contract was made by parties in roughly equal bargaining positions, as two large corporations would be.

Chapter 18

True-False Questions

1. F. Courts usually do enforce shrink-wrap agreements. The reasoning is that the shrink-wrap terms constitute an offer, proposed by a seller and accepted by a buyer after the buyer had an opportunity to review the terms.
2. T
3. T

4. F. Under the Electronic Signatures in Global and National Commerce (E-SIGN) Act, which Congress passed in 2000, no contract, record, or signature can be denied legal effect simply because it is in an electronic form (although some documents are specifically excluded).
5. F. The UETA, like the Uniform Computer Information Transactions Act (UCITA), was drafted by the National Conference of Commissioners on Uniform State Laws and the American Law Institute as a proposal of legislation for the states to enact individually. Most states have enacted the UETA. (Only a couple of states have enacted the UCITA.)
6. F. Parties to a transaction can waive or vary any or all of the provisions of the UETA (that is, they can opt out or choose not to have it apply), but the UETA applies in the absence of an agreement to the contrary. The parties must have agreed to conduct their transaction electronically, however.
7. T
8. T
9. T
10. F. Electronic self-help occurs when a licensor undertakes to enforce the licensor's rights through electronic means, typically on a breach of the license agreement by the licensee. The UCITA allows this practice but limits its use, and these limits cannot be waived by contract.

Fill-in Questions

UCITA and the UETA; UCITA and the UETA; UETA; UETA

Multiple-Choice Questions

1. B. The terms of a shrink-wrap agreement typically concern warranties, remedies, and other issues. The other answer choices in this question represent locations of the terms in click-on agreements, in "fine print," and in computer code that may not be readable by humans. A shrink-wrap agreement is typically between the manufacturer of hardware or software and its user.
2. A. Shrink-wrap agreements have not always been enforced. The most important consideration is the time at which the manufacturer communicated the terms to the end-user. If they are proposed after a contract is entered into, they can be construed as proposals for additional terms, to which the consumer must expressly agree.
3. C. A binding contract can be created by clicking on, for example, an "I agree" button if an opportunity is provided to read the terms before the button is clicked. If the terms are not revealed until after an agreement is made, however, it is unlikely that, as in cases involving shrink-wrap agreements, they would be considered part of the deal. Here, the problem states that the button referred to the terms, meaning the buyer knew, or should have known, what was being agreed to.
4. B. Under the E-SIGN Act, no contract, record, or signature may be denied legal effect solely because it is in electronic form. An e-signature is as valid as a signature on paper, and an e-document is as valid as a paper document. One possible complication is that state laws on e-signatures are not uniform. Most state have enacted the Uniform Electronic Transactions Act (UETA) but with individual modifications.
5. A. The UETA does not apply unless the parties agree to use e-commerce in their transaction (unlike the Uniform Computer Information Transactions Act (UCITA), which applies to any agreement that falls within its scope). The UETA does support all electronic transactions, but it does not provide rules for them (again unlike the UCITA, which covers only contracts concerning computer information, but imposes rules on those contracts).
6. D. To fall under the UETA, the parties to a contract must agree to conduct their transaction electronically. The UETA then applies in the absence of an agreement between the parties to the contrary, although they can waive or vary any or all of its provisions. Whether the contract involves computer information is irrelevant under the UETA. To fall under the UCITA, however, a contract must involve, in whole or in part, computer information, as defined by the act, unless the parties to the deal opt in or opt out of the UCITA's application.
7. C. To be "sent," an e-record must be properly directed from the sender's place of business to the intended recipient, in a form readable by the recipient's computer, at the recipient's place of business. This location is the recipient's place of business with the closest relation to the transaction. If a party does not have a place of business, the party's residence is used. An e-record is received when it enters the recipient's processing system in a readable form, even if no person is aware of the receipt
8. B. If the parties to a deal subject to the UETA agree to a security procedure and one party fails to detect an error because it does not follow the procedure, the other party may be able to avoid the effect of the error. To do so, the conforming party must (1) promptly notify the other party of the error and of his or her intent not to be bound by it and (2) take reasonable steps to return any benefit or consideration received. If there can be no restitution, the transaction may not be avoidable. (If the parties do not agree on a security procedure, other state laws determine the effect of the mistake.)
9. C. The UCITA covers, besides the contracts mentioned in this problem, contracts to access online databases, to create computer programs, for computer games, and to distribute information on the Internet, via disks, and other similar contracts. These are all

contracts involving computer information, as that term is defined in the UCITA.

10. D. The UCITA is like most other uniform acts that apply in the business context. For contracts that fall within its scope, it applies in the absence of an agreement to the contrary, and parties can also bring contracts under it that would not otherwise be governed by it. Parties who would otherwise be covered by the UCITA can also agree to opt out of all or part of the act and agree not to be covered by it. Exceptions include the rules that concern good faith, unconscionability, and related principles.

Issue Spotters

1. The effect of an e-record is determined from its context and circumstances. Any relevant evidence can prove that an e-record is, or is not, the act of a party to a deal. A party's name or "signature" on an e-record is not necessary to give effect to it, although a party's name typed on, for example, an e-mail purchase order, qualifies as a "signature" and is attributable to the party.

2. According to the UCITA, computer information is "information in electronic form obtained from or through use of a computer, or that is in digital or equivalent form capable of being processed by a computer" [UCITA 102(10)]. Generally, this includes software and electronic databases in any format that a computer can read.

3. First, it might be noted that the UETA does not apply unless the parties to a contract agree to use e-commerce in their transaction. In this deal, of course, the parties used e-commerce. Unlike the UETA, the UCITA applies to any agreement that falls within its scope. The UCITA also addresses e-commerce issues that the UETA does not. The UETA supports e-transactions, but it does not include rules for those transactions. The UCITA, however, imposes rules, although it does so only for contracts that come under it—contracts that involve computer information.

Cumulative Hypothetical Problem for Unit Three—Including Chapters 9–18

1. D. An offeror can revoke an offer for a bilateral contract, which is what this offer is, any time before it is accepted. This may be after the offeree is aware of the offer.

2. C. Courts impose an objective, or reasonable, analysis in determining whether or not a contract was made and in interpreting its terms. This is known as the objective theory of contracts.

3. B. A mutual mistake of fact may be a ground for relief, but it is not the only mistake for which relief may be granted. Although a party to a contract is not normally granted relief for a unilateral mistake, if the other party knew, or should have known, of the mistake, the law allows for relief.

4. C. A novation completely discharges a party to a contract. Another party assumes the discharged party's obligations. If a party has assigned his or her rights under a contract, he or she may still be liable in the event the assignee defaults. A *executed* accord would allow a party to avoid liability under a contract, but an *unexecuted* accord does not.

5. A. Damages, the remedy at law, is the usual remedy for a breach of contract. Specific performance is granted only if the remedy at law is inadequate, as it is when, for example, the goods that are the subject of a contract are unique. Courts are also reluctant to award specific performance in cases involving contracts for services.

Questions on the Focus on Legal Reasoning for Unit Three—*Ford v. Trendwest, Inc.*

1. C. In the *Ford* case, the court reasoned that "[w]hen the parties contracted for at-will employment, Ford had no greater expectations than an at-will employee, and Trendwest had no fewer rights than an at-will employer. . . . Nothing in this contract changed the at-will employment relationship." The court concluded that "lost earnings cannot measure damages for the breach of an employment at-will contract because the parties to such a contract do not bargain for future earnings. By its very nature, at-will employment precludes an expectation of future earnings."

2. A. The majority in the *Ford* case stated that "[a]n employee's expectations under an employment at-will contract are no different from the employment itself." An at-will employee may be terminated at any time for any reason. Nothing in an agreement to hire an individual for employment at-will "change[s] the at-will employment relationship."

3. D. The dissent in the *Ford* case reasoned that if an employer "promises . . . specific treatment in specific situations and an employee is induced thereby to . . . not actively seek other employment, those promises are enforceable." If they are breached, "the mere fact an employer could have fired the employee without liability the next day or under some other circumstance not amounting to breach of contract does not render . . . a claim for lost wages speculative."

Questions on the Focus on Ethics for Unit Three—Contract Law and the Application of Ethics

1. A. If a contract is unconscionable, it is so unfair and one-sided as to "shock the conscience" of a court and be unenforceable. Unconscionability, which represents an attempt by the law to enforce ethical behavior, is a common law concept that is not precisely defined. Even UCC 2–302, which adopts the doctrine, does not define the term with specificity. Instead, it is

the prerogative of the courts to determine its application in contract cases.
2. D. If, in contracting, an individual fails to look after his or her own interest, the party with whom he or she contracts arguably does not have a responsibility to look after the other's interest. It can be acceptable to take advantage of the circumstance, although if there is a suit, the court might consider the relative bargaining positions of the parties to decide whether the deal is too one-sided.
3. C. In the interests of fairness and justice, a court may estop the subcontractor from denying the existence of a contract, in the circumstances presented in this question. A party who reasonably relies on such a promise to his or her detriment can then obtain some measure of relief for any ensuing injury or damage. Ethical standards underlie this doctrine.

Chapter 19

True-False Questions

1. T
2. T
3. F. If a transaction involves only a service, the common law usually applies (one exception is the serving of food or drink, which is governed by the UCC). When goods and services are combined, courts have disagreed over whether a particular transaction involves a sale of goods or a rendering of service. Usually, a court will apply the law that applies to whichever feature is dominant. Article 2 does not cover sales of real estate, although sales of goods associated with real estate, including crops, may be covered. A contract for a sale of minerals, for example, is considered a contract for a sale of goods if the severance is to be made by the seller.
4. F. Unlike the common law rule that contract modification must be supported by new consideration, the UCC requires no consideration for an agreement modifying a contract.
5. F. A contract will be enforceable, and a writing will be sufficient under the UCC's Statute of Frauds, if it indicates that a contract was intended, if it includes a quantity term, and—except for transactions between merchants—if it is signed by the party against whom enforcement is sought. Most terms can be proved by oral testimony or be supplied by the UCC's open term provisions (for example, price, delivery, and payment terms). A contract is not enforceable beyond the quantity of goods shown in the writing, however, except for output and requirements contracts.
6. T
7. T
8. F. A seller can accept an offer to buy goods for current or prompt shipment by promptly *shipping* the goods or by promptly *promising* to ship the goods. Of course, under the mirror image rule, an offer must be accepted in its entirety without modification, or there is no contract. Under the UCC, additional terms may become part of the contract if both parties are merchants (though not if at least one party is a nonmerchant).
9. T
10. F. Under the UCC, oral contracts for specially manufactured goods may be enforceable. Also, an oral contract for a sale or lease of goods may be enforceable if the party against whom enforcement is sought admits in court pleadings or proceedings that a contract was made. Partial performance of a contract for a sale or lease of goods may also support the enforcement of an oral contract, at least to the extent of that performance.

Fill-in Questions

Course of dealing; Usage of trade; trade; consistent; terms in the agreement

Multiple-Choice Questions

1. D. A sale is defined as "the passing of title from the seller to the buyer for a price." The price may be payable in money or in goods, services, or real estate.
2. C. A merchant is a person who acts in a mercantile capacity, possessing or using expertise specifically related to the goods being sold. A merchant for one type of goods is not necessarily a merchant for another type, however. The test is whether the merchant holds himself or herself out by occupation as having knowledge or skill unique to the goods in the transaction.
3. A. Under the UCC, a sales contract will not fail for indefiniteness even if one or more terms are left open, as long as the parties intended to make a contract and there is a reasonably certain basis for the court to grant an appropriate remedy. If the price term is left open, for example, and the parties cannot later agree on a price, a court will set the price according to what is reasonable at the time for delivery. If one of the parties is to set the price, it must be set in good faith. If it is not fixed, the other party can set the price or treat the contract as canceled.
4. B. A lease involves a lessor who leases (or buys) goods from a supplier and leases (or subleases) them to a lessee. In other words, a lessor sells the right to the possession and use of goods under a lease. Sales are subject to Article 2 of the UCC. Gifts are not subject to the UCC.
5. C. The contract is subject to the Statute of Frauds, and thus should be in writing to be fully enforceable. A contract that is subject to the Statute of Frauds but is not in writing will be enforceable, however, if payment is made and accepted—but only to the extent of the payment actually made.
6. D. In a transaction between merchants, additional terms in the acceptance of an offer become part of a contract *unless* they qualify as one of these exceptions.

7. A. A contract in writing that was intended to be a final expression cannot be contradicted by evidence of prior agreements or contemporaneous oral agreements. Some evidence outside the contract is admissible, however. Besides the evidence noted in the correct answer, evidence of what the parties did under the contract (their course of dealing and their course of performance) and the usage in their trade (commercial practices) is also admissible.
8. C. A firm offer can only be made by a merchant in a signed writing. The other party does not need to be a merchant. Consideration is not necessary, and no definite period need be specified. This question and answer are based on a question that appeared in the CPA exam in November 1995.
9. D. An unconscionable clause is one that is so unfair and one-sided that it would be unreasonable to enforce it. When considering such a clause, a court can choose among the answers choices in this problem. To assess unconscionability, a court may weigh such factors as a high price, a consumer's level of education, and his or her capacity to compare prices.
10. D. Contracts without specified quantities are not enforceable under the UCC. The UCC includes a number of open-term provisions that can be used to fill the gaps in a contract. Terms for delivery, payment, and price can be proved by evidence, or whatever is reasonable will be determined. The quantity of goods must be expressly stated, however, or a court cannot award a remedy.

Starbucks Coffee Co. International Sales Contract Applications

1. B. As stated in the "Breach or Default of Contract" clause on the second page, this contract is subject to Article 2 of the UCC. If the parties to a sales contract do not express some of the terms in writing, including the price term, the contract is still enforceable. A sales contract that must be in writing is only enforceable, however, to the extent of the quantity stated in writing. If these parties did not state the amount of product ordered, the contract may not be enforced because if a quantity term is left out, the court would have no basis for determining a remedy.
2. B. When a seller, as a party to a sales contract, states or otherwise expresses what the goods will be, then the goods must be that. The goods must at least conform to the seller's description of them, wherever that descriptions is, whether in the contract, in promotional materials, on labels, by salespersons, by comparison to a sample, etc. A seller's subjective belief is not the standard. The buyer's subjective belief may be the standard if the contract specifies that the goods must personally satisfy the buyer.
3. C. This clause states the terms for payment under this sales contract and indicates that the buyer has two days after the day of tender in which to pay for the goods or will be considered in breach. The "BREACH OR DEFAULT OF CONTRACT" clause sets out what happens "if either party hereto fails to perform." These are all incentives for the buyer to pay on time.
4. A. This clause allows the buyer to reject nonconforming product, although this is limited to a specific number of days. (Note that the buyer' right to reject does not need to be stated in a contract for the buyer to have that right.) This clause details the procedures that the parties may follow if the product does not meet its description. These are incentives for the seller to deliver conforming goods.
5. D. This is a destination contract, as indicated by the "ARRIVAL," "DELIVERY," "INSURANCE," and "FREIGHT" clauses. This means that the seller bears the risk of loss until the coffee is delivered to its destination (a "Bonded Public Warehouse" in Laredo, Texas). Risk of loss is discussed in more detail in the following chapter.

Issue Spotters

1. Yes. Under the UCC, if a merchant gives assurances in a signed writing that an offer will remain open, the offer is irrevocable. The car dealer in this problem is a merchant who promised to keep an offer open for seven days and did not do so.
2. A shipment of nonconforming goods constitutes an acceptance and a breach, unless the seller seasonably notifies the buyer that the nonconforming shipment does not constitute an acceptance and is offered only as an accommodation. Without the notification, the shipment is an acceptance and a breach. Thus, here, the shipment was both an acceptance and a breach.
3. Yes. In a transaction between merchants, the requirement of a writing is satisfied if one of them sends to the other a signed written confirmation that indicates the terms of the agreement, and the merchant receiving it has reason to know of its contents. If the merchant who receives it does not object in writing within ten days after receipt, the writing will be enforceable against him or her even though he or she has not signed anything.

Chapter 20

True-False Questions

1. T
2. F. Title passes at the time and place at which the seller delivers the goods—unless the parties agree otherwise, which is always an option under the UCC.
3. T
4. F. This is the definition of a sale or return.
5. F. A buyer has an insurable interest in goods the moment they are identified to the contract by the

seller. A seller has an insurable interest in goods as long as he or she has title. After title has passed, a seller who has a security interest in goods retains an insurable interest. Thus, a buyer and a seller can both have an insurable interest in goods at the same time.

6. T

7. F. In a sale on approval, the risk of loss remains with the seller until the buyer accepts the goods.

8. F. Generally, a buyer acquires whatever title the seller has to the goods. If a seller (or lessor) stole the goods, he or she has no title, and the buyer (or lessee, who might otherwise acquire a valid leasehold interest) gets nothing. The real owner can reclaim the goods from the buyer or the thief.

9. F. Under a *shipment* contract, title passes at time and place of shipment. Under a destination contract, title passes when the goods are tendered at a certain destination.

10. T

Fill-in Questions

F.O.B.; F.O.B.; F.O.B.; F.A.S.

Multiple-Choice Questions

1. C. These are the requirements for identification. Title and risk of loss cannot pass from seller to buyer until the goods are identified to the contract. Other actions on the part of a seller, such as arranging for shipment or obtaining insurance, do not determine when an interest in goods passes.

2. B. Under a shipment contract, risk passes when the seller puts the goods into a carrier's possession. Under a destination contract, risk passes when the seller tenders delivery to the buyer. This question and answer are based on a question that appeared in the November 1995 CPA exam.

3. A. When goods are to be picked up by a buyer, if a seller is a nonmerchant, risk passes on the seller's tender of delivery (unless the parties agree otherwise). The goods were tendered before the theft, so the buyer suffers the loss. If the seller is a merchant, the risk of loss passes when the buyer takes possession of the goods.

4. A. If a bailee holds goods for a seller and the goods are delivered without being moved, under a negotiable document of title, the risk of loss passes when the buyer receives the document. If the document is nonnegotiable, however, more is required to transfer the risk: the buyer must also have had a reasonable time to present the document and demand the goods. In either case, the risk can also pass on the bailee's acknowledgment of the buyer's right to possess the goods. In any case, if the bailee refuses to recognize the buyer's right, the loss stays with the seller.

5. A. Entrusting goods to a merchant who deals in goods of the kind gives the merchant power to transfer all rights to a buyer in the ordinary course of business. The owner of the car has good title against the dealer, but a buyer in the ordinary course of business can acquire, in good faith, good title from the merchant. This title is good against even the original owner. Note that had a thief stolen the car from the original owner and left it with the dealer, the later buyer would not have good title against the original owner.

6. B. When goods are to be picked up by a buyer, if a seller is a merchant, the risk of loss does not pass to the buyer until the buyer takes possession of the goods (unless the parties agree otherwise). The goods were tendered before the theft, but the buyer did not take possession.

7. B. Under a destination contract, the risk of loss passes when the seller tenders delivery at the specified destination. Here, the destination was the buyer, and the goods were destroyed before they reached that location. Also, note that "F.O.B." indicates that the seller bears the cost of the transport to the specified destination.

8. C. A buyer has an insurable interest in goods as soon as they are identified to the contract, even before the risk of loss passes. A seller has an insurable interest as long as he or she still has title to the goods. More than one party can have an insurable interest at the same time.

9. A. Generally, the party who breaches a contract bears the risk of loss. Here, the buyer breached by shipping defective goods. The risk would have passed to the buyer if the buyer accepted the goods in spite of their defects. (If the buyer had accepted the goods and then discovered the defects, the buyer could have revoked its acceptance, which would have transferred the risk back to the seller.)

10. B. Under a shipment contract, if the contracting parties do not specify a time for title to pass, then it passes on delivery of the goods to the carrier.

Issue Spotters

1. The result would be the same as if the contract stated, "F.O.B. New York." For the risk of loss to remain with the seller, a seller must specifically agree to deliver goods to a particular destination. Remember, all contracts are assumed to be shipment contracts unless they state otherwise.

2. The seller suffers the loss. If goods are so nonconforming that a buyer has the right to reject them, the risk of loss will not pass from the seller to the buyer until the defects are cured or the buyer accepts the defective goods. Here, the defects had not been cured and the buyer had not yet accepted the goods. Note that if the goods were shipped and arrived at the buyer's location, the risk would remain with the seller because the goods were defective.

3. No. A seller has voidable title if the goods that he or she is selling were paid for with a bad check (a check that is later dishonored). Normally, a buyer acquires only the title that the seller had, or had the power to transfer, but a seller with voidable title can transfer good title to a good faith purchaser (one who buys in good faith without knowledge that the seller did not have the right to sell the goods). Under those circumstances, an original owner cannot recover goods from a good faith purchaser. Here, the ultimate buyer is a good faith purchaser.

Chapter 21

True-False Questions

1. T
2. T
3. T
4. F. If the parties do not agree otherwise, the buyer or lessee must pay for the goods at the time and place of their receipt (subject, in most cases, to the buyer or lessee's right to inspect). When a sale is on credit, a buyer must pay according to credit terms, not when the goods are received. Credit terms may provide for payment within thirty days, for example. A credit period usually begins on the date of shipment.
5. F. After having had a reasonable opportunity to inspect, a buyer has only a reasonable time within which to reject goods. Also, once goods are accepted, they cannot be rejected. (Acceptance can be revoked, however.)
6 F. Merchants are held to a higher standard than nonmerchants are. For a merchant, good faith means honesty in fact and the observance of reasonable commercial standards of fair dealing in the trade.
7. F. If, before the time for performance, a buyer or lessee clearly communicates his or her intent not to perform, the seller or lessor can suspend performance and wait to see if the other will perform, or the seller or lessor can treat the anticipatory repudiation as a breach, suspend performance, and pursue a remedy.
8. T
9. F. If a contract does not state where goods are to be delivered, and the buyer is to pick them up, the place for delivery is the seller's place of business (unless the parties know that the goods are elsewhere, in which case the place of their delivery is their location). Shipment and destination contracts are subject to different rules that depend on their terms.
10. F. A buyer can reject an installment only if its value is *substantially impaired* by a nonconformity that cannot be cured (in which case, the seller has breached the contract).

Fill-in Questions

conforming; and; buyer; receipt; unless

Multiple-Choice Questions

1. C. In an installment contract, a buyer can reject an installment only if a nonconformity substantially impairs the value of the installment and cannot be cured. Thus, among the answer possibilities here, the rejection of the first installment is the best choice. This deviation might be curable, however, by an adjustment in price or by a shipment of conforming goods, so an answer that suggested these alternatives might represent an even better choice.
2. A. If a contract that involves a sale of identified goods does not specify a place of delivery, and the buyer is to pick up the goods, and the parties know when they contract that the goods are located somewhere other than the seller's place of business, the location of the goods is the place for their delivery.
3. D. When tender is rejected because goods are nonconforming, a seller cannot exercise the right to cure by offering other nonconforming goods after the contracted time for performance. In this problem, the seller has breached the contract, and the buyer may seek a remedy.
4. C. The buyer must designate defects that are ascertainable by reasonable inspection, or those defects cannot be used to justify rejection or to establish breach if the seller could have cured them on being seasonably notified. In this problem, the seller could have cured quickly if it had known the reason for the buyer's rejection, and thus, the buyer cannot win a suit for damages.
5. A. If, before the time of performance, a party to a contract informs the other party that he or she will not perform, the nonbreaching party can treat the repudiation as a final breach and seek a remedy or wait, for a commercially reasonable time, hoping that the breaching party will decide to honor the contract. In either case, the nonbreaching party can suspend his or her performance.
6. D. In this problem, the seller is the beneficiary. Under a letter of credit, if the documents presented by the beneficiary comply with the terms, the issuing bank must pay the beneficiary. The buyer (or account party) has promised to repay the issuer for amounts it pays to the beneficiary in these circumstances.
7. C. The parties to a contract can stipulate the time, place, and manner of delivery. In the absence of specified details, however, tender of delivery must be at a reasonable hour and in a reasonable manner. The buyer must be notified, and the goods must be kept available for a reasonable time. This question and answer are based on a question that appeared in the CPA exam in November 1995.
8. B. Unless the contract provides otherwise, a buyer (or lessee) has an absolute right to inspect tendered goods before making payment, to verify that they are as ordered. If they are not as ordered, the buyer has no duty to pay, and the seller cannot enforce any right to payment.

9. C. Acceptance of goods under a sales contract can be express or implied. A buyer can accept goods by words ("I accept," "the goods are what I ordered," etc.) or conduct (any act, such as using the goods, inconsistent with the seller's ownership).
10. C. It is the seller's obligation to tender delivery of goods. Under a shipment contract, a seller must make a reasonable contract for the transportation of goods, tender to the buyer whatever documents are necessary to obtain possession of goods from the carrier, and notify the buyer that shipment has been made.

Issue Spotters

1. Yes. Normally, goods must be tendered in a single delivery, but the parties can agree otherwise or the circumstances may be such that either party can rightfully request delivery in lots. The seller's proposal to work around the circumstances in this problem seems reasonable.
2. Yes. A seller is obligated to deliver goods in conformity with a contract in every detail. This is the perfect tender rule. The exception of the seller's right to cure does not apply here, because the seller delivered too little too late to take advantage of this exception.
3. Yes. In a case of anticipatory repudiation, a buyer (or lessee) can resort to any remedy for breach even if the buyer tells the seller (the repudiating party in this problem) that the buyer will wait for the seller's performance.

Chapter 22

True-False Questions

1. F. Ordinarily, specific performance is considered inappropriate if damages will place the buyer or lessee in the position that he or she would have been in if the seller or lessor had fully performed. In other words, in most cases only if damages is an inadequate remedy is specific performance awarded.
2. T.
3. T
4. T
5. T
6. F. When a seller delivers nonconforming goods, the buyer can reject the goods with timely notice. The buyer can then recover any payments for the goods, as well as the expense of keeping or returning them. Or, in some circumstances, the buyer can resell the goods.
7. F. If a seller breaches a contract, under the UCC the buyer can cancel it and retains all rights to any other remedy against the seller.
8. F. A buyer or lessee who accepts nonconforming goods can revoke the acceptance, but only by notifying the seller or lessor, which must occur within a reasonable time and before goods have, for example, spoiled. If the goods are perishable, the buyer or lessee must follow any reasonable instructions of the seller or lessor regarding the goods. (This is also the case when the buyer or lessee rejects the goods.)
9. F. Before goods are delivered, a seller can cancel a contract only if the buyer breaches it. And even in that circumstance, the seller must notify the buyer.
10. F. Under the United Nations Convention on Contracts for the International Sale of Goods (CISG), remedies include damages, the right to avoid the contract, and the right to specific performance. These are similar to remedies available under the UCC.

Fill-in Questions

an automobile under warranty; value or use; within a certain number of opportunities; a new car, replacement of defective parts, or return of all consideration paid

Multiple-Choice Questions

1. C. If a buyer repudiates a contract or wrongfully refuses to accept goods, a seller can cancel the contract, which discharges the seller's obligations, or sue for damages: the difference between the contract price and the market price at the time and place of tender. The seller can also recover incidental damages. If the market price is less than the contract price, damages include the seller's lost profits. This question and answer are based on a question from the November 1995 CPA exam.
2. C. If a buyer is forced to obtain substitute goods for those that were due under a contract, the buyer can recover from the seller the difference between the cost of the cover and the contract price, plus incidental and consequential damages, less whatever expenses (such as delivery costs) were saved as a result of the seller's breach.
3. C. Depending on the circumstances, when a seller or lessor delivers nonconforming goods, the buyer or lessee can reject the part of the goods that does not conform (and rescind the contract or obtain cover). The buyer or lessee may instead revoke acceptance, or he or she may recover damages, for accepted goods.
4. D. Under the UCC, contracting parties can provide for additional remedies or different remedies, including a change in the measure of damages. There are some limits. If a buyer is a consumer, for example, limiting consequential damages may be unconscionable.
5. B. Replevin is an action to recover specific goods in the possession of a party who is wrongfully withholding them. When a seller (or lessor) refuses to deliver (or repudiates the contract), the buyer or lessee may maintain an action to replevy the goods. The buyer or lessee must show, however, an inability to cover.

6. C. If the quantity shipped is a truckload or more, a seller can stop delivery of goods if the buyer is insolvent or in breach of the contract. Of course, if the buyer is in possession of the goods, the buyer's rights to the goods have been acknowledged by the carrier or another bailee, or the buyer has received a document of title to the goods, the seller must use some other remedy.
7. C. When a seller has delivered goods that are in the possession of the buyer and the buyer refuses to pay, the seller has two choices: he or she can bring an action for the price or reclaim the goods. There are limits on the availability of the right to reclaim, however, and use of this remedy bars the seller from pursuing other remedies.
8. C. A buyer (or lessee) can sue for damages when a seller (or lessor) repudiates the contract or fails to deliver the goods, or when the buyer has rightfully rejected or revoked acceptance of the goods. The place for determining the price is the place at which the seller was to deliver the goods. The buyer may also recover incidental and consequential damages, less expenses saved due to the breach.
9. C. To use this remedy, the buyer must give the seller seasonable notice and tell the seller what the defect is. The buyer must then follow the seller's instructions as to what to do with the nonconforming goods. Of course, the buyer should be reimbursed for the expense of storage or return and so on.
10. A. If a lessee (or buyer) wrongfully refuses to accept, the lessor (or seller) can recover the difference between the contract price and the market price (at the time and place of tender), plus incidental damages. If the market price is less than the contract price, the lessor (or seller) can recover lost profits.

Issue Spotters

1. Yes. Withholding delivery is a remedy available to a seller when a buyer wrongfully rejects goods. Wrongful rejection is a breach of contract. If a breach is material and deliveries are to be made in installments, the seller can withhold the entire undelivered balance of the goods.
2. The buyer can recover the difference between the market price—at the time that the buyer learned of the breach, at the place for tender—and the contract price, plus incidental damages (reasonable expenses incident to the breach) and consequential damages (of which the seller knew at the time of the breach), less any expenses saved by the breach. Thus, in this problem, the buyer can recover $2,000 ($10,000 x $.20), plus incidental damages and consequential damages (for the halt to the buyer's operation), less any expenses saved by the breach.
3. If a buyer wrongfully refuses to accept conforming goods, the seller can recover damages. The measure is the difference between the contract price and the market price (at the time and place of tender), plus incidental damages. If the market price is less than the contract price, the seller gets lost profits.

Chapter 23

True-False Questions

1. T
2. F. Warranties are not exclusive. A contract can include an implied warranty of merchantability, an implied warranty of fitness for a particular purpose, and any number of express warranties.
3. F. Unless the circumstances indicate otherwise, the implied warranty of merchantability (and the implied warranty of fitness for a particular purpose) can be disclaimed by such expressions as "as is" and "with all faults." Express warranties can also be disclaimed.
4. T
5. T
6. T
7. T
8. F. A seller's statement of opinion or recommendation about the goods is an express warranty only if the seller who makes it is an expert and gives the opinion as an expert.
9. T
10. F. There is no implied warranty with respect to defects that a reasonable examination would reveal if a buyer examines goods before entering a contract. This is also true if the seller demands that the buyer examine the goods and the buyer refuses.

Fill-in Questions

can; can; can; need not; must

Multiple-Choice Questions

1. C. An implied warranty of merchantability arises in every sale of goods by a merchant who deals in goods of the kind. It makes no difference whether the merchant knew of or could have discovered a defect that makes a product unsafe. The warranty is that the goods are "reasonably fit for the ordinary purposes for which such goods are used." The efficiency and the quality of their manufacture, and the manufacturer's compliance with government regulations, are not factors that directly influence this determination.
2. C. An implied warranty of fitness for a particular purpose arises when any seller—merchant or nonmerchant—knows a particular purpose for which a buyer will use goods and that the buyer is relying on the seller's skill and judgment. Here, the buyer was relying on the seller to choose a dependable vehicle for off-road driving, and the seller knew it.
3. A. This phrase, or similar language, will generally disclaim most implied warranties. To specifically

disclaim an implied warranty of fitness for a particular purpose, a writing must be conspicuous, but the word *fitness* does not have to be used. A specific disclaimer of the implied warranty of merchantability must mention *merchantability*. Note that warranties of title can be disclaimed only by specific language (for example, a seller states that it is transferring only such rights as it has in the goods), or by circumstances that indicate no warranties of title are made.

4. D. When an express warranty is made in a sales contract, the Magnuson-Moss Warranty Act prevents sellers from disclaiming or modifying the implied warranties of merchantability and fitness for a particular purpose. Also, with respect to the time limit in an express warranty, sellers can impose a time limit on an implied warranty, but it must correspond to the duration of the express warranty.

5. C. The other warranties of title are that the goods are free of the security interest of a third party of which the buyer has no knowledge and that the goods are also free of any third party's copyright, patent, or trademark claim. The choice concerning the quality of the goods at the price is a statement of opinion, and a seller's statement of opinion is not a warranty.

6. A. A label is an affirmation of fact, which is an express warranty and a standard that the labeled goods must meet. Regarding the other choices, an implied warranty is not express. An implied warranty of merchantability arises in every sale (or lease) in which the merchant selling the goods deals in goods of the kind. An implied warranty of fitness for a particular purpose arises when the merchant knows (or has reason to know) the particular purpose for which the customer is buying the goods.

7. A. As part of the warranty of title, sellers warrant that they have good and valid title and that, in a sale, the transfer of title is rightful. This warranty may be disclaimed, but only by specific contractual language.

8. A. The statement in the brochure is an affirmation of fact and thus a warranty that the goods will meet that standard. Statements that attest to the quality of the goods ("the best on the market") would not qualify.

9. D. This is a statement of opinion (puffing, or puffery). Puffing creates no warranty. If the salesperson had said something factual about the vehicle (its miles per gallon, its total mileage, whether it had been in an accident, etc.), it would be more than puffing and could qualify as an express warranty.

10. A. Showing a sample to a customer creates a warranty that the goods delivered to the customer will in fact match the sample. A sample represents a standard that the goods must meet. Warranties of fitness for a particular purpose, merchantability, and usage of trade are implied warranties. This question and answer are based on a question that appeared on the CPA exam in 1997.

Issue Spotters

1. No. A creditor with a valid security interest can repossess goods from a subsequent purchaser. If a creditor repossesses goods, however, a buyer who had no actual knowledge of the security interest can recover from the seller for breach of warranty. Thus, the creditor in this problem can repossess the car from the ultimate buyer, who can recover from the seller-borrower.

2. No, at least not on this ground. Merchantable food means food that is fit to eat. Food containing cholesterol is merchantable—that is, it is fit to eat—if it is similar to all other food of the kind on the market.

3. No. The seller's description of the item as a "truck" creates an express warranty that it is a truck, and selling the item "as is" cannot disclaim this warranty—a seller cannot normally deliver a truck without wheels and avoid liability.

Cumulative Hypothetical Problem for Unit Four—Including Chapters 19–23

1. C. The modification would not be considered a rejection. Under UCC 2–207, a merchant can add an additional term to a contract, with his or her acceptance, as part of the contract, unless the offeror expressly states otherwise.

2. C. If nothing is stated in a contract about the risk of loss, then the UCC determines when the risk of loss passes. Under the UCC, if there are no contract terms to the contrary, the risk of loss passes on delivery, if the seller is a merchant.

3. B. Under UCC 2–709, a seller can demand enforcement of a contract if the buyer breaches, the goods have been identified, and the seller cannot resell the goods for a reasonable price. From the perspective of the seller, recovery of the contract price is specific performance.

4. C. A seller makes an express warranty by providing an assertion, an affirmation, a promise, or a similar statement about the quality of the goods that becomes a part of the basis of the bargain. The promises may be oral, and the seller's intent is not relevant.

5. B. To be subject to the UCC's implied warranty of merchantability, goods must be fit for their ordinary or intended use, but they do not need to be fit for ALL of the possible purposes that a buyer might have in mind. The other choices are part of this implied warranty.

Questions on the Focus on Legal Reasoning for Unit Four—*Parker Tractor & Implement Co. v. Johnson*

1. A. In the *Parker* case, the court reasoned that "it is enough that sufficient facts are given from which the [court] may safely make at least a minimum estimate" of the amount of damages. Damages are speculative "only when the cause is uncertain, not when the amount is uncertain."

2. A. The majority in the *Parker* case held that lost business profits can be awarded if the data of their estimation are so definite that they can be ascertained reasonably by calculation. In estimating those damages, the court reasoned that they could be calculated using the testimony of the injured party if that was the best evidence available.

3. D. The dissent in the *Parker* case reasoned that more substantial proof is necessary to obtain damages. The weight to be given the proof—the scarcity of documentary evidence, the arguably self-serving testimony of the plaintiff, the non-existent proof of some points—was the issue over which the court in the *Parker* case disagreed.

Questions on the Focus on Ethics for Unit Four—Domestic and International Sales and Lease Contracts

1. B. Besides good faith, read into every contract is the concept of commercial reasonableness. These two concepts impose certain duties on the contracting parties. Also underlying the application of the UCC provisions are reasonability in the formation, performance, and termination of contracts. To determine what is commercially reasonable, a court may look to the course of dealing, usage of trade, and the surrounding circumstances.

2. C. This doctrine is an application of the concept of commercial reasonableness. Under this doctrine, performance may be excused but only if the nonperforming party has made every effort to meet his or her obligations under the contract.

3. D. In the interests of fairness, even though a party has agreed to a term, it may be held to be so unfair as to be unenforceable. Under this doctrine, a court may decline to enforce the entire contract, enforce the contract without the clause, or limit the enforcement of the clause to avoid an unfair result. The court would look at the circumstances as of the time the contract was made in the context of its commercial background. Ethical standards underlie this doctrine.

Chapter 24

True-False Questions

1. T
2. T
3. T
4. T
5. F. To be negotiable, an instrument must be payable on demand or at a definite time. Instruments that say nothing about when payment is due are payable on demand.

6. F. The length of the extension does not have to be specified if the option to extend is solely that of the *holder*. After the specified date passes, the note becomes, in effect, a demand instrument. The period of an extension must be specified, however, if the option is given to the maker.

7. F. This is an order instrument. Order instruments that meet the requirements for negotiability are negotiable. An instrument that contains any indication that does not purport to designate a specific payee (for example, "payable to bearer") is a bearer instrument. A bearer instrument that meets the requirements for negotiability is also negotiable. When an instrument is not negotiable, it may be transferred by assignment.

8. T
9. T
10. F. To be negotiable, an instrument must be payable in a fixed amount of money. Money includes a "medium of exchange authorized or adopted by a domestic or foreign government as a part of its currency." An instrument payable in an amount stated in foreign currency can be paid in that currency or in U.S. dollars.

Fill-in Questions

drawer; drawee; payee; maker; payee

Multiple-Choice Questions

1. A. One of the requirements of negotiability is that an instrument be payable to order or to bearer. An instrument that is payable to the order of an identified person is an order instrument. An instrument that is payable to bearer is a bearer instrument. A bearer instrument can be negotiated further without a payee's signature. References to other agreements do not affect an instrument's negotiability. Conditioning payment would render an instrument nonnegotiable, however. This question and answer are based on a question from the May 1995 CPA exam.

2. A. An instrument that is not payable to the order of an identified person is a bearer instrument. Although this instrument uses order language, it does not designate a specific payee.

3. A. To be negotiable, an instrument must state with certainty on the face of the instrument a fixed amount of money to be paid when the instrument is payable. When an instrument states simply that it is payable "with interest," the interest rate is the judgment rate of interest, which is fixed by statute.

4. D. A draft is created when the party creating it orders another party to pay money, usually to a third party. The drawee (the party on whom the draft is drawn) must be obligated to the drawer, either by an agreement or through a debtor-creditor relationship, for the drawee to be obligated to the drawer to honor the draft. A trade acceptance is a draft; a check is a draft.

5. B. The drawer is the party who initiates a draft, which orders the drawee (the bank in this problem) to pay. A check orders the payment of a certain amount of money to the holder on demand. The party to whom a check (or any instrument) is made payable is the payee.
6. D. A negotiable instrument that has only two parties is a promissory note: a written promise made by one person (the maker) to another (the payee). A certificate of deposit is a type of note issued when a party deposits funds with a bank that the bank promise to repay with interest. A draft (a check is a draft) involves three parties (drawee, drawer, and payee).
7. D. All of the other answer choices are among the requirements for negotiability. The other requirements are that an instrument must be in writing (on something permanent and portable—a shirt might be acceptable but not, for example, a cow), must state a fixed amount of money, and must be payable to order or to bearer, unless it is a check.
8. A. The location of the maker or drawer's signature does not affect the negotiability of an instrument. Also, a signature may, among other things, be a trade name or may consist of thumbprint, a handwritten statement, or a rubber stamp.
9. A. A promise or order is conditional, and nonnegotiable, if it does what any of the other answer choices state. This instrument, however, only makes a reference to another writing (as it would if, for example, it stated, "this debt arises from the performance of delivery services"), which does not make the instrument conditional. Similarly, a statement that an instrument is payable only from a particular fund or source does not affect its negotiability.
10. A. That an instrument is undated does not affect its negotiability, nor does postdating or antedating an instrument affect negotiability. Also, the omission of the name of the bank on which an instrument is drawn or payable will not render an instrument nonnegotiable.

Issue Spotters

1. Yes. To be negotiable, an instrument must be in written form and have a relative degree of permanence and portability. To be negotiable, an instrument must also be signed by the drawer. Rubber stamps bearing signatures are common in business.
2. A statement that "I.O.U." money (or anything else) or an instruction to a bank stating, "I wish you would pay," would render any instrument nonnegotiable. To be negotiable, an instrument must contain an express promise to pay. An I.O.U. is only an acknowledgment of indebtedness. An order stating, "I wish you would pay," is not sufficiently precise.
3. The check is a bearer instrument. Although the drawer gave the check to a specific person, the check itself does not designate a specific payee, which it would need to do to be an order instrument. Either way, the check is negotiable, however.

Chapter 25

True-False Questions

1. F. A negotiable instrument can be transferred by assignment or negotiation. When a transfer fails to qualify as a negotiation, it becomes an assignment and is governed by the rules of assignment under contract law.
2. T
3. T
4. F. Bearer instruments can be negotiated by delivery alone. That is why a bearer instrument is considered payable to whoever is in possession of it.
5. F. To be a holder, a person must have possession and good title. The definition of a holder, from UCC 1–201(20), is "the person in possession if the instrument is payable to bearer, or in the case of an instrument payable to an identified person, if the identified person is in possession."
6. F. Despite taking an instrument for value, in good faith, and without notice, a transferee cannot be a holder in due course (HDC) unless he or she is a holder.
7. T
8. F. If a holder is an HDC, all other parties' claims to an instrument and most other parties' defenses against payment on the instrument cannot be successfully asserted against the HDC.
9. T
10. T

Fill-in Questions

can; cannot; cannot

Multiple-Choice Questions

1. A. A party can convert a blank indorsement to a special indorsement "by writing over the signature of the indorser in blank any contract consistent with the character of the indorsement." In other words, the instrument in this question is a bearer instrument and the payee can convert it to an order instrument by doing what is stated in the answer choice.
2. A. Before the payee indorsed the back of the check, it was an order instrument. It could be negotiated further only with the payee's signature (and with delivery). After the check was indorsed, it became a bearer instrument and could be negotiated by delivery alone. If a bearer instrument is lost, it can be payable to whoever finds it.
3. C. The first step in becoming a holder in due course (HDC) is that a party must be a holder. To be a holder, the instrument must be negotiable. The re-

quirements for HDC status are that a party takes the instrument for value, in good faith, and without notice of any claims to it or defenses against payment on it. This question and answer are based on a question that appeared in the CPA exam in May 1995.

4. C. An instrument that is payable to the order of a specific payee is negotiated by delivery of the instrument to that payee. The payee negotiates the instrument further by indorsing it and delivering it to the transferee.

5. C. A restrictive indorsement requires the indorsee to comply with certain instructions regarding the funds involved (but it does not restrict the negotiation of the instrument). A blank indorsement specifies no particular indorsee and can be a simple signature. A qualified indorsement disclaims contract liability on the instrument (for example, an indorser adding "without recourse" to his or her signature is a qualified indorsement). A special indorsement names the indorsee ("pay to Adam") with the signature of the indorser.

6. B. A holder takes an instrument for value when he or she pays cash for it, gives a negotiable instrument for it, or makes an irrevocable commitment to a third person. He or she is an HDC to the extent that he or she gives value for the instrument (and meets the other requirements for HDC status).

7. C. A holder of a time instrument who takes it after its due date is "on notice" that it is overdue. Such a holder cannot become an HDC. Nonpayment by the due date should indicate to any purchaser who is obligated to pay that there is a defense to payment.

8. A. A bank can become an HDC when honoring other banks' checks to the extent it has given value. Thus, a bank becomes an HDC when it permits a customer to draw against a credited instrument, but only to the extent that the customer draws on the credit.

9. C. A thief cannot be a holder. A party who takes in good faith and without notice from a thief is an HDC, however. A party in the situation of the drawer of this check might also avoid liability to an ordinary holder by asserting the personal defense of unauthorized completion of an incomplete instrument (discussed in the next chapter).

10. A. A party who takes an instrument with knowledge of one defense that the maker or drawer has against payment on the instrument prevents the party from attaining HDC status as to all defenses. The party does not satisfy the requirement for HDC status that he or she must take the instrument without notice.

Issue Spotters

1. A payee negotiates an instrument further by indorsing it and delivering it. A specific payee's indorsing a check (which is, as explained above, an order instrument initially) converts the check to a bearer instrument. A bearer instrument can of course be negotiated by delivery alone (indorsement is not necessary).

2. When the payee signed the back of his check, he converted it to a bearer instrument. Because a bearer instrument can be negotiated by delivery alone, the check was negotiated to the finder. To avoid such a loss, the payee might not have indorsed it until he reached the bank. Or he could have indorsed it "For deposit only," and in this way, the check would have remained an order instrument.

3. This party is an HDC to the full extent of the note. One of the requirements for becoming an HDC is taking an instrument for value. A party may attain HDC status to the extent that he or she gives value for the instrument. Paying with cash or with a check is giving value.

Chapter 26

True-False Questions

1. T

2. F. Some parties are secondarily liable.

3. T

4. F. All transferors of negotiable instruments, including those who present instruments for payment, make certain implied warranties regarding the instruments. For example, a person who transfers an instrument for payment warrants to any other person who in good faith accepts or pays the instrument, with some exceptions, that the instrument has not been altered.

5. T

6. T

7. F. The loss in such a case falls on the drawer against whom the check is effective if it has been transferred to an innocent party. However, comparative negligence may be available as a defense against liability to a drawee bank, for example, which may thus be partially liable for the amount paid on the instrument.

8. F. Personal defenses can be used to avoid payment to an ordinary holder, but only universal defenses can defeat the claims of all holders, including HDCs.

9. F. An unauthorized signature can be binding, however, if the person whose name is signed ratifies it. The person's negligence may also prevent him or her from denying liability. Usually, when there is a forged or unauthorized indorsement, the burden of loss falls on the first party to take the instrument with the forged indorsement.

10. T

Fill-in Questions

presentment; presenter; presenter; the maker or the drawer; materially altered

Multiple-Choice Questions

1. A. Forgery of the signature of the maker of a note is a real defense and thus good against an HDC. This is only if the person whose signature was forged has not ratified it or is precluded from denying it. The other choices are personal defenses, which are good against ordinary holders but not HDCs. This question and answer are based on a question that appeared in the November 1992 CPA exam.
2. D. If a check has been materially altered and the alteration is clearly visible, a party who takes the check has notice of a defense against payment on it and cannot become an HDC. He or she can recover nothing on the check. (If the alteration was not visible and the party could otherwise become an HDC, he or she could enforce the check according to the original terms.)
3. B. If a drawer believes an imposter to be the named payee at the time the drawer issues an instrument, the imposter's indorsement is effective (not considered a forgery) as far as the drawer is concerned. This is also true when there are other parties between the drawer, the imposter, and the drawee (for example, when the imposter negotiates the check to a third person who presents it to the drawee for payment).
4. D. If a person is deceived into signing a negotiable instrument, believing that he or she is signing something other than a negotiable instrument, fraud in the execution is committed against the signer, who has a valid defense against payment even if the instrument is negotiated to an HDC.
5. A. When there is a breach of warranty concerning the underlying contract for which a negotiable instrument (the note) was issued, the maker can refuse to pay the note. This is a personal defense, not good against an HDC, but the party who accepted the note was not an HDC, but the other contracting party who took the note with knowledge of the claim against it. The other choices are also personal defenses, but they do not fit the facts in this problem.
6. B. Makers of notes and acceptors of negotiable instruments are primarily liable. (Drawers—and indorsers—have secondary liability.) A drawee (the bank in this problem) becomes primarily liable becomes an acceptor, which occurs when, as here, it accepts a check for payment.
7. C. Based on their signatures on an instrument, a drawer and a payee-indorser have secondary liability. Parties who are secondarily liable promise to pay only if the following events occur: (1) the instrument is properly and timely presented; (2) the instrument is dishonored; and (3) notice of dishonor is given in a timely manner to the secondarily liable party.
8. A. When a drawee fails to accept or pay a draft, including a check, the drawer's (secondary) liability arises. The party holding the draft can then attempt to obtain payment from the drawer.
9. A. All of the parties on a note are discharged if the maker of a note (the party primarily liable on it) pays to a holder the amount due in full. Payment by any other party, however, discharges only that party and later parties, however.
10. B. The issuer of the check in this problem was authorized to use an employer's checks to pay for certain items. Assuming the seller knew of this agency relationship, the principal (the employer) is liable for the amount of the check. There is nothing in the facts here to suggest that the seller had notice of a defense to payment on the check, or notice that the amount of the check was materially altered, either of which would have prevented it from becoming an HDC and changed the liability of the parties.

Issue Spotters

1. Yes. As in cases of forgery, in which the person whose name is used is not liable, this firm can assert the defense of the unauthorized signature against any HDC, because the employee exceeded authority in signing the check on behalf of the firm.
2. No. Material alteration is a partial defense against an HDC. An HDC can enforce an instrument that has been materially altered against the maker or drawer according to the original terms only. Of course, if the alteration had been visible, the result would be different—the party would be on notice and could not recover anything on the instrument.
3. No. When a drawer's employee provides the drawer with the name of a fictitious payee (a payee whom the drawer does not actually intend to have any interest in an instrument), a forgery of the payee's name is effective to pass good title to subsequent transferees.

Chapter 27

True-False Questions

1. T
2. F. If a bank pays a check over a customer's proper stop-payment order, the bank is obligated to recredit the customer's account, but only for the amount of the actual loss suffered by the drawer because of the wrongful payment.
3. F. A bank's duty to honor its customer's checks is not absolute (although when a bank receives an item payable from a customer's account, but there are insufficient funds in the account to cover the amount, the bank can choose to pay it and charge the customer's account). Failing to pay an overdraft will not subject the bank to criminal prosecution, though a person who writes a bad check may be prosecuted (and sued).
4. T
5. T

6. T
7. T
8. F. Under the Expedited Funds Availability Act of 1987, there are different availability schedules for different funds, depending on such factors as the location of the bank on which an item is drawn, what type of item it is, the age and activity of an account, and the amount of the item.
9. T
10. F. A forged drawer's signature on a check has no legal effect as the signature of the party whose name is signed. If the bank pays the check, the bank must recredit the customer's account (unless the customer's negligence contributed substantially to the forgery).

Fill-in Questions

drawer; creditor; principal; drawee; debtor; agent

Multiple-Choice Questions

1. C. Each bank in the collection chain, including the depositary bank, must pass the check on before receipt. Under the deferred posting rule, a check received after a bank's cutoff hour, can be considered received the next day.
2. D. When a bank pays a check on a drawer's forged signature, generally the bank is liable. This is particularly true when the bank's negligence substantially contributes to the forgery. If the customer's negligence contributed to the forgery, however, the bank may not be liable. The amount of the check does not affect liability.
3. D. This is assuming the drawer's state allows oral stop-payment orders. If a drawee bank pays a check over a customer's stop-payment order, the bank is obligated to recredit the account of the customer, but the bank is liable for no more than the actual loss suffered by the drawer.
4. A. A bank that pays a customer's check bearing a forged indorsement must recredit the customer's account or be liable to the drawer customer for breach of contract. A customer has a duty to examine returned checks and corresponding bank statements, however, and must report any forged indorsements within three years.
5. B. A drawee bank's contract is with its customer, not with those who present its customers' checks for payment. Thus, a drawee bank is not liable to a holder who presents a check for payment, even if the drawer has sufficient funds on deposit to pay the check. The holder's recourse is against the drawer, who may subsequently hold the bank liable for a wrongful refusal to pay.
6. A. A bank is not obligated to pay a stale, uncertified check. If the bank decides to pay it, however, the bank might consult the customer first or simply pay it an d charge the customer's account of the amount.
7. A. The certification of a check by the bank on which it is drawn discharges the drawer, who was secondarily liable on the check. The bank remains primarily liable and has now guaranteed payment. This question and answer are based on a question that appeared in the November 1981 CPA exam.
8. C. The customer is liable for this amount because the bank was not notified that the card was missing until after the withdrawal. If a customer does not inform the institution within less than two business days after learning of a card's loss or theft, the customer's liability for unauthorized transactions is up to $500.
9. C. If a drawee bank cashes a customer's check over the customer's (drawer's) forged signature, the bank is liable for the loss. (Of course, this is assuming that the customer's negligence did not cause the loss—the customer's negligence can shift the loss, as noted above.) The bank may be able to recover at least some of the loss from the forger, however.
10. A. Though it is not yet entirely clear which laws apply to e-money, the Federal Trade Commission (FTC) Act, as well as the other statutes mentioned here, and common law principles (such as contract law) do extend to new forms of debits and credits. The FTC Act applies to the facts in this problem—this act prohibits unfair or deceptive practices. The other statutes apply in other circumstances.

Issue Spotters

1. Yes, to both questions. In a civil suit, a drawer is liable to a payee or to a holder of a check that is not honored. If intent to defraud can be proved, the drawer can also be subject to criminal prosecution for writing a bad check.
2. Yes, to the first question. The general rule is that a bank must recredit a customer's account when it pays on a forged signature. The bank has no right to recover from a holder who, without knowledge, cashes a check bearing a forged drawer's signature, but in this question, the party who cashed the check was the thief who forged the signature. Thus, the bank in this problem cannot collect from its customer, but it can collect from the party who cashed the check. The bank's recourse is to look for the thief.
3. The drawer is entitled to $6,300—the amount to which the check was altered ($7,000) less the amount that the drawer ordered the bank to pay ($700). The bank may recover this amount from the party who presented the altered check for payment.

Cumulative Hypothetical Problem for Unit Five—Including Chapters 24–27

1. B. A promissory note is a written promise by one party to pay money to another party. This instrument is not a draft: there is no drawee. Because it is not a

draft, it cannot be a sight draft, a check, or a trade acceptance, all of which are drafts.

2. B. This instrument meets all of the requirements for negotiability: it is in writing, it is signed by the maker, it is an unconditional promise to pay a fixed amount of money, it is payable to bearer, and it is payable at a definite time. The extension clause does not affect its negotiability because, although the right to extend is given to the maker, the period of the extension is specified.

3. C. The instrument is negotiable, but it can be negotiated further only by the bank's indorsement, because it was converted from a bearer instrument to an order instrument with the indorsement to pay to the order of the bank. Because it was a bearer instrument, it could have been negotiated by delivery only, without indorsement. The indorsement "without recourse" does not affect the negotiability of the instrument.

4. A. The bank is an HDC because it took the instrument (1) for value, (2) in good faith, and (3) without notice that any person had a defense against payment on it. The party from whom the bank bought the instrument was not an HDC, however, because that party did take the instrument with knowledge of the contract dispute.

5. D. No party to a check has primary liability with respect to payment on it. The drawer is secondarily liable to the payee. If the drawer has sufficient grounds, he or she may sue the drawee for wrongful dishonor, but the payee cannot successfully sue the drawee.

Questions on the Focus on Legal Reasoning for Unit Five—*Scalise v. American Employers Insurance Co.*

1. A. In the *Scalise* case, the court held that if a check is honored and paid on presentment, the date of the payment of the underlying obligation is the date of the delivery of the check. The court acknowledged that the debt is not discharged until the check is paid, but reasoned that once that happened, payment occurred as of "the moment of the delivery of the check."

2. A. The majority in the *Scalise* case held that if a check is honored and paid on presentment, the date of the payment for the underlying obligation is the date of the delivery of the check. The majority cited the principle that "the giving of a draft by a debtor to his creditor does not discharge the debt itself until the draft is paid, it being a means adopted to enable the creditor to obtain payment of the debt and remaining, until honored or paid, but evidence of the indebtedness." But the majority reasoned that "payment by check is ordinarily understood to constitute payment for an obligation as of the moment of delivery of the check, provided that the check is honored upon its presentment."

3. D. Contrary to the majority, the dissent in the *Scalise* case reasoned that "[t]he giving of a check by a debtor to his creditor does not discharge the debt until the check is paid" and indicated that this is when "payment" occurs. Otherwise, "the plaintiff's time to exercise his rights . . . begins to run before he even has any such rights."

Questions on the Focus on Ethics for Unit Five—Negotiable Instruments

1. A. The maker's reliance on the fraudulent party's assurance that the note was not a note constitutes negligence. UCC 3-305(a)(1)(iii) states that fraud is a defense against an HDC only if the injured party signed the instrument "with neither knowledge nor a reasonable opportunity to obtain knowledge of its character or essential terms." The HDC doctrine reflects the philosophy that when two or more innocent parties are at risk, the burden should fall on the party that was in the best position to prevent the loss.

2. B. Under UCC 4–402(b), a bank that wrongfully dishonors a customer's check "is liable to its customer for damages proximately caused by the wrongful dishonor of an item. Liability is limited to actual damages proved and may include damages for an arrest or prosecution of the customer or other consequential damages." In other words, on wrongful dishonor, a bank's liability may be considerable.

3. D. Electronic fund transfers (EFTs) have often given rise to evidentiary issues. Because an EFT leaves no "paper trail," proof of a transaction may consist only of an impulse in a computer database. Proof that a transaction did not occur may consist mostly of contradicting testimony. The Electronic Fund Transfer Act (EFTA) resolved some related issues, but not all, particularly not those involving a disagreement between a customer and a computer. Under the EFTA, courts sometimes rule in favor of banks and sometimes decide in favor of their customers.

Chapter 28

True-False Questions

1. F. Perfection is the process by which secured parties protect themselves against the claims of third parties who may wish to have their debts satisfied out of the same collateral. In most situations, this process involves filing a financing statement with a state official. That filing may be accomplished by a paper filing or electronically.

2. T

3. F. A security interest in proceeds perfects automatically and remains perfected, in most cases, for at least twenty days after the debtor's receipt of the proceeds.

4. F. The financing statement must include the names of the debtor and creditor, and describe the collateral. Also, to avoid problems arising from different descriptions, a secured party can repeat the security agreement's description in the financing statement or file the two together.
5. T
6. T
7. T
8. T
9. F. A debtor who has defaulted has redemption rights. Before the secured party decides to retain the collateral or before it is disposed of, the debtor can take back the collateral by tendering performance of all secured obligations and paying the secured party's expenses. (Other secured parties have this same right.)
10. F. When more than one creditor claims a security interest in the same collateral, the first interest to be filed takes priority. The first to attach has priority if none of the interests has been perfected.

Fill-in Questions

1. creditor; creditor
2. first; first

Multiple-Choice Questions

1. C. A *financing statement* must provide the names of the debtor and the creditor and describe the collateral covered by the security agreement. Filing a financing statement (which is the most common means of perfecting a security interest) gives notice to other creditors of the secured party's interest. Why the debtor and the creditor entered into the deal is not relevant to others' interests in this context.
2. B. In those cases in which it is otherwise available, the right of self-help repossession can generally be exercised so long as the secured party does not commit trespass onto land, assault, battery, or breaking and entering. Here, the repossession occurred on a public street and did not involve any commission of the other crimes.
3. C. To be effective, a written security agreement must (1) be signed by the debtor, (2) contain a description of the collateral, and (3) the description must reasonably identify the collateral. This meets one of the three requirements for an enforceable security interest. The other requirements are that creditor's giving something of value to the debtor, and the debtor having rights in the collateral. Once these requirements are met, the interest attaches. A security interest is enforceable when attachment occurs.
4. C. To retain collateral that a secured party repossessed on a debtor's default, the secured party must notify the debtor and (in all cases except consumer goods) any other secured party of whom the party has notice of a claim, as well as junior lien claimants who filed their liens or security interests ten days before the debtor consented to the retention. If the debtor or other secured party objects within twenty days, the collateral must be sold, or otherwise disposed of. If the collateral is sold, the first priority of the proceeds are the fees stemming from the secured party's preparation for the sale.
5. B. The secured party has fourteen days to reply. More frequent requests must be paid for. Among other rights and duties of the parties, if the secured party assigns its interest in the debtor's collateral, the assignee can become the secured party of record through the filing of a uniform amendment form, which is also required for the secured party's release of the debtor. If the debtor pays the debt and asks for a termination statement, the secured party has twenty days to comply.
6. C. A secured party's security interest in collateral includes an interest in the proceeds (whatever is received) from the sale, exchange, or other disposal of the collateral. This interest perfects automatically and remains perfected for twenty days. Ways to extend this period are listed in the answer. It should be noted, too, that the initial effective term of the filing of a financing statement is a period of five years, and this can be extended for another five years by the filing of a continuation statement before the expiration of the original filing.
7. C. The first security interest to be filed or to be perfected has priority over other filed or perfected security interests. Although the first lender was not the first to provide funds to the debtor, it was the first to file its financing statement. Priority between perfected security interests is nearly always determined by the time of perfection (which is usually by filing). Note, though, that perfection may not protect a secured party's interest against the claim of a buyer in the ordinary course of business, and some others.
8. C. A purchase-money security interest (PMSI) is created (1) when a seller retains or takes a security interest in collateral to secure part or all of the purchase price of property serving as collateral, or (2) when some other party (such as a bank) takes a security interest in the collateral to secure the party's advances or other obligation that is actually used by the debtor to acquire rights in or to use the collateral.
9. A. The filing of a security interest in a corporate debtor's collateral should be done in the state in which the debtor is incorporated. For individual debtors, however, the place of filing is the state of the debtor's principal residence. Of course, the perfection of an interest in some types of collateral, such as negotiable instruments, can only be accomplished by taking possession of the property.
10. D. In most states, filing is in a central office (of the state in which the debtor is located). When collateral consists of timber to be cut, fixtures, or collateral to be extracted, a filing in the county in which the col-

lateral is located is typically required. Of course, if perfection is by a pledge (possession), no filing is necessary.

Issue Spotters

1. A creditor can put other creditors on notice by perfecting its interest: by filing a financing statement in the appropriate public office, or by taking possession of the collateral until the debtor repays the loan.
2. The PMSI has priority. When two or more secured parties have perfected security interests in the same collateral, the first to perfect has priority (unless a state statute provides otherwise). There are exceptions to this general rule, however, concerning a PMSI. As in this question, a PMSI has priority, even if it is second in time of perfection when it attaches to inventory, it is perfected, and proper written or authenticated notice is given to other security-interest holders on or before the time that the debtor takes possession of the inventory. All of these occurred in this question.
3. When collateral is consumer goods with a PMSI, and the debtor has paid less than 60 percent of the debt or the purchase price, the creditor can dispose of the collateral in a commercially reasonable manner, which generally requires notice of the place, time, and manner of sale. A debtor can waive the right to notice, but only after default. Before the disposal, a debtor can redeem the collateral by tendering performance of all of the obligations secured by it and by paying the creditor's reasonable expenses in retaking and maintaining it.

Chapter 29

True-False Questions

1. F. A mechanic's lien involves real property. An artisan's lien or an innkeeper's lien involves personal property.
2. F. This is prohibited under federal law. Garnishment of an employee's wages for any one indebtedness cannot be a ground for dismissal of an employee.
3. T
4. T
5. T
6. T
7. F. Under an assignment for the benefit of creditors, a debtor transfers title to his or her property to a trustee or assignee, who sells the property and offers payment to each of the debtor's creditors in proportion to what is owed. Each creditor can accept the tender, and discharge the debt, or reject it, and attempt to collect in another way.
8. T
9. F. This is the most important concept in suretyship: a surety can use any defenses available to a debtor (except personal defenses) to avoid liability on the obligation to the creditor. Note, though, that a debtor does need not to have defaulted on the underlying obligation before a surety can be required to answer for the debt. Before a *guarantor* can be required to answer for the debt of a debtor, the debtor must have defaulted on the underlying obligation, however.
10. T

Fill-in Questions

contract of suretyship; surety; surety; guaranty contract; guarantor

Multiple-Choice Questions

1. B. The jeweler can keep the necklace until the customer pays for the repair. If the customer fails to pay, the jeweler has an artisan's lien on the necklace for the amount of the bill and can sell the necklace in satisfaction of the lien.
2. A. The creditor in this problem can use prejudgment attachment. Attachment occurs at the time of or immediately after commencement of a suit but before entry of a final judgment. The court issues a writ of attachment, directing the sheriff or other officer to seize property belonging to the debtor. If the creditor prevails at trial, the property can be sold to satisfy the judgment. (A writ of execution can be used after all of the conditions represented by the answer choices in this problem have been met.)
3. D. The creditor can use garnishment, a collection remedy directed at a debtor's property or rights held by a third person. A garnishment order can be served on the employer so that part of debtor's paycheck will be paid to the creditor. This question and answer are based on a question that was part of the CPA exam in 1996.
4. B. The debt is $200,000. The amount of the homestead exemption ($50,000) is subtracted from the sale price of the house ($150,000), and the remainder ($100,000) is applied against the debt. Proceeds from the sale of any nonexempt personal property could also be applied against the debt. The debtor gets the amount of the homestead exemption, of course.
5. C. A guarantor is secondarily liable (that is, the principal must first default). Also, in this problem, if the president were, for example, the borrower's only salaried employee, the guaranty would not have to be in writing under the main-purpose exception to the Statute of Frauds. A surety is primarily liable (that is, the creditor can look to the surety for payment as soon as the debt is due, whether or not the principal debtor has defaulted). Usually, also, in the case of a guarantor, a creditor must have attempted to collect from the principal, because usually a debtor would not otherwise be declared in default.
6. C. A guarantor has the right of subrogation when he or she pays the debt owed to the creditor. This

means that any right the creditor had against the debtor becomes the right of the guarantor. A guarantor also has the right of contribution, when there are one or more other guarantors. This means that if he or she pays more than his or her proportionate share on a debtor's default, the guarantor is entitled to recover from the others the amount paid above the guarantor's obligation. This problem illustrates how these principles work.

7. D. At the request of a creditor who obtains a judgment against a debtor, a writ of execution is issued after the entry of the judgment if the debtor still does not pay. A sheriff, or other officer, executes the writ by seizing the debtor's nonexempt property, selling it, and using the proceeds to pay the amount of the judgment.

8. C. When a debtor defaults on a mortgage, the mortgagee can foreclose on the property. The usual method of foreclosure is a judicial sale. The property is sold, and the proceeds are applied to the debt. The mortgagor can pay the debt and redeem the property before the sale. If the proceeds do not cover the debt, the mortgagee can recover the difference by obtaining a deficiency judgment in a separate legal action after the foreclosure.

9. D. A surety agrees to be primarily liable to pay a debtor's debt. If the debtor and the creditor materially alter the terms of their contract without the surety's consent, a surety who agreed to act without being compensated is discharged completely. (A surety who accepted payment is discharged to the extent that he or she suffers a loss under the contract as modified.)

10. C. If a creditor in possession of a debtor's collateral surrenders it without the guarantor's consent, the guarantor is released to the extent of any loss attributable to the surrender. This protects a guarantor who agrees to the obligation only because the debtor's collateral is in the creditor's possession.

Issue Spotters

1. Larry and Midwest can place a mechanic's lien on Joe's property. If Joe does not pay what he owes, the property can be sold to satisfy the debt. The only requirements are that the lien be filed within a specific time from the time of the work, depending on the state statute, and notice of the foreclosure and sale must be given to Joe in advance.

2. Yes. In this problem, the party who assured the lender of payment on behalf of the debtor is a surety. A surety has a right of reimbursement from the debtor for all outlays the surety makes, as here, on behalf of the suretyship arrangement.

3. Co-sureties may be required to reimburse any co-surety who pays more than his or her proportionate share on a debtor's default. In such a case, the co-sureties are liable in proportion to their promise to pay the debt. If co-sureties have agreed to be obligated for the debt in equal proportions, then that is the amount for which they are indebted to the surety who pays the debt. In this problem, Dian and Ernie can each be held liable to pay $300 to Carol.

Chapter 30

True-False Questions

1. F. Any individual can be a debtor under Chapter 7, and any debtor who is liable on a claim held by a creditor may file for bankruptcy under Chapter 7.

2. F. The filing of a bankruptcy petition, voluntary or involuntary, automatically stays most litigation and other actions by creditors against the debtor and his or her property. A creditor may ask for relief from the stay, but a creditor who willfully violates the stay may be liable for actual damages, costs, and fees, as well as punitive damages.

3. T

4. T

5. F. Under Chapter 13 (and 12), a bankruptcy may be commenced only by voluntary petition. Involuntary petitions may be used to start bankruptcy proceedings under either Chapter 7 or Chapter 11.

6. T

7. T

8. F. Under Chapter 11, the creditors and the debtor formulate a plan under which the debtor pays some of the debts, the other debts are discharged, and the debtor is then allowed to continue in business.

9. F. Some small businesses—those who do not own or manage real estate and do not have debts of more than $2 million—can choose to avoid creditors' committees under Chapter 11. Those who choose to do so, however, are subject to shorter deadlines with respect to filing a reorganization plan.

10. T

Fill-in Questions

7; 11; 13; 7; 11; 13; 7; 11; 13

Multiple-Choice Questions

1. D. Under Chapter 11, creditors and debtor plan for the debtor to pay some debts, be discharged of the rest, and continue in business. Under Chapter 13, with an appropriate plan, a small business debtor can also pay some (or all) debts, be discharged of the rest, and continue in business. A petition for a discharge in bankruptcy under Chapter 11 may be filed by a sole proprietor, a partnership, or a corporation; a petition for a discharge under Chapter 13, however, may be filed only by a sole proprietor, among these business entities.

2. D. Under Chapter 13, a debtor can submit a plan under which he or she continues in possession of his or her assets, but turns over disposable income for a three-year period, after which most debts are discharged. When applicable, a Chapter 13 plan must provide for the surrender of all collateral to the creditors. Note that a court will not refuse to approve a Chapter 13 plan on the objection of a creditor or a trustee if the property to be distributed under the plan is ore than the amount of the creditors' claims.
3. D. Under Chapter 7 or Chapter 11, a corporate debtor (or an individual debtor or a partnership, but not a farmer or a charitable institution) who has twelve or more creditors can be forced into bankruptcy by three or more of them, who collectively have unsecured claims for at least a certain amount. (The amount is periodically increased.) A debtor with less than twelve creditors can be involuntarily petitioned into bankruptcy by one or more of them, if the petitioner (or petitioners) has a claim for at least a certain amount.
4. D. Claims that are not dischargeable in bankruptcy include the claims listed in the other answer choices: claims for back taxes accruing within three years before the bankruptcy, claims for alimony and child support, and claims for most student loans (unless their payment would result in undue hardship to the debtor, as stated in the correct answer choice). There are many others.
5. A. Any individual can file a petition for bankruptcy under Chapter 7, and this is the chapter most commonly used by individual debtors. The individual does not have to be insolvent. A court can dismiss a petition, however, if granting it would constitute substantial abuse or if the court finds that the debtor could pay off his or her debts under Chapter 13. Most debtors eligible under Chapter 7 could also file under Chapter 11, although the latter is more commonly used by corporate debtors. Under Chapter 11, some of the debts are paid. Chapter 13 is a possibility under the circumstances described in the problem, but a debtor is more likely to prefer a Chapter 7 discharge, which does not require payment of many debts. Chapter 12 is an option only for certain farmers.
6. A. Other grounds on which a discharge may be denied include concealing property with the intent to defraud a creditor, fraudulently destroying financial records, and refusing to obey a lawful court order. Having obtained a discharge in bankruptcy six years earlier is also a ground for denial. The other choices represent individual debts that are not dischargeable in bankruptcy. This question and answer are based on a question from the 1997 CPA exam.
7. A. The first unsecured debts to be paid are the administrative expenses of the bankruptcy proceeding. Among the debts listed in this problem, the order of priority is then unpaid wages, consumer deposits, and taxes. Each class of creditors is fully paid before the next class is entitled to anything.
8. B. Other transfers that a trustee can set aside include a transfer made with the intent to hinder, delay, or defraud a creditor; transfers made to an insider within a year of the debtor's filing a petition in bankruptcy; payments within days before the petition for a preexisting debt; any reason that the debtor could use to get the property back.
9. D. Most corporations can file for bankruptcy under Chapter 7 or 11. The same principles that govern liquidation cases also govern reorganizations. Corporate debtors most commonly file petitions for bankruptcy under Chapter 11. One important difference between the two chapters is that in a Chapter 11 proceeding, the debtor can continue in business.
10. D. A bankruptcy trustee has the power to avoid preferential payments (preferences), fraudulent transfers, and transactions that the debtor could rightfully avoid (such as transactions founded on fraud or duress). Other transfers that a trustee can set aside include those listed in the answer to question number 8 above.

Issue Spotters

1. The order of their priority is the party with the mechanic's lien, the party with the perfected security interest, and, lastly, the party with the unperfected security interest. Mechanic's liens (and artisan's liens) have priority over perfected security interests. Secured parties have the next highest priority. Unsecured creditors are generally paid last, if at all.
2. Yes. A debtor's payment to a creditor made for a preexisting debt, within ninety days (one year in the case of an insider or fraud) of the bankruptcy filing , can be recovered if it gives a creditor more than he or she would have received in the bankruptcy proceedings.
3. No. Besides the claims listed in this problem, the debts that cannot be discharged in bankruptcy include amounts borrowed to pay back taxes, goods obtained by fraud, debts that were not listed in the petition, alimony, child support, certain cash advances, and others.

Cumulative Hypothetical Problem for Unit Six—Including Chapters 28–30

1. C. A creditor can place a mechanic's lien on real property when a person contracts for labor to repair the property but does not pay. An artisan's lien entitles a creditor to recover from a debtor for the repair of personal property. In both cases, the property can be sold to satisfy the debt, but notice of the foreclosure and sale must first be given to the debtor.
2. D. With the right of subrogation, a surety, or a guarantor, may pursue any remedies that were available to the creditor against the debtor. These rights

include collection of the debt. A right of contribution is available to a co-surety, who pays more than his or her proportionate share of a debt, to recover from any other co-sureties. An exemption, in the context of a debt, is property that a debtor can protect from being used to pay the debt. Exoneration is not a term that applies to this circumstance.
3. A. If a buyer in the ordinary course of business does not know that a purchase violates a third party's rights, the buyer takes the goods free of any security interest. This is an exception to the general rule that a security interest in collateral continues even after the collateral is sold.
4. B. Only a debtor can file a plan under Chapter 11, but for the court to confirm it, the secured creditors must accept it. There is another condition that the plan must meet. It must provide that creditors retain their liens and the value of the property to be distributed to them is not less than the secured portion of their claims, or the debtor must surrender to the creditors the property securing those claims.
5. A. A Chapter 11 plan must provide for the full payment of all claims entitled to priority and the same treatment of each claim within a particular class. After the payments are completed, all debts provided for by the plan are discharged.

Questions on the Focus on Legal Reasoning for Unit Six—*In re Stanton*

1. D. In the *Stanton* case, the court held that the creditor's lien was not avoidable by the bankruptcy trustee because it was not the corporation that filed a petition in bankruptcy. In other words, the automatic stay provision did not apply. The court in that case reasoned that when money is loaned to a non-bankrupt corporation that the debtor owns, "[a] business relationship of stock ownership does not . . . extend the automatic stay to non-bankrupts."
2. C. The majority in the *Stanton* case reasoned, regarding a lender's lien's priority in these circumstances, that "where the advances of promised loan moneys are, under an agreement to lend money, largely optional," as they would be in this problem, "liens attaching prior to an optional advance would thus be superior." In other words, the bankruptcy trustee would be senior to the bank's lien for advances made after the debtor filed for personal bankruptcy because the trustee would "attach" before those later advances.
3. B. The dissent in the *Stanton* case reasoned in this context that the Bankruptcy Code's automatic stay provision "barred the debtors' attempt to use their house as collateral without prior court approval because, in continuing to use their house as collateral for [the corporation's] debts on post-petition advances, the debtors incurred debt within the meaning of" that provision.

Questions on the Focus on Ethics for Unit Six—Creditors' Rights and Bankruptcy

1. A. The opposite of all of the rest of the answer choices is true: self-help repossession is stressful for debtors, because it is often done in the middle of the night or otherwise attempted clandestinely; the repossession can be risky, in part because it may encourage violent confrontations with debtors; and the UCC does not define "breach of the peace," which can add to the complications. That self-help repossession can be done without involving the courts, however, is the reason that it is permitted.
2. D. One way the law protects creditors is by making it possible for a creditor to have a security interest in the proceeds from the collateral. There have been cases, however, in which proceeds disappeared. For example, proceeds have been held to have disappeared when they were eaten by farm animals and were thus not "traceable."
3. A. The bankruptcy laws—including the automatic stay provision, and the provisions as to which and how much debt can be discharged—can make a creditor's secured or unsecured obligation worthless, while enhancing the debtor's position by freeing secured assets from the obligations that they secure. This situation and the ease with which debtors can file for bankruptcy fuels the agitation for reform of the bankruptcy laws to at least make it less easy for debts to be discharged.

Chapter 31

True-False Questions

1. T
2. T
3. T
4. T
5. F. In most states, a minor can be an *agent* but not a principal.
6. T
7. F. When an agent breaches an agency contract, the principal can choose to avoid the contract.
8. F. If an agent is negligent and harms a third party, the injured third party can successfully sue the principal. In some circumstances, the principal may also sue the agent. The same principles apply when an agent violates a principal's instructions.
9. T
10. T

Fill-in Questions

performance; notification; loyalty; obedience; accounting

Multiple-Choice Questions

1. A. The problem states that the two persons are hired as employees. The employer is the principal. Normally, all employees who deal with third parties are deemed to be agents.
2. D. This is an agency relationship. An agency agreement does not have to be in writing, and an agent does not need to indicate that he or she is an agent. The business of the agent is not a determining factor in whether an agency relationship exists.
3. C. If an agent is not a gratuitous agent (one who does not perform for money), a principal owes the agent compensation for his or her services rendered. In this problem, if nothing had been agreed to, the principal would owe the agent the customary amount for his or her services. Also, payment must be timely. Another of a principal's duties is to reimburse an agent for expenses related to the agency, unless the parties have agreed otherwise. This question and answer are based on a question that appeared in the CPA exam in 1996.
4. A. An agent's duties to a principal include a duty to act solely in the principal's interest in matters concerning the principal's business. This is the duty of loyalty. The agent must act solely in the principal's interest and not in the interest of the agent, or some other party. It is also a breach of the duty of loyalty to use a principal's trade secrets or other confidential information (but not acquired skills) even after the agency has terminated.
5. A. There is a long list of factors that courts can consider in determining whether an individual is an employee or an independent contractor, and all of the choices in this question are among those factors. The most important factor, however, is the degree of control that the employer has over the details of the work.
6. D. Neither consideration nor a written agreement is required to form an agency relationship. Normally, an agency relationship must be based on an agreement that the agent will act for the principal, but the agreement does not have to be in writing—it can be oral or it can be implied from the parties' conduct.
7. D. If a principal causes a third person to believe that another person is his or her agent, and the third person deals with the supposed agent, the principal is estopped to deny the agency relationship. The third person must reasonably believe that the relationship existed and that the agent had authority. An ordinary, prudent person familiar with business practice and custom would have been justified in making the same conclusion.
8. B. In performing an agency, an agent is expected to use reasonable diligence and skill, which is the degree of skill of a reasonable person under similar circumstances. If an agent claims special skills, such as those of in this problem, he or she is expected to use those skills.
9. B. A failure to disclose material information bearing on an agency relationship is a breach of an agent's duties. In that circumstance, the agency is voidable at the option of the principal. When the principal transfers the property that was the object of the agency, as in this problem, the agency relationship has been voided.
10. A. Agency law is essential to the existence of most business entities, including corporations, because without agents, most firms could not do business. A corporate officer who serves in a representative capacity, as in this problem, is an agent. The corporation is the principal. For a contract to be binding on the firm, it needs only to be signed by the agent and to be within the scope of the officer's authority.

Issue Spotters

1. Yes. A principal has a duty to indemnify an agent for liabilities incurred because of authorized and lawful acts and transactions and for losses suffered because of the principal's failure to perform his or her duties.
2. No. An agent is prohibited from taking advantage of the agency relationship to obtain property that the principal wants to purchase. This is the duty of loyalty that arises with every agency relationship.
3. As set out in the problem, the truck driver is an employee, and the lighting technician and the booking agent are independent contractors. The booking agent is an agent, but either the employee or the independent contractor may at times also act in the capacity of an agent.

Chapter 32

True-False Questions

1. T
2. F. An agent is liable for his or her own torts, but a principal may also be liable under the doctrine of *respondeat superior*. The key is whether the tort is committed within the scope of employment. One of the important factors is whether the act that constituted the tort was authorized by the principal.
3. T
4. T
5. T
6. F. Criminal acts by an agent are not the responsibility of the principal, who will not thus be liable to a third party for any consequent harm.
7. F. The parties to an agency may always have the *power* to terminate the agency at any time, but they may not always have the *right*. If a party who terminates an agency does not have the right to do so, he or she may be liable for breach of contract.

8. F. One of the main attributes of an agency relationship is that the agent can enter into binding contracts on behalf of the principal. When an agent acts within the scope of his or her authority in entering a contract, the principal is bound, whether the principal's identity was disclosed, partially disclosed, or undisclosed to the other party to the contact.
9. T
10. F. An e-agent is a semi-autonomous Computer program that is capable of executing specific tasks, including responding to "electronic messages or performances without review by an individual," according to the Uniform Computer Information Transactions Act.

Fill-in Questions

is; an undisclosed; undisclosed; tort injuries; generally does not result

Multiple-Choice Questions

1. C. Implied authority can be conferred by custom, inferred from the agent's position, or inferred as reasonably necessary to carry out express authority. In determining whether an agent has the implied authority to do a specific act, the question is whether it is reasonable for the agent to believe that he or she has the authority.
2. C. When an agent acts within the scope of his or her authority to enter into a valid contract on behalf of an undisclosed principal, the principal is liable on the contract. Ratification is not necessary. The agent may also be liable on the contract. This question and answer are based on a question included in the May 1995 CPA exam.
3. C. Under the doctrine of *respondeat superior*, an employer (or principal) is vicariously liable for the wrongful acts of his or her employee (or agent) committed within the scope of employment (or agency).
4. A. Unless an agency is in writing—in which case, it must be terminated in writing—an agent can learn of a termination through any means. Until an agent is notified of the principal's decision to terminate the agency relationship, the agent's authority continues. Similarly, third parties with whom the agent deals must be informed of the termination to end the agent's apparent authority, as regards those third parties.
5. C. When an agent acts without authority and a third party relies on the agency status, the agent may be liable for breach of any contract purportedly signed on behalf of a principal. The agent may not be liable, however, if the third party knew that the agent did not have authority to contract on behalf of the principal. In either case, the principal is not liable, unless he or she ratifies the contract.
6. A. Apparent authority exists when a principal causes a third party reasonably to believe that an agent has the authority to act, even if the agent does not otherwise have the authority to do so. If the third party changes positions in reliance on the principal's representation, the principal may be estopped from denying the authority. Thus, here, the principal could not hold the customers liable for failing to pay.
7. C. Until an agent is notified of the principal's decision to terminate the agency relationship, the agent's authority continues. Similarly, third parties with whom the agent deals must be informed of the termination to end the agent's apparent authority, as regards those third parties. Unless an agency is in writing, in which case it must be terminated in writing, an agent can learn of a termination through any means.
8. B. An employer is liable for harm to a third party by an employee acting within the scope of employment. Here, the question is whether the employee was acting within that scope. Factors that indicate he was not include that the act (theft) was not authorized, did not advance the employer's interest, is not commonly performed by employees for their employers, and involved a serious crime. The employer might be liable if it knew that the employee would commit a tort or allowed it. In this problem, the employee acted without the employer's knowledge.
9. C. An agent (or employee) is liable for his or her own torts, whether or not they were committed within the scope of a principal's employment. The principal is also liable under the doctrine of *respondeat superior* when a tort is within the scope of the employment. One of the important factors in determining liability is whether the agent was on the principal's business or on a "frolic of his or her own."
10. A. When an agent is employed to accomplish a particular objective, the agency automatically terminates when the objective is accomplished.

Issue Spotters

1. A person in whose name a contract is made by one who is not an agent may be liable on the contract if he or she approves or affirms that contract. In other words, the employer-principal would be liable on the note in this problem on ratifying it.
2. Third persons injured by an employee's negligence can sue the employee or the employer, if the tort was committed while the employee was acting within the scope of employment. Thus, the employer is liable unless the driver's sidewalk driving is found to be outside the scope of his employment. The driver is liable, because an individual is always liable for his own torts.
3. Probably. A principal is liable for a loss due to an agent's knowing misrepresentation if the representation was made within the scope of the agency and the agent's scope of authority.

Chapter 33

True-False Questions

1. T
2. F. Employment "at will" means that either party may terminate the employment at any time, with or without good cause. There are many exceptions to this doctrine, enacted by state legislatures and Congress, or created by the courts. These include exceptions based on contract or tort theories, or public policy.
3. F. Employers are free to offer employees no benefits. Federal and state governments participate in insurance programs designed to protect employees and their families by covering some of the financial impact of retirement, disability, death, and hospitalization.
4. T
5. F. A "whistleblower" is one who reports wrongdoing. Whistleblower statutes protect employees who report their employers' wrongdoing from retaliation in the form of discharge, and sometimes other adverse employment conditions, on the part of those employers.
6. F. The Electronic Communications Privacy Act prohibits the interception of telephone (and other electronic) communications. Some courts recognize an exception for employers monitoring employee business-related calls, but monitoring personal conversations is not permitted.
7. F. Secondary boycotts, including hot-cargo agreements, which are described in the question, are illegal.
8. F. It is the central legal right of a *union* to serve as the bargaining representative of employees in negotiations with management.
9. T
10. F. Employees' right to engage in collective bargaining through elected representatives, like their right to organize and their right to engage in concerted activities for those and other purposes, was established in the National Labor Relations Act.

Fill-in Questions

either; unless; may; Some; A few states; may not

Multiple-Choice Questions

1. A. Child-labor, minimum-wage, and maximum-hour provisions are included in the Fair Labor Standards Act (also known as the Wage-Hour Law), covering virtually all employees. The employer may also be subject to the other laws given as choices in this problem, but those laws concern other rights and duties of employees and employers. This question and answer are based on a question that was included in the May 1995 CPA exam.
2. B. Investigating theft is the only circumstance in which an employer may require polygraph tests. Drug tests are prohibited by some states, and restricted by others or by collective bargaining agreements. Their use may also be subject to tort actions for invasion of privacy. An employer may monitor employees' *business* phone conversations but not their *private* ones.
3. B. Intentionally inflicted injuries are not covered by workers' compensation. Many states cover problems arising out of preexisting conditions, but that is not part of the test for coverage. To collect benefits, an employee must notify the employer of an injury and file a claim with the appropriate state agency.
4. C. Under the Immigration Act, employers recruiting workers from other countries must complete a certification process with the U.S. Department of Labor. Part of the process is to show that there is a shortage of qualified U.S. workers in the particular area and that hiring aliens will not have a negative impact on the labor market in the area.
5. B. The Federal Unemployment Tax Act of 1935 concerns the system that provides unemployment compensation. The Employee Retirement Income Security Act (ERISA) of 1974 concerns the regulation of private pension plans.
6. A. The Employment Retirement Income Security Act (ERISA) covers such employers. The Labor Management Services Administration of the U.S. Department of Labor enforces ERISA. The other laws mentioned in the choices in this problem regulate other areas of retirement and security income.
7. B. Under the Family and Medical Leave Act (FMLA) of 1993, employees can take up to twelve weeks of family or medical leave during any twelve-month period and are entitled to continued health insurance coverage during the leave. Employees are also guaranteed the same, or a comparable, job on returning to work.
8. C. Under the Consolidated Omnibus Budget Reconciliation Act (COBRA) of 1985, most workers' medical, optical, or dental insurance is not automatically eliminated on termination of employment. The workers can choose to continue the coverage at the employer's group rate, if they are willing to pay the premiums (and a 2 percent administrative fee).
9. D. The National Labor Relations Act protects employees who engage in union activity and prohibits employers from refusing to bargain with employees' designated representative. Violations of these provisions are employer unfair labor practices.
10. D. An employer can hire permanent replacement workers during an economic strike. After the strike, the replacement workers do not have to be fired to make way for the strikers. Temporary replacement workers may be hired during any strike.

Issue Spotters

1. Probably. Some courts have held that an implied employment contract exists between employer and

employee under an employee handbook that states employees will be dismissed only for good cause. An employer who fires a worker contrary to this promise can be held liable for breach of contract.

2. No. Generally, the right to recover under workers' compensation laws is determined without regard to negligence or fault. Unlike the potential for recovery in a lawsuit based on negligence or fault, however, recovery under a workers' compensation statute is limited to the specific amount designated in the statute for the employee's injury.

3. No. A closed shop (a company that requires union membership as a condition of employment) is illegal. A union shop (a company that does not require union membership as a condition of employment but requires workers to join the union after a certain time on the job) is illegal in a state with a right-to-work law, which makes it illegal to require union membership for continued employment.

Chapter 34

True-False Questions

1. T

2. F. An employer may be liable even though an employee did the harassing, if the employer knew, or should have known, and failed to take corrective action, or if the employee was in a supervisory position and took a tangible employment action against the injured employee.

3. F. Just as an employer may be liable for an employee's misconduct, the employer may be liable for harassment by a nonemployee, if the employer knew, or should have known, of the harassment and failed to take corrective action.

4. T

5. T

6. T

7. F. If the Equal Employment Opportunity Commission (EEOC) decides not pursue a claim, the victim can file a suit against alleged violator. The EEOC can pursue a claim in federal district court, however, in its own name against alleged violators (and this is true even if the employee has agreed to submit the dispute to arbitration). The EEOC can also intervene in a suit filed by a private party.

8. F. Title VII covers only employers with fifteen or more employees, labor unions with fifteen or more members, labor unions that operate hiring halls, employment agencies, and federal, state, and local agencies. In other words, small employers are generally exempted from the application of this federal statute.

9. T

10. T

Fill-in Questions

can; may sue if a settlement between the parties is not reached; reinstatement, back pay, and retroactive promotions

Multiple-Choice Questions

1. A. Before filing a lawsuit, the best step for a person who believes that he or she may be a victim of employment discrimination is to contact a state or federal agency to see whether the claim is justified. The appropriate federal agency is the Equal Employment Opportunity Commission. Most states have similar agencies that evaluate claims under state law.

2. A. Sexual harassment occurs when, in a workplace, an employee is subject to comments or contact that is perceived as sexually offensive. An employer may be liable even though an employee did the harassing. If the employee was in a supervisory position, as in this problem, for an employer to be held liable, a tangible employment action may need to be proved. Here, the employee's pay was cut.

3. A. The other choices would not subject the employer to liability under the Age Discrimination in Employment Act (ADEA). Discrimination is prohibited against persons forty years of age or older, even if the discrimination is unintentional. Mandatory retirement may be instituted, but not on account of an employee's age, and an employee may be discharged for cause at any age. This question and answer are based on a question that appeared in the CPA exam in 1996.

4. C. An employer who is subject to the Americans with Disabilities Act cannot exclude arbitrarily a person who, with reasonable accommodation, could do what is required of a job. A disabled individual is not required to reasonably accommodate an employer. Also, the standard is not "significant additional costs," to either the employer or the disabled individual.

5. C. Title VII prohibits employment discrimination on the basis of race. This includes discriminating against members of a minority with darker skin than other members of the same minority. Title VII also prohibits using physical characteristics that are typical of some races to distinguish applicants or employees.

6. C. Title VII prohibits showing a preference for members of one minority over members of another. Title VII also prohibits making distinctions according to the race of a person's spouse, friends, or other contacts. The other laws mentioned in the answer choices prohibit discrimination on the basis of age and disability, respectively, as suggested by their titles.

7. C. The Equal Pay Act of 1963 prohibits gender-based discrimination in wages for equal work. Different wages are acceptable because of any factor but gender, including seniority and merit.

8. C. Here, the employer would seem to have a valid business necessity defense. It appears reasonable

that administrative assistants be able to type. An employer can insist that, to be hired, a job applicant possess the actual skills required for a job. Except for an applicant's willingness or unwillingness to acquire certain skills, the other answer choices might be legitimate defenses in other circumstances.
9. A. The Age Discrimination in Employment Act (ADEA) of 1967 requires, for the establishment of a *prima facie* case, that at the time of the alleged discrimination, the plaintiff was forty or older, was qualified for the job, and was discharged or otherwise rejected in circumstances that imply discrimination. The difference between a *prima facie* case under the ADEA and under Title VII is that the ADEA does not require a plaintiff to show that someone who is not a member of a protected class filled the position at the center of the claim.
10. C. The employer's best defense in this problem would be that being able to pass the tests is a business necessity—it is a necessary requirement for the job. Discrimination may be illegal even if it is not intentional, and whether or not all men pass the tests is not relevant to whether there is discrimination against women. If the employer hires some women for the job, it could not argue successfully that gender is a BFOQ for the job.

Issue Spotters

1. Yes, if he is a member of a protected class. These circumstances would then include all of the elements of a *prima facie* under Title VII of the Civil Rights Act of 1964: (1) the applicant is a member of a protected class, (2) he applied and was qualified for an open position, (3) he was rejected, and (4) the employer continued to seek applicants or filled the position with a person who is not in a protected class. The employer would then have to offer a legitimate reason for its action, and the applicant would have to show that this is a pretext, that discriminatory intent was the motivation.
2. Yes. One type of sexual harassment occurs when a request for sexual favors is a condition of employment, and the person making the request is a supervisor or acts with the authority of the employer. A tangible employment action, such as continued employment, may also lead to the employer's liability for the supervisor's conduct. That the injured employee is a male and the supervisor a female, instead of the other way around, would not affect the outcome. Same-gender harassment is also actionable.
3. Yes, if she can show that she was not hired solely because of her disability. The other elements for a discrimination suit based on a disability are that the plaintiff (1) has a disability and (2) is otherwise qualified for the job. Both of these elements appear to be satisfied in this problem.

Cumulative Hypothetical Problem for Unit Seven—Including Chapters 31–34

1. B. The requirements for recovery under state workers' compensation laws include the existence of an employment relationship and an accidental injury that occurs on the job or within the scope of employment. Accepting benefits precludes an employee from suing his or her employer, but it does not bar the employee from suing a third party for causing the injury.
2. D. The Social Security Act of 1935 provides payments for persons who are retired or disabled. The Social Security Administration is a federal agency that also administers the Medicare program. Unemployment benefits, however, are part of a state system created by the Federal Unemployment Tax Act of 1935.
3. D. One of the agent's fiduciary duties to the principal is the duty of loyalty. This means that the agent must not engage in conflicts of interest, and the agent cannot compete with the principal without informing the principal and obtaining the principal's consent.
4. A. Title VII of the Civil Rights Act of 1964 covers many forms of discrimination, including discrimination based on gender, race, religion, color, and national origin. But Title VII does not prohibit discrimination based on age, which is the subject of the Age Discrimination in Employment Act of 1967.
5. B. The Age Discrimination in Employment Act of 1967 prohibits discrimination against persons aged forty or more. This includes mandatory retirement of such individuals. In most circumstances, however, an employer can discharge an employee for cause, regardless of his or her age, without running afoul of this, or any other, federal anti-discrimination law.

Questions on the Focus on Legal Reasoning for Unit Seven—*Redi-Floors, Inc. v. Sonenberg Co.*

1. D. In the *Redi-Floors* case, the majority explained out that "if an agent buys in his own name, without disclosing his principal, and the seller subsequently discovers that the purchase was, in fact, made for another, he may, at his choice, look for payment either to the agent or the principal." In the words of the court, a seller "who has once elected, can claim no right to make a second choice," however.
2. A. It would likely depend on the grounds for the verdict. In the reasoning of the majority in the *Redi-Floors* case, however, "it is the plaintiff who is entitled to elect against which of the defendants, principal or agent, to take the judgment." In this *Redi-Floors* case, "the trial court's erroneous granting of a directed verdict deprived the plaintiff of its right to elect which defendant it would proceed against."
3. D. The dissent in the *Redi-Floors* case reasoned that the seller made its decision against whom to pursue an action when the contracting party "procured a judgment order which was reduced to writing

against" the principal. Obtaining that judgment "constituted an election of alternative remedies that precluded plaintiff from pursuing the excluded remedy against" the agent. "As the plaintiff may not obtain judgment against both, he must make an election *prior to judgment*."

Questions on the Focus on Ethics for Unit Seven—Agency and Employment

1. D. The conduct stated in the answer choices is permitted by legal and ethical considerations. Other actions that may be proscribed by ethics include secretly profiting from the agency relation, and failing to disclose the agent's interest in property that the principal is buying.
2. C. Agents and principals owe each other fiduciary duties. The law mandates for a principal duties of compensation, cooperation, and reimbursement of agency-related expenses. A principal is not legally bound to a duty of loyalty, however, although a sense of loyalty may be based on ethical obligations.
3. D. Under the employment-at-will doctrine, an employer may terminate an employee for any reason or no reason at any time. Without an employment contract, or anything from which an employment contract can be implied, and without the protection of a federal or state statute, there are only limited common law grounds on which an action against such a termination can be maintained. The set of facts in this problem do not state a violation of public policy that would support such an action.

Chapter 35

True-False Questions

1. F. A sole proprietorship is the simplest form of business organization. In a sole proprietorship, the owner and the business are the same. Anyone who creates a business without designating a specific form for its organization is doing business as a sole proprietorship.
2. T
3. T
4. T
5. F. The parties to a franchise (the franchisor and the franchisee) determine its termination. Generally, the parties provide in the franchise contract that termination is "for cause" and notice is required. Of course, in the case of a dispute, litigation may ensue and the parties may end up in court, which may then have to determine whether or not to terminate the franchise arrangement. That is not the usual course, however.
6. T
7. F. A franchisor can exercise greater control in this area than in some other areas of the business, because the *franchisor* has a legitimate interest in maintaining the quality of the product or service to protect its name and reputation.
8. F. There is state law covering franchises, and it is very similar to federal law on the subject, requiring certain disclosures, limiting termination without cause, and so on. State deceptive practices acts and UCC Article 2 may also apply to franchises.
9. F. Federal laws covering franchises include the Automobile Dealers' Franchise Act of 1965, the Petroleum Marketing Practices Act (PMPA) of 1979, the federal antitrust laws, and the Franchise Rule of the Federal Trade Commission (which requires certain disclosures and a meeting between the parties to a franchise agreement).
10. T

Fill-in Questions

distributorship; chain-style; manufacturing

Multiple-Choice Questions

1. D. There are no limits on the liability of the owner of a sole proprietorship for the debts and obligations of the firm. A sole proprietorship has greater organizational flexibility, however, than other forms of business organization.
2. B. Antitrust laws are most likely to be violated if the franchisor requires the franchisee to purchase exclusively from the franchisor. A franchisor's setting of prices at which products may be sold may also violate antitrust laws.
3. C. Under a contract between the franchisor and the franchisee, the latter may be required to pay a fee for the franchise license, fees for products bought from or through the franchisor, and a percentage of advertising and administrative costs.
4. C. In this type of franchise, a franchisor typically requires a franchisee to pay it a fee for the right to sell its products. The franchisor also usually requires that the franchisee pay the franchisor a percentage of the receipts from the sales of the products.
5. C. Of the choices here, again the franchisor can set the terms. There may be little for a franchisee to negotiate with some franchises, but perhaps the chief advantage of a franchise is that the franchisee is obtaining the opportunity to profit from the sales of a proven product or service.
6. C. Franchise agreements typically provide that the franchisor can terminate a franchise for cause. If no set time for termination is provided, a reasonable time will be implied. A franchisor cannot usually terminate a franchise without notice.
7. C. A franchisee may have some protection under the Franchise Rule of the Federal Trade Commission

with respect to what the franchisor must disclose, and how and when the disclosure must be made, before the franchisee invests in a franchise. A franchisee may have additional protection under federal law, depending on the nature of the products or services being sold. State protection, while similar to federal law, may include more protection under deceptive practices acts or Article 2 of the UCC.

8. A. A disadvantage of the sole proprietorship form of doing business is that the ability to raise capital while maintaining control, and retaining the same form, is limited chiefly to borrowing funds. The trade off in this situation is that a sole proprietorship provides greater organizational flexibility—no one needs to be consulted in making business decisions. Bringing in partners would convert the business to a partnership. Issuing stock would require incorporating or establishing another form of business. Selling the business would of course sacrifice all control.

9. C. A franchise is an arrangement through which the owner of a copyright, a trademark, or a trade name licenses others to use it in selling goods or services. Most franchises can also be characterized as distributorships, chain-style business operations, or manufacturing or processing-plant operations.

10. B. A franchisee is a purchaser of a franchise. The seller of a franchise is the franchisor. Although economically dependent, or at least related, these parties are usually otherwise independent of each other.

Issue Spotters

1. When a business is relatively small and is not diversified, employs relatively few people, has modest profits, and is not likely to expand significantly or require extensive financing in the immediate future, the most appropriate form for doing business may be a sole proprietorship.

2. Yes. If the franchisor is acting in good faith, "cause" may also include the death or disability of the franchisee, the insolvency of the franchisee, and a breach of the franchise agreement.

3. Too much control may result in the franchisor's liability for torts of a franchisee's employees. For example, if the employee performs in a manner that is attributed to the control of the franchisor, and this performance results in an injury to another, the franchisor may be held liable.

Chapter 36

True-False Questions

1. F. A partnership is formed through an agreement among the partners. If this agreement satisfies the definition of partnership, nothing more is needed for a partnership to exist. The partnership agreement does not need to be in writing, except as otherwise required under the Statute of Frauds.

2. F. Partners are subject to personal liability for the debts and obligations of a partnership, and this is whether or not they have participated in its management. On the firm's dissolution, its creditors have the top priority in the distribution of the firm's assets. If those assets are not sufficient to pay the creditors, the partners are liable for the difference.

3. F. Other situations that do *not* cause the dissolution of a partnership include an involuntary sale of a partner's interest in the firm, a partner's insolvency. Circumstances that will dissolve a partnership include the addition of a new partner, the withdrawal of a partner, and the death of a partner.

4. T

5. T

6. F. Unless otherwise set out in the partnership agreement, profits are shared equally, and losses are shared in the same proportion as the profits, under the UPA.

7. T

8. F. The members of a joint venture may be sued individually, but the joint venture cannot be sued as an entity.

9. T

10. F. Partners in a partnership can bind other partners to contracts and other obligations to third parties. The members of a joint venture have limited power to bind other members.

Fill-in Questions

are; obligation; sued; cannot; releases; must

Multiple-Choice Questions

1. A. Under a partnership by estoppel theory, a person who is not a partner, but who represents himself or herself as a partner, is liable to a third person who acts in reasonable reliance on that representation. If one of the actual partners had consented to the misrepresentation, however, the firm would also be liable.

2. A. A partner holds all partnership property (and proceeds from its sale) as a tenant in partnership with all of the other partners. Each partner has equal rights to the property for the firm's purposes, but not for other reasons without the consent of all of the partners. Also, a partner's fiduciary duty requires him or her to hold in trust for the others all funds realized from transactions connected with the business of the partnership and to account for the profits.

3. C. This arrangement for the payment of an employee (a base wage and a sales commission) does not make the employee a partner in the employer's business. There are three attributes of a partnership: sharing profits, joint ownership of a business, and an equal right in the management of the business. None of these are present here.

4. C. There are many ways to cause the dissolution of a partnership. Partners may expressly agree to dissolve their partnership, or the addition of a new partner or the transfer of a partner's interest (with or without all other partners' knowledge or consent) may cause a firm's dissolution. Depending on a particular state's law, dissolution may also result from the withdrawal of a partner. Of the choices in this problem, however, the only one that would cause dissolution is a partner's bankruptcy. Dissolution is, of course, only the first step towards the termination of the firm's legal existence. The winding up of the partnership's affairs cover the other steps. This question and answer are based on a question from a CPA exam in 1998.

5. C. In all states, partners are jointly and severally liable for torts and breaches of trust. This means that any or all of the partners may be held liable. This is true even if, as in this problem, they did not participate in the tort or breach of trust.

6. B. For most purposes, a partnership is regarded as an entity. A partnership can sue and collect judgments in its own name (rather than in the names of the individual partners). A partnership can own real estate in its name. For federal income tax purposes, however, a partnership is considered an aggregate: the firm files an informational return with the Internal Revenue Service, but does not pay taxes on its profits. The income is passed through to the partners, who pay taxes on it on their individual returns.

7. B. After a partner informs the other partners that he or she is withdrawing from the partnership, the withdrawing partner is not liable for contracts entered into by his or her former partners. In fact, the partnership has dissolved and is also not liable. The parties who sign the contract are, of course, liable, however, as is any new partnership formed to carry on the business.

8. C. This definition is like the definition of a partnership. A joint venture is similar to a partnership, and is generally subject to partnership law, but unlike a partnership, a joint venture is created in contemplation of a limited activity. A joint venture may have more than two members, and a joint venture is not a corporate enterprise, although its members may be corporations. This question and answer are based on a question that appeared in the November 1989 CPA exam.

9. D. A syndicate may exist as a partnership, a corporation, or no legally recognized form. As in this problem, a syndicate is a group of individuals financing a project.

10. A. A business trust is similar to a corporation. Like corporate shareholders, the owners hold shares in the trust and they are not personally liable for the organization's debts and obligations.

Issue Spotters

1. No. A widow (or widower) has no right to take a dead partner's place. No one can become a partner without the unanimous consent of the partners. Also, if a partner dies, the surviving partners, not the heirs of the deceased partner, have the right of survivorship to the specific partnership property, such as inventory. Surviving partners must account to the decedent's estate for the *value* of the deceased partner's interest in the property, however.

2. No. Under the partners' fiduciary duty, a partner must account to the partnership for any personal profits or benefits derived without the consent of all the partners in connection with the use of any partnership property. Here, the leasing partner may not keep the money.

3. There are differences between these forms of business organization, but all of them are treated under the law like partnerships. The differences include that the members of joint ventures have less authority than partners, and the members of a joint stock company are not agents of each other. Also, a joint stock company has many of the characteristics of a corporation: (1) ownership by shares of stock, (2) managed by directors and officers, and (3) perpetual existence.

Chapter 37

True-False Questions

1. T
2. F. A corporation formed in a country other than the United States, but that does business in the United States, is an alien corporation. A foreign corporation is a corporation formed in one state, but doing business in another state.
3. T
4. F. Powers set out in corporate documents (and in the laws of the state of incorporation and state and federal constitutions) are express powers. Acts of a corporation that exceed its express and implied powers are called *ultra vires* (which means "beyond the powers"). Legal and illegal acts can be *ultra vires*.
5. T
6. T
7. F. An S corporation has tax imposed only at the shareholder level. Other corporations are subject to double taxation, however, which was one of the reasons for the enactment of the S corporation statute. Only corporations with seventy-five or fewer shareholders can qualify for S-corporation status, although in some circumstances, a corporation can be an S-corporation shareholder.
8. T
9. F. Each state has its own body of corporate law, and these laws are not identical. Most states have

adopted, at least in part or at least in principle, the Model Business Corporation Act or its revision, the Revised Model Business Corporation Act. There is still variation among the states, however, some of which do not follow either act.

10. T

Fill-in Questions

promoters; unless; an incorporator; need not

Multiple-Choice Questions

1. D. State incorporation laws vary, so looking for the state that offers the most favorable provisions for a particular firm is important. There are some principles that states commonly observe, however. For example, in all states a firm can have perpetual existence, but cannot do business under the same, or even a similar, name as an existing firm.

2. D. Implied powers attach when a corporation is created. These powers include the power to borrow money, to lend money, to extend credit, and to make charitable contributions. The other powers listed here are typically expressed in state statutes.

3. A. Corporate directors manage the business of a corporation. The directors normally employ officers, who oversee the daily operations. The directors may be initially designated by the incorporators or promoters, but are later elected by the shareholders (the owners of the corporation).

4. A. This firm has the characteristics of a close corporation. A close corporation is also generally allowed to restrict the transfer of its stock. Firms represented by the other answer choices could also be close corporations. To be a professional corporation, a firm must be a corporation formed by professionals (and the firm is designated by "P.A." for "professional association," or some other appropriate abbreviation). S corporations and nonprofits corporations have other requirements.

5. C. All corporations issue bonds (and stocks). Bonds are also known as debt securities. Types of bonds include callable bonds, debentures, and mortgage bonds.

6. C. To obtain capital, a corporation issues securities, principally stocks and bonds. Essentially, a security represents either an ownership interest in a firm or a debt owed by the firm.

7. A. Articles of incorporation serve as a primary source of authority for its organization and functions. The information contained in the articles includes the firm's operating name, its duration, its nature and purpose, its capital structure (including the value and classes of corporate stock), its registered office and agent (who receives legal documents on the firm's behalf), and the date of its annual shareholders' meeting (which is not likely to appear in the corporation's charter).

8. C. Common stock represents an interest in a corporation with regard to all of these aspects in proportion to the number of shares owned out of the total number of shares issued. Common stock represents the true ownership of a corporation. Preferred shareholders have priority to the payment of any dividends (they do not have a right to dividends) but may not have the right to vote. Common stockholders are the last to receive payment for their investment, however, on the dissolution of the corporation.

9. C. The certificate of incorporation is viewed as evidence that the firm has met the requirements for corporate existence. A *de facto* corporation is one as to which there is a defect in complying with state law, but among other things, there was a good faith attempt to comply. A firm that does not have a certificate of incorporation may be held to be a corporation by estoppel when a third party contracts with it and it should not otherwise by allowed to avoid liability.

10 A. Other factors that a court may use to pierce the corporate veil include that a party is tricked or misled into dealing with the firm rather than the individual, that the firm is too thinly capitalized (not overcapitalized), and that the firm holds too few (not too many) shareholders' meetings.

Issue Spotters

1. Yes. A foreign corporation must have sufficient minimum contacts with a state for it to exercise jurisdiction. Doing business within a state is generally considered to constitute sufficient contact, as a firm does when it sells or advertises in a state, or otherwise places goods in the stream of commerce. Thus, a court in which a firm does business can exercise jurisdiction over it even if it was not incorporated in that state.

2. Yes. Small businesses that meet certain requirements can qualify as S corporations, created specifically to permit small businesses to avoid double taxation. The six requirements of an S corporation are (1) the firm must be a domestic corporation, (2) the firm must not be a member of an affiliated group of corporations, (3) the firm must have less than a certain number of shareholders, (4) the shareholders must be individuals, estates, or qualified trusts (or corporations in some cases), (5) there can be only one class of stock, and (6) no shareholder can be a nonresident alien.

3. Yes. Broad authority to conduct business can be granted in a corporation's articles of incorporation. For example, the term "any lawful purpose" is often used. This can be important because acts of a corporation that are beyond the authority given to it in its articles or charter (or state statutes) are considered illegal, *ultra vires* acts.

Chapter 38

True-False Questions

1. T
2. T
3. F. Preemptive rights consist of preferences given to shareholders over other purchasers to buy shares of a new corporate issue in proportion to the number of shares that they already hold. This allows a shareholder to maintain his or her proportionate ownership share in the corporation. Generally, these rights are granted (or withheld) in the articles of incorporation.
4. T
5. F. Any damages recovered in a shareholder's derivative suit are normally paid to the corporation on whose behalf the shareholder or shareholders exercised the derivative right.
6. T
7. F. Officers and directors owe the same fiduciary duties to the corporations for which they work. They both owe a duty of loyalty. This duty requires them to subordinate their personal interests to the welfare of the corporation.
8. F. The business judgment rule immunizes directors (and officers) from liability for poor business decisions and other honest mistakes that cause a corporation to suffer a loss. Directors are not immunized from losses that do not fit this category, however.
9. T
10. T

Fill-in Questions

but ownership is not; can; recorded as the owner in the corporation's books

Multiple-Choice Questions

1. B. Dividends may be paid from the other sources listed here. Once declared, a dividend becomes a debt enforceable at law like any other debt. Generally, state law allows dividends to be paid as long as a corporation can pay its other debts as they come due and the amount of the dividend is not more than the net worth of the corporation.
2. A. There is no such right. This is also not a right of directors, except as specified in the articles of incorporation. The ownership of a corporation by shareholders also does not include rights of actual ownership of specific corporate property.
3. A. Officers and other executive employees are hired by a corporation's board of directors. The rights of the officers and other high-level managers are defined by their employment contracts with the corporation.
4. C. Directors must exercise care in their duties. For example, they are expected to use a reasonable amount of supervision over corporate officers and employees when they delegate work. Their liability for breach of this duty could be grounded in negligence or mismanagement of corporate personnel. They are also expected to be loyal: faithful to their obligations and duties.
5. D. The other choices do not represent proper purposes for which a shareholders' derivative suit may be filed. A shareholder's derivative suit is a claim filed on behalf of the corporation. Such a suit may allege, for example, that officers or directors misused corporate assets. Of course, any damages that are awarded must be paid to the corporation. This question and answer are based on a question that appeared in a CPA exam in 1998.
6. C. Cumulative voting can often be used in the election of directors to enhance the power of minority shareholders in electing a representative. In calculating a shareholder's votes under the cumulative voting method, in this problem, Mary's number of shares is multiplied by the number of directors to be elected.
7. B. Unless a state statute provides to the contrary, a quorum of directors must be present to conduct corporate business, such as the declaration of a dividend. A quorum is a majority of the number of directors authorized in the firm's articles or bylaws. The rule is one vote per director.
8. A. The board of directors hires the company's officers and other managerial employees, and determines their compensation. Ultimate responsibility for all policy decisions necessary to the management of corporate affairs also rests with the directors.
9. B. Directors' main right is their right to participate in board meetings. Directors also have a right to inspect corporate books and to be indemnified in defense of some lawsuits (regardless of the outcome of the suit). Rights that directors do not have include a right to compensation. That is, directors may be compensated for their efforts, but they have no inherent right to it. "Preemption" is not a right.
10. C. Under their duty of loyalty, directors cannot compete with their corporation or have an interest which conflicts with the interest of the corporation. Owning the stock of a competitor would also constitute an interest which conflicts with the interest of the corporation on whose board a director serves.

Issue Spotters

1. Under these circumstances, a minority shareholder can petition a court to appoint and receiver and liquidate the assets of the corporation.
2. Yes. A shareholder can bring a derivative suit on behalf of a corporation, if some wrong is done to the corporation. Normally, any damages recovered go into the corporate treasury.
3. Yes. A single shareholder—or a few shareholders acting together—who owns enough stock to exercise

de facto control over a corporation owes the corporation and minority shareholders a fiduciary duty when transferring those shares.

Chapter 39

True-False Questions

1. T
2. F. Appraisal rights are available only when a statute specifically provides for them. The rationale for appraisal rights is that shareholders should not be forced to become owners of corporations that are different from the ones in which they originally invested
3. F. Shareholder approval is required to amend articles of incorporation (and to undertake other extraordinary business matters, such as selling all of a corporation's assets outside the ordinary course of business).
4. F. Shareholder approval is not normally required to buy all, or substantially all, of another corporation's assets. It is necessary, however, that the selling corporation's shareholders approve the sale of all or substantially all of its assets to another corporation.
5. T
6. F. Dissolution can occur by this means, but there are many other ways to bring about the dissolution of a corporation. Also, liquidation, which is the other step in the termination of a corporation, can be performed without court supervision.
7. T
8. F. Ordinarily, a corporation that purchases the assets of another corporation does not assume the other's liabilities. In some cases, however, the purchasing corporation may be held responsible for the seller's liabilities (for example, if the purchasing corporation continues the seller's business with the same personnel).
9. T
10. F. In those states that provide for shareholder appraisal rights, they are usually available in sales of substantially all of a corporation's assets. Note that once a shareholder chooses to exercise appraisal rights, he or she loses his or her status (to vote, receive dividends, and so on) in many jurisdictions.

Fill-in Questions

extraordinary; shareholder; before; before; the vote is taken.

Multiple-Choice Questions

1. A. In a merger or consolidation, the surviving corporation acquires all the assets of both corporations without a formal transfer. In a merger, the surviving corporation's articles of incorporation are considered to be *amended* by the articles of merger, and in a consolidation, the articles of consolidation *replace* the previous corporations' articles.
2. C. Directors and shareholders must approve a consolidation (or a merger). Corporate officers do not have to approve either a merger or a consolidation. In both cases, a state must also issue a certificate of consolidation or merger. A court approval's is not required, however.
3. C. In either a merger or consolidation, the surviving corporation acquires all of the assets and assumes all of the debts of its predecessors (the corporations that formed it).
4. B. Without shareholder approval, one corporation may buy all, or substantially all, of the assets of another corporation. The other choices are actions that a board of directors cannot undertake without shareholder approval. This question and answer are based on a CPA exam question that appeared in a 1997 exam.
5. C. A corporation's failure to comply with administrative requirements could also result in a court-ordered dissolution. Filing an annual report is an administrative requirement. Dissolution may be ordered if a corporation fails to commence business operations after forming. Other reasons include obtaining a corporate charter through fraud and abuse of corporate powers. Failure to declare a dividend and failure to earn a profit are not grounds for which a court would order a dissolution, if the directors are otherwise complying with their fiduciary duties
6. B. This combination is a merger (one, but only one, corporation continues to exist). In a consolidation, an entirely new corporation acquires all of the assets and liabilities of the consolidating, disappearing corporations.
7. C. In a merger, the surviving corporation assumes all of the debts and liabilities of the disappearing corporation. Of course, the surviving corporation also inherits all of the disappearing corporation's rights. These rights and liabilities include those arising from litigation. (When one firm "absorbs" another, the firm doing the "absorbing" will be the survivor.)
8. A. This combination is a consolidation (a new entity takes the place of the consolidating, disappearing firms). In a merger, one of the merging entities continues to exist.
9. C. These articles must first be approved by the corporations' directors and shareholders. If this were a consolidation, the procedure would be the same.
10. C. A statute must provide for these rights before they can be exercised. If it does, however, and the parties cannot agree on a fair appraisal value, a court will determine it. Note that appraisal rights are usually not available in cases of short-form mergers or sales of substantially all a corporation's assets.

Issue Spotters

1. The first combination is a merger. One of the previously existing corporations absorbed the other. The second combination is a consolidation. Neither of the combining corporations continue after the combination: a new firm continues in their place.
2. Shareholders who disapprove of a merger or a consolidation may be entitled to be paid fair value for their shares. These are known as appraisal rights.
3. To retain control over itself, a target corporation can take any one or more of a number of defensive measures. The target may attempt to take over the acquiring corporation, it may sell off its most attractive assets, or it may seek to be taken over by a more desirable acquiring corporation, among other courses of action.

Chapter 40

True-False Questions

1. T
2. T
3. T
4. T
5. F. Rule 506, issued under the Securities Act of 1933, provides an exemption for these offerings, if certain other requirements are met. This is an important exemption, applying to private offerings to a limited number of sophisticated investors.
6. T
7. T
8. F. *Scienter* is not a requirement for liability under Section 16(b) of the Securities Exchange Act of 1934, but it is required for liability under Section 10(b) and under Rule 10b-5.
9. F. Anyone who receives inside information as a result of an insider's breach of his or her fiduciary duty can be liable under Rule 10b-5, which applies in virtually all cases involving the trading of securities. The key to liability is whether the otherwise undisclosed information is *material*.
10. F. Most securities can be resold without registration. Also, under Rule 144 and 144A ("Safe harbor" provisions), there are specific exemptions for securities that might otherwise require registration with the SEC.

Fill-in Questions

prosecution; triple; twenty-five; may

Multiple-Choice Questions

1. B. Under the Securities Exchange Act of 1934, the Securities and Exchange Commission all of the other duties and more, including regulating national securities trading, supervising mutual funds, and recommending sanctions in cases involving violations of securities laws. This question and answer are based on a question that was included in a 1996 CPA exam.
2. A. This purchase and sale is a violation of Section 16(b) of the Securities Exchange Act of 1934. When a purchase and sale is within a six-month period, as in this problem, the corporation can recover all of the profit. Proof of *scienter* is not required.
3. D. Under the Securities Act of 1933, a security exists when a person invests in a common enterprise with the reasonable expectation of profits derived primarily or substantially from the managerial or entrepreneurial efforts of others (not from the investor's own efforts).
4. A. Because of the low amount of the issue, it qualifies as an exemption from registration under Rule 504. No specific disclosure document is required, and there is no prohibition on solicitation. If the amount had been higher than $1 million but lower than $5 million, this offer might have qualified for an exemption under Regulation A, which requires notice to the SEC and an offering circular for investors.
5. D. The amount of this offering is too high to exempt it from the registration requirements except possibly under Rule 506 or Section 4(6). This issuer advertised the offering, however, and Rule 506 prohibits general solicitation. Thus, without filing a registration statement, the issuer could not legally solicit *any* investors (whatever it may have believed about the unaccredited investors). This offering does not qualify under Section 4(6), because unaccredited investors participated.
6. D. This issue might qualify under Rule 505 or Section 4(6), except that again, the issuer advertised the offering, which it cannot do and remain exempt from registration. In other words, the amount of this offering disqualified the issuer from advertising it without filing a registration statement.
7. B. A registration statement must supply enough information so that an unsophisticated investor can evaluate the financial risk involved. The statement must explain how the registrant intends to use the proceeds from the sale of the issue. Also, besides the description of management, there must be a disclosure of any of their material transactions with the firm. A certified financial statement must be included.
8. C. A corporate officer is a traditional inside trader. The outsider in this problem is a tippee who is liable because the tippee knew of the officer's misconduct. Liability here is based on the fact that the information was not public. Liability might be avoided if those who know the information wait for a reasonable time after its public disclosure before trading their stock.
9. A. Of course, the offering must be registered with the SEC before it can be sold, and this requires a registration statement. Investors must be given a prospectus that describes the security, the issuing corpo-

ration, and the risk of the security. A tombstone ad tells an investor how and where to obtain the prospectus.
10. A. Most resales are exempt from registration if persons other than issuers or underwriters undertake the resales. Resales of restricted securities acquired under Rule 504a, Rule 505, Rule 506, or Section 4(6) may trigger registration requirements, but the original sale in this problem came under Rule 504.

Issue Spotters

1. The average investor is not concerned with minor inaccuracies but with facts that if disclosed would tend to deter him or her from buying the securities. This would include facts that have an important bearing on the condition of the issuer and its business—liabilities, loans to officers and directors, customer delinquencies, and pending lawsuits.
2. No. The Securities Exchange Act of 1934 extends liability to officers and directors in their personal transactions for taking advantage of inside information when they know it is unavailable to the persons with whom they are dealing.
3. Yes. All states have their own corporate securities laws.

Chapter 41

True-False Questions

1. T
2. F. Similarly, a limited partnership will not dissolve on the personal bankruptcy of a limited partner. These same events occurring to a general partner can dissolve the firm, however.
3. F. State law applies. Like the formation of a corporation and other forms of limited liability organizations, the formation of a limited liability company (LLC) requires that articles of organization be filed in the state of formation. Otherwise, an LLC will not be held to exist, and its members will not enjoy the features that they wanted.
4. T
5. F. One of the chief advantages of a limited liability company (LLC) is that it offers the limited liability of a corporation. Because an LLC also offers the tax advantages of a partnership, many businesses are using this form of organization.
6. F. A feature that makes a limited liability partnership attractive to professionals is that its partners can avoid liability for the malpractice of other partners. Of course, each partner is liable for his or her own wrongful acts. All of the partners may be held liable for other obligations of the partnership, however.
7. F. The liability of the limited partners in a limited partnership is limited to the amount of their investment in the firm, but the liability of the general partners is the same as that of the partners in a general partnership (unlimited).
8. T
9. T
10. T

Fill-in Questions

members; limited liability company; limited partners; limited partnership

Multiple-Choice Questions

1. D. Ordinarily, limited partners are liable for the debts of their limited partnerships only to the extent of their capital contributions to the firms. A general partner, in contrast, may be held personally liable for the full amount of the firm's obligations. Similarly, a limited partner, unlike a general partner does not have a right to control the partnership. This question and answer are based on a question that appeared in the November 1989 CPA exam.
2. B. A partner (general or limited) pays personal income taxes on his or her share of the firm's income, regardless of whether or not it is distributed to him. The other partners pay taxes on their shares of the firm's income. Note that each partner is liable for a pro rate share of the taxes even if they are not distributed.
3. B. A limited liability company (LLC) can be taxed as a partnership, a sole proprietorship (if there is only one member), or a corporation, but when there is more than on member, electing to be taxed as a partnership is generally preferable. The income can be passed through to its members without being taxed at the company level. Generally, there is no particular advantage to being taxed as a corporation. In fact, avoiding the double corporate tax is one reason for forming an LLC.
4. B. Normally, the members of a limited liability company are liable for the debts of their company only to the extent of their investment in the firm, like corporate shareholders or limited partners. Sole proprietors and general partners, in contrast, may be personally liable for the full amount of their firms' obligations.
5. C. One of the advantages of the limited liability company (LLC) form of business organization is that its members are not personally liable for the debts of their firm regardless of the extent of their participation in management (unlike a limited partnership). In fact, unless agreed otherwise, an LLC's management will be considered to include all members. Another advantage is that there is generally no limit on the number of members that a firm can have (unlike an S corporation).
6. D. Limited partnerships may be dissolved by many causes but not by any of these choices. Partners may expressly agree to dissolve their partnership, or

dissolution may be caused by the withdrawal, death, or mental incompetence of a general partner (unless the others agree to continue the business). A *general* partner's death or bankruptcy causes the firm to dissolve, as would an event that makes it impossible to operate the partnership lawfully. Dissolution can also result from a court decree.

7. B. Professionals who organize as a limited liability partnership avoid personal liability for the wrongdoing of other partners. They have only the same liability as a limited partner in a limited partnership. That is, their liability does not extend beyond the amount that they have invested in the firm.

8. A. Also, the partners must sign a certificate of limited partnership, which must then be filed with the appropriate state official, usually the secretary of state.

9. A. Limited partners essentially have fewer rights than general partners. (In return, they assume less liability for the debts of the firm.) One of the important rights of general partners that limited partners usually do not have is the right to participate in the management of the firm.

10. C. It is expected that eventually, state laws governing limited liability companies (LLCs) will be made relatively uniform. As for the other choices, the members are not subject to personal liability for the firm's obligations. Also, unlike corporate income, LLC income can pass through the firm and be taxed only once.

Issue Spotters

1. A partner who commits a wrongful act, such as fraud, is liable for the results. The partner who supervises the party who commits the act may also be held liable. Some states limit this liability so that each partner is liable only up to the proportion of his or her responsibility for the result.

2. There is no law that expressly bars the participation of limited partners in the management of a limited partnership. Limited partners are, however, normally exempt from personal liability for partnership debts, torts, breaches of contract, and breaches of trust. This exemption rests primarily on the limited partner's not participating in the management of the partnership. Thus, it is the threat of personal liability that deters their participation.

3. The members of a limited liability company (LLC) may designate a group to run their firm, in which situation the firm would be considered a *manager*-managed LLC. The group may include only members, only nonmembers, or members and nonmembers. If instead, all members participate in management, the firm would be a *member*-managed LLC. In fact, unless the members agree otherwise, all members are considered to participate in the management of the firm.

Chapter 42

True-False Questions

1. T
2. T
3. T
4. F. According to utilitarianism, it is the consequences of an act that determine how ethical the act is. Applying this theory requires determining who will be affected by an act, assessing the positive and negatives effects of alternatives, and choosing the alternative that will provide the greatest benefit for the most people. Utilitarianism is premised on acting so as to do the greatest good for the greatest number of people. An act that affects a minority negatively may still be morally acceptable.
5. T
6. F. In situations involving ethical decisions, a balance must sometimes be struck between equally good or equally poor courses of action. The choice is often between equally good alternatives—benefiting shareholders versus benefiting employees, for example—and sometimes one group may be adversely affected. (The legality of a particular action may also be unclear.)
7. T
8. F. Simply obeying the law will not meet all ethical obligations. The law does not cover all ethical requirements. An act may be unethical but not illegal. In fact, compliance with the law is at best a moral minimum. Furthermore, there is an ethical aspect to almost every decision that a business firm makes.
9. T
10. F. Bribery is also a legal issue, regulated in the United States by the Foreign Corrupt Practices Act. Internationally, a treaty signed by the members of the Organization for Economic Cooperation and Development makes bribery of public officials a serious crime. Each member nation is expected to enact legislation implementing the treaty.

Fill-in Questions

Religious standards; Kantian ethics; the principle of rights

Multiple-Choice Questions

1. C. Business ethics focus on the application of moral principles in a business context. Different standards are not required. Business ethics is a subset of ethics that relates specifically to what constitutes right and wrong in situations that arise in business.

2. A. Traditionally, ethical reasoning relating to business has been characterized by two fundamental approaches—duty-based ethics and utilitarianism, or outcome-based ethics. Duty-based ethics derive from religious sources or philosophical principles. These standards may be absolute, which means that an act may not be undertaken, whatever the consequences.

3. A. Under religious ethical standards, it is the nature of an act that determines how ethical the act is, not its consequences. This is considered an *absolute* standard. But this standard is tempered by an element of compassion (the "Golden Rule").

4. D. In contrast to duty-based ethics, outcome-based ethics, or utilitarianism, involves a consideration of the consequences of an action. Utilitarianism is premised on acting so as to do the greatest good for the greatest number of people.

5. D. Utilitarianism requires determining who will be affected by an action, assessing the positive and negatives effects of alternatives, and choosing the alternative that will provide the greatest benefit for the most people. This approach has been criticized as tending to reduce the welfare of human beings to plus and minus signs on a cost-benefit worksheet.

6. A. A corporation, for example, as an employer, commonly faces ethical problems that involve conflicts among itself, its employees, its customers, its suppliers, its shareholders, its community, or other groups. Increasing wages, for instance, may benefit the employees and the community, but reduce profits and the ability of the employer to give pay increases in the future, as well as decreasing dividends to shareholders. To be considered socially responsible, when making a decision, a business firm must take into account the interests of all of these groups, as well as society as a whole.

7. B. In any profession, there is a responsibility, both legal and ethical, not to misrepresent material facts, even at the expense of some profits. This is a clear ethical standard in the legal profession and in the accounting profession. This question and answer are based on a question that was included in the CPA exam in November 1994.

8. A. In part because it is impossible to be entirely aware of what the law requires and prohibits, the best course for a business firm is to act responsibly and in good faith. This course may provide the best defense if a transgression is discovered. Striking a balance between what is profitable and what is legal and ethical can be difficult, however. A failure to act legally or ethically can result in a reduction in profits, but a failure to act in the profitable interest of the firm can also cause profits to suffer. *Optimum* profits are the maximum profits that a firm can realize while staying within legal and ethical limits.

9. D. The principle of rights theory of ethics follows the belief that persons have fundamental rights. This belief is implied by duty-based ethical standards and Kantian ethics. The rights are implied by the duty that forms the basis for the standard (for example, the duty not to kill implies that persons have a right to live), or by the personal dignity implicit in the Kantian belief about the fundamental nature of human beings. Not to respect these rights would, under the principle of rights theory, be morally wrong.

10. C. The Foreign Corrupt Practices Act prohibits any U.S. firm from bribing foreign officials to influence official acts to provide the firm with business opportunities. Such payments are allowed, however, if they would be lawful in the foreign country. Thus, to avoid violating the law, the firm in this problem should determine whether such payments are legal in the minister's country.

Issue Spotters

1. The answer depends on which system of ethics is used. Under a duty-based ethical standard, it may not be the consequences of an act that determine how ethical the act is; it may be the nature of the act itself. Stealing would be unethical regardless of whether the fruits of the crime are given to the poor. In contrast, utilitarianism is premised on acting so as to do the greatest good for the greatest number of people. It is the consequences of an act that determine how ethical the act is.

2. Maybe. On the one hand, it is not the company's "fault" when a product is misused. Also, keeping the product on the market is not a violation of the law, and stopping sales would hurt profits. On the other hand, suspending sales could reduce suffering and could stop potential negative publicity if sales continued.

3. When a corporation decides to respond to what it sees as a moral obligation to correct for past discrimination by adjusting pay differences among its employees, an ethical conflict is raised between the firm and its employees and between the firm and its shareholders. This dilemma arises directly out of the effect such a decision has on the firm's profits. If satisfying this obligation increases profitability, then the dilemma is easily resolved in favor of "doing the right thing."

Cumulative Hypothetical Problem for Unit Eight—Including Chapters 35–42

1. A. A partnership is an association of two or more persons who manage a business and share profits. Here, the partnership began when the parties combined their assets and commenced business. Before that time, there was no sharing of profits, no joint ownership of a business, and no equal right in the management of a business (because there was no business). The execution of a formal partnership agreement is not necessary, nor is the consent of creditors.

2. B. Unlike general partnerships, which can come into existence even when the parties do not intend to form a partnership, a limited partnership can only be created pursuant to the provisions of a state statute. This statute sets out exactly what partners must do to form a limited partnership, which must include at least one general partner who assumes personal liability for the debts of the firm.

3. D. The information that each state requires to be in articles of incorporation differs somewhat, but the information represented by the choices in this problem is generally required. It is not necessary to name the initial officers in the articles. Other information that might be required includes the number of authorized shares. Other information that is not required includes quorum requirements.

4. D. Other information that must be included in a registration statement, under the Securities Act of 1933, includes a description of the issuer's business, a description of the security, the capital structure of the business, the underwriting arrangements, and the certified financial statements.

5. B. Rule 504 exempts certain stock offerings from the registration requirements of the Securities Act of 1933. To qualify, a non-investment company offering may not exceed $1 million in any twelve-month period, the Securities and Exchange Commission must be notified of the sale.

Questions on the Focus on Legal Reasoning for Unit Eight—*In re Miller*

1. A. In the reasoning of the majority in the *In re Miller* case, fraud in such cases as this problem "could be imputed only on a finding of agency." The court held, however, that "Section 20(a) extends liability well beyond traditional [agency] doctrines, providing expansive remedies in a highly regulated industry."

2. D. The dissent in the *In re Miller* case reasoned that a finding of agency is not necessary to impose liability under Section 20. The dissent would have imputed liability in the circumstances described in these questions, and would have held that the debt represented by that liability was not dischargeable in bankruptcy.

3. C. In the *In re Miller* case, the majority reasoned that there is "nothing in the Bankruptcy Code or the securities laws indicating that these two separate provisions of law should be combined" to impose liability on a fraudulent broker's innocent employer and declare that liability a non-dischargeable debt under the Bankruptcy Code. "Section 20(a) [of the Securities Exchange Act] extends liability well beyond traditional doctrines, providing expansive remedies in a highly regulated industry." However, "the Bankruptcy Code addresses actual, traditional fraud, and we are not persuaded that it should be read in such a way as to encompass the nontraditional liability imposed under [Section] 20(a)."

Questions on the Focus on Ethics for Unit Eight—Business Organizations

1. D. This duty arises from the legal principles of agency, and applies to all corporate officers, managers, and directors. When personal interests conflict with the interests of the corporation, the corporate party must not act against the interest of the corporation. If an officer usurps a corporate opportunity by, for example, setting up a competing firm to take advantage of an opportunity that might have otherwise been utilized by his or her corporation, a successful claim against the individual can result in the individual giving up an interest in the new company to the shareholders of the corporation.

2. C. Corporate directors have a fiduciary duty to exercise care when making decisions that affect their corporations. Fiduciary duties may, in some extraordinary circumstances, be owed to other directors, officers, or the firm's creditors, particularly if a director's corporation is nearly insolvent. In normal situations, however, the duty of care extends chiefly to the corporation's shareholders, and may include a duty to implement a program to uncover and prevent wrongdoing by corporate personnel.

3. B. When a franchisor's control over the operations of its franchisee is too extensive, the franchisor may be held liable for the torts of the franchisee's employees under agency principles. This may occur even if the franchise agreement between the parties specifies that the individuals are independent contractors, or otherwise.

Chapter 43

True-False Questions

1. T
2. T
3. T
4. F. Agencies formulate and issue their rules under the authority of Congress. These rules are as legally binding as the laws enacted by Congress. It is for this reason, in part, that rulemaking procedures generally include opportunities for public comment, that the rules are subject to review by the courts, and that agencies are subject to other controls by the three branches of government.

5. F. Appeal is not mandatory, and if there is no appeal, the initial order becomes final. Either side may appeal the determination in an agency adjudication, however, to the commission that oversees the agency or ultimately to a federal court.

6. F. Congress can influence agency policy in several ways. These include that Congress can create or abolish an agency, or influence policy by the appropriation of funds for certain purposes. Congress can also revise the functions of an agency.

7. T

8. T

9. F. State and federal agency actions often parallel each other. (State and federal court review of state and federal agency decisions, respectively, is also similar.) When there is a conflict between state and federal agencies, the supremacy clause of the Constitution requires that the federal agency's operation prevail over an inconsistent state agency's action.

10. F. In most circumstances, a warrant is required for a search or the agency will be held to have violated the Fourth Amendment. Warrants are not required, however, to conduct searches in businesses in highly regulated industries, in certain hazardous operations, and in emergencies.

Fill-in Questions

Federal Register; anyone; must; *Federal Register*

Multiple-Choice Questions

1. D. Agency powers include functions associated with the legislature (rulemaking), executive branch (investigation), and courts (adjudication). Under Article I of the U.S. Constitution and the delegation doctrine, Congress has the power to establish administrative agencies and delegate any or all of these powers to those agencies.

2. C. Agencies may obtain information through subpoenas or searches. A subpoena may compel the appearance of a witness (a subpoena *ad testificandum*) or the provision of certain documents and records (a subpoena *duces tecum*). In some cases, particularly searches of businesses involved in highly regulated industries, searches may be conducted without warrants.

3. C. Procedures vary widely among agencies, even within agencies, but under the Administrative Procedure Act, rulemaking typically includes these steps: notice, opportunity for comment, and publication in the *Federal Register* of a final draft of the rule.

4. C. An agency has the authority to issue subpoenas. There are limits on agency demands for information, however. An investigation must have a legitimate purpose. The information that is sought must be relevant. The party from whom the information is sought must not be unduly burdened by the request. And the demand must be specific.

5. D. The president's veto is a method by which the authority of an agency can be checked or curtailed. The limits listed in the other responses in this question are choices available to Congress to limit the authority of administrative agencies.

6. B. The Government-in-the-Sunshine Act requires "every portion of every meeting of an agency" that is headed by a "collegial body" to be open to "public observation." The Freedom of Information Act requires the federal government to disclose certain records to persons on request, with some exceptions. The Regulatory Flexibility Act requires, among other things, analyses of new regulations in certain circumstances. The Small Business Regulatory Enforcement Fairness Act covers several matters important to businesses, including the federal courts' authority to enforce the Regulatory Flexibility Act, but it does not cover the opening of agency meetings to the public.

7. C. The Administrative Procedure Act provides for court review of most agency actions, but first a party must exhaust all other means of resolving a controversy with an agency. Also, under the ripeness doctrine, the agency action must be ripe for review: the action must be reviewable (which agency actions presumably are), the party must have standing, and an actual controversy must be at issue.

8. A. This is the "arbitrary and capricious" test under which acts committed willfully, unreasonable, and without considering the facts can be overturned. (The other choices are not legitimate grounds for judicial review.) A court may also consider whether the agency has exceeded its authority or violated any constitutional provisions. Depending on the circumstances, when a court reviews an act of an administrative agency, the court may also determine whether the agency has properly interpreted laws applicable to the action under review, acted in accord with procedural requirements, or reached conclusions that are not supported by substantial evidence.

9. B. After an agency publishes notice of a proposed rule, any interested parties can express their views in writing, or orally if a hearing is held. The agency must respond to all significant comments by modifying the final rule or explaining, in the statement accompanying the final rule, why it did not modify the rule in response to the comments.

10. B. An administrative law judge (ALJ) presides over hearings when cases are brought to the agency. Like other judges, an ALJ has the power to administer oaths, take testimony, rule on questions of evidence, and make determinations of fact. It is important to note that an ALJ works for the agency but must not be biased in the agency's favor. There are provisions in the Administrative Procedure Act to prevent the bias, and to otherwise promote the fairness, of the ALJs, for example by prohibiting *ex parte* comments to the ALJ from any party to the proceeding.

Issue Spotters

1. Checks against the arbitrary use of agency power include the courts' power to review agency actions. Congress also has considerable power over agencies. Among other things, Congress can create, restrict, or abolish an agency. Congress can also limit the funds that it appropriates to an agency. The president can exercise control over a federal agency through the appointment of its officers.

2. Under the Administrative Procedure Act (APA), the ALJ must be separate from the agency's investigative and prosecutorial staff. *Ex parte* communications between the ALJ and a party to a proceeding are prohibited. Under the APA, an ALJ is exempt from agency discipline except on a showing of good cause.

3. A formal adjudicatory hearing resembles a trial in that, in both types of proceedings, the parties can undertake extensive discovery (involving depositions, interrogatories, and so on), and during the hearing they may give testimony, present other evidence, and cross-examine witnesses. An administrative proceeding differs from a trial in that in the former, more information, including hearsay, can be introduced as evidence.

Chapter 44

True-False Questions

1. T
2. T
3. F. Under certain circumstances, consumers have a right to rescind their contracts. This is particularly true when a creditor has not made all required disclosures. A contract entered into as part of a door-to-door sale may be rescinded within three days, regardless of the reason.
4. T
5. F. A consumer can also include a note in his or her credit file to explain any misinformation in the file. Under the Fair Credit Reporting Act, consumers are entitled to have deleted from their files any misinformation that leads to a denial of credit, employment, or insurance. Consumers are also entitled to receive information about the source of the misinformation and about anyone who was given the misinformation.
6. T
7. F. The Fair Debt Collection Practices Act applies only to debt collectors that attempt to collect debts on another party's behalf. Typically, the collector is paid a commission—a percentage of the amount owed or collected—for a successful collection effort.
8. F. The Federal Trade Commission (FTC), the Federal Reserve Board of Governors (Fed), and other federal agencies regulate the terms and conditions of sales. For example, the FTC issues regulations covering warranties and labels, and the Fed regulates credit provisions in sales contracts.
9. F. One who leases consumer goods in the ordinary course of their business must disclose *all* material terms in writing—clearly and conspicuously—if the goods are priced at $25,000 or less and the lease term exceeds four months. The Consumer Leasing Act of 1988 requires this.
10. T

Fill-in Questions

$50; before; prohibits; from billing; if

Multiple-Choice Questions

1. D. The FTC has the power to issue a cease-and-desist order, but in some cases, such an order is not enough to stop the harm. With counteradvertising (also known as corrective advertising), an advertiser attempts to correct earlier misinformation by admitting that prior claims about a product were untrue.
2. C. A regular-size box of laundry soap, for example, cannot be labeled "super-size" to exaggerate the amount of product in the box. Labels on consumer goods must identify the product, the manufacturer, the distributor, the net quantity of the contents, and the quantity of each serving (if the number of servings is given). Other information may also be required.
3. B. In a door-to-door sale, a consumer generally has at least a three-day cooling-off period within which to rescind the transaction. Salespersons are required to give consumers written notice of this right. If a sales presentation is to a consumer who speaks only Spanish, the notice must be in Spanish, too.
4. C. Under the Fair Debt Collection Practices Act, once a debtor has refused to pay a debt, a collection agency can contact the debtor *only* to advise him or her of further action to be taken. None of the rest of these choices would be legitimate possibilities.
5. B. This is required under Regulation Z (which was issued by the Federal Reserve Board under the Truth in Lending Act) and applies to any creditor who, in the ordinary course of business, lends money or sells goods on credit to consumers, or arranges for credit for consumers. The information that must be disclosed includes: the specific dollar amount being financed; the annual percentage rate of interest; any financing charges, premiums or points; the number, amounts, and due dates of payments; and any penalties imposed on delinquent payments or prepayment.
6. D. When contracting parties are subject to the Truth-in-Lending Act (TILA), Regulation Z applies to any transaction involving an installment sales contract in which payment is to be made in more than four installments. Normally, such loans as those described in this problem require more than four installments to repay. In any transaction subject to Regulation Z, the lender must disclose all of the credit terms clearly and conspicuously.
7. C. The Fair Packaging and Labeling Act requires that products include a variety of information on their labels. Besides the information specified in the answer to this problem, manufactures must identify them-

selves and the packager or distributor or the product, as well as nutrition details, including how much and what type of fat a product contains.

8. B. Under the Smokeless Tobacco Health Education Act of 1986, packages of smokeless tobacco products must include warnings about the health hazards associated with the use of smokeless tobacco similar to warnings contained on cigarette packages.

9. C. The Consumer Product Safety Commission (CPSC) has sufficiently broad authority to remove from store shelves any product that it believes is imminently hazardous and to require manufacturers to report on products already sold. Additionally, the CPSC can ban the make and sale of any product that the CPSC deems to be potentially hazardous. The CPSC also administers other product safety legislation.

10. D. The Truth-in-Lending Act includes rules covering credit cards. There is a provision that limits the liability of a cardholder to $50 per card for unauthorized charges made before the creditor is notified, and exempts a consumer from liability if the card was not properly issued. When a card is not solicited, it is not "properly issued," however, and thus a consumer, in whose name unauthorized charges are made, is not liable for those charges in any amount.

Issue Spotters

1. Yes. The FTC has issued rules to govern advertising techniques, including rules designed to prevent bait-and-switch advertising. Under the FTC guidelines, bait-and-switch advertising occurs if the seller refuses to show the advertised item, fails to have in stock a reasonable quantity of the item, fails to promise to deliver the advertised item within a reasonable time, or discourages employees from selling the item.

2. Under the Truth-in-Lending Act, a buyer who wishes to withhold payment for a faulty product purchased with a credit card must follow specific procedures to settle the dispute. The credit card issuer then must intervene and attempt to settle the dispute.

3. Under an extensive set of procedures established by the FDA, which administers the Federal, Food, Drug and Cosmetic Act, drugs must be shown to be effective as well as safe before they may be marketed to the public. In general, manufacturers are responsible for ensuring that the drugs they offer for sale are free of any substances that could injure consumers.

Chapter 45

True-False Questions

1. F. Common law doctrines that were applied against polluters centuries ago may be applicable today. These include nuisance and negligence doctrines.

2. T

3. F. There are different standards for different pollutants and for different polluters. There are even different standards for the same pollutants and polluters in different locations. The standards cover the amount of emissions, the technology to control them, the notice that must be given to the public, and the penalties that may be imposed for noncompliance.

4. F. The Toxic Substances Control Act of 1976 regulates substances that the production and labeling of substances of that potentially pose an imminent hazard or an unreasonable risk of injury to health or the environment. The Comprehensive Environmental Response, Compensation, and Liability Act (CERCLA) of 1980 regulates the clean up of leaking hazardous waste disposal sites.

5. T

6. T

7. F. To penalize those for whom a violation is cost-effective, the EPA can obtain a penalty equal to a violator's economic benefits from noncompliance. Other penalties include criminal fines. Private citizens can also sue polluters. It is generally more economically beneficial for a business to comply with the Clean Air Act.

8. T

9. F. Under CERCLA, a party who transports waste to a hazardous waste site may be held liable for any and all of the cost to clean up the site. There is a variety of "potentially responsible parties" who may also be held liable, including the party who generated the waste, and current and past owners and operators of the site. A party assessed with these costs can bring a contribution action against the others, however, to recoup the amount of their proportion.

10. T

Fill-in Questions

federal; federal; environmental impact that an action will have; environment; an action might cause to the environment; and reasons

Multiple-Choice Questions

1. D. An environmental impact statement (EIS) must be prepared when a major federal action significantly affects the quality of the environment. An action that affects the quality of the environment is "major" if it involves a substantial commitment of resources and "federal" if a federal agency has the power to control it.

2. C. Under the 1990 amendments to the Clean Air Act, different standards apply to existing sources and major new sources. Major new sources must use the maximum achievable control technology (MACT) to reduce emissions from the combustion of fossil fuels. Other factories and businesses must reduce emissions of hazardous air pollutants with the best available technology.

3. D. Sport utility vehicles are now subject to the same standards for polluting emissions as automobiles. If new motor vehicles do not meet the emission standards of regulations issued under the Clean Air Act, the EPA can order a recall of the vehicles and a repair or replacement of pollution-control devices.

4. C. A polluter can be ordered to clean up the pollution or to pay for the clean-up costs, and other penalties may be imposed. For example, fines may be assessed and imprisonment ordered.

5. C. Under the Resource Conservation and Recovery Act of 1976, producers of hazardous waste must properly label and package waste to be transported. Under the Comprehensive Environmental Response, Compensation, and Liability Act of 1980, the party who generated the waste disposed of at a site can be held liable for clean-up costs.

6. C. Under the Resource Conservation and Recovery Act of 1976, the EPA monitors and controls the disposal of hazardous waste. Under the Comprehensive Environmental Response, Compensation, and Liability Act, the EPA regulates the clean up of hazardous waste sites when a release occurs.

7. B. An action that affects the quality of the environment is "major" if it involves a substantial commitment of resources. Minor landscaping does not qualify because it does not involve such a commitment. The landscaping in this problem is "federal," however, because a federal agency controls it, and any landscaping can affect the quality of the environment.

8. C. Under the 1990 amendments to the Clean Air Act, different standards apply to existing sources and major new sources. Major new sources must use the maximum achievable control technology to reduce emissions from the combustion of fossil fuels. Other factories and businesses must reduce emissions of hazardous air pollutants with the best available technology. This question and answer are based on a question that appeared in the CPA exam in 1996.

9. B. One of the goals of the Clean Water Act is to protect fish and wildlife. In part, this goal is met by protecting their habitats, such as swamps and other wetlands. Protecting these areas can also protect navigable waters into which wetlands drain and other surrounding resources. Before dredging and filling wetlands, a permit must be obtained from the Army Corps of Engineers.

10. C. Any potentially responsible party can be charged with the entire cost to clean up a hazardous waste disposal site. Potentially responsible parties include former owners and may, under certain circumstances, include a lender to the owner. Of course, a party held responsible for the entire cost may be able to recoup some of it in a contribution action against other potentially responsible parties.

Issue Spotters

1. The Comprehensive Environmental Response, Compensation, and Liability Act of 1980 regulates the clean up of hazardous waste disposal sites. Any potentially responsible party can be charged with the entire cost to clean up a hazardous waste disposal site. Potentially responsible parties include the person who generated the waste (ChemCorp) the person who transported the waste to the site (Central), the person who owned or operated the site at the time of the disposal (Intrastate Disposal), and the current owner or operator of the site (ABC). A party held responsible for the entire cost may be able to recoup some of it in a lawsuit against other potentially responsible parties.

2. Yes. On the ground that the hardships to be imposed on the polluter and on the community are greater than the hardships suffered by the residents, the court might deny an injunction—if the plant is the core of a local economy, for instance, the residents may be awarded only damages.

3. The Environmental Protection Agency (EPA) was established to administer most federal environmental policies and statutes. Although not identified in the text, other federal agencies with authority to regulate specific environmental matters include the U.S. Departments of the Interior, Defense, and Labor, the Food and Drug Administration, and the Nuclear Regulatory Commission.

Chapter 46

True-False Questions

1. F. This is a vertical restraint.
2. F. This is a horizontal restraint.
3. T
4. F. Exclusive dealing contracts are those under which a seller forbids a buyer from purchasing products from the seller's competitors.
5. F. Price discrimination occurs when sellers charge competitive buyers different prices for identical goods.
6. F. This is a *vertical* merger. A horizontal merger is a merger between firms that compete with each other in the same market.
7. F. This is a *horizontal* merger. A vertical merger occurs when a company at one stage of production acquires another company at a higher or lower stage in the chain of production and distribution.
8. T
9. T
10. T

Fill-in Questions

A restraint of trade; Monopoly power; monopoly power

Multiple-Choice Questions

1. A. An agreement to set prices in the manner described in the problem is a price-fixing agreement, which is a restraint of trade and a *per se* violation of Section 1 of the Sherman Act.
2. C. Conduct that is blatantly anticompetitive is a *per se* violation of antitrust law. This is the most important circumstance in determining whether an action violates the antitrust laws. If an action undercuts competition, a court will not allow a party to undertake it. Such conduct typically includes price-fixing agreements, group boycotts, and horizontal market divisions. The U.S. Department of Justice can prosecute violations of the Sherman Act as criminal or civil violations, but can enforce the Clayton Act only through civil proceedings. The Federal Trade Commission can also enforce the Clayton Act (and has sole authority to enforce the Federal Trade Commission Act). A private party can sue under the Clayton Act if he or she is injured by a violation of *any* antitrust law.
3. C. Territorial or customer restrictions, like the restriction described in the problem, are judged under a rule of reason. The rule of reason involves a weighing of competitive benefits against anticompetitive harms. Here, the manufacturer's restriction on its dealers would likely be considered lawful because, although it reduces *intra*brand competition, it promotes *inter*brand competition.
4. D. In applying the rule of reason, courts consider the purpose of the conduct, the effect of the conduct on trade, the power of the parties to accomplish what they intend, and in some cases, whether there are less restrictive alternatives to achieve the same goals.
5. C. The elements of the offense of monopolization include monopoly power and its willful acquisition. Market domination that results from legitimate competitive behavior (such as foresight, innovation, skill, and good management) is not a violation.
6. C. Price discrimination occurs when a seller charges different buyers different prices for identical goods. To violate the Clayton Act, among other requirements, the effect of the price discrimination must be to substantially lessen competition or otherwise create a competitive injury.
7. C. Of course, a U.S. firm is subject to the jurisdiction of a U.S. court. For a U.S. court to hear a case against a foreign entity under U.S. antitrust laws, the entity's alleged violation of the law must have a substantial effect on U.S. commerce (or be a *per se* violation). In other words, foreign and domestic firms may be sued for violations of U.S. antitrust laws.
8. A. Conduct subject to the rule of reason is unlawful if its anticompetitive harms outweigh its competitive benefits. Conduct typically subject to a rule of reason analysis includes trade association activities, joint ventures, territorial or customer restrictions, refusal to deal, price discrimination, and exclusive-dealing contracts.
9. B. Similar exemptions from the antitrust laws include cooperative research among small business firms, cooperation among U.S. exporters to compete with comparable foreign associations, and joint efforts by businesspersons to obtain legislative, judicial, or executive action.
10. A. An important consideration in determining whether a merger substantially lessens competition and hence violates the Clayton Act is market concentration (the market chares among the firms in the market). If a merger creates an entity with more than a small percentage market share, it is presumed illegal.

Issue Spotters

1. A unilateral refusal to deal violates antitrust law if it involves offenses proscribed under Section 2 of the Sherman Act. This occurs if the firm refusing to deal has, or is likely to acquire, monopoly power and the refusal is likely to have an anticompetitive effect on a particular market.
2. Size alone does not determine whether a firm is a monopoly—size in relation to the market is what matters. A small store in a small, isolated town is a monopolist if it is the only store serving that market. Monopoly involves the power to affect prices and output. If a firm has sufficient market power to control prices and exclude competition, that firm has monopoly power. Monopoly power in itself is not a violation of Section 2 of the Sherman Act. The offense also requires an intent to acquire or maintain that power through anticompetitive means.
3. This agreement is a tying arrangement. The legality of a tying arrangement depends the purpose of the agreement, the agreement's likely effect on competition in the relevant markets (the market for the tying product and the market for the tied product), and other factors. Tying arrangements for commodities are subject to Section 3 of the Clayton Act. Tying arrangements for services can be agreements in restraint of trade in violation of Section 1 of the Sherman Act.

Cumulative Hypothetical Problem for Unit Nine—Including Chapters 43–46

1. D. Advertising that consists of vague generalities is not illegal. This is also true of advertising that includes obvious exaggerations. Advertising that may lead to sanctions by the Federal Trade Commission is deceptive advertising: advertising that misleads consumers.
2. A. An administrative agency has a number of options to determine whether a manufacturer is complying with the agency's rules, but the agency may not use its powers arbitrarily or capriciously or abuse its

discretion. The options that an agency may choose include those in the other answer choices, as well as obtaining a search warrant to search the premises for a specific item and return it to the agency.

3. D. Under the Comprehensive Environmental Response, Compensation, and Liability Act of 1980, any "potentially responsible party" can be charged with the entire cost to clean up a hazardous waste disposal site. Potentially responsible parties include the party who generates the waste, the party who transports the waste to the site, and the party who owns or operates the site.

4. C. A business firm may be subject to regulations issued by federal, state, and local administrative agencies. The firm is no less subject to those regulations if they are conflicting or if the firm does not know of the regulations. Federal agencies include the Federal Trade Commission, the Environmental Protection Agency, and the U.S. Department of Justice, all of which have counterparts at the state level in most states. A business firm is also subject to regulations at the county, city, and other local governmental levels.

5. C. It is price discrimination when a seller charges different buyers different prices for identical products. Price discrimination is a violation of the Clayton Act if the effect of the pricing is to substantially lessen competition or otherwise create a competitive injury.

Questions on the Focus on Legal Reasoning for Unit Nine—*Pfennig v. Household Credit Services, Inc.*

1. B. In concluding that such fees as the charge in this problem are finance charges requiring disclosure, the majority in *Pfennig v. Household Credit Services, Inc.,* explains that the Truth-in-Lending Act (TILA) defines a finance charge "as the sum of '*all charges*' paid by the person to whom credit is extended and assessed by the creditor 'as an incident to the extension of credit.' " Under this definition, a finance charge "is intended to provide an accurate price tag for credit, and TILA demands that it be disclosed more conspicuously than other items."

2. C. The dissent in *Pfennig v. Household Credit Services, Inc.,* reasons that an over-limit fee is not mentioned in the TILA, and is excluded from the definition of a finance charge by Regulation Z, which excludes "[c]harges for actual unanticipated late payment, for exceeding a credit limit, or for delinquency, default, or a similar occurrence." The conflict between the majority and the dissent in the *Pfennig v. Household Credit Services, Inc.,* case is over how to interpret the TILA and Regulation Z.

3. C. In the *Pfennig v. Household Credit Services, Inc.,* case, the majority reasoned that "[t]he purpose of TILA is to assure a meaningful disclosure of credit terms so that the consumer will be able to compare . . . the various credit terms available to him and avoid the uninformed use of credit and to protect the consumer against inaccurate and unfair credit billing and credit card practices." A "finance charge is intended to provide an accurate price tag for credit, and TILA demands that it be disclosed more conspicuously than other items."

Questions on the Focus on Ethics for Unit Nine—Government Regulation

1. D. Of course, this outcome is debatable, and the issue is contentious. The questions, which do not have certain answers, concern the extent to which the government goes in regulating individuals and businesses in the interest of protecting the environment. At what point are the costs of environmental regulations too much for an individual, a business, or society as a whole to bear? How much are we willing to sacrifice to ensure that future generations have a healthful world?

2. A. This conduct would be a violation of the Fair Debt Collection Practices Act (FDCPA) if the party engaging in it is a collection agency. Under the FDCPA, collections agencies are allowed to contact only a debtor at his or her workplace and only with the permission of the employer. Some observers believe that the FDCPA does not offer consumers enough protection, because it does not cover creditors that collect their own debts.

3. A. Professional baseball players can sue team owners for anticompetitive practices that include collusion to blacklist players, cap players' salaries, or forcing players to play for certain teams. Baseball may be otherwise exempt from the application of the antitrust laws. Although originally a holding of the United States Supreme Court, the Court has recently held that this situation can be changed only through an act of Congress.

Chapter 47

True-False Questions

1. T

2. F. If goods are confused due to a wrongful act, it is the *wrongdoer* who must prove what percentage of the whole belongs to him or her to acquire title to any of the goods. Otherwise, the *innocent party* gets title to the whole.

3. F. The essence of a gift is that it is a voluntary transfer *without* consideration. The elements of a gift are donative intent, delivery, and acceptance.

4. F. If an accession is performed in good faith, ownership depends on the change in the value of the property. The greater the increase in the value of the property, the more likely it will be that the improver will be considered the owner of the property.

5. T
6. F. To constitute a bailment, a delivery must be of possession without any transfer of title and there must be an agreement that the property be returned or otherwise disposed of according to the owner's directions.
7. F. In most cases, a bailee is subject to a reasonable standard of care. Depending on the specific type of bailment, that standard may range from slight care (bailment for the sole benefit of the bailor) to great care (bailment for the sole benefit of the bailee).
8. F. A bailee has *two* basic responsibilities: to take proper care of the property and to surrender or dispose of the property at the end of the bailment.
9. T
10. T

Fill-in Questions

inter vivos; causa mortis; causa mortis; causa mortis; inter vivos

Multiple-Choice Questions

1. A. Personal property includes such items as computer software and home pages. Those who produce personal property have title to it. Because the creator of the property produced it, she owns it. There is an exception, however. Employees do not own what they produce for their employers. Here, she was hired to create property for another; the other owns what she created.
2. B. A right of survivorship, in which a deceased joint tenant's interest passes to the surviving joint tenant, is the distinguishing feature of a joint tenancy. Generally, to acquire or own property as joint tenants, the owners must specify that as the form they want their ownership to take. If these buyers had not specified that form, they would own the property as tenants in common.
3. A. The three elements for an effective gift are donative intent, delivery, and acceptance. Here, the giver had the intent, and the recipient clearly accepted, if delivery was effective, which it was. Delivery of the key to the box was constructive delivery of the earrings. Thus, the gift would have been effective even if the giver had died before the recipient had taken them from the box.
4. A. The finder found what appears to be lost property. Generally, the finder of lost property has good title against all *but the true owner.* Therefore, the finder in this problem has title.
5. A. When goods are commingled, and the goods are lost, the owners bear the loss in the same proportion that they contributed to the whole. This is assuming that they can prove how much they contributed to the whole. Thus, the parties take out the same proportions that they put in.
6. B. The three elements for an effective gift are donative intent, delivery, and acceptance. Here, the giver had the intent and clearly delivered the object of the gift (by constructive delivery). Thus, the gift would have been effective if the recipient accepted it. Acceptance is generally presumed unless proven otherwise. In the problem, the recipient announced that she did not want the gift and left they key in the possession of the donor. In this case, there was no gift. The property belongs to the donor's heirs.
7. A. A bailee must be given exclusive possession and control of the property and knowingly accept it. Here, there is no delivery of possession. Regarding the other choices, money does not need to be involved for a transaction to be a bailment, a car is personal property, and a signed contract is not necessary for a bailment (the bailment agreement may be oral).
8. B. The wallet appears to have been placed behind the plant intentionally and thus is classified as mislaid property. The owner of the premises on which mislaid property is found is entitled to possession as against the finder.
9. A. A bailment involves delivery of personal property in such a way that the bailee is given, and knowingly accepts, exclusive possession and control over it. By accepting the coat, the restaurant is given exclusive possession and control over the purse, but it the restaurant does not *knowingly* accepts the purse.
10. B. A common carrier is liable for damage caused by the willful acts of third persons or by an accident when the goods are in the carrier's possession. Thus, the carrier is liable for most of the losses among these answer choices. The other loss is caused by an act of the shipper, however, and thus must be borne by the shipper. This question and answer are based on a question that appeared in the November 1995 CPA exam.

Issue Spotters

1. Yes. A bailee's right of possession may be temporary, but it permits the bailee to recover damages from any third persons for damage or loss to the property.
2. Yes. An ordinary bailee owes a duty to take proper care of the clothes left in its charge. To recover from a party who does not fulfill his or her duty of care, the injured party must normally prove a lack of care. In this case, that would be difficult, because the bailor is unaware as to why the property was returned in bad condition. Under the law of bailments, proof of damage or loss raises a presumption that a bailee is guilty of negligence (or conversion), and the bailee must prove that he or she exercised due care.
3. The shipper suffers the loss. A common carrier is liable for damage caused by the willful acts of third persons or by an accident. Other losses must be borne by the shipper (or the recipient, depending on the terms of their contract). This shipment was lost due to an act of God.

Chapter 48

True-False Questions

1. T
2. F. The owner of a life estate has the same rights as a fee simple owner except that the value of the property must be kept intact for the holder of the future interest.
3. F. An easement merely allows a person to use land without taking anything from it, while a profit allows a person to take something from the land.
4. T
5. F. Under the Fifth Amendment to the U.S. Constitution, when taking private property, the government is required to pay the owner just compensation.
6. F. The government has the power to take private property, but the purposes for which such property may be taken must be *public*.
7. F. This is a tenancy for years. A periodic tenancy does not specify how long it will last.
8. F. To be entitled to a variance, a landowner must show that a granting of the variance would *not* substantially alter the essential character of the zoned area.
9. T
10. T

Fill-in Questions

warranty; special warranty; quitclaim

Multiple-Choice Questions

1. C. A *profit* is the right to go onto land in possession of another and take away some part of the land itself or some product of the land. In contrast, an easement is a right to make limited use of another person's land without taking anything from the property. A license is a revocable right to come onto another person's land.
2. C. The rights that accompany ownership in fee simple include the right to sell the land or give it away, as well as the right to use the land for whatever purpose the owner sees fit, subject, of course, to the law's limitations.
3. C. Warranty deeds include a number of promises, including a covenant of quiet enjoyment, which guarantees that the buyer will not be disturbed in his or her possession of the land by the seller or any third persons. If this covenant is breached, the buyer can recover from the seller the purchase price and any damages for the eviction.
4. A. A covenant runs with the land so that the successors to the original parties are entitled to its benefit (or burdened with its obligation) if it meets four requirements. It must be created in writing (in the problem, the deeds). The parties must intend that it run with the land (in the problem, each successive owner agreed to maintain the fence). The limits on the "burdened" land (maintaining the fence) must have a connection to the land (the fence is built on the land and marks the common boundary). The original parties must have been in privity of estate when the covenant was created. All of these requirements are met here.
5. B. An easement is a right to make limited use of another's real property without taking anything from it. In this problem, it is an easement by necessity—the owner needs access to his property. The right to take something from the property is a profit. A revocable right to come onto the property is a license.
6. C. Besides a legally sufficient description of the property and the price, a valid deed must contain the names of the grantee (buyer) and grantor (seller), words evidencing an intent to convey the property, and the grantor's (and usually the spouse's) signature. This question and answer are based on a question that was included in the CPA exam in November 1995.
7. A. A lease that does not specify how long it is to last but does specify that rent is to be paid at certain intervals creates a periodic tenancy. The tenancy is automatically renewed for each rental period unless it has been properly terminated.
8. A. Under a notice-race statute, a good faith purchaser who records his or her deed first can claim priority. In this problem, the result would be the same if the state had a pure race statute. In that circumstance, the first person to record a deed would have superior rights to the property, whether he or she knew of another previous, unrecorded transfer. Under a pure notice statute, however, the result might be different. In that circumstance, a person who does not know of a previous, unrecorded transfer can claim priority, whether or not he or she records first.
9. C. Sellers of most new houses are subject to an implied warranty of habitability. That means that the house is fit for human habitation (in reasonable working order and of reasonably sound construction). A seller of any house—old or new—may be liable for fraud or misrepresentation, particularly if, as in this problem, the buyer relied on the statements of the seller or the seller's agent.
10. C. This situation meets all the requirements for acquiring property by adverse possession: the possession was (1) actual and exclusive; (2) open, visible, and notorious; (3) continuous and peaceful for the statutory period; and (4) hostile, against the whole world, including the original owner.

Issue Spotters

1. Yes. An owner of a fee simple has the most rights possible—he or she can give the property away, sell it, transfer it by will, use it for almost any purpose, possess it to the exclusion of all the world, or as in this

case, transfer possession for any period of time. The party to whom possession is transferred can also transfer his or her interest (usually only with the owner's permission) for any lesser period of time.

2. This is a breach of the warranty deed's covenant of quiet enjoyment. The buyer can sue the seller and recover the purchase price of the house, plus any damages.

3. Probably not. A zoning ordinance is considered discriminatory if it affects one parcel of land in a way unlike surrounding parcels if there is no rational basis for the difference. The facts as stated in the problem do not indicate any basis for zoning this land differently.

Chapter 49

True-False Questions

1. T
2. T
3. T
4. F. On the termination of a lease, a tenant is no longer liable for rent, but the tenant is also no longer entitled to possession of the property. A lease can terminate when its term ends or by other methods, including timely notice (for a periodic tenancy), a landlord's release and a merger of the tenant's interest into the title to the property, a surrender by agreement, an abandonment, a forfeiture, or the destruction of the property by a cause beyond the parties' control.
5. F. A tenant can withhold rent only under a breach of the lease or, in most states, the implied warranty of habitability. Typically, this requires a major defect.
6. F. In most states, a tenant can make any use of property that is legal, relates to the purpose for which the property is adapted or ordinarily used, does not create a nuisance, and *does not injure the landlord's interest*. This last requirement means that a tenant cannot make alterations without the landlord's consent.
7. T
8. T
9. F. A landlord can sell, give away, or otherwise transfer his or her property without affecting a tenant's obligations under a lease, except that the tenant becomes the tenant of the new owner.
10. F. If an assignee (or a sublessee) later defaults on the obligation to pay rent, the tenant must pay it. (Also, before a tenant can assign or sublet the property, he or she must have the landlord's consent if the lease requires it).

Fill-in Questions

residential; tenant's; residential; residential; tenant's

Multiple-Choice Questions

1. A. A residential lease, to be enforceable, must include a description of the leased property. The other choices are only options. Note, too, that this lease is for a two-year term. A lease that cannot be completed within a year must be in writing to be enforceable (under the Statute of Frauds). This question and answer are based on a question that was part of the November 1995 CPA exam.
2. A. An assignment does not relieve an assigning tenant from the obligation to pay rent during the original term or during an extension under an option in the original lease.
3. B. A court would likely declare this clause unconscionable. The clause attempts to exculpate a residential landlord from fulfilling the important duty of providing habitable premises. Of course, a tenant has a duty to notify the landlord of a failure of a heating system, if the landlord has no other way of knowing of it (but this is not the same as a duty to mitigate damages).
4. B. If a tenant can prove that a landlord's primary purpose in attempting to evict the tenant is retaliation for complaining about the condition of leased premises, the tenant can stop the eviction proceedings. He or she can then collect damages, terminate the lease, or regain possession of the premises.
5. D. A tenant has exclusive possession until a lease expires, but the tenant must pay rent even if he or she moves out (assuming the move is unjustified). A landlord may treat a tenant's moving out with no intent of returning (as evidenced, for example, by a failure to pay rent) as an offer of surrender. The landlord's retaking of possession relieves the tenant of any further duty to pay rent, although the landlord may sue for previously unpaid rent.
6. C. A landlord is liable for injuries occurring on property within the landlord's control (common areas). A tenant must maintain in a reasonably safe condition those areas under his or her control. Here, the area where the injury occurred was under the tenant's control. (Depending on the terms of a commercial lease, a tenant's duty may coincide with the landlord's and both may be liable. The obviousness of a condition, its cause, and the requirement to give notice may be taken into consideration).
7. D. A landlord may treat a tenant's moving out with no intent of returning before the end of the term as an offer of surrender (assuming the move out is unjustified). The landlord's retaking of possession is considered acceptance of the surrender. A landlord can be considered to retake possession of the property by moving into it, or by changing the lock and renting it to a new tenant. In any case, this relieves the tenant of the duty to pay rent.
8. A. Despite the clause in the lease agreement, the landlord will be held liable for negligence. This type of clause is known as an exculpatory clause, and is unen-

forceable when the landlord fails to fulfill her or his duties, as in this question.

9. A. The difference between an assignment and a sublease is that an assignment involves a tenant's entire interest under the lease (the right to possession for the rest of the term), while a sublease involves all or part of the premises for a shorter term (only one of two rooms for the sixth and seventh months of a one-year lease, for example). Unless the lease prohibits it, a tenant can assign or sublet without the landlord's consent.

10. C. When a landlord transfers his or her interest in leased property, the tenant becomes the tenant of the new owner. It is to this new owner that the tenant owes rent. Both parties must continue to follow the terms of the lease.

Issue Spotters

1. In many states, a landlord who responded like the landlord in this problem would be wrong. Those states require a landlord to provide actual physical possession of the property that a tenant has agreed to lease. Other states require a landlord to transfer only the legal right to possession, and a new tenant is responsible for removing a previous tenant. In those states, of course, the landlord in this problem would be correct.

2. Probably not. If the landlord had taken no steps against crime, in an area in which there had been some crime, the landlord may have been liable if an injury resulted. In the problem, however, the landlord installed an alarm and hired a security guard. Unless there was some other reasonable precaution that the landlord should have taken, there would likely be no liability for an injury in the building due to crime.

3. When a landlord transfers his or her interest in leased property, the tenant becomes the tenant of the new owner. The new owner is entitled to any subsequent rent but must follow the terms of the existing lease.

Cumulative Hypothetical Problem for Unit Ten—Including Chapters 47–49

1. B. The most important factor in determining whether an item is a fixture is the intent of the owners. Other factors include whether the item can be removed without damaging the real property, and whether the item is sufficiently adapted so as to have become a part of the real property. If removal would irreparably damage the property, the item may also be considered a fixture.

2. C. If a joint tenant transfers his or her interest by deed to a third party, the third party becomes a tenant in common with the remaining joint tenant or tenants. (If there is more than one remaining joint tenant, they are still joint tenants among themselves.)

3. A. The elements for a transfer of real property ownership by deed include the names of the grantor and grantee, the intent of the grantor to convey ownership, the legal description of the property, the signature of the grantor, delivery, and acceptance. Elements that are not required include consideration, the signature of the grantee, a recording of the deed, and a purchase price.

4. C. The purpose of a recording statute is to determine the priority of two deeds to the same property. Under a race-notice recording statute, the party who records his or her deed first has priority if he or she did not have notice of a prior conveyance. Because the second transferee in this problem had notice of the first transfer, she does not have priority.

5. B. If a tenant transfers only part of a lease—that is, if the tenant transfers the right to occupy leased premises for less than the whole term—the arrangement is a sublease. (If the transfer is for the whole term, it is an assignment.) In a sublease, the original tenant is still liable to the landlord for the rent and other conditions of the original lease despite the transfer of the right to occupy the property.

Questions on the Focus on Legal Reasoning for Unit Ten—*Tahoe-Sierra Preservation Council, Inc. v. Tahoe Regional Planning Agency*

1. C. The majority in *Tahoe-Sierra Preservation Council, Inc. v. Tahoe Regional Planning Agency*, reasons that "a temporary restriction that merely causes a diminution in value is not" a taking of property. "Logically, a fee simple estate cannot be rendered valueless by a temporary prohibition on economic use, because the property will recover value as soon as the prohibition is lifted." Moratoria "are used widely among land-use planners." The Court added, however, that factors such as "the good faith of the planners, the reasonable expectations of the landowners," and "the actual impact of the moratorium on property values" should be weighed in the balance.

2. A. The dissent in *Tahoe-Sierra Preservation Council, Inc. v. Tahoe Regional Planning Agency*, argues that when a property owner is forced "to leave his property economically idle, he has suffered a taking," whether that idleness is "temporary" or "permanent." The dissent fears that if this principle is not applied, a government has "every incentive" to label a ban on development "temporary" and "repeatedly [extend] the 'temporary' prohibition into a long-term ban on all development" This would let a government "do by regulation what it cannot do through eminent domain—i.e., take private property without paying for it."

3. D. Under the holding in *Tahoe-Sierra Preservation Council, Inc. v. Tahoe Regional Planning Agency*—which is that a building moratorium like that described in these questions is not a taking and does not require compensation—property owners are not owed compensation for a local government's temporary ban on further development of their property. A property owner might thus have to bear the financial burden of undeveloped land as long as a local regulatory body deems.

Questions on the Focus on Ethics for Unit Ten—Property

1. C. Domain names have value, and they are commonly bought and sold in the market. There is no right to use a domain name that belongs only to a party whose real name is similar to the domain name. It has been held, however, that the right to use a domain name is inextricably bound to the services provided by a domain name registrar, because the name cannot function on the Internet without those services. Because services cannot be the subject of a garnishment, the right to use a domain name cannot be subject to a garnishment.
2. A. A finder of lost property can acquire good title to the property against everyone except its true owner. A rightful owner of lost property has rights to the property superior to all others persons. If two non-owners vie for title, the first to possess the property will prevail. There is an exception that applies in cases of abandoned property: if a trespasser finds abandoned property, better title may vest in the owner of the land on which the property was found.
3. C. When a bailment is for the sole benefit of the bailee, as in this problem, a greater standard of care of the bailed property rests with the bailee. The opposite would of course be true if this were a bailment for the sole benefit of the bailor. In all cases, bailees have a duty to exercise at least reasonable care over bailed property, though what constitutes reasonable care depends on the circumstances.

Chapter 50

True-False Questions

1. T
2. F. Insurance is classified according to the nature of the risk involved.
3. F. A broker is normally the agent of the applicant. If the broker fails to obtain coverage and the applicant is damaged as a result, the broker is liable for the loss.
4. T
5. T
6. F. The application is part of the contract. Misstatements in the application can void a policy, especially if the insurer would not have issued the policy if it had known the facts (although under an incontestability clause, the insurer may have a limited time within which to void a policy on that basis).
7. T
8. F. Coinsurance provisions are standard clauses in fire insurance policies, but they reduce recovery only in cases of *partial* loss and then only if the insured has less insurance than a specified percentage. The dollar amount of recovery is equal to the dollar amount of loss multiplied by the quotient of the dollar amount of insurance and (the total value of the property multiplied by the specified percentage). In other words, if the specified percentage is 80 percent, the total value of the property is $100,000, the amount of insurance is $40,000, and the loss is $30,000, the amount of recovery is $15,000—$30,000 x [$40,000/ ($100,000 x 80 percent)].
9. T
10. F. An antilapse clause provides a grace period for an insured to pay an overdue premium. A typical period is thirty days, and even then notice may be required to cancel the insurance.

Fill-in Questions

ordinary; nature of the coverage; insurance company; insurance company; is; insurance company

Multiple-Choice Questions

1. D. When applying for insurance, an applicant must disclose all material facts, which include all facts that would influence an insurer in determining whether to charge a higher premium or to refuse to issue a policy altogether. The correct response to this problem requires determining whether the misstatement was material. Under the circumstances stated in the problem, it was not.
2. C. An insurance company evaluates risk factors based on the information in an insurance application. For this reason, misrepresentation can void a policy, especially if the company can show that it would not have extended insurance if it had known the facts.
3. A. The insurable interest in life insurance must exist at the time the policy is obtained. Under a key-person life insurance policy, it will not matter if the key person is no longer in the business's employ at the time of the loss (the person's death).
4. C. To recover for a loss under a property insurance policy, an insurable interest in the property must exist when the loss occurs. It does not make any difference whether or not the property is owned in fee simple, or by an individual, or when an insurance policy is issued. This question and answer are based on a question that was included in the CPA exam in November 1995.
5. C. Property insurance can be canceled for gross negligence that increases the hazard insured against. Other reasons for canceling insurance include non-payment of premiums, fraud or misrepresentation, and conviction for a crime that, like gross negligence, increases the hazard insured against.

6. C. When a coinsurance clause provides that if an owner insures the property up to a specified percentage of its value (80 percent, in this problem), he or she will recover any loss up to the face amount of the policy. Because, in this problem, the insured's coverage was up to the specified percentage ($160,000), and the loss was for less, the insured can recover the entire amount of the loss.
7. B. Liability insurance protects against liability imposed on a company resulting from injuries to the person or property of another. Coverage under a liability policy may also include expenses involved in recalling and replacing a product that has proved to be defective.
8. A. If policies with several companies cover the same risk and the amount of coverage exceeds the loss, under a multiple insurance clause the insured collects from each insurer its proportionate share of the liability to the total amount of insurance. If each insurer covers the full value of the property, each insurer's share of the loss will be equal.
9. C. Under an appraisal and arbitration clause, if the insurer and the insured disagree about the amount of recovery (the value of a loss), they can demand separate appraisals. If they still cannot come to terms, the appraisals are assessed and resolved by a third party (called an umpire).
10. D. To obtain insurance, one must have a sufficient interest in what is insured. In this problem, the insured had a sufficient interest in the property when the policy was obtained. That is, when the policy was taken out, the insured would have sustained a monetary loss from the property's loss. To collect for a property loss, the insured must likewise have an insurable interest in the property *when the loss occurs.* Here, the insured sold the property *before* the loss.

Issue Spotters

1. Insurance companies use the principle of risk pooling. The risk that an event will occur requiring payments under an insurance contract is spread among a large number of people to make the premiums small compared with the coverage offered.
2. No. To obtain insurance, one must have a sufficiently substantial interest in whatever is to be insured. One has an insurable interest in property if one would suffer a pecuniary loss from its destruction. This interest must exist *when the loss occurs.* To obtain insurance on another's life, one must have a reasonable expectation of benefit from the continued life of the other. The benefit may be founded on a relationship, but "ex-spouse" alone is not such a relationship. An interest in someone's life must exist *when the policy is obtained.*
3. Those who are dissatisfied with the maximum liability limits offered by regular insurance coverage may want to buy separate coverage under an umbrella policy. Umbrella policies often cover personal liability in excess of an automobile or a homeowners' policy's liability limits.

Chapter 51

True-False Questions

1. F. A will is revocable by the testator (or by operation of law) at any time during his or her life.
2. T
3. F. Intestacy statutes regulate how property is distributed when a person dies without a will. These statutes typically provide that after payment of the decedent's debts, the remaining property passes to the decedent's surviving wife, children, or other relatives. If there are no living relatives, the property passes to the state.
4. T
5. T
6. F. A will can appoint a guardian for minor children or incapacitated adults and can also appoint a personal representative to settle the affairs of the deceased.
7. F. The spouse—or child, if a child is born after a will is executed—is entitled to receive whatever portion of the testator's estate that he or she is permitted to take under the state's intestacy laws.
8. T
9. T
10. F. Unless the trust expressly provides otherwise, it will not terminate on the trustee's death. Normally, a trust does specify its own termination date. If its purpose is fulfilled before that date, a court may order termination. If no date is stated, a trust terminates when its purpose is fulfilled, or becomes impossible or illegal.

Fill-in Questions

executor; administrator

Multiple-Choice Questions

1. D. When assets are insufficient to pay in full all that a will provides, the gifts of general property, such as sums of money, are reduced proportionately. Thus, the gifts to the testator's daughters will be reduced. This is known as abatement.
2. B. Under intestacy statutes, each state regulates how property is distributed when a person dies without a will. These statutes attempt to carry out the likely intent of the decedent, setting out rules by which the deceased's natural heirs (such as children, siblings, parents, or other family members) inherit his or her property. This question and answer are based on a question that appeared in the CPA exam in 1997.

3. C. If an express declaration of revocation is missing from a second will, the wills are read together, and if a disposition in the second will is inconsistent with the prior will, the language of the second will controls.
4. C. A surviving spouse usually receives a share of the estate—one-half if there is also a surviving child and one-third if there are two or more children, and the remaining property passes to the children and the children of deceased children.
5. D. Under a testamentary trust, which is set up in a will, a designated, court-approved trustee would manage the property for the daughters' benefit.
6. B. A gift of personal property by will is a legacy (or a bequest)—its recipient is a legatee. A gift of real estate by will is a devise—its recipient is a devisee. Gifts can be specific, general, or residuary (paid out of the assets remaining in the estate after all taxes and bills have been paid, and specific and general gifts have been made.
7. D. On the death of a joint tenant, property held in joint tenancy passes to the surviving joint tenant or tenants without probate. In the other instances, probate is not avoided, and in the case of the trust, ongoing court supervision is required. (Note—property held in joint tenancy is not subject to a will or to probate, but it is subject to estate taxes.)
8. C. Among a trustee's duties is the responsibility to dispose of assets that do not represent prudent investments. A trustee must also distribute the risk of loss from investments by diversification. Thus, when a trustee is granted discretionary investment power, he or she must *not* invest *only* in conservative securities. (If *no* discretion is granted to a trustee, however, most states require conservative investments.)
9. C. A trust's ordinary receipts and expenses, such as rent, are chargeable to trust income (unless the trust provides otherwise). Extraordinary expenses and receipts, such as proceeds from the sale of property, are allocated to principal.
10. B. A durable power of attorney authorizes a person to act on behalf of an incompetent person.

Issue Spotters

1. No. The general test for testamentary capacity is that the testator comprehend and remember the "natural objects of his or her bounty" (usually family members and others), that the testator comprehend the kind and character of the property being distributed, and that the testator understand and formulate a plan for disposing of the property. In this problem, the testator passes the test.
2. The specific gifts will pass as directed. When estate assets are insufficient to pay in full all that a will provides, the gifts of general property, such as the sums of money, are reduced proportionately. Thus, the gifts to Emily, Fred, and Greg will be reduced.
3. The estate will pass according to the state's intestacy laws. Intestacy laws set out how property is distributed when a person dies without a will. Their purpose is to carry out the likely intent of the decedent. The laws determine which of the deceased's natural heirs (including first the surviving spouse, second lineal descendants, third parents, and finally collateral heirs) inherit his or her property.

Chapter 52

True-False Questions

1. T
2. T
3. F. Compliance with GAAP and GAAS may be required, but it is no guarantee of freedom from liability. Also, there may be a higher standard of conduct under a state statute or judicial decision.
4. F. The majority view is that accountants are subject to liability for negligence to foreseeable users. In some states, however, the view is to extend liability only to users whose use of, and reliance on, an accountant's statements or report was reasonably foreseeable.
5. F. Under the securities acts, an accountant may be subject to criminal penalties for willful violations.
6. T
7. F. Tax preparers may be subject to penalties if they fail to furnish a taxpayer with a copy of the return.
8. T
9. T
10. F. No, privity is not required. To recover, a plaintiff must prove five elements, including *scienter*, a fraudulent act or deception, reliance, materiality, and causation.

Fill-in Questions

will not; may; may

Multiple-Choice Questions

1. B. Working papers are the property of the accountant whose work they represent, but working papers cannot be released without the permission of the client for whom they were accumulated.
2. C. Generally, an auditor can be held liable to a third party for negligence. In most states, however, an accountant is liable only to users whom the accountant knew or should have known about. In some states, privity is required; in others, "near privity" is the requirement. This question and answer are based on a question that appeared in the CPA exam in 1997.
3. D. Under the Securities Act of 1933, an accountant may be liable for any false statement of mate-

rial fact or omission of a material fact in a registration statement. The other elements indicated in the other choices are not requirements for liability under this statute.

4. C. Under the Securities Exchange Act of 1934, an accountant may be liable for any false statement of material fact or omission of a material fact made with the intent to defraud. An accountant may also be liable for failing to disclose to a client facts that give reason to believe misstatements have been made or fraud has been committed.

5. A. In most states, under a court order an accountant must disclose information about his or her client, including communications between the accountant and the client.

6. A. The client assigned the employee who was committing the wrongful act to assist the accountant, who failed to discover the wrongdoing because the employee covered it up. The client's loss was thus due to the client's own error. This generally reduces or eliminates any potential liability on the part of the accountant.

7. C. Besides the cost to obtain the accountant's contracted-for services elsewhere and the amount of any penalties for failing to meet deadlines, the client may recover other reasonable and foreseeable losses.

8. C. In this problem, the attorney failed to exercise reasonable care and professional judgment, thereby breaching the duty of care owed to clients. If a statute of limitations runs out, a client can no longer file a suit and loses a potential award of damages.

9. B. In a number of states, working papers remain the property of the accountant. These papers may act as crucial evidence in case the accountant needs to defend himself or herself against charges of negligence or fraud. At the same time, because the working papers reflect the client's financial situation, the client has the right of access to them. Also, in some circumstances, audit papers must be retained for as long as five years.

10. C. Another possible defense that an accountant or other professional may assert against a charge of negligence, in a state that allows contributory negligence as a defense, is that the client was negligent.

Issue Spotters

1. Unintentionally misstating a material fact may lead to liability based on constructive fraud. A professional may be liable for constructive fraud whether or not he or she acted with fraudulent intent. Constructive fraud may exist, for instance, if a professional intentionally fails to perform a duty in reckless disregard of the consequences.

2. Yes. In these circumstances, when the accountant knows that the bank will use the statement, the bank is a foreseeable user. A foreseeable user is a third party within the class of parties to whom an accountant may be liable for negligence.

3. No. In the circumstances described in the problem, the accountant will not be held liable to a purchaser of the securities. To avoid liability, however, the accountant must prove that he is free of fraud and negligence.

Chapter 53

True-False Questions

1. F. According to the principle of comity, however, a nation will give effect to the laws of another nation if those laws are consistent with the law and public policy of the accommodating nation.

2. F. The act of state doctrine tends to immunize foreign nations from the jurisdiction of U.S. courts—that is, foreign nations are often exempt from U.S. jurisdiction under this doctrine.

3. F. As with the act of state doctrine, the doctrine of sovereign immunity tends to immunize foreign nations from the jurisdiction of U.S. courts

4. F. The Foreign Sovereign Immunities Act sets forth the major exceptions to the immunity of foreign nations to U.S. jurisdiction.

5. T

6. T

7. F. Legal systems in all nations can be generally divided into *common* law and civil law systems.

8. T

9. F. Some contract law has been internationalized through the CISG, but parties contracting internationally can agree to apply other law to their contract disputes.

10. T

Fill-in Questions

An expropriation; A confiscation; an expropriation; a confiscation

Multiple-Choice Questions

1. C. Under certain conditions, the doctrine of sovereign immunity prohibits U.S. courts from exercising jurisdiction over foreign nations. Under the Foreign Sovereign Immunities Act, a foreign state is not immune when the action is based on a commercial activity carried on in the United States by the foreign state.

2. A. Under the act of state doctrine, the judicial branch of one country will not examine the validity of public acts committed by a recognized foreign government within its own territory. The awarding of a government contract under the circumstances described in the problem meets this criterion.

3. C. U.S. courts give effect to the judicial decrees of another country under the principle of comity, if those decrees are consistent with the laws and public policies of the United States.
4. C. The U.S. Congress cannot tax exports, but it may establish export quotas. In particular, under the Export Administration Act of 1979, restrictions can be imposed on the export of technologically advanced products.
5. C. Unlike exports, imports can be taxed. A tax on an import is a tariff (generally set as a percent of the value). Imports can also be subject to quotas, which limit how much can be imported.
6. B. Although increasingly influenced by codified (statutory) law and in some observers' opinions overwhelmed with administrative rules and regulations, common law legal systems are based on judicial decisions and precedent. Despite this general frame of reference, common law courts in different nations have developed different principles.
7. C. Civil law systems are based on codified (statutory) law. Administrative rules and regulations and judicial decisions are, of course, part of the operation of a civil law system. In a civil law system, courts are permitted to interpret the statutes that make up the code and to apply the rules, but unlike a common law system, in which judicial precedent plays a significant role, the courts in a civil law system are not expected to develop their own body of law.
8. B. In many countries, however, judges are actively involved in trials, such as by questioning witnesses. In the United States, besides a less participatory role at trial, a federal judge is less likely to be influenced by politics, in part because he or she cannot be removed by impeachment except in extreme cases.
9. A. For example, mutual assent (offer and acceptance) is a common element for an enforceable contract. But the details of its application varies in different countries. In Germany, for instance, a written offer must be held open for a reasonable time, unless the offer states otherwise, and oral offers must be accepted immediately or they expire. In Mexico, if a time for acceptance is not stated in an offer, the offer is deemed to be held open for three days (plus whatever time is necessary for the mails).
10. C. In some countries, employers cannot discriminate against employees or job applicants, to varying degrees. The prohibited bases for discrimination differ among nations. Discrimination is not prohibited in all countries, however.

Issue Spotters

1. Under the principle of comity, a U.S court would defer and give effect to foreign laws and judicial decrees that are consistent with U.S. law and public policy.
2. A U.S. firm—or any domestic firm—can license its formula, product, or process to a foreign concern to avoid its theft. The foreign firm obtains the right to make and market the product according to the formula (or the right to use the process) and agrees to keep the necessary information secret and to pay royalties to the licensor.
3. The practice described in this problem is known as dumping. Seen as an unfair international trade practice, dumping is the sale of imported goods at "less than fair value." Based on the price of those goods in the exporting country, an extra tariff can be imposed on the imports. This is known as an antidumping duty.

Chapter 54

True-False Questions

1. F. Important considerations in selecting a lawyer include the attorney's knowledge as to what a client needs, the attorney's willingness to investigate the relevant law, the attorney's ability to communicate with the client, and the attorney's perception of what issues are of foremost concern.
2. T
3. F. A business's name must be different from those of other businesses, to avoid, among other things, misleading consumers. A corporation's name should also include the word *corporation, company,* or *incorporated.* To protect a corporate name as a trade name within a state in which the firm does business, the name should be filed with the appropriate state office.
4. T
5. F. By means of what is called a private offering, a limited amount of money can be raised from a limited number of investors without first registering the shares with the Securities and Exchange Commission. The requirements include a limit on how much money can be raised, how many investors are asked to buy, and how sophisticated (knowledgeable about investments) the investors are.
6. T
7. F. A contract *should* be in writing in case of a dispute, and in some cases, a contract *must* be in writing to be enforced. The requirement of a writing comes under the Statute of Frauds, which is part of the basic contract law principles that apply to be business.
8. T
9. F. An employer is bound to its promises of employment. Such promises may even be implied from statements in employment manuals. For this reason—and for the reason that other disputes may arise—all terms of employment should be put in writing, including grounds for termination.
10. T

Fill-in Questions

employees; employees; employees

Multiple-Choice Questions

1. D. The benefits of retaining an attorney at any point in a business relationship, but particularly during the start-up of a business, include the responses to this question. Besides providing *legal* advice, a lawyer may be able to direct a new business to potential investors, provide *business* advice, and act as a sounding board for business ideas. Another benefit is the flexibility of payment plans.
2. D. Sole proprietorships and general partnerships avoid the formalities of incorporating or of creating a limited partnership, but there is no business form that avoids all legal requirements. All businesses must meet such requirements as business name registration, occupational licensing, state tax registration, health and environmental permits, zoning and building codes, import/export regulations, and laws governing the workplace.
3. B. At the initial meeting of a corporation's board of directors, the directors adopt bylaws, appoint corporate officers, and take other necessary steps. Those steps do not include the "adoption" of articles of incorporation, which must be drafted and filed before a corporation exists, or the selection of a corporate name, which is also done before a corporation exists (of course, the name can be changed later).
4. C. Registering a trademark with the U.S. Patent and Trademark Office gives the mark national protection if it is in use or will be within six months. Of course, there are other requirements—the mark must be distinctive, for example, so as not to mislead customers, and must remain in use. The owner must protest others' use of the mark, and the registration must be renewed after five years (and every ten thereafter).
5. C. When an entrepreneur (or any business) wants to exchange an interest in an enterprise for capital and the interest consists of shares of stock, it is subject to securities laws. A limited amount of money can be raised from a limited number of investors without registering the shares with the Securities and Exchange Commission. Offering shares to the public, however, requires that the securities be registered. (There is a simplified registration form for small businesses, known as the Small Corporate Offering Registration, or SCOR.
6. C. The Fair Labor Standards Act (FSLA) requires the payment of the minimum wage, as well as time-and-a-half for overtime. The FLSA also requires employers to keep wage and hour records. (The FLSA applies to businesses with $500,000 or more in sales or those engaged in interstate commerce. In this problem, the firm is engaged in interstate commerce, although the dollar amount of the firm's sales is not stated.) State law, not the FLSA, may require a meal break. This question and answer are based on a question that was included in the November 1994 CPA exam.
7. A. If a firm is not organized as a sole proprietorship, anyone who signs contracts or negotiable instruments (drafts or notes) on the firm's behalf must do so as an agent to avoid personal liability. Otherwise, if the contract is breached, or the instrument is not honored or paid, the party may be held liable on it.
8. B. A contract may require a buyer to pay all costs to collect overdue accounts. State debt-collection laws prevent the use of abusive efforts to collect the accounts, however. Other legal incentives that a seller might use to get a buyer to pay on time include price discounts, late charges, and interest.
9. C. An employer who makes a *negative* statement to other employers about the reason for a former employee's termination may be liable to the *employee* for defamation if the statement is false. An employer who makes a *positive* statement to other employers about the reason for a former employee's termination may be liable to the *employer* for misrepresentation if the statement is false. The safest course might be to make only a neutral statement, confirming little more than the dates of employment.
10. B. A buy-sell agreement enables shareholders to buy others' shares and provides for the price to be paid. A buy-sell agreement that includes a right of first refusal prevents the sale of shares to a third party without first giving the other owners a right to buy. A "take-along" clause allows an investor to participate in a sale of shares to a third party. (This clause may provide an incentive for a venture capitalist to invest in the firm.) A key-person *insurance policy* provides benefits to a firm if the key person dies.

Issue Spotters

1. Forms of business organization that limit the personal liability of their owners include corporations, limited partnerships, limited liability corporations (LLCs), and limited liability partnerships (LLPs).
2. Customer lists, pricing policies, and similar trade secrets can be protected. An employer can require employees to agree not to divulge trade secrets if the employees go to work for a competitor or go into the business for themselves. An employer can also insist that employees *not* go to work for competitors or set up a competing business, in which the company's trade secrets will likely be disclosed. These latter agreements (covenants not to compete) must, of course, be reasonable in time and geographic limits, or they will not be enforced.
3. Although a loan is possible, most businesses raise capital by exchanging ownership rights (equity) for capital. A plan describing the firm, its products, and its anticipated performance is presented to potential investors who examine the firm's books and assets. Terms of financing, how much ownership and control

the investor will receive, the type and quantity of stock (if any) the investor will get, and other issues are part of the negotiations. Depending on the form of the business seeking the investment, the investor may be called a shareholder, a partner, or a member. Depending on the amount of the investment, how that amount is solicited, and what the investment buys, a firm's attempt to attract investors may have to be registered with the Securities and Exchange Commission.

Cumulative Hypothetical Problem for Unit Eleven—Including Chapters 50–54

1. A. Under a coinsurance provision, the amount of recovery is the amount of the loss multiplied by the quotient of the amount of insurance and (the total value of the property multiplied by a specified percentage). Here, the specified percentage is 80 percent, the total value of the property is $500,000, the amount of insurance is $300,000, and the loss is $60,000. The amount of recovery is $45,000—$60,000 x [$300,000/($500,000 x 80 percent)]. (Note that a coinsurance provision reduces the amount of a recovery only in a case of partial loss and then only if the insured has less insurance than the specified percentage.)
2. D. Ordinary expenses, such as rent and depreciation, are chargeable to income. Extraordinary expenses, such as principal payments on mortgages, are allocated to principal. This is also the allocation for receipts.
3. D. The elements of fraud include misrepresentation of a material fact, *scienter* (knowledge of the charged party that the statement was false), intent to deceive, justifiable reliance on the part of the charging party, and damages. Without reliance, the circumstances in this problem would not amount to fraud.
4. C. The Internal Revenue Service (IRS) has the power to enforce the federal tax laws. Against a tax preparer who aids and abets in the falsification of tax information and tax evasion, the IRS can seek fines, injunctions, and criminal sanctions.
5. D. A plaintiff does not need to show either intent or reliance to succeed under this law. (Reliance is am element of fraud and is important under the Securities Exchange Act of 1934.) The plaintiff also does not need to show privity. The plaintiff does need to show that he or she suffered a loss. Defenses that the defendant might use in this case is that he or she used "due diligence," he or she used generally accepted accounting principles, the plaintiff knew of the misstatements, the misstatements were not material, there were no misstatements in the registration statement, or there was no connection between the misstatements and the loss.

Questions on the Focus on Legal Reasoning for Unit Eleven—*Overton v. Consolidated Insurance Co.*

1. D. The majority in *Overton v. Consolidated Insurance Co.* reasons that to collect a claim filed under an insurance policy, "an insured must show some form of harm caused by an 'occurrence,' " which is a "harmful event" that is "neither expected nor intended from the standpoint of the insured." Property damage is expected if the insured is "put on notice. If an event causing loss is not contingent or unknown prior to the effective date of the policy, there is no coverage." This notice is enough, holds the majority, for an insurer to avoid liability under an insurance policy for property damage.
2. A. The dissent in *Overton v. Consolidated Insurance Co.* reasons that persons obtain insurance to cover risks of all kinds, and that the situation described in the problem would be no different, likely arguing that the insured knew only of a risk of pollution. At most, the dissent might state, "reasonable minds could conclude" the property owner knew that pollution was present; not that the owner knew the pollution would cause a loss or liability.
3. D. When a property owner does not have insurance coverage, the owner might have to personally bear the financial burden of the cost to clean up environmental pollution of the property. Under federal and state law, this expense may be assessed against other responsible parties. But that does not necessarily exempt a current owner, particularly one who knew of the pollution, from liability altogether.

Questions on the Focus on Ethics for Unit Eleven—Special Topics

1. C. As in this problem, an incontestability clause provides that after an insurance policy has been in force for a specific period of time, the insurer cannot contest statements in the application. That is, the insurer cannot later refuse to pay a claim on the basis of a material misrepresentation in the insured's application for the policy. This and other issues of fairness often arise when insurance companies attempt to avoid payment of claims under policies.
2. D. An insurance agent owes fiduciary duties to the insurer but not to the insured. The agent's duties to the insured are only contractual. Although they may seem unfair, a contrary rule could result in an insurance agent being held liable for failing to advise a client of every possible insurance option and removing the insured's responsibility to take care of his or her own financial circumstances.
3. D. Accountants face potential liability under federal and state securities laws, tax laws, and, consumer protection statutes. This liability may be civil, criminal, or both. There may be different standards of proof under different causes of action, and in some instances, there may be strict liability. Accountants are also held to a common-law duty of care.